The GLASGOW ENCYCLOPEDIA

Not houses finely roofed or the stones of walls well built, nor canals or dockyards make the city, but men able to use their opportunities.

ARISTIDES THE JUST, *c*.490 BC

The **GLASGOW** ENCYCLOPEDIA

Joe Fisher

MAINSTREAM PUBLISHING

EDINBURGH AND LONDON

GLASGOW
DEVELOPMENT AGENCY

TO MOLLY

First published in Great Britain in 1994 by MAINSTREAM PUBLISHING COMPANY (EDINBURGH) LTD
7 Albany Street
Edinburgh EH1 3UG

ISBN 1 85158 212 6

Produced with support from Glasgow City Council and Glasgow Development Agency.

A catalogue record for this book is available from the British Library

Design by Michael Dancer
Typeset by Saxon Graphics Ltd, Derby
Printed in Great Britain by Butler and Tanner Ltd, Frome

Contents

Introduction

The activities of an encyclopaedist, as he goes about his labours, resemble in some ways those of Mary Shelley's famous Dotor. First comes the unearthing of other men's creations and the removal of some of their parts. This process is followed by their reassembly into a similitude of life which the encyclopaedist anxiously hopes will not betray its origins, and further that the joins will not show nor the absence of an odd limb or two be noticed. In other words the encyclopaedist does not originate, he collates.

This might be thought a mechanical task, fit, as Dr Johnson said of dictionary-making, only for drudges. There are, however, sizeable pitfalls in the way of the harmless drudge. For instance, the history of Glasgow (like that of many other old communities) has so far received surprisingly scant attention from scholarly historians – most extant works concerned with its past could, with little exaggeration, be regarded as companion volumes to D. Macleod Malloch's *The Book of Glasgow Anecdote*, and the continued repetition of customary anecdotes through book after book has left untouched many important themes – gaps which are unfortunately mirrored in any compilation.

Another pitfall is the Law of Reverse Certainty – the effects of the rough usage of time and posterity, for instance, have worn down and polished our knowledge of Prince Charles Edward Stewart's 1745 passage through the city to half-a-dozen or so words – *Clementina Walkinshaw, thorn tree, shoes, hose, waistcoats and shirts,*

Cameron of Lochiel – while an elucidation of the Glasgow Trades Council attitude towards the city's post-First World War elections would require an as yet unwritten book. This factor has the unfortunate result of making it very easy to gather material on the late 18th century and very difficult to do so on the late 20th cetury.

The layout of the Encyclopedia is, I hope, straightforward and self-evident. There are about 180 articles or themes, some small, others quite large, arranged in alphabetical order by their titles – BUSES, EXHIBITIONS, GLASGOW TRADES COUNCIL, MAPS, PARKS, RAILWAYS, STREAMS. In a few cases, subordinate themes have been placed under a related main article – fiction and poetry under LITERATURE. At the end of many of the articles indications have been given of other articles whose topics are related – *See also* TENEMENTS at the end of the article on HOUSING, for example.

It should not be forgotten that this is an encyclopedia and not a dictionary. Whereas the latter has thousands of entries, each on a specific fact, encyclopedic entries attempt to encompass larger and more general themes. To gain access to discrete items of information within these, recourse should be had to the detailed index following the text, by which individual persons, places and things can quickly be located. The index also directs enquiries made under a synonym to the equivalent term used – burns *see* STREAMS, statues *see* MONUMENTS. Names of articles are always shown in CAPITALS.

Whatever merits this encyclopedia may possess, there is no doubt that it owes its existence, in a fundamental sense, to the Glasgow Room of the Mitchell Library. On its shelves, available to all, can be found a collection of printed material of all kinds relating to the city. This has been gathering since 1877; the collection is now second to none and very few recent books about Glasgow lack an acknowledgement to it and to its staff. I am profoundly grateful for the opportunity of having been associated with it (and them) for almost a half-century.

The illustrations come from two notable sources – I take this opportunity to express my thanks to both. One is an institution, the Glasgow Room in the Mitchell Library, the other a person, Cordelia Oliver, who most generously allowed me to choose freely from the riches of the collection of Glasgow photographs made by her late husband, George Oliver.

About seven miles south-west from Glasgow, on the south bank of the Clyde, the average height of the flood plain is no more than 20ft above sea-level, an ideal site for an airport.

The first airport in this area was located on the outskirts of the burgh of Renfrew. During the First World War it was used by the Royal Flying Corps and continued to serve as a training station for the Royal Air Force (in particular for 602 (City of Glasgow) Squadron of the Royal Auxiliary Air Force) until the 1930s when it was transferred to another site at Abbotsinch, about two miles to the west of the burgh.

The Renfrew airfield then became a civil airport, control passing from the Ministry of Civil Aviation to the Renfrew Corporation. It soon came to be regarded, unofficially, as Glasgow's airport, but by the late 1950s its limitations were becoming increasingly obvious. Its 6,000ft-long main runway was now too short for the new powerful passenger aircraft coming into service, and yet the airport's location so near a built-up area made any expansion difficult, if not impossible.

Interest now turned to the Abbotsinch airfield as a much more promising site. Consisting of some 700 acres of flat, peaty soil lying between the Black Cart and the White Cart, it had no nearby built-up area to hinder expansion. In 1943 it had passed from the RAF to the Royal Navy as Royal Naval Air Station HMS *Sanderling*, and continued in use until 1963. After much discussion and argument over the respective merits of Abbotsinch, Renfrew and Prestwick, the Ministry of Civil Aviation announced in 1960 that the replacement for Renfrew would be Abbotsinch. (Prestwick's 30 miles from Glasgow ruled it out.) It was commissioned as the new terminal in 1962, and in 1963 Glasgow Corporation, with some degree of reluctance, agreed to become responsible for running it. Work started in April 1964 and the new Glasgow Airport was opened, on schedule, in May 1966.

At that time its main runway was 6,720ft long but increasing use brought about a much needed extension to 8,720ft in 1973, followed by a massive £2 million expansion of its facilities in June 1976. Earlier, in 1971, the Corporation had wanted to extend the runway to 9,500ft, only 300ft shorter than Prestwick Airport's, but the government, for political reasons, was anxious to retain Prestwick for long-range, transatlantic traffic, limiting Glasgow to domestic and short-haul flights. By the early 1970s the airport's finances began to slide into the red, and Glasgow Corporation became anxious to transfer its responsibilities to the British Airport Authority.

Finally, in April 1975, just before local government reorganisation took place, the city handed over its airport to the BAA for £7,600,000. Its use continued to grow and by 1986 it had become the fourth busiest airport in Britain. One factor in its success has been its close proximity to the M8 motorway.

The next major step in its history was

the decision by the Ministry of Transport in March 1989 which altered the existing Scottish Lowland Airports policy and cleared Glasgow Airport for transatlantic flights; in less than a year it was offering direct flights to New York, Boston, Chicago and Toronto.

1992 saw the completion of the first of two £60 million projects which has increased its capacity by 70 per cent and will enable it to handle up to six million passengers a year by the mid-1990s. The second phase will provide the handling capacity for more than ten million passengers (more than double its current capacity) by the end of the century.

Archaeology

The spread of Glasgow as a built-up area has meant that very few archaeological remains have come to light within the city. By far the largest group of such remains has been the extensive number of single-tree dug-out canoes which have been found embedded in the Clyde drift which fills the river valley in and around the city. Twenty or so, some dating back over 4,000 years, have been unearthed, lying mostly between the north bank of the river and the beginning of the 100ft ancient raised beach or terrace marked by the Rottenrow. Constructed from oak trees, all but one have been made by scooping out (in two cases by fire) the interiors of the tree trunks. The exception was a clinker-built specimen (its transverse ribs were covered by rows of 8in broad deals overlapping each other) which measured 18ft by 5ft.

The earliest of these canoes was found in 1780 in St Enoch's Sq, 25ft down and 45ft from the river-bank. The following year another one was dug up at the Cross where the Tontine building was being constructed. In 1824 one was disinterred in Stockwell St and the next year another was found 10ft below London St. About the same time one was unearthed in the Drygate, behind the Duke St Prison. A small example, only 4ft long, was discovered 6ft down in the Candleriggs in 1857. That year, during the deepening of the Clyde, no less than 12 dug-outs were uncovered (one of these was the clinker-built specimen). During the construction of the Queen's Dock in 1875 one was found 15ft down. Another was found in the river in 1879 just below Rutherglen Bridge and a second one in 1880 from the river-bed at Glasgow Green. The locations of all these canoes suggest that in prehistoric times the Clyde extended northwards to the edge of the 100ft beach.

When Agricola was Governor of Roman Britain he marched north into Scotland in AD81 and it is in Tacitus's account of his campaign that the Clyde first appears in Roman literature, as *Clota*. After Hadrian's Wall was built in AD120 (from the Solway to the Tyne), the Emperor Antoninus Pius decided to move the military boundary further north into Scotland and about AD140 had the Antonine Wall built. It consisted of a turf wall on a stone base which ran from Bridgeness on the Forth to Old Kilpatrick on the Clyde and which had at least 13 forts along its length. In its course it passed about four miles to the north of the city, with forts at Bearsden and Balmuildy. Despite this closeness to the city no conclusive proof has ever been found suggesting that there was ever any Roman settlement where Glasgow now stands.

One of the main Roman routes through the Scottish lowlands from the south passed through Carlisle and on up the valley of the Annan. About Carstairs it apparently forked, one fork going north-east and the other west along the north bank of the Clyde, through Bothwellhaugh. Major-General William Roy recorded *c.* 1790 that 'traces of it were lately to be seen particularly a little to the eastward of Tollcross'. It has been supposed that this road was making for the major fort at Balmuildy (one of only two stone forts along the wall) and that it would pass through the site of the city in doing so. A possible route may have followed Duke St, Drygate, Dobbie's Loan, Port Dundas, Possilpark and Lambhill. The exact date of

the departure of the Romans from around Glasgow is not known but the wall was evacuated sometime towards the end of the second century.

Roman finds within the area of the city are extremely scanty. Some time before 1856 a denarius of Constantine II (minted 317–40) with some other coins and medals was dug up from the bed of the river near Govan. A coin of Crispina (*c.*180) was found near Petershill (Springburn district) and an unidentified coin was discovered 25ft below Clyde St (Bridgeton district) in 1892. In 1876 a good specimen of a red-glazed Gaulish pottery bowl of Samian ware (*c.*100–300) was found in the Provost's Haugh (Glasgow Green) 4½ft below the surface, and cinerary urns have been dug up in Partick and Whiteinch.

The area around the Cathedral must have been one of the earliest to be built on. Excavations here have uncovered the meagre remains of medieval buildings, but subsequent building has effectively destroyed anything of consequence.

GOVAN SARCOPHAGUS

The ancient burgh of Govan (now part of Glasgow District) lies on the south bank of the Clyde a mile or so downstream from Glasgow. Its history goes back almost as far as Glasgow's, and it has been said that it may have been almost as important an ecclesiastical centre as its neighbour. Its distant religious past was confirmed in 1855 when an important archeological discovery was made in the churchyard of Govan Old Parish Church. A series of monumental structures was uncovered, consisting of a sarcophagus made from a

single block of hollowed-out sandstone with its sides and ends decorated with panels of interlaced and figured ornaments dating from *c.*10–11 AD, two cross shafts, two cross slabs, five hog-back tombstones, bowed and gabled blocks in a Scandinavian style and a large number of recumbent grave-markers dating from the early 10th to early 12th centuries. The group forms one of the finest collections of such material in Scotland, and adds cogency to the theory that by the early 10th century the site was a major religious centre.

Archives

In 1964 the Corporation established the Glasgow City Archives as part of the Town Clerk's Department, with a remit to collect, store, control and make available all historically important material produced by the Corporation in the course of its activities. As well as carrying out this official function, the City Archives has also accepted some responsibility for collecting other archival matter relating to the city – for example, records of business firms and industrial concerns (particularly those relating to the Clyde shipyards and to the Clyde Port Authority, formerly the Clyde Navigation Trust), of prominent landed families connected with the city and of churches within the presbyteries of Glasgow and Ayr.

Following local government reorganisation, in 1975 the archives became part of the new Strathclyde Region. It thus became responsible for the maintenance of the archives of the largest region in Scotland, but the Glasgow District and its archives, as part of the region, still remain a close concern of the new Archives. In 1984 it moved from its cramped quarters in the City Chambers to accommodation in the Mitchell Library. Its presence in the building, which also houses the Library's Glasgow Collection, serves to bring together under one roof a unique collection of written and printed material relating to the history of the city.

CITY RECORDS

The city's early records were those of the Cathedral (whose bishop was the city's temporal lord). When the last Catholic archbishop, James Beaton, fled the city in 1560 at the time of the Reformation, he took all the records with him, including two cartularies, a protocol book and a` rental, along with 500–600 original charters. Most of these he deposited in the Scots College in Paris, while a few went to the Carthusians. In 1692 Father Thomas Innes (c.1667–1744), brother of the college principal, put them into order. He also managed to produce a transcript of them in two large volumes, of which there is no longer any trace. Knowledge of their existence attracted some attention in Scotland at the beginning of the 18th century, particularly from the Jacobites who were motivated by the lack of

documentary evidence for the legitimacy of King Robert II's marriage, and in the course of the 18th century several other transcripts were made. During the French Revolution almost all the original documents disappeared, the only survivors being the two medieval cartularies, and the protocol and rental books (all of which were later to reappear in Scotland).

It is said that Father Innes alone remained behind at the college and managed to pack some records into barrels and dispatch them for safety to St Omers. The Abbé MacPherson selected the most important of those still remaining and carried them off to London where they were seen by George Chalmers, author of *Caledonia*, who then mislaid many of them! What remained were taken to Scotland and passed into the keeping of the Roman

Catholic Church. The protocol book and the rental are now part of the Scottish Catholic Archives – both were published in 1875. The older of the two cartularies, known as the *Registrum Vetus Ecclesia Cathedralis Glasguensis* (the Ancient Register), is also with the SCA, while the other, the *Liber Ruber* (the Red Book), is in the Scottish Record Office. In 1843 Cosmo Innes prepared from these and from other sources (mainly transcripts) a chronological ordering of all extant and known muniments of the bishopric of Glasgow, which was published by the Maitland Club in two volumes in 1843 as the *Registrum Episcopatus Glasguensis*. The Maitland Club also published, in 1846, the *Liber Collegii Nostre Domine* which contained the *Book of the Collegiate Church of the Blessed Virgin Mary and Saint Anne* (this church later became the Tron or Laigh Church) and the *Charters of the Friars Preachers of Glasgow* (their place of worship became, after the Reformation, the Blackfriars Church).

Three of the 18th-century transcripts are also extant: one of 633 pages, made for the Earl of Panmure in the 1720s, is in Brechin Castle; one made for the Glasgow Town Council by Innes in 1739 is in the Town Clerk's Office (141 pages covering the text of 60 documents, mainly of interest to the city); and the third, made in 1766, is held by Glasgow University (two volumes of 1,216 pages, including material from both cartularies).

Athenaeum

About the middle of last century a number of young businessmen in the city decided to fill the educational vacuum which existed between the Mechanics' Institute and the Glasgow University. Under the title of the Glasgow Educational Association they began to meet early in the morning to study logic. Later, classes in political economy were added, but the association soon collapsed through lack of support.

The idea was taken up again, however, and in 1847 the Athenaeum was formally constituted. The new body, based on the Manchester Athenaeum, described itself as a literary and scientific institution for organising commercial classes in Glasgow. It began life in the Assembly Rooms in Ingram St – the opening ceremony in 1847 was chaired with considerable dash by Charles Dickens. Soon some 2,000 students had enrolled at one guinea a year. There were public lectures and regular classes; at first these were designed for commercial students but later more cultural classes were added. Unusually for the times, the evening classes were co-educational. The numbers attending fluctuated considerably. Early classes barely reached 400 and fell to 200 in the 1850s and 1860s but by 1897 were up to 2,600.

The Assembly Rooms were run on the principle of a Tontine Society, and the Athenaeum bought a quarter share on a Tontine member's life for £70. By an extraordinary stroke of luck, the site of the Assembly Rooms was required by the government for Glasgow's new General Post Office and the £70 share realised the sum of £6,500. Along with other contributions this windfall enabled the Athenaeum to purchase a site on the north side of Mandela Pl (then St George's Pl) and the new building was opened there in 1888. It provided a library and a reading-room, organised lectures on science, philosophy, history, geology and literature, and held classes (attended by some 1,000 students) in English grammar, French, German, drawing, shorthand, music and art, for both men and women. An extension was opened in 1893 which included a gymnasium, a concert hall and a theatre.

In 1903, it was raised to the status of a Central Institution for Commercial Education in Glasgow and the West of Scotland, taking the name of the Athenaeum Commercial College. By 1905 it had become a combination of a club and an educational establishment. As a club it offered its members the use of a library, reading-room, magazine room, writing-room, dining-room, buffet, smoking-room and billiard room. Educationally, it was now split into three sections: a commercial college, a school of music and a civil service and professional department.

After reorganisation in 1915 it became primarily concerned with running vocational courses, although a few cultural courses were still offered. By 1930 the school of music had become the Scottish College of Music (now the Royal Scottish Academy of Music and Drama in Renfrew St) and the commercial college evolved into the Glasgow and West of Scotland Commercial College in Pitt St, becoming part of the new Strathclyde University in 1964.

Following the recent departure of the College of Music and Drama to Renfrew St, most of the building in Mandela Pl has been converted to flats.

Ballooning

Vincenzo Lunardi (1759–1806), the famous Italian balloonist, came north after making his first balloon flight in Britain from London in 1784, and in November 1785 he made an ascent from St Andrew's Sq (not then built upon) in the east end of the city. His balloon passed over an enormous crowd gathered in the Green to see his ascent, and descended two hours later at Hawick, 70 miles distant. So great was the interest in his demonstration of aerial navigation that previous to his flight he exhibited the balloon (tethered by a net) floating in the choir of the Cathedral – admission, one shilling.

The following month he made a second ascent. This time he chose a large and enclosed garden not far from his previous take-off point, but one which allowed him to restrict spectators to those prepared to pay for the privilege. His second journey was much shorter; he only reached as far as Campsie, a distance of a mere ten miles, and was back in the city the same evening at 8 o'clock.

Banks

Until the middle of the 18th century Glasgow had no bank, for the level of the city's trade and commerce was such that adequate banking facilities for the city's small traders could easily be provided by local wealthy merchants. At this time the only Scottish banks were the three Edinburgh located public banks, the Royal Bank of Scotland, the Bank of Scotland and the British Linen Company. Their traditional approach to banking matters did not make them popular in the west of Scotland; their bank notes had little currency there and most financial transactions in Glasgow were carried out in specie. There had been two early attempts to plant branches in Glasgow (1696 and 1731) but both had failed, mainly because the Edinburgh banks had made no attempt to adjust the banking facilities they offered to the needs of a rising mercantile community; for instance, they would not accept bills of exchange – the life blood of a merchant city – stating that 'they found it very troublesome, unsafe, and improper'.

However, the rapidly increasing volume of the city's transatlantic trade with the tobacco-producing areas of North America required improved banking and several of the city's most wealthy and influential merchants decided to set up their own Glasgow bank. The six involved in this first venture included Alexander Houston of Jordanhill and Andrew Buchanan of Drumpellier, both prominent in the tobacco trade. The bank, under the name of the Ship Bank, opened its doors in January 1750 and went on to become one of the most successful of the Glasgow private banks.

Its rapid success led to the immediate formation of a second bank in the same year. Almost 30 merchants were involved in the launch of the Glasgow Arms Bank; the tobacco-trading activities of two of them, John Glassford and Archibald Speirs of Elderslie (along with William Cunninghame of Lainshaw and James Ritchie of Busbie), were later said to have laid the foundations for Glasgow's mercantile success. The fact that seven of the subscribers were, at one time or another, provosts of the city, is a clear indication of the close connection between the trading community and the burgh's administration.

What is remarkable about the setting up of these banks was that both of these apparent Glasgow enterprises were, in fact, underwritten by the two Edinburgh public banks. The Ship Bank was founded as a private co-partnery with unlimited liability under the aegis of no less an institution than the Bank of Scotland, while the Glasgow Arms Bank opened with cash backing supplied by the Royal Bank of

Scotland. It can only be supposed that the Edinburgh banks mistakenly chose to consider these western institutions as their agencies rather than as their rivals. They were quickly disillusioned, for, with alarming rapidity their two 'offspring' committed the heinous crime of issuing their own notes. In the face of these western upstarts the Edinburgh banks laid aside their traditional enmities and joined in a sustained and forceful attack on what they obviously regarded as puny rivals. This attack was carried through on three fronts. First, they took the Glasgow banks to law, a move which did not meet with success. Then they withdrew all credit facilities, again to no avail. Finally, they carried the attack on to the enemies' own ground. For five years one of their agents assiduously presented notes issued by the offending banks (it was the printing of these that annoyed the Edinburgh banks more than anything else) and demanded *specie* in return – again unsuccessful. One very effective counterstroke was to make the demanded payments in silver; in one marathon exercise it took the Glasgow bank 34 laborious days to pay out £2,893 in sixpences. Twice the teller kept back one sixpence to force the agent to count the amount three times!

Soon, in November 1761, Glasgow had its third bank, the Thistle, which was usually regarded as catering for the 'aristocracy'. Once again its financial backing came from the Royal Bank of Scotland!

A fourth bank, the Merchant Banking Company, was launched in 1769. Its particular object was to provide a service for the growing number of small shopkeepers and tradesmen in the city who apparently found the existing three unwelcoming. These 'aristocratic' banks regarded the Merchant Banking Company's arrival with a degree of distaste, and some attempts were made to hinder its activities.

Completely reversing its previous policy, the Royal Bank of Scotland had taken the plunge and finally set up its own branch in the city in September 1783 with David Dale and Robert Scott Moncrieff as joint agents. Despite the increasing activities of the local banks, by the close of the 18th century it was this Glasgow agency and not the local private banks which became the the biggest banking businesses outside England, its discounts in the city amounting to £1,000,000.

In 1785 a small bank was opened by Messrs Andrew, George & Thomson. The only memorable event connected with this bank that has come down to us, apart from its demise in 1793, is that a mahogany chest containing £1,600 in guineas and notes addressed to it was stolen, later to be found, unopened, on a dungheap in the Saltmarket.

But all was not plain sailing in Glasgow banking circles. Distant events, then as now, have a bad habit of intervening from time to time in local affairs, and when Britain declared war on revolutionary France in February 1793, the demand for money was so great throughout the country that both the Glasgow Arms Bank and the Merchants Bank failed in the same year (the former for £113,000), although with the saving grace that each managed to pay their depositors in full.

The last of the city's private banks was formed in 1809, under the name of the Glasgow Bank. Curiously enough, the moving force behind its setting up came from outside the city entirely, from banking circles in Dundee and London. Their financial strength enabled it to start off with the large paid-up capital of £100,000, a considerably greater amount than those ever possessed by the now somewhat quiescent Ship and Thistle. As a result of this generous backing, and also because of its willingness to respond to commercial opportunities, it soon acquired the largest business of any of the Glasgow private banks.

A new type of bank now began to make its appearance in Glasgow. The already established private or provincial banks had on the average about £50,000 of capital and somewhere in the region of a dozen shareholders. The banks which now began to appear on the scene, generally called joint-stock banks, operated at a much higher level, with about eight times the amount of capital and over a hundred shareholders. Between 1830 and 1844 no fewer that four of these joint-stock banks started up in Glasgow – the Union Bank (1830), the Western Bank (1832), the Clydesdale Bank (1838) and the City of Glasgow Bank (1839). Some of these new ventures took over the responsibilities of the older Glasgow banks. In 1836 the Thistle merged with the Union Bank, and in the same year the very first Glasgow bank, the Ship, joined with the Glasgow Bank to form the Glasgow & Ship, which in its turn merged in 1843 with the Union Bank.

The fortunes of all these banks varied widely. Only one of them, the Clydesdale Bank, still has an independent existence. Of the others, the Union Bank, after following a successful course for many years, finally merged with the Bank of Scotland in 1955. The three other banks did little to maintain the prestige of Glasgow banking. The Edinburgh & Glasgow Bank was badly managed and was soon absorbed into the Clydesdale Bank in 1858.

The Western and the City of Glasgow banks both had short but extremely colourful lives, and became well-articulated skeletons in the financial cupboards. During the course of the 19th century the Scottish banking system had shown itself to be in many ways more advanced than the English. In several areas it was a pioneer – in the early adoption of joint-stock banking and of limited liability, the widespread use of notes instead of *specie*, the setting up of a widespread network of numerous branches and the adoption of cash credits (overdrafts), for example. In all this Glasgow showed itself to be the exemplar, and had, indeed, now become the second greatest commercial centre in Britain. This rapid growth, however, brought its perils, including a fair amount of hubris. Soon that apparently inevitable concomitant of the capitalistic system began to show itself, the now all-too-familiar 'boom and bust' cycle.

The first victim was the Western Bank. It became more and more deeply involved in the 1830s and 1840s railway mania and quickly expanded until it soon had over a hundred branches. Then it began to dabble in hair-raising speculative adventures in the Far East and in Latin America, until finally its involvement in the American commercial panic of 1857 brought about its downfall. When its affairs were wound up in 1877 its total liabilities came to over £6,000,000.

The City of Glasgow was equally aggressive in its financial dealings, but its ultimate downfall – and degree of guilt – was so much greater in that it compounded with its financial speculations a considerable amount of fraud. It was commonly regarded as a progressive bank and could point to over 130 branches throughout Scotland as evidence of its good standing. It was, however, deeply involved in complicated dealings in the Far East and North America and, even more ominously, had a very heavy concentration of loans to a few privileged firms and individuals. Everything appeared normal until, suddenly, on 2 October 1878, it closed its doors permanently and went into liquidation. Upon investigation it was found that its total losses amounted to over £6,000,000 and worse still, that it had been endeavouring to conceal this fact by what nowadays might be called 'creative accounting'. In commercial terms its collapse was disastrous, bringing about the fall of many large business concerns; even worse was its effect in terms of ordinary human misery. The fortunes of its shareholders (many of whom had invested life savings, small and large) were almost totally wiped out, for the bank's charter did not limit their liability in any way. Out of a total of 1,819 shareholders only 250 survived solvent. Six of the directors and the industries manager were convicted of criminal fraud – two received 18 months imprisonment, the rest eight months. The repercussions of this lamentable affair were felt throughout Glasgow and the whole of Scotland; not the least of the effects was a prolonged and not unnatural diffidence among Scottish bank managers to become involved in anything which could be labelled speculative.

However, despite these two notable disasters, the last 20 years of the century brought Scottish banking to its peak, a position almost totally due to the flourishing of Glasgow banks and banking. The progress of Glasgow banking over the next hundred years or so is perhaps best demonstrated by the history of the city's sole surviving bank, the Clydesdale. During the 19th century its lending activities involved it in such traditional industries as fishing, farming, cattle-trading, paper-making, flax-spinning, sailcloth manufacture, cotton-spinning and weaving, textile-dyeing and general merchanting. More specialised activities began to attract the bank's attention, one example of which was the rapidly growing warehousing firms such as Wylie and Lochhead. Lending to many new industries such as whisky distilling and railway contracting and running, also grew. The largest loans went to the most rapidly growing business of all – iron manufacturing. Money was also lent to local authorities and to charities, including for instance the Glasgow Barony Parochial Board. The period between 1870 and the end of the First World War was one of great achievement for the city, earning for it the soubriquet of 'The Second City of the Empire', and much of this success was due to the city's banking facilities; but the interwar years of slump and decay brought little comfort to Glasgow's banks for, depending as they did on the staple of west central Scotland, they inevitably shared the effects of the area's industrial decline.

One significant development of this period is worthy of note. In 1918 various mergers of English banks brought into being the Big Five clearing banks with the Midland as the largest. The latter, seeking to extend outside England, began 'affiliating' with various Scottish banks and, in 1920, the Clydesdale was taken over by the Midland. Many people in Glasgow regretted this English connection and the consequent loss of independence but the new, enlarged sphere of activities worked well for the Clydesdale. Interestingly, this English alliance helped ultimately to end one constant source of Scottish financial irritation, the English habit of charging for changing Scottish banknotes – for in 1943 the London banks waived this annoying surcharge, an action which, peculiarly, took a great many years to become common knowledge. In 1950 the Clydesdale became the Clydesdale & North of Scotland Bank Ltd, a cumbersome name which, for the sake of familiarity, was changed back to its original form in 1963. The same year saw the removal of the bank's old coat-of-arms mark, replaced by the well-known symbol formed from the bank's initials. Its sensitively phrased 'affiliation' with the Midland Bank had at least kept it within the United Kingdom. Its purchase by the National Australia Bank in 1987 has weakened its connection with Glasgow to such an extent that it is difficult to avoid the conclusion that, after almost two and a half centuries, Glasgow banking is no more.

One other aspect of banking in Glasgow should not be overlooked. The upheaval of commerce and trade which followed the Napoleonic Wars and their aftermath created a pressing need for some way in which the more humble members of society could store up small nest-eggs to tide them over adversity. The ordinary commercial banks did not want to become involved in small deposits and would not normally accept less than £10 – a huge sum for a working man. So, in 1810, a Dumfriesshire minister started the first savings bank for his parishioners with the express purpose of accepting as deposits any sum no matter how small. Its usefulness was so amply demonstrated that similar banks sprang up all over the country. Glasgow was once again in the forefront and, in 1836, the National Security Savings Bank of Glasgow, formed by the amalgamation of a number of smaller savings banks, began in Hutchesons' Hospital in Ingram Street, later to change its name to the much more familiar Trustee Savings Bank of Glasgow. For over a hundred years it was one of the most influential of all the TSBs in the United Kingdom. When it amalgamated with its neighbours in the 1980s to form the West of Scotland TSB it was the largest

grouping in Scotland, and when it subsequently merged in 1983 to become the TSB Scotland it was the largest of the four regional TSBs. Now a national bank, it has travelled a long way from its origins as the working man's friend.

PRINCIPAL GLASGOW BANKS

Ship Bank merged with Glasgow Bank	1750–1836
Glasgow Arms Bank failed	1750–1793
Thistle Bank merged with Union Bank	1761–1836
Merchants Bank failed	1769–1793
Thomsons Bank failed	1785–1793
Glasgow Bank merged with Ship Bank	1809–1836

Glasgow Union Banking Co
  merged with Royal Bank
  of Scotland
	1830–1955

Western Bank failed	1832–1857
Glasgow & Ship Bank merged with Union Bank	1836–1843
Clydesdale Bank	1838–
City of Glasgow Bank failed	1839–1878
Bank of Glasgow to National Bank of Scotland	1843–1844
Glasgow Banking Co., to Western Bank	1843–1844

Bells

Glasgow was once well-known for its bells. Even as late as the start of the 20th century the absence of personal and private time-keepers was compensated for by a fairly elaborate system of bells. Every morning at 5.30 a.m. the morning or workers' bell was rung, then at 6 p.m. came the evening bell, followed by the curfew bell at the surprisingly late hour of 10 p.m.; each bell was usually rung for about five minutes. Curfew comes from the French *couvre-feu*; the ringing of the curfew bell was a signal for the extinction of all domestic fires at nightfall. When the city's houses were built of wood and thatch, untended fires were particularly dangerous. The need for a strict curfew disappeared when Council regulations required houses to be built of stone and slate. Glasgow's pre-eminence in campanology was even celebrated in four lines of doggerel of somewhat outspoken vigour:

> *Lithgo' for Wells,*
> *Glasgow for Bells,*
> *Falkirk for Beeves,* *
> *Edinburgh for Whores and Thieves.*

The most famous of all the Glasgow bells no longer exists in its original form. In Scotland's Celtic Church each priest called his flock to worship by the ringing of his own hand-bell, and after St Kentigern's death his must have become a much revered holy relic. We can still see a fairly exact depiction of it in the city's coat-of-arms as a square bell made from a hammered metal plate riveted into shape with an open handle attached to the square flat top. St Kentigern's bell had an added sanctity as it was said to have been given to

him by the Pope when the saint visited Rome. Any mention of the original bell is absent from inventories of the Cathedral's treasures so it can be assumed that the bell purporting to be his which made its appearance about the beginning of the 14th century was a pious copy. It was used as the 'Deid Bell', to be rung through the streets for the repose of the souls of the dead. This bell in turn disappeared after the Reformation but came to light again in 1577. By 1612 it was apparently worn out and a new one was made in 1640 – this time a cast bell. Once again it was lost but, most surprisingly, it came to light centuries later in 1867 in the possession of an old woman in Gretna and was returned to the city. It measures 7in at the mouth and bears a relief of the city's arms and the date 1641.

The next most famous bell is undoubtedly the great bell which used to ring from the steeple of the Cathedral. Before the western towers were demolished in the 1840s, it and a smaller companion hung in the north-west tower or campanile. It is thought to have been placed there in compliance with the 1548 will of Archbishop Gavin Dunbar who directed that two bells were to be hung in that tower – the larger one was over 11ft in circumference. About 1593 it was cracked or otherwise damaged and recast by Arthur Allan. At that time the Council treasurer was Marcus Knox who no doubt authorised the payment for the repair. Unfortunately, John McUre in his gossiping history of the city (1738) stated that the bell had been cast in Holland and gifted by Knox, so that when the bell was again recast in 1790 by

Thomas Mears of London these two errors were included in the bell's new inscription. One of its most important functions was to ring the curfew every night at 10p.m. After suffering further damage it was removed from the steeple (where it had hung since the destruction of the campanile) and replaced by a new bell, through the generosity of Major John Garroway of the chemical manufacturers R. & J. Garroway. The new bell was cast by J. C. Wilson, Glasgow bellfounder; it weighs 25 cwt, measures 4ft in diameter and produces the musical note F. It was first rung in October 1896.

Another historic Glasgow bell is the one made for the Tron Church steeple. It was cast in Holland in 1631 and its inscription is of considerable importance as it is the first recorded appearance of the city's arms to be accompanied by the city's full motto: 'LORD, LET GLASGOW FLOVRISCHE THROUGH THE PREACHING OF THY WORD AND PRIASING [sic] THY NAME', 'SOLI DEO GLORIA, MICHAEL BVCERHVYS ME FECIT, ANNO DOMINI 1631', 'FIDES EST EX AUDITUS ET AUDITUS EX VERBO DEI, FAITH COMMES BY HEAING [sic] AND HEARING BY THE WORD OF GOD, ROM, X. 17'.

The fourth Glasgow bell is one which used to hang in the Tolbooth steeple at the Cross, and is the oldest of the city bells. It carries the inscription 'KATHELINA-BEN-IC-GHEGOTEN-VAN-JACOP-WAGHEVNS-INT-JAER-ONS-HEEREN-MCCCCCLIIII' (Catherine, I am cast by Jacob Waghevens in the year of our Lord 1554). As early as the middle of the 15th century a Tolbooth building stood at one corner of Glasgow Cross and sometime in the following century its steeple acquired, probably at second hand, the Waghevens bell. When the new tolbooth was erected in 1626 the old bell was transferred to it, thus involving it in the complicated history of the various bells which have at various times hung in that steeple.

A fifth Glasgow bell is the old Calton Bell. In 1849 the Calton chapel-of-ease (Calton was a small burgh which lay immediately to the east of the city) which had been founded in 1792 was granted the status of a *quoad omnia* church. It looked for a bell befitting its new status and its bigger neighbour kindly gave it one of its old bells. This was another Dutch bell, measuring 2ft 3in across the mouth and weighing 408lb. It bore the inscription 'FLOREAT GLASGUA PRAEDICATIONE EVANGELI [Let Glasgow flourish by preaching the Word]. GERARD KOSTER ME FECIT AMSTELDAMI ANNO 1663'. Its date and provenance identify it as the only one remaining of the peal ordered by the Council and placed in the Tolbooth. It cracked in 1881 but was saved from destruction by the exertions of J. F. S. Gordon, antiquarian and outspoken priest of the episcopal church St Andrews-by-the-Green.

In 1663, just after the Restoration of Charles II and the return of episcopacy to Scotland, the Town Council decided to get a 'paill of belles' from Holland, then famous for bell-casting. At first it was intended to set the new peal in the steeple of the Merchants' House in the Briggait, but when the bells arrived in 1665 the Council changed its mind and installed them in the steeple of the new Tolbooth along with the old 1554 bell. The latter was restricted to striking the hours, but the new peal entertained the citizens with various tunes which were played from two o'clock to three o'clock every day except Saturdays and Sundays.

In 1736 a new set of chimes was installed. Originally consisting of 19 bells (costing £316 from London) which were played by a musician hired by the Council, they soon proved a bad buy. The clockwork was unsatisfactory and, even worse, the bells were out of consort. They were retuned by chiselling and were then augmented by 14 bells from Edinburgh. The new bells, as well as being playable by hand, were also equipped with a clockwork mechanism programmed to play a selection of national airs. Every two hours a different Scottish melody was played:

Sunday – 'Easter Hymn';
Monday – 'Gilderoy';
Tuesday – 'Nancy's to the greenwood gane';
Wednesday – 'Tweedside';
Thursday – 'The lass o' Patie's Mill';
Friday – 'The last time I cam' o'er the muir';
Saturday – 'Roslin Castle'.

By 1816 the clock mechanism had become worn out and Miller & Russell, Glasgow, substituted a new one at a cost of £325, which also played the quarters and the hours.

The new mechanism began to deteriorate and soon only ringing by hand could be allowed. In 1843 the clock itself was replaced but by 1880 the whole set of

chimes was past repair and the Council resolved to install a completely new carillon of 16 bells. When the steeple was cleaned out preparatory to the installation of the new bells, 32 old bells were removed, among them the great bell of 1554, 12 dated 1735 (survivors of the London bells), 14 Edinburgh bells (six dated 1738, the others undated), three of 1843 and two dated 1845.

The new set was cast by J. C. Wilson, Gorbals bellfounder, and cost £1,165. It weighed 4½cwts and encompassed the musical notes G, A, B, B, C, D, E, E, F, F, G, A, B, B, C, D. The bells were hung from light crossbars and connected by stout copper wires to a double row of large keys. The carillon was inaugurated in December 1881; it played at 6 p.m. each day (5 p.m. on Saturdays and 9 a.m. and 1 p.m. on Sundays).

For more than 250 years the Herbert family were the hereditary bell-ringers in the Tolbooth. The last of them, Miss Jessie Herbert, succeeded her uncle about 1940 and played the bells every Hogmanay for some 30 years.

Bowling

The earliest reference to the playing of bowls in Glasgow is in 1595, when the game was forbidden during the Sabbath. The next reference is 1695, when Mungo Cochrane set up one of the city's earliest public bowling greens in the Candleriggs, then on the westernmost edge of the town. It had a long life, disappearing only when the Candleriggs Bazaar took over its site in 1817.

A Society of Bowlers was formed in 1804, with a green behind the Town's Hospital, and by 1817 the Candleriggs green had been replaced by three other public greens. One lay at the top of the High St in Kirk St, another in Hutchesontown, but the best known of the three was the Willowbank or Sauchiehall Green. It was established by William Harley in Blythswood Sq, and, like many others of the early greens, moved fairly frequently. In 1833 it transferred to Elmbank St, then to Willowbank Cres (off Woodlands Rd) in 1859 and finally, in 1897, to Dowanhill (off Byres Rd) where it still flourishes.

The Albany Bowling Club started in 1833 in Stirling Rd. It moved to Glebe St and then to Chatham Pl until, in 1900, its site was taken over by the Glasgow School Board and the club disbanded. The rapid development of the city centre in the 19th century forced many of the early clubs either to disband or relocate, and the second generation of clubs (1850s onwards) were located in the suburbs.

In 1835 the Wellcroft Bowling Club began in Surrey St, Laurieston, moving to Eglinton St in 1851 from where railway construction compelled it to shift in 1876 to Queen's Dr, Crosshill. The year 1836 saw the beginning of the Whitevale

Bowling Club in Whitevale, moving in 1921 to Golfhill. The Bridgeton Bowling Club started up about 1853; it was obliged to disband in 1890 when the School Board acquired the site.

From the middle of the century a proliferation of bowling clubs appeared: Partick Bowling Club (1845); Govan Bowling Club (1847); Hillhead Bowling Club (1849); Kingston Bowling Club (1850); St Rollox Bowling Club (1857); Bellahouston Bowling Club (1858); Cathcart Bowling Club (1889); Giffnock Bowling Club (1895).

Many survived well into the 19th century. In 1936 there were 75 bowling clubs affiliated to the Glasgow Bowling Association and currently the city has 107 clubs, 78 of which are privately operated and 29 in the city parks.

Boys' Brigade

One of the first of modern youth organisations was the brain child of a Glasgow businessman, William Alexander Smith (1854–1914). While involved in running Sunday School classes for children from working-class backgrounds, he recognised the need for an organisation for boys over 12 years of age which would be based on two concepts, discipline and *esprit de corps*, which he hoped would attract such young boys. So, in 1883, with two friends, he set up in a hall in North Woodside Rd the first ever company of what he called The Boys' Brigade. Its tenets were simple and clear – obedience,

punctuality and cleanliness – and he set out to achieve these aims through elementary drill, physical exercises and a close association with a place of worship.

The Brigade's stated object was 'The advancement of Christ's kingdom among boys and the promotion of habits of reverence, discipline, self-respect ['obedience' was added in 1893] and all that tends towards a true Christian manliness'. Its crest was an anchor with the words 'Sure and Steadfast'. Taking into account the background from which many of the Brigade's members were to be drawn, the uniform was kept very simple; worn over ordinary clothes it consisted of a brown leather belt with the BB crest on its buckle, a white haversack over the right shoulder and a small, round, dark blue pill-box cap with two narrow rings of white braid. In the 1970s the pill-box gave way to a blue Terylene 'forage' cap. Officers wore a dark blue civilian suit, a glengarry cap and tan gloves and carried a cane.

The first company consisted of only three officers (Smith being the Captain) and 28 boys, but it was obvious that he had struck a chord for, within a year, a second company was started, to be followed quickly by two more. By 1885 there were five companies; at a meeting held that year the new organisation took its now established form and felt strong enough to venture out as a national institution. Already a company had been formed in Edinburgh and it was now laid down that each locality would have its own brigade with its constituent companies distinguished by running numbers.

By 1886 there were 44 companies with 136 officers and about 2,000 boys. Four of the companies were in England – London, Manchester, Armitage Bridge and Penzance. That same year the Glasgow battalion held its first annual inspection, and by 1887 the movement had spread to New Zealand and the USA. Its extraordinary growth over the succeeding years is well illustrated by its Jubilee parade in 1933 in Glasgow in which 30,000

boys from all over the British Isles and elsewhere took part, and by the 1950s there were in Great Britain about 3,000 companies with an individual membership of over 80,000, while overseas there were almost 20,000 in 30 different countries.

In 1888 Smith gave up his business activities to become the full-time secretary of a movement which was rapidly becoming a British institution. Some criticism was directed against it for what was said to be its strong militaristic spirit as exemplified by its use of dummy rifles in elementary arms drill, a practice which, however, was never insisted on and gradually fell into disuse.

On its 21st birthday the Glasgow battalion was inspected by Lord Baden-Powell and Smith urged him to rewrite a little treatise he had prepared for training soldiers for use by the Brigade. This he did, under the title *Training for Boys*. So great was the interest in the book that in 1908 Baden-Powell was practically forced to set up a movement based on it to which he gave the name The Boy Scouts. As these two youth organisations developed over the years they developed a certain complementary quality – the Boy Scouts came to be thought of as outdoor and comparatively unregimented, while the Boys' Brigade, as befitting its Glasgow origins, exhibited a more urban and disciplined form.

Bridges

The Victoria Bridge, 1851-54, took the place of the old medieval Glasgow Bridge. The tower in the background is all that remains of the Merchants' House in the Bridgegate; it now rises from what was the Fish Market, before becoming the Briggait Centre. (George Oliver)

Until the end of the 18th century the city's single medieval bridge sufficed for all its cross-river transport needs. Glasgow's spreading area and influence then brought about a spate of bridge-building and at the present time the Clyde as it flows through the city is crossed by no less than 14 bridges – four pedestrian, seven general traffic, one motorway and two railway:

c.1450	Glasgow Bridge (afterwards known as the Victoria Bridge)
1772	Jamaica St Bridge
1775	Rutherglen Bridge
1821	Dalmarnock Bridge
1833	South Portland St Bridge (first, pedestrian)
1834	Hutchesontown Bridge (after-wards known as the Albert Bridge)
1855	St Andrews Suspension Bridge (pedestrian)
1870	St Enoch Station Bridge (first)
1878	Central Station Bridge (first)
1901	King's Bridge (first)
1901	Polmadie Bridge (first, pedestrian)
1928	King George V Bridge
1970	Kingston Bridge (motorway)
1988	Bell's Bridge (pedestrian)

Dalmarnock Bridge

This is the furthest east of all the city bridges and joins the Glasgow district of Dalmarnock on the north bank to the former royal burgh of Rutherglen. Its predecessors were two wooden bridges erected in 1821 and 1848. The second of these lasted until 1887; the present structure was opened in

1891. It is a five-span bridge of steel-plate girders resting on granite-faced sandstone piers, and was the first Glasgow bridge to have a perfectly flat road surface.

Rutherglen Bridge

With five arches, and 16ft wide with a pronounced humpback, it was said to have been designed by James Watt after the style of the Glasgow Bridge. It was erected in 1775 in order to join the ancient and royal burgh of Rutherglen more directly with Glasgow; in 1765 the Glasgow Bridge had been closed to carts, to the great inconvenience of the inhabitants of Rutherglen. Its existence changed the name of the settlement at its northern end from Barrowfield to Bridgeton. It cost £1,800, of which sum Rutherglen paid £1,000 to free the bridge from toll charges. It suffered badly from erosion caused by the completion of a weir at Glasgow Green in 1880 and a new three-arch bridge, 60ft wide, and faced with granite, was opened in 1896.

Polmadie Bridge

This pre-stressed concrete bridge (1955, 12ft wide) crosses the river between Glasgow Green and Richmond Park. It replaces a structure put up in 1901 from wood salvaged from a temporary Jamaica St bridge.

King's Bridge

A bridge was erected here (King's Drive to Ballater St) in 1901 with wood from a temporary bridge put up while the Jamaica St Bridge was being built. In 1933 it was replaced by the present concrete and girder five-span bridge, which is 303ft long and 70ft wide.

St Andrews Suspension Bridge

This wrought-iron bridge was opened in 1855 to take the place of a ferry which ran between McNeil St (Hutchesontown) and Glasgow Green and which conveyed workers to and from Calton and Bridgeton. Sometimes called Harvey's Bridge, after Bailie Harvey who was responsible for its erection, it was closed in 1870 but reopened after necessary repairs. It is 220ft long and 13ft wide.

Albert Bridge or Hutchesontown Bridge

The trustees of Hutchesontown, on the south bank of the Clyde, being legally obliged to provide a river crossing, in 1794 engaged John Robertson, a Pollokshaws mason, to build a bridge from Hutchesontown to the foot of the Saltmarket. It had five arches and was 400ft long and 26ft wide, but the foundations proved to be far from adequate and a high flood in 1795 totally destroyed the uncompleted bridge. Eight years later a replacement wooden bridge was built slightly upstream, and in 1829 the foundations of a new bridge were laid. The engineer responsible was Robert Stevenson (grandfather of Robert Louis Stevenson) and the bridge was opened in 1834. It had five arches and a width of 35ft. In 1864 it was discovered that the increased water-flow resulting from the removal of the second weir was scouring the soil covering the bridge's foundations, and four years later it was demolished, with the customary timber replacement until the present Albert Bridge (Saltmarket to Crown St) was opened in 1871. Its cast-iron superstructure stands on granite piers which are founded on huge concrete pillars encased in iron caissons – the first use of this technique in connection with the Glasgow bridges. It has three arches, is 410ft long and 60ft wide.

Glasgow Bridge (also known as Bishop Rae's Bridge, Great Bridge, Old Bridge, Stockwell St Bridge, and now **Victoria Bridge** (Clyde St to Gorbals St)

Traditionally said to have been built by

Bishop Rae *c*.1350 (replacing an earlier wooden structure), it was for some 400 years the city's only cross-river communication (save for fords). It is said that a Lady Lochow bore the expenses of the third arch from the north end; she is also said to have founded a lepers' hospital, St Ninian's, at the south end of the bridge.

The site of the bridge was probably selected in the first place as being the furthest downstream point which the technology of the time could bridge. It had eight stone arches, its roadway was 12ft wide and 415ft long, and it had a pronounced humpback which rose 40ft above low-water level. Its longevity was surprising considering the number and nature of the repairs it underwent. In 1658 the town council ordained that, in order to avoid rutting the surface, the bridge tackmaster was 'not to suffer ony cairtis with wheilleis go alongst the brig untill that the wheilleis be taken off and the boddie of the cairt alon harled [dragged] by the hors'.

In 1671 the southernmost arch collapsed, providentially during the Glasgow Fair when the bridge lacked its normal busy traffic. It was quickly repaired, but by 1758 the old structure was becoming more and more ruinous. In an endeavour to reduce the wear and tear on it the town council, in 1765, placed removable barriers at either end to prevent carts from using the bridge. With a delicate sense of what was proper, they arranged for the posts to be removed to allow the passage of the coaches and chaises of gentlemen. The inhabitants on the south side, particularly those in Rutherglen, protested vigorously, took the council to law, and forced it to repair the weakened structure and to reopen it.

The two northern arches were filled in so as to confine the breadth of the river and to prevent to some extent the constant flooding of the lower parts of the town. In 1776 the bridge was widened on the eastern side by 10ft, and the third northern arch, with the two at the opposite end, was also filled in (leaving only the three central arches open). At the same time the road surface was lowered. The roadway was again widened in 1821 when Thomas Telford added elegant cast-iron footpaths (spanning the old bridge's protruding cutwaters) to increase the width to 34ft – an extraordinary transmogrification of a bridge at least 450 years old!

It was finally and sadly demolished in 1847, to be replaced by the Victoria Bridge, opened in 1854 and now the oldest of the city bridges. Built by James Walker (London), it has five segmental arches and is faced with granite from Kingstown near Dublin. It was the last Glasgow bridge to be built by traditional method of driving wooden piles into the river-bed as supports for the superstructure – all subsequent bridges were founded on large concrete columns constructed on the river-bed by means of enveloping iron caissons.

Carlton Place Suspension Bridge was built (1851) to connect the city proper with Portland St on the south bank. Its graceful curves provide a counterpoint to the solidity of the river's other bridges. (George Oliver)

South Portland St Suspension Bridge

A wooden bridge was erected from Carlton Place about 1833 and proved so serviceable that when it became unsafe in 1846 the heritors of Gorbals erected in its place – and at their own expense – a wrought-iron suspension bridge, the first of its kind in the city. Its ashlar pylons were designed by Alexander Kirkland and the engineering work was carried out by George Martin. It was opened in 1853 and was 410ft long and 15ft wide. At first a small charge of one bawbee or one halfpenny was made for using it, but this was soon discontinued. It seems to have suffered from various defects: shortly after being completed one of the masonry towers split and had to be rebuilt, and later still serious faults were found in some of the iron supporting chains. In 1871 it was largely reconstructed.

Jamaica St Bridge (also known as Glasgow Bridge and Broomielaw Bridge)

As Glasgow continued to grow westwards there was an increasing need for a river-crossing at the west end of the city, and in 1767 the foundation stone of a new bridge (at first known as the Broomielaw Bridge, from its proximity to the Broomielaw Harbour) was laid at the foot of Jamaica St which had been opened up a few years before. Built by John Smeaton to a design of William Mylne of Edinburgh, it was opened in 1772. It was about 500ft long and 32ft wide with seven arches and was deservedly called the 'Bonny Brig'. It had distinctive circular holes (or ox-eyes) through the haunches over the piers which were meant to carry off excess flood waters. Although regarded as spacious for its time it was still old-fashioned enough to have a most awkward humpback, and within a comparatively short time, having quickly proved to be the city's most important bridge, it became incapable of accommodating the rapid increase in its traffic. Even its stability was questioned; to counteract the scouring action of the water-flow a weir had been erected close beside it but this had not been entirely effective.

The decision was made to replace it, and the foundation stone of a new bridge, designed by Thomas Telford, was laid in 1833. Opened in 1836 it was 560ft long and 60ft wide with seven arches. The traffic using it was measured the year it was opened and it was found that in one week in December some 20,826 pedestrians, 253 horse-riders, 160 carriages, 634 carts and 166 wheelbarrows used it. Although its foundations were 10ft deeper that its predecessor, it still suffered from river-scour, it was still too narrow and its arches were found to be too close together for the easy passage of vessels, so once again, in 1894, a replacement was decided on. The first design was for a 100ft-wide, four-arch structure, but such was the public demand for as near a replica of Telford's bridge as possible, that the new bridge was redesigned to have the seven arches of its predecessor, its width was reduced to 80ft, and Telford's granite facings, his balustrades and his copestones were re-used. The 'new' bridge was opened in the last year of the old century and still takes much of the city's north and south-bound traffic. It runs from Jamaica St to Bridge St.

George V Bridge

Opened in 1928 and running from Oswald St to Commerce St, this is a reinforced concrete bridge with an 80ft-wide roadway and a length of 412ft. With a parapet similar to its neighbour, the Jamaica St Bridge, it appears to have three arches but these are, in fact, three disguised spans of concrete box girders. Its height of 18fift above high-water was designed to allow small coasting vessels to pass under it on their way to and from the Broomielaw.

Kingston Bridge. The Western flank of the Inner Ring Road crosses the Clyde on this multi-lane highway. (George Oliver)

Kingston Bridge

A major element in post-war Glasgow's road system, this bridge, besides forming part of the western flank of the the city's Inner Ring Road system, also links the northern and southern parts of the M8 motorway. It took three years to build, cost £6.5 million, and was opened in 1970. It consists of two parallel bridges each 85ft wide and each carrying five lanes of motorway traffic. The total deck structure is 880ft long with a river span of 470ft. Its highest point is 60ft above high-water, thus allowing dredgers to pass under it.

Bell's Bridge

This footbridge was designed and completed in 1988 to join the Scottish Exhibition Centre on the north bank to the site of the Glasgow Garden Festival. It has three spans: one is fixed and the other two are cantilevered about a central pier. This allows the two-span section to pivot around this pier and thus enable vessels to pass.

In addition, two railway bridges cross the Clyde. The St Enoch Station Bridge, located between the Victoria and Albert Bridges, carries four lines of tracks which once took trains into the now demolished St Enoch Station. The present bridge replaced in 1899 a two-track bridge built in 1870, at the opening of the station.

The second railway bridge, closely neighboured by the Jamaica St and George V Bridges, leads north into Central Station. It was built in 1899–1905 when the station was enlarged and reconstructed, and can carry ten tracks. On its east side can be seen the piers of the first bridge, all that is left of its two-track structure, built in 1876–78 and removed 1966–67.

The only major tributary entering the Clyde within the city boundaries is the Kelvin. It flows from the north and marks the old boundary between Glasgow and the former burgh of Patrick. Its bridges are:

Queen Margaret Bridge

The most northerly of the Kelvin's major bridges, it carries Queen Margaret Drive over the river on a skewed concrete arch with a span of 135ft and a width of 80ft. It was built in 1926–29 to a design by the City Engineer, T. P. M. Somers, and is faced with finely finished Corncockle sandstone; its parapet is of polished red Peterhead granite.

Great Western Bridge

A splendid example of late (1889–91) Victorian bridge-building, it crosses the Kelvin on two massive cast-iron arches with a total span of 182ft.

Kelvin Way Bridge

This single-arch red sandstone bridge carries the roadway which passes through the Kelvingrove Park. Designed by the City Engineer, A. B. McDonald, in 1914 it is chiefly remarkable for the four elaborate bronze sculpture groups at the corners of the span which were designed by Paul R. Montford.

Partick Bridge

A single cast-iron arch which crosses the Kelvin at an angle, carrying Dumbarton Road. On its upstream side is visible an earlier freestone three-arched bridge, built in 1800 and now disused.

Buildings

St Vincent St Church. The unorthodox steeple of Alexander 'Greek' Thomson's masterpiece displays his extraordinary ability to combine seemingly conflicting styles and motifs into a commanding whole.
(George Oliver)

With remarkable consistency Glasgow's 17th and 18th-century visitors praised the city's buildings – its stately, well-constructed, stone-built and slate-roofed houses and its broad, straight streets. They seldom ignored its three notable public buildings of an earlier age – the Cathedral, the College (as the University was usually known) and the Tolbooth – but their praise was mainly directed towards the contemporary scene.

The viewpoint of the city's 19th-century visitors suffered a remarkable reversal. For them the contemporary scene was largely ignored and the emphasis was now laid on Glasgow's growing pollution (smoke, smell, sewage and slums). This disregard of the city's built environment continued, surprisingly, well into the 20th century.

Glasgow, whether from ignorance of the past or faith in the future, has never hesitated to demolish and rebuild, and as a consequence very few pre-18th-century buildings now remain – the 12th-century Cathedral, the 15th-century Provand's Lordship, the 17th-century Tolbooth and Merchants' Hospital steeples being notable exceptions.

However, as the Victorian age ceased being merely 'old-fashioned' and instead became the subject of scholarly interest, Glasgow's hitherto neglected examples of Victorian and Edwardian buildings began to attract belated recognition, so that by 1971 Lord Esher was able to say in his *Conservation in Glasgow* that 'Glasgow is now the finest surviving example of a great Victorian city'. Evidence that this recognition is being sustained is clearly seen in the recent burgeoning of books on the city's singular architectural legacy.

Two of Glasgow's architects have achieved more than local fame, even if, like the city's buildings, it has been long in coming. First in date is Alexander 'Greek' Thomson, whose churches and houses combine subtle asymmetries with bold vertical and horizontal contrasts, and whose terraces and warehouses exhibit classical regularity and idiosyncratic detail. The second, Charles Rennie Mackintosh, is a greater and more influential figure, bringing together as he did traditions deriving from Scottish vernacular architecture with innovations which were the forerunners of the Modern style. His magisterial School of Art is now regarded as a seminal work of international importance.

Aikenhead House (1806)
King's Park.
David Hamilton.
Built as a mansion for John Gordon, tobacco merchant, its extensive wings were added by architect David Hamilton in 1826. Until recently it was a municipal museum within the park but was converted into 14 residential flats in 1986.

Buck's Head Building (1862–63)
Corner of Argyle St and Dunlop St.
Alexander Thomson.
An unusual building, it was 'Greek' Thomson's first large commission. Vertical stone pilasters with iron stanchions form an apparently insubstantial curtain wall into which the glazing is directly inserted. It takes its name from the Buck's Head Hotel, the previous building on the site, the mansion of Provost Murdoch.

Ca d'Oro (1872)
Corner of Gordon St and Union St.
John Honeyman.
Built originally as a furniture warehouse in the form of a cast-iron palazzo, and comp-

arable to the Gardner building. Despite the claim that its name comes from the Venetian 'Golden House', it was the name of a restaurant set up in it in 1927. It caught fire in 1987, but has been reconstructed in its original form (without, fortunately, the obtrusive added mansard roof).

Caledonia Rd Church (1856–57)
Caledonia Rd.
Alexander Thomson.
Now only a burnt-out shell on one of Glasgow's many gushet sites, Thomson's first church (and thought by many to be his finest achievement) is an amalgamation of three simple ideas: a tall Lombardic tower and a Greek portico both standing on a broad, deep plinth or podium, and arranged in picturesque asymmetry.

Carlton Place (begun 1802)
Peter Nicholson.
This fine riverfront residential terrace on the south bank of the Clyde was begun in 1802 by Nicholson (who left it unfinished – it was completed by John Baird I). It was designed as the prestigious showpiece of John Laurie's failed attempt to create a high-class residential area south of the river and was named after the Prince Regent's London dwelling. Laurieston House, which is the main centre feature of the terrace, was the joint dwellings of the two brothers, John and David Laurie. It was the first time a Glasgow street had been designed as a single architectural concept.

City Chambers (1883–88)
George Square.
William Young.
Intended to confirm the city's burgeoning importance and wealth at the end of the century, the new City Chambers was built to the award-winning design of a young London Scot. The grandeur of the main west façade, looming above the square and dominated by its elaborately sculptured

Jubilee Pediment, is well matched by the opulence of its interior, with its polished granites, ornate staircases of figured marble and alabaster, colourful mosaics, mahogany-panelled rooms and its vast Banqueting Hall decorated with murals by many of the city's most distinguished artists.

Country Buildings, Wilson St, c.1850. Occupying an entire block in the heart of the Merchant City, this complicated structure housed the Sheriff Courts, the Municipal Buildings, the County Offices and the Merchants' House. The last of these to vacate the building for other premises was the Sheriff Court, and it now awaits a new occupier. As so often in Glasgow the vista up Hutcheson St (on the left) is closed by a public building, appropriately in this case by Hutchesons' Hospital.
(Robert Carrick, c.1852, Mitchell Library)

County Buildings and Courthouse (begun 1844)
40–50 Wilson St.
William Clarke and George Bell.
A large, Greek-style building, filling an entire street block and with a truly monumental south-facing portico. The first part of it was built in 1841 to provide accommodation for the county offices and the Sheriff Court (fronting Wilson St) along with the Merchants' House. The façade of the latter was on the west face of the building, looking along Garth St towards its historic counterpart, the Trades' Hall in Glassford St (the Merchants' House moved to George Square in the 1870s). In 1868–71 an addition was built at the north end of the block, fronting on Ingram St, to house the municipal offices (removed from the foot of

the Saltmarket) and an extension on the east side facing Brunswick St for additional court accommodation. In 1892 when the City Chambers moved to its new quarters in George Square the area it vacated was rebuilt as part of the courts. Since the departure of the Sheriff Court to south of the river, there have been various proposals for its use, including a museum of fashion.

Crown Arcade (*c*. 1819)
31 Virginia St.
Architect unknown.
Designed as the Tobacco Exchange, and later the Sugar Exchange, the Arcade still retains its original and complicated layout of three tiers of pilastered galleries and glass roof.

Customs House (1840)
298 Clyde St.
John Taylor, customs officer.
Its neat Greek Doric design is complemented by an elaborate and finely sculptured coat-of-arms on the roof above the entrance. Considering the city's commercial eminence it is surprisingly small. It is now the Procurator Fiscal's Office.

David Livingston Tower (1963)
94/168 George St.
Covell, Matthew and Partners.
Part of Strathclyde University; an interesting, complex arrangement of medium height groups in orange framing, punctuated by an irregular 17-storey tower in dark green walling.

The Double Villa (1856)
25/25a Mansionhouse Drive.
Alexander Thomson.
By ingeniously combining two fairly small houses into one architectural unit, 'Greek' Thomson gave himself sufficient scope to set out fully his subtle asymmetrical design.

Fish Market (1873)
64–76 Clyde St.
William Clarke and George Bell.
Appropriately situated a few hundred yards from the river, it was extended in 1886 and again in 1903, in the process enveloping the old steeple of the Merchants' Hall. It is in the French Empire style and particularly noticeable are the two pairs of winged seahorses above its twin arches. When the market moved to Blochairn in 1977 the building was imaginatively refurbished (1985–1986) as the Briggait Shopping Market, but it never attracted sufficient visitors to make it a success.

A. Gardner & Sons Warehouse (1855–56)
36 Jamaica St.
John Baird, senior.
'The Iron Building' (now Martin & Frost) has been described as 'one of the great landmarks of Western architectural history' and 'one of the most remarkable cast-iron warehouses of its date anywhere in Britain'. Baird erected the structural frame by using a combination of wrought- and cast-iron beams and stanchions made by Robert McConnell, iron-founder. The use of iron enabled the span of these beams to be exceptional for their time; between them were inserted delicately proportioned windows, the whole being virtually a wall of glass.

Glasgow School of Art (1897–99, 1907–9)
167 Renfrew St.
Charles Rennie Mackintosh.
Despite the popular recognition awarded to the Cathedral, the Tolbooth and Glasgow University as architectural symbols of Glasgow, there can be no doubt that the School of Art is the city's architectural crown and a seminal masterpiece. The School's Head, Fra Newberry, laid down a number of exacting conditions regarding the requirements for a brand new School of Art (including a cost limit of £21,000). Many of the city's leading architects entering the architectural competition; the commission went to Mackintosh's design as it matched most closely these demanding requirements. The financial exigencies meant that the building went up in two parts – first from the east gable to the main entrance and afterwards from the entrance to the west gable. It amply illustrates all those features for which Mackintosh has become famous – the masterly use of Scottish vernacular forms, the foreshadowing of the Modern Movement, the innovative arrangements of the interior space and its subtle mirroring in the external walls, and the minute attention paid to every use of wood, stone, glass and iron throughout the building. Its position on the southern slope of one of the city's ubiquitous drumlins (very similar to 'Greek' Thomson's St Vincent St Church) gives it the commanding site it deserves.

Glasgow University (1866–70)
Gilmorehill.
Sir George Gilbert Scott.
By the middle of the 19th century much of old Glasgow had become a slum. The University's High St site was part of it, and since the early 1840s the University had been looking westwards for a new location. In 1863 it sold its old site to the North British Railway Co for £10,000 and bought the lands of Gilmorehill, in the fashionable west end, for £65,000 in 1865. Instead of setting up the expected architectural competition the University offered the commission to an English architect, Sir George Gilbert Scott, to the intense chagrin of the local architectural establishment – in particular Alexander 'Greek' Thomson, who detested Sir George's favourite style, the Gothic.

Work began on the Gilmorehill site in

1866 and was completed in time for the University to move in 1870. Basically it consists of two east and west courtyards united by a central tower, which serves as a ventilation duct. For many Glaswegians it is one part of the city's architectural triumvirate, along with the Cathedral and the Tolbooth, with its 600ft south-facing façade dominating the skyline above the valley of the River Kelvin. Sir George called its style one 'which I may call my own invention', and which is usually referred to as 'Scottish Gothic'. He intended the central tower to be capped by a lead-covered solid spire but it was completed in 1887–91 (after his death) by his son who added the kenspeckle open-work spire.

Two relics of the Old College are incorporated into the Gilmorehill building – the Lion and Unicorn Staircase (William Riddell, 1690) in the west courtyard, and the Pearce Lodge (1887–88) at the north-east corner, contrived from fragments saved from the façade of the old High St building (commemorating Sir William Pearce of the Fairfield Shipbuilding Co).

Grosvenor Terrace (1855)
Great Western Rd.
J. C. Rochead.
Based on the lines of a Venetian palace, this extended terrace is one of the city's architectural marvels. Three long storeys of repetitive semicircular-headed windows are closed at either end by slightly advanced end bays. The Grosvenor Hotel at the east end of the terrace was badly damaged by fire in 1978, but has been successfully rebuilt by using glass-reinforced concrete details taken from the originals.

Hatrack Building (1899–1902)
142a/144 St Vincent St.
James Salmon II.

One of Glasgow's most unusual pieces of architecture, involving the imposition of a ten storey building on a plot only 29ft 6in wide. It is basically a façade formed of three intricately interlocking glazed bays upheld by an exiguous framework of red sandstone. At one time it was surmounted by a series of projecting finials, from which it derived its nickname.

Hutchesons' Hall (1802–5)
158 Ingram St.
David Hamilton.
Another *point de vue* facing south down Hutcheson St, it replaced an older building located on the north side of the Trongate, demolished when Hutcheson St was opened up. It is a clever amalgam of 18th-century French, English baroque and late Adam styles. The first-floor hall was largely the work of John Baird in 1876.

George and Thomas Hutcheson were two 17th-century philanthropic Glasgow lawyers who left funds in trust to build a hospice for impoverished old men and a school for poor boys – another name for the building was Hutcheson's Hospital. Two statues of the brothers, carved by James Colquhoun in 1649, were taken from the tower of the old building to stand in alcoves on the Hall's façade.

Alexander 'Greek' Thomson's Grecian Buildings (1865) in Sauchiehall St. In the left background is the Dental Hospital, and to the right the Mackintosh School of Architecture. (George Oliver)

Justiciary Court House (1809–14)
Saltmarket.
William Stark.
When the accommodation afforded by the old Tolbooth at the Cross became inadequate, the town council, the Courts and the Jail moved south to a new building at the foot of the Saltmarket. The austere Greek Doric style (its first appearance in Glasgow) was in complete contrast to the other contemporary public buildings in the city. It was largely reconstructed by J. H. Craigie in 1913.

Kelvingrove Art Gallery and Museum (1901)
Kelvingrove Park.
Sir J. W. Simpson and Milner Allen.
Despite local submissions to the architectural competition, the commission to build this gallery went to two English architects – a decision which aroused considerable local feeling. Despite conforming to the city's penchant for red sandstone, its incredible architectural exuberance (Spanish Baroque) has no parallel among the city's other buildings. Its construction was partly financed by the profits from the International Exhibition of 1888. The main entrance faces north across the Kelvin valley, but the most used entrance is off Sauchiehall St, a situation which has given rise to one of the most persistent of the city's urban myths - i.e. that the architect committed suicide when he discovered that his building had been built the wrong way round!

Kirklee Terrace (1845–64)
Great Western Rd.
Charles Wilson.
Originally known as Windsor Terrace, it was designed in an Italianate style by Charles Wilson, a pupil of David Hamilton, and was the first of Great Western Road's famous terraces, built to provide suitable residences for the city's commercial, manufacturing and professional middle classes.

The Knowe (*c*.1851–53)
301 Albert Drive.
Alexander Thomson.
This is one of Alexander 'Greek' Thomson's earliest houses and illustrates several of his well-known architectural characteristics such as its square tower and low-pitched roof, the main roofs similarly pitched and with overhanging eaves, and the overall asymmetrical design. However, it lacks his later emphasis on continuous fenestration.

Langside Halls (1847)
1 Langside Avenue.
John Gilbert Graham.
Unusually, this building began life as the National Bank of Scotland at 57 Queen St. Its Palladian style is richly ornamented with swags of fruit, bearded faces on the keystones, tasteful finials and the Royal Arms on the roof, flanked by Peace and Plenty. In 1901 it was moved stone by stone to its present site and re-erected as a suite of halls by A. B. McDonald, City Engineer, in 1902–3.

Lion Chambers (1905)
170/172 Hope St.
James Salmon II and John Gaff Gillespie.
The Chambers rise for 90ft from a site only 33ft by 46ft. Its 4in thick walls and floors are of reinforced concrete, one of the earliest uses in Scotland of the Hennebique system. The building is supported on 21 continuous columns varying in width from 13in to 8in.

Merchants' Steeple (1665)
Bridgegate.
The steeple, which now protrudes from the old Fish Market, is all that remains of the Merchants' Hall built in 1659. The tower was erected in 1665 and has been ascribed, without foundation, to Sir William Bruce.

The style is Gothic, with Renaissance touches in the upper parts.

Park Circus (1855–63)
Charles Wilson.

Situated on a piece of ground which rises gently from Charing Cross westwards, culminating in a high-standing bluff overlooking Kelvingrove Park and the valley of the Kelvin, with the University of Glasgow on the opposite height. The architecture, mainly in the form of French-roofed terraces which follow the area's contour lines, and the layout are unsurpassed in the city (and perhaps elsewhere). Its skyline is dramatised by the three towers of Trinity College (formerly the Free Church College, designed and built by Charles Wilson in 1856–61) now converted into flats, and the single tower of J. T. Rochead's Park Church (1858) – the rest of the church was demolished in 1968.

Pollok House (1747–52)
Pollok Park, Pollokshaws.
William Adam?

The Maxwell family of Pollok can be traced back to the 13th century when they had two fortified dwellings in the area. Pollok House, on the banks of the White Cart, is said to have been built from designs made by William Adam, senior, for Sir John Maxwell, the second baronet. The actual building work began just before Adam's death in 1747, and was completed by his son in 1752, although it is not known if he worked exactly to his father's designs. The building was added to extensively, mainly in the 19th century, to provide accommodation for the large library and collection of master paintings acquired by the ninth baronet. It is approached by an elegant 18th-century bridge across the Cart.

Provan Hall (15th century)
Auchinlea Rd, Garthamlock.

The Hall stands in all that is left of the lands of the Prebendary of Lanark (a member of the Chapter of Glasgow Cathedral), and would have been his country house. The northern part dates from the late 15th century and faces, across a medieval walled courtyard (with a gateway bearing the date 1647), an 18th-century dwelling-house. When it passed from ecclesiastical ownership in 1565 it was bought and then sold by the burgh, eventually passing back into private ownership in 1778, where it remained until 1938 when it was sold to the National Trust for Scotland. The Trust leases it to the district council who maintain a small museum in it.

Renfield St Stephens Church (1849–52)
256 Bath St.
J. T. Emmett, London.

One of the few city churches still thriving. It was the first example in Glasgow of 'Tractarian' Gothic, and the first and most elegant of the tall church spires which once dominated the skyline of central Glasgow. It was formerly known as St Matthew Blythswood Church.

Royal Bank of Scotland (1) (1827)
Royal Exchange Square.
Archibald Elliot.

The bank moved to this site in 1827 after vacating the Cunninghame mansion. The exterior is a pure Greek style; the interior has been refashioned several times. It is linked to the other buildings on the west side of the square by two triumphal arches, which provide pedestrian access to Buchanan St.

Royal Bank of Scotland (2) (1930)
92–98 West George St.
James Miller.

A superb neo-classical building – tall, slender and white with almost no decoration, it achieves its effect by scrupulous attention to proportion and fine craftsmanship.

Royal Scottish Academy of Music and Drama (1982–88)
Renfrew St.
Sir Leslie Martin.

The RSAMD's thorough use of brick is by no means in keeping with the Scottish preference for stone, but its monumental aspect is more than solid enough. Its chief feature is the deep, continuous and bevelled colonnade which runs in front of both the Renfrew St and Hope St façades, and its grand staired entrance.

St Andrew's Parish Church (1739–56)
St Andrews Square.
Mungo Naismith, mason, to a design of Allan Dreghorn, Glasgow merchant and amateur architect.

In order to demonstrate his belief in its safety, Naismith was said to have slept under the portico after its centring was removed. The oldest church in the city after the Cathedral. It has been described as the finest church of its generation in Scotland, and is the only surviving relic which fully displays the taste and style of Glasgow's 18th-century tobacco lords. The style is based on James Gibb's St Martin's-in-the-Fields, London, albeit on a smaller scale, and its interior amply matches its exterior in opulence and grandeur. Its future is uncertain but it has been proposed to use it as a joint church and arts centre. The building's situation is an early example of the Glasgow habit of surrounding large pieces of architecture with a residential square.

St Andrew's RC Cathedral (1814–17)
172 Clyde St.
James Gillespie Graham.

Built as a chapel for Glasgow's growing Irish Catholic population, the church marked the significant introduction into the city's architectural styles of revival Gothic. It became a cathedral in 1889, when its interior was upgraded by Pugin & Pugin. It is said that the reason for the huge cost of £16,000 was partly due to the then unfamiliar style and construction.

St Andrew's-by-the-Green (1750–51)
33 Turnbull St. (the north edge of Glasgow Green)
William Paull and Andrew Hunter, masons, and Thomas Thomson, wright.

It is the oldest surviving Episcopal church in Scotland, and was known as the 'English Church' in its early years. A rectangular box with pediments on each façade, it is surrounded by a tiny burying-ground. It was nicknamed the 'Whistlin' Kirk' because of its organ (by Donaldson of York, 1795, and transferred from the Cathedral in 1812) – at that time organs were not allowed in Presbyterian churches. For his part in building it, Hunter, who belonged to one of the Seceding churches, was excommunicated.

No longer a church, its future was threatened because it lay in the track of the proposed east flank of the Inner Ring Road; in 1988 it was converted to office use.

St Andrew's Halls (1873–77)
Granville St.
James Sellars.
The Halls were financed by a public company in response to the need for hall accommodation in the west end; financial problems forced the company to sell out to Glasgow Corporation. The building takes the form of a massive and powerful classical façade with four immense sculptured groups by John Mossman. The Halls were totally gutted by fire in 1962, leaving only the Granville St façade intact. This was incorporated into an extension of the Mitchell Library (which occupies the eastern half of the island site) which, as well as housing the major part of the library, contains the Mitchell Theatre and the James Moir Hall.

St David's (Ramshorn) Church (1824–26)
98 Ingram St.
Thomas Rickman (with the assistance of James Cleland, Superintendent of Public Works).
It replaced a previous church on the same site, built in 1720 to accommodate the western movement of the city's merchants. In

Early English Gothic, it is particularly high and narrow, mainly because Cleland insisted on a crypt. As with so many Glasgow public buildings, it stands as a focal point at the north end of the Candleriggs. It is now the property of Strathclyde University.

St Enoch Underground Station (1896)
St Enoch's Square.
James Miller.
Like a lost stranger this little essay in red sandstone, a fanciful blend of Baronial and Jacobean influences is dominated by the enormous bulk of the St Enoch Centre and other, older, commercial buildings. Formerly the surprising entrance to the city's subway, it was temporarily suspended above the gaping hole caused by the reconstruction of its associated station, and now serves as a bijou city travel information centre.

St George's Tron (1807–9)
165 Buchanan St.
William Stark.
It occupies an island site in Mandela Place, affording a *point de vue* looking west along George St. The upper parts seem to have been based on Wren, the lower portion on Hawksmoor. The church is mainly a magnificent façade, and the actual church building is distinctly meagre. The four obelisks around the tower should have been gigantic statues but there was not enough money.

St Jude's House (1838–39)
278 West George St.
John Stephen.
Built as a Scottish Episcopal church, it later became St Jude's Free Presbyterian Church, and since 1975 offers itself as office accommodation. Its chief feature is a very large 'battered' door inserted into a tall Greek pylon (reminiscent of 'Greek' Thomson) which was originally crowned with a miniature version of the Lysicrates monument (removed in the 1960s).

An extraordinary confrontation of architecture, ranging from the bijou Greek-style Unitarian Church on the left (demolished), by way of the bravura of 'Greek' Thomson's St Vincent St Church to the modern geometrical severity of Heron House (c.1971). (George Oliver)

Sheriff Court of Glasgow and Strathkelvin (1980–86)
Gorbals St.
Keppie, Henderson and Partners.
A riverside building, its dour and fortress-like exterior belies the many-faceted division of its interior with its numerous galleries and bridges producing surprising vistas.

The Royal Exchange building, Queen St, began as the 18th-century town-house of Cunninghame of Lainshaw, a wealthy tobacco lord, then became the Royal Bank of Scotland's Glasgow branch, and in 1832 opened as the Royal Exchange after many alterations inside and out (including the superb portico) by the architect David Hamilton. Until recently it housed the Glasgow District's Stirling's Library. (George Oliver)

St Vincent St Church (1857–59)
265 St Vincent St.
Alexander Thomson.
Built on a drumlin site which slopes steeply to the south, this church is composed essentially of a rearrangement of the same elements found in the Caledonia Rd church – a Greek temple, a tall, asymmetrically placed tower, and a massive plinth – and makes full use of its commanding position. Unlike the plain tower of the previous church, this one is an exotic combination of Egyptian, Greek and Roman motifs (some even see an Indian influence), and the astounding overall effect defies criticism. With the destruction of his Queens Park church and the vandalism of his Caledonia Rd church, this now represents Thomson's only piece of ecclesiastical architecture of European standing.

Stirling's Library
Royal Exchange Square.
This building is an example of a peculiarly Glasgow architectural style – locating a prestigious building in the centre of a residential square. Here the building came first, in the form of the magnificent town-house of William Cunninghame of Lainshaw, rich tobacco lord, built in 1778 from an unattributed design. It was bought in 1817 by the Royal Bank of Scotland; when the bank moved to new premises on the west of the square, it was largely reconstructed (1827–32) as the Royal Exchange by David Hamilton. He added a huge double portico of Corinthian pillars to the Queen St façade, a cupola above, and a lofty newsroom hall to the rear of the old house (previously given over to gardens) which is probably Glasgow's greatest early 19th-century interior. Another prevalent

Glasgow architectural feature of the building is its position as the focus of the vista looking west along Ingram St. A mansard storey was added in 1880, which housed the city's first telephone exchange. In 1954 Glasgow District Libraries took it over, converting it to accommodate Stirling's Library when it had to vacate its premises in Miller St. It has been proposed that it should now become the city's gallery of contemporary art.

Stock Exchange (1875–77)
Buchanan St.
John Burnet senior.
This is a fantastic exercise in secular Gothic (early French) of which there is very little in Glasgow. The interior was removed in 1969–71 and rebuilt as office accommodation.

Templeton's Carpet Factory (1889)
Glasgow Green.
William Leiper.
One of the city's most exotic buildings, its glowing façade facing the Green is a curtainwall of multicoloured bricks in an elaborated design modelled on the Venetian Doge's Palace. Lack of agreement between the architect and the engineer as to how the façade should be pinned to the main structure behind it caused it to collapse, but it was successfully rebuilt in 1892. The factory was converted to the Templeton Business Centre in 1984.

Trades' Hall (1791–94)
85 Glassford St.
Robert Adam.
Built for the Trades' House, the federation of Glasgow's 14 trades, it is Palladian in style and very characteristic of Adam's best work. It was designed to face east down Garth St. It is Glasgow's only surviving Adam building, his other major work, the Royal Infirmary, having been demolished before the First World War. The interior

was extensively remodelled in the late 19th and 20th centuries.

Tron Steeple (*c.* 1593)
Trongate.
The building takes its name from the tron or public weigh-beam which was kept in it. The tower dates from *c.* 1593 and the steeple from 1630–36; this is all that is left of the original Tron Church which began in 1484 as the Collegiate Church of St Mary and St Anne and was converted to a burgh kirk in 1586. The church itself was destroyed in 1793 by a fire started by vandals, and was later rebuilt in the form of a nondescript box by James Adam, south and independent of the steeple. In 1855, in order to provide through pedestrian access, ground arches designed by John Carrick were inserted in the steeple.

Western Club (1839–42)
147 Buchanan St.
David and James Hamilton.
A good example of David Hamilton's later experimental style and an early appearance of the Italianate in Glasgow – a true palazzo. In 1968–72 its palatial interior was reconstructed to suit it for office accommodation. The fine lines of its exterior have been obscured by a thick 'protective' coating.

See also HOUSING
PROVAND'S LORDSHIP
TENEMENTS
TOLBOOTH
TONTINE

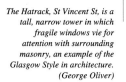
The Hatrack, St Vincent St, is a tall, narrow tower in which fragile windows vie for attention with surrounding masonry, an example of the Glasgow Style in architecture. (George Oliver)

Burgesses

The inhabitants of early Glasgow were divided into two classes, the burgesses or freemen and the unfreemen or serfs. In time the state of servitude of the second category was forgotten, but for many centuries the day-to-day government of the burgh was in the hands of the first category. In the beginning the burghal qualification was the ownership of one rood of land within the burgh, which had to be built upon within one year. Women were not admitted to the ranks of burgesses but widows enjoyed certain rights to their husbands' privileges.

The duties of the burgesses were essentially two: to 'watch and ward', that is, to guard the town against external attack or internal disorder; and to bear their share of taxation. Admission was usually by payment of what was for the time a large sum of money. This payment was reduced if the applicant was 'near hand', that is, the son or son-in-law of a burgess, and increased if the applicant was 'far hand', not so related. The behaviour of the burgh and all those in it was ordered by the burgesses for it was they who formed the self-electing Town Council, a state of affairs which continued until the reform of local government in Scotland in 1833. At the beginning of the 19th century there was estimated to be about 5,000 burgesses in the city.

The power to create burgesses rested in the hands of the Town Council and was jealously guarded. Within the burgess rank there were two classes – merchants (traders, shopkeepers, etc) and craftsmen (wrights, tailors, etc), and whereas merchants only required entry on the roll,

craftsmen had additionally to have served an apprenticeship and to be members of one of the city's 14 incorporated trades. After the establishment in 1605 of a guild which included both merchants and craftsmen, the customary description on a ticket read that so-and-so was a burgess and a guild brother.

With the passage of time the main reason for being a burgess was to qualify for admission to one of the incorporations, and, until the late 19th century, to become a member of the Town Council. The Glasgow burgess oath was involved in the creation of two of the main branches of the Secession Church. The oath required intending burgesses to pledge themselves to uphold the religion by law established, and exception was taken by many to this intrusion by the state into affairs of the church; the Secession Church split into two fractions, the 'Burghers' and the 'Anti-Burghers'. In 1819 the Glasgow magistrates cut the Gordian knot by deleting the offending statement from the Glasgow oath.

From early times it became customary to admit gratis to the burgess roll persons whom the municipality wished to honour. Visiting noblemen (and their chief servants), clergymen, army officers and politicians were the usual recipients of this honour, and the custom still continues. Sometimes called the Freedom of the City, it of course confers no special privileges whatsoever. The largest body of such honorary burgesses was created after the Boer War when all returning soldiers from the city were placed on the roll.

The wide range of recipients can be gauged by a few random names – Edward

Jenner (discoverer of smallpox vaccination), Richard Cobden (19th-century
politician), David Livingstone, Gladstone,
Disraeli, Lord Kelvin, Sir Thomas Lipton,
Henri Poincaré (mathematician), Edward
VIII (when Prince of Wales) and George VI
(when Duke of York).

The legal necessity to become a
burgess for the purpose of carrying on a
business or trade began to fall into desue-
tude at the beginning of the 19th century
and in 1846 the Burgh Trading Act
removed the legal obligation altogether.
After that date both the Merchants House
and the Trades House became in essence
philanthropic institutions, although membership of both these bodies still requires
the possession of a 'burgess ticket'.

See also MUNICIPALITY

Robert Burns in Glasgow

Burns's links with Glasgow, either direct
or indirect, were few and of little
importance – the city which brought him
fame and fortune was Edinburgh.

In June 1787 Burns went north on a
jaunt through the West Highlands and he
seems to have journeyed by way of
Glasgow, meeting there George Grierson, a
Glasgow medical man. Grierson, who had
subscribed for 36 copies of the Kilmarnock
edition of Burns's poems (by far the largest
Glasgow subscription), accompanied the
poet on the trip and left a manuscript
account of it, *Hints respecting Burns the
Ayrshire Poet*. He became a friend of Burns
and was said to have had an extensive
correspondence with him. This correspondence came into the hands of John Reid
in Kingston (a district of Glasgow near the
river). Unfortunately, when the Clyde rose
in 1831, the collection was destroyed by
the flood waters. According to his sister
Isobel, Burns bought several bolts of silk
on this visit which he sent back to his
mother and sisters to have made into 'a
bonnet and a cloak to each'. The same
month he wrote asking Creech, his
Edinburgh publisher, to send 50 copies of
the second edition of his poems to John
Smith, one of Glasgow's leading book-
sellers (in all there were 133 Glasgow subscribers). In September of that same year
he mentioned in a letter that his famous
autobiographical letter to another Glasgow
doctor, Dr James Moore, had been 'forgot
among other papers at Glasgow on my way
to Edinburgh'.

His actual recorded visits to the city
were usually overnight stays while going to
and from the capital city. The earliest of
these was in 1788, during which year he
seems to have passed through the city
several times. In February he wrote to
Captain Richard Brown saying that he
hoped to meet him in Glasgow on his way
home from Edinburgh, and informing him
that he would be staying at George Duthie's
Black Bull Inn in Argyle St. (There is a
plaque attached to the wall of Marks &
Spencer in Argyle St which commemorates

this visit.) In a March letter he mentioned that he proposed setting out from Edinburgh for Mauchline by way of Glasgow. The same month he apologised to Brown for not having obtained a copy of 'the Directory' (presumably Jones's Glasgow Directory, published the previous year) while in Glasgow. Later that same year he picked up a packet of books for Mrs Agnes (Nancy) Maclehose in Edinburgh from Dunlop & Wilson, booksellers in the Trongate. Then in a letter to William Cruikshank he said that he had tracked down in Glasgow the cocoa the former was so partial to and had sent off a supply by the carrier. Also during 1788 he placed another order with the same Glasgow silk-merchant, Robert McIndoe, Horn's Land, off Virginia St, for 15 yards of his finest black lutestring silk, this time as a present for his wife, Jean Armour, at a cost of over four pounds.

There is a completely unsubstantiated story – or rather myth – of Burns coming to Glasgow to have his first collection of poems printed in the city. This account says that he came to Glasgow in the spring of 1786 with his poems in his pocket and a letter of introduction to William Reid, resident poet of the Duck Club of Partick,

then an apprentice with Dunlop & Wilson, city printers and publishers, and later a partner in Brash & Reid, well-known Glasgow publishers, printers and book-sellers. Nothing came of the visit, it is said, except for some exchange of letters between Reid and the poet.

Elizabeth Burns, the poet's illegitimate daughter by Annie Park, married a Pollok-shaws weaver, John Thomson, in 1808. She died in 1873, having been a widow for four years, and was buried beside her husband in the old Vennel Burying Ground.

Mrs Nancy Maclehose (1759–1841), the grass widow with whom Burns enjoyed a singular epistolary passion under the respective pseudonyms of Clarinda and Sylvander in Edinburgh in 1787, was the daughter of Andrew Craig, a prominent Glasgow surgeon; at the age of 15, she had been toasted by the members of the Hodge Podge Club, one of the city's many convivial 18th-century clubs, as 'pretty Miss Nancy'. After separation from her Glasgow lawyer husband, her straitened circumstances were alleviated by two small annuities from the Glasgow Royal Faculty of Physicians and Surgeons and by the Glasgow Royal Faculty of Procurators.

Burying-Grounds

Within the boundaries of present-day Glasgow over 40 burying-grounds can be traced. They fall roughly into three categories: (1) those associated with establishments of the national church (and its sects); (2) those which accommodated members of other branches of the Christian faith; and (3) those set up by private companies. Over the years most of the extant grounds exemplifying these three categories have been taken over by the Glasgow District Council's Parks and

Recreation Department, Cemeteries and Crematoria.

For countless centuries the dead were buried in the grounds associated with the church parishes in which they had lived, and this method proved sufficient until the combined effects of the industrial and agricultural revolutions brought about a vast increase in the urban population. As late as the 1830s Glasgow's parish burying-grounds, some 16 in number, could just cope. Even then, in 1830, there were over 1,700 interments in the High Church burying-ground and over 5,000 people were dying each year.

For many, many years the only burying-ground in Glasgow was the historic one which lay on the south side of the Cathedral or High Kirk, sloping down to the Molendinar Burn. Legend has it that it had been consecrated in the 4th century by St Ninian himself. In its present state it consists of a large number of flat, almost totally illegible tombstones, with a number of tombs in various states of ruin round the boundary walls. One interesting tomb is that of Dr Peter Lowe, who was responsible for setting up Glasgow's Faculty of Physicians and Surgeons, c.1612. In addition, the Cathedral interior contains many plaques and inscriptions indicating the last resting places of many of the city's most eminent citizens. In 1801 and 1832 land was laid out for burial purposes to the north of the Cathedral. The District Council took it over in two stages, in 1914 and 1958.

One unusual burying-ground associated with the Cathedral was that belonging to the old Barony Kirk (which used to meet in the Cathedral crypt). Moving out of the crypt in 1798, the congregation filled it with earth and used it as a burying-ground until 1835.

Another burying-ground of an early date was Blackfriars (or College) Church which was situated in the grounds of the old College in High St, and was demolished after the College moved to Gilmorehill in 1870.

From time to time, excavations close to or on the sites of churches long gone have given evidence of old and forgotten burying-grounds. For instance, when the Saracen's Head Inn in the Gallowgate was being built in 1755, many human remains were found. Similarly, excavations in Howard St (close to the vanished St Enoch's Church) brought to light many skeletons. No doubt many more lie unseen and forgotten below present-day Glasgow.

There were five other long-established parish churches with burying-grounds which lay outside old Glasgow – Govan Church, Cathcart Old Church, Rutherglen Church, Shettleston Church and Tollcross Church – which now lie within the city boundaries.

In 1719 a new burying-ground was opened up on the north side of Back Cow Loan (now Ingram St) and a new church added to it the following year. At first called the North West Church, it later became known as St David's (Ramshorn). The ground was initially reserved for Glasgow merchants, and although this distinction was soon removed, it remained Glasgow's most fashionable burying-ground throughout the last half of the 18th century and the first half of the 19th, with many members of the city's mercantile aristocracy finding their last resting-place there. One singularity of it is that it holds the body of Pierre L'Angelier, the unfortunate lover of Madeleine Smith who was tried for murdering him with arsenic, and escaped by the Scottish verdict of 'Not Proven'. Another is the presence on the pavement in front of the church of the inscribed initials AFRF. When Ingram St was widened, part of the front of the burying-ground was taken over, and the initials indicate the lair of Robert and Andrew Foulis, two eminent Glasgow printers and publishers at the end of the 18th century. In 1825 the church crypt was opened for burials, but by the end of the century the general use of the burying-ground had been discontinued.

Other than pre-Reformation burials around the Cathedral, there were no early Roman Catholic burying-grounds in Glasgow; the first post-Reformation one recorded was St Mary's, established in Abercrombie St in 1839. It was hemmed in on all sides by tenement buildings and entry was through a pend close. It was demolished some time in the 1960s. The two other Roman Catholic burying-grounds are St Peter's, Dalbeth, London Rd (1851), still the responsibility of the Church, and St Kentigern's, Maryhill (1882) under the control of the District Council.

Two of the early Episcopal city churches had burying-grounds associated with them. St Andrew-by-the-Green, Greendyke St, was established in 1750, and Christ Church, Brook St, in 1837, but both are now no more.

The Quakers had two burying-grounds, one in Partick (Keith St) which was opened in 1711 and had its last burial in 1857, and another in Stirling Square (Albion St) from the 1730s to about 1800.

Many of the bewildering proliferation of Scottish Secession churches had burying-grounds attached, and the Glasgow ones included Anderston Old (Anderston Relief, Anderston UP) in Heddle Place (1770, crypt 1839, demolished in 1967); St Mark's (Anderston Associate, Anderston Anti-Burgher) in Cheapside St (1792, demolished in 1967). Both these churches and burying-grounds were removed to make way for the western flank of the city's Inner Ring Road.

Although the third category (burying-grounds not linked with any religious body) date mainly from the second quarter of the 19th century, there were a few earlier examples. A burying-ground of 2.25 acres in the Gorbals (Rutherglen Rd) was opened in 1715. It was acquired by the district council in 1885 and was developed in the early 1950s as a garden and play area.

Another non-denominational burying-ground was the one associated with the Town's Hospital, 1733 ('Hospital' in the sense of a hospice or shelter for the needy, i.e. the City Poorhouse) which dates from 1733 and had a burying-ground associated with it in Dunlop St (closed round c.1830 and later removed entirely).

In the city's east end the Calton Incorporation of Weavers opened a burying-ground in Abercrombie St in 1786. Its 1.25 acres were taken over by the district council in 1885. This burying-ground contains memorial stones erected c.1837 to honour the Calton weavers buried there, killed in 1787 when troops were ordered to fire on workers protesting against conditions and wages. The stones were rededicated by the Glasgow Trades Council in 1931, and later moved to a place on the ground's wall.

There can be little doubt that after the High Church the most notable of the city's burying-grounds is the Glasgow Necropolis. East of the Cathedral and on the other side of the ravine down which the Molendinar flows, a rocky eminence rises 200ft above the surrounding ground. This ground had been in the possession of the Merchants House of Glasgow since 1650; copiously planted with trees, it was popularly known as the Fir Park. The summit was occupied by a monument erected in 1825 to John Knox, consisting of a 58ft Doric column, designed by Thomas Hamilton, surmounted by a 12½ft-tall standing statue of the famous Reformer, designed by William Warren. It was on this site that the Glasgow merchants decided to lay out the city's first planned burying-ground; the results of their labours has been claimed as one of the greatest Victorian cemeteries in Britain. Particular care was taken with the landscaping, and much attention was paid to the proper choice of trees and shrubs and to the quality of the burying-ground's sculptural ornaments. Considerable work had to be undertaken to prepare the rocky, sloping site and many tombs had to be blasted out of the solid stone. The various compartments into which the Necropolis was divided were distinguished by letters of the Greek alphabet – usually written out as 'Alpha' or 'Sigma'. At its peak, the burying-ground covered 37 acres (15ha).

The Necropolis was formally opened in 1833 (though the first interments had actually taken place the previous year – one being of a Jew who was buried in a section of the burying-ground set aside for members of his faith). It was purposely modelled on the famous Père Lachaise cemetery in Paris, and the families of deceased Glasgow merchants, businessmen and academics vied with each other in the opulence of the tombs and mausoleums of their departed, which in design run the architectural gamut from chaste Greek to flamboyant Gothic – out of 50,000 burials, tombs were constructed for no less that 3,500. It was completely undenominational, accepting the bodies of Protestants, Catholics, Lutherans, Jews, Quakers and any others. A few years after it opened a 60ft span bridge, commonly called the 'Bridge of Sighs', was thrown over the Molendinar (culverted over in 1877 as Wishart St) connecting the burying-ground with Cathedral Square.

Its monumental splendours are so many as to defy detailed listing, but two oddities are perhaps worth noting: the presence of a cenotaph to the Laureate of the Nursery, William Miller, the author of 'Wee Willie Winkie' who died in 1872 and was buried in Tollcross Church burying-ground, and the tombstone (a Celtic cross) of Andrew McColl (*d.* 1888), which is said to be an early and undistinguished design by the famous Charles Rennie Mackintosh.

After the beginning of the 20th century the Necropolis became less fashionable and began to decline in use. In 1966 the Merchants House handed it over to the district council, along with £50,000 for its upkeep.

The Necropolis was only the first of several large burying-grounds in Glasgow not connected with a particular church, for the still increasing population required ever more cemeteries. The next one was located in the city's north-east, in Springburn, on the west side of the steeply rising Springburn Rd. Its name, Sighthill, succinctly describes the site and its outlook. Its 48 acres were opened in 1840, and its clientèle was drawn largely from the middle classes – which perhaps explains the lack of the architectural exuberance displayed in the Necropolis. The system of locating individual lairs (or grave plots) was distinctly odd: every lair was identified by a compass-bearing from a central point and by a distance measured along that bearing; it is most unlikely that such a cumbersome system existed for long.

Within the cemetery is located a monument in memory of John Baird and Andrew Hardy, executed for treason after the Radical Rising of 1820. Their bodies were exhumed and secretly buried directly in front of the monument, and the ground around it became sought after as a place of sepulture by other and later radicals! In 1954 the district council took over the burying-ground and for ease of maintenance converted it into a lawn cemetery (i.e. all edgings and boundaries of individual lairs were removed to facilitate mowing).

In the same year, 1840, the first new burying-ground was opened south of the Clyde, where a large and increasing workforce lacked any suitable places of burial. Named the Southern Necropolis, its three sections, Central, West and East, were opened in 1840, 1846 and 1850 respectively. At that time the lower elements of society could hope for little more than interment in a mass or common grave, and the Southern Necropolis was the first attempt to provide the working man with the opportunity for a cheap but dignified burial. It is the last resting-place of Sir Thomas Lipton, grocer, yachtsman and millionaire, and of Hugh Macdonald, author of *Rambles around Glasgow*. It was taken over by the District Council in 1954.

The growing population of the east end of the city, an area of tenements and factories, was catered for by the opening of the Eastern Necropolis (sometimes known as Janefield). Opened in 1847, it measures 24.7 acres and was acquired by the district council in 1969.

Maryhill, in the north of the city, has several large burying-grounds which together cover some 85 acres – Lambhill Cemetery, 1881, and St Kentigern RC Cemetery, 1882 (Balmore Rd) and the Western Necropolis, 1882 (Tesla St). In the latter burying-ground is the first of Glasgow's four crematoria, erected by the Scottish Cremation Society in 1895. The others are the Daldowie Crematorium (1955, Glasgow District, Broomhouse, Uddingston), Linn Crematorium (1962, Glasgow District Council, Lainshaw Drive) and Craigton Crematorium (1957, Craigton Crematorium Co. Ltd, Berryknowes Rd).

The district council is also responsible for Cardonald Cemetery (Mosspark Boulevard), Eastwood Cemetery (Thornliebank Rd), Riddrie Park Cemetery (Cumbernauld Rd), Rutherglen Cemetery (Mill St), Sandymount Cemetery (Gartocher Terr), Tollcross Cemetery (Corbett St), and Westburn Cemetery (Old Mill Rd, Cambuslang).

Other Glasgow burying-grounds not the responsibility of the district council are Cathcart Cemetery, 1878 (Clarkston Rd) and Craigton Cemetery, 1873 (Berryknowes Rd).

Buses

The use of motor-buses to provide public transport in Glasgow began before the First World War when several private companies started to run services from the centre of the city. One of the earliest of these was introduced in 1914 and went out to Cumbernauld. At first, the central terminus for all these services was George Square,

but because of congestion the magistrates allocated services to Carlton Place, Cathedral St and Renfrew St, although not all of the private companies chose to adopt this sensible arrangement.

Because of the city's excellent tram system these early bus services made little headway, but after the war, the trams' lack of flexibility and their inability to expand into the new suburbs allowed the bus companies to increase – by the end of the 1930s there were 1,157 licensed vehicles operating in Glasgow, owned by 159 different proprietors.

As early as 1905 the Corporation Tramways Department had secured powers enabling it to run an omnibus service but as long as the trams continued to be profitable these powers were not used. However, when the post-war situation made it clear that the monopoly of the tram was disappearing, the Corporation decided to institute its own bus services. The necessary Provisional Order was passed in 1921 but it was not until December 1924 that an experimental service began. Starting from Monteith Row (next to Glasgow Green), it ran west to Partick and then north-east to Maryhill.

In the following years other Corporation bus services were introduced. The early development of the tramway system, designed to serve an older Glasgow, meant that the new municipal housing developments (begun after the 1914–18 War) lacked public transport and so these new services were purposely designed to act as feeders from the large and growing developments to nearby tram termini – for example, Knightswood to Anniesland and Kelvindale to the Botanic Gardens.

In 1925 an ominous note was struck when, for the first time, a tram route (Stobcross Ferry to Finnieston) was converted to a bus route. Bus journeys became more comfortable at the beginning of 1926, when all the buses were fitted with pneumatic tyres, and at the end of 1928 the first double-decker took to the streets, its livery of green and orange soon to become an increasing presence in the Glasgow streets.

More links were now inaugurated between various housing schemes – Carntyne to Croftfoot, Knightswood to King's Park, Mosspark to Kelvindale.

In August 1930 the Corporation obtained parliamentary powers which forbade private bus companies to set down passengers within the city on outward journeys or to uplift passengers on inward journeys, a monopoly which was maintained for over 40 years.

After the Second World War the tramcars entered a terminal decline as more and more of their routes were replaced by buses, until in September 1962 the last tram service (Dalmuir West to Auchenshuggle) was replaced by bus service no. 64.

The 1970s saw changes in bus transport greater than any before. In 1972 the Greater Glasgow Passenger Transport Authority was set up to provide 'a properly integrated and efficient system of public transport'; in turn the authority set up the Greater Glasgow Passenger Transport Executive (after local government reorganisation in 1975 the duties of the PTA were transferred to Strathclyde Regional Council) and in June 1972 the new PTA adopted the running of the Corporation bus system. The 1,300-bus fleet taken over by the PTE was in considerable need of overhaul. First came a new livery, verona green on the bottom panels, sunglow yellow between the decks and white window surrounds and roofs. By a more practical move (cutting down the street-life of a bus from 17 to 12 years) the overall efficiency of the fleet was improved – many of the city's withdrawn buses were now sold to other operators. In 1974 the introduction of Transcards allowed limitless travel, and by 1979 all city buses were running under one-person operation.

The city buses' biggest upset was undoubtedly the Transport Act of 1980 which swept away almost all the existing regulatory and licensing procedures. One of the first effects was the removal, in 1982, of the monopoly exercised within the city boundaries by its bus system, and soon many outside operators were running services into the city centre.

In 1981, in an effort to reduce painting costs, bus liveries were again changed, becoming dark green, black, and yellow. A final change produced the standard, all-over Strathclyde orange. Control now passed from public to private ownership in the form of Strathclyde Buses Ltd, although the Strathclyde PTE still oversees all public transport in the Strathclyde area.

Canals

Of the five Scottish canals whose useful lives extended into the 20th century, Glasgow had links with three – the Forth and Clyde Canal, the Monkland Canal and the Glasgow, Paisley, Johnstone and Ardrossan Canal.

As a result of the union of the English and Scottish parliaments in 1707, for the first time Scottish merchants and manufacturers had legal access to the growing trade with the American colonies. The building of a canal which would join the two great Firths of Clyde and Forth and bring together the two cities of Glasgow and Edinburgh, now became a project offering considerable advantages to their burgeoning trade. This opportunity was of particular importance to Glasgow for it was beginning to find that the splendid prospects in the New World were likely to more than make up for the geographical barriers which had barred her from Scotland's traditional trade across the North Sea. Daniel Defoe, a man who greatly regarded Glasgow as a commercial city, pointed out in his *Tour of Great Britain* (1724–26) 'How easy a Work it would be to form a Navigation . . . from the Forth to the Clyde'.

Three surveys were carried out, the last in 1762 by John Smeaton, the most eminent engineer of the day. In 1768 an Act was passed giving powers to construct a canal based on his survey which would run from the Forth to the Clyde at Bowling. The Glasgow town council subscribed £1,000 towards the undertaking, much of this sum coming from the tobacco lords who would particularly benefit from the increased trading opportunities.

Construction was begun from the eastern termination, but difficulties were experienced in extending the Glasgow end. By 1773 work had only reached Kirkintilloch, by 1775 to Stockingfield (three miles north of the city), and by 1777 to Hamiltonhill (on the outskirts). The collapse of the tobacco trade following the American War of Independence brought about a halt due to lack of funds, but an additional Act in 1784 made available fresh finances (from the Forfeited Estates – estates of Jacobite supporters confiscated by the government) and at last, in 1790, the

Clyde was finally reached at Bowling. This last stretch of 11 miles was famous for including the Kelvin Aqueduct, which carried the waterway across a broad valley. It was 245ft long and 50ft high and was the largest structure of its kind in Britain at that time.

A collateral cut extended the canal nearer to the city where a large set of basins with numerous wharves was constructed and was named Port Dundas in honour of Lord Dundas of Kerse, governor of the company. The total length of the Forth and Clyde Canal was 39 miles, it had 39 locks, was 63ft wide on average, and had a depth of 9½ft. The purpose of the canal

The Forth and Clyde Canal, c.1850. The transport facilities of the canal enabled many small factories to establish themselves along its banks. This is probably a view near Maryhill, with a bridge over the River Kelvin visible in the valley. (Robert Carrick, c.1852, Mitchell Library)

was three-fold: (1) to allow sea-going vessels to pass from sea to sea; (2) to act as an inland waterway for the movement of agricultural produce, mineral resources and local manufactures; and (3) to be a main highway for travellers across the width of Scotland.

Its success in the early days was largely due to the great and continuing increase in Glasgow's trade and commerce at the beginning of the 19th century, and the area around Port Dundas (at that time quite separate from Glasgow) must have resembled an early industrial estate. The wide range of activities carried on there witnessed to its invigorating effect – factories of all sorts sprang up: colour-works, chemical-works, dye-works, grinding mills, mills for logroot, dye and bread stuffs, foundries, machine-shops, potteries, engine-works, grain mills, distilleries and soap-works, while the traffic carried on the canal itself consisted chiefly of coal, ironstone, pig-iron, timber, castings, grain, salt, sugar, oil, stones and slates – generally speaking all bulk cargoes.

This local vigour probably owed something to the the fact that in 1816, when Lord Dundas and his partners resigned from the management, the governorship was taken over by the redoubtable Glasgow entrepreneur, Kirkman Finlay, and, most unusually, the seat of power was moved from London to Glasgow. Finally, in 1822, the opening of the Edinburgh and Glasgow Union Canal made possible for the first time direct communication between the two great cities, but the attainment of that peak actually marked the beginning of the end for the canal.

The irresistible and rapidly expanding forces of the infant railway systems doomed all canals to a process of slow attrition and decay, and the death-knell of the Forth and Clyde Canal was sounded by the opening of the Edinburgh and Glasgow Railway in 1842. For both passengers and freight the railway became practically the only choice and in 1867 the company bowed to the inevitable: the canal became the property of the Caledonian Railway

Company. It persisted on into the 20th century but eventually its only users were a few fishing boats and an occasional barge full of timber. It was taken over by the British Transport Commission in 1948 who in turn passed it on to the British Waterways Board in 1962. Finally, on 1 January 1963, the Board closed it down as a navigational water; henceforward it would be a 'remainder' waterway, to be used as a leisure adjunct.

The increasing demand by the city for coal for domestic and industrial uses at the end of the 18th century soon disclosed a monopoly situation. The many city pits and those in the immediate neighbourhood could charge what they liked, for although there were abundant supplies of cheap coal in the Monklands district a score of miles to the east of Glasgow, the poor roads of the time were not able to cope with the necessary transport required to bring this coal to the city. The solution was obvious – build a canal.

So in 1770 an Act was obtained which authorised such a project, and by 1790 the Monkland Canal, built under the superintendence of James Watt, was ready. It was 12 miles long, 25ft wide and 4½ft deep, without a single lock. Initially it did not prove a success mainly because the lack of locks involved the considerable annoyance of having to trans-ship cargoes of coal at least twice. Eventually, though, locks were built and, even more importantly, the canal was extended by a cut of junction beyond its terminal basin in Townhead to Port Dundas and so on to Stockingfield to join the Forth and Clyde Canal.

One noteworthy oddity connected with this canal was the means adopted to negotiate the sudden difference in levels (almost 100ft) at Blackhill, near Riddrie. A series of locks had eventually been built

here to avoid the need to unload and reload coal shipments, but the loss of water in operating them was so great that often the canal had to be closed. In 1850 the locks were replaced by a huge iron tank which could be filled with water and raised or lowered on an inclined plane. It was calculated that this device, known as a 'gazoom', reduced the time taken by nine-tenths and the amount of water by five-sixths.

Inevitably, the Monkland Canal came to share the decline of the Forth and Clyde Canal and in 1867 it too was taken over by the Caledonian Railway Company. The gazoom went for scrap about 1887 and for many years after that the waterway existed as a stagnant and reed-covered encumbrance until it finally closed in 1952. By an ironic symbolism, its filled-in course became the foundation for part of the eastern approach to Glasgow of the M8 motorway.

The early movement of seaborne cargoes up and down the Clyde was considerably impeded by the shallowness of the upper reaches of the river and by the many delays imposed by the vagaries of time and tide. At the beginning of the 19th century a grandiose scheme to circumvent these problems brought into existence Glasgow's third canal, the Glasgow, Paisley, Johnstone and Ardrossan Canal. The intention of its planners was that cargoes would be unloaded in Ardrossan Harbour in the lower reaches of the firth and brought safely and speedily to the Tradeston district of Glasgow along this waterway. A route was surveyed by Telford and powers were obtained in 1806 to construct a 32-mile navigation between these two places. Work began the following year at the Glasgow terminus (called Port Eglinton in honour of the Earl of Eglinton, one of the prime movers in the affair) and by 1811 the canal had reached Johnstone, a few miles west of Paisley. It was 4½ft deep and 10 miles long, and by following a circuitous route dispensed with locks altogether. One of its most popular uses was as the conveyance of passengers between the two burghs, in fast, light fly-boats pulled by trotting horses – in 1813 some 425,000 persons enjoyed this quick, comfortable method of transport. It is obvious, with hindsight, that the canal was much too late on the scene; the section from Johnstone to Ardrossan was replaced by a railway line – the canal itself was never a financial success. In 1869 it was bought by the Glasgow & South Western Railway Company who closed it down in 1885, filled it in and built a railway line along it – which was given the name of the 'Paisley Canal Line'!

Castles

Crookston Castle

Towerside Cresc.

About 1168 Sir Robert de Croc received the lands of the Leven Valley from the High Steward of Scotland, and built the first Crookston Castle on a knoll a little to the south of Paisley. It subsequently passed through several hands until about 1400 when Sir Alexander Steward built the extant castle in the form of a rectangular block of three storeys with higher square towers at each corner. It suffered a siege in 1488 during which all but one of the towers were destroyed. Although its later owners, the Stewarts, left it for Inchinnan, the castle was occasionally occupied till the end of the 16th century. In 1757 the then owner, the Duke of Montrose, sold it to the Maxwells of Pollok. In 1847 Sir John Maxwell restored the surviving north-east tower and carried out some other repairs. Sir John Stirling Maxwell presented it to the National Trust for Scotland in 1931. It is the only castle in the Glasgow area to be classified as an Ancient Monument.

Haggs Castle was restored in the middle of the 19th century as a private residence. In 1972 it became the District Council's Museum of Childhood. (William Graham, Mitchell Library)

Haggs Castle

St Andrew's Dr.

Situated at the north-east corner of the Pollok County Park, Haggs Castle was built in 1585 by Sir John Maxwell of Pollok as an L-shaped fortalice of three storeys. It was abandoned in 1753 and soon became a ruin, but by 1860 it had been somewhat fancifully restored. During the Second World

War it was taken over by the Army, then converted into flats, and finally acquired in 1972 by the Corporation who converted it into Glasgow's Museum of Childhood.

Cathcart Castle

The eminently defensible site of this now demolished castle may date back to the Dark Ages, but its first recorded appearance was during the 14th century, when it was associated with Rainald de Ketkert. In form a simple rectangular keep five storeys high, it was later occupied by Sir Alan, first Lord Cathcart, who sold it in 1467 to the Sempills of Ladymuir. In the middle of the 19th century it was bought by a Glasgow tradesman who intended to demolish it and use the stone as building material, but was frustrated by its solidity. In 1801 the tenth Lord Cathcart bought it back. He intended to restore it but failed to do so. Glasgow Corporation took it over in 1927 but its condition continued to deteriorate until by the 1950s it had to be closed to the public because of its dangerous state. It was finally demolished in 1980, leaving only 7ft of its walls still standing above ground.

Castlemilk Castle

A late 15th-century rectangular tower, this castle now exists only as a stump surrounded by the Castlemilk housing scheme. It had been considerably modernised in the 19th century, and in 1938 was bought by Glasgow Corporation who used it (till 1969) as a children's home.

Gilbertfield Castle

This castle is located a mile south of Cambuslang on the slopes of the Dechmont Hill. An L-shaped tower house dating from 1607, it is now in a ruinous condition.

Mugdock Castle

An important early stronghold of the Grahams, its ruins stand on the edge of Mugdock Loch two miles north of Milngavie. Built before the end of the 14th century in the form of a courtyarded castle (of which two towers survive), it was extensively used and added to until the beginning of the 18th century. In 1875 John Guthrie Smith had a large modern mansion built beside (and connected to) the restored surviving tower, but both the mansion and the castle have now deteriorated to the same ruinous state.

Bishop's Castle

This castle was located immediately to the south-west of the Cathedral, more or less in the space now occupied by Cathedral Square. Possibly erected when the Cathedral was rebuilt in the 12th century, it is first mentioned in the records in 1258. In its beginnings it was probably no more than a strong place for the protection of the bishops, but successive bishops and archbishops added to its structure and grandeur until its alternative name, the Bishop's Palace, became increasingly appropriate. During the Scottish Wars of Independence it was garrisoned *c.* 1300 with 1,000 English troops. It was this force which Blind Harry described as being defeated by William Wallace at the Battle of the Bell o' the Brae. In 1430 Bishop John Cameron added the five-storey quadrangular Great Tower to the southernmost point of its triangular shape, and about 1510 Bishop James Beaton added a smaller tower and established the surrounding 15ft-high curtain wall. An elaborate gatehouse and arched gateway were built by Bishop Gavin Dunbar (*d.* 1547). We can catch a glimpse of its civilised appearance in 1553 when Archbishop James Beaton instructed the provost and council as to his choice of bailies, in 'the inner flower garden' of the castle. Following the departure in 1560 of Beaton, the Cathedral's last Roman Catholic archbishop, it declined into a semi-ruin under the succeeding Protestant archbishops. In 1611 Archbishop John Spottiswoode restored it to something like its former state, but by the beginning of the 18th century it had reverted to a ruin. It served as a convenient quarry for the town's masons, particularly in 1755, when its stones were largely used in the construction of the new Saracen's Head Inn. In 1786 the city's place of execution moved from the Howgate Head to the north-east corner of the castle yard. Its few remaining vestiges were finally swept away in 1792 by the erection of the Glasgow Royal Infirmary.

Although by no means an important stronghold it suffered several attacks in its long history. During a rebellion in 1517 against the Queen Dowager acting as Regent, Mure of Caldwell and several others stormed and plundered the castle but were compelled to surrender. The Archbishop brought an action against Mure for 'Wrangwis spoliatioun' and detailed the goods taken from his castle. These included 'xxviii feddir bedds, v dusan of peuder veschell, tua kists, tua kettills, xii tunnes of wynne' and much more. Then in 1544,

during the minority of Mary Queen of Scots, the Earl of Arran acting as Regent was attacked by the Duke of Lennox who took up his position in the Bishop's Castle. After a siege of ten days it was retaken by the Regent's forces. Despite promises to the contrary all but two of the garrison were massacred. Lennox sought revenge and met the Regent's forces at The Butts (a piece of ground outside the city's boundaries on the east where the citizens held their wapinschaws) but was again defeated. Considering that the citizens had supported the Duke of Lennox, Arran gave the city over to plunder. In 1570 the castle was again attacked by the adherents of Queen Mary, but despite being held by only 24 men it did not surrender. When Cromwell was approaching Glasgow after his victory at Dunbar (1650), he was informed that the vaults beneath the Bishop's Castle had been filled with gunpowder which was to be exploded as he entered the city. Whether this was true or not, Cromwell decided not to run any risks and came into the city by way of Cowcaddens and the Cow Loan. After the Battle of Drumclog in 1679 it is said that the victorious Covenanters came to Glasgow and forcibly entered the castle, destroying much property.

Cathedral

For more than half its recorded history Glasgow's importance came from the fact that the little community was the seat (or *cathedral*) of a bishop; it was the presence of St Mungo's Cathedral on the west bank of the Molendinar burn that ensured its pre-

eminence throughout the whole of south-west Scotland; its citizens were the bishop's freemen and it was his officers who ruled in his name and who collected the town taxes and stent.

Although the origins of this ecclesiastical rule lay so far back in the city's life as to be largely a matter of legend, certain facts are quite clear. It was during the Roman occupation of south and central Scotland that Christianity first made its presence felt, for it is related that when St Ninian, returning from France to Galloway at the end of the 4th century, passed through Cathures (an early name for Glasgow) he consecrated a Christian cemetery there. After the Roman withdrawal from Britain at the beginning of the 5th century, however, the mists of the Dark Ages descend and we know nothing of Cathures for almost 200 years.

The *fons et origo* of the city now appeared on the scene. St Kentigern (a Celtic personal name which probably comes from *ceann* meaning 'head' or 'chief', and *tighearn*, 'lord' or 'ruler') was born of a princely family in south-east Scotland. He spent the early part of his life in a religious foundation in Culross, but was forced to flee because, it was said, of the jealousy he aroused amongst his brothers-in-God. Travelling westwards he came across a dying holy man Fergus who when dead Kentigern placed on a cart pulled by two oxen. When the cart eventually came to rest at Glasgow he buried Fergus there in St Ninian's cemetery and founded a church on the banks of the Molendinar dedicated to the Holy Trinity. After living in Wales for some time he returned to Glasgow in 581 and remained there till his death in 603, being buried in his own church. So great was the affection felt for him by his people that they gave him the nickname Mungo meaning 'Dear One'.

After the saint's death there followed a long period of obscurity, for we know practically nothing about the little community on the banks of the Clyde for the next 200 years. With Earl David, Prince of Cumbria (later to become King David,

the 'sair sanct for the croon'), the curtain lifts and the history proper of the church of Glasgow begins. When he became king in 1124 he introduced a new aristocracy into the kingdom – Saxons, Normans and Flemings from south of the Border to whom he gave grants of land and who brought into Scotland the first taste of feudalism.

It was not only the temporal power which suffered a change; the spiritual power also changed as the old Celtic form of ecclesiastical government, in the form of loose groupings of monastic settlements with undefined and irregular boundaries, gave way to a parochial and much more regular system. About 1120, while still only an earl, David prepared a full record of the extensive property of the Cathedral, the 'Register or Inquisition of the Bishopric of Glasgow'. This important document confirmed and established the Cathedral's ancient rights and possessions, which now spread from the Antonine Wall to the Solway Firth. In all, it exercised jurisdiction over 31 temporal possessions, most of them located in the immediate neighbourhood of the church, though others lay as far afield as Dumfries, Roxburgh and Peebles.

This Inquisition marked the beginnings of 440 years of growing prosperity and power for St Mungo's Cathedral. One indication of this growth was the bull of Pope Innocent VIII, obtained in 1492 by Bishop Blacader, which elevated the See of Glasgow to the dignity of an archbishopric.

The most brilliant epoch of the Cathedral was during the latter half of the 15th century. Bishop Cameron (1426–46) increased the number of canons from 25 to 32, making the Cathedral chapter the largest in the kingdom. Nine of these canons held special offices – dean, archdeacon, sub-dean, chancellor, precentor, treasurer, sacristan, bishop's vicar and sub-precentor. Under the rule of Bishop Turnbull (1447–54) and by favour of James II, it was raised in status from a burgh of barony to a burgh of regality; for the *reddendo* of a red rose it now enjoyed almost all the considerable powers of a royal burgh. It could also boast of its brand new *studium generale* or University set up by a bull of Pope Nicholas V in 1451. It did not reach that position, however, without a struggle. For instance it had to fight to free itself from ecclesiastical dependency on the English church. As early as 1122 the See of York claimed the right to supremacy over the Glasgow bishopric, and it was not until 1188 that Bishop Jocelin finally obtained a rescript from Pope Alexander III which declared that the See of Glasgow was subordinate only to Rome itself.

It also shared in the troubles and devastation of the Wars of Succession. The attempts of the English king, Edward I, and his successors, to establish themselves as the Overlords of Scotland and thus to dictate who should be King of Scotland, were met by no greater opposition than from Glasgow Cathedral. Robert Wischard, who occupied the chair of Kentigern for 45 years from 1271 to 1316, fought the English invaders with every means at his command, even including the breaking of oaths and the donning of armour. He misappropriated wood for constructing the Cathedral spire, using it instead to build catapults to be used in besieging the Castle of Kirkintilloch, and it was he who absolved Robert the Bruce for his slaughter of the Red Comyn. While taking the part of a warrior he was captured by the English and imprisoned in chains. He was freed in 1314, one of the first to be redeemed after the Battle of Bannockburn.

The high days of the see did not last long, however. The disastrous Battle of Flodden (1513) was an ominous curtain-raiser to a long period of strife in Scotland both for Church and State, and Glasgow had its share. The spread of the doctrines of the Reformers brought widespread dissension and as early as the episcopacy of Gavin Dunbar (1524–47) two heretics were burned near the east end of the Cathedral. His successor, Alexander Gordon, resigned after only a year and joined the Protestants. Finally, when it became clear that the ruling powers accepted the Reformed faith, Archbishop James Beaton gathered together the records and treasures of the Cathedral and retired to Paris in 1560. Before he fled he took the precaution of appointing the Earl of Arran as Bailie of the Regality for a period of 19 years, presumably hoping that when the storm blew over he would be able to resume without trouble the temporalities of the see. Fate declared otherwise and James Beaton became the last Roman Catholic Archbishop of St Mungo's Cathedral. There is a story, often repeated, that tells how the craftsmen of the city, when it was proposed in 1588 by some perfervid supporters of the new religion to raze the Cathedral, leapt to its defence and saved the building – a good story, but one without foundation.

The lay powers, now bereft of the authority which had ruled them for centuries, declared that since they could not find the Archbishop they were forced to elect themselves, thus marking the beginning of the dissolution of the church's temporal powers and possessions. The Earl of Arran, no doubt to the great disappointment of Beaton, turned Protestant himself and many of the temporalities were seized by lay owners. The four archbishops who followed Beaton – John Porterfield, James Boyd, Robert Montgomery and William Erskine – were given the fitting title of 'tulchan' bishops. This was the name given to the device by which the stuffed skin of a cow's own calf was used to trick her into letting down her milk, symbolising the passing of Church lands into the hands of lay persons via the complaisant clerics.

In 1557 the greater part of the Cathedral's lands were conveyed to Walter Stewart of Minto.

The first Protestant minister, and for some time the only minister in the city, was David Wemyss, appointed in 1565. The sequence of minsters was broken when Charles II restored Episcopacy in 1660; the bishops then appointed were in turn ousted in 1688 when William of Orange brought back the Presbyterian form of worship, restarting a line of Ministers of the Gospel which has continued without a break to the present day.

There was a period, however, when the ministers of the High Kirk did not enjoy the huge building undisturbed. The radical change in the style of worship following the Reformation called for buildings where the whole population could gather and hear the Word of God – essentially meeting places to accommodate a speaker and an audience. So there began a process which split up the Cathedral into three separate parishes. (Had it not been for this phenomenon Glasgow's Cathedral might not have survived intact, for its fabric might have been used, as was done elsewhere, as a quarry from which to construct separate and smaller churches.) Walls were thrown up and galleries inserted with a supreme disregard for the building's architectural fitness.

First, in 1595, the lower church was allocated to the Barony congregation (the area surrounding the city). Then in 1648 the nave was walled off from the choir to become the Outer High, where the eastern part of the city met for worship. This left to the High Kirk itself the choir and the name Inner High. In 1798 the Barony left its subterranean quarters and moved to a new building erected a short distance away. When Queen Victoria asked her chaplain, the famous Dr Norman McLeod, for a photograph of the new Barony, he told her it was 'the ugliest Kirk in all Europe'!

When the congregation had finally departed, the Barony heritors filled the under-church with soil halfway up the pillars and used it as a burying-ground! This bizarre practice was only discontinued in about 1844. The congregation which met in the nave, the Outer High, left in 1835 to become St Paul's, leaving the High Kirk in sole possession. With increasing knowledge of the building's long history and a

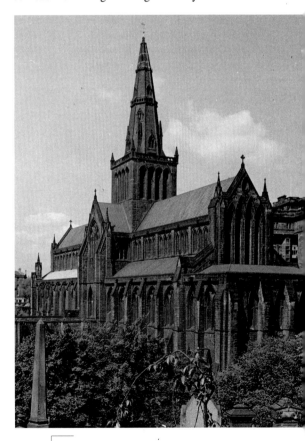

Glasgow Cathedral from the Necropolis. The unusual depth of its east end is the direct result of building on the steep slope descending to the Molendinar Burn. (George Oliver)

growing appreciation of its place in the city's history, the 19th century saw a series of adjustments which have brought the Cathedral back to a better condition than at any time since the Middle Ages. Urged on by Archibald McLellan's 1833 plea for its restoration, the authorities returned the interior to its original condition by the removal of the disfiguring party wall; unfortunately, an excess of zeal and lack of knowledge led, in 1846 and 1848, to the removal of two old towers which had stood at the two corners of the west wall. Their removal also destroyed a considerable quantity of documents relating to the history of the Cathedral and the city which had been stored in one of them. After a dispute over admission fees (even then!) full control of the building passed in 1857 from the town council to the Crown, and St Mungo's Cathedral is now held in trust for the nation by the Secretary of State for Scotland.

THE BUILDING

No remains earlier than the late 12th century have been found, but it can be assumed that the Celtic monastery buildings of which the city's first church formed the principal part would have been of the simplest character – wood, wattle and daub or undressed stone, with thatched roofs. The one unusual circumstance of the church's site was that the tomb of St Kentigern lay on a steep eastern slope running down to a small burn, the Molendinar. So, in order to keep the saint's grave within the building and to place it in the centre of a large open area, and at the same time to keep the choir at the east end on the same level as the nave to the west, a most extraordinary underpinning had to be constructed directly below the choir. Sometimes described as a crypt, it is more

properly an under or lower church. It gives Glasgow's Cathedral a unique feature, which has been described as one of the greatest architectural treasures of the medieval period in Scotland.

The first definite building date we have is 1136 when a new, almost certainly mortared stone church was dedicated. No trace whatsoever of this Norman church has been uncovered.

Some time towards the end of the 12th century this building was destroyed by fire and Bishop Jocelin (in office 1175–99) erected a new Cathedral in 1197. It is probable that at this time the east end was considerably extended to provide a more fitting setting for the high altar and for the saint's tomb directly below it. Nothing remains of Jocelin's work but a single vaulting shaft in the south aisle of the lower church.

The third phase was largely completed during the episcopate (1233–58) of William de Bondington. The east end was once again remodelled and extended not only further to dignify St Kentigern's tomb but also to provide the necessary space for the many chapels and altars required by the liturgical usages of the time.

The disastrous times of the Scottish War of Independence afforded little opportunity to proceed with the renewal and expansion of the nave, still relatively untouched, but sometime about 1330 work seems to have begun on this part of the structure. The style adopted is somewhat heavy and pedestrian and seems to suggest a certain dullness of spirit, harking back as it does to the style of an earlier period.

By this time the building had assumed the shape we see today, Scotland's greatest and best-preserved church of the Gothic period, the end of an architectural history of some 300 years.

It is in essence a simple rectangle

divided by a transept which does not project beyond the north and south walls, and a crossing surmounted by a square tower and a stone steeple. At the east end the vaulted lower church lies beneath the choir, and at the north-east corner in an annexe is the chapter house. The other major structure is a chapel projecting south from the transept, of which only the lower part was completed. It is known as the Blacader Aisle after Archbishop Blacader (in office 1483–92).

BISHOPS

Michael, 1115.

John Achaius, 1117–47. Rebuilt the Cathedral church, which was consecrated on 7 July 1136, in the presence of King David.

Herbert, 1147–64. Introduced the Use of Sarum (Salisbury) which continued until the Reformation.

Ingelram, 1164–74. For defending the cause of the Scottish church against the claims of York he was appointed Bishop of Glasgow on the death of Herbert.

Jocelin, 1175–99. Abbot of Cistercian monastery at Melrose before becoming Bishop. Obtained for Glasgow, from William the Lion, the grant of burgh status, a market on Thursday and the right of a fair. In 1188 he obtained, by a rescript from Pope Alexander III, a declaration that his see was subordinate only to Rome.

Hugh de Roxburgh, 1199. Died after two months in the seat.

William Malvoisine, 1200–2. Translated to the See of St Andrews, becoming primate of Scotland in 1202.

Florence, 1202–7. Son of Count Florence of Holland, his uncle was William the Lion.

Walter, 1208–32.

William de Bondington, 1233–58. Built the lower church and the choir.

Nicholas de Moffat, 1259. Prevented from obtaining consecration by King Alexander III.

John de Cheyam, 1259–68. An Englishman and very unpopular with the King and the Chapter.

Nicholas de Moffat, 1268. Again elected but not consecrated.

William Wischard, 1270. Was translated to St Andrews soon after consecration.

Robert Wischard, 1271–1316. Supported the national cause against Edward I. Preached against him and armed and fought against him. Captured in 1306, he remained a prisoner till 1314.

Stephen de Donyouer, 1316–17. Died on the way to Rome.

John de Lindsay, 1317.

John de Egglescliffe, 1318. Never got possession.

John de Lindsay, 1323–35. Mortally wounded in a sea battle with the English when returning from France.

John Wischard, 1335–38.

William Rae, 1338–67. Said to have built the stone bridge over the Clyde which was not replaced till 1850.

Walter Wardlaw, 1367–87. He and David Beattie were the only Scottish bishops to become cardinals.

Matthew de Glendonwyn, 1387–1408. Was said to have had stones hewn for the central tower but died before building began.

William Lawedre, 1408–1425. Erected the central tower and partly built the chapter-house.

John Cameron, 1426–46. Completed the spire above the tower.

James Brewis, 1447. Died after a few months in office.

William Turnbull, 1447–54. Founded the University in 1451.

Andrew de Muirhead, 1455–73.

John Laing, 1474–83.

George de Carmichael, 1483.

Robert Blacader, 1483–92. Became Archbishop in 1492.

ARCHBISHOPS

Robert Blacader, 1492–1508. Stood high in favour of James IV. Last to contribute to the building of the Cathedral. Died on the way to the Holy Land.

James Beaton, 1509–22.

Gavin Dunbar, 1524–47. During his episcopate two heretics were burnt at the east end of the Cathedral.

Alexander Gordon, 1550–51. Resigned, became a Protestant.

James Beaton, 1551–70. Last Roman Catholic archbishop. Retired to France in 1560, taking with him the treasures and archives of the Cathedral.

The various records which supply the dates and sequences of the bishops and archbishops listed above are not always consistent and discrepancies are unavoidable.

REFORMATION ARCHBISHOPS

John Porterfield, 1571–72. First of the titular or 'tulchan' prelates.

James Boyd of Trochrig, 1573–81.

Robert Montgomery, 1581–85.

William Erskine, 1585–87.

Walter Stewart, 1587.

James Beaton, 1587–1602. Despite never returning to his see he was restored its revenues. After his death the church's lands became a temporality in favour of the Duke of Lennox.

John Spottiswoode, 1603–15. A strong Episcopalian.

James Law, 1615–32.

Patrick Lindsay, 1633–38.

Andrew Fairfoul, 1661–1663. During his episcopate the persecution of the Covenanters reached its height.

Alexander Burnet, 1664–69.

Robert Leighton, 1671–74. Tried in vain to bring the Presbyterians and Episcopalians together.

Alexander Burnet, 1674–79.

Arthur Ross, 1679–84. Many Covenanters were hanged during his episcopate.

Alexander Cairncross, 1684–87.

John Patterson, 1687–1689.

MINISTERS

David Wemyss, 1565–1615.

Archibald Douglas, 1571–93.

Robert Scott, 1616–29.

John Maxwell, 1629–39. Deposed for opposing the 1638 General Assembly Covenant.

Edward Wright, 1641–46.

Robert Ramsay, 1647–51.

Cathedral Square, c.1850. On the left is the facade of the Robert Adam-designed Glasgow Royal Infirmary. On the right is the Barony Church (said to be the ugliest church in the city) with the Cathedral in between. In the foreground an early horse-bus is passing a twin-barrelled milk-cart. (Robert Carrick, c.1852, Mitchell Library)

James Durham, 1651–58.

Ralph Rodger, 1659–62. Deprived of his living for opposing Episcopacy.

Arthur Ross, 1664–75. Promoted to Archbishop in 1679.

Richard Waddell, 1682–84. Translated to St Andrews.

Archibald Inglis, 1685–87.

Ralph Rodger, 1687–89. Returned on being granted Toleration.

James Brown, 1690–1714.

George Campbell, 1715–48.

John Hamilton, 1749–80.

William Taylor, 1780–1823.

Duncan Macfarlan, 1824–57. Moderator of the General Assembly in 1843, the year of the Disruption.

John Robertson, 1858–65.

George Stewart Burns, 1865–96.

Pearson McAdam Muir, 1896–1915.

James McGibbon, 1916–22.

Lauchlan Maclean Watt, 1923–34.

Neville Davidson, 1935–67.

William J. Morris, 1967–

DIMENSIONS

Length of nave 128ft
Width of nave 62ft
Length of lower church 128ft
Height of spire 216ft
Total length of Cathedral 280ft
Length of Blacader Aisle 55ft
Width of Blacader Aisle 26ft
Length of choir 128ft
Width of choir 23ft
Number of pillars 147

See also　CHURCHES
　　　　　　RELIGIOUS GROUPS
　　　　　　ST KENTIGERN

Chamber of Commerce

By the end of the 18th century Glasgow's growing trade (particularly with North America and the West Indies) and its increasing manufacturing capabilities had created a need for some co-ordinating body for its businessmen and factory-owners, and in 1783 the Glasgow Chamber of Commerce and Manufacture was set up (the first in the United Kingdom) mainly through the urgings of Patrick Colquhoun, Lord Provost and tobacco merchant. It began with 216 members, 168 in the city, with the rest coming from Paisley, Greenock, Port Glasgow and Kilbarchan, and Colquhoun was its first president. Its membership declined to 73 in 1803 but rose again during the course of the century to reach 900 in 1883.

It met in the Tontine Tavern till 1822, then at various places till 1877 when it moved into the Merchant's House in George Sq. Its primary interest was the protection of the city's trade; from the beginning its aims were to raise standards of production, especially in the cotton industry, and to ease the burden of taxation on its members. Two of its earliest campaigns were against the Corn Laws (which forced up the price of the workers' food) and against the antiquated Scottish bankruptcy laws (which seriously discommoded the city's commercial activities). It was also involved in improving the city's postal service and, in 1831, helping to break the East India Company's trading monopoly.

Towards the end of 1788 the Chamber established a Commerical Agent in London. Colquhoun, who was leaving Glasgow for the capital, undertook this important task. He also acted as a link (in modern terms, perhaps a 'lobbyist') between the Chamber and Westminster, keeping an eye on the flood of legislation coming out of Parliament which might affect its members, and putting the Chamber's views to the legislators.

Before the First World War, its membership was limited to the city's more important businessmen and it had considerable influence with both local and central government.

In 1937 the Junior Chamber of Commerce was established, accepting members between the ages of 20 and 40.

Keeping its members informed has always been an important function of the Chamber, and this is the principal task of the *Journal of the Glasgow Chamber of Commerce* (begun in 1918). It provides an analysis of business trends likely to affect its members, it constantly updates changes in commercial law through its case notes, it supplies up-to-date company notes and, mindful of its long history, it reminds its members (currently over 1,000) of the Chamber's eventful past.

Children's Pursuits

Not unusually, Glasgow children's pastimes are ill-recorded and only fleeting glimpses can be had of their activities. A short list of early 19th-century games suggests that only the names have changed – 'Wully, Wully, Wastle, I'm up on your Castle', 'Robbers and Rangers', 'Scotch and English', 'Smugglers and Gaugers', 'I Spy', 'Roundabout, Roundabout, Merrymatansey', marbles, dragons (or kites), peeries (or tops), skipping-ropes and shinty. Peevers (or beds) only became possible when paving stones allowed the chalking of beds and the sliding of peevers.

An old-fashioned girls' game was the Lottery Book. Small, square woodcut pictures were hidden between the pages of a thick book and participants were invited to stick a pin between the closed pages; the

Traffic-free Dalmally St, off Maryhill Rd, provides a safe play area, outside the dark openings of the communal closes. (John S. Logan, Mitchell Library).

lucky ones choosing the right page received a 'dabbity' while the unlucky ones lost a pin – pins seem to have been a universal children's currency.

A game not possible before the common use of tin cans was 'Kick the Can'. A 'home' or 'den' had a tin can placed in it. This was kicked (preferably by a boy wearing tackety boots) as far away as possible, while all but the one who was 'het' ran away and hid. Those captured and imprisoned in the den could be freed if a hider could come and kick away the can again.

Not so much a game as a hazard took place in the back-courts. Each tenement back-court had its own washing-house separated from adjoining ones by high, narrow walls, and children (almost always boys) would teeter dangerously from washing-house to washing-house along these slender paths, running the gauntlet of volleys of abuse from the occupants of the tenements.

A large number of rhymes have been sung and recited by the city's children, but many of them are of Scottish rather than Glasgow provenance. Some, however, can be positively identified as genuine Glasgow, such as:

Born in a tenement at Gorbals Cross,
Of all the teddy boys he was the boss,

Got him a razor five feet wide;
Chopped up his mother and dumped
   her in the Clyde.

Collie, collie dug,
Lift up yer lug
And let the gentry by ye.
    lug – ear
In yonder green valley
There lived a wee Tallie,
Ah gave her some biscuits tae start a
   wee shop.
Before the shop started
The wee Tallie farted
And blew a' the biscuits away up a 'kye
   Tallie – Italian
   up a 'kye – up in the sky

Oor wee school's the best wee school,
The best wee school in Glesga,
The only thing that's wrang wi' it
Is the baldy-heided maister.
He goes tae the pub on a Setturday night,
He goes tae church on Sunday,
And prays the Lord tae gie him strength
Tae belt the weans on Monday.
   baldy-heided – bald-headed
   weans – children

Paddy on the railway, pickin' up stanes,
Alang came an engine, and brak

Paddy's banes.
'Oh!' said Paddy. 'That's no' fair.'
'Well!' said the driver, 'ye shouldny
   huv been there!'
   stanes – stones

Sugarally watter, black as the lum,
Gether up preens an ye'll a' get some.
   preens – pins
   Small, cut-up pieces of liquorice are placed in an empty medicine bottle along with water and sugar. The bottle is then firmly corked and vigorously shaken for as long as possible, thus producing a muddy, brownish liquid. For the price of a pin the purchaser is allowed one swallow.

Tell-tale tit,
Yer mammy canny knit,
Yer daddy canny go tae bed
Withoot a dummy tit.

Wee chookie burdie, tol, lol, lol,
Laid an egg on the windy sole,
The windy sole began tae crack,
Wee chookie burdie roared and grat.
   chookie – hen, chicken
   windy – window
   sole – sill
   grat – wept

Glasgow has produced one nursery rhyme whose first verse has become famous throughout the English-speaking world. It was written by William Miller (1810–72), a Glasgow wood-turner.

Wee Willie Winkie
Rins through the toun,
Up stairs and doon stairs
In his nicht-goun,
Tirlin at the window,
Crying at the lock,
'Are the weans in their bed?
For noo it's ten o'clock.'
   tirlin – rattling
   weans – children

Churches

For many centuries the cathedral provided for the religious needs of the city and of the immediate landward areas beyond its boundaries. In addition, there were a number of small chapels in or near it, some dating from at least the 13th century. St Thenew's Chapel, dedicated to the mother of St Kentigern, was located outside the old West Port and survived until 1597, while nearby was a chapel to Thomas a Beckett. On the north side of the Trongate, not far from the Cross, stood a chapel dedicated to our Lady and mentioned as early as 1293. At the east end of the Drygate there was a chapel dedicated to St John the Baptist. Also on the city's east side was Little St Mungo's Chapel, with an associated burying-ground and draw well. Built about 1500, it lay north of the Gallowgate on the east bank of the Molendinar. In 1754 the burying-ground became the site of the well-known Saracen's Head Inn, and stones from the chapel's ruins went to the building of the inn. Outside the city's northern gate, on the common muir, was St Rollox's (Roche) Chapel. St Roche was the patron saint against pestilence and it was common, for obvious reasons, to find chapels dedicated to him *outside* city walls. Glasgow plague-sufferers were usually ejected from the city to this muir and the chapel's burying-ground was used for the victims of the 1645–46 visitation of the plague.

With the Reformation (1560) a profound change came over the religious needs of citizens. The Protestant emphasis on the preaching of the Word required auditoria, not theatres, and the pulpit, not the high altar, became the focus. In order to meet these new needs many smaller buildings were required and a process of church erection began in Glasgow which, keeping pace with the developing city, eventually led in 1820 to the presence within its boundaries of the ten *city* (or *burgh*) churches. These ten continued to minister to the spiritual needs of the old city's adherents to the national religious organisation, the Church of Scotland, despite the upheavals of the 1843 Disruption and two World Wars. However, the growing decay and desertion of the inner city eventually took its toll and the past few decades have witnessed the departure of all but two of the ten (St Andrew's and St George's Tron), either by termination or by uniting with some suburban church.

A collegiate church, St Mary and St Anne (Our Lady College), had been founded *c.*1484 by James Henderson, Subdean of the Cathedral, near the south-west corner of the Cross. Neglected after the Reformation, it was rebuilt about 1592 as the city church for the South Parish. First known as the Laigh Kirk ('Low Church') to distinguish it from the High Kirk (the Cathedral), it later took the name of the Tron Church because the tron or public weighing apparatus was stored in the base of its tower. Its session-house was regularly used as a guard-house by burgesses on night watch-and-ward duties. One evening in 1793, while they were out on patrol, some young members of a local Hell-fire Club entered and, to test their ability to endure heat (useful in their after-life!), fed the fire to such an extent that the resulting conflagration totally destroyed both the session-house and the church, leaving only the steeple. In addition, the blaze destroyed the first volume of the presbytery minutes and damaged 13 other volumes. A replacement church, located further to the south, was built in 1794. The old steeple, quite separate from the new building, was retained and in 1855 ground arches were inserted in it to allow through-access by pedestrians. In 1946 the congregation was transported to a new church in Balornock. In 1980 the church building was leased by the District Council to the Glasgow Theatre Club and was opened as the Tron Theatre in 1982.

The district known as the Barony was that part of the Archbishop's lands lying immediately outwith the city's boundaries. In 1595 it was disjoined from the cathedral and erected into a new parish. It took possession of the cathedral crypt (where its situation was described as 'dark, dirty and incommodious'). The congregation of the Barony Kirk continued to meet in its gloomy depths until 1798, when a new church was erected in Cathedral Square, slightly to the east of the cathedral. In 1890 it moved again, to the west side of High St, into a handsome building costing £20,000 (now a ceremonial hall for Strathclyde University). An early Barony minister was Zachary Boyd (1623–53), best known for preaching a vehement sermon against Oliver Cromwell in 1650 as the latter sat amongst the congregation. Cromwell is said to have stopped one of his officers from pistolling the preacher, taking his own revenge by bidding Boyd dine with him and keeping him on his knees while Cromwell prayed from midnight to 3 a.m. Another notable Barony minister was Donald Cargill (c.1619–81), who joined the extreme wing of the Covenanters and was executed for treason. In 1982 the Barony joined with St Paul's and St David's (Ramshorn) as the Barony Ramshorn.

A convent of Dominicans or Black Friars was founded on the east side of the High St in 1246. Its chapel was gifted to Glasgow University by the Crown after the Reformation, but by 1635 it was in such a ruinous condition that the University resolved to give it to the Town Council for use as one of the city churches. In 1670 Blackfriars Church (or the Old College Church, as it was known) was struck by lightning and more or less rendered unusable. It was rebuilt and reopened in 1702. When the university moved to Gilmorehill in 1870 the church fell out of use and the congregation moved to a new building in Westercraigs, Dennistoun. In 1982 it terminated on uniting with Dennistoun Church and Dennistoun South Church as Dennistoun Blackfriars.

In 1648 the nave of the cathedral was partitioned off from the choir under the name of the Outer High Kirk to serve the East Parish. This division left the choir to the High Church (as the Inner High). In 1835 the Outer High moved to St Paul's Church, built for the congregation in Frederick St. In 1907 it moved again to a new site at the top of John St and terminated in 1953 on uniting with St David's (Ramshorn) and later with the Barony as the Barony Ramshorn.

Under the Toleration Act of 1687 a building was erected for Presbyterian worship (at that time the state had imposed Episcopalianism on Scotland) in King St (also known as the Wynd). In 1691 this church, known as the Wynd Church, was taken over by the Town Council as one of the city churches, but in 1761 the Wynd Church congregation was transferred to the new St Andrew's Church off the Saltmarket in St Andrew's Square. For a while in the latter half of the 18th century, an area to the south-west of the Cross became fashionable. The mansions in St Andrew's

Square and Charlotte St were occupied by many of the city's merchants and manufacturers and the district eventually acquired an appropriately prestigious church. It was a long time a-building (1739–56) and became the parish church in 1761. (It united with St James's Glasgow Cross in 1939 and with Gillespie Central in 1953.)

Until the middle of the 18th century the organisation of the city churches had been on a voluntary basis, but in 1763 the magistrates and council took to themselves the sole right of patronage of all the churches within the city with the exception of the cathedral.

As the area to the north and west of the old city centre became increasingly built over, the need for a new church there was met by the erection in 1720 of the North West or Ramshorn Church on the north side of the Cow Loan, later Ingram St – *Ramshorn* was the name of the land thereabouts. It was rebuilt in 1825 when Ingram St was extended further west and became St David's (Ramshorn). It is the only one of the extant city churches still surrounded by its own burying-ground. It terminated in 1953, joining with St Paul's and the Barony as the Barony Ramshorn. The building now belongs to Strathclyde University.

The westward movement of the city continuing, a West Parish was set up in 1761. At first it used the restored Wynd Church (vacated by its previous congregation which was now worshipping in St Andrew's Church), but in 1807 a new parish church was built at the north end of Buchanan St; and the church name, St George's, then became the parish name. In 1940 it united with the Tron St Agnes (in the same building) as St George's Tron.

St Thenew, the mother of St Kentigern, was supposed to have died in Glasgow, her burial-place and associated chapel lying to the south-west of the Cross outside the West Port. When a new parish was being marked out for this growing area, its church was built (1780) on or near the site of the ancient chapel and hence took the name of St Enoch's Church (a corruption of St Thenew). It was rebuilt in 1827, retaining the old spire, and one of the new windows carried the innovatory representation of the symbol of the Church of Scotland, the Mosaic burning bush. This novelty was regarded by many as the cloven hoof of papistry and one reverend gentleman had to be restrained from smashing it to pieces with his staff. St Enoch's Church, to considerable protest, was demolished in 1925, the congregation moving to St Enoch's Hogganfield.

When Thomas Chalmers became minister of the Tron Kirk in 1815 he brought with him his strong belief that the poor of each parish should be looked after by the parish church. In 1820 he was given a test-bed for his theory when he was appointed to a new parish, St John's. Its church, designed by David Hamilton and costing £9,000, had its opening delayed by the collapse of its tower. It was located off Graeme St (later Bell St) in one of the poorest areas of the city. Chalmers and his church elders tried hard to put his theory into action, but without long-term success. It terminated in 1953 on uniting with Chalmers church, now part of Calton New. In 1962 the building's dangerous condition led to its demolition.

St James's Church was the tenth and last of the 'city churches'. The Methodists had erected a church in Great Hamilton St in 1817 far beyond their means, and when it was vacated by them it became in 1820 the parish church for the St James's Parish. It terminated in 1949 in uniting with Pollok St Aidan's as St James's (Pollok).

By the 1830s the city was expanding so fast that the old city churches could no longer minister to the needs of all its inhabitants. Thomas Chalmers was quick to recognise this and his campaign for church extension in the city was ably supported by several wealthy laymen, including William Collins, publisher and printer. In 1834 it was proposed to set up 20 new churches in Glasgow, each to seat 1,000 members and each to cost not more than £2,000. Unlike the burgh churches, these new places of worship were either chapels of ease (and therefore not able to act independently) or *quoad sacra* churches (and restricted to purely religious matters). The last of these extension churches was erected in Springburn in 1842.

Although the statistical survey (see below) seems to indicate a considerable growth in the various branches of the Church of Scotland in the city, Glasgow has suffered, like other Scottish burghs, from an oversupply of church buildings. One reason for this has been its share in the general Scottish overgenerous secession church construction; the other has been the drift outwards to the suburbs of the inner-city population, leaving behind many churches of architectural significance in a state of ravaged emptiness.

The Gaelic Church

A combination of events, particularly the Highland Clearances and the city's pressing need for factory workers, pushed or pulled many Highlanders into Glasgow from the end of the 18th century onwards, and it became obvious that to meet the religious needs of these incoming Gaels, Gaelic-speaking churches would need to be set up. As early as 1727 a Highland Society had been instituted in the city with the principal aim of attending to the education and welfare of the young Highlanders in

Glasgow. A later offshoot of this body was the Gaelic Chapel Society (1768), which was responsible, about 1770, for the erection of a Gaelic-speaking church in Ingram St – Gaelic sermons in the morning, English in the afternoon. In 1833 the Glasgow Presbytery recognised it as a *quoad sacra* church, its parish being the whole city. About this time a census of Highlanders in the city was taken which established that there were 20,000 of them of whom 16,000 could speak only Gaelic – by now there were three Gaelic chapels in the city (a Gaelic chapel of ease had been set up in Duke St in 1798) which could between them accommodate 3,600. In 1837 the original Ingram St building was sold for the 'fabulous' sum of £12,000 and a new one erected in Hope St in 1851, which took the name of St Columba. Once again the church was forced to move, this time because the Caledonian Railway Co required the site in connection with its new Central Station (opened 1879). A sum of £44,700 was received and about £33,000 was spent on erecting in 1904 a handsome and architecturally prestigious church on sloping ground at the western end of St Vincent St. The new church has continued to serve a congregation which has kept shrinking, mainly due to the rapid fall in immigration from the Highlands.

The Secession Churches

In 1738 an association of Praying Societies in and about Glasgow petitioned to be accepted by the Associated Synod (i.e. the original Secession Church, formed in 1733). Their first meeting-place was at Crosshill, near Cathcart, then in a tent erected on the north side of Rottenrow, until their first meeting-house was erected in 1742 in Shuttle St, near the High St. As the result of a dispute over the religious significance of the oath taken by new burgesses, the Associated Synod split in 1747 into two branches, Burgher and Anti-Burgher, and the Shuttle St congregation became known as the Burgher Church. In 1821 it moved to a new church building (costing £8,000) in Albion St, and took the name of Greyfriars Church, after an ancient establishment of Grey Friars near its site. In 1847 Greyfriars joined with another secession church, the Relief Synod, to form Greyfriars UP (United Presbyterian) Church. After a further union with the Free Church of Scotland in 1900, the union being known as Greyfriars UF (United Free) Church, the congregation returned to the Church of Scotland in 1929.

When the Anti-Burghers separated in 1747, they established a meeting-house in the Havannah (a street running east from the High St, below and parallel to Duke St). Later, when the building was enlarged and an entrance made to the north, it became known as the Duke St Anti-Burgher Church. In 1820 the Burghers and the Anti-Burghers amalgamated and eventually, in

1880, the church moved to Cathedral Square as the Cathedral Square UF Church.

STATISTICAL SURVEY OF DENOMINATIONS			
	1850	1900	1992
Church of Scotland	29	83	128
Free Church	32	95	9
United Presbyterian	27	74	*
Other Secession Churches	14	5	–
Roman Catholic	6	26	76
Episcopalian	6	20	14
Baptists	5	15	17
Methodists	2	8	3
	121	326	247

* The United Presbyterian joined with a majority of the Free Church in 1900 as the United Free (UF) Church which in turn joined with the Church of Scotland in 1929.

See also　CATHEDRAL
　　　　　　　RELIGIOUS GROUPS

City of Culture

In 1986 it was announced by the cultural ministers of the European Commission that out of nine submissions (which included Bath, Bristol, Cambridge and Edinburgh) Glasgow had been chosen to be the European City of Culture in 1990. With a typical degree of courage and optimism the city decided that, unlike previous chosen cities, its celebrations would last the entire year and that it would encompass the whole range of manifestations of the city's life and times.

The main sources of funding were the Councils of Glasgow District and Strathclyde Region. Of the estimated total cost of around £50 million, about half came from these two bodies. It was decided that the pivotal event of the year would be a multimedia celebration of the city's history, 'Glasgow's Glasgow'. Its working title, 'The Words and the Stones', emphasised its twin approaches, by way of the city's written and spoken records and through its buildings and artefacts. It was staged in the totally refurbished 22 massive brick-vaulted arches which support the high-level railway tracks leading to Central Station. The layout of the exhibition was unusual being based on the geography of the city, so that the north-east corner of the exhibition, for example, represented the events, people and buildings associated with the north-east part of the city. There were 102 different subdivisions in 12 main areas, six representing the city north of the river and six representing the south. Emphasis was laid on the worldwide search for material associated with the city, and there were 3,000 objects from over 300 lending institutions. The exhibition was criticised by some, mainly as being responsible for a loss of some £4 million (representing 30 per cent of the District's cultural budget for the year), and for its initial high-price admission policy. Nevertheless, 509,000 people visited it; and its intense concentration, into a comparatively small space, of such a vast conglomeration of the material substance of the city's past and present, afforded a vivid and memorable reminder of Glasgow's rich and varied history.

Among the other major events of the year was the exhibition 'Glasgow Girls: Women in Art and Design, 1880–1920'. This was a major retrospective exhibition of over 400 items of decorative and fine art by more than 30 artists, all of whom had studied at Glasgow School of Art; it provided a reassessment of the part played by early 20th-century women artists. A huge theatrical production, *The Ship*, by Bill Bryden and William Dudley, celebrated the erstwhile pre-eminence of Clyde shipbuilding, the Bolshoi Opera visited the city and the Burrell Collection housed a prestigious display of 'The Age of Van Gogh'.

During the year one major venue was opened – the Royal Concert Hall – and several others substantially refurbished, among them the Tramway Theatre, the King's Theatre, the Citizens' Theatre, and, in particular, the McLellan Galleries, which were completely redesigned.

Along with the Garden Festival of two years earlier, the City of Culture Year helped considerably to confirm the city as an established tourist centre.

Cleansing

Until the city's size made positive action a necessity, the history of the cleansing of Glasgow's streets was a struggle between the Town Council – with its indignant and ineffectual remonstrations (1599: 'na middingis be wpoun the Hiegate fra sydwall to sydwall'; 1656: 'na maner of persoune lay fulyie [noisome substances] on the calsayis [causeways] whill first they have horssis redie to tak away the samyne')– and the citizens who were fully aware of the market value of their individual middens.

The Council's weary repetitions indicate clearly that nothing was being done. Certainly during times of plague, as in 1646, extraordinary measures were taken – special cleansers employed, horses purchased to remove sweepings, bailies to inspect all work done – but in normal times, expediency ruled.

It was not until the passing of the 1800 Police Act that the cleansing of streets became a public duty. At first the cleansing was undertaken by the city's night-watchmen as part of their ordinary duties, but by 1816 there were 16 full-time scavengers employed, and the sale of manure was bringing in an annual sum of £418 to the Council's coffers. Until 1868, the cleaning of courtyards with their noisome middens and ashpits was supposed to be carried out by the landlords, but in that year a Cleansing Department was established with overall responsibility for all cleansing. In a city largely built of tenements, back-court cleansing was a major responsibility. Though nowadays much reduced because of tenement demolition, in 1933, for example, there were more than 24,000 back-courts to be kept clean.

With the increasing use of the water closet, the proportion of excrementitious matter in the collected refuse fell off dramatically and it became possible to sort the sweepings and ashpit contents. Towards the end of the century several refuse works were opened where the rubbish was divided – manure went for sale to farmers and for use on the Corporation's farms, the rest (in those days, largely ash from domestic fires) was pressed into aggregate to form concrete. More recently, Refuse Disposal Works have been constructed – Polmadie Works in 1958, Govan Works in 1964 and Dawsholm Works in 1970. Most rubbish now goes direct to incineration, after tins and other metal items have been extracted, while the grit, dust and ash become clinker.

The cleansing of the city is still the responsibility of the District Council through its Cleansing Department. It collects more than 260,000 tonnes of rubbish each year through its street-sweeping and refuse collection services.

See also SEWAGE SYSTEM

Climate

The general climate of Glasgow is much the same as that of the rest of the west of Scotland. Although it lies in the broad and extensive plain of the Clyde basin it is almost completely surrounded by sheltering high ground. To the north lie the Campsie Fells and Kilsyth Hills (1,900ft), north-west are the Dumbartonshire Hills (over 2,000ft), west and south-west are the hills of Renfrewshire and Ayrshire, and to the south is high moorland (1,200ft).

The prevailing westerlies as they journey across the warmer currents of the Atlantic ocean bring with them cool, wet weather, so that the climate tends to be equitable with cool summers and mild winters. One difference is that within the city's built-up area the phenomenon of 'urban warmth' tends to keep the temperature one or two degrees higher than in the surrounding countryside. In addition, lying as it does within its large howe or valley, Glasgow is particularly sheltered from the cold north and east winds.

The winter temperature lies between 0.4°C and 6.3°C and the summer between 10.6°C and 19°C, but it is not too exceptional for the warmest day of winter to equal the coldest day of summer, and domestic heating is generally thought necessary between mid-September and mid-May. It is popularly believed that the healthiest month is September and the most fatal March.

Until quite recently the city suffered badly from industrial smog (so voluminous were the emissions that on occasions its smoke pall could be traced all the way to England) but the effects of the Clean Air Acts and the loss of smoke-producing industries have practically eliminated this climatic effect.

The average yearly rainfall is 40in (seldom falling below 30in) and in general there are about 230 days with rain each year. The driest months are generally March to June, and the wettest December and January. The average wind velocity is 10 mph (appreciably less than the average for Edinburgh), and the range of humidity falls between 74 per cent and 86 per cent – a fairly high figure.

Because of its northerly altitude the city's longest day is one hour longer than that of the south of England, while its midwinter day is correspondingly 1fi hours shorter; its average annual total of sunshine is 1,308 hours.

Clubs

During the latter half of the 18th century, when the profits from Glasgow's growing economy had created a class with leisure, many of the city's merchants and manufacturers filled at least part of their time by forming social clubs. Lacking other accommodation, these small gatherings met in one of the many city 'change-houses' or taverns, each one being associated with a different tavern. Some met daily, most weekly, a few at still longer intervals. One distinguishing feature was their all-male membership.

One of the earliest of these clubs was the Anderston Club, which took its name from the little village of Anderston where it met, then lying outside the city boundaries. It was founded about 1750 by Robert Simson, Professor of Mathematics at Glasgow University, and many of his university colleagues were members, among them Adam Smith, at that time Professor of Moral Philosophy. Its members also included many of the city's chief merchants and it has been said that it was Smith's social intercourse with these that helped to plant the seeds of his great work, *The Wealth of Nations*.

As new clubs formed they tended to attract members with common interests. For instance, the Hodge Podge Club, founded about the same time as the Anderston, began its life as a literary club but soon became the recognised venue for the city's tobacco aristocracy, while the Meridian Club, which met when the city's banks closed for dinner in the middle of the day, attracted the city's money-men.

In 1780 the Gaelic Club was established. Its aim was 'to remind them of Ossian . . . [and] to converse as friends in the bold and expressive language of the heroes in ages past' – an aim soon conveniently forgotten. Although regarded as one of the most hospitable of the Glasgow clubs, it always remained very much an aristocratic brotherhood.

The 18th-century volunteer movement was very active in Glasgow, and it too had its own club. Founded about 1790, it took its name, the Grog Club, from its favourite tipple. Its members were mainly bachelors and golfers.

Probably the most bizarre was the Face Club (c.1795). Its sole reason for existence was to allow its members the opportunity to meet for dinner, at which each member sat down face-to-face with his own individual boiled sheep's head.

The nearest to a political club was probably the Camperdown Club. Formed in 1797, and named after the famous naval victory of that year, it was a hotbed of rampant Toryism.

No excuse seems to have been thought necessary to form a club, and two which started in 1798 exemplify this. The Pig Club took its name from the figure of a pig which hung from the president's chain of office, and the What-You-Please Club had no membership qualifications of any kind – a possible reason for the large number of actors who joined it.

Probably the most professional of all these clubs was the Medical Club (c.1800), whose members were mainly drawn from the Faculty of Physicians. It did much to spread the use of vaccination against smallpox.

Another club which began at the turn of the century was the Packers' Club. Exporters of textiles had to supervise the packing of their goods in order to ensure that various taxes had been paid, and those involved in this process formed their own club.

Like the Face Club the Partick Duck Club (1810) existed for one purpose only. The grain mills which lined the banks of the Kelvin provided rich feeding for the many ducks which bred on the river and it was these birds which provided the main item on the club's weekly agenda. It was said that by October (when the club closed) there was scarcely a duck left on the river! The club's members were mainly drawn from the deacons of the city's various Incorporated Trades.

The Sma' Weft Club (*sma' weft* was the rather contemptuous term applied to a small textile manufacturer) was formed about 1830 when the agitation for political reform was at its height. It was part of the attack by the city's Whigs on the old self-serving and unreconstructed Town Council and had a reputation for inquisitive probing into the misdeeds of the City Fathers.

Almost all of these clubs had short lives, generally lasting no longer than the interest (or the life) of their progenitor, but one Glasgow club, the Western, has successfully survived down to the present. In 1825 a Major Monteith founded the Badger Club, which later became the Western Club. One common feature of all the Glasgow clubs had been their custom of meeting in taverns or inns; the standing of this club's members is clearly indicated by the fact that in 1842 they moved out of their howff into a palatial new building at the north-west corner of the crossing of Buchanan St and St Vincent St. Commissioned by the club from the famous Glasgow architect David Hamilton, it is now one of the city's architectural treasures. The club no longer meets there, having transferred to an address in Royal Exchange Sq.

The Clyde

Idle cranes on the north bank of the Clyde, symbols of the almost complete disappearance of the river's shipbuilding capacity. (George Oliver)

Broomielaw, 1828. Looking east from the Jamaica St Bridge. Clyde St, on the extreme left, shows St Andrew's Cathedral (RC), with the steeple of the Merchants' House beyond it. Visible behind the north end of the old medieval Glasgow Bridge is the Nelson Monument in the Glasgow Green with Gorbals Parish Church at its south end. In the foreground is Smeaton's bridge with its distinctive ox-eyes (designed to carry off flood water) and an early paddle-steamer moored to the Broomielaw Quay.

There is an old rhyme which says:

Annan, Tweed and Clyde
Rise a' oot o' ae hillside.
Tweed ran, Annan wan,
And Clyde fell
And brak its back owre Corra Linn.

The first part of this rhyme is not quite true, but the sources of the three rivers do indeed lie within a short distance of each other. A north-facing amphitheatre of hills about 20 miles north of Dumfries contains the Daer Reservoir into the southern end of which flows a stream which rises on the northern slopes of the Gana Hill (2,191ft). From the northern end of the reservoir issues the Daer Water which is joined after a short distance at Watermeetings by the Powtrail Water. The resulting stream is the embryonic Clyde. (From this point onwards the Ordnance Survey labels the combined Waters as the Clyde.) The matter is complicated by the fact that Clyde Law (1,790ft), a short distance away to the north-east, is the source of *two* burns called Clyde (sometimes known as Clyde's Burn or Little Clyde's Burn). One of these was diverted by the construction of a railway line into a tributary of the Annan but the other enters the combined Daer and Powtrail Waters a little to the south of Elvanfoot and from that point on the watercourse is indubitably the Clyde.

The river's length from source to Greenock is about 100 miles, during which journey it falls some 2,000ft. It drains an area of about 1,600 square miles and the boundaries of its catchment basin are identical for much of their length with those of the shire of Lanark. It is unique amongst the larger Scottish rivers in that its course runs mainly to the north-west.

From Elvanfoot to Thankerton it meanders peacefully northwards, being diverted slightly to the east by the mass of Tinto (2,334ft). After skirting its northern slopes the river begins its accelerated north-west course towards Glasgow. About Carstairs junction it receives the contributions of a major stream, the Douglas Water, and then near Lanark, in the course of just over four miles, it descends from 400ft to 170ft and in doing so forms the famous Falls of Clyde – Bonnington Linn, Corra Linn, Dundaff Linn and Stonebyres Falls. Slowing down now, the river passes through open farmland and the remnants of the once-famous Lanark orchards.

At Motherwell it enters what was once Glasgow's industrial hinterland, the former source of the coal and iron ore which were the sinews of the city's industrial strength in its heavy engineering works, shipyards and factories. Rutherglen Bridge, a short distance upstream from the city centre, is the point at which the river becomes tidal and the river level here is controlled by a weir upstream from the last city centre crossing, the Albert Bridge. From here until well past Whiteinch to the west of the city, the river is virtually canalised (the work of the Clyde Navigation Trust).

As it passes through the city the Clyde receives another two major inflows, first from the River Kelvin which has its source in the Kilsyth Hills north-east of the city, and then on the south, at Renfrew, from the combined waters of the Black Cart and the White Cart, both of which rise in the Renfrewshire hills. Further downstream the western end of the Forth & Clyde Canal joins the river at Bowling. At Dumbarton the Leven flows down into it from Loch Lomond. Now, as it approaches the port of Greenock, the river of Clyde ends and the Firth of Clyde begins.

See also CLYDE NAVIGATION
STREAMS

Gorbals from the north bank of the Clyde, with its high-rise flats advancing of an earlier Gorbals. (George Oliver)

The Broomielaw. On the far side of the river the paddle-steamers are about to start their journey 'doon the watter' to the many small resorts lining the Clyde estuary. Those in the foreground demonstrate the steamers' fine lines, which helped to make them some of the fastest vessels of their day. (William Graham, Mitchell Library)

Clyde St looking west of the second Glasgow (Jamaica St) Bridge. Rafts of wood (part of the city's timber trade) can be seen floating in the river, while the crowded masts of vessels in the Broomielaw Harbour are visible behind the bridge. (Robert Carrick, c.1852, Mitchell Library)

ISLANDS

Until the deepening of the Clyde during the 18th and 19th centuries, its wide, sandy-bottomed and shallow course was considerably impeded by a number of islands. These little islands moved positions, changed names and in some cases became absorbed into the river-bank, but a rough tally from early maps (in particular Blaeu's 17th-century *Theatrum Scotiae*) would give:

Point Isle – nearly opposite Nelson's Monument in Glasgow Green.
Dowcot Island (i.e. pigeon house) – between the old bridge and Jamaica St bridge. The capture of this isle was the aim of the stone battles waged between the boys of Glasgow and Gorbals.

Water Inch – at the mouth of the Kelvin.
White Inch – now the name of the district on the north bank.
King's Inch (or Inch of Renfrew) – this island, with Sand Inch, diverted one arm of the Clyde to run close to Renfrew.
Buck Inch – a small islet between King's Inch and Sand Inch.
Sand Inch.
Newshot Isle – a large island below the mouth of the Cart.
Inch Innan and **Collin's Isle** – two unlocated islands lay further downstream.

These islands all disappeared at various dates as the scouring and deepening of the river went ahead.

Clyde Navigation

The Firth of Clyde is a sheltered, deep-water estuary with depths of up to 200 to 300ft. It offers excellent access to transatlantic routes but the 20-mile stretch between Glasgow and Greenock afforded, at low water, depths of little more than 2ft, when it was still in a 'state of nature', and the successful efforts of the city to turn this muddy trickle into a passage for ocean-going ships has given rise to the saying 'Glasgow made the Clyde, and the Clyde made Glasgow'.

The shallowness of the Clyde was early noted as a significant impediment to the city's developing sea-going trade. In the middle of the 17th century the Glasgow merchants were forced to unload their cargoes at Ayrshire ports such as Irvine and Cunningham, and to transport them overland on packhorses. In 1656 the Commissioner for Customs and Excise in Scotland reported that Glasgow was 'kept under by the shallownesse of her river, every day growing more and more increaseing and filling up, soe that noe vessells of any burden can come nearer up then within fourteene miles, where they must unlade and send up theyr timber . . . in rafts or floats and all other commodityes by 3 or 4 tonnes at a time in small cobbles or boats'. Indeed, until the beginning of the 19th century ocean-going ships had no alternative but to dock downriver at Greenock or Port Glasgow and unload their cargoes into lighters or 'gabbarts' which were then sailed or poled up river to Renfrew, from thence to be towed by men and horses to the city.

Even so, there was still enough traffic to warrant the erection in 1662 of a small landing-stage, the Broomielaw Quay. A more radical solution to the problem was taken in 1668 when 22 acres of land near Newark Castle (18 miles downriver on the south bank) was purchased by the Town Council who had a deep-sea port built on it. At first called Newport, in 1774 it became Port Glasgow and by the end of the century it had become an efficient and useful adjunct to the city's sea trade. In 1710 it was appointed the principal customs port on the Clyde but it never fully realised the expectations of its builders; the adjacent port of Greenock stole a march on it, and its berthages began to silt up.

During this period, little or no attention was given to the possibility of actually deepening the river. But as the opportunities of the city's merchants began to increase following the Union of the Parliaments in 1707 (which allowed Scottish merchants to take part in the lucrative trade with the North American colonies), so their increased power in the city's affairs caused the Town Council to give serious consideration to methods of improving the upper navigation of the Clyde.

In 1725 James Stirling, mine manager at Leadhills, suggested that a system of weirs and locks, by impounding the freshwater flow, would form a much deeper channel. Thirty years later the Town Council commissioned James Smeaton, civil engineer, to draw up plans for such a scheme. For the site of the main dam or weir he selected Marlin Ford (four and a half miles west of the Old Glasgow Bridge). Parliamentary permission was obtained and work was begun, but by 1762 it was found that the silt and sand at the ford was insufficient foundation for the massive dam and the whole project was abandoned.

In 1768 John Golborne from Chester, experienced in civil engineering projects, was asked by the Town Council to report on how the river might be deepened. In his report he pointed out that 'The River Clyde is at present in a state of Nature' and that the solution would be found by 'proceeding on the Principle of assisting Nature'. His simple method was to build out at right-angles to the banks and from opposite sides pairs of long jetties or dykes; the resulting narrowing of the channel would increase the velocity and strength of the water-flow and the vastly increased scouring action would erode the river-bed (fortunately for the city's maritime future, almost all the river-bed was of a friable nature). He promised a depth in every part of 7ft if this was done.

The Council wasted no time; the Second Act for the Improvement of the Clyde Navigation, which appointed the members of the Town Council as the Statutory Trustees of the Clyde, was passed in 1770. Soon over 100 jetties had been constructed (some as long as 500ft, a clear indication of the breadth of the old river) and the beneficent effects were noticed in a remarkably short time. By the end of 1772 a depth of 5ft had been reached and vessels of 70 tons burthen were now, for the first time, able to sail into the city. In 1775 the Town Council declared itself satisfied that Golborne had 'fully implemented his contract'.

The wide, shallow Clyde had always been subject to periodic flooding and it soon appeared that the new, deeper river was not immune. In 1795 a flood so severe that it swept away the almost completed Hutchesontown Bridge devastated the ships

SHIPPING NEWS

The embarkation of one of the early Clyde paddle-steamers from the little Broomielaw Harbour, bound for Liverpool. On the opposite bank of the Clyde rises one of the city's many steam-powered spinning mills. (Glasgow Looking Glass, 1825, Mitchell Library)

in the harbour and flooded the merchants' and traders' warehouses. In 1798 John Rennie, river and canal engineer, reported that the increased flooding was caused by a greater run-off into the river upstream and that the only solution would be to further deepen the channel by dredging. At this time it was still not possible to bring ships over 100 tons up to Glasgow Harbour and larger ships were still having to unload at Greenock.

In 1805 Thomas Telford, civil engineer, was commissioned to report on the state of the river. In his report he advocated joining up the ends of Golborne's jetties with low transverse rubble training walls and filling in the space behind them with the spoil dredged from the river. This was taken in hand, thus beginning the process of 'canalising' the river. The improvement was such that ships of 150 tons were now able to dock in the Harbour; an added bonus was that the land being created behind the training walls now became valuable additions to the riparian landowners.

The organising body became, in 1809, the River Improvement Trust. Murmurs of complaint began to come from the city's merchants; the Trustees were still drawn only from the Town Council and the traders felt that they should be represented.

For the first time, ships could now be registered in Glasgow, and in 1815 the city was declared to be the head port for Customs purposes.

The advent of the steam-powered vessels, in the shape of the *Comet* in 1812, enabled the combination of Glasgow and the Clyde to assume a leading place in the new industrial world. By 1818 there were 17 steamboats active on the river, carrying both passengers and cargo, and the rapid development of shipbuilding in the growing number of Clyde yards gave the city a long-maintained lead. From the point of view of the Trust, one of the most significant developments of steam-power was the use of the steam dredger – the first made its appearance as early as 1824. Its vast superiority over the older manual type meant that eventually the Trust would be able to rely on straightforward dredging to maintain and improve the Clyde navigation.

Nevertheless, the Clyde was still too shallow for many ocean-going vessels and the Trustees sought new ways of improving it. In 1834 a neglected report from ten years before by Joseph Whidbey was re-examined by the River Improvement Committee. He had maintained that the principal agent in scouring the river-bed was not the downflow of river water but the force of the ebbing tide and that instead of restricting the width of the river it should instead be widened. The Committee admitted that the fact that ships drawing more than 12ft could still not come up to Glasgow suggested that the deepening action of the restricting jetties was no longer apparent. So the process was reversed and the river was progressively widened, from 400ft in the Harbour to 1,200ft off Dumbarton, by the removal of many of the old walls and dykes.

In 1840 the Fifth Clyde Navigation Act set the number of trustees as 33 and introduced representatives from the Merchants' House, the Trades House, the Chamber of Commerce and the neighbouring burghs of Gorbals, Calton and Anderston. Dredging of the lower reaches continued apace: by 1845 ships with an 18ft draught were able to dock in the Harbour, as could ships of up to 1,000 tons five years later. Most of the river's steamship traffic was to Dublin, Belfast and Liverpool, along with considerable river and estuarine trade.

In 1854 a totally unexpected obstruction was discovered in the river-floor at Elderslie. It proved to be a huge bed of volcanic lava lying only 8ft below low water. It stretched from bank to bank and extended almost 1,000ft along the river. There was only one way to remove such an obstruction – underwater blasting. At first by gunpowder and then by dynamite the struggle to remove it continued for 53 years, and by 1907 almost 20ft of solid lava (over 108,000 tons) had been removed.

The Clyde Navigation Act of 1858 set up a new body, the Clyde Navigation Trust, in place of the River Improvement Trust. It was now composed of nine councillors, nine elected shipowner ratepayers and two representatives each from the Merchants' House, the Trades House and the Chamber of Commerce.

At various times and places weirs had been placed across the river, either to protect the bridge piers from erosion or to deepen the water by impounding it. The first Broomielaw Bridge (1772) had its own weir but it proved to be both inefficient and incommoding, for it prevented easy access to the upper reaches of the harbour. In 1842 it was moved to the east side of the Old Bridge and in 1851 to the east side of the Albert Bridge. It took the form of a rough bank of stones and boulders covered at high-water with a lock for the passage of ships at its north end. Its ill-considered removal in 1880 did considerable damage: upriver silt reduced the level of water in the Harbour, sewage was carried upriver, long stretches of river-bank above the site of the weir were eroded so much that they collapsed and the foundations of several bridges were damaged (Rutherglen Bridge suffered so badly that it had to be replaced). So, parliamentary powers were obtained by the Corporation in 1894 and a new movable weir was erected in 1901 at the same place, where it remains to this day. It has three large sluice gates each 80ft long, 12ft deep and weighing about 45 tons. At high-water the gates are lowered to impound water upstream, and at low-water they are raised to allow vessels to pass upstream. The weir suffered considerable damage in 1941 when heavy and continuous rain damaged both the weir and the banks above and below it.

As larger and larger ships came down the slipways of the Clyde shipyards, much of the resources of the Trust were used to ensure that the river was able to receive them and that ancillary capabilities also were available. In 1875 the Trust set up the Govan Dry Dock, at that time the largest in the United Kingdom, later adding two others. Then in 1878, to assist in the fitting-out of new vessels, it erected at Finnieston a 50-ton crane, to be followed later by one of 75-tons lifting capacity and later still by two 130-ton giants. Between the wars the need for a high-level downriver bridge was widely canvassed and it was found that the probable site of such a

bridge would require the removal of the Trust's 130-ton crane; a new 175-ton crane, largely financed by Glasgow Corporation, was erected at Stobcross. It is 175ft high, with a jib 152ft long; besides assisting in the fitting-out of new ships it was also much used for loading on-ship steam-engines manufactured for overseas customers by the North British Locomotive Co.

The need for cross-river vehicular ferries downstream from city centre bridges was recognised by the Trust, and between 1890 and 1912 it established moving platform ferries at Finnieston and White-inch, as well as replacing the old Govan ferry. It also acquired the chain ferries at Erskine (1904) and Renfrew (1911). As well as providing cross-river services, the Trust also set up a series of small passenger vessels plying up and down the river between Victoria Bridge and Whiteinch. This service started in 1884 with four vessels built by T. B. Sneath in Rutherglen. They measured 72ft in length and had bluff bows to enable them to land passengers at the existing ferry stairs. This was found to be too dangerous and later models had conventional bows and landed their cargoes at floating platforms. They were called 'Cluthas' (an old name for the Clyde) and were numbered serially from 1 to 12; '5' and '6' were also built at Rutherglen but later numbers were built at Dumbarton and Port Glasgow. They carried from 230 to 350 passengers (some Cluthas were 100ft long) at 15-minute intervals, and proved to be both popular and profitable. They were particularly useful to the inhabitants of Govan and Partick who found them to be a quick and easy way to reach the city centre. In 1897, their peak year, they carried over three million passengers, but the inauguration of electric tramcars and the opening of the Subway rapidly killed them off and they were withdrawn in 1903.

In 1905 what proved to be the last Clyde Navigation Act was passed. The Trust was now to consist of 42 trustees (a large and, some thought, unwieldy number) – 18 to be elected by shipowning ratepayers, 16 to come from the Corporation and eight to represent the adjacent burghs and counties. The chairman was no longer to be *ex officio* the Lord Provost but would be elected. This was to be the final form of the Clyde Navigation Trust, until its dissolution in 1965.

The navigation of the channel was by now almost entirely maintained by continuous dredging, carried out by a combination of bucket dredgers and self-propelled hoppers. In the early days the dredged material had been used to consolidate the spaces behind the trans-verse dykes. In 1862, when these were all filled, the hoppers began to dump the spoil downstream in deep water at the mouth of Loch Long. After complaints and a court case, the Trust was obliged to move its dumping-ground to a site off Garroch Head, to the south of the Isle of Bute. Dredging is a costly procedure, and with the almost complete disappearance of shipping activity from the river, the need for this expensive process has, like the ships, disappeared and there is growing evidence that the river is beginning to silt up.

Thanks to the Trust's efficient labours it was now possible to launch very large ships into the river. The *Lusitania*, at that time the largest ship in the world (785ft long), was launched in 1907 and taken down the river with 30ft of water under her, a feat only possible by extensive pre-launch dredging. In 1914 the *Aquitania*, a much larger ship, went carefully down a channel which the Trust had spent two whole years dredging and straightening specifically for the launch. Symbolically, this launch can

be seen as representing the apogee of the Navigation, for after it came a miserable and inexorable decline. The post-war maritime nations had too many ships already, and the Harbour saw its shipping tonnage decline from almost seven million tons to little more than five million.

The launch of the *Queen Mary* with a draught of 35ft (and the two later 'Queens') and of the battleship *Vanguard* (1946) demonstrated that the Clyde could still build and launch great ships, but both of these, in their own way and for different reasons, represented ship types which were no longer viable. For a while during the Second World War some of the harbour's old prosperity returned – in 1944 nine million tons of shipping used it – but this improvement could only be temporary.

In 1961 the Rochdale Report recommended that all ports within one river or estuary should be managed by one authority, and in 1966 the Clyde Navigation Trust, the Greenock Harbour Trust and the Clyde Lighthouses Trust came together to form the Clyde Port Authority.

The fate of the Glasgow Harbour itself was made certain by the rise of the modern bulk carrier with its unacceptable 40ft draught and its containerised cargo. The port soon became a vista of weed-grown quays, filled-in docks and empty berths. The new Trustees, accepting the inevitable, turned to the neglected lower reaches. In 1969 the Clydeport Container Terminal came into operation at Prince's Dock, Greenock. Unfortunately the trend is now to unload container ships at UK southern ports and then distribute cargoes by road transport, so that Greenock's initial success has not been maintained; in 1979 the Hunterston Ore Terminal, Ayrshire, was opened.

From the time of the little Broomielaw Quay in the 17th century the

Glasgow Harbour was in a state of continual expansion. At first the need for more berths was accommodated by extending the existing quays, but this expedient was constrained by the need to keep the overall harbour size within reasonable limits, and soon vessels were tying up five or six abreast. The solution was to open up the river-banks in a series of docks (more properly described as tidal basins) offering off-river berthages. The first of these was the Windmillcroft Basin, better known as Kingston Dock. It was opened in 1867 on the south bank next to the Broomielaw Bridge, and had five acres of water space. It proved very popular, especially with the smaller coastal vessels, and was rebuilt in 1917. The Clyde has a small tidal range (about 10ft) so that the Kingston Dock and all later Clyde docks never required dock gates to control water levels and could thus offer unimpeded access. It was infilled in the late 1960s to make room for the new Kingston Bridge (opened 1970).

Next to open, in 1877, was the 34-acre Queen's Dock, at Stobcross, on the north bank. Its two basins, with their 10,000ft of quay, became the Trust's major berthage and provided accommodation for both passenger and cargo ships sailing to Australia, Canada, East Africa, Burma, the West Indies, South America and the Mediterranean. It closed in 1969 and was infilled with material from demolished tenements, St Enoch's Station and Cathcart Castle. Its site became in 1985 the Scottish Exhibition and Conference Centre.

The Prince's Dock (three basins, at Cessnock on the south bank) was finished in 1897 and was mainly used for cargo trade. It was the first dock to have a complete range of dockside cranes, including one capable of 130-ton loads on its west quay, used to install engines and boilers in recently launched ships. It was complemented by a similar crane on the Finnieston Quay on the opposite bank. It was closed in the 1970s; its infilled site was used for the Glasgow Garden Festival in 1988 and is expected to become a housing development. Six miles downriver at Clydebank the Rothesay Dock was opened in 1907 for coal and ore shipments, but its function was later taken over by the General Terminus Quay. In 1931 the King George V Dock was opened at Shieldhall, four miles downriver on its south bank. Little used in its early years, it proved a boon during the Second World War when it was claimed to be one of the most used shipping facilities in the country.

More specialist accommodation was also provided. In 1878 lairages for the increasing livestock trade (mainly from Ireland) were opened at Yorkhill, and in 1907 were moved to the Merkland Animal Lairages. The Meadowside Quay and Granary for grain cargoes was opened in 1914, enlarged in 1937 and doubled in size in 1960.

The General Terminal Quay was established on the south bank in 1849. From an extensive railhead just behind it, Scottish coal was loaded directly into ships moored at its quay. In 1957 it was transformed into a facility for unloading iron ore (via three giant transporters) for the ill-fated Ravenscraig Steelworks, 11 miles away at Motherwell. Even discounting the closure of Ravenscraig, the facility was ill-conceived, for the increase in size of the new ore carriers prevented them from using it.

The historical continuity of the organisation which made the river which made the city is best expressed by its headquarters building. Beginning in 1820 in Robertson St as the offices of the Harbour Police, it was resplendently transmogrified by the architect J. J. Burnett in 1908 into what has been described as 'one of Glasgow's most important and impressive buildings', and now houses the Trust's successor, the Clyde Port Authority.

See also THE CLYDE

Coat-of-Arms

Although Glasgow had no official coat-of-arms until 1866, the various objects which made up that armorial bearing had their origins back in the time of the city's earliest history, all of them being associated with its patron saint, Kentigern: the bird represented the robin redbreast which he brought back to life; the fish with its golden ring was the salmon which helped to save Queen Languoreth from the wrath of her cuckolded husband, King Rydderch Hael; the tree was originally a hazel branch which Kentigern caused miraculously to burst into flame; and the bell was supposed to have been the small hand-bell used by the saints of the Celtic Church to call their flocks to worship.

It had always been the custom to authenticate documents by appending seals to them and it was on the seals used by the ecclesiastical and civil authorities of Glasgow that these various items first appeared. Between the end of the 13th century and the middle of the following century they all found their way on to the city's seals, in various combinations; the first time they were all present much as they are today was in 1647, when 'John Grahame product ane new seale maid be directioun of the toune, for which was payit xlii lib 1s' (£42.05). There was as yet no motto attached to the arms, but in 1637 a bell cast in Holland for the Tron Kirk steeple, as well as carrying the city's arms, carried a lengthy inscription: 'Lord Let Glasgow Flovrichse Throvgh The Preaching Of Thy Word And Priasing [*sic*] Thy Name'. The next stage is illustrated in a book printed by the Glasgow printer Robert Sanders in 1663 in which the motto is shortened to 'Lord let Glasgow flourish through the Preaching of thy Word'. Later still, in 1699, an ornamental stone over the entrance to Blackfriars' Church shortened it still further to the present form, 'Let Glasgow flourish'.

During the 18th and early 19th centuries many variations on these themes appeared – the fish lay on its back or its stomach, the bird looked to the left or to the right, the bell was fastened to the tree or floated free, the tree showed its roots or grew from a little mound. At length, in 1866, at the request of the Lord Provost, John Blackie junior, a local historian

Andrew Macgeorge published an exhaustive work of research entitled 'An inquiry as to the armorial insignia of the city of Glasgow' in which he gave more than adequate reasons for suggesting that the Town Council ask the Lord Lyon King of Arms to grant and authorise proper arms for the city according to his findings. This was done, and on 26 October 1866 the Lord Lyon granted a patent in the following words:

> Argent on a mount in base Vert an oak tree proper, the stem at the base thereof surmounted by a salmon on its back also proper, with a signet ring in its mouth Or; on the top of the tree a red-breast, and in the sinister fess point an ancient hand bell, both also proper; above the shield is placed a suitable helmet, with a mantling Gules doubled Argent, and, issuing out of a wreath of the proper liveries, is set for crest the half-length figure of St Kentigern affronté, vested and mitred, his right hand raised in the act of benediction, and having in his left hand a crozier, all proper; in a compartment below the shield are placed for supporters two salmon proper, each holding in its mouth a signet ring, Or; and in an escrol entwined with the compartment this motto, 'Let Glasgow flourish'.

Some of the more obscure terms used can be explained as follows:

'Argent' – a white or silver background to the shield.

'a mount in base Vert' – a little green mound from which the tree grows. It has been said, without any evidence, that this mound represents the little hill which miraculously raised up St Kentigern so that his voice could be heard clearly by his congregation.

'an oak tree proper' – although originally a hazel branch, it came to be described as an oak tree. 'Proper' indicates that the object is be represented realistically, not symbolically.

'Gules doubled Argent' – the cloth cover of the helmet is striped red and white.

'a signet ring, Or' – a gold ring.

'Supporters' – none of the early versions had supporters, Macgeorge came across a seal used by the City Chamberlain's Department which showed two salmon upright on either side of the shield and adopted them as heraldic supporters.

The version of the city's coat-of-arms now in use differs in a few particulars from that of 1866. Following the restructuring of Scottish local government brought about by the Local Government (Scotland) Act 1973, a new coat-of-arms was granted to the City of Glasgow District Council on 6 February 1975. This new version has one major change – the helmet has disappeared and in its place is 'a coronet appropriate to a statutory District videlicet: a circlet richly chased from which are issuant eight thistle heads (three and two halves visible) Or'

Probably the best-known statement regarding the city's coat-of-arms is the child's rhyme (not of any great antiquity):

Here's the Bird that never flew,
Here's the Tree that never grew,
Here's the Bell that never rang,
Here's the Fish that never swam.

There is a last line which is not so well known:

That's jist the drucken Salmon!

Common Good

The city's common good has been defined as 'such property and funds as are held for behoof of the community by the Council, unfettered by any restriction as to its dispersal save conformity to common law and the promotion of the public weal of the burgh'.

In medieval times and earlier, various parcels of land in and around Glasgow were possessed in common by the burgesses. These lands were the burgh's patrimony and it was on them that the citizens pastured their cattle, cut their firewood, dug their peat and quarried their building stone. To this were later added receipts taken in by the town's officers by way of fines, dues and customs. In short, all the town's revenue was paid into the Common Good and all its communal expenditure was met out of it.

As the burgesses changed from being farmers to merchants these lands were no longer required for tillage, and beginning about the time of the Reformation sales of burgh land to private individuals began to become quite common. One acceptable reason for this was that as the land was the community's wealth, then when extraordinary expenditure was incurred the only source of ready money was to sell some of the common land. For instance, in 1588 when the town decided to buy the Kelvin Mill for £600, the cash was found by feuing some of the burgh land.

The problem was that the closed and self-perpetuating nature of the Town Council afforded splendid opportunities for self-gratification. In 1568 the bailies 'condiscendit to set ane pairt of oure common muris amangis ourselfis'. This practice became a vicious circle as more land had to be sold to make good earlier misappropriations, and in 1691 the Council was forced to petition the Convention of Royal Burghs for permission to sell off three large portions to make good debts incurred by former magistrates 'misapplying of the tounes patrimony in their own sinistrous ends' – in 1690 Provost Barns had been held in the Edinburgh Tolbooth for maladministration of the Common Good.

The alienation of the town lands to the east of Glasgow – known as the East Common or Gallowmuir – began at the end of the 17th century. One of the largest purchasers here was John Walkinshaw (who became 'of Barrowfield' through purchasing the 'Burgh Fields' – which much later was to become Bridgeton. Other lands surrounding the old town were similarly disposed of – Cowcaddens passed into the hands of Patrick Bell in the 1660s, and the lands of Stobcross on the west were bought at an earlier date by the Anderson family. The 470 acres of the Blythswood lands (north of Anderston) were acquired by Provost Colin Campbell (these were not actually common land but had belonged originally to the Church). When this process was completed the city was ringed by land possessed by those governing it.

The Old Green and the New Green, also part of the burgh's patrimony, came under threat. A major part of the Old Green (which lay on the banks of the Clyde west of Stockwell St) was bought by Alexander Oswald of Shieldhall, and parts of the New Green (the present Glasgow Green) were also sold off, but the citizens' deep-rooted feelings about alienating the Green caused most of it to be bought back later.

For some time now the Common Good has become almost entirely a matter of investment rather than property, but even from early times surplus money has been disbursed in many ways. From the time of the Reformation on, the stipends of the ministers of the city churches were paid from it. The Corporation markets were financially administered under it and till 1878 the Green was maintained by it. In 1876 it contributed £5,000 towards the erection of the new Glasgow University on Gilmorehill, its funds enabled the Corporation to purchase the St Andrew's Halls in 1890 and it has always contributed towards the city's charities, in particular its hospitals and infirmaries. The most unusual use of its funds was to finance loans towards the construction and equipping of the Corporation's tramway system in 1894.

In return the Tramways agreed to pay back at the minimum rate of £9,000 yearly until the loan was extinguished; before the First World War it was these regular (and increasing) repayments which kept the Common Good solvent.

In 1895 the surplus came to £360,000 (with assets of over £1,000,000). In 1924 this surplus increased to about £500,000. In 1980 the market value of its assets had reached over £5,000,000 and in 1990 over £7,000,000 (mainly investments, although a small proportion is still derived from various properties throughout the city). Nowadays, almost half the surplus is expended on civic ceremonies and on hospitality to distinguished visitors as well as on worthwhile single projects such as the recent refurbishment of the McLellan Galleries and improvements to the Citizens' Theatre.

See also MUNICIPALITY

Courts of Law

Until comparatively recently the city's legal needs were supplied by a bewildering multiplicity of courts. The oldest of these was probably the Burgh Court which came into being in the Middle Ages when the Bishop of Glasgow was the territorial Lord of Glasgow and its judges were his bailies. When the city became a Burgh of Regality in 1450, a Regality Court was set up in which, once again, the bailies of the Town Council exercised jurisdiction over the

city, the Barony parishes, and Monkland and Govan. The Consistory or Commissary Court completed the triumvirate. This also was a bishop's court, one which concerned itself with testamentary affairs and matters of scandal, and which met in one of the western towers (demolished in 1845) of the Cathedral. It lingered on until 1826 when whatever of its duties were still relevant were taken over by the Sheriff Court. The scope of all these courts changed gradually over the centuries, constantly widening their respective (and often overlapping) jurisdictions.

The city's law agents who represented clients in the city's inferior courts were known as procurators. Their principal arena was the Commissary Courts and they could thus date their beginnings back some 500 years to the days of the medieval church. In 1668 they formed themselves into a society, the Faculty of Procurators in Glasgow, mainly to examine and regulate the admission of new members. They enjoyed exemption from certain burghal duties, such as having soldiers billeted on them and having to watch and ward. Although the term 'procurator' is now, in this sense, obsolete, the Royal Faculty of Procurators in Glasgow still exists as a society representing those solicitors practising in the city.

The abolition of Scottish heritable jurisdiction in 1747 (the government's reaction to the convenience this power had offered to the Jacobite clan chiefs in the rebellions of 1715 and 1745) brought major changes in the city's administration of justice. The Regality Court disappeared, but more importantly, the judicial powers of the hereditary Sheriffs now passed into the more professional control of the Deputy Sheriffs, and the Sheriff Court was on the way to becoming an effective source of justice.

Glasgow's Sheriff Court was active by 1758, with a jurisdiction covering the burgh, the parishes of the Barony and somewhat beyond. It had considerable powers and could adjudicate in all cases of capital crime except the four pleas of the Crown – murder, rape, robbery and fire-raising. The last time a Glasgow Sheriff passed the death sentence was in 1788. The court met twice a year (from May to June and from November to March) in the old

Tolbooth at the Cross till 1814, after which it moved to the new Justiciary Buildings at the foot of the Saltmarket. About 1844 it moved back to the city centre, to the County Buildings in Wilson St.

Cases requiring judgment by a superior court came before the High Court of Justiciary on Circuit. Twice a year itinerant Lords of Justiciary from the central courts in Edinburgh held court in Glasgow, and their solemn procession along the Gallowgate from their lodgings in the Saracen's Head Inn to the Tolbooth was a recognised part of the city's ceremonial year. The High Court moved in 1812 to the new Justiciary Buildings and Courthouse at the foot of the Saltmarket, sharing it with the Council, the Jail and the Sheriff Court. After 1842 the removal of the Sheriff Court and the Council then left it with the occupancy of the whole building. By 1867 it was holding three sessions in the city; of the 70 Glasgow cases coming before it in 1955, some 58 were tried on circuit.

For the first half of the 19th century, many litigants, because of the Sheriff Court's antiquated and time-consuming procedures, preferred to use the more efficient Burgh Court – by this time divided into the Town or Bailies Court, the Summary Court, the Inferior or Conscience Court and the Small Debt Court. By the middle of the century, however, the Sheriff Courts had been reorganised and the Glasgow Court's business grew at such a rate that its accommodation had to be enlarged five times between 1844 and 1900, until it was occupying almost the whole County Building.

Between them, the Sheriff Court and the Police Courts eventually took over all the former functions of the old Burgh Court, which quietly expired about 1870. The Police Courts were particularly busy dispensers of justice, trying over 1,000 criminal cases in 1820, for example.

By the middle of the 20th century the principal criminal courts in Glasgow were the High Court of Justiciary, the Sheriff Court (before which serious cases were tried, either with a jury or in summary form by the Sheriff alone) and the Police Courts (chiefly involved in more trivial cases – in 1954 these were reduced from seven to three, Central, Marine and Govan). Apart from those requiring to go before the Court of Session, civil cases were taken care of by the Sheriff Court and the Justices of the Peace Court. The JP Court originally had jurisdiction over the whole of the Lower Ward of Lanarkshire (which included Glasgow) but when the city became the county of a City in 1867 it acquired its own JP Court. In 1986 the Sheriff Court (now officially the Sheriff Court of Glasgow and Strathkelvin) moved out of its disintegrating and malodorous quarters to a new and prestigious building on the south bank of the Clyde.

One of Glasgow's courts was concerned, in a legal sense, with neither criminal nor civil lawbreakers. This was the Dean of Guild Court, which from an early period became the arbiter in all matters concerning the positioning and construction of new buildings within the city.

See also DEAN OF GUILD COURT

Craft Guilds

In its early years Glasgow's importance came from being the seat of a Bishop and as such the source of ecclesiastical authority in Strathclyde – its citizens lived by ' sowing and reaping, herding and slaughtering. Two classes lived within its slight defences, burgesses and unfreemen – the latter servants, casual workers and labourers, the former landowners, merchants, craftsmen, priests, lawyers, the Bishop's freemen. These various groups within the burgess class, however much they may have differed from each other, shared one common characteristic – a constant, unremitting effort to protect their own interests.

The strength and influence of these groups tended to increase with the growth of the city, and one group in particular, the merchants, seized every opportunity for self aggrandisement. From an early period they managed to exercise an increasing influence on the municipal administration. There was a strong suggestion (on the part of the merchants, naturally) that they belonged to a socially superior class and as such could not allow socially inferior classes of burgesses, those who worked with their hands, to share administrative power with them. What this meant in practice was that right down to 1688 the rule of the city was in the hands of a mercantile clique largely composed of about half a dozen families (the Bells, Campbells, Andersons, Walkinshaws and Hamiltons, all related by blood or marriage) who shared out the municipal offices of provost and bailie amongst themselves, to the almost total exclusion of the craftsmen. However, as the city expanded (in the 50 years following the Reformation its population increased from 4,500 to 7,644) its character began to change more and more rapidly from an agricultural community to a manufacturing and trading community. In these circumstances the craftsmen of the city found it increasingly unsupportable that they were denied a proper share in the government of their city and yet had to pay in full their share of tax and stent.

Almost from their first appearance on the scene, craftsmen throughout Scotland had banded themselves together into fraternities and guilds. Before the Reformation these were primarily religious bodies involved in maintaining altars to their patron saints, having burial prayers said for their deceased members and helping their poor, old or disabled members, but soon they began to exercise more and more control over the work activities of their members. The earliest list of crafts demonstrates clearly the wide range of activities carried out by these Glasgow craftsmen, including as it did hammermen (covering blacksmiths, lock-smiths, swordmakers, clockmakers, etc), tailors, cordiners (cobblers or shoemakers), maltsters, weavers, baxters (bakers), skin-ners, fleshers, masons (wrights, coopers, sawyers, slaters, plasterers), surgeons and barbers, bonnet-makers, litsters (dyers), mariners and fishers. As the needs of the city changed over time, the activities of the craftsmen also changed, and by the time a definitive list came to be compiled it differed slightly from this one.

What brought the struggle between the merchants and the craftsmen to a head was the power vacuum left by the flight of the last Roman Catholic archbishop, James Beaton, at the Reformation in 1560. By its charter, the city's religious head had always been its ruler. It was the officers he

appointed to collect his taxes from his freemen that by degrees became the provost and bailies of the city – always, however, selected finally by himself. Following his disappearance no one was sure where the new seat of power lay and the age-old dispute between the merchants and the craftsmen now reached fresh heights. Such was the tension and confusion that finally the Crown stepped in and forced the disputing parties to go to arbitration. The outcome of this royal intervention was the famous *Letter of Guildry* (1605). This created two new offices – a Dean of Guild (a merchant) and a Deacon Convener (a craftsman) (both *ex officio* members of the Council) and established an authoritative list or roll of burgesses which included both merchant and craft. The following year it was decided that 12 merchants and 11 craftsmen be admitted to the Town Council. Although this decision finally gave a degree of power to the crafts, they were still in the minority, a position they were forced to occupy until the Burgh Reform Act of 1833 finally swept away all remnants of restrictive practices. This very first Burgess Roll set out the following list of crafts and the corresponding numbers of craftsmen belonging to each one: tailors (65), maltsters (55), cordiners or shoe-makers (50), weavers (30), hammermen (29), baxters or bakers (27), coopers (23), skinners (21), wrights (21), mariners and fishers (17), masons (11), bonnet-makers (7), litsters or dyers (5) and surgeons (2), a total of 363 against 213 merchants.

It soon became apparent that the crafts were as jealous of each other as they were of the merchants, and for almost 200 years they fought continually amongst themselves for precedence. The main reason for this was that the various Seals of Cause under which they had become incorporated were either of doubtful provenance or gave chronological pre-eminence to minor crafts. Finally, in 1777, it was agreed for all time coming that the ranking was to be hammermen, tailors, cordiners and maltmen (the most considerable of all the crafts), followed by weavers, baxters, skinners, wrights, coopers and fleshers (of middling importance), with the masons, gardeners, barbers and bonnet-makers bringing up the rear and completing the grand count of Glasgow's Fourteen Incorporated Trades.

Generally the first step in becoming a craftsman was for the youth to be entered by his father as a booked apprentice to a master craftsman. For seven years, unpaid, he worked and learned the craft until he was finally discharged by his master. Then he bought his burgess-ship. For sons or sons-in-law of burgesses this was a purely nominal sum, considerably more for strangers. This in turn allowed him to submit an 'essay' or trial piece and so to obtain admission to the craft. For another two years he remained a simple burgess and could not employ anyone to work under him. Finally, after another four years (13 in all), he became a guild brother and a fully fledged member of his craft. Those who were never booked apprentices or who came from elsewhere could serve the full term but never became anything more than journeymen (i.e. hired by the day or week) or servants.

There was another way to become a burgess, a way which existed from the earliest days, and that was 'gratis'. It was always within the Town Council's power to create anyone a burgess without condition if they so wished. This was usually a reward for someone who had done them – the craft or the town – a service, and brought with it all the ordinary benefits of burgess-ship. Another form was the 'honorary' burgess. This was given to those

whom Glasgow wished to honour, and so we find members of the nobility (and their servants), ministers of the gospel, visiting celebrities, high-ranking military men, statesmen, members of the Royal family, and so on, being given what is now generally described as the 'freedom of the city' – a purely ceremonial position which brought to its holder nothing but the honour.

For 70 years the various crafts continued their various ways – some, like the hammermen and the wrights moving ahead on the floodtide of the Industrial Revolution, others, like the weavers and bonnet-makers, falling prey to advancing technology or fashion changes.

As the 18th century gave way to the 19th, however, it was obvious that the monopolistic, paternalistic outlook of a regulatory system which looked back to the Middle Ages had no place in a capitalistic world, and by the beginning of the 19th century there was a growing disregard for its regulatory powers. Finally, in 1846, an Act was passed abolishing the exclusive trading privileges of the Scottish guilds and incorporations. In many Scottish burghs the outcome of this act was that the incorporations divided their funds amongst their members and broke up the Societies. This did not happen in Glasgow, however, where instead the Fourteen Incorporated Trades threw open their doors to any burgess of repute, and continued to thrive as semi-private corporations, administering their properties for the benefit of their members and families and for the benefit of all kinds of charitable, educational, social and benevolent schemes for the public welfare. Some years ago it was estimated that £60,000 was paid out in the form of pensions to widows, unmarried daughters and bursars, and the combined funds of the Trades House and the Incorporated Crafts ran into six figures. Admission is now open to those who wish to qualify, irrespective of trade or profession – for example, the Hammermen's roll now includes doctors, lawyers, chemists, professors and other professional and academic persons. It has been claimed that the House has become a kind of electoral college for selecting

directors for many of the city's public institutions – at one time it supplied more than 30 such institutions.

See also MERCHANT GUILD
MUNICIPALITY

Crosses

Old Glasgow possessed a variety of crosses. The earliest was probably the Great Cross of St Mungo, which was located in the Cathedral yard. Despite its size it was said to be all of one piece, and had been miraculously transported to its place in the saint's cemetery. It possessed curative properties:

> *They bring mad men, on fuit and
> horss*
> *And byndis thame to Sanct Mungoes
> cross*

There was another Great Cross in the Rottenrow which was taken down in 1575. Two other Glasgow crosses were Otterburne's Cross (1430) in Dobbie's Loan and the Twa (or Brither) Crosses on the Easter Common. To the north-west of the Cathedral stood the Girth Cross; the 'girth' (or 'garth') was the area round a sacred building within which sanctuary could be found, usually marked by four crosses.

The most significant of the city's crosses was the Mercat Cross or *crux foralis*. A burgh's market cross was a visible sign of its legal right to hold a market, and as of right Glasgow possessed

such a symbol; the problem is to establish where exactly it stood. The old layout of Glasgow's streets gave it *two* crossroads (the usual places for market crosses). One was located at the head of the High St near the Cathedral, where the east and west thoroughfares of the Drygate and the Rottenrow met. The other was at the foot of the High St at the conjunction of the Trongate and the Gallowgate. This unusual dichotomy has been explained by assuming that the upper quadrivium marked the centre of the very early ecclesiastical development, while the lower one indicated the later growth of a trading and residential area. If this is correct, then slight indications of a stone pillar at the north end could be explained as no more than another sanctuary marker, a companion Girth Cross, while the later and fuller accounts will refer to the Trongate/Gallowgate, High St/Saltmarket crossing.

The earliest reference in the Town Council minutes to the market cross is in 1590 when two servant boys were convicted of 'clymming upoun the Croce and breking of samin' and of 'playing upoun the heid thairof with ane pyp'. The next reference records its disappearance. In

1659 the Council decided to remove not only the Guard House which had been built round the cross but the cross itself. It is recorded that this was done and that the site of the old Mercat Cross was causewayed over. Despite this plain record of its removal, a supposed account in the *Glasgow Courant* some time in the middle of the 17th century is said to describe a *second* removal of the Cross; and Daniel Defoe is reported as having seen it before 1726.

The whereabouts of the cross became a matter of some interest in 1869, when two old residents firmly declared that in their respective boyhoods the old cross had lain (1) on the north side of St Andrew's Parish Church and was later buried *in situ*, and (2) on ground where St John's Parish Church then stood. The latter gentleman had measured his cross and described it as being octagonal in cross-section, 12½ft long and 17in in diameter. Excavations were carried out at both sites (and, for good measure, a few others) but no trace of the old Mercat Croce was found.

In 1930 a replacement cross was erected at the Cross, designed by Edith Burnet Hughes. It takes the form of a single-storey stone octagonal structure surmounted by a balustraded platform from which rises a central pillar surmounted by a heraldic unicorn. Its platform is used for ceremonial proclamations.

Dean of Guild Court

After the departure in 1560 of James Beaton, the last Roman Catholic Archbishop of Glasgow, the city's merchants and craftsmen disputed over who should bear the government of the burgh. Their overt disagreements were at last overcome in 1605 when both agreed to the terms of a Letter of Guildry, which set up a guild of merchants and craftsmen under a Dean of Guild. The Dean was provided with a Court composed of four merchants and four craftsmen – originally it had various regulatory functions, but eventually all but one of these disappeared.

Seventeenth-century urban life meant living cheek by jowl with several neighbours all intent on encroaching on one anothers' living space. To control such depredations, officials called 'lyners' (i.e. liners) had been given power by the Town Council to establish the proper extent of properties by calculating with the aid of measuring lines their true boundaries, and this function now became the new Court's concern.

Through time the Court's responsibilities grew. In 1728 it was given the power of prohibiting the erection, alteration or demolition of any building within the city without its warrant. Then in 1788 the Town Council entrusted it with the lining of the city's streets (i.e. the control of the the line of buildings fronting the public streets). A further significant step was taken in 1790 when plans and elevations of proposed buildings had to be submitted to it. (The plans from 1861 were preserved in various depositories – what remain, from

1885, are now in the custody of the Strathclyde Region Archives.) Other powers were granted: the Glasgow Police Act of 1800 increased the Court's powers by giving it authority to deal with dangerous or ruinous buildings; the 1862 Police Act added powers to compel proprietors to provide adequate (by the standards of the time) sanitary provisions; and the Glasgow Building Regulations Act (1892) greatly extended its control over the provision of space, light and ventilation of new buildings.

And so the Dean of Guild Court carried out its work for over 350 years, as the city expanded and developed. By the 1970s it was dealing with some 2,500 cases of dangerous buildings each year and its achievements and efficiency were still increasing when, suddenly, it disappeared. By the terms of the Local Government (Scotland) Act, 1973, all Dean of Guild Courts throughout Scotland ceased to exist, their functions passing to the building control departments of the appropriate new authorities. The Glasgow Dean of Guild Court held its last sitting in May 1975. The Act also brought to an end the *ex officio* presence of the Dean of Guild and of the Deacon Convener as unelected members of the Glasgow Corporation.

See also   COURTS OF LAW

Directories

The first Glasgow directory was published in 1783 by John Tait. It consisted of 103 pages and contained the names of over 1,700 persons and firms – these included 18 Ministers of the Gospel, 16 professors, 16 medical practitioners and no less than 52 law agents. In his preface Tait states that 'the publisher did make an actual survey of a great number of houses, shops, warehouses, etc, [but] many had scruples of giving information'. The next directory was published by Nathaniel Jones in 1787 as a 'Directory, or Useful Pocket Companion' with 1,552 names. He listed himself in its pages as being a 'Keeper of Servants' Register Office, 2nd stair, left hand, Presbyterian Close'. He also produced issues for 1789 to 1792. From 1799 on it became an annual publication. Until 1827 it was published by Walter McFeat, who also complained of having trouble collecting information. In 1815 it listed over 4,000 names, increasing to over 6,000 by 1825.

In 1828 it became the *Glasgow Post Office Directory*. According to its title page it included '. . . merchants, traders, manufacturers and principal inhabitants'. Its new title served to indicate that it had been printed 'for the letter-carriers of the Post Office.' At that time the staff of the Post Office consisted of a postmaster, two clerks and two letter-carriers. In 1833 a section under trades and professions was added, and in 1844 a street directory was included. The issue for 1847 carried a city map; and similar maps, growing in size over the years, appeared in all subsequent directories. These maps, although not claiming the accuracy of Ordnance Survey maps, have the great merit of providing a year-by-year record of the many alterations and additions to the city's layout. The copious appendices at the back of the directory supplied details of the members of the Corporation, the University, the Law and the churches, as well as information on the city's banks, insurance offices and charitable institutions, and for a couple of decades before the First World War it included self-contained suburban directories for several of the independent small burghs surrounding the city.

The series continued to appear for well over 130 years, providing raw data relating to the city's commercial, business and manufacturing enterprises, as well as recording its street-by-street expansion; but by the late 1960s it had fallen upon difficult times and by its last issue, 1977, it was no more than a shadow of its former self.

A few other Glasgow directories, all short-lived, had struggled for a year or two, but Kelly's Glasgow Directory supplied a useful supplement to the Post Office Directory, running from 1923 to 1974. The Post Office Directory was essentially a business-orientated publication, but Kelly's achieved a wider range, particularly with its large section listing 'private residents'.

Districts

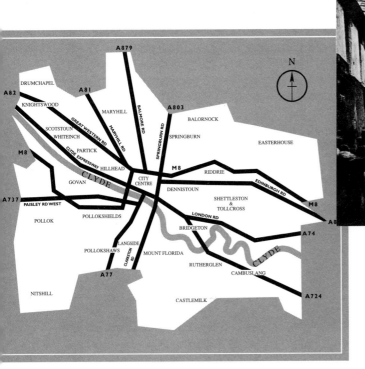

Gorbals Main St, looking north. This small burgh was once the property of Sir George Elphinstone, Glasgow Provost at the beginning of the 17th century. He built his baronial hall in its main street, seen here on the right. At the time of the photograph the architecture is still a mixture of the old cottages, double-storey houses, and the newer three or four-storey tenements.
(Thomas Annan, 1871, Mitchell Library)

Anderson

This community began downriver from Glasgow in the 1720s as a weaver's village. As the 18th-century city expanded, its topography obliged it to spread east and west along the north river-bank, and Anderston's expansion in the west was matched by that of Calton and Bridgeton in the east. It and the Calton were the first of the city's industrial villages. Its name came from the Andersons of Stobcross (a wooden stob or cross) who had been there since the 16th century. The land occupied by the weaving village was feued out originally by James Anderson and one of its attractions was that as it lay outside the jurisdiction of the city it was therefore outside the jurisdiction of the city craft incorporations. By the middle of the century its weavers had earned a reputation for producing high-quality cambrics and lawns from yarn brought in from France and Holland. The Andersons' family mansion, Stobcross House, disappeared when the Queen's Dock was excavated in 1875.

By 1794 the population of Anderston was about 4,000 and its industries now included two large potteries, Delftfield and Verreville. The latter had been established at Finnieston, a small hamlet set up in 1768 by the Orr family and named after the family tutor, the Revd John Finnie.

Glasgow's growing cotton industry effectively changed Anderston from a rural village to an industrialised district. In 1799 Henry Houldsworth came north from Manchester to manage a water-powered spinning mill in the village. He succeeded so well that he soon set up his own mill in Cheapside St, powered by a 45hp steam-engine. He was a hard taskmaster and when he reduced his workers' wages in 1837 there followed a strike exacerbated by the employment of scabs (or 'nobs'). One of the nobs was shot and killed, and at the ensuing trials five of the leaders of the Glasgow Association of Operative Cotton-spinners were sentenced to seven years' transportation. In the late 1830s Houldsworth moved out of cotton and became an early ironmaster in Lanarkshire.

In 1824 the district became self-governing as a Burgh of Barony, with a population of more than 7,000. It did not enjoy its independent state for long, however: in 1846 it was one of the first of the small burghs surrounding the city to be taken over by it.

With the deepening of the Clyde the quayage of the Glasgow Harbour began to extend downriver, and by the 1840s the Hydepark, Lancefield and Finnieston Quays had all been constructed within the Anderston district. A local landmark here was and still is the 175ft high hammerhead Finnieston Crane, erected in 1932 and used to install boilers and engines in new-built ships. Walter Neilston set up his Hydepark Locomotive Works in Anderston before moving them to Springburn in 1861 and it was here, in Stobcross St, that Sir Thomas Lipton, grocer *extraordinaire*, opened his first bacon and cheese shop in 1871.

Anderston's industrial heritage contributed to its two disastrous fires. In 1960 a bonded warehouse went on fire, exploded, and killed 19 firefighters, while in 1968 some 22 workers in an upholstery factory (formerly a bonded warehouse) were trapped and died behind its barred windows.

The westwards movement of Glasgow's centre has now reached Anderston and many of the city's new international-style hotels are located just within its boundaries.

Blythswood

Shortly before Colin Campbell junior (three times Provost of the city) died in 1690, he acquired from the creditors of Sir George Elphinstone (a former Provost) the 470-acre lands of Blythswood, which then lay a short distance west of the burgh. The value of these lands, as the city's development moved steadily westwards, increased many times over in later years, and by the beginning of the 19th century was reputed to yield upward of £25,000 per annum. Feuing of the lands, on a strict grid plan, had begun in the 1790s, and in 1830 Glasgow's jurisdiction was extended over the estate. Along with earlier developments nearer the city centre (now known as the Merchant City) this became Glasgow's New Town, at first a residential area for the city merchants but later a business and commercial centre. It still retains much of its early architecture, but obtrusive examples of mirror glass and polished stone casing are increasing.

Bridgeton

When the old Glasgow Bridge was closed for a period to wheeled traffic in 1765, the neighbouring burgh of Rutherglen (a mile or so east of the city and south of the river) found it expedient to build its own access bridge upstream. Opened in 1776, it required a road into the city from its north end and by 1778 the small community which had grown up around this bridgehead was being called Bridgetown, later Bridgeton. It soon became an industrial suburb of the city and by the middle of the 19th century it was full of power-loom weaving factories and had a population which had increased to 64,000. In 1846 it shared Anderston's fate and was annexed by Glasgow.

When the cotton industry declined, Bridgeton turned for a while to the manufacturers of thread; in 1872 Sir William Arrol set up in the district his Dalmarnock Iron Works, the source of

many famous bridges such as the Forth Railway Bridge, the London Tower Bridge and the second Tay Bridge. It closed in 1986.

When the City Improvement Trust demolished some old properties in the centre of Bridgeton in the 1870s, the replacement buildings formed Bridgeton Cross (completed about 1900) and at its centre the Sun Foundry erected a cast-iron pavilion which has since become famous as the Bridgeton Umbrella.

Calton

Immediately to the east of the city, the Calton was laid out in 1705 by the Walkinshaws of Barrowfield. Being outside the city it escaped the regulatory powers of the city's craft guilds. At first known as Blackfaulds it was renamed the Calton in 1723 when the Town Council repurchased it. Resold by the city in 1731 to John Orr, merchant, it had to wait till 1817 to become a Burgh of Barony. Then in 1846, along with the burgh of Anderston, it was taken over by Glasgow. When the billeting of soldiers on private citizens came to an end, the city's first infantry barracks were erected in the Calton in 1795 on an area known as the Butts, where formerly the city's wapinschaws (military displays) had been held.

By the 1820s its population had grown to more than 16,000, mainly hand-loom weavers or workers in cotton factories. In 1787 it had been these weavers who took to the streets in protest against wage cuts. In the course of the resulting riots, six weavers were killed by the military, and three of them were buried in the weavers' lair in the Calton Burying-Ground.

There were large outcroppings of clay in the district and several local potteries were established. Later, the manufacture of clay pipes became an important local industry – in 1891 William White's factory was producing 14,000 pipes daily. The district also included chemical works and breweries.

Matt McGinn (1928–77), Glaswegian, humorist, renowned folk singer and writer, was born in the area's Ross St. Following the Scottish lairds' custom of using their territorial name, he was proud to call himself Matt McGinn of the Calton.

Cambuslang

Cambuslang (located east of Rutherglen) took shape as a gathering of miners' and weavers' rows, with a few small estates. By the late 19th century it was mainly accommodation for the workers in the neighbouring steelworks, dyeworks and heavy engineering concerns and is now a victim of industrial blight. It became part of Glasgow following the 1975 local government reorganisation.

Castlemilk

This is one of the four vast peripheral housing schemes which were built by the Corporation during the 1950s and 1960s and it shares with them the unfortunate heritage of unemployment and vandalism. The Castlemilk estate, which lies to the south-east of the city, was bought in 1938 but building did not start on it till 1954. Its most prominent feature is its 20-storey high-rise flats.

Cathcart

Like Govan and Eastwood, Cathcart is an ancient parish lying on the south side of Glasgow. Its early history differed in no way from other small settlements around the city (agriculture and weaving) apart from the development of several papermills which utilised the waters of the Cart. It was the opening of the Cathcart District

Railway in 1884 that caused the spread of tenements and villas which housed its growing number of commuters and which increased its population to well over 16,000. It was annexed to Glasgow in 1912.

Cowcaddens

The many cowfeeders (dairymen) in the city used to drive their cattle northwards out of the city along the Cow Loan (now Queen St) to the rich grazing land in the Cowcaddens, but with the opening of the Forth and Clyde Canal and the development of Port Dundas on its banks in 1790, Cowcaddens became a thriving industrial estate with chemical industries, sugar refineries, malting, brewing, dyeing, foundries, and so on. When the canal was superseded by the railways the area lost its industrial impetus, long before the closure of the canal in 1962.

Crosshill

Created a police burgh in 1871 (population, 3,798; 82 acres), it was and is a residential suburb. It became part of Glasgow in 1891.

Drumchapel

The Corporation purchased the Drumchapel estate (lying north-west of the city) in 1939 but building did not begin until after the Second World War. At its height it housed over 30,000 people; like the other peripheral schemes, 'The Drum', as it is popularly known, has suffered the ills of high unemployment and the resulting delinquency and vandalism. A Council Housing Department report spoke of its 'unattractive, uninspired and often oppressive environment'.

Easterhouse

The land (lying to the north-east of the city) on which this housing scheme is built was annexed by the Corporation from

Lanarkshire in 1938 for the specific purpose of house-building. It was not until 1954 that the project got underway. Its poor reputation is probably the best known of the four great post-war schemes. Its exposed position provided a far from ideal site. It was some time before the basic facilities appeared, and it soon became a byword for decay and deprivation. Since the 1980s various schemes to bring in private developers and housing associations have been tried, with some degree of success.

Gorbals

In the middle of the 14th century, when the first stone bridge was thrown over the Clyde, the only habitation at its southern end was St Ninian's Chapel and Leper Hospital, erected by Lady Lochow and conveniently lying outside the burgh. The district increased in size over the centuries, at first known as 'Little Govan' (to distinguish it from 'Meikle Govan', the Govan of today) but more usually called Gorbals. It was under the jurisdiction of the See of Glasgow and its name was said to be derived from an ecclesiastical Latin word *garbale* meaning teinds (tithes) paid to the Church in the form of sheaves of grain.

In 1571 the Archbishop feued the little village and the land about it to Sir George Elphinstone, merchant and provost of Glasgow, who had it erected into a Burgh of Barony and Regality, but Sir George fell upon hard times and the Town Council, in partnership with Hutchesons' Hospital and the Trades House, bought it from him – one half to the Hospital and one quarter each to the Town and the Trades.

One early industry in Gorbals was coal-mining – as early as 1655 two of its inhabitants were given the right to mine its coal by the Town Council. It also earned a reputation for the manufacture of guns and

of worsted plaids. In 1661 it was annexed to Glasgow, and for the next 200 years, despite being a burgh in its own right, it suffered the indignity of being ruled by a Glasgow bailie. The annexation of Gorbals marked the city's first acquisition of territory on the south bank of the Clyde. Its rate of growth was such that by 1770 it was disjoined for ecclesiastical purposes from 'Meikle Govan' and erected as an independent parish under the patronage of the Glasgow University.

Twenty years later the Trades House became aware of the possibilities of the district – it had become a fashionable area for those wanting to leave the old city centre – and began feuing out their westward part in the 1790s, giving it the unimaginative name of Tradeston. The Trustees of Hutcheson's Hospital followed suit and laid out their eastward half, calling it, with equal lack of imagination, Hutchesontown. In 1801 the Trustees feued a strip along the bank of the Clyde to James Laurie, on which he and his brother laid out what they intended to be an elegant residential suburb, Laurieston, but which foundered on the uncontrollable intrusion of industry and its concomitant pollution.

In 1808 Gorbals obtained its first set of police powers, and in 1846 it became an integral part of Glasgow. Throughout the 19th century it steadily lost its reputation as a fashionable district. Although some good tenements were erected by the City Improvement Trustees, the well-built houses which lined its broad streets were rapidly subdivided again and again to accommodate the city's latest indigent incomers. By 1891 there were more than 40,000 people crammed into the area. The Irish were to be first, followed later by the Jews and later still by the Indians and Pakistanis. As a post-war Comprehensive Development Area, the old Gorbals was largely demolished and rebuilt with some of the city's first high-rise flats. Unfortunately, the fact that they had been designed by Sir Basil Spence did not prevent them suffering from intractable dampness and they have, in their turn, been demolished.

Flying in the face of all expectation, the Citizens' Theatre, in the converted Royal Princess's Theatre building on Gorbals Main St, has achieved a theatrical reputation sustained well beyond the city.

Bridgegate, 1834. The steeple is part of the Merchants' House or Hospital – although the Hospital has disappeared, the steeple is still extant. A milk-cart stands outside a tavern, with one of the city's many public wells behind it.
(J. Scott, Glasgow Illustrated, 1834, Mitchell Library)

Govan

There is some evidence that Govan's early importance may date from a period even before the advent of Christianity, and that the rise of Glasgow as an ecclesiastical centre may have deprived Govan of its due place. Early records state that towards the close of the 6th century, Constantine (said to have been the son of Queen Languoreth, for whom St Kentigern worked the miracle of the ring and the salmon) founded a religious house at, and was buried in, Govan. Later, when the new stone-built Glasgow Cathedral was consecrated in 1136, David I presented the Bishop of

Glasgow with the lands of Partick and the church of Govan. The presumed site of the old parish church is, unusually, circular in shape – often an indication of a pre-Christian holy place. Its name is, unconvincingly, derived by some from *gudhbhan*, a school-house, by others from *cu faen*, dear rock. A third etymology associates its name with 'smith' or the 'land of the smith'. Its position, opposite the confluence of the Kelvin and the Clyde, caused the early establishment of a ford here. An old route, Water Row, led down to the ford and stepping-stones, and from the 16th century on a ferry made contact with that part of Govan across the river even easier.

For centuries Meikle Govan (as it was sometimes known, to distinguish it from Little Govan or Gorbals) was no more than a little village with an old church. One of its earliest industries was coal-mining and the Govan collieries were probably the most profitable ones in the district – in 1822 nearly 300 vessels were loaded at the harbour with Govan coal. Later, weaving became a staple industry and in 1839 it had over 340 hand-loom weavers. The produce of its gardens and orchards found a ready sale in nearby Glasgow.

Far-reaching changes came about in 1850 when the brothers James and George Thomson opened a shipbuilding yard in Govan. They called it Clyde Bank; later, when it was transferred across the river the name became a single word, Clydebank. The changes accelerated when in 1858 Charles Randolph and David Elder opened another shipyard in the burgh, which became one of the most important and innovative yards on the Clyde. Their first yard was at Old Govan; later they moved to an adjacent site called Fairfield, from which the yard took its name of Fairfield Shipbuilding & Engineering Co. At one time it was the largest private shipbuilding yard in the world, employing over 4,000 workers, and about half the Clyde-built tonnage came from Govan yards. After many vicissitudes it has now become Kvaerner Govan Ltd. John Elder (and his wife Isabella) left their mark on the burgh in other ways, giving to it the Elder Park, the Elder Library and the Elder Cottage Hospital.

In 1862 Govan became a burgh but it did not retain its independence for long, being taken over by Glasgow in 1912. Its prosperity, largely based on shipbuilding, continued through two world wars, but the decline in shipbuilding following the Second World War brought about a corresponding decline in its prosperity. Its population fell and it became one of the earliest of the city's Comprehensive Development Areas and many of its old buildings and streets have been swept away. Despite its annexation, despite its changing face, it still cherishes memories of its past, when it was the fifth-largest burgh in Scotland. It still celebrates its own annual fair, the Govan Old Fair, it boasts of its Govan Old Victualling Society, 1777, which it claims is the oldest co-operative system in Britain, and, till 1983, boasted of its own newspaper, the *Govan Press*, founded in 1885.

Govanhill

The ownership of a small area of residential land measuring about 140 acres which lay between Govan and Crosshill was disputed by the two burghs, and was consequently known as 'No Man's Land'. The dispute was solved in 1877 by making 'No Man's Land' a burgh (population, *c*.7,000). Its distinguishing feature is its retention of much of its late Victorian tenements. It was annexed by Glasgow in 1891.

Hillhead

Hillhead is located north-west of the city with the Kelvin bounding it to the south and east. It was set out to feu as early as 1820 but was slow to develop and it was not till the 1850s that its grid plan of streets began to fill up. It was constituted a police burgh in 1869 (population, 3,634; 130 acres). It was, and has remained, purely residential, mainly business and professional people. The close proximity of Glasgow University has contributed much to its character. It was annexed to Glasgow in 1891.

Kinning Park

Kinning Park, at the east end of the Govan district, developed quickly as an industrial suburb with the opening of the Kingston Dock in 1867 and Prince's Dock in 1897. It became a police burgh in 1871 (population, 6,634; 109 acres) and a part of Glasgow in 1888.

Maryhill

Before the Forth and Clyde Canal had reached all the way to the Firth of Clyde, it stopped short at Stockingfield, a mile or two north of the city, and sometime after 1775 the area around it was laid out as a sort of early industrial estate by Robert Graham. His wife was Mary Hill and the district became known as 'Maryhill' after her. As the canal traffic grew so did Maryhill and by 1850 it had a population of about 3,000. It had print fields, weaving-mills, paper-mills, saw-mills, boatyards and iron foundries. It became a police burgh in 1856 (109 acres) and was annexed by Glasgow in 1912.

Part of Maryhill was called Kelvin Dock, where little boatyards built the small steam cargo ships or puffers which traded throughout the Highlands and Islands. Because of the narrowness of the canal most were launched broadside on – from the 1860s to 1921 more than 60 of them left the little yards. An unusual name given to part of Maryhill was the Botany Feus (locally corrupted to 'The Butney'). The name was said to have come from the choice given to convicts – either to go to Botany Bay, Australia, or work on the canal.

After the old infantry barracks in the Calton closed, the new barracks was erected in Maryhill in 1876. Demolished in 1960, the site became the Wyndford Housing Estate, completed in 1968, within the old barracks wall.

Maryhill has the only church designed by Charles Rennie Mackintosh. His Queen's Cross Church (in a style sometimes described as Art Nouveau Gothic) was opened in 1899; in 1977 it became the headquarters of the Charles Rennie Mackintosh Society.

Parkhead

About two miles east of Glasgow Cross a number of easily accessible coal seams were used by John Reoch, ironmaster, in a forge he set up in 1837 and which took its name from a small nearby weaving hamlet, Parkhead. Four years later the forge was taken over by David Napier, the shipbuilder and engineer. In 1863, it passed into the possession of William Beardmore, senior, and the history of Parkhead became the history of the Parkhead Forge. William Beardmore, junior, took over in 1887, just as the forge began the production of high-quality steel. It continued to expand and began supplying the Admiralty with steel-plate. Next it bought land downriver at Dalmuir and established a shipyard there where the forge's products could be turned into ships. It soon became the largest single employer in the west of Scotland. Although a main contributor to the nation's arma-

ments during the First World War, by the 1920s it was getting into increasing financial difficulties. Despite a reprieve granted by the Second World War it had to stop trading in 1975, and its cleared site has become a large shopping market, The Forge.

Parkhead is also the home of A. G. Barr & Co, makers of the popular drink, Irn Bru. Barr's took over a local firm in 1887 and by 1987 had become one of Britain's leading soft-drink manufacturers. Parkhead has long been associated with Celtic Football Club, begun in 1887 by a Roman Catholic priest as a charity organisation. Its first pitch was close beside the Eastern Necropolis (also known as Janefield Cemetery) and when the club moved to an adjacent site it was described as having left a graveyard for Paradise – a name by which it is still popularly known.

Partick

The name Partick can be traced back to 1136 when the lands of *Perdeyc* (said to mean 'little wood') were granted to the Bishop of Glasgow by David II. The River Kelvin, which marked its eastern boundary, was used from an early date to drive a number of water-mills; most were corn-mills but there were also paper-mills, flint-mills and slit-iron-mills, many of which were still working in the 19th century.

In 1611 George Hutcheson, a leading Glasgow lawyer, money-lender and philan-thropist, built a large house on the west bank of the Kelvin. For a long time it was mistakenly supposed to have been the bishop's country residence and so was called the Bishop's Castle. It disappeared sometime in the 1840s.

The Kelvin was crossed by a ford and stepping-stones until a stone bridge was erected in 1601 (removed in 1897). When the west end of Argyle St was extended, a new bridge was opened in 1797 to join the new thoroughfare to Partick. This old bridge now lies within Kelvingrove Park. Another realignment of Argyle St was the occasion for the erection of the present bridge in 1878.

The lands on either side of the Kelvin's mouth were developed as shipyards in the 1840s, Tod & MacGregor at Meadowside on the west bank and T. B. Sneath at Pointhouse on the east bank. The yards changed hands several times over the years but by the 1960s they had all gone – the last dry dock was filled in with debris from the demolished Grand Hotel at Charing Cross.

The burgh received some notoriety in 1875 when a procession in celebration of Daniel O'Connell, the Irish patriot, was attacked by Orange supporters, starting a violent riot which lasted for two days. It was brought under control after the Riot Act had been read and a contingent of the Glasgow police had been called in.

Like most of these small communities surrounding Glasgow, Partick achieved a short period of independence in the latter half of the 19th century, becoming a police burgh in 1852 and a part of Glasgow in 1912.

Pollok

This was the first of the city's enormous peripheral housing schemes and lies to the south-west of the city. Its construction, unlike the others, began just before the Second World War, on ground purchased from the family of the Maxwells of Pollok. Of the four border schemes (Pollok, Drumchapel, Easterhouse and Castlemilk) it still exhibits some remnants of the Corporation's interwar schemes, with its range of housing going from cottages to four-storey tenements.

Pollokshaws

It began as an early 18th-century weaving community on the White Cart. It had one of the earliest print works in Scotland in 1742, and its cotton-mill was the first in the country to be lit by gas, at the end of the 18th century. Calico printing was for long carried on in the burgh, followed by turkey-red dyeing up until 1837. It also possessed paper-mills and iron foundries. It has been considerably redeveloped, particularly from the 1960s on, and is a mixture of old and new, including some obtrusive high-rise flats. A daughter of Robert Burns, Betty (Mrs John Johnstone), is buried in the Kirk Lane Burying-Ground, which belonged to one of the burgh's early churches.

Pollokshields East

The feus here were less rigorous than in its neighbour, Pollokshields West, and allowed tenements, shops, schools, churches, and so on. A police burgh in 1880 (population 2,800; 84 acres), it became part of Glasgow in 1891.

Pollokshields West

This district was feued by Sir John Maxwell of Pollok at the beginning of the 1850s. The conditions of the feus were particularly strict, prohibiting shops and trade, and limiting the type of houses to villas in their own grounds, and with its well-looked-after mansions and wide tree-lined streets it has successfully fought off the 20th century. It became a police burgh in 1876 (population 1,864; 166 acres) and was taken over by Glasgow in 1891.

Rutherglen

This ancient community was an early Royal Burgh and its charter, traditionally dated 1126, gave it jurisdiction over much of Glasgow itself. Its location just above where the tidal flow of the Clyde ceases made it an important medieval port, and its trading activities till the late 12th century eclipsed those of Glasgow. After that date the importance of Rutherglen's harbour and the extent of its trade diminished and it became little more than a village, involved in weaving and the coal trade. Between the Union of Parliaments in 1707 and the Reform Act of 1832, Rutherglen was one of the Clyde Burghs (the others were Glasgow, Dumbarton and Renfrew) who jointly elected one member to Parliament.

In the 19th century T. B. Sneath established a busy little shipyard in the burgh, and Lord Overton's chrome works, subjected to a vigorous campaign by Keir Hardie for the deleterious effects it had on the workforce, has left an awkward legacy of contaminated land.

Shettleston and Tollcross

A record, dated 1226, refers to a place described as '*villam filie Sedin*' – the settlement of Sedin's son or daughter – and there is a later reference to Schedinestun. This is taken to be the original form of Shettleston, a village lying about three miles east of Glasgow Cross. Folk etymology, however, insists that the name comes from the weaving propensities of the district and should be 'Shuttlestown', while another theory derives it from the 'Sheddings', where the old and new Shettleston roads diverge. Apart from having a recorded early beginning, its chief claim to fame is its number of coal-pits, some of which were in use as early as the 16th century. With its immediate neighbour, Tollcross, it provided labour for the Clyde Ironworks, opened in 1786. Its mining, agricultural and weaving activities were supplemented in the 19th century by some minor industries – textile machinery manufacturing, a ropeworks and a bottleworks, a laundry and a Co-operative creamery.

Tollcross, which lies about three-quarters of a mile to the south, was a typical small weaving village, separated from Shettleston by a large public park, Tollcross Park. This belonged to the Dunlops of Garnkirk and Tollcross, who lived in its mansion-house till the Corporation bought it in 1897. The burying-ground of the parish church contains the grave of William Miller, the 'laureate of the nursery' as author of *Wee Willie Winkie*. Like its neighbour, Tollcross also has its etymological curiosity, a district, a farm and a brae all called Egypt. The simple explanation is that the occupant of the farm had served in Egypt with the army and so named his farm.

Springburn

To the north of the Cathedral the ground rises fairly steeply, and at the top of this rise, about 1½ miles from the city, stood a few cottages, past which flowed a small *burn* from a nearby *spring*.

The prosperity and well-being of this Springburn rose and fell with the railway – at its height, three out of every four railway workers in Britain were employed in Springburn. In 1831 the city's first railway, the Glasgow & Garnkirk, was constructed to bring cheap coal into the city from the Monkland coalfields, and its thriving St Rollox terminus lay at the foot of the Springburn incline, advantageously located by the cut which connected the Monkland Canal with the Forth and Clyde Canal. Then in 1842 the Edinburgh & Glasgow Railway Co opened its Queen St Station and established its workshops at Cowlairs, near the centre of Springburn. (The company passed into the hands of the North British Railway Co in 1865, then into the LNER in 1923, finally closing down under British Rail in 1968.) In 1856, the Caledonian Railway Co set up its workshops at St Rollox; eventually these also were closed down in 1988. In 1861 Neilston & Co, locomotive builders in Hydepark St, Anderston, transferred to Springburn where, after various amalgamations and changes in ownership, it became the North British Locomotive Co, one of the largest manufacturers of locomotives in Europe, employing well over 8,000 men and exporting to more than 60 countries. Its effortless supremacy in the building of steam locomotives seems to have rendered it incapable of moving on from steam to diesel and electric and it closed down in 1962.

So, in a little over 20 years, Springburn lost the mainspring of its existence, its main street was turned away from its centre, an expressway diverted other traffic round it, most of its tenements were demolished and its shopping centre now takes its customers from the high-rise flats of the vast adjacent Council housing scheme of Balornock. Symptomatic of its decline as a community, its nine churches were replaced by a single new one.

On the falling ground to the south of Springburn lies the 46-acre Sighthill Cemetery. It was opened in 1840, one of several privately owned Glasgow buryinggrounds starting up at this time. For some, its chief claim to fame is its memorial obelisk to John Baird and Andrew Hardie, two of the leaders of the abortive Radical Rising of 1820, who were convicted of treason and beheaded. Their bodies were exhumed from Stirling (where they had been executed) and reinterred at Sighthill in 1847.

Education

From medieval times till the 19th century Glasgow had, and needed, only one school. The Burgh or Grammar School, later the High School, provided the sons of well-to-do Glaswegians with a grounding in Latin grammar, and little else. The rapid progress of the city during the course of the 19th century created the need for a new type of education which would prepare the city's youth for entry to the universities and professions, and in response the High School in the 1830s radically enlarged its curriculum to include English, Mathematics, Geography, Modern Languages, Physics and Chemistry.

The need was so great that a spate of new schools (eventually some 300) began to appear on the scene, ranging from the deplorable to the excellent. At the bottom were a large number (about 200) of so-called private or adventure schools – small, ill-housed and with teachers who could barely teach the rudiments of reading and writing. Then came about 100 church, charitable or free schools, run either directly by the parish churches or through some charitable institution, which provided the educational fundamentals with a ballast of religious instruction. Above these came about 40 'Higher Class' schools which strove to emulate the standards of the High School. They charged fees (generally in excess of 9d. a week) and, like the High School, could coach for entry to the academic and professional worlds, and to the burgeoning business world.

By the end of the 1860s it was estimated that two out of every five Glasgow children did not attend any school and that only half of those receiving any education went to a reasonably efficient school. This unsatisfactory situation was brought to an end by the passing of the Education (Scotland) Act of 1872. Under it, education for all children under 13 became compulsory and School Boards were set up throughout Scotland to run this new system of state education. The Glasgow School Board was established in 1873 and, like all the other boards, its 15 members were chosen by popular vote, from an electorate of over 100,000. The School Board ballots (unlike the parliamentary ones of the time) were secret, and women were able to vote. The Glasgow Board was faced with a task of monumental proportions, for the educational conditions of the city were the worst in Scotland; but it still managed to maintain a significant lead over most of the other Scottish Boards – for instance, it eliminated half-time education even before Parliament required it; it set high standards for its teachers by employing only those properly trained; and, at a practical level, it took over from the various charitable institutions the onerous task of distributing boots and clothing to necessitous children. Unfortunately, until the Board's demise in 1918, deep-seated religious differences between Glasgow Protestants and Roman Catholics occupied much of their time and marred much of their work.

The new system changed the face of education in Glasgow beyond all recognition. The disreputable adventure schools disappeared almost immediately. Unlike England, the Church in Scotland was only too willing to have the state take over its age-old educational duties, and even the number of 'Higher Class' schools began to diminish.

The Glasgow Board had about 87,000 children in the city of school age. There were about 200 schools capable of accommodating some 57,000 pupils, so the Board's first task was an intensive building programme, with 30 new schools as the immediate target. The first of these new schools was built in the Gorbals in 1874 (it was demolished in 1966). Another of these Board schools, Scotland St School (1906), had as its architect the famous Charles Rennie Mackintosh and is now preserved as a listed building.

The new Board schools were funded by a government grant, by fees and by a school rate set and levied by the boards. In Glasgow the fees ranged from 2d. a week to 5/- a month; in addition school-books and jotters had to be bought. In 1892 all fees were abolished in the city's elementary schools, but were still charged in the secondary schools. Over time these, too, were steadily reduced and eventually most Glasgow State schools offered free education.

By 1893 the board had established five excellent secondary schools – City School, John St School, Kent Rd School, Whitehill School and Woodside School – locations all carefully chosen so as to cover the whole city. These were classified as Higher Grade Schools and to them were added the High School and Garnethill School (later the Glasgow High School for Girls). By 1908 the Glasgow School Board had a roll of some 80,000 pupils attending over 70 schools.

By the First World War the expansion of the city had meant that its educational system was now being administered by *five* different school boards. This impossible situation was resolved by the 1918 Education (Scotland) Act which substituted for almost a thousand Scottish boards a score of local education authorities, bringing into being the unitary Glasgow Education Authority. The GEA was in turn replaced, during the 1929 shake-up of local government in Scotland, by Glasgow Corporation. In 1954 the concept of comprehensive education came to the city which, by this time, had 256 schools (177 primary and 79 secondary).

Following the 1872 Act the city's Roman Catholic schools, faced by the Protestant insistence on carrying out school religious instructions according to the tenets of the Protestant faith, had opted to stay out of the new system. Thus forgoing state funding, they had found great difficulty in maintaining adequate standards. Now, under the 1918 Act, this sectarian problem was 'solved' – the Roman Catholic schools now became the responsibility of the new GEA but retained their privilege of maintaining the religious nature of their schooling.

The city had, at this date three types of fee-paying schools within its boundaries:

Education Authority	
Allan Glen's (boys)	1853
High School (boys)	(1824)
High School for Girls	1894
Notre Dame (girls, RC)	1897
Direct Grant Schools	
Hutchesons' Boys' Grammar	1650
Hutchesons' Girls' Grammar	1876
St Aloysius College (boys, RC)	1859
Independent Schools	
Receiving contributions from GEA	
Kelvinside Academy (boys)	1878
Laurel Bank (girls)	1903
Park School (girls)	1880
Westbourne (girls)	1877
Not receiving contributions	
Glasgow Academy	1845

Apart from the city's distinctive position regarding Roman Catholic schooling, Glasgow's educational history now became that of Scotland as a whole, but in the 1970s the Corporation decided that the city's selective, fee-paying secondary schools in receipt of funding from the authority should become comprehensive, free, co-educational schools with intakes drawn from the area in which they were located. This immediately called forth a widespread and vigorous opposition, and in 1972 the Court of Session declared that the Corporation's claim of thus fulfilling the terms of the 1962 Education Act was null and void. However, the following year the Secretary of State for Scotland overturned this opinion, giving the schools concerned until the 1973–74 session to make the necessary changes. The city's oldest educational establishment, the High School, shook off the dust of the city and set up as an independent school outwith the city boundaries. Allan Glen's School (that unique experiment in elementary and secondary technical education), after an unsuccessful attempt to amalgamate with the City School, expired. The others accepted the Corporation's *fiat*.

The education of its children was yet another function lost by the city under local government reorganisation, when its educational needs became the responsibility of Strathclyde Region.

In the 1820s Glasgow, in the person of David Stow, a Glasgow merchant, pioneered the first British institution specifically designed to inculcate teaching skills (the Normal School for the Training of Teachers) which became so highly regarded that Glasgow-trained teachers became much sought after.

See also ATHENAEUM
UNIVERSITIES

SCHOOLS

Allan Glen's School

Allan Glen, a Glasgow wright who died in 1850, left £20,000 to endow a free charitable industrial school in the city. It was opened in 1853 on a site at the corner of North Hanover St and Cathedral St with a roll of 50 boys. Initially only the three Rs were taught, but in 1876 laboratories, workshops and lecture rooms were added and the range of subjects expanded, although for a time all 'cultural' subjects (except for one foreign language) were dropped at the end of the third year.

In 1882, when the Glasgow and West of Scotland Technical College was set up, Allan Glen's was placed under the governors of that institution. The school's success (it had become the first establishment in Scotland to supply an elementary technical education) required it to be extended in 1888, and the College authorities found it had become a financial burden, so in 1912 it was transferred to the Glasgow School Board as a Science High School and to new premises in North Montrose St (previously Provanside School) in 1926.

It continued preparing its pupils for entry into the disciplines of science and technology for more than half a century and in 1958 began an ambitious programme of rebuilding on a site to the north of Cathedral St. The new school was formally opened in 1965 with accommodation for 870 pupils, but in less than ten years it became apparent that Glasgow Corporation's proposal to admit to all schools within its boundaries on a co-educational, comprehensive, non-fee-paying and territorial basis could only mean the end of Allan Glen's distinctive educational contribution. There was a proposal in 1972 to amalgamate it with the City Public Secondary School but any further plans were halted in 1973

when the Secretary of State for Scotland agreed that after the remaining classes had finished their courses the school would close. This closure took place in 1989 under the restructuring policy of the new education authority, Strathclyde Region.

Glasgow Academy

At a meeting of leading Glasgow citizens it was decided to establish an academic institution designed to meet the needs of the expanding western area of the city in which 'secular knowledge would be taught on evangelistic principles'. As a result, in 1847, Glasgow Academy was opened in an Elmbank St building designed by Charles Wilson. In 1877 the building was bought by the Glasgow School Board for the use of the High School of Glasgow, and the Academy moved further west to a site next to the Kelvin Bridge on the Great Western Rd, into accommodation for some 800 boys. In 1920 control passed from the old Glasgow Academy Company to a new educational trust. In 1991 the Academy joined with the Westbourne School for Girls to become a co-educational school with a combined roll of 1,000 pupils.

Glasgow High School for Girls

At the end of the 19th century the district of Garnethill (north of Sauchiehall St) was fast developing into a lower-middle-class residential area but it lacked a good school. So in 1878 the School Board opened the Garnethill Public School in Cecil St, for 'the children of less wealthy parents'. It was designed from the beginning as a centre of educational excellence and became the prototype for public secondary schools throughout Scotland. So successful was it that for a while it seriously reduced the rolls of both Glasgow Academy and

Kelvinside Academy.

In 1894 the upper department set up separately as the Glasgow High School for Girls – at the time it was probably the largest girls' school in the country – and in 1899 it was officially designated a Higher Class School for Girls, on a level with the High School.

The pressure on the school's limited accommodation was such that pupil numbers in some classes almost reached 100. In 1915 a site in Oakfield Ave was acquired as an extension, but the onset of the First World War delayed building till the 1930s. In 1968, after a delay caused this time by the Second World War, new premises were opened in Cleveden Rd, Kelvindale.

In 1973, along with other Glasgow fee-paying selective schools, it was required by the Corporation to become a free, territorial, comprehensive and co-educational school, taking the name of Cleveden Secondary School.

High School of Glasgow

The High School of Glasgow was, until 1976, one of the city's oldest surviving institutions. In the medieval period the Church was responsible for education and it is probable that as early as the 12th century the Cathedral of Glasgow had some sort of grammar school under its care. The first direct evidence of the school's existence is a document of 1460 recording a donation made to it. This record is also the earliest evidence that by that date the school's patrons were the burgh councillors and not the church authorities, and that it was no longer situated within the Cathedral but in a narrow street (Grammar School Wynd, later Greyfriars Wynd, now Nicholas St) opening off the west side of the High St near its junction with George St.

By 1600 the school building had become dilapidated and the Council decided to repair it. Above the restored building's entrance the bailies proudly carved 'Schola Grammaticor. A Senatu Civibusque Glascuansis Bonar. Literar. Patronis Condita' – The Grammar School built by the Town Council and the citizens of Glasgow, patrons of sound learning.

The school was under the control of a rector or master who had below him several doctors or undermasters, all appointed by the Town Council. By the 18th century there were three undermasters and a supernumerary. The latter was required 'to carry forward the boys of slow genius'. Classes were, by today's standards, very large; at the beginning of the 17th century there were only two teachers for over 300 children. Educational theories had nothing to do with this state of affairs – it was the only way the teachers' earnings could reach a reasonable degree of sufficiency.

The curriculum, from the school's earliest days until the start of the 19th century, was what its name would suggest – the teaching of Latin and Greek grammar, prose and composition.

At the end of the 18th century it was decided to do away with the office of rector, all the masters being considered of equal authority. Each master took the same class through its four years at the school so that the new system had in effect created four separate schools. Also at this time it was decided to move the school to a new site on the north side of George St. Foundations were laid in 1787 but by 1807 the new school's accommodation was already found to be inadequate, and in 1820 the roll was to reach 580. A new site was found in John St and a new building opened there in 1821.

A rector had finally been reappointed in 1815; until his death in office in 1830 the educational needs of the pupils were assumed to be what they had been for centuries – i.e. to be taught Latin and Greek and, rather oddly, writing. But the roll continued to increase (it now stood at 800), new educational ideas were abroad, and in the next decade many new departments started up – English, Mathematics, Geography, Modern Languages, Natural Philosophy and Chemistry. Symptomatic of the change in outlook was the decision in 1834 to rename the institution the High School of Glasgow. Old habits died hard, however, and as late as 1866 it was not thought unusual that the Classical Department was still considered to be the most important.

In 1872 control of the High School, as one of the city's burgh schools, was transferred to the newly created Glasgow School Board. One of the Board's first actions was to propose moving the school to Elmbank St, off Sauchiehall St. There was some opposition to this relocation which would take the school away from the old town where it had been for centuries, but the opportunity to transfer to modern buildings (left vacant by Glasgow Academy going to Hillhead) and to move to the 'better' side of the city could not be disregarded, and the move was made in 1878. One of the first actions was to erect on four empty pedestals statues of Homer, Cicero, Galileo and James Watt.

Over the years many additions were made to the original buildings – a Junior Department in 1897, dining accommodation in 1904, a hall block in 1906 and the New Building in 1934 (to accommodate Science, Carpentry, Physical Education and Art).

The move to Elmbank St seems to have marked a change in the ethos of the school, resulting in a move away from the 'burgh school' to something resembling more an English public school. Organised games were begun in 1878 and in 1919

ground at Anniesland on the city's north-west boundary was acquired and set up as the school's sports ground (enlarged in 1924). School colours were also introduced. First, in the 1870s, came maroon and yellow with the motto 'Virtus Sola Nobilitas'. The colours changed in 1903 to green, blue and white (said to be the colours of the Cameronian tartan), being altered again, in 1912, to chocolate and gold with the motto 'Haec Summa Est' (irreverently translated as 'This is the limit'), and finally, the motto was changed to 'Sursum Semper'. In 1910 a house system was begun, the names of the four houses being those of masters; these were later changed to the names of politicians and soldiers.

The School's curriculum continued to widen and its standing to improve throughout the next 60 years. It was the 1970s, however, which brought about the greatest and most significant change in its entire history. The Corporation decided that all schools under its control should not charge fees and should not select their pupils on any other basis than territoriality. In 1970 it abolished fees and in the following year did away with selectivity. Strenuous efforts were made by the High School and its supporters to avert their fate but the Corporation's decision, supported by the Secretary of State for Scotland, was final: the High School of Glasgow must either drop selectivity or break with the local authority. The second alternative was chosen and plans were made to amalgamate with Drewsteignton School in Bearsden. Work began on a new school complex at Old Anniesland, the sports ground, the last session in Elmbank St began in 1975 and in the summer of 1976 the two merged schools (still under the old name of the High School of Glasgow) moved into their new complex.

Hutchesons' Grammar School

George Hutcheson's charitable foundation for the care of the aged, Hutchesons' Hospital, was added to by his younger brother Thomas, who made provision for extra funding to lodge and educate 'tuelf maill children indigent orphanes or uthers of lyk conditions'.

The first pupil was enrolled in 1643 and by 1650 the full complement of 12 had been achieved – the boys (aged from seven to 11 years) were boarded in the back wing of the Hospital. The school soon fell into financial difficulties, largely caused through overspending by the Hospital Patrons in 1650 when they bought the lands of Gorbals, and it was forced to close in 1652. It was reopened successfully in 1661 and six years later the roll had again reached its one dozen. A radical and permanent change, however, was that the pupils were no longer boarded, receiving in lieu maintenance money and clothes.

When the Hospital building in the Trongate was sold in 1795 the pupils were temporarily accommodated in rented premises, but with the building of the new Hospital in Ingram St permanent accommodation again became available. The floor above the new building's Great Hall was designated the schoolroom, but another, rather mean room erected at the east end of the Hospital was used for this purpose instead.

The number of enrolments began to rise. Between 1740 and 1840 the number of pupils had risen from 20 to 120, and it was decided to build a new school in Crown St in the Gorbals. The site was described as possessing 'quietness of situation, good air and a roomy and open site', and the new building was opened in 1841.

Boys coming into the school, usually at the age of seven or eight, received four years' elementary schooling, consisting of the 3 Rs (with a little Latin for the cleverer boys) in classes sometimes numbering as many as 80 pupils. They were then apprenticed to a trade – in the words of Thomas Hutcheson, 'to be chapmen or mariners or any other lawful trade'. Pupils showing more than usual promise would be sent on to the High School.

A complete change came over the school's educational outlook in 1872, when the Act setting up compulsory education in Scotland came into force. Now entrance was no longer to be limited to found-ationers, moderate fees were to be charged, and schooling provided up to University entrance standard. Hutchesons' School would now become a secondary school and would be open to both boys and girls.

In the event a separate Girls' School was set up in Elgin St, and it and the considerably refurbished Boys' School were opened in 1876. Towards the end of the century the two schools, particularly the Boys', ran into trouble, and by 1902 the latter's roll had declined from over 1,000 to 161, a lamentable drop attributed in part to the building's worsening environment and to the competition of the free School Board schools.

In 1912 the Girls' School moved to new premises in Kingarth St (now the junior school) where it began a very successful career, and the Boys' School began to revive under several very able Rectors. But by 1914 it was clear that the only way forward was a new building on a new site.

Continuing financial problems and a lack of entrants rendered this move impossible for a time, but in 1938 the Scottish Education Department approved the purchase of a site at Crossmyloof (part of the Nether Pollok estate). Further progress was stopped by the outbreak of the Second World War, but work was resumed in 1956 and the new Hutchesons' Boys' Grammar School was officially opened in 1960. In 1976 the Boys' and Girls' Schools combined to form one educational establishment on the new site, as Hutchesons' Grammar School, with a roll of over 1,500.

Kelvinside Academy

The continuing expansion of Glasgow's west end as a high-class residential area led to the opening of Kelvinside Academy (Kirklee Rd) in 1878 with 155 boys on the roll. When the Glasgow Academy moved into the neighbourhood that same year, the new school suffered from the competition. By 1913 it had run into financial difficulties and its roll was down to 142. After the First World War it increased to 314 but the academy experienced another financial crisis in 1928, caused, it was said, by the appointment of an *English* rector! More likely causes were the increase in local private elementary schools and a tendency for parents to send boys off to boarding-schools. Its financial difficulties increasing and its roll continuing to fall, in the late 1930s it sought to alleviate its problems by obtaining a grant from the Glasgow Education Authority, in return for setting aside some free places for Glasgow schoolboys. During the Second World War the school was evacuated, not returning to the Kirklee Rd building until 1944. In 1959 the arrangement with Glasgow Corporation was stopped as the roll began to increase, reaching 700 by 1978. Currently it has 650 boys on its roll.

OTHER SCHOOLS

Park School (started in 1870 as a boys' school, in Lyndoch Place, Park Circus, and becoming a girls' school ten years later with about 180 pupils) joined with two other Glasgow girls' schools in 1976, forming the West of Scotland School Company. One of the other two was **Laurel Bank School**, founded in 1903 and by 1919 established in a group of converted terraced houses in Lilybank Terrace. The second was **Westbourne School**, begun in 1877 to 'educate young ladies' in a terraced house in Westbourne Gardens. In 1991 Westbourne joined with the Glasgow Academy; Laurel Bank and Park continue successfully, each with rolls of some 400 pupils.

In the 19th century the rising middle-class element in the city's Roman Catholics began to look for a suitable education for their sons, and in the middle of the 19th century two schools were established to satisfy this demand – *St Aloysius' College* and **St Mungo's Academy**. Both fell foul of the reorganisation of the Glasgow schools in the 1970s, but both, by different routes, solved the problem and continue in being.

Electricity Supply

The earliest use of electricity (as an illumination source) was in 1879 when the newly opened St Enoch's Railway Station was lit by six arc lamps, followed by a similar installation at Queen St Station the following year. In both cases the supply was generated specifically for the stations.

About the same time, two Glasgow pioneers, Muir and Mavor (later to become Mavor & Coulson Ltd), equipped the General Post Office with electric lighting, and in 1884 set up a power station in Miller St to provide a public supply. Their early customers included Arthur & Co, warehousemen, the Telephone Co, and Kate Cranston's Ingram St tea-room. So successful was this venture that a larger installation began operating in John St in 1889, with a 400–500hp engine providing 2,400 volts AC.

As it had previously done with the gas supply, the Corporation now became interested, and in 1890 acquired powers under a Parliamentary Act to supply electricity throughout the city.

In 1892 the Corporation, using its new powers (at first under the control of the Gas

Pinkston Power Station, 1955. The electricity which powered the Corporation's tramcars was supplied by the Corporation's own power station. (John S. Logan, Mitchell Library)

Department) bought out Muir and Mavor for £15,000 and immediately began to erect a new power station in Waterloo St. This opened in 1893 (the earlier stations were now closed down); one of its first projects was to supply arc lighting in some of the city's principal streets – Trongate, Argyle St, Jamaica St, Union St, Renfield St, Buchanan St, St Vincent St and George Sq.

The success of the new service (since 1897 run by the Electricity Department) ensured a very rapid expansion of the supply area, from Park Circus to Glasgow Cross. Two temporary sub-stations had to be opened to cope with the new demand, but in 1900 two new generating stations were opened, at Port Dundas in the north (operating capacity 45,000hp) and at Eglinton Toll in the south (20,000hp). The previous year the Corporation had used its powers to purchase the generating station of the Kelvinside Electric Co, which had been set up to supply the city's west end.

Two neighbouring burghs, Govan and Partick, also erected power stations, the former in 1900 (120hp, later increased to 4,200hp) and the latter in 1905. When these burghs were annexed by Glasgow in 1912, their electricity supply systems came with them.

About this time the Corporation adopted 250 volts as its regulation supply pressure. It was now becoming apparent that industry was beginning to realise the superiority of electricity over steam or manual power, and by the First World War almost two-thirds of the Corporation's electricity was being used for power. The number of domestic consumers was also growing, and there were now some 50,000 users in this category, a figure which had increased to 145,000 by the 1930s.

The demand was now growing at such a rate that in 1910 a 100,000kw station was planned for Dalmarnock, but it did not become operational till 1920. When the electricity supply was taken over by the British Electricity Authority in 1948, 45 per cent of the output was used for power and the number of consumers had reached more than 240,000.

Entertainments

CINEMAS

When motion pictures were still little more than a curiosity, the Glasgow cinema existed only as a sideshow. In 1896 they could be seen during the Christmas season in an unlit Sauchiehall St shop and at Walter Wilson's Jamaica St Colosseum Warehouse. In 1897 E. H. Bostock showed moving pictures as an extra attraction in his Circus, and in a slightly more permanent form Arthur Hubner, who had come to Glasgow to manage an ice-skating rink at Hengler's Circus in Sauchiehall St, added motion pictures to its variety performances; later, he transferred them to the Britannia music-hall in Argyle St (afterwards the Panopticon). George Green, later to play a prominent part in setting up picture houses in Glasgow and the surrounding area, introduced motion pictures at the carnival in the Old Barracks Yard and at Vinegar Hill.

The first custom-built picture houses were probably the Vitagraph, which opened in 1901 in Sauchiehall St, near Charing Cross, and the Electric Theatre, almost next door. On the opposite side of Sauchiehall St was the West End Electric Theatre and at 140 Sauchiehall St, the Glasgow Picture House, which opened in 1910.

The curiosity value of these early shows had led to their being located near the city centre, but as their reliability and familiarity increased, they began to open up over a much wider area, a move hastened by the status confirmed on them by the 1909 Cinematograph Act – in the years 1910 and 1911 the Glasgow magistrates granted licences for over 50 picture houses. The working classes were finding in the cinema a replacement for the music-hall, and most of these new venues were located in the congested east end and south side of the city. In the east end could be found Pringle's Picture Palace (known as the 'Three Ps'), the Annfield Halls and Green's Whitevale Theatre (both in the Gallowgate), while on the south side were the Gorbals Picturedrome (Govan St) and the Paragon (Tobago St).

Soon the cinemas became more respectable and began moving back to the city centre – in 1912 La Scala (with seating for 1,000 people) opened in Sauchiehall St. Sumptuously appointed picture houses with 1,500 capacities, like the B. B. Cinerama in Victoria Rd, began to appear in middle-class suburbs. The years of the Depression saw the picture house become an established part of life – Glasgow had over 130, more cinemas per head of population than any city outside the USA. Green's Playhouse in Renfield St, with seating for 4,200, was said to be the biggest in Europe.

After the Second World War, the Glasgow cinemas shared in the industry's general attrition, most of the suburban ones either closing or becoming bingo halls. The city centre cinemas that have survived have been those which could be converted to the multi-screen mode.

CIRCUSES

Travelling wild beast shows made regular appearances at the annual Fair on the Glasgow Green, along with acrobats, clowns and jugglers. One of the earliest of these was Wombwell's Circus; when his lioness gave birth it was seen as the fulfilment of a prophecy of Alexander Peden, a famous Covenanting minister, that a lioness would whelp on Glasgow Green.

By the middle of the 19th century circus companies began to take up permanent stances in the city. One of these was Newsome's Circus which opened on a site in Ingram St in 1877, but a more famous circus family had already established itself in 1863 in what had been the Prince's Theatre Royal in West Nile St. This was Hengler's Cirque which had previously visited the city in the shape of a travelling tented circus on Glasgow Green. The Henglers were Danish in origin and had been performing in Britain since the late 18th century. In 1885 it moved to custom-built premises at the corner of Washington St and Wellington St. When its lease came to an end it sold out to the General Post Office and moved in 1904 to an existing building in Sauchiehall St. In 1888 a rotunda had been built there to exhibit a large-scale panoramic painting of the Battle of Bannockburn. This structure was renovated as the Hippodrome in 1904 and the same year opened as the new Hengler's Circus. For the next 20 years it became one of the city's best-loved entertainments, especially during the festive season. Two acts in particular caught the audiences' fancy: the employment of large numbers of child-actors in the ring (until the authorities prohibited this), and, above all, the celebrated water spectacle. A 'sinking stage' enabled a lake to be formed in the ring and 23,000 gallons of water flooded it within a few minutes to a depth of almost 10ft. Many water scenes were devised, but the most popular with the Glasgow audiences was 'The Sioux' in which bands of Red Indians in their frail canoes plunged over rapids into the lake to be shot by cowboys.

By the beginning of the century, however, tastes were changing – musical revues and the 'moving pictures' were becoming more and more popular – and the Circus ran into severe financial problems. Eventually it was forced to close down, giving its last performance in December 1924. The building was gutted and reopened as the Waldorf Palais de Danse. In 1927 it became the Regal Cinema and is now the ABC 2 Cinema.

When Hengler's closed the Glasgow Corporation arranged that the Kelvin Hall would become the new venue for the annual Christmas circus, a tradition that has been continued at the Scottish Exhibition and Conference Centre, after the Kelvin Hall was converted to accommodate the Museum of Transport and a modern sports complex.

The Wombwell concern linked up with a prominent member of another old travelling menagerie family, E. H. Bostock, to become Bostock & Wombwell's travelling menagerie and circus, paying its first visit to Scotland in the early 1870s. The company's usual Glasgow site was in the New City Rd area, or sometimes in the Saltmarket. Eventually permanent quarters were established at the former site in 1897 as the Scottish Zoo & Variety Circus or the Scottish Zoo and Glasgow Hippodrome. Bostock himself settled in Glasgow, becoming a Councillor and a JP and was popularly known as 'Scotland's Barnum'. By 1905 he had relinquished the management of the zoo to Thomas Barrasford.

MUSIC HALLS
AND PANTOMIME

Glasgow's music halls grew out of the city's singing saloons, combinations of theatres and public houses, which had no admission charge. They were mainly found in the Saltmarket and the best known included the Shakespeare, Odd-Fellows and Jupiter. While the singing saloons offered professional entertainment, amateur performances were to be found at the much rougher Free-and-Easies, some equipped with protective screens between the audience and the performers!

It was an Englishman, James Bayliss, who built the first proper music hall, the Scotia in Stockwell St, near the bottom of the Saltmarket. He also opened the Royal Colosseum Theatre in the Cowcaddens (later to become the Theatre Royal). When he died his widow took over the running of the Scotia, and it was under her management that Harry Lauder made his first appearance in Glasgow.

The four top music halls were the Royal Princess's Theatre (Gorbals), whose owner, Harry McKelvie, has been credited with creating modern pantomime; the Colosseum (also on the south side); the Pavilion (Renfield St) – still in business; and the Theatre Royal (Cowcaddens) – now Scottish Opera. Next in rank came the Metropole, Empire and Empress. The Queen's Theatre, near Glasgow Cross, stood alone in its glory. It was said that the only way its scripts passed the censor was because he could not translate them into English!

The appearance of the Scotch comic as a distinct genre owes much to Harry Lauder. Once established, most of its finest practitioners seemed to be Glaswegians and most belonged to the generation born just before the First World War.

Tommy Lorne (Hugh Corcoran) (1890–1935) was born in Kirkintilloch but was brought up in Glasgow and became a draughtsman in a steelworks. He began his career as a comedian at the Royal Princess's under Harry McKelvie. Such was his success that he moved, first to the Pavilion and then to the Theatre Royal, where he became the first Scotch comic to take a principal role. Dissatisfied with what he thought a meagre salary, he left. He took to drink, conquered it, but died before he could make a comeback.

Dave Willis (David Williams) (1895–1973) became the leading Scotch comic after Lorne died. Because of his appearance and costume he was known as the Scottish Charlie Chaplin. He stayed faithful to his Glasgow audience, and reached the peak of his popularity just before the Second World War. He retired in 1951 while still successful and bought a hotel in Rothesay (a strange procedure followed by other Scotch comics). Unfortunately, the hotel business was a failure and he died penniless.

Tommy Morgan (1898–1958) became the principal comic at the Metropole in 1931. His well-known nickname – 'Clairty' – came from a saying of his mother, 'Clare to goodness'. His 19 successive shows at the Pavilion were something of a record, and his appearances at the lavishly produced pantomimes at the Alhambra and the Empire make him a rival of Dave Willis for the title of the greatest of all the Glasgow comics.

Although Will Fyfe (1885–1947) was born in Dundee, his 'I belong to Glasgow' has become the one song connected with the city which is known throughout the world. It celebrates the 'common working man' and his escape from his harsh existence through drink. It also, in its own words, 'points the scinger of forn' at the rich Glaswegians who also indulge but who escape notice and censure as they drive past in their motor-cars.

Other Glasgow comedians would include Lex McLean, who succeeded Tommy Morgan at the Pavilion and earned himself the nickname of 'Sexie Lexie' for his use of blue material; Chic Murray, a complete original whose inconsequential patter turned ordinary speech into surrealism; Alex Finlay who took over from Will Fyfe as partner to Harry Gordon and was known as the pocket Lauder;

George West, a close friend of Lorne who performed at the Royal Princess's for over 20 years in Christmas and New Year pantomimes (which often lasted till Easter!); Jimmy Logan, who comes from a well-known Glasgow theatrical family and who has had aspirations as a theatrical entrepreneur; and Stanley Baxter, who moved from the Citizens' Theatre's pantomine *Tintock Cup* first into radio, then pantomine, then south to London to TV and films, where he has won fame for his unrivalled impersonations. He has also created an unusual linguistic niche for himself through his humorous publications on Glasgowese, *Parliamo Glasgow*.

THEATRES

The earliest reference to theatrical entertainment in Glasgow concerned a visit to the city in August 1728 by some of Anthony Aston's Edinburgh company of comedians. With the permission of one of the city's bailies, they tried to stage a performance of *The Beggars' Opera* in the Weigh House, which was stopped in the face of vociferous objections from the town's Calvinist ministers.

In 1753 Glasgow's first theatrical structure was erected in the shape of a temporary wooden booth put up against the wall of the Bishop's Palace (close to the Cathedral). It is one of Glasgow's most persistent urban myths that the preaching of the celebrated English evangelist George Whitefield so enraged the mob that they proceeded to level the offending theatre to the ground. Whitefield himself pointed out that it was the playhouse manager who removed the theatre's roof when the players had finished.

In 1764 a group of liberal-minded

Glasgow citizens tried again. No magistrate would authorise a theatre, nor would any private individual sell ground for one to be built within the city, so they bought, at an exorbitant price, a piece of land in Alston St, Grahamston, a small village outwith the city boundaries (on the site of Central Station) and erected their theatre there. Even before it opened, a mysterious fire consumed all its scenery and theatrical machinery along with the extensive wardrobe of the celebrated actress Mrs Bellamy; it was rumoured that a visiting Methodist minister had urged on a crowd inflamed by his preaching to commit the deed of arson. Rebuilt and refurbished, it ran until 1782, when it suffered the fate of so many of Glasgow's theatres and met its end – in flames.

The next attempt at setting up a theatre marked the proper beginning of the city's continuing theatrical tradition. Although a few ministers sought to have it stopped, changing attitudes allowed the new theatre to be erected within the city, on a site which lay on the east side of Dunlop St (leading south off Argyle St). It had the backing of several eminent citizens, cost £3,000 and had as its manager John Jackson, lessee of the Grahamston Theatre as well as of theatres in Aberdeen, Edinburgh and Dundee. At this time theatres were still regarded as the resort of vagabonds and rogues, and the law required that letters-patent be obtained from the magistrates before a theatre could perform 'major drama'. Jackson obtained the necessary authority so that the new building was entitled to call itself the Theatre Royal, Glasgow. At first the stage was occupied by the company of the Edinburgh Theatre Royal but soon it acquired its own company. Many famous actors appeared on its boards, such as the celebrated Mrs Siddons in 1795.

Despite Jackson's efforts (including an enlargement of the structure in 1801) the theatre under his management was never entirely successful, and by 1804 its glory had departed. Some of the *bon ton* of the city thought it too small and unprepossessing, and so a group of rich merchants financed the building of a magnificent new theatre in Queen St (opened 1805) of which Jackson was the first manager. The Dunlop St Theatre continued to decline and was sold at auction in 1807 to a West Indies trader who used most of it for warehousing his merchandise; the rest of the building was let for circuses, pugilistic displays and public meetings of all sorts. Then, about 1822, Frank Seymour took it over, renovated the building and named it the Caledonian Theatre (the letters-patent having been lost to the new Queen St theatre).

About the same time John Henry Alexander, lessee of the Theatres Royal in Dumfries and Carlisle, who had tried for the Caledonian, took over the cellar accommodation in its basement and turned it into a theatre which he called the Dominion of Fancy. So low was its ceiling that the boxes and galleries were no more than areas marked off by ropes. The rivalry between the two establishments was so intense – each outdoing the other in noisy interruptions – that the magistrates ordered them to perform on alternate nights!

When Seymour moved to the Queen St theatre in 1825, Alexander bought the Caledonian for £5,000. He also paid £1,000 for the letters-patent, following the destruction by fire of his Queen St rival in 1829, and was thus able to restore to the Dunlop St theatre the name Theatre Royal. Under his energetic management Dunlop St became *the* Glasgow theatre. He rebuilt the structure three times; after a fire in 1840 the front elevation was increased by one storey, with niches for the statues of Shakespeare, Garrick – and John Henry Alexander! His eccentricities as actor-manager (he would argue with the audience from the stage, or would leave it to check the takings at the door) endeared him to the city's playgoers, but one major disaster marred his management. In February 1849 a small fire, soon extinguished, caused such a panic that 65 persons (mainly young folk) died of suffocation trying to leave the building, an incident which still ranks as Glasgow's greatest theatrical disaster. Alexander retired in 1851 and was succeeded by Edmund Glover, who successfully catered to the changing tastes of his audiences by staging very successful pantomimes, Italian operas and melodramas.

Not surprisingly, Glasgow's first proper theatre, the Theatre Royal in Dunlop St, was not immune to the fate of most of the city's theatres, and it was almost totally destroyed by fire in January 1863 – only the façade was left after the blaze. It had been rebuilt by the end of the year only to disappear forever under the vast bulk of St Enoch's Railway Station in 1869 when it was purchased by the City Union Railway Company.

A group of well-to-do Glasgow merchants considered that the Dunlop St theatre was too small and paltry for the city and decided to finance the construction of a new and much grander theatre. They chose a site near the top end of Queen St, and in 1803 obtained the necessary patent (thus depriving the Dunlop St theatre of its Theatre Royal title). In April 1805, the Theatre Royal, Queen St, was opened. At 70ft wide and 158ft long, it could seat 1,500 persons; its interior had been designed by the eminent Glasgow architect David Hamilton, it had cost £18,500 (much of which had come from the sale of £25 shares) and it was said to be the finest theatre outside London. It played four nights every week and was said to bring in £250 each night. The first lessee was John Jackson, but he went bankrupt and died in 1806. The theatre was never the success its founders had hoped for, perhaps because its size was disproportionate to the needs of the city. Despite the novelty of installing gas illumination in 1818, it still did not prosper. In 1825 Frank Seymour of the Caledonian Theatre took it over and brought about some increase in its popularity. The brilliancy of the new lighting was chiefly demonstrated by a large chandelier, and it was said to be due to a fault in its gas supply that the building was totally destroyed by fire in January 1829. So great was the financial loss that a benefit ball was held on behalf of Seymour, who then decamped with the money, leaving his unpaid creditors behind. He returned later the same year to build and run the short-lived York St theatre.

In the early 1840s legislation removed the monopoly of the letters-patent system and Glasgow theatres proliferated to such an extent that it is impossible even to list them all. What follows instead is a chronology of the more important of the city's theatres.

1829 – York St Theatre
An ill-designed, temporary theatre built by Frank Seymour when the Theatre Royal, Queen St burnt down. He unsuccessfully claimed letters-patent for it and it closed in 18 months.

c.1840 – Charles Calvert's Wooden Booth
(Also known as the Royal Hibernian Theatre)

It was located at the foot of the Saltmarket and was typical of the many old theatres which enjoyed much noisy patronage from the denizens of the overpopulated wynds and closes around it. It provided comedy and tragedy three times a night, with four performances on a Saturday.

1842 – Adelphi Theatre
A wooden construction in the Saltmarket. It was one of the city's two licensed theatres during the first half of the 19th century. It was destroyed by fire in 1848.

1845 – City Theatre
A massive brick building in Jail Square with a capacity of 5,000. It was built and run by John Henry Anderson, usually known as Professor Anderson, Wizard of the North, a colourful character who earned his fame as a prestidigitator and who was constantly being taken to court for infringing the rights of the patent-holder. The theatre lasted only five short months before being destroyed by fire.

1849 – Queen's Theatre
A brick building with a cement façade in Greendyke St (north side of Glasgow Green), it was erected by Charles Calvert in commemoration, he said, of the recent visit

to the city by Queen Victoria. In 1860 it was bought over and used as a Sunday mission and weekday education centre. It ended up as part of the Hides and Skins Market.

1857 – Britannia Music Hall

The remarkable survival of this Argyle St theatre means that, after the Dumfries Theatre Royal, it is the oldest theatre still extant in Scotland. An architecturally Grade A listed structure, it occupies the second and third floors of a building erected as a warehouse. It was in use until the 1930s and still retains its proscenium and galleries. Its many names have included Campbell's Music Saloon, Trongate Theatre, Hubner's Cinematograph, Fell's Waxworks, and the Tron Cinema. In 1897 it showed early silent films, then in 1906 became the Panopticon (amusements, museum, waxworks, family fair). In the 1920s it was taken over by A. E. Pickard, an eccentric Glasgow showman and property-owner, who named it the Panopticon.

1862 – Scotia Music Hall

It was originally built in Stockwell St by James Bayliss as a temperance music-hall, but burnt down in 1875. It was rebuilt by his widow (with seating for 3,500), remaining temperance till 1892. It was bought over and in 1897 was renamed the Metropole. It specialised in 'Drama of the Day', usually of a particularly lurid cast, but returned to a music-hall in 1922 featuring Scottish-flavoured variety and gory melodrama. Sir Harry Lauder made one of his earliest appearances as an amateur performer on its boards. It was taken over by the Logans (a well-known Glasgow theatrical family) in the late 1930s until its destruction by fire in 1961, when the title was transferred to the Empress (1913) at St George's Cross.

1867 – Royal Colosseum Theatre and Opera House

Built in Hope St, Cowcaddens, by Bayliss (from stones quarried on the site), it was taken over by the proprietors of the Dunlop St Theatre Royal when the latter closed in 1869, and renamed the Theatre Royal. In its heyday it was considered to be the most prestigious of all the Glasgow theatres. Twice destroyed by fire (in 1879 and 1895) and twice rebuilt, the building erected after the first fire was said to be the largest theatrical building in Scotland, with accommodation for more than 4,000 spectators. In October 1956 it was bought by Scottish Television for use as studios. Most of the interior was left intact (apart from slight damage caused by a fire in 1970). In 1974 it was bought by Scottish Opera, lavishly restored and opened the following October with a gala performance of *Die Fledermaus*. Although their legal significance has disappeared, the letters-patent originally granted to its 18th-century forerunner are still held by the theatre.

1870s – Queen's Theatre

While many Glasgow theatres considered themselves 'west end' the Queen's in Watson St, near Glasgow Cross, was defiantly east end. It enjoyed many names in its career, such as the Star Music Hall (1881), Shakespeare Music Hall, New Star Theatre of Varieties, People's Palace of Amusements (1894–98), Pringle's Picture Palace (1898–1908), Queen's Picture Palace (1908–18), and Queen's Variety Theatre (1918–52). In 1884 panic caused by a false fire alarm killed 14 and injured 18 of its audience. During the Second World War it was famous for the utterly Glasgow comics Frank and Doris Droy. It was said that the only reason their scripts were passed by the Lord Chancellor was because no non-Glaswegian could understand them!

In 1946 and 1947 it afforded shelter to the Unity Theatre. It was destroyed by fire in 1952.

1878 – Royal Princess's Theatre
Originally known as Her Majesty's, this Gorbals theatre (Main St) was famous for its melodramas, its national dramas, but above all for its pantomimes. The latter often ran for as long as 20 weeks and effected a revolution in the art of pantomime by stressing the comedian rather than (as had been the custom) the Principal Boy. One idiosyncrasy was that all its pantomime titles had exactly 13 letters – its last pantomime was *Hi, Johnny Cope*. Its façade was graced by Doric columns and statues said to have been taken from David Hamilton's Union Bank in Ingram St. In 1945 it was sold to the Citizens' Theatre.

1879 – Royalty Theatre
Until 1884 it was mainly used by touring repertory companies, but is best known as the home of the Glasgow Repertory Company (1909–14). After the First World War the theatre (in Sauchiehall St) was bought by the YMCA and renamed the Lyric, with capacity for 847 people. Many of Glasgow's best-known amateur theatrical companies used it as their venue. After suffering fire damage in 1953, it was rebuilt at a cost of £126,000. It was sold in 1959 but demolished in 1962 to make way for a monolithic office block of unrelieved monotony.

1897 – Empire Theatre
It was built in Sauchiehall St on the site of an earlier theatre, the Gaiety (demolished 1896), and was originally called the Glasgow Empire Palace. It soon became the leading variety theatre of the city, taking over from the Scotia. Almost every British or American performer of note appeared on its boards. It is alleged that its discriminating Glasgow audiences (of 1,676 people) were quick to indicate their displeasure at inadequate acts and the theatre became known as 'the English comics' grave'. On the third appearance of Morecambe and Wise some slight sporadic applause was heard (their two previous appearances had been met with silence) and a stage-hand told them, 'Aye, boys, they're beginning to like you!' It closed in 1963.

1904 – King's Theatre
Built in Bath St as the fashionable theatre for the West End, for many years it was used by prestigious touring plays, musical comedies and variety shows. In 1962 it became the first home of Scottish Opera. Two years later it was bought by the Glasgow Corporation for £150,000 and now offers its hospitality to a mixture of professional touring companies, local amateur theatrical groups, opera and, at Christmas, a lavish pantomime. It has seating for 2,000 and is a Grade A listed building.

King's Theatre, Bath St (1904). One of the few major theatres left in Glasgow, it is owned by Glasgow District Council and is used largely by professional touring companies and by local amateur theatrical groups. (George Oliver)

1904 – Palace Music Hall
It enjoyed a short life as a variety theatre, being converted to a cinema in 1914 and

then in 1962 to a bingo hall – a common declension for Glasgow theatres. It stood immediately to the right of the Citizens' Theatre (in Main St, Gorbals) and was suddenly demolished in 1977.

1904 – Pavilion Theatre

Renfield St. Originally named the Palace of Varieties, it is now one of the few completely unsubsidised, independent theatres in Britain. In the 1940s and 1950s it became famous for its long-running pantomimes. Then in the 1970s and 1980s it put on a wide range of solo performers of note, from Billy Connolly and Sidney Devine (famous, at least in Glasgow, for his individual style of singing), to Robert Halpern, a stage hypnotist. Recently it has staged a number of well-known Scottish dramatic pieces, including Hector MacMillan's *The Sash* (a play based on the Scottish Orange Order, an ultra-Protestant organisation), Wildcat's production of *The Celtic Story* (the dramatised history of Celtic Football Club) and Tony Roper's *The Steamie* (about life in a public washhouse).

1905 – Coliseum Theatre

A large variety theatre in Eglinton St which became a cinema in 1929, when it showed the city its first talking picture *The Talking Fool*. Its acoustics were considered to be amongst the best in Glasgow and so was chosen for a 1920s performance of Wagner's *The Ring*. Its combination of size (seating for 2,893) and distance from the city centre meant that it could not be filled profitably every evening – hence its early change to a cinema. It was closed in 1969.

1909 – Glasgow Repertory Players

Sauchiehall St. The GRP was established to 'encourage the initiation and development of a purely Scottish drama' and as such was a forerunner of the early Citizens' Theatre. It used the Royalty Theatre at the east end of Sauchiehall St and had its short career terminated by the outbreak of the First World War.

1910 – Alhambra Theatre

Waterloo St. Began with an emphasis on straightforward music-hall, but from 1926 on found more success in musical comedies, revues and plays, often with a Scottish slant, and its pantomimes starred all the leading Scottish entertainers. In the 1940s it was used regularly by the Wilson Barrett Repertory Company, whose season tickets were in great demand amongst the city's middle-aged, middle-class matrons. After vain attempts to save it, the theatre was demolished in 1969.

1913 – Metropole Theatre

With a capacity of 1,286, this theatre in St George's Rd began life as the West End Playhouse, but closed after six months through lack of support. It then became the Empress Variety Theatre and Picture House in 1914 and later still the New Empress. In 1956 it was damaged by fire, but was restored and opened in 1960 as the Falcon Theatre, an unsuccessful arts centre. Offered to Glasgow Corporation in 1962, it was refused, and was bought by Alex Fruitin who opened it as the New Metropole (the original Metropole in Stockwell St had burned down in 1961). It was taken over in 1964 by Jimmy Logan for £80,000 who hoped to use it as a venue for Scottish farce. This venture proving unsuccessful, it was again offered to the Corporation, and again refused. The building lay vacant for several years, finally being demolished in 1990 to make way for a clump of Glasgow's new and ubiquitous brick-built flats.

1927 – Green's Playhouse

Renfield St. For a while in the 1940s it claimed to be Europe's largest cinema. About 1971 it changed its name to the Apollo Centre, a monstrous discothèque, concert-hall and cinema, closing down in 1985. In 1987 parts of the huge structure began to collapse and it was demolished.

1937 – Glasgow Workers' Theatre Group

Set up by the Keir Hardie Trust in Renfrew St, it proved to be the forerunner of the Glasgow Unity Theatre.

1940 – Park Theatre

Opened in a converted private house in Woodside Terrace with a capacity of 106; its plans to expand into a neighbouring dwelling-house were thwarted by lack of planning permission. It was criticised for being unadventurous and not supporting native drama, but its activities helped to bridge the gap between amateur and professional theatre. It closed in 1949.

1941 – Unity Theatre

This group was set up as an amalgamation of five amateur groups which included the Glasgow Workers' Theatre Group, the Transport Players and the Jewish Institute Players. It had a decided left-wing bias and, unusually, tried to run a professional group and an amateur group in parallel. Its aim was to become a people's theatre group and to draw working-class audiences. It played first in the Athenaeum Theatre and then in the Queen's Theatre (1946). Its unusual set-up probably contributed to its demise in 1947.

1945 – Citizens' Theatre

Gorbals St. Established in 1943 through the initiative of the Scottish playwright James Bridie, the Citizens' Theatre took its title from a phrase in the manifesto of the Glasgow Repertory Group (1909–14). Its first production was Bridie's own *Holy Isle*. In its early days it had many talented Scottish actors well equipped to carry out its original aim, namely to provide a venue for Scottish dialect plays and to help create a National Theatre, but Bridie always

Citizens' Theatre, Gorbals Main St. Originally the 19th-century Royal Princess Theatre, it appears here when both its surroundings and itself had been stripped to the bare essentials, but in 1989 the exterior was completely remodelled. (George Oliver)

doubted its capacity to perform English plays – a discerning glimpse of its later troubles. In 1945 it was offered, and accepted, a ten-year lease of the Princess's Theatre in the Gorbals; when the lease ran out in 1955, Glasgow Corporation bought the theatre for £17,000 and rented it back to the administration. By the end of the 1960s it was beginning to lose its way – it had had five Artistic Directors since 1962, and audiences were dwindling as standards fell.

Then, in 1969, Giles Havergal was appointed artistic director (along with his designer Philip Price) and the direction of the theatre changed completely. Indicative of the new approach was their first production – an all-male Hamlet with breech clouts. It has been said that their motto seemed to be 'If nobody likes what we do, then let's do what we like!' The result of this iconoclastic approach was, and continues to be, a riveting series of exercises to *épater les bourgeois*, and plays are generally chosen not for being Scottish or English but European.

In 1965 the Close Theatre (150 capacity) was opened in a converted dance-hall and casino next door to the Citizens', run by the parent theatre as a venue for late-night films, poetry readings and theatre workshops but, like so many others, it was destroyed by fire in 1973.

Major renovations were begun in 1978 in the course of which the façade of the old theatre disappeared. As part of the renovation, the six statues which had stood on the pediment of the theatre were carefully removed and placed within the new entrance area. These effigies (Shakespeare, Burns and four Muses) were supposed to have come from the old Union Bank building in Ingram St, although there is some debate about the reliability of the evidence; Shakespeare and Burns now decorate the foyer while the Muses stand in a row behind an extremely large and long plate-glass window.

1980 – The Mitchell Theatre

Granville St. After the St Andrew's Halls burned down in 1962, the site was taken over by the adjacent Mitchell Library for an extension, and the plans included a small theatre. With a capacity of 418, it offers a venue for productions which find the other city theatres too large or too expensive.

1982 – Tron Theatre

Trongate. After the demise of the Close Theatre, the Glasgow Theatre Club was set up in 1978, and in 1980 the Glasgow District Council leased to it, at a nominal rent, the old Tron church building which, after considerable alteration, was opened as a club theatre in 1982. As the Tron Theatre Club it had a membership of some 5,000, and in 1989 it began to operate as a public theatre under the name of the Tron Theatre. It specialises in contemporary Scottish and international theatre.

1988 – Tramway Theatre

Albert Drive. Built originally as a tramcar depot, it was much later converted to accommodate the Museum of Transport. When the latter moved to the Kelvin Hall, the old building was again changed, this time to a stage capable of taking Peter Brook's large-scale version of the Indian classic, *The Mahabharata*.

During the greater part of the 19th century the Glasgow 'geggies' were the venues for what could truly be called the working man's theatre. These structures were built from wood or canvas and were usually of a temporary nature. They sprang up in the city wherever there were vacant spaces – Morrison St south of the river, the Cowcaddens on the north, Vinegar Hill to the east, for example – but they were clustered thickest around the foot of the Saltmarket, where they formed an important part of Glasgow's annual Fair, and on sites off the High St. Their audiences were largely composed of young men and boys and the admission prices charged and the pieces presented were tailored to suit such audiences. The bigger geggies could seat several hundred people. They charged 1d. and 2d. for pit and gallery respectively; those of a rougher nature charged only 1½d. and 1d. Although they flourished most in the summer season, those which were more substantially built operated during the winter when naphtha flares supplied the illumination and charcoal braziers the heating. There were usually two performances each evening at 6 p.m. and 8 p.m., but sometimes three could be crammed in, and there were usually four on a Saturday.

The pieces staged were either the more gory and martial parts of Shakespeare (*Macbeth* and *Richard III* were favourites) or 'horror' performances such as 'Sweeney Todd, the Demon Barber', or 'Burke & Hare, the grave-robbers', the whole affair being leavened with farces and popular songs and dances. There was usually an 'orchestra' of a fiddle and a cornet, sometimes augmented by six violins, two cornets, a banjo and a drum.

Unlike the legitimate theatres the geggies were usually known by their proprietors' names – for example, Glenroy's Geggie, Mrs O'Brien's Geggie, Ferguson's Geggie, Prince Miller's Geggie, Colin's Geggie – undoubtedly the best known being Mumford's Geggie at the foot of the Saltmarket. William Mumford, born in Bedfordshire, had come to Glasgow about 1834 with a puppet show, and although he disappeared from the scene about 1843 his geggie continued in his name until the 1870s, after which it became a clothes market, and was demolished in 1902. One of his 1839 playbills promised moving mechanical figures 5ft high depicting participants in the famous Eglinton Tournament of that year, along with 'singing, dancing and other amusements'.

The most popular 'turn' in any piece was the 'deid man's drap'. This required the actor involved to drop 'lifeless' to the stage in a particularly exaggerated manner. One actor who specialised in this theatrical *tour de force* often had to repeat it several times until he was forced to exclaim 'Hoo' can ye expec' a fella tae drap deid when the stage is a' covered wae wulks [cooked whelk shells]?'

The closure of the Glasgow Green Fair more or less marked the end of the Glasgow geggie although a few lingered on in the Fair's short-lived new venue, Vinegar Hill. By the end of the century the geggies were no more.

Ethnic Groups

ASIANS IN GLASGOW

Glasgow's trade with the East Indies (which grew rapidly during the latter half of the 18th century) must have brought individual members of the Asian races to the city either as sailors or servants, but there is almost no direct evidence of their presence in the city. A painting from this period showing John Glassford of Dougalston (one of the most eminent of Glasgow's 18th-century tobacco merchants) with his family, has a dark smudge behind his chair which, on close examination, turns out to be a young negro servant.

Glasgow's continuing development throughout the 19th century as a deep-sea port with strong Empire connections

Glasgow's mosque (1985), with its green-glazed and faceted dome, adds a touch of exotic colour to the south bank of the Clyde. (George Oliver)

inevitably brought into the heart of the city increasing numbers of lascar seamen. Paid off between voyages they began to form small, largely unnoticed communities in the dockland area. Their numbers went on growing up to and during the First World War, so much so that in 1919 white seamen objected so violently to their employment that rioting broke out in the Broomielaw, and 130 black British seamen were forced to leave the city.

By the 1920s Indian immigrants were no longer servants or sailors but were coming from the distressed areas of India to find employment; by 1925, several houses near the river were permanently occupied by about 30 Indians. These individuals were in the main either poor peasant farmers or young unattached males, mostly Muslims from the Punjab although their numbers included a few Sikhs. They soon found a comparatively empty niche in the social system, taking to the roads as hawkers, mainly of clothes, and few areas in the city and its vicinity were not visited by their own particular 'Indian Johnny'. The success of these early pioneers brought others, and their numbers rose rapidly, reaching about 200 by the 1930s, almost all living in and working from Glasgow. There were surprisingly few religious or class distinctions amongst these early immigrants, with Muslims, Sikhs and even Untouchables living amicably together in the same households. Few Hindus came over at this period, for being the élite of Indian society they were under no great pressure to emigrate. Also, probably because of their small numbers, the immigrants suffered little intolerance from the general public. Soon the community was large enough to require a formal structure, and the Indian Association was set up in Glasgow in 1937.

During the Second World War almost the entire Indian population of Scotland gathered in Glasgow and many found work in wartime factories in and around the city. Their numbers (by now about 400) were sufficiently large for the community to be

able to establish a permanent religious centre, and in 1940 the Muslims (still the largest group) set up the Muslim Mission in a temporary mosque in Gorbals St. The following year saw the Sikh Association established with a temple in South Portland St. As the locations of these streets indicate, the Asian community was occupying the area lying just south of the Clyde which had been vacated by the city's Jewish community.

After the war many returned to the traditional business of peddling and hawking. Because of high unemployment in India and Pakistan at this time the number of immigrants began to increase and the size of the Asian community grew sharply – by 1955 there were about 1,300 in Scotland. A change in the pattern of immigration became noticeable for now wives and children began for the first time to form part of the influx, and this brought about the formation of deeper, permanent roots.

Although peddling continued to be almost the expected occupation (most of the pedlars' licences in Glasgow in the 1950s and 1960s were taken out by Asians), many of the new immigrants found work elsewhere, generally at the bottom of the social scale. The community also found itself increasing as the relatively greater unemployment in England forced many English Asians north, and by 1960 about 3,000 were to be found in Glasgow.

Emigration from the Indian subcontinent practically ceased in 1962 with the Commonwealth Immigration Act, but by now the community was self-sustaining and thriving. Less and less was peddling an acceptable job, and many found employment as drivers and conductors in Glasgow Corporation tramcars and buses – at one time they formed more than half the workforce.

By the late 1960s the majority of the Scottish Asian community were living in and around Glasgow and were earning their livelihood by some form of shopkeeping, either wholesale or retail. A still more recent development has been the increase in the number of Asian doctors and nurses who have helped to make up shortfalls in the NHS.

The followers of Islam and Sikhism were not long in establishing religous centres in the city. In 1940 the Muslims set up a Muslim Mission in a temporary mosque in Gorbals St, and later, in 1984, opened their Central Mosque (the first custom-built mosque in Scotland and one of the biggest in Europe) on the south bank of the Clyde with accommodation for some 2,000 wortshippers. The Sikh community, in 1941, established a temple in South Portland St, and now have a Cultural and Welfare Centre in the city's west end.

Within the last decade the Asian community in Scotland has almost doubled, and the bulk of these – over 17,000 – are to be found in and around Glasgow. Although few expressions of overt bad feeling have been recorded by the native Scots (probably due to the small numbers involved), the younger Asian generation is beginning to expect more and more to take part in all aspects of the everyday life of the city. They are not as prepared as their fathers were to accept a subservient place, and some signs of stress are beginning to show.

CHINESE IN GLASGOW

The Chinese community in Glasgow dates from the 1950s and its members, some 10,000, are mainly Cantonese from the Hong Kong New Territories and their descendants. They came to Glasgow as the result of the direct invitation of the Corporation, and many originally found employment in the city's hospitals. Now almost all work in the catering trade. Many stay in the Garnethill district, adjacent to the numerous Chinese restaurants along the entire length of Sauchiehall St, while a more affluent group have moved out to Bearsden.

ITALIANS IN GLASGOW

The earliest Italians to reach Glasgow arrived at the end of the 19th century and the beginning of the 20th. Italian immigrants to Scotland came mainly from three separate regions: the town of Barga and the surrounding countryside in Tuscany; the town and countryside of Picinisco in Lazio; and Borgo Val di Taro in Emilia-Romagna. Those who came to Glasgow were mainly from Barga and Picinisco.

Most of these early immigrants set themselves up as fish-and-chip and ice-cream vendors, a good example of finding and developing areas of opportunity not previously occupied. Many of their descendants are involved in various retail businesses and in catering; it is noticeable that almost none have become involved in local politics. It is estimated that 20,000 Glaswegians are of Italian descent.

The city's Italian community suffered (as did that of the whole country) when Italy entered the Second World War on the side of Germany in 1940. At the popular level there were many acts of vandalism against Italian shops and establishments in the city, while the authorities marched off at gunpoint all the adult males to internment camps in the Isle of Man, and when the *Arandora Star* was torpedoed off Ireland on her way to Canada, 29 of the 446 drowned came from Glasgow.

JEWS IN GLASGOW

There is almost no recorded evidence of any Jewish presence in Scotland before the end of the 18th century, when references become increasingly plentiful to Jews in Edinburgh, although the first proper Jewish community was not set up there until the 1820s. A permanent settlement of Jews in Glasgow came slightly later than in Edinburgh although there had been a few earlier visitors. In the 1790s the advertisement columns of the *Glasgow Herald* announced the passing ministrations of two Jewish quack-doctors, William Brodum and Samuel Solomon (the latter famous for his patent medicine, *The Balm of Gilead Cordial*), and the famous Jewish prize-fighter, Daniel Mendoza, gave boxing displays in the city in 1791.

The rise of Glasgow's permanent Jewish community, mainly merchants and traders, mirrored closely the city's own explosive growth throughout the 19th century. The first recorded reference is to an Isaac Cohen, hatter, who was admitted burgess and guild brother in September 1812. The introduction into Scotland of the silk hat was said to be due to him; his admittance (and presumably his being excused from the normal burgess religious oath) suggests that the citizens of Glasgow had no strong objections to the presence of Jews in the business community. Other early Jewish names were P. Levy (furrier, 1817), Samuel Michael (burgess hammerman, 1823) and Salis Schwabe (member of the Merchants' House, 1832).

By 1823 there were sufficient Jews in the city to set up a small community which met for worship in a little synagogue in the High St, and in the following year the first circumcision was carried out. A census in 1831 recorded the presence of 47 Jews in Glasgow. One puzzle of this early period was where the fledgling community buried its dead, for the first Jewish cemetery did not come into use until 1831. A small portion of the new Necropolis, next the Cathedral, was bought by the Jews in 1830 for 100 guineas, and the first interment in it was of Joseph Levi, a 62-year-old quill merchant, who had died of cholera, then rampant in the city.

As their numbers increased they moved in 1842 to a new synagogue in George St. A small dissenting group remained behind, however, calling themselves the Old Hebrew Congregation. The dispute was due in part to disagreement over the ownership of the burying-ground, but eventually in 1849 the two groups reunited in consequence of the purchase of a new cemetery plot in Janefield Cemetery in 1853, necessary because of the filling up of the Necropolis site by 1850 after only 51 burials.

By 1850 the community numbered around 200. Once again a larger synagogue was needed and one was set up at the corner of John St and George St in 1858. Once again there was a break-away congregation, this time calling itself the Glasgow New Hebrew Congregation, but it quickly returned (after only three years of independence) and brought with it its own burying-ground in Craigton Cemetery.

Up until this time Jews settling in Glasgow had been largely shopkeepers and businessmen, many of whom were from Holland or Germany, but in the 1870s and 1880s circumstances brought into the city large numbers of Jews from Russia and Poland. One reason was the rise of anti-Semitic feeling in Russia, where the spread of pogroms caused many Jews to flee to the west. Another reason was that one of the biggest warehouse concerns in Glasgow, Arthur & Co, introduced new methods of bulk tailoring, and recruited largely amongst the London Jewish tailors. Most of these new arrivals found accommodation south of the river in the Gorbals. This new settlement upset the balance of gravity of Glasgow's Jewry for it brought into being two communities, one north of the river, the other south, each with a slightly different outlook.

Again, increasing numbers required increased accommodation for worship. A piece of ground at the corner of Hill St and Garnet St, in the Garnethill district (lying to the immediate north of Sauchiehall St) was purchased for £3,500. On it a splendid new synagogue (the first purpose-built synagogue in Scotland) was erected at a cost of £13,000 and was consecrated in 1879. Once again, however, the noise of dissent was heard. It was said that the better-off Jews were taking the opportunity to move (like their counterparts amongst the Gentiles) westwards away from the old built-up city centre, where increasing numbers of poorer Jews were settling. There was also a feeling among the more

orthodox that the new synagogue was exhibiting reformist notions; it was called the '*Englischer Shul*' by the southside Jews and was patronised, so it was said, mainly by academics and professional men (strange to say, the same criticism was expressed 100 years later when it was said that its members 'included leading figures in medicine, law, accountancy, science, commerce and the arts' – it even set up a mixed-voice choir, quietly abandoned in 1882).

There were now about a thousand Jews north of the river and some 300 to the south in the Gorbals. The latter felt strong enough to open their own prayer-house in Commerce St in 1880, and soon this new synagogue (called the Glasgow New Hebrew Congregation) had over 80 members. In 1884 the two congregations agreed to unite under the title of the Glasgow Hebrew Congregation, the northern group taking the name of the Garnet Hill Congregation (as the name was then spelt) while the Gorbals group called itself the Branch Congregation, a title indicating that it was still thought of as dependent on Garnet Hill, even although its population was beginning to overtake the latter. The increasing population caused it to move to new premises in Main St, Gorbals, in 1887 with room for 150 male and 120 female worshippers.

About this time a nationwide investigation into the notorious sweat-shop practices which were so prevalent in the tailoring trade produced evidence that there were over a thousand Jews in Glasgow engaged in this trade. It was also calculated that an equal number were employed as peddlers and small shopkeepers. At the same time over 200 Jews came to work in the tobacco manufacturing firm of Stephen Mitchell & Sons, many of them recent immigrants taken on by the firm's Jewish-born Glasgow manager.

Between the 1890s and the outbreak of the First World War the Jewish population of Glasgow increased from about 2,000 to nearer 6,000, most of the increase coming from eastern Europe. This was the period when the Gorbals presented its most Jewish appearance, with Yiddish names and signs in shop windows, barrels of herring outside grocers, a proliferation of Jewish bakeries and butchers, and, at street corners, bearded and ringleted men discussing with much gesticulation abstruse points from the Torah. It was during this period that the first signs of Zionism began to appear amongst Glasgow Jewry – always stronger south of the river.

The Garnethill synagogue, after about 20 years of under-use, began to benefit as a number of families chose to move west instead of south. The Gorbals synagogue along with two of the smaller congregations in the area came together in 1907 to form the Jewish Community Council – a body which the northern congregation refused to join. A later attempt was made in 1914 to set up a Glasgow Jewish Representative Board.

New Jewish arrivals in the city just before the First World War included several whose names became locally famous. Bernard Fruitin, from 1908 on, gained control over a number of Glasgow places of entertainment, including the Metropole, the Bedford Picture Theatre, the Queen's Theatre at the Cross and the Oatlands Hippodrome. From Dublin in 1908 came Abraham Goldberg who by the early 1920s had established himself in the Candleriggs as A. Golberg & Co, warehouseman.

Once again the Gorbals synagogue was becoming inadequate for its growing population and, in 1892, its structure was largely rebuilt. At the same time the supervision exercised by the Garnethill congregation was becoming increasingly irksome; in 1898 a United Glasgow Synagogue was constituted which allowed the Gorbals community more responsibility. In 1900 in its continued search for adequate accommodation it bought a site at 93 South Portland St at a cost of £2,400. The desire to raise a worthy building brought with it profound financial problems which plagued the congregation well into the 20th century. The ability and ease with which small differences resulted in break-away congregations (a situation not unfamiliar in other Scottish religious circles) ensured that the Great Synagogue (as the South Portland St building was known) had its rivals. Two of the most important of these were the Chevra Kadisha (Holy Congregation) which met in an old Baptist church in Buchan St from 1889 to 1972, and the Bes Hamedrash Hagadol (Great House of Study), which closed in 1956.

As early as the first years of the 20th century it became apparent that as fast as the community prospered it continued its southwards movement, first into Govanhill and then into Queen's Park (where a congregation was established in 1907). The movement increased in momentum after the First World War and soon the Gorbals community found itself in a position somewhat similar to its northern neighbour – i.e. that of a rapidly declining population aggravated by an excess of synagogue accommodation. Many Jews, it was true, returned for a while to pray in the synagogues and to shop at the Jewish bakers and butchers, but the decline continued. In the 1950s the smaller synagogues were forced to amalgamate and the end came in 1974 when the Great Synagogue itself closed its doors. By the 1980s there was hardly a Jew left in the Gorbals, and not a single Jewish building remained.

Although the district of Newton Mearns, several miles south of the city, is now regarded as the main Jewish centre in the west of Scotland, the Garnethill synagogue still continues its ministrations, and when it celebrated its centenary in 1979, it thought fit to name three of its congregation as deserving special mention as an indication of the integration of Glasgow's Jewish community into the life of the city. First was Bailie Michael Simons (1842– 1929), the first Jew elected to the Town Council, on which he served for many years. It was said that he declined the office of Lord Provost, but became a Deputy Lieutenant of the County of the City of Glasgow. Second was Ernest Greenhill, who, although born in Liverpool, had a long and successful career in the Glasgow Corporation, finishing up as its Treasurer and eventually going to the House of Lords in 1967 as Lord Greenhill of Townhead. Councillor Sir Myer Galpern was the third name. He also served in the Town Council, becoming the city's Lord Provost. He then went on to the House of Commons, where he represented the Shettleston and Tollcross Ward. After serving as Deputy Speaker he went to the House of Lords as a life peer.

Executions

The main thoroughfare leading east from Glasgow Cross is named the Gallowgate (i.e. the road to the Gallows) and at one time led out to the Gallowmure, a clear indication of where the city's early place of execution had been located. Ladywell St in the Drygate passes through what was once the Gallowmure and was formerly known as Hangman's Brae.

In 1765 the place for executions was changed to the Howgatehead, which lay to the north of the cathedral – six hangings took place on this spot. This same site had seen the martyrdom of three Convenanters at the end of the 17th century.

The next move was to the ruins of the Bishop's Castle, lying on the south side of the Royal Infirmary. The first execution took place here in 1784 (in all, nine hangings), then a fourth move took the gibbet down to the Cross, just outside the prison in the old Tolbooth (19 executions).

When the new jail was built at the foot of the Saltmarket (and gave its name to the Jail Sq), the gallows went with it in 1814. This site saw by far the largest number of public hangings – 52 were carried out here from 1814 to 1865. The gibbet faced east and its viewpoint gave rise to the popular saying 'Ye'll dee facin' the Monument' (i.e. on the gallows, looking at Nelson's Monument in the Green). The last person to die 'facing the Monument' was the notorious Dr Pritchard who poisoned his wife and mother-in-law – it was estimated that over 80,000 spectators saw him die.

In 1875 Duke St Prison became Glasgow's place of execution, moving to Barlinnie Prison in 1928, where the last hanging took place in 1960.

The necessary post of hangman was always a difficult one to fill, though in 1605 the Town Council found an ingenious method. Although John McLelland lay under sentence of death, 'nevertheles the proveist bailleis and counsall, desolat of ane executor . . . hes acceptit . . . the said John to be thair executour . . . and he [be] dispensit with the said act crymis of thift committit by him'!

The normal procedure was for the condemned man, the hangman and a carter to proceed to the place in a cart. After the hangman had adjusted the noose, the carter lashed his horse and the cart moved away from under the victim. Andrew Marshall, a murderer who was executed at Howgatehead in 1769, was the last body to hang in chains.

In 1818 Matthew Clydesdale, collier and murderer, was executed in Jail Sq. Part of his sentence was that his body was to be delivered to Dr James Jeffrey, Professor of Anatomy at Glasgow University. A most extraordinary story soon arose, alleging that when his corpse was subjected to an electric current and the action of a pair of bellows a horrid semblance of life returned to it. It was said to have sat up and opened its eyes. This might have had disastrous consequences, but Jeffrey had the presence of mind to plunge his lancet into the body's jugular vein! Matthew's cadaver had indeed been subjected to some medical experimentation but the original accounts make no reference whatsoever to his 'resurrection'.

An unusual place of execution was used in 1841. Two Irish navvies employed on the construction of the Edinburgh–Glasgow railway were convicted of murdering one of their overseers and were hanged at the scene of the crime, Crosshill in Bishopbriggs.

Exhibitions

The enormous success of the innovative 1851 Crystal Palace Exhibition in London encouraged several other European cities to set up similar events. Glasgow decided, rather late, to take the plunge and in 1888 inaugurated what was eventually to become a series of five major exhibitions; what is even more remarkable was that the first three all took place within the short period of 23 years. The aim of the Glasgow International Exhibition of 1888 was to 'promote and foster the sciences and the arts, and to stimulate commercial enterprise', and the profits (there were sure to be profits) were to go towards setting up a new Art Gallery, Museum, and School of Art.

Glasgow at this time had two large central open spaces – the Glasgow Green in the east and the West End Park in the west. These two urban spaces symbolised many things to Glaswegians – above all the division between the working classes and the professional classes.

The best site must have been obvious from the start, for the West End Park lay in a natural amphitheatre, with Glasgow University on its heights to the west, the architectural splendour of Park Circus to the east, while in the residential area surrounding it lived most of the business and academic élite of the city from whom the exhibition's organisers were drawn.

The overall design of the exhibition buildings struck a note which was to become something of a trademark for the Glasgow exhibitions – a decidely oriental style. As the Glasgow architect, James Sellars, explained in a matter-of-fact way, such a style was 'readily executed in wood'! The exhibition's progress towards completion was speedy and uneventful and on 8 May 1888, a day of brilliant sunshine, the Prince of Wales turned the elaborate gold key and declared Glasgow's first International Exhibition open.

Following the example of the Crystal Palace Exhibition, almost all the activities were brought together under one roof. The Main Building had a floor area of over 470,000 sq ft and was set out in a cruciform shape with a broad central avenue running east and west. At the west end was the reverberating Machine Section, full of pulley-belts, steam and pistons, immensely popular with the men and the boys, while at the east end was the 'Women's Industries', where home industries and crafts such as woodcarving, wall-hanging designing and needlework were well represented.

The Fine Arts Section was large, containing some 2,700 exhibits (painting, sculpture, architecture and photography). Prominent in this section were many paintings and other examples of fine art loaned by local industrialists.

It is not surprising that in an area which could boast of almost 40 shipbuilding yards, the Naval Architecture and Marine Engineering Department was extensive and well patronised with its lavish display of models representing every possible type of ship.

Although described as an international exhibition, there were very few foreign goods on display; if it had not been for an excellent display of the products of the Empire, such a soubriquet would have been definitely unmerited; in keeping with the city's strong trading connections with India many displays (and demonstrators) came from that subcontinent.

The amusement area was placed significantly some distance away from the 'serious' side, on the far bank of the Kelvin, but nevertheless was a great success, especially the switchback railway, a new experience for Glaswegians.

The old Queen honoured the exhibition with a state visit in August and later returned to pay a private visit (during which the exhibition was closed), a royal cachet which served to draw even more folk through its gates.

On the last day, 10 November 1888, it was triumphantly announced that the total figure for visitors was 5,748,379 – easily beating Manchester's 4,765,137. The success of Glasgow's first, and some would say its best, exhibition had more than confirmed the city's immense pride in itself – 'here's tae us, wha's like us!'

The great success of the 1888 Exhibition seems to have awakened in the municipality a latent desire to exhibit itself, for after less than 13 years had passed another one was mooted. The last one had, after all, left a handsome profit of some £46,000. Why not use these profits to erect a large gallery in which to display the city's growing art collection, and why not hansel the new edifice by making it the centre of another International Exhibition. Glasgow, 'the first municipality in the world and the second city of the Empire', now felt secure enough in the first light of the Edwardian era to lay on another gigantic 'party'.

Because of an inability to think of anything particularly new and of a fond nostalgia for the style of the first, the International Exhibition of 1901 was very like its predecessor. There was one difference, however – this time there were two separate and distinct buildings, the new

Museum and Art Gallery and the Industrial Hall. One example of the lack of new ideas was the repeated use of the same vaguely oriental architecture – it is scarcely surprising that a design submitted by Charles Rennie Mackintosh was unsuccessful. The constructional technique employed was mainly prefabricated plaster panels on a sacking base.

It was advertised as the largest and most important exhibition ever staged in Britain, and there was a feeling of considerable loss of face when only a comparatively minor Royal, the Duchess of Fife, came north to open it on 2 May 1901. As befitted its new premises, the Fine Art Section took pride of place, and the noisy, smelly Machinery Hall was now exiled across Argyle St, to a site later to house the Kelvin Hall.

One significant advance on the previous exhibition was the inclusion of a number of pavilions from abroad and there can be no doubt that the star of this section was the Russian contribution. It consisted of four large pavilions entirely constructed from wood in a 'picture-book' Russian style with many-sided spires covered with fretted arches, bulbous and steeply-pitched roofs along with lengthy stretches of cleverly articulated windows.

The most splendid of the exhibition buildings was the Grand Concert Hall which could accommodate an audience of more than 3,000, and which was used mainly for seemingly endless brass band music!

The exhibition closed on 9 November 1901, having been visited by 11,497,220 persons, and the respectable profit it realised went towards restoring the West End Park to its original condition and to further enriching the new Art Galleries.

It was only ten years later that another Glasgow exhibition was set up. This time it was to be called the Scottish Exhibition of National History, Art and Industry, 1911. Its aim was to fund a chair of Scottish history and literature at Glasgow University, and as 'internationalism' had been the key word of the two previous exhibitions, this time it was to be 'nationalism', for the new century was bringing to Scotland a renewed sense of its nationhood. A less flattering explanation could be that the nostalgic glances of this exhibition towards the nation's past rather than its future perhaps saw the coming loss of Glasgow's industrial pre-eminence.

The weather on the opening day, 3 May 1911, was most determinedly wet. Gone was the flamboyant, assertive oriental architecture of the past. This time the exhibition's thorough-going emphasis on things Scottish and things past brought about a a virulent attack of 'Scottish mist', both in the styles and the exhibits. The main building, the Palace of History, was a vast historical fake – a steel-framed, asbestos-covered simulacrum of the Palace of Falkland which housed over one thousand items, from Queen Mary's scissors to Covenanters' swords and pistols, while in the wood, plaster and canvas 'Auld Toon', guides dressed-up in 'old-fashioned' costume ushered the visitors into the 'Auld Tartan Shop' and the 'Olde Toffee Shoppe'. Once again there was a Palace of Industry but on a much lesser scale than previously and with fewer exhibits, and once again a prominent Fine Arts Palace. The trend towards separate buildings continued, with palaces or pavillions for history, industry, art, music, decorative arts, electricity and engineering, along with many other smaller kiosks.

The amusement section was substantially increased and one of the notable items was an aerial railway which conveyed excited passengers across the Kelvin at the dizzy height of 130ft. An unusual element in this entertainment area was the large number of displays of members of native races living in mock-ups of their 'ethnic' habitats. Scotland's own aborigines were similarly treated, for the amusement section also housed An Clachan, a Highland village on the banks of the Caol Abhain (the river Kelvin)!

Despite the wet opening, the exhibition weather was the best in living memory, and the gratifying total of 9,369,375 visitors passed through the exhibition's turnstiles and £15,000 was set aside from it to endow a chair of Scottish history.

The latter half of the 19th century saw a number of exhibitions mounted in the city's industrialised east end. Not surprisingly, these were all industrial exhibitions. One of the earliest was the Industrial Exhibition at 99 Argyle St, which had 500 exhibits, 400 of which, its placards announced, were by working men. The East End Industrial Exhibition of Manufactures, Science and Art took place in 1890–91. Its profits were to go towards establishing 'an institute for the intellectual and social improvement and recreation of the inhabitants of the east end of Glasgow' – this object was realised by the erection of the People's Palace. It had been intended to hold it on the Glasgow Green, but when this proved impracticable its venue was moved to vacant Reformatory buildings in Duke St. The National Trades and Industries Exhibition took place in 1895–96 on the same site. One of its attractions was billed as a 'real treat for lovers of music' – a more or less non-stop series of brass band concerts. In 1896–97 the Trades and Industries Exhibition was held in the same place; it included Edison's Kinetophones and cinematographic shows.

Glasgow had to wait 27 years for its next major exhibition, for the city had other things on its mind. First, the 1914–18 War revived, artificially and temporarily, Glasgow's flagging heavy industries, particularly its shipyards. Next, the ensuing worldwide slump, directly in the very areas of Glasgow's strength, plunged the city deep into the miseries of the 1920s' depression. It was therefore almost in a mood of defiance that Glasgow became the venue for an Empire Exhibition, to take place in 1938 (a date which marked the 50th anniversary of its first International Exhibition). It was a brave effort, all the more so in the light of hindsight, for this exhibition, based on peace and the concept of empire, was followed by the world's most devastating war and the dissolution of the world's greatest empire.

All but one of its five aims were couched in rather vague and general terms, but the one Scottish aim – 'to direct attention to Scotland's historical and scenic attractions' – prophetically suggested that the country's salvation lay with the cultivation of its tourism industry.

This exhibition was to be the biggest yet seen in the city – its estimated cost was about £10,000,000 – and the usual site, Kelvingrove Park, was far too small, so Bellahouston Park, to the south-west of the city centre, was chosen. The two reasons which directed this choice was that it could offer 150 acres of flat ground and, as an island site, was accessible from all sides.

Thomas Smith Tait, the exhibition's architect-in-chief, decided to divide the exhibition's buildings into three distinct categories – those connected with the Empire (both Dominions and Colonies), those illustrating the affairs of Great Britain and those representing Britain's industrial and manufacturing achievements. The arrangement of these three areas was based on a simple plan: the two largest buildings, the Palaces of Engineering and

Industry, faced each other at either end of the exhibition's main thoroughfare. This consisted of two parallel ways, Dominions Avenue and Colonial Avenue, lined by the pavilions of Canada, Australia, Ireland, Southern Rhodesia, West Africa, and so on. On a right-angled offshoot at the west end of the main axis was located the United Kingdom pavilion, and the two Scottish pavilions lay on a further right-angled avenue. These three principal avenues all but circled a 150ft hill in the centre of the park and on its top was erected what came to be the exhibition's trademark, the Tower of Empire. Known more familiarly as Tait's Tower, it was essentially a 300ft lift shaft with an observation platform at its top, but its clean lines and interlocking shapes were architectural features which came to represent the essential form of the whole enterprise and which were mirrored over and over again in almost all the other exhibition buildings.

Two recurring features of Glasgow exhibitions were not ignored in the Empire Exhibition. Tucked away in the empty east end of Bellahouston Park were the Highland Clachan and the Amusement Park, their contiguity again suggesting the Lowlander's appreciation of the proper level at which to display the Highlander!

There were more than 200 pavilions within the confines of the park. Most were designed as temporary buildings and made full use of the conveniences of clad steel frameworks and copious glazing. Architecturally, they eschewed the luxurious grandiloquence of the earlier Glasgow exhibitions, using simple low flat or curving planes, often locking together ingeniously and often punctuated by vertical forms which echoed the central tower.

The Empire Exhibition was opened on 3 May 1938 by George VI. It was hoped that by the closing date of 29 October some 20 million visitors would have gone through its turnstiles. To considerable disappointment, however, the final total was only 12½ million; the main reason for this low figure was put down to a summer of unprecedented wind and rain.

Despite widespread protests, Tait's Tower was dismantled during the summer of 1939, and the only traces of the exhibition still visible are the Palace of Arts, now used mainly for educational purposes (unlike the other exhibition buildings it had been built in stone with the intention of continuing as an art gallery), a granite memorial slab on Bellahouston Hill which had been unveiled by the king in 1937, and, ironically, the Peace Cairn. One other building was saved – the Palace of Engineering was purchased by the government and re-erected at Prestwick International Airport.

Fairs

Some time between 1189 and 1198 King William the Lion granted to Jocelin, Bishop of the See of Glasgow, the privilege of holding an annual fair within his city. A few years earlier he had confirmed to the bishop the right to maintain a weekly market on Thursdays, but the ability to hold an annual fair was much more important.

Whereas the former restricted those taking part to city burgesses, an annual Fair was open also to merchants furth of the burgh to whom were granted the King's Peace and remission from tolls – as a later proclamation put it, 'nane of ovr souerane lordis legis cumand to this fair, reparing thairin, or gangand thairfra do ony hurt or trublend ane to ane . . . bot leif peacablie and vse thair merchandice . . . under goddis pece and our souerane lordis protectioun'.

The period of the Fair was declared to be the octave of the apostles Peter and Paul and as the feast of these two saints was held on 29 June, so the Fair began on 7 July and ran for one week. There can be little doubt that this particular date was chosen because it was on this day that the Cathedral had been dedicated in 1136.

For centuries the Fair continued to start on 7 July no matter what day of the week this might be, but following the Reformation the city magistrates thought fit to avoid desecrating the Sabbath by declaring in 1577 that if 7 July fell on a Sunday then the Fair should begin on the previous Saturday. The effect of this was that the first Monday in July became the recognised start of the Fair proper. Then following 1752, when eleven days were omitted in order to correct the cumulated errors of the old Julian Calendar, Fair Monday now fell on either the second or third Monday. Gradually, by nothing more legal than informal sanction, it became accepted that the second Monday in July was Fair Monday and so it has remained ever since.

For many centuries the Fair was held at the top of the High St in the neighbourhood of the Wyndhead, not far from the west end of the Cathedral. As the lower part of the burgh which stretched up north from the river grew in importance, so the Fair moved down south from its first site

Glasgow Fair, 1825. By the end of the 18th century the Fair had become less a market and more an occasion for working-class jollifications. This view, from the roof of the Justiciary Building at the foot of the Saltmarket, shows the Fair in the 1820s – a series of circuses and theatres ranged along the west end of the Glasgow Green with smaller booths dotted here and there. (Glasgow Looking Glass, 1825, Mitchell Library)

and settled at the north end of the old Glasgow Bridge which was for many centuries the only access to the town from the south. Here at the foot of the Stockwell, around the Water Port, the Fair carried on in its old form up until the beginning of the 19th century. The two principal events were the horse market on Wednesday and the cattle market on Friday. The horse market extended west from Stockwell St along Clyde St and up Glassford St, while the animals were put to the test by being run along the Trongate and Argyle St. The cattle market occupied most of Stockwell St in company with the feeing market where the local farmers engaged their farm labourers and servants. Because of the presence of the latter it was the custom to set up entertainment booths where the gathering crowds could enjoy themselves with swings and roundabouts, giants and fat boys, learned pigs and dwarves. In 1818 a new Cattle Market was opened near Graham St off the Gallowgate, and the old Fair saw the last of its bestial.

This departure changed the nature of the Fair in a radical manner, for it now became merely an occasion for merry-making and licence by the urban working classes. No longer were the participants country servants looking for masters but rather young lasses from the spinning and weaving manufactories and young lads from the engineering shops and printworks. Now when the bellman in his red coat cried out at the Cross, 'Glesca Fair is noo open!', a new type of Fair sprang up along the western end of the Glasgow Green facing the Justiciary Building at the foot of the Saltmarket (there was now insufficient space for the Fair at its old location).

Shows, menageries, circuses, theatres, fortune-tellers, games of chance and wheels of fortune lined the east side of Jail Square and enticed the pale denizens of the city's stinking closes and wynds out for a brief spell of freedom and hectic pleasure. While the major booths occupied the street edge, the smaller fry were placed along the north side while the 'hobby horses' and 'Waterloo flies' formed the fair's southern boundary next to the river. Inside this square were four quadrilateral rows of drinking booths for the consumption of whisky, then a fairly new institution in the city. For a while the showmen were allowed to occupy the ground free of charge, but in 1815 a ground rent was instituted, the proceeds of which were initially used to improve the condition of

the city's public wells. This charge was continued till 1870 and exercised an increasingly restrictive effect on the size of the fair. Finally, in 1871, the Town Council, in a fit of Victorian prudery, decided to allow no more ground rents and thus brought to an end the centuries-old association between Glasgow's Fair and the banks of the Clyde.

In response to this fiat the showmen moved lock, stock and barrel to Vinegar Hill, an open space on the north side of Camlachie. There for a while the scenic railway, the merry-go-rounds, coconut shies, shooting saloons and boxing booths continued to represent all that was left of an age-old tradition.

But as the old-type Fair died a new one arose to take its place. The cheap, efficient and frequent services offered by the fleets of Clyde paddle-steamers brought the burgeoning Clyde resorts within the reach of the ordinary Glasgow working man and his family, and the Fair was reborn under the guise of holidays 'doon the watter'. Indeed, for many Glaswegians, the 'Fair Fortnight' spent in digs at Rothesay, Dunoon, Millport, Largs, Girvan, Campbeltown or Arran is the real, authentic Glasgow Fair.

Return Home.

New Year's Day has always had in Scotland all the freedom of the Saturnalia. Drunkenness and liberty reigned in the streets of Glasgow. (Northern Looking Glass, 1826, Mitchell Library)

Ferries

Before Glasgow began spreading into the area south of the river there were only two substantial communities on that bank, Govan and Renfrew, so that cross-river communications were adequately served by the Old Bridge at the foot of the Saltmarket and by the two small Govan and Renfrew ferries. As industries began to proliferate along both banks of the river in the 19th century, however, there was a growing need to increase cross-river access. Bridges were not suitable as they would have seriously restricted ship-access to the Broomielaw, Glasgow's busy harbour, and so a service of ferries began to criss-cross the river, from the west side of the Broomielaw Bridge down to Govan and beyond to Whiteinch. An Act of 1840 allowed the Clyde Navigation Trustees to establish and operate such ferries, and from the 1840s on the Trust took over and extended the existing ferries downriver. By the end of the century no charge was made for their use. There were about eight, many beginning as oar-driven vessels, progressing to steam, and finally diesel. In descending order from Jamaica St Bridge they were:

York St/West St (Kingston)
A rowing boat in the 1840s, it was replaced by the Clyde Navigation Trust with a steam-powered vessel in 1868 and discontinued in 1913.

Clyde St/entrance to Kingston Docks
Its 1840s' rowing-boat was taken over by the Clyde Navigation Trustees in 1848; in 1865 it gave way to one of the earliest Clyde steam ferries, which was double-ended and could carry about 60 passengers.

It had a vertical boiler (to increase deck space) and became the pattern for all later passenger ferries. At first it was equipped with water-jet propulsion and steering, but the experiment was not successful and the conventional propeller drive was restored. The busiest of the city ferries, it carried almost 6,000 passengers per day. It closed in 1967 following the construction of the Kingston Bridge.

Hydepark St/foot of Springfield Quay
Begun in 1849 and discontinued in 1884; it was throughout a rowing-boat.

Finnieston Ferry, Finnieston St/ Mavisbank Quay
One of the city's three major ferries (along with the Govan Ferry and the Whiteinch Ferry). A rowing-boat in 1846, it was taken over by the Clyde Navigation Trust in 1848 and replaced by a steam ferry in 1868. The city's first high-level vehicular ferry boat came into use at Finnieston in 1890. The carrying deck was supported by four massive corner pillars and could adjust itself to the state of the tide by rising and falling. It was able to carry eight carts and horses and 300 passengers and was one of the city's busiest crossings. About 1936 it was moved slightly upstream in order to ease access to adjoining quaysides. The 24-hour ferry's last trip was made in 1977.

Kelvinhaugh St/Maxwell St (Govan)
A rowing-boat from 1851, it was replaced by a steam ferry in 1876. The longest-lived ferry of all, it carried on until 1980, operating from 5 a.m. till 11 p.m.

Govan Ferry
As a long-established and populous com-

munity on the Clyde's south bank, Govan must have had some sort of ferry from an early period but the first recorded is a 1734 hand-operated chain ferry (Pointhouse to Water Row, Govan) which could accommodate both vehicles and passengers (in this type of ferry a long chain was laid from bank to bank across the river-bed along which the ferry pulled itself). The Govan Ferry was taken over in 1857 by the Clyde Navigation Trust which introduced one of the Clyde's first steam-driven ferries here in 1865. Two years later a steam-driven double-chain ferry took its place, to be followed in 1875 by a new ferry with movable ramps at both ends which could accommodate eight carts and 140 passengers. It in turn was superseded in 1912 by a new type of ferry in which the deck could be raised and lowered to accommodate different tide levels (this ferry had first been installed at Finnieston in 1890). In the 1930s the ferry became diesel-powered. The last run took place in 1965.

Govan West Ferry
Ran between Meadowside and Govan Wharf, from 1881 to 1965. Was later known as the Meadowside Ferry.

Whiteinch Ferry
The furthest downriver of all the city's ferries, it began in 1857 as a rowing-boat, was converted to steam-power in 1891 and to high-level vehicular transport in 1900–5. The opening of the Clyde Tunnel led to it being shut down in 1963.

Triangular Ferry
This unusual and short-lived (1895–1909) ferry ran from the mouth of Queen's Dock across to the mouth of Prince's Dock, downriver to Highland Lane, Govan, and then back across to Queen's Dock.

Meadowside Ferry
Not a cross-river ferry, but a rowing-boat which conveyed passengers across the mouth of the Kelvin at Partick (1867–90).

Fire Fighting

All early communities, with their wooden walls and thatched roofs, were continually at risk from fire, and old Glasgow suffered from several serious conflagrations. The most disastrous of these early fires happened in 1652, some 14 years before the Great Fire of London, and, like that catastrophe, was preceded by an outbreak of plague. It started in the house of James Hamilton in the High St on 17 June and the flames, fanned by a north-west wind (an uncommon direction for the city), spread south to the Saltmarket and east and west along Trongate and Gallowgate. Completely out of control, it reached as far south as the Bridgegate and it took 18 hours before the flames began to die down. By that time, one third of the city had been destroyed; the Town Council reported that 'thair will be neir four scoir closses all burnt, estimat about ane thousand families'. The damage was assessed at £100,000 sterling, and although Cromwell disobligingly remarked that 'we recommend them as high objects of charity to such pious and well-disposed people as shall be willing to contribute', Parliament eventually allocated £1,000 sterling to the distressed city.

Probably as a result of this conflagration, Glasgow acquired its first fire engine four years later. The Council caused the Edinburgh 'ingyne for slockening of fyre' to be examined and a copy built and installed in the city. Although it now had its own fire engine, the city's main defence against outbreaks was still chains of water buckets and long hooked poles for pulling down thatch or walls to prevent fires from spreading.

Another precaution was taken in 1658 when dangerous trades were banished from the town. This regulation brought about the expulsion of four candle factories to fields just beyond the city's western boundaries; their new location was given the name 'Candleriggs' which it still bears today.

There was another major outbreak of fire in November 1677. This was the result of arson; a disgruntled blacksmith's apprentice set fire to his master's premises at the corner of Saltmarket and Trongate in revenge for a beating, and over 130 houses were destroyed in the resulting fire.

This incident was followed by a Council regulation that all houses whether new or repaired were to be built 'from heid to foot, bak and foir' of stone. This ordinance, and others requiring slate instead of thatch, had some effect, although some of these old wooden houses managed to survive into the middle of the 19th century. One beneficial effect of these regulations was to change Glasgow into that well-built, handsome city so often praised by later visitors.

In 1725 a second fire engine was brought all the way from London at a cost of £50 sterling, and in 1744 the city

appointed its first full-time firefighter in the person of Robert Craig, smith. A further step was taken three years later when Craig was put in charge of 24 part-time firemen who managed the city's three fire engines. Each man was equipped with a strong leather cap 'having the Glasgow arms printed on the front thair of that he may be known upon occasioune of fire'.

From 1767 on, fire insurance offices began to fix their individual 'marks' to buildings insured with them. This practice, however, led to such arguments about the respective responsibilities of the different firefighting teams that in 1787 the Town Council took over full control and the marks gradually fell out of use.

The year 1793 saw a destructive fire in the Tron (or Laigh) Kirk in the Trongate. Its Session House was used by the nightly Town Guard or Watch as its headquarters and one evening, when the Town Guard was out on patrol, a group of high-spirited young drunks (said to be members of a local 'Hell-fire Club') invaded the premises and stoked up the fire to see how well they could withstand an imitation of the heat which would be their ultimate destination! So fierce was the blaze that the Session House and the church were both set alight and destroyed, leaving only the steeple (still straddling the pavement west of the Cross). The fire also destroyed the records of Glasgow's General Kirk Session and badly damaged the Presbytery Registers.

By the close of the 18th century, the style of fighting fires had changed very little; but the beginning of the new century brought about many changes. In 1807 a regular police force was set up and the city's firefighting duties were passed over to this new organisation. With the responsibilities came six manual pumping engines and about 1,000ft of sewn leather hose. The engines were kept at strategic points throughout the town – the Meat Market, the Potato Market (King St), Wynd Church, south side of the Trongate, Hutchesons' Hospital, and Laing's Callander Close (Gallowgate).

One of the difficulties in fighting city fires had always been the lack of water – obtained as best it could be from burns, wells and the river – but with the establishment of several early water companies, the fire service could access a network of fire cocks throughout the city. These numbered 40 in 1811 and 152 in 1816.

In 1829 the Superintendent of Fire Engines had 48 firemen under his charge, eight to each engine. These were pulled to the fire by the firemen themselves, whilst the large water butts (one for each engine) were drawn by horses belonging to selected carters who lived near the fire points. One of the early superintendents, in an excess of zeal, built to his own specifications a monster fire engine called *Clyde* which unfortunately suffered from two faults – it required 40 men to operate it and, as it weighed three tons, it could not be moved!

Although Glasgow burnt down its theatres with surprising regularity, on only one occasion was there serious loss of life. In February 1849 at the Theatre Royal, Dunlop St, a small gas leak was accidentally ignited but safely extinguished. The cry of 'Fire!' was raised, however, and in the ensuing panic 65 members of the audience, mostly young people in the galleries, were crushed to death on the stairs.

A new custom-built Central Fire Engine Station was built in College St (off High St) in 1851 with full stabling facilities within the building. Another important improvement came with the introduction in 1858 of water from Loch Katrine. So powerful and copious was this new supply that it was possible to place

over 1,000 hydrants throughout the city streets. This was followed by another important innovation in 1861 when telegraphic communication was introduced between the fire stations and the central police headquarters, which still controlled the fire service.

The city's first steam fire engine was purchased in 1870 for £500 and immediately did away with the old manual engines – it could do the work of five of the latter and could deliver 400 gallons every minute. In 1873 another 'steamer' was bought and was ingeniously fitted to one of the Clyde's steam ferries. This proved most useful in tackling fires on or near the river, a very built-up area with many warehouses. About this time the firefighting personnel were all put on a full-time basis and a stud of horses maintained for the sole use of the fire service.

In 1878 some 82 public fire alarms were set up at the corners of the city's principal streets. By breaking a glass disc and pressing a knob the alarm was instantly raised; the ornamental boxes housing this apparatus became a familiar sight in the city's main streets.

A Salvage Corp Committee (later the Glasgow Rate and Salvage Association) was formed in 1877, quite separate from the fire service. Its purpose was to inspect premises for fire risks and to reduce losses by moving and covering the contents of buildings on fire, and was maintained by the insurance companies.

In 1891 the fire service was at last detached from the police and set up as an independent force. By this time there were over 4,000 fire hydrants throughout the city.

In 1898 a fire in the Renfield St premises of W. & R. Hatrick, wholesale chemists, was quickly brought under control; but while firemen were still in the building a disastrous explosion brought down the remains of the building and killed four firemen. This was the first occasion on which a firefighter had been killed in action, and an early example of fire hazards due to dangerous substances.

The fire service was responsible for creating one of the city's better-known legends. In 1894 a dog, 'Wallace', followed a fire engine back to the fire station and, despite his owner's efforts, refused to return home. The dog remained with the service for the rest of his life. His claim to fame was his curious habit of running in front of an appliance proceeding to a fire. It was popularly believed that the dog was able to tell where the fire was located, but the more mundane explanation was that the leading appliance's driver indicated by his gestures which way Wallace should turn. When a visitor to the station noticed the dog's sore paws he had a set of four small rubber boots made for him, but Wallace always preferred his unadorned paws. When he died in 1902 his body was stuffed and placed in a glass case along with his boots.

By the turn of the century, fire service personnel numbered 120 and appliances and apparatus consisted of 11 steam engines, 12 hose and ladder carriages, 42 horses, 1,800ft of leather hose and 28,600ft of canvas hose. In addition, there were now 144 street alarms and over 5,000 hydrants.

Another milestone was the purchase in 1905 of the service's first motor appliance – a 4-cylinder, 24hp engine with a maximum speed of 22mph – from the Wolseley Tool & Motor Car Co of Birmingham. This spelt the end of the picturesque horse-drawn appliances, and in 1913 the last two horses, Kelvin and Tweed, were honorably retired.

There were few changes in the service between the wars, but an important improvement in the service, in 1942, was the introduction of radio communication between the appliances and the stations. For the duration of the Second World War Glasgow's distinctive service was lost in the anonymity of the National Fire Service. Although the city suffered little serious war-damage, two incidents involved the fire service particularly. The cruiser HMS *Sussex*, moored at Yorkhill Quay, was hit by a 250lb bomb and it took the service 12 hours to extinguish the resulting blaze. Although the effect of the Clydebank Blitz (March 1941) on the city was relatively small, 250 of the pumps were called out and five of the fire stations were hit.

Like any large city, Glasgow has recently suffered several major fires, and two of these were particularly serious outbreaks. In 1960 a bonded warehouse in Cheapside St, Anderston, holding over one million gallons of whisky and rum, went on fire. The first problem was that the narrow and congested streets in the area made it very difficult to bring sufficient firefighting power to bear on the conflagration. The other was the extremely volatile nature of the liquids in store, for the building literally exploded, and the collapsing walls buried and killed 14 members of the Glasgow Fire Service along with five personnel from the Glasgow Salvage Corps.

The second incident occurred in the same area and in the same type of building. In 1968 a fire broke out in an upholstery factory which was housed in an old bonded warehouse in James Watt St. As was customary for such high-security buildings, its windows were barred, and 22 workers were trapped and died behind those barred windows.

In 1960 the long-established system of street fire alarms was discontinued, as the increasing availability of the telephone emergency service was rapidly rendering them unnecessary.

In 1975, along with many other functions of the old Corporation, the Glasgow Fire Service passed out of its control into that of Strathclyde Region, with its new headquarters at Hamilton.

Football

Apart from the obvious fact that it required the minimum of equipment, three other circumstances ensured that the establishing of football as the Scottish national sport took place in Glasgow. These were first the enormous increase of the city's working-class population in the 19th century (thus providing a ready-made audience); second, the shortening of the working week (enabling supporters to attend matches on Saturday afternoons); and third, Glasgow's cheap and comprehensive system of trams (making it possible for fans to travel to matches anywhere in the city).

A significant date in the city's sporting history is 13 March 1873, when a group of local clubs with Queen's Park in the lead (the oldest Scottish club, formed in 1867 by members of the Glasgow YMCA) met in Dewar's Temperance Hall in Bridge St, Glasgow, and set up the Scottish Football Association. (The other clubs involved were Clydesdale, Dumbreck, Vale of Leven, Eastern, Third Lanark Rifle Volunteers, Rovers and Granville – where are they now?) One of its first actions was to provide a trophy: known at first as the Challenge Cup, it is still being played for today as the Scottish Cup.

Around this time another two momentous events took place in the history of Glasgow football: the formation of a team in 1872 by some young men on the Glasgow Green, who called themselves the Rangers, and the efforts of a Roman Catholic priest to alleviate the poverty in the city's east end by forming, in 1887, a football team called Celtic. And when the newly founded SFA finally came to rest in Carlton Place on the south bank of the Clyde, it ensured that the premier organising body for Scottish football was firmly linked with Glasgow. Indeed, by 1870, the city had 35 clubs registered with the Association and had become the main centre for the rapid increase in Scottish clubs.

The next development was the setting up of a Scottish League during the 1890–91 session, a development in which Rangers and Celtic played an important part. Although the League met with some opposition, in particular from Queen's Park, because of the introduction into the sport of what one contemporary critic called 'money making and money grubbing', its rules, which brought professionalism into Scottish football, were finally legalised by the SFA in 1893.

By the concluding years of the 19th century it was clear that Glasgow Rangers and Glasgow Celtic were becoming what they still remain, the game's biggest names in the city and beyond. They first came face to face officially in 1894 when Rangers defeated Celtic 3–1. Even at this early stage the seeds of football as big business had been sown; for example, that year Rangers' income increased from around £1,000 to over £5,000. More and more clubs, with Celtic leading the way, began to form themselves into registered limited liability companies.

How much the prominence of these two clubs was due to circumstances unconnected with football would be difficult to say, but it would be impossible to deny that Celtic supporters, in an elegant Glasgow euphuism, 'kick with their left feet' (i.e. are Roman Catholics), nor that the colour most commonly associated with Rangers is Protestant blue. Although in their early years both teams had players of the 'wrong' religion, Rangers had a reputation for never employing a Roman Catholic player under any circumstances; their decision in 1989 to break this rule shook the foundations of Glasgow football. A whole range of anecdotes and urban myths have grown up around these two teams, assisted and augmented by the odd circumstance that their ritual meeting once a year on New Year's Day, has caused this Auld Firm match to be regarded more as a religious observance than a mere game of football.

Glasgow football in the early years of the 20th century was not marked by any great players or great games – the city's claim to footballing fame during this period rested on the building of what was in its heyday the greatest stadium in the world. Queen's Park's quixotic devotion to the spirit of amateurism would have undoubtedly sunk them without trace but for the incredible gamble the club took – they built Hampden Park. Twice they had been forced to move, and they determined that their third 'Hampden Park', opened in 1903, would be a truly ambitious (and expensive) gesture. Their behaviour was no doubt influenced by the fact that a stadium of superior accommodation would stand a good chance of becoming the venue for all future international matches.

The late 1920s and the 1930s continued to be dominated by the Auld Firm sides, with Rangers probably the greater, winning the Cup six times and the League 15 times. One important factor in their success was their ability to pick able new players, and for some 20 years after the Second World War they continued to maintain that leading position. For instance, after the League Cup was instituted, Rangers in the season 1948–49 were the first team to achieve the Treble (the Scottish League, the Scottish Cup and the League Cup). They were also the first Scottish team to reach the final of a major European competition when, in 1961, they were beaten 2–1 by Fiorentina in the Cup Winners' Cup.

But the post-war years brought the unwelcome realisation that Britain no longer had a monopoly in the game it had given to the world. The adoption on the continent of fresh ideas and new approaches was giving opportunities to other countries. An early example of this trend was when the Hungarians, the first continental team to beat England at Wembley in 1953, met Scotland at Hampden the following year. Their fluid play and superb ball-control enabled them to run rings round their old-fashioned opponents to the tune of 4–2.

Another unfortunate change was brought about by forces external to the football world. After the war it became increasingly easy to travel about the country, by train, bus or car. This began to erode the local allegiances of football enthusiasts in small burghs throughout Scotland who now found it as easy to travel to Ibrox Stadium or Celtic Park as to their local teams' fields. With the media's attention being regularly directed towards Glasgow's 'big boys', it now became fashionable (and easy) to support one of the two Auld Firm teams whether you came from Kilmarnock or Falkirk, Dumbarton or Lanark.

Celtic had never really recovered its old *élan* during the 20 years which followed the First World War, despite beating Rangers in the League Cup 1957–58 by 7–1. The team's revival dated from the arrival on the scene of Jock Stein as manager. A former Celtic player, he had gone on to manage Hibernian before returning to Celtic in 1965. The first sign of his magic was Celtic's 3–2 win against Dunfermline Athletic in the Scottish Cup final of that year. Undoubtedly his greatest achievement, however, was taking his team to Lisbon in May 1967 where they beat Inter Milan 2–1 in the final of the European Cup – the first, and so far the only, Scottish football team to win this trophy. They then went on to win an unsurpassed nine League titles in a row (1965–66 to 1973–74).

It was during Stein's reign at Parkhead that Rangers found themselves relegated to playing the same role that Celtic had endured in the 1940s and 1950s. But with the appointment of Willie Waddell as manager in 1969 things began to improve for Rangers. This was demonstrated clearly in the 1971–72 season when, in the final of the European Cup Winners' Cup, they beat their old rival of 1945, Moscow Dynamo, by 3–2, thus achieving their first European trophy. Currently they have been showing considerable financial acumen which has enabled them to bring Ibrox Stadium close to the new rigorous standards. They have even taken on a Catholic player.

Recently, for the first time, it has seemed that the ascendancy of the two Glasgow giants might be threatened – for in 1970 Aberdeen beat Celtic in the Scottish Cup final, went on to take the European Cup Winners' Cup from Real Madrid with a score of 2–1 and became only the second team to win in succession the Scottish Cup for three years 1982, 1983 and 1984.

Whatever the reasons for the dominant positions occupied in Glasgow football by Celtic and Rangers, there can be no doubt that their pre-eminence had anything but a discouraging effect on the other Glasgow-based teams which struggled along in their shadow.

Of the three which survived – Clyde, Partick Thistle and Queen's Park – the latter occupied, and continues to occupy, a peculiar place in Scottish football. Possibly because it was the the prime mover in organising the beginnings of football in Scotland Queen's Park has always taken up a position beyond mere sectarianism – more of an institution than a club. It has two particular claims to fame. First was its steadfast aversion to professionalism; it would be amateur or nothing. Unfortunately, the result of this attitude was that it became a training ground for young would-be professionals and year after year its position was weakened as its best players left for paying positions with other teams – a weakness which brought about their relegation from Division One time and time again. In 1948, for instance, Queen's Park were relegated for the third time, then staged a come-back till the end of the 1955–56 season, only to suffer relegation again after a couple of years. Second, of course, is their playing field, Hampden Park – a name known wherever football is played. The first Hampden (the name was taken from a block of nearby houses) was a field rented from Glasgow Corporation for £20. When the rent rose to £100 they moved a few hundred yards to the second Hampden. It soon became the favoured venue for Cup finals and staged the first ever all-ticket match in 1884. However, becoming dissatisfied with the short lease, the club moved for a third time, leaving the second Hampden to become Third Lanark's park under the name of New Cathkin. The completion of the third Hampden Park in 1903 gave Glasgow three of the world's finest football parks – Hampden, Ibrox and Parkhead. The new park could hold 40,000 standing and 4,000 sitting, and despite the steady decline in the club's playing powers the income it received from the prestigious matches which took place on its ground enabled it to continue to expand its magnificent headquarters. In 1927 a further 25,000 places were added, and, with an additional 4,500 in 1937, it had reached its peak. From then on it broke almost every attendance record possible. The Scotland versus England match of 1937 drew in an incredible 149,415 spectators, said to be the highest official attendance ever recorded in Britain.

By the late 1940s, however, it began to go downhill rapidly. For safety reasons its capacity had to be reduced, and by 1972 its upkeep had become well beyond the club's resources. Over the next decade Glasgow's premier stadium became a political shuttlecock between competing forces, which included the SFA, regional and district authorities and central government. When these bodies eventually withdrew their financial support it set up an appeal and, with the aid of lotteries and private and public money, was saved – for the moment. Its future is uncertain, particularly in view of FIFA's insistence on all-seated stadiums for international games.

Partick Thistle, founded in 1876 and one of Scotland's oldest football clubs, has been described as 'the friendly team', the alternative football club. When it started, its home town of Paisley was an independent burgh immediately to the west of Glasgow, and it may have been this strong local identity which prevented it from rising out of Division Two. In their early days they moved several times; their fifth park was at Meadowside, on the banks of the Clyde, and it was said that two men in a rowing boat were stationed in the river to retrieve wandering balls. After being forced to get out in 1908 to make way for a shipyard the club eventually ended up at Firhill, an out-of-the-way district to the north of Glasgow. It may have been nearer the city centre, but it was notoriously hard to find! The team's most notable achievement was undoubtedly winning the Scottish Cup in 1920–21 by beating Rangers 1–0, while another peak was their 4–1 win against Celtic in 1971 which brought them the League Cup.

Clyde FC started its career in 1877 and, rather like Partick Thistle, it has always remained a domestic club with strong local ties, in this case with Bridgeton. Its first pitch was in Barrowfield Park, near the north bank of the Clyde, a location which probably supplied it with its name. In 1898 it moved south of the river to Shawfield Park. Always in dire financial straits, the club now took a course of action which finally drove it from its ground. In 1932, to augment its funds, it inaugurated greyhound racing on its pitch. Unfortunately, this venture proved so successful that the Shawfield Greyhound Racing Company took over the stadium, leaving Clyde FC mere tenants. Worse was to follow when, in 1971, the Greyhound Racing Association bought over Shawfield and disposed of it to developers 13 years later. Clyde was given notice to quit, and in 1986–87 was lucky to be able to share Firhill with Partick Thistle.

Presently it has a ground-share arrangement with Hamilton FC and expects to move to a purpose-built all-seated stadium in connection with Cumbernauld Development Corporation. The club's unfortunate distinction is never to have won the Cup or the League.

Third Lanark began life about 1868 as the regimental team of the Third Lanark Rifle Volunteer Reserves. It soon opened its ranks to 'civilians' and in 1872 moved to a private ground in the Glasgow district of Crosshill. The following year it was one of the group of clubs which came together to set up the Scottish Football Association. In 1903 it took over Queen's Park's vacated second Hampden, renaming it Cathkin Park. For obvious reasons, its local nickname was the 'Warriors' and its colours scarlet. Despite its long and eventful history the club had very few successes in national competitions – it won the Cup twice, in 1888–89 and 1904–5, and the League once, in 1903–4. After the Second World War it suffered more than most from the national decline in football support. To this were added financial difficulties, boardroom battles and plain mismanagement and, in the summer of 1967, the club found itself being wound up by order of the Court of Session, thus ending the career of the oldest professional football club in Scotland.

Glasgow has not escaped its share of football disasters; two of the most tragic occurred at Ibrox. During an exciting moment in an England v. Scotland match being played at Ibrox Stadium on 5 April 1902, the crowd on the west terracing leaned forward, causing a large part of the wooden stand suddenly to give way; 24 spectators plunged to their death 50 feet below, 24 others were seriously injured and another 493 had to be treated for more minor injuries. The hard lesson taught by this tragedy was that only solid earth or reinforced concrete can withstand the weight of crowds.

The second major accident happened at an Auld Firm match on 2 January 1971, again at Ibrox. A late goal was scored by Rangers just as many spectators were already making their way down the various outside stairs. It was said that many tried to turn back and reach the terracing although this was discountenanced by the official inquiry. For whatever reason, the crowd on Stairway 13 (the scene of three previous incidents) panicked and in the ensuing crush 66 people died and hundreds more were injured.

At a national level, for many reasons, football is finding the modern world of mass-media entertainment a difficult place to fit into. How well will Glasgow meet this challenge? Moves by Rangers in 1989 may indicate a way ahead. By signing a Catholic player they have begun to break down the barrier of sectarianism while their ongoing plans for upgrading Ibrox to the highest of international standards (including seated accommodation for over 40,000 spectators) suggest that a willingness to change with changing times may be the key. As far as Celtic is concerned, their successes of the 1960s and 1970s have not been repeated and financial problems combined with an urgent need to find a new ground (Celtic Park has fallen far behind the required new standards, particularly as regards seated accommodation) seem to have badly affected the team's playing qualities.

The Taylor Enquiry, set up in 1989 following the Hillsborough Stadium disaster, produced recommendations which are affecting all the Glasgow clubs' forward-planning, particularly the requirement that spectators should be admitted only to seated accommodation at all matches played at sports grounds designated under the Safety of Sports Ground Act, 1975.

CELTIC

Address: Celtic Park, 95 Kerrydale St
Founded: 1888
Stadium Capacity: 53,330 (8,534 seated)
Nickname: The Bhoys
Record Attendance: 92,000 (v. Rangers, January 1938)
Record Victory: 11–0 (versus Dundee, Division One, October 1895)
Most League Points: 72 (Premier Division, 1987–88)
Most League Goals: 116 (Division One, 1916–17)
Strip: Green and white hooped shirts, white shorts and socks

CLYDE

Address: Firhill Park (shared), 90 Firhill Rd
Founded: 1878
Stadium Capacity: 17,393 (3,000 seated)
Nickname: The Bully Wee
Record Attendance: 52,000 (v. Rangers, November 1908)
Record Victory: 11–1 (versus Cowden-beath, Division Two, October 1951)
Most League Points: 64 (Division Two, 1956–57)
Most League Goals: 122 (Division Two, 1956–57)
Strip: White shirts with red and black trim, black shorts, white socks

PARTICK THISTLE

Address: Firhill Park (shared), 90 Firhill Rd
Founded: 1876
Stadium Capacity: 17,393 (3,000 seated)
Nickname: The Jags

Record Attendance: 24,500 (versus Hearts, February 1952)
Record Victory: 11–1 (versus Stranraer, January 1932)
Most League Points: 55 (Division Two, 1985–86)
Most League Goals: 99 (Division Two, 1931–32)
Strip: Amber shirts with red shoulders and sleeves, red shorts with amber stripes, red socks

QUEEN'S PARK

Address: Hampden Park, Mount Florida
Founded: 1867
Stadium Capacity: 64,110 (seated 11,376)
Nickname: The Spiders
Record Attendance: 95,772 (v. Rangers, January 1930) (Stadium record is 149,547, Scotland versus England, 1937)
Record Victory: 16–0 (versus St Peters, August 1885)
Most League Points: 57 (Division Two, 1922–23)
Most League Goals: 100 (Division One, 1928–29)
Strip: White and black hooped shirts and socks, white shorts

RANGERS

Address: Ibrox Stadium
Founded: 1873
Stadium Capacity: 42,000 (35,000 seated)
Nickname: The Gers
Record Attendance: 118,567 (versus Celtic, January 1939)
Record Victory: 14–2 (versus Blairgowrie, Scottish Cup, January 1934)
Most League Points: 76 (Division One, 1920–21)
Most League Goals: 118 (Division One, 1933–34)
Strip: Royal blue shirts with red and white trim, white shorts, red socks

Foulis Academy of Fine Arts

From as early as 1738 Robert Foulis (university printer, with his brother Andrew) had considered setting up an academy of fine arts in Glasgow, and while travelling through the Continent in 1751 he bought paintings, prints and sculptures for the use of the proposed academy (it is said that there were some 500 pictures in the Academy's collection, including ones by Raphael, Correggio, Titian, Rubens and Van Dyck). He also brought back artists and craftsmen – a painter, an engraver, a copperplate printer and two plaster moulders.

As could have been expected, Foulis received little help from his fellow citizens, but three wealthy Glasgow merchants – John Glassford of Dougalston (1715–83), tobacco merchant; Archibald Ingram (1704–70), his brother-in-law, calico printer and banker, provost 1762–64; and John Coats Campbell of Clathic, merchant, provost 1784–86 – contributed sufficient funds to start up his Academy in 1754 (15 years before the opening of the Royal Academy of Arts in London).

There is little information regarding the actual working of the Academy; Robert himself described its activities as 'modelling, engraving, original history painting and portrait painting'. A few pupils were enrolled, and every year during the King's Birthday celebrations their works were exhibited on the walls of one of the University quadrangles. It has been said that in the course of its first ten years the Academy produced over 1,000 prints, as well as statues, busts and paintings. Few of its pupils made names for themselves but among those who did were David Allan and James Tassie. Allan, known as the Scottish Hogarth, entered the Academy in 1755 at the age of 11, and left in 1762. Two years later he was sent to study in Rome, largely at the expense of the Academy, and on his return he achieved a successful career as a portrait painter in London and Edinburgh. Tassie, from Paisley, graduated from the Academy in 1763 and went to Dublin where he invented a form of vitreous paste with which he made imitation cameos – using it he produced over 500 portrait medallions of famous contemporaries. Robert Paul showed early promise but died while still a pupil. He left behind a large, impressive but unfinished engraving of a view of the Trongate from the Cross, which was eventually completed in 1777 by fellow pupil, William Buchanan.

The work of the Academy was constantly impeded by lack of money, and much of the profits from the printing house were swallowed up in maintaining it. When Ingram, the principal benefactor, died in 1770 the end of the Academy was near, and after Andrew Foulis' death in 1775 Robert gave up the struggle to keep it going. He printed a catalogue of its 459 paintings and went to London to sell them at auction. The times were not auspicious – eventually Christie's disposed of them at a price far below their true value – and it is reported that after the charges of the auction were met only 15/- remained. A disappointed man, Robert died at Edinburgh in 1776 on his way back to Glasgow, leaving debts of over £6,000.

Galleries and Museums

The City of Glasgow District Council is responsible through its Museums and Art Galleries Department for several museums/galleries throughout the city, the most prestigious of which is undoubtedly the **Kelvingrove Art Gallery and Museum**, located at the west end of Sauchiehall St in the Kelvingrove Park.

Although the old Town Hall at Glasgow Cross boasted of a set of portraits of British royalty, the founding contents of this Corporation Art Gallery and Museum came mainly from two sources. First, the art collection of Archibald McLellan (1796–1854), a Glasgow coach builder who had an artistic taste somewhat beyond that of his time and had amassed a remarkable collection of paintings (mainly Dutch, Flemish and Venetian) which he bequeathed to the Corporation along with the gallery he had built to house it.

Earlier, the city's *cognoscenti* apparently enjoyed a different reputation – Sir Henry Raeburn, the celebrated portrait painter, declared that 'To say that the Gentlemen of Glasgow pay like Princes would be doing them the highest injustice, for theÿ pay infinitely better . . .' Some 20 years later another two large bequests were made, one in 1874 by William Ewing (more than 30 pictures) and another in 1877 by John Graham Gilbert, himself a popular portrait painter. When Sir Charles Robinson, HM Surveyor of Pictures, described the city's art collection as being of exceptional quality, the Corporation suddenly became aware of the treasures they owned. Now other donations followed – from James Reid of Hydepark Locomotive Co, from Adam Teacher,

The District Council's Art Gallery and Museum seen from across the River Kelvin, 1973. (George Oliver)

Graham Young of Kelly, Thomas Smellie and others.

In 1870 the Corporation acquired a mansion, Kelvingrove House, Kelvingrove (named after the River Kelvin which flows through it and built in 1783 from a design by Robert Adam for Patrick Colquhoun, a former Glasgow provost), and began to use it to house various collections of historical, scientific and technical objects belonging to the city.

It was decided to erect a single building to house both this collection and the city's growing art collection (along with a concert hall and art school), and it was agreed that the profits from Glasgow's 1888 International Exhibition should be devoted to this task. These profits (£46,000) were augmented by over £70,000 from a few prominent citizens. The

Corporation added a further £46,000 plus a free site in Kelvingrove Park, and in 1891 the Association for the Promotion of Art and Music held an architectural competition for the new building. From the 62 designs submitted, that of John W. Simpson and E. J. Miller Allan was selected, and work began. Unfortunately, costs escalated and in 1896 the Corporation was obliged to take over from the bankrupt Association, and the new art gallery and museum (the concert hall and art school were quietly dropped) was opened in 1902.

A succession of worthy superintendents and directors increased the scope of its various collections by purchase and bequest; the most memorable of these was Dr Tom J. Honeyman, during whose time of office (1938 to 1971) the fine art collection was considerably augmented, probably on account of his close acquaintance with Sir William Burrell (of the Burrell Collection). Now the Kelvingrove Art Gallery and Museum is considered to be among the foremost civic collections in Britain.

It is divided into four departments: Natural History and Zoology; Archaeology, History and Ethnography; Decorative Art; and Fine Art. Displays are distributed through some 20 public galleries in an ornate two-storey building.

The Natural History Department embraces geology, botany and zoology and contains a wide range of exhibits from minerals to butterflies, insects to fossils and herbariums to environmental displays of local and exotic flora and fauna.

The Department of Archaeology, Ethnography and History is responsible for displays of all kinds of artefacts from an Egyptian mummy to a Scottish dancing master's violin, but its most noteworthy collection is probably the Scott Collection of European Arms and Armour. Robert Lyon Scott (1871–1939) was the chairman of the Scott Shipbuilding & Engineering Co of Greenock, and he bequeathed to the museum his superb collection (described as 'one of the choicest ever made') of over 800 important examples of armour, along with a valuable library of more than 3,000 volumes.

The Department of Decorative Art is comparatively new, having been set up in 1973. It contains important collections of metalwork, ceramics, glass, furniture, costumes and textiles. Its silverware collection is rich in Scottish examples, with a natural emphasis on Glasgow items (until 1964 Glasgow had its own Assay Office).

The Fine Art Department has over 3,000 oil paintings, 12,500 prints and drawings and 300 pieces of sculpture. Its greatest strengths are Dutch 16th-century paintings, French 19th and early 20th-century paintings and all forms of Scottish art from the 18th century onwards – in particular the Glasgow School and the Scottish Colourists. In popular terms, its best-known pictures would include *St Victor and Donor* by the Master of Moulins, Giorgione's *Adultress brought before Christ*, Whistler's *Portrait of Carlyle* and Dali's *Christ of St John of the Cross* (which was recently moved to the St Mungo Museum of Religious Life and Art), but it also has major works by such painters as Rubens, Corot, Courbet, Millet, Pisarro, Monet, Degas, Seurat, Van Gogh and Matisse, while its Scottish collection includes works by Ramsay, Raeburn, Horatio McCulloch, McTaggart, Hornel, Fergusson, Peploe, Cadell and Eardley.

The Department of Museums and Art Galleries is also responsible for other museums throughout the city.

The McLellan Galleries, Sauchiehall St. Archibald McLellan built, in the year of his death, a large gallery to house his collection, consisting of a frontage of shops and houses behind which was a suite of three exhibition rooms. Unfortunately he died insolvent in 1856 and the Corporation grudgingly found itself obliged to pay off his creditors and to purchase the collection for £15,000 and the building for £29,500. After many vicissitudes the gallery became a useful venue for exhibitions of all kinds. Following a disastrous fire in the 1980s it was completely refurbished (at a cost of £3.4 million) to the highest standards in time for Glasgow's year as the City of Culture in 1990, and now provides the Glasgow Museums and Art Galleries with a major venue for large-scale travelling shows of international standing and other exhibitions.

The People's Palace was opened in the Glasgow Green in 1898 and is now an extremely popular museum depicting the social and political life of the city (*see* PEOPLE'S PALACE).

The Burrell Collection (Pollokshaws Rd) was gifted to the Corporation in 1944 by Sir William Burrell, shipowner and art collector, and is located in its custom-built gallery (opened 1983) in Pollok Country Park (*see* BURRELL COLLECTION).

The Museum of Transport was opened in 1964 in a former tramcar depot in Albert Drive. It illustrates the history of Glasgow's shipbuilding, locomotive-building and motor-car manufacturing industries by means of a comprehensive collection of tramcars, buses, carriages, bicycles, railway engines, motor-cars and a remarkable collection of model ships. It contains a reproduction of a 1939 Glasgow street with shops typical of the period and a small cinema. In 1987 it was transferred to new and enlarged premises located within the refurbished Kelvin Hall (off Dumbarton Rd).

Pollok House (Pollok Country Park) was built between 1748 and 1752 as the family home of the Maxwells of Pollok, and was presented to the city in 1966 by Mrs Anne Maxwell Macdonald. It houses a magnificent collection of Spanish paintings gathered by Sir William Stirling Maxwell last century.

Haggs Castle (St Andrew's Drive) was opened in 1976 as a museum with the aim of showing today's children how the children of the past lived and played, with period rooms and a reconstructed Victorian nursery. It is housed in a much restored castle built for John Maxwell of Pollok in the late 16th century.

Provand's Lordship (High St) is the oldest domestic building in Glasgow, dating from 1471, and is now a small museum exhibiting medieval furniture in period room settings (*see* PROVAND'S LORDSHIP).

Rutherglen Museum of Local History (King St, Rutherglen) displays the long history of a royal burgh which only came into Glasgow in 1975.

Camphill House (*c.*1818), located in the Queen's Park, was converted into a museum in 1895 and is now a museum of costume containing a large collection of costumes and textiles.

St Mungo Museum of Religious Life and Art (Castle St) opened in 1993 and is the first museum in the world to be entirely devoted to the study of religious life and art. It contains priceless works of art depicting aspects of the world's six major religions, and features the only permanent Zen garden in the United Kingdom.

The Hunterian Art Gallery (University Ave) part of Glasgow University, is based on the benefaction of William Hunter (1718–83), a celebrated London anatomist and physician who had received his early education at the University. Its main strength lies in its paintings, which include three Chardins, a Rembrandt and a Ramsay.

Other later gifts include works by Reynolds and Raeburn, and its collection of prints is the largest in Scotland. Its 15,000 items range from Dürer to Hockney, by way of Rennie Mackintosh and Picasso. Another of its strengths is its very important collection of drawings and personalia of James McNeill Whistler (1834–1903). It also contains a superb reconstruction of Charles Rennie Mackintosh's house at 6 Florentine Ave (now 78 Southpark Ave), Hillhead, his home for eight years, with many items of his furniture and fittings – a measure of Mackintosh's artistic importance can be gauged by a mahogany writing cabinet which cost £10 in 1933 and which was bought by the University in 1979 for £80,000.

The Hunterian Museum (University Ave) is Scotland's oldest public museum, opening in 1807. Hunter was an assiduous coin collector and his coin cabinets form an important part of the museum. There is a considerable collection of the archaeology of Scotland from the earliest period to Roman times, as well as ethnographic material brought back by Captain Cook and displays of the geology of Scotland.

Springburn Museum (Atlas St), located in the premises of Springburn Library, is a local museum, and reflects in visual form the past and present conditions of the district, once the largest locomotive manufacturing centre in Europe.

Royal Highland Fusiliers, Regimental Museum (Sauchiehall St) houses uniforms, pictures and other military memorabilia, much of it belonging to the history of Glasgow's own regiment, the Highland Light Infantry (now part of the RHF).

BURRELL COLLECTION

Sir William Burrell's grandfather came from Northumberland to Glasgow *c.*1830 and some 20 years later set up in business with his son, William senior, as Burrell & Son, shipping and forwarding agents at Port

The main entrance to the Burrell Collection, Pollok Country Park, in the shape of a 14th-century arch from Hornby Castle, Yorkshire, set into a quite plain stone gable. A part of the main galleries is visible in the background. (George Oliver)

Dundas, Glasgow, on the Forth and Clyde Canal. The business prospered, and by 1870 the firm had become involved in owning and running deep-sea merchant shipping. On the death of William, senior, in 1885, his two young sons, William, junior, and George, took over the business. By careful buying and selling of their merchant fleets at opportune moments they amassed very considerable fortunes and when they finally disposed of their business interests in 1916 William was able to devote his money and the rest of his life to building up his art collection, a pursuit for which he had shown an early taste.

Burrell was self-trained and his resources were never as great as his American rival collectors, nor was he ever a leader of taste, and yet he eventually brought together a collection equalled by few for its scope and breadth – Sir John

Rothenstein (former Director of the Tate Gallery) described him as 'a collector of vast perception'. He kept a careful account of all his purchases, which shows that between 1911 and 1957 he spent each year about £20,000 adding to his collection. In 1927 he and his art treasures moved to Hutton Castle, Berwickshire, although by then the collection's size was such that much had to be put out on loan. Sometime in the 1930s he decided that his collection should become a permanent one under some form of public ownership. It has been said that he offered it to the Tate Gallery, who turned it down for lack of space. Eventually, in 1944, he made it over to Glasgow, the city of his birth and of his business.

He attached to the gift certain conditions, one of which became a vexatious stumbling-block: the site of the building housing his collection must be not less than 16 miles from the Royal Exchange, Glasgow, and not more than four miles from Killearn, Stirlingshire – Sir William feared the destructive power of atmospheric pollution and wanted a rural setting. Strenuous efforts were made to find an appropriate place – Mugdock Castle and the Dougalston estate, both a few miles north of the city, were both considered – but before a decision could be made Burrell died in 1958 in his 97th year. Finally the Trustees, swayed no doubt by various Clean Air Acts and smokeless zones, agreed in 1963 to allow the collection to be housed in a building within the 360-acre Pollok estate. This was a large area of open landscaped ground three miles south of the city centre. For centuries the property of the Maxwells of Pollok, it was generously donated, along with Pollok House, to the Corporation by Mrs Anne Maxwell Macdonald in 1967. An international competition to design a gallery was announced, and out of 242 entries the

winners, announced in 1972, were three unknown architects Barry Gasson, John Meunier and Brit Andreson, then tutors in the Cambridge University School of Architecture.

The completed building, opened in 1983 by the Queen, has been described as 'deceptively simple' and 'modest, practical and poetic'. Located in the corner of a large field it is roughly triangular in plan. It is clad in Dumfries red sandstone (one of the city's traditional building materials) combined with glass and stainless steel. It covers over 130,000ft square and includes a restaurant, two libraries, study rooms, a lecture theatre, and conservation work-shops. It incorporates 15 historical archways bought by Sir William mainly from the collection of Randolph Hearst, the American millionaire newspaper-owner; as well as reproductions of three rooms from Hutton Castle, complete with fittings and furniture. It cost £20 million (shared equally between Glasgow Corporation and the government).

Although Burrell collected widely, his acquisitions fall into certain clearly defined categories, the most important of which are the fields of North European late Gothic art, oriental ceramics and bronzes, and 19th-century French paintings:

19th-century paintings
Degas (22 paintings, including *Edwin Duranty in his Study* and *The Rehearsal*), Cezanne, Renoir, Manet, Géricault, Boudin, Daumier, Pissarro, Crawhill, MacTaggart, Lavery, Whistler, Millais.

North European medieval art
Stained glass, sculpture and, in particular, tapestries (one of the finest collections extant).

European Post-medieval art
Silver, table glass, needlework.

Oriental art
Chinese ceramics, bronzes and jade, a small

collection of Japanese prints. This accounts for one quarter of the whole collection.

Near East

Carpets from an area stretching from India to Turkey.

Artefacts

From Mesopotamia, Assyria, Egypt, Greece, Rome.

The collection is not a closed one and items continue to be added. The most important of these is undoubtedly the Warwick Vase, a huge Roman marble vase weighing 8¼ tons, which the Trustees purchased in 1978 for £253,808, and which now adds lustre to the Courtyard of the Burrell Collection Gallery.

Pollok House, 1740s. The house and its surrounding parklands were given to the city by the Maxwell family in 1966. Its plain but well-proportioned front faces on to the White Cart. The matching garden pavilions and terrace were added in 1904. (George Oliver)

PEOPLE'S PALACE

The east end of Glasgow, as happened in many large British towns, early became an area given over to industrial buildings and working-class housing. It lacked most municipal amenities, but as early as 1866 the erection of a building to be devoted to the recreation and improvement of this area's inhabitants had been mooted, and eventually, in 1898, the People's Palace was opened in the Glasgow Green by Lord Rosebery. The building cost about £32,000. Over £7,000 came from the Caledonian Railway Co for permission to dump soil excavated from its tunneling activities, about £3,300 from the profits of the 1891 East End Exhibition and some £4,400 from the sale of a bleaching ground in Bridgeton; the balance came from the Corporation. The facilities consisted of a suite of reading and recreation rooms, a

museum and a picture gallery.

The three-storeyed museum and gallery is constructed in red sandstone in the French Renaissance style from designs by the City Engineer, A. B. Macdonald, while its entire southern façade is enclosed by a huge winter garden or conservatory, four times the size of the museum. It is traditionally said to be based on the inverted hull of Nelson's *Victory* – a theory lent some credence by the close proximity of the first monument erected to him.

The museum is now devoted to presenting the social history of the city. Until 1940 this function was carried out by a Glasgow Room in Kelvingrove Art Gallery and Museum but it was transferred to the People's Palace in 1940. The design of the building is not suitable for modern displays and its small size has had a cramping effect, but it holds the key to the city's past in its wide range of artefacts. These include, for example, the Tontine Faces from Glasgow Cross, Regality boundary stones, a Roman Samian ware bowl (c.AD150) found in the adjacent Fleshers' Haugh, the 1554 Katherine bell from the Tolbooth Steeple, the 18th-century Saracen's Head Inn five-gallon pottery punch bowl, and the family portrait of John Glassford, a famous 18th-century tobacco lord. It has a series of imaginative three-dimensional reconstructions of medieval and 18th-century Glasgow and a large collection of paintings of the city and its people. It also holds many relics of Glasgow's labour history, including an excellent and extensive group of trade union banners, as well as a large collection of stained glass, much of it from redundant city churches.

Recently it has commissioned paintings from several contemporary Glasgow artists, including Alasdair Gray (also the author of *Lanark*), John Byrne (also a playwright) and a striking set of eight panels by Ken Currie illustrating Glasgow's radical history.

Gangs

Every city, throughout history, has suffered from semi-organised groups of youths and young men indulging in riotous behaviour. Glasgow has by no means escaped, and for a short period in the 1920s and 1930s its gangs became unjustifiably notorious.

The earliest Glasgow gang on record was the Penny Mob in Townhead, about 1880. Its name came from its members' subscriptions, and its main victims appeared to have been anyone not of the gang's nebulous religious affiliations. At the turn of the century other names are recorded – the Hi Hi, Ping Pong, San Toy, Tim Malloy and Village Boys, but apart from having memberships of about 100, nothing more is known of them.

The heyday of the Glasgow gangs was undoubtedly the period of the post-First World War Depression. The operational areas of the gangs of this period (as of the earlier ones) were the crowded streets in and around the city centre. Two of the earliest were the Redskins and the Black Hand Gang in 1919 and 1920, their names suggesting adolescent reading. Later, gangs began to proliferate in an alarming manner – some of the better known included the Norman Conks, Billy Boys, Beehive Gang, South Side Stickers, Calton Entry, Briggate Boys, Bedford or Parlour Boys, Antique Mob (Shettleston), Calton Entry Mob (Tollcross) and the Butney Boys (Maryhill). Many of the names came from east-end streets or districts.

The first large-scale conflict between gangs was on the Albert Bridge (which links north and south Glasgow) in 1928, between the South-Side Stickers and the Calton Entry (a district north of the river). The locus of the battle and the respective 'turfs' of the two gangs suggest a dim folk-memory of the once notorious stone battles which took place between groups from north and south of the Clyde for possession of one of the small islands then found on the river in the early 19th century.

The best-known gang rivalry was that between the Norman Conks (from Norman St, and 'Conquerors') and the Billy Boys. The leader of the former was Bull Bowman, and of the latter, William Fullerton. In this case the rivalry was greatly overheated by Glasgow's religious bigotry, for the Conks were Roman Catholic and the Billy Boys (named after the folklore version of the life of William III) owned a nebulous but nevertheless perfervid allegiance to Protestantism – Dans and Billys. These two gangs were of considerable size (the Billy Boys could muster 800) and they attracted more than the merely criminal. Their attacks and counter-attacks in and around Bridgeton were frequently major incidents. Their weapons were not usually razors (ineffective in mass combats) but rather beer bottles (intact or broken), pickstaves and sharpened bicycle chains, and their war chests were kept filled by terrorised local shopkeepers.

During the 1930s a combination of various methods gradually reduced the gangs to impotence. Sir Percy Sillitoe, a

reforming Glasgow Chief Constable, set up an organisation specially to deal with them, equipped with situation maps, pre-knowledge of likely fights, radio-controlled patrol cars, etc. He constantly harried the two important gangs, the Conks and the Billy Boys, laying carefully planned ambushes and allowing them no time to recoup. Action of a different kind was bravely taken by some church authorities and eventually the gangs disappeared from sight.

After the Second World War, in the late 1950s and early 1960s, exposure by newspapers and television again brought the Glasgow gangs to public attention. New names appeared – Calton Tongs, Gorbals Cumbie (Cumberland St), Maryhill Fleet, and Possilpark Uncle (after a TV series, *The Man from U.N.C.L.E.*). These more prominent gangs were themselves split up into various subgroupings; the Maryhill Fleet, for instance, had at least 20 subdivisions. Once again, preventative police action took its toll; now the effects of the ruthless pursuit of drug-dealing profits have made Glasgow's early gangs a matter of past history.

Garden Festival

The first British Garden Festival was held in Liverpool (1984), the second in Stoke-on-Trent (1986) and the third in Glasgow. The Glasgow Festival, which ran from April to September 1988, was located for the most part on the 100-acre site resulting from the filling in of the Prince's Dock on the south bank of the Clyde. The same year

that Glasgow's proposal was made, 1983, Laing Homes Ltd purchased the site for £2.5 million. In November the city's proposal was accepted and the Scottish Development Agency, the event's main funding body and organiser, leased the site from Laing. Total costs, less income from expected visitors, were estimated to be about £70 million. In the event there were 4.3 million visitors which was 40 per cent above target.

The pioneer German festivals laid particular stress on the horticultural aspects of the concept but Glasgow continued the emphasis of the earlier British festivals in bringing leisure pursuits into more prominence, underlining the idea of a complete family day out. With this object in view there were five easily identifiable 'rides' – the tramcars, the Festival railway, the 240ft Clydesdale Bank Anniversary Tower, the Mississippi Steamboat and the Coca-Cola White Knuckle Roller-Coaster.

Several thousand tons of soil and more than 300,000 trees and bushes were used to landscape the site, and six theme sectors were set out – science and technology, health and well-being, plants and food, landscape and scenery, water and maritime activities, recreation and sport. Two special features were the specially created 'High St', decorated with outlines of the city's best-known spires and towers which housed over 20 single-storey shops, and Bell's Bridge, an opening foot-bridge which crossed the river from the Scottish Exhibition and Conference Centre on the north bank to the Festival on the south.

Along with the City of Culture activities in 1990, the success of the Festival played an important part in establishing Glasgow as one of Scotland's leading tourist destinations.

Gas Supply

The use of coal gas as an illuminant began in Glasgow about 1805 when a few of its citizens experimented by heating small retorts of coal in a fireplace and using the resultant gas for lighting purposes. Its commercial use began in 1817 with the formation of the Glasgow Gas-Light Co, a joint venture between the Corporation and some private investors to light the streets and other public places. The first works, the Townhead Gas Works, were located not far from the Cathedral, and its gas holder (capacity 25,000 cubic ft) was reputed to be the largest in the country. The actual supply of gas began the following year and one of the first to use it was a grocer who installed six gas 'jetties' in his Trongate shop. It was also used the same year to illuminate the Dunlop St Theatre Royal, and by the following year there were over 1,500 public gas lamps throughout the city's streets. In 1827, when the output was about 80 million cubic ft, the first gas meters were introduced; about 15 years later the output had risen to 217 million cubic ft, and the darkness of the tenement closes began to give way to gas jets.

So profitable did this venture become that in 1843 another company, the City and Suburban Gas Company of Glasgow, began to manufacture gas. It was also during this year that the clock faces on the Tolbooth Steeple were lit by gas. Despite the supposed competitiveness of two suppliers the customers constantly protested about high prices, and the Corporation also began to complain that almost 25 per cent of the gas was being allowed to leak away. Eventually, in 1869, the Corporation bought out the two companies and set up its own Gas Department. To supplement the large gas works it had taken over at Townhead, Dalmarnock and Tradeston, it erected an even larger one at Dawsholm (1871). In 1891 it took over the Temple Gas Works (which had belonged to the Partick, Hillhead & Maryhill Gas Co, and whose gas holder was the third largest in the world). The Townhead Gas Works closed down in 1874, and when the Provan Gas Works opened in 1904 the Dalmarnock Works also ceased to operate. In 1885 the Corporation opened a depot for the sale and hire of gas cooking stoves and the sale of gas fires.

Following the Corporation's take-over the consumption of gas went up by leaps and bounds. In 1870 it had been 1,295 million cubic ft, by 1913 it had risen to 7,733 million cubic ft, supplied to over 280,000 consumers within an area of 98 square miles.

In 1948, under the Gas Act, the Corporation Gas Department (by then serving over a million consumers) handed over to the nationalised Scottish Gas Board its four large gas works, its four chemical works and various workshops and showrooms. At that time the area covered by the Gas Department was about 138 square miles and the total length of mains was 1,585 miles.

Gates

Although Glasgow had no defensive walls it had a number of city gates or ports. These were mainly for administrative or regulative purposes, to monitor the passage of goods and produce and to help to maintain public order. In time of plague entry to the burgh was strictly controlled by means of the gates.

Glasgow had four main entry points, corresponding to the four points of the compass. On the north side of the city there was a pair of gates. First was the Stable Green Port (North Port), which lay on Castle St above where the Royal Infirmary now stands. It took its name from being near the stables of the Bishop's Castle. The second northern gate was the Castle Gate Port (Castle Yett* Port) which controlled a road running along the east side of the same castle past its gateway. It was

sometimes known as the Kirk Port from its proximity to the old Barony Church.

On the eastern boundary was the Gallowgate Port (East Port) which was situated on the Gallowgate, to the east of Charlotte St. Traffic from Edinburgh and beyond, up the Scottish east coast from England, came through this gate.

To the south the Brig or Briggait Port barred the north end of the old Glasgow Bridge. It was the busiest of all the gates for through it passed much of the traffic, trade and produce of south-west Scotland.

On the west the Wester Gait or Trongate Port crossed Argyle St at Stockwell St and controlled the route west to Dunbarton through Partick. It had originally been placed nearer the Cross but was moved west *c.*1588.

As the city lacked walls it could of

course be entered by other ways, wherever gaps between the boundary houses allowed, and these secondary entries were sometimes given the dignity of being named a port. Thus, in addition to the Gallowgate Port, the city's eastern boundary could be crossed through the Drygate Port, located at the eastern extremity of the Drygate, or through two lesser gates – Lindsay's Port and the Stinking Vennel, both allowing entry directly into the High St. Also giving access to the High St, but from the western side, were the Greyfriars Port and the School Wynd. Old records mention other ports, not now traceable, such as Colin's Port and Findlay's Port.

The southern entry was complicated by two other gates in addition to the Brig Port. First, at right angles to it, was the Water Port through which passed traffic entering the city from the west along the north bank of the Clyde. There was also another gate which barred the way north

into the Saltmarket from immediately to the south of where the Bridgegate joined it. It had a number of names – Walker Gate (from the Saltmarket's earlier name of Waulker Gait), Porta Inferior or Nether Barras Yett.

On the west side there were two additional ports. One was at the corner of Bell's Wynd and the Candleriggs, and was said to have been the most handsome of all the city gates. The other was on the line of the Rottenrow and was called the Rottenrow Port.

The main gates seem to have remained in use until the beginning of the 18th century. Possibly with the setting up of a ring of tollgates around the city where the various turnpike roads entered it, the need for the gates disappeared. The two east–west gates lasted into the 1750s – the Gallowgate Port was removed in 1749 and the West Port in 1751, while the southern gates went in 1788.

Ghosts

Glasgow never appears to have been attractive to ghosts and there are very few stories about them in the city.

One story which Glasgow shares with many other sites is the Piper and the Tunnel. A piper and his dog entered a tunnel which was said to run from the Cathedral to the old church in Rutherglen. They were never seen again, but his voice has been heard declaiming, 'Ah doot, Ah doot, Ah'll ne'er get oot'.

In 1670 a 'devil' was reported to be troubling a house in Keppoch, a district to the north of the city. It cast peats and dropped stones from the roof but hurt no

one – behaviour usually associated with a poltergeist.

Robert Dreghorn, known as 'Bob Dragon', was the son of a rich Glasgow merchant and was reputed to be the ugliest and most profligate man in the city. He committed suicide about 1806, and his spirit was said to haunt his Clyde St mansion.

Sir William MacEwen, a pioneering 19th-century brain surgeon, refused to operate on a young artist who then committed suicide. As a result, Sir William's ghost roams the corridors of the Western Infirmary.

The city's Underground has attracted a few stories. In 1922 a woman and a young girl fell in front of a train – the girl was saved but the woman died and her spirit, the 'Grey Lady', haunts the tunnels. Cleaners working in the tunnel between Kelvinbridge and Hillhead stations have heard the disembodied voices of women singing, while a seemingly ordinary man discovered in empty carriages being cleaned disappears when led to the exit.

Glasgow

NAME

The roots of 'Glasgow' as a place-name have proved difficult to establish with any certainty. The earliest record is Jocelin's statement in his life of St Kentigern (12th century) in which he states that the saint set up his church *'in villa dicta* deschu *quod interpretator* cara familia *que nunc vocatur* glaschu'; that is, 'the place was called *deschu* which means "dear place", and is now called *glaschu'*. It would appear that Jocelin derives the name from two Welsh words, *clas*, 'close' or 'cloister', in the sense of a religious community, and *cu*, 'dear', to give 'Dear Place'. The problem with this derivation is that normally the first part of such a phrase would be adjectival. It has been suggested, with some probabilty, that Jocelin's *deschu* is a scribal error for *cleschu*, equating it with his later name *glaschu*, and that the city's name derives from the joining of two Gaelic words, *glas*, 'green' and *cau*, 'hollow' or 'valley', meaning 'Green Hollow'. Popular etymology has decided on an amalgam of parts of both of these, in the form 'Dear Green Place'.

At various times other, odder, meanings have been suggested, including dark glen, black church, beloved water, grey dog, deserted road, valley of prayer, sacred glen, green field, eloquent voice, grey water and green wood!

OTHER GLASGOWS

A number of settlements in North America are called Glasgow, but few of them provide clear evidence of the origin of their name.

Two Canadian examples are **New Glasgow** in **Nova Scotia**, founded in 1805, population 10,500, and **Glasgow**, a little village on **Cape Breton Island** with a population of about 100.

The United States of America has several more examples.

Glasgow, in **Delaware**, was originally called Aikentown but changed its name to Glasgow about 1800. It is a busy crossroads on Route 40.

Glasco, New York, has two possible origins, either a misspelling of Glasgow or from the letters GLASS CO displayed on the roof of the Woodstock Glass Co.

Glasgow in **Kentucky** was named by James Mathews after his hometown, and has a population of 13,000.

Glasco, Kansas, is said to be the result of poor spelling by the local postmaster in 1870. Population, 700.

Glasgow, Montana, began as Siding 45 of the Great Northern Railway. Its new name was a random choice by a railway clerk. Population, 7,000.

Glasgow in **Illinois**, a small settlement but

big enough to have its own post office.

Glasgow Village, Missouri, is a suburb of St Louis and has adopted Glasgow's coat-of-arms.

Glasgow, Missouri, was named after James Glasgow, one of a group of St Louis merchants in 1836. Population, 100.

Glasgow, Virginia, was a boom town in the 1890s and is located near the Blue Ridge Mountains. It has a population of 1,300.

Glasco, Connecticut, was founded by a blacksmith, Isaac Glasco. Population, 600.

Glasgow Eastern Area Renewal

The years of deterioration and deprivation suffered by the central areas of the city led the Corporation to set up in Hutchesontown in 1957 the first of 29 Comprehensive Development Areas which were intended eventually to cover one–twelfth of the city's area. The programme was to run for 20 years and the main emphasis was to be the thorough clearance of older working-class housing, but by 1969 only nine CDAs had been approved. By 1975 five more had been approved and over 95,000 demolitions had taken place. It became apparent however, that the social cost of such widespread demolition was proving unacceptable – parts of Govan, Partick and Springburn were torn apart – so the CDA programme was allowed to wind down. Its place was taken by Local Plans which sought closer co-operation with local communities through mutual decisions. By 1980 the city had 48 of these.

In 1976 a fresh approach was adopted by setting up the Glasgow Eastern Area Renewal GEAR scheme. The city's east end

had always been an area of factories and factory-workers' dwellings and, an obvious example of inner-city deprivation, it was considered to be an eminently suitable area for a new approach – an integrated and large-scale planning initiative – covering the districts of Bridgeton, Dalmarnock, Parkhead, Calton, Camlachie, Shettleston, Tollcross, Sandyhills and Cambuslang. As befitted its multi-purpose aims it was formed from a partnership which included Glasgow District Council, Strathclyde Regional Council, Scottish Special Housing Association, Greater Glasgow Health Board and the Scottish Development Agency. The District was to provide £52 million, the SDA £39 million, the SSHA £39 million and the SRC £13 million.

The area covered by GEAR was 4,000 acres and held a population of 45,000 in some 17,000 homes. The whole concept was the largest of its kind in western Europe. Officially its activities terminated in 1987 but the partners undertook to continue for another three years. It has achieved most success in rehabilitating the environment (more than 200 gap sites were landscaped – inhabitants have been heard to remark on the apparent activity of the Forestry Commission, to judge by the extensive tree-planting) and in the provision of new quality housing stock – of the £200 million committed, 60 per cent went on housing. By 1985 some 200 factories and workshops had been built, about 1,800 houses erected, 5,000 houses modernised, and 1,400 private houses built. But the area's social and economic problems have proved to be much more intractable.

Glasgow Humane Society

In 1787 James Coulter left £200 in the care of the Faculty of Surgeons in Glasgow in order to establish a society for the rescue and recovery of persons drowning in the Clyde and other Glasgow watercourses, the start in 1790 of the Glasgow Humane Society.

In 1795 a dwelling-house and a boat-house were erected for the Society's use on the edge of the Clyde in the Green of Glasgow. Although none of the Society's early records are extant, it would appear that several of the Clyde ferrymen were paid by the Society for retrieving bodies from the river; it was also claimed in 1825 that some 600 persons had been saved by its activities.

Like similar societies in other large cities, the Glasgow Humane Society seems in its early period to have limited its activities largely to the awarding of medals and certificates to individual rescuers, but in 1859 it took the unusual step of appointing a full-time officer. The first to take up this post was George Geddes I (it is interesting to note that amongst the earlier individuals mentioned as assisting the Society were a James and a John Geddes, probably ferrymen). George Geddes was active from 1859 to 1889 and was succeeded by his son, George Geddes II,

who held the post till 1932. It was said that for two generations, whenever there was a fatality connected with the river, the cry 'Send for Geordie Geddes!' went up. When Geddes died in harness in 1932, his assistant, Ben Parsonage, took over. Parsonage, who had been appointed in 1928, proved to be the longest-serving officer of the Glasgow Humane Society, working on the river until his death in 1979. During his employ it has been reckoned that he was responsible for saving more than 1,000 lives and for recovering at least 2,000 bodies. After his death his son, George Parsonage, took over as officer on a part-time basis.

In 1867 the Society's house was extended and updated, and in 1937 was replaced by a new building. The officers have always worked from a timber wharf a few yards from the Society's house, fitted with pontoons and with about a dozen boats to call on. Despite the inclusion of motor-boats, for the purposes of rescue work and underwater dragging, the slower but more manoeuvrable rowing-boats have more than held their own. The Glasgow Humane Society still operates as an autonomous society, independent of both the Glasgow District and Strathclyde Region.

The Glasgow School

In the last two decades of the 19th century a group of about 20 artists – not all Scots, but all associated with the country in one way or another, mainly through the Glasgow School of Art – came together to form a loose and informal group known as the Glasgow School but more popularly as the Glasgow Boys. Their aim was to make a break with the conventional styles of contemporary Scottish painting and to acknowledge the artistic changes which had taken place on the continent. They never made revolutionary claims and were content, indeed anxious, to have their works accepted and displayed in academies and institutes. Only a handful of the 20 really achieved critical acclaim.

Their artistic development was assisted to a degree by the famous art dealer, Alexander Reid, who brought many examples of influential European paintings to Glasgow. They were also strongly influenced by Whistler; it was two of their number who persuaded Glasgow Corporation to purchase his *Carlyle* portrait in 1891.

Around 1878 James Guthrie (1859–1930) of Greenock and E. A. Walton (1860–1922) of Renfrewshire, both at the Glasgow School of Art, formed a strong friendship which became the nucleus of the Group. The following year Joseph Crawhall (1861–1913) of Northumberland joined them, and in 1883 John Lavery (1858–1941) of Belfast settled in Glasgow as one of the School. George Henry (1858–1943) of Irvine, another Glasgow School of Art student, became an important member of the Group, along with his close friend E. A. Hornel (1864–1933), an Australian expatriate.

Guthrie is usually regarded as the Group's leader. His early *plein-air* paintings gave way to portraits, and between 1885 and his death he portrayed many of the important and successful people of his day.

Walton was also a leading figure amongst the Boys. He experimented with a wide range of materials and techniques; in 1899 he painted one of the panels in the City Chambers' Banqueting Hall – Glasgow Fair in the 15th century – in which he used real sand.

Crawhall was particularly proficient in pen and ink (and brush), often with vivid watercolour washes. He was fond of hunting and shooting and these activities often appeared in his almost cartoon-like pictures.

Lavery, after an early landscape period, went to London to become one of the most successful portrait painters of the time, particularly noted for his society portraits. He also painted one of the Banqueting Hall murals – a somewhat uncharacteristic shipyard scene.

Henry and Hornel tend to be bracketed together and their visit to Japan strongly influenced their style. A joint-work, *The Druids – Bringing in the Mistletoe* (1890), in the Glasgow Art Gallery is an important Group piece, as is Henry's deceptively simple *Galloway Landscape* (1889), also in the gallery.

At their height over 600 of their paintings were exhibited in Europe, but by the beginning of the 20th century their fire had dimmed, and convention, from which they had striven to escape, claimed them.

The western elevation of Charles Rennie Mackintosh's most celebrated building, the Glasgow School of Art, demonstrates his ability to blend intricately sculpted masonry with soaring columns of small-paned windows. (George Oliver)

Glasgow School of Art

In the 1840s the government set up several Schools of Design to 'influence and improve design in manufactures' by providing training for textile industry designers. Glasgow, with its thriving textile industry, was an obvious choice for such a school and one was established in 1840 in Ingram St. An early head was Charles Heath Wilson, who had to be forcibly 'retired' in 1863 and was followed by Robert Greenless, a local landscape painter. He retired in 1881 and was succeded by Thomas C. Simmonds the same year.

As its original purpose became irrelevant with the decline of the city's textile industry, the School began to cater for fee-paying students and amateurs, and in 1869 it moved from the city centre to the McLellan Galleries in Sauchiehall St, becoming known as the Glasgow School of Art and the Haldane Academy (the reference to 'Haldane Academy' – added when the Governors of Haldane's Trust, set up by James Haldane, a Glasgow engraver, supplied financial support – was later dropped). The results it achieved were such that it was soon receiving a larger grant than any other similar school in Great Britain.

Towards the end of the century, however, its financial position was becoming critical. Originally its committee had been self-electing but in 1892 its governors began to be elected from various

Glasgow public institutions, and it registered itself under the Companies Act. These changes, enabling it to receive parliamentary grants, removed much of its financial insecurity, and the appointment in 1885 of Francis ('Fra') Newbery (1853–1946) as headmaster or director continued and strengthened the revitalising process. He involved the School closely with the burgeoning Arts and Crafts movement, and just before and after the First World War it had no equal in metalwork and embroidery. His wife set up the section of Needlecraft and Embroidery, along with Ann Macbeth, in 1894. These classes in what were described as Applied Arts Studies gave women an increasing prominence in the school, and by 1901 some 47 per cent of the students were women. Newbery also encouraged the development of the school's painting and sculpture classes, particularly by bringing in as visiting lecturers and assessors members of the Glasgow School (more popularly known as the 'Glasgow Boys'). Some of this group had actually trained at the School, and its European recognition helped to enhance the School's reputation. In 1901 it became the Central Institution for Higher Art Education for Glasgow and the West of Scotland, and in 1902 Newbery, who had been asked to supervise the Scottish section of the prestigious International Exhibition of Decorative Arts at Turin, further improved the school's standing by selecting almost entirely works by its students.

Newbery devoted much of his time and energy towards raising funds to allow the relocation and rebuilding of the School, and by 1896 he was in a position to invite 12 local architects to submit plans for a new building located in Renfrew St, a short distance away from the old site. The award went to the firm of Honeyman & Keppie,

and the new structure, a pioneering architectural masterpiece, was the work of the young Charles Rennie Mackintosh, himself a student at the School. At first there was only enough money (some £14,000) to allow the eastern half to be erected (from Dalhousie St to the main doorway) and the whole building was not completed till 1910. Newbery's efforts laid the foundations for the School's continuing success, but his health was badly damaged by his strenuous work both in and out of the school, and he was forced to retire in 1918.

The School's students were trained in a wide range of artistic work, including landscape and figure painting, architecture, modelling, sculpting, designing and decoration. It also produced art masters and mistresses as well as teachers of drawing in primary schools. Those who attended the day classes were generally professional art students, while the evening classes attracted what were termed 'artisans and art workers'.

As one of the largest and oldest schools of art in Great Britain it continues to hold a premier place in the teaching of art and has recovered a great deal of its earlier industrial and market-oriented outreach. Douglas Bliss, the well-known wood-engraver, was director from 1946 to 1964 and was followed by Sir Harry Barnes, under whose direction the Mackintosh School of Architecture was established (it and the School of Planning are both degree-awarding bodies, in co-operation with the University of Glasgow) and the School continued to grow both physically and academically. It offers instruction in drawing and painting, architecture, planning, ceramics, embroidered and woven textiles, photography, sculpture, jewellery, printmaking, environmental art and graphic design.

Its reputation has been enhanced by a number of young painters trained at the School who have all recently established international reputations – any list of them would include Steven Campbell, Adrian Wiszniewski, Ken Currie, Peter Howson, Alison Watt and Stephen Conroy.

Glasgow Style

In 1908 the Lady Artists Club in Blythswood Sq decided to renew their front door and commissioned Charles Rennie Mackintosh to design the replacement. Although it carries all the hallmarks of a Mackintosh design, they have been successfully modulated and subordinated to its classic surroundings. (George Oliver)

A group of artists and designers, with a shared connection through the Glasgow School of Art, came together just before and after the First World War and created a comprehensive system of interior decoration which came to be known as the Glasgow Style.

Some of the group were, or became, important figures in their own right – Charles Rennie Mackintosh (architect), George Walton (artistic designer), Talwin Morris (book designer and binder), and Jessie M. King (book illustrator); other group members have remained more background figures – Herbert McNair (teacher and designer), Jessie Newbery (embroiderer and wife of the dynamic head of the Glasgow School of Art, Francis Newbery), John Ednie (interior design), George Logan (furniture design) and Ann MacBeth (embroiderer).

Mackintosh and MacNair became close friends, an association made still closer when they married the sisters Margaret and Frances Macdonald. Both Margaret and Frances were talented designers and embroiderers, and they all worked so closely together that they became known as 'The Four'.

The group's distinctive style, as applied to interior decoration, was characterised by simple, elongated and highly stylised forms derived from plants or emaciated human forms – the use of the latter gave the group its nickname of the 'Spook School'. Surfaces tended to be smooth, and the colours were always muted shades of mauve, pink and green. A Scottish response to continental Art Nouveau, it achieved a surprisingly popular success – probably because a tamer version of it was taken up by some of the large furniture stores (such as Wylie &

Lochhead) for their middle-class customers. Individual contributions from the various members of the group would result in a co-ordinated design which included furniture, fabrics, carpets, light fittings and orna-ments for individual customers.

Glasgow Trades Council

The earliest minute-books of the Glasgow Trades Council are dated 1858, although previous stirrings can be discerned as far back as 1811. Unfortunately there is then a gap till 1884. The Glasgow Trades Council always had an importance far beyond the confines of the city, for it represented the workers of the second city of the United Kingdom and one with a well-developed industrial base.

It was in April 1858 that a cotton-spinner, a baker, a carter, a mason and a sawyer set up the Glasgow Council of Trade Delegates (later to become the Council of the United Trades of Glasgow and finally the Glasgow Trades Council). For many years it was barely kept alive by a small group of activists, but the severe industrial depression of the 1870s and the increasing assertiveness of the proliferating left-wing groups of the time brought about a resurrection in 1871; between 1888 and 1889 its affiliated societies increased from 49 to 71.

The Council's disillusion with the Liberal movement (which had represented the city in Parliament for much of the 19th century) led to increasing support for the ILP (formed in 1894) and in the 1896 municipal elections eight Labour candidates were elected to the Corporation with support from the Glasgow Trades Council.

In 1912 Emanuel Shinwell became its chairman — at this time its interests included working-class housing, women's suffrage, state medical service and baby clinics.

Close links now began to develop between the Council and Labour group (now numbering 18) in the Corporation, and in 1918 the Glasgow Trades Council became the Trades and Labour Council (representing 93 trade union branches, 11 ILP branches, 2 Co-operative Societies, the Fabian Society and the British Socialist Society) with Shinwell in the chair. The Council's part in the famous 40-hour strike at the beginning of 1919 brought it into national prominence and consigned Shinwell and others to terms of imprisonment.

By the mid-1920s the Council had come under the influence of a group of Communist Party sympathisers, and it came to adopt a distinctly far left of centre attitude, refusing, for instance, to send delegates to the Scottish Council of the Labour Party. Eventually the moderates prevailed and a decision to adopt the rules of the Labour Party was carried overwhelmingly. Following this, the link between the industrial section of the Council and the Borough Labour section was broken in the late 1920s.

Throughout the 1930s most of the efforts of the Glasgow Trades Council were directed towards fighting for the unemployed, and later, by the end of the decade, towards combatting fascism and fighting for peace. The efforts to promote peace led to some opposition to war preparations (such as air-raid precautions).

With Russia's entrance into the Second World War, there was a growing resurgence of the influence of Communist Party supporters in the Council, and its attitude hardened well to the left of the Labour Party. So pronounced did this attitude become that in 1951 the General Council of the Scottish Trade Union Congress went so far as to disaffiliate the Council. A pragmatic solution was found – in 1952 the Glasgow Trades Council was wound up, and then restarted under the aegis of the STUC.

Golf

Although golf, that quintessentially Scottish game, originated on the sandy machairs of the country's east coast, it was being played in Glasgow as early as the 16th century. For over 200 years it took the form of unregulated play over the Glasgow Green, the city's only open space; by 1777 its existence was noticeable enough to be mentioned in John Gibson's history of the burgh.

Shortly before 1786 a group of well-to-do Glasgow gentlemen regularised the situation by setting up the Glasgow Golf Club (with rules based on those of the Honourable Company of Golfers at Edinburgh), the first (and for a long time the only) golf club in the west of Scotland. Like their proletarian predecessors, the members of the new club perforce played over the Green, at that time very much in a state of nature and consequently full of 'hazards'. The original purpose of the club was to enable its members to compete for the Silver Club trophy. Played for each spring, its winner became captain for the ensuing year and supplied a silver ball with his name and the date to be hung from the metal club.

In 1789 (when the members numbered 25) the city magistrates were asked for permission to build a clubhouse at or near the old Herd's House on the Green, for the convenience of the members. At first this was refused but in 1792 leave was given to take down the 'present herd's house or golf-house' and to build a new one. It must have been a fairly substantial building for the members used it for drinking, eating and gambling. By the end of the century its membership had almost doubled.

The course consisted of seven holes, and a match was made up of three rounds or 21 holes in all. The names of only two holes have survived: the Monument Hole (after an obelisk in memory of Lord Nelson, a prominent feature of the Green), and the Humane Society House Hole. Members playing were obliged to wear the club uniform of a grey jacket or pay a bottle of rum. The spirit, popular in Glasgow through its connection with the West Indies trade, was the club's betting currency, and not all the wagers placed were connected with golf. In February 1821 the minute book carried the following wager: 'Major Maclay bets that his toast will be the best of the whole. Mr Lindsay bets the contrary, a bottle of rum. Major Maclay, when it came to his toast, gave "The best of the whole" and all the members gave it as their opinion that Mr Lindsay had lost the bet.'

Some records remain of scores and lengths. The lowest winning score for the Silver Club was 109 strokes, an average of 5 strokes per hole, while the highest was 134, explained as being caused by 'An excessive wet day and grass very long'. In 1786 John Gibson drove a ball for the record distance of '201 yards, 1 foot, 11 inches'.

The club lapsed between 1794 and 1809 and disappeared in 1833. Almost a generation later, in 1870, its name was revived and the reconstituted club became the city's most exclusive golf club. By 1901 there were 33 other golf clubs in and around the city, and almost a hundred by the start of the First World War. Many catered for what were then called 'respectable members of the working class'; indeed, in Glasgow (as its municipal courses bear witness) and elsewhere in Scotland, the game has never entirely lost sight of its classless origins. The club asked permission from the Corporation to lay out a course in Queen's Park; four years later it had to move to Alexandra Park. Then, again at the insistence of the Corporation, the club moved in 1895 a mile or so to the north and set up a third course at Blackhill, but their stay there was equally short. By now, 1909, the club had over 700 members with a subscription set at 12 guineas. Finding these constant changes irksome, their next move, in 1904, took them outside the city to Killermont, just over the city boundaries on the north bank of the Kelvin. Despite a threat from the Corporation to buy up their lease the club managed to obtain a perpetual feu on their grounds in 1922. The world's oldest open amateur tournament, the Tennant Cup, is held there.

After its abandonment by the club, the Corporation continued to maintain the 9-hole Alexandra Park course as the first of their municipal courses. Its success encouraged them to open a second one in Bellahouston Park in 1899, and at present the District Council maintains four 18-hole courses at Deaconsbank, Lethamhill, Linn Park and Littlehill. Within Greater Glasgow there are now around 82 golf courses (72 of which are 18-hole and 10 of which are 9-hole).

Halls

City Halls

For many years the city's only public hall had been what was usually called the King's Hall in the Tolbooth building at the Cross, which measured only 44ft by 24ft. A separate Town Hall was erected in 1734 as an annexe to the Tolbooth and, until the middle of the 19th century, these rooms were the only venues for civic entertainment or social intercourse. As the city grew in size and complexity it became apparent that there was now no accommodation big enough to allow for the meeting together of large numbers of its citizens.

A solution to this problem was the opening in 1841 of the City Halls in the Candleriggs. When completed, it contained five halls, the largest of which (the Grand Hall) was 94ft by 60ft and could accommodate 3,500 – such numbers would now be considered dangerous and after reconstruction in 1968 its authorised accommodation is little over 1,000. The suite of rooms was carried on iron columns above the bazaar and fruitmarket located on the ground floor. In 1855 an organ was added at a cost of £1,600. City Halls proved to be a considerable asset both to the Corporation and to the citizens, and became the regular venue for any meeting of size and importance: it was here that Charles Dickens gave his celebrated readings, that Thackeray lectured, and that David Livingston was honoured by the city. All the great political gatherings took place in it, and it was also extensively used for such mundane events as concerts, social tea meetings, balls, dances, entertainments and lectures.

It had some disadvantages. It was surrounded by narrow streets which made access difficult and the area around it was no longer residential, most of its inhabitants who could afford to having moved west. It has still proved useful on many occasions, however – from being the Glasgow headquarters of the wartime Ministry of Food from 1939 to 1954, to providing an assembly hall for the Glasgow College (now the Scottish Caledonian University). After the destruction of the St Andrew's Halls in 1962 it came back into its own again for a while, but the opening of the Royal Concert Hall in 1990 has limited its use. As well as running the City Halls, the Council's Performing Arts and Venues Department is also responsible for

a dozen public halls throughout the city.

St Andrew's Halls

The steady rise of the city's west end as a residential area served to make apparent that locality's lack of decent hall space, so a private company was formed to erect a set of halls at the top of North St. The building, designed by Campbell, Douglas and Sellars, was opened in 1877 at a cost of some £100,000. The Grand Hall measured 108ft by 75ft and could hold 4,500 persons – a figure reduced to some 2,500 in later more safety-conscious days. There were two minor halls, the Berkeley Hall (72 × 39ft) and the Kent Hall (51 × 39ft), each usefully named after the streets running alongside them. There were several other lesser halls within the complex, including a 72ft by 50ft ballroom.

During the 1870s the city was in the throes of severe commercial depression and the owners soon found that they could no longer finance the running costs. Accordingly, in 1890, they were obliged to sell it to the Corporation for £37,000.

The St Andrew's Halls continued to act as a commodious venue for many large gatherings in the city, from political meetings to musical performances. The acoustics of the Grand Hall were said to be the equal of any concert hall in Europe – in fact, on a visit to the city the eminent tenor, Enrico Caruso, remarked that he had never found anything better.

In 1962 it was totally gutted by a fire which left only the Granville St entrance and the façade intact. After considerable discussion, the Corporation agreed that the site should become an extension of the immediately adjacent Mitchell Library. The splendid façade with its four sculpture groups has been incorporated into the new structure and a small 400-seat auditorium, the Mitchell Theatre, is part of the new complex.

Kelvin Hall

Facing the Kelvingrove Art Gallery and Museum, the present Kelvin Hall was erected in 1927 to take the place of a previous hall, opened in 1917 and burnt down in 1925. With 170,000 square feet all on one floor, it was regularly used for large-scale exhibitions such as the city's contributions to the Festival of Britain in 1951. Unusually, during the Second World War, it became the country's chief factory for producing barrage and convoy balloons.

The Kelvin Hall is probably best remembered by Glaswegians as the site of the Corporation's annual Christmas circus and carnival. In 1987 the complex was converted and opened as two self-contained units, the Kelvin Hall International Sports Arena and the Museum of Transport. Its other functions have now been transferred to the Scottish Exhibition and Conference Centre.

The Scottish Exhibition and Conference Centre, Finnieston St, 1987, broods like an exercise in geometry. It stands on the north bank of the Clyde on the filled-in site of the Queen's Docks, surrounded by acres of tarmacadamed carparks.
(George Oliver)

Scottish Exhibition and Conference Centre (SECC)

The Kelvin Hall was no longer a suitable venue for modern large-scale events, and as early as 1983 planning began for the construction of a major exhibition and conference centre of international standing. The site finally chosen was the infilled and reclaimed Queen's Docks, located between the Clydeside Expressway and the river, about one mile from the city centre.

Covering an area of 19,000 square metres it takes the form of five interlinked halls of varying sizes and capabilities, Hall 1 (concert auditorium/conference venue) is the largest – it is capable of housing, on the same day, a pop concert with an audience of 10,000, a music festival for 2,000 and a trade exhibition catering for 3,500 visitors. Its carpark can accommodate 3,500 vehicles; 100,000 pines and larches have been planted to provide windbreaks. It is the third-largest venue in the United Kingdom after the NEC and Earl's Court, Olympia. All the Kelvin Hall's exhibition activities have been transferred to it, including the Christmas circus.

It was opened in 1985 and its cost of £36 million was equally shared between Glasgow District and Strathclyde Regional Councils, and the Scottish Development Agency, with contributions from the private sector.

Royal Concert Hall

The loss of the St Andrew's Halls as a major venue for large-scale events in the city was keenly felt, though it was almost 30 years before it was replaced. The site chosen for the new hall looks down from the north end of Buchanan St (conforming to the Glasgow propensity to place important buildings at the ends of streets) and the Royal Concert Hall was erected there (at a cost of £29 million) as one of Glasgow's main contributions to its role as City of Culture in 1990. The site was a difficult one, part solid rock, part a filled-in quarry. Building was further complicated by the presence only 60ft below it of the access tunnel to the busy Queen St Railway Station, which necessitated mounting the auditorium on a system of isolating rubber pads. The main auditorium, horseshoe in shape, can seat an audience of over 2,400, with choir accommodation for 250, and has a computer-controlled stage which can be altered to provide 36 different layouts. The hall contains conference facilities, exhibition areas, a restaurant and bars. It is run by an independent company, Glasgow Cultural Enterprises, set up by the District Council.

Historians

Four histories of Glasgow appeared during the 18th century. The very first was by John McUre, who brought out his *The city of Glasgow; or, an account of its origin, rise, and progress, with a more particular description thereof than has hitherto been known* in 1736, when he was 85. He had been Clerk to the Register of Sasines in Glasgow and as such had access to 'many antient records, charters, and other antient vouchers, and from the best historians and private manuscripts'. Nineteenth-century historians tended to regard him as an old-fashioned gossip. Certainly his accounts of the early period of his history is far from reliable, but for the city of his own time he is accurate and useful. A very serviceable reprint came out in 1830 with illustrations, notes and appendices.

In 1777 John Gibson, merchant, published his *History of Glasgow from the earliest accounts to the present time*. The value of his book lies in his informed and detailed account of the growth of Glasgow commerce at the end of the century. He makes the interesting point that the American War of Independence (1775) was not an unmitigated disaster for the city as it forced its merchants and manufacturers to look elsewhere for markets.

Andrew Brown produced his two-volume *History of Glasgow, Paisley, Greenock and Port Glasgow* in 1795–97. He was a failed Tobacco Lord who died in poverty, and his history is particularly good on the city's late 18th-century trade and commerce.

The fourth is *An historical account and topographical description of the city of Glasgow and suburbs* by James Denholm, published in 1797. A polished work in the best style, it ran to three editions, each bigger than its precursor. It was extremely popular, probably because it catered for the growing demand for a guide rather than a history, and its chief interest is in the author's meticulous descriptions of the social and industrial conditions of the city and its many new buildings.

James Cleland was by trade a cabinetmaker and by inclination a statistician of some note (he was census-taker for the burgh on two occasions). He was appointed Superintendent of Public Works in Glasgow in 1814, and as such was much involved with the city's new streets and buildings. He brought out his *Annals of Glasgow* in two volumes in 1816. It covers general and statistical information on many of the city's public services, institutions and societies. It is quite disordered and his dates cannot always be relied on, but there are a great deal of miscellaneous facts in his *Annals*. His *Rise and progress of the city of Glasgow* (1820) was a *réchauffé* of his earlier work.

The Revd James F. S. Gordon, Episcopalian priest at St Andrew's-by-the-Green, brought out an unusual type of history. Entitled *Glasghu facies, a view of the city of Glasgow* (1872) its two volumes embodied the substance of McUre's history along with the matter of 30 other Glasgow writers, along with explanatory notes and critical comments.

Old Glasgow . . . to the eighteenth century (1880) by A. Macgeorge is a straightforward and readable standard 19th-century history of Glasgow's earlier years.

G. McGregor was a journalist with the *Glasgow Herald*, and his *History of Glasgow from the earliest period to the present time* (1881) is an excellent piece of journalism; its annalistic layout is useful for 'events of the year' research.

Robert Reid (1773–1865) was a successful Glasgow merchant from a long line of successful Glasgow merchants, and in the 1850s and 1860s he published, under the pseudonym 'Senex', several books based on his reminiscences. These were gathered together, along with miscellaneous information from other hands, and published as three large volumes in 1884 under the title *Glasgow, past and present*. Reid himself describes it, reasonably, as 'a mass of hodge-podge'. Although deriving mainly from his own memories, he could call on family lore to extend its scope (involving information personally given to him by his grandmother, born in 1715, the year of the first Jacobite Rebellion). Because his family's position and his occupation involved him in all the commercial affairs of a commercial city, it is an irreplaceable historical treasure for the city's late 18th and early 19th centuries. It is further helped by an excellent index.

Another idiosyncratic historical account was provided in 1865 by Peter Mackenzie (1799–1875). He had started his career in a Glasgow law office but gave this up for the life of a radical politician and publisher. In 1831 he founded *The Reformers' Gazette* and continued it for 34 years. It was devoted to drawing attention to the many political grievances of the day, in particular to the need for parliamentary reform. From it he made a selection relating to the burgh and published it in two volumes in 1865 as *Old reminiscences of Glasgow*. It provides a valuable insight into the social and political aspects of what might be termed the 'alternative' Glasgow, but is occasionally marred by gossipy and unfounded accounts of events. It also lacks an index, one reason why it is so seldom referred to.

1876 saw the first instalment of an important source work for Glasgow, the first volume of *Extracts from the records of the burgh of Glasgow* (1876–1916), edited by Sir James D. Marwick (later volumes by Robert Renwick) under the auspices of the Scottish Burgh Records Society. Although described merely as 'extracts', the 11 volumes of the series are very full transcripts of the minutes of Glasgow Town Council from 1573 to 1833, and include helpful introductions, full indexes and useful maps.

Although entitled *The people's history of Glasgow*, John McDowall's book is rather a mini-encyclopedia. Published in 1899 it is a topic-arranged précis of city facts, from 'Armorial Bearings' to 'Prominent Men'. For a quick fix on most Glasgow people, places and things before the 20th century it makes a good start.

The beginning of the 20th century saw the publication of an unusual paperback history of the city. *Glasgow in 1901* appeared under the authorship of James Hamilton Muir, which was a portmanteau phrase hiding the identities of the brothers James and Muirhead Bone, and John Hamilton Charteris. An impressionistic view of middle-class Glasgow by three of its own members (a journalist, an artist and a lawyer), it is quite unlike any contemporary account of the city, and its effect is considerably enhanced by the many atmospheric vignettes of city scenes by Muirhead Bone.

In 1909 Sir James D. Marwick produced his *The river Clyde and the Clyde burghs* which deals very fully with the relations of the city with its rival burghs on the river – Rutherglen, Renfrew and Dumbarton.

Glasgow's pre-Reformation period, when the city was ruled by its archbishops, is not well represented. James Primrose's *Medieval Glasgow* (1913) is the only work which gathers together from scanty sources an account of this era.

In 1917 the Corporation agreed that Robert Renwick, then Town Clerk Depute, should be commissioned to research and prepare an 'authentic, accurate and well-documented history of the burgh'. The commission was accepted, and the first volume published in 1921. On Renwick's death the task was taken over by George Eyre-Todd, journalist and Scottish man-of-letters, who brought out another two volumes (1931, 1934), taking the history up to the reform of local government in 1833. The expectation that a burgh official and a journalist would be capable of producing a worthwhile history was not realised, and the city still awaits an authentic, accurate and well-documented history.

The first volume of David Murray's scholarly *Early burgh organisation in Scotland* (1924) is devoted to Glasgow, and ably traces the evolution of the city's burghal organisation from the earliest times to the end of the 17th century.

J. Cunnison and J. B. S. Gilfillan edited the Glasgow volume (1958) of the *Third Statistical Account of Scotland*. This worthy offspring of Sir John Sinclair's *Statistical Account of Scotland* (1791) is a 1,008-page compendium which covers, albeit briefly, every aspect of the city from the site and its development to social relations, from theatres to municipal transport. It is an essential introduction and bird's-eye view for anyone interested in the city.

In 1967 John R. Kellett, then senior lecturer in economic history at Glasgow University, published *Glasgow, a Concise History*. Although purposely written as a school textbook, the author's intimate acquaintance with the source material and its significance makes this slight book an excellent introduction (and a foil to the *Third Statistical Account*) to the city's history.

The popularity of C. A. Oakley's *The Second City* is amply illustrated by the number of editions it has run through since 1946. With no pretensions, but showing a considerable knowledge of the city and its character, this is a readable description of the main events of its history, accompanied by many illustrations.

Andrew Gibb, from Glasgow University's Department of Geography, published his *Glasgow, the Making of a City* in 1983. Although geographical in concept, it is based on a firm historical framework and its dependence on original sources (not always a feature of city histories) makes it a useful guide.

There is now a group (growing but

still small) of specialist histories of the city, such as T. M. Devine's *The Tobacco Lords* (1975); J. M. Roxburgh's *The School Board of Glasgow, 1873–1919* (1971); R. A. Cage's *The Working Class in Glasgow, 1750–1914* (1987); I. McLean's *The Legend of Red Clydeside* (1983); W. Eadie's *Movements of Modernity: the Case of* *Glasgow and Art Nouveau* (1990); H. B. Peeble's *Warshipbuilding on the Clyde* (1987) and J. Kinchen's *Glasgow's Great Exhibitions* (1988). There is also a fairly large group of popular accounts of the city, including those by J. M. Reid, Jack House, Maurice Lindsay, Cliff Hanley, David Daiches and Alan Massie.

Hospitals

By the close of the 19th century there were three main types of hospital in Glasgow:

(1) **Voluntary Hospitals** – These hospitals were financed generally by public subscription and were run by Boards of Managers. They mainly admitted patients suffering from acute non-infectious illnesses.

(2) **Public Health Authority** – Under the Police Act of 1866 municipalities, including Glasgow, were obliged to maintain permanent fever hospitals for the treatment of all kinds of infectious diseases.

(3) **Parish Council** – This body was responsible for the relief of the sick poor. By 1890 approximately 900,000 were looked after of whom 2 per cent (18,000) were officially classed as paupers. The Parish Councils were set up in 1894 as the successors to the old Parochial Boards who had previously administered the provisions of the Scottish system of poor relief.

VOLUNTARY HOSPITALS

Glasgow Royal Infirmary

This was the sixth of the Scottish city infirmaries to be set up (Edinburgh, Aberdeen, Dumfries, Montrose and Paisley had been opened at various dates between 1729 and 1786). Most of the earlier establishments had been erected through the concern of the citizens but the Glasgow infirmary came into being through the endeavours of one individual, George Jardine, Professor of Logic at Glasgow University, in 1787. A site located to the west of the Cathedral, and which had been occupied for hundreds of years by the Bishop's Castle, was bought from the

Crown; a royal charter was granted in 1791 and in the following year the foundation stone was laid with full masonic honours. The architects were the famous brothers, Robert and James Adams (Robert died the same year the work commenced). Many contributions were received, from £150 from a theatre benefit night to £1,200 from the Royal Glasgow Volunteers. It was a well-proportioned building in the rococo style, with a plain lower base and an ornamental upper façade. It was surmounted by a dome beneath which was located the operation room with space for 200 students; later this area became the Hospital Chapel.

The rapid increase in the city's population meant that from time to time additions were made to the original building – there had been only 136 beds at the start but by 1861 this figure had increased to 572. The need to separate fever cases from the main surgical wards was early recognised, and in 1832 a 'fever hospital' was erected north-east of the main building, initially to accommodate the victims of the cholera epidemic of that year. By 1886, however, all fever cases were being sent to the fever hospital at Belvidere.

By the end of the 19th century it became clear that the infirmary as it stood (more than a hundred years old by then) could not cope with its increasing use unless some drastic alterations were made. In 1897 it was agreed that the front block should be rebuilt 'on the lines of the most approved views' and money was collected for this purpose. But it soon became apparent that nothing short of a complete rebuilding would solve the infirmary's pressing problems. From several submitted designs, that of James Miller was selected – in defiance of the views of many architectural authorities. Apart from criticism of the internal layout, the Board of Management was attacked vehemently for selecting the one design whose vast bulk would utterly dwarf the nearby medieval cathedral; there was also an acrimonious debate regarding the use of funds originally meant for the rebuilding scheme.

Eventually, in 1907, the foundation stone was laid and the completed building was opened in July 1914 by King George V. At the time it was reckoned to be the largest public building in the United Kingdom.

The close teaching connection which existed between the infirmary and the old University in the High St was broken in 1874 after the University removed to its present site at Gilmorehill in the city's west end, but the link was restored in 1911 with the founding of four new university chairs in medicine, obstetrics, surgery and pathology. The infirmary continued to be supported by voluntary contributions – one of the best known of these voluntary sources was the money collected each year by the city's students through the streets of Glasgow – and in 1938 its ordinary expenditure amounted to £133,433.

After the Second World War, the Corporation's plans to rationalise the city's road network included extensive changes in Townhead (the infirmary lay on its southern boundary). Once the details of the expected alterations became known, it was decided that the future of the infirmary could only be assured by building a completely new structure to the north of the old building, on the edge of the M8 motorway. The architects Basil Spence, Glover & Ferguson were engaged to design a brand new hospital. The estimated cost was £18 million but it came as no great surprise, presumably, when the final figure turned out to be in excess of £40 million.

The earth removed in 1973 in connection with its foundations was providentially used as the fill-in for the Queen's Dock. The infirmary was finally handed over to the Greater Glasgow Health Board in December 1981, although some parts of the building had been in use since 1977. During this preliminary phase the old building still continues to be the main ward block.

Two names famous in the history of medicine are connected intimately with the Royal Infirmary. It was in its Surgical House (built 1859) that Joseph Lister (1827–1912) discovered and made effective the revolutionary principle of antiseptic surgery. Unfortunately, the intention to retain the House as a memorial was frustrated when the building was demolished in the mid-1920s. The second name is that of Sir William MacEwan, Professor of Surgery, who carried out his epoch-making work in connection with the surgery of the brain during his period at the infirmary and further extended Lister's work by originating the concept of aseptic surgery. It has also been claimed that the infirmary was the first hospital in the country to use x-rays for diagnostic purposes.

Western Infirmary

The initiative to erect a new hospital in the city's west end came from Glasgow University, the main reason being the need to provide teaching opportunities for medical students at the new university site on Gilmorehill (overlooking the West End Park and the River Kelvin – the University had moved from its original location in the High St in 1870), but there was also a need to provide hospital facilities for the rapidly growing population west of the city centre.

It was decided to erect a 350-bed infirmary to a design by the architects John Burnet Son & Campbell on a site immediately to the west of the University. The original plans, prepared in 1869, had to be downgraded to only 190 beds because of financial restrictions. The infirmary was opened in 1874; seven years later, thanks to a substantial donation by John Freeland, Glasgow merchant, it was completed according to the original design, doubling the ward accommodation.

A minor Glasgow mystery involves two reliefs and a statue of an animal of the cat family which appear on these additions. One theory is that they represent pumas, while another states that they are leopards, said to form part of the Freeland family crest.

One sad event in the infirmary's history happened on 5 April 1902 when all the spectators injured in the collapse of a wooden stand at the nearby Ibrox Park, home of Glasgow Rangers Football Club, were brought to the infirmary – 223 were treated in the hospital, 150 were admitted and 14 died.

In 1948 the Secretary of State for Scotland became responsible for the hospital services of the city and, accordingly, the Western Infirmary became part of the National Health Service, its running costs now becoming a charge on the public funds.

By the late 1950s it was apparent that there was a pressing need to rebuild the hospital (which was now around a hundred years old). Accordingly, a contract was given to the Glasgow architects Keppie, Henderson & Partners in 1968. Work on the new building began in 1970 and by 1973 the first patients were being admitted, although the official opening was not until the October of that year.

Maternity Hospitals

Glasgow's first hospital for the care of expectant mothers opened about 1792, but was closed at the demand of the

Magistrates. However, in 1834, more than 80 of its most prominent citizens urged the Lord Provost to re-establish the Lying-in Hospital. It opened up in the vacated old Grammar School building in Grammar School Wynd, but the accommodation proved unsuitable and a move was made in 1841 to premises in St Andrews Sq (off the Saltmarket). Its genteel neighbours complained about its nuisance value and it moved again, in 1858. This 'nuisance value' may have derived from the fact that, unlike most other similar institutions, it opened its doors to, simply, 'poor and homeless lying-in women' with no bar on the unmarried. It returned to the area it had started from, finding accommodation in an old house and grounds at the corner of the Rottenrow and Portland St (at the top of the long ridge which runs parallel with and to the north of George St), where it was to remain for over 130 years. It changed its name in 1866 to the **Glasgow Maternity Hospital**, and in 1879 the old house was taken down and a new building erected, built in the 'Early English Domestic Gothic' by the architect, Robert Baldie.

In 1888 Dr Murdoch Cameron brought fame to the hospital. The abominable living conditions and totally inadequate diet of much of the city's working population had produced a notorious skeletal malformation called the 'Glasgow Pelvis', and out of necessity he was obliged to deliver afflicted expectant mothers by caesarean birth. So meticulous and expert was Cameron in this hitherto 'last extremity' operation that it rapidly became a routine speciality of 'Rottenrow'. In 1908 it once again expanded into newly built premises, and again changed its name to the **Glasgow Royal Maternity and Women's Hospital**, Rottenrow.

Like all the other voluntary Glasgow hospitals, Rottenrow was involved in a perpetual struggle for funds, a struggle which reached exhaustion point when in March 1948 it was only saved from insolvency by a bank loan. This enabled it to continue its services until July when, with all the other medical services, it was taken over by the NHS.

The opening of the **Queen Mother's Maternity Hospital** at Yorkhill in January 1964 has helped to hasten the implementation of a scheme by which Rottenrow will be relocated in the new Royal Infirmary complex.

PUBLIC HEALTH AUTHORITY HOSPITALS

Belvidere

This was the first permanent hospital in Scotland set aside for the treatment of infectious diseases – until the discovery of antibiotics such illnesses were a continuing scourge in all large communities. The estate of Belvidere near the north banks of the Clyde about two and a half miles east of the city was acquired and a fever hospital opened there in 1829. By 1832 it had 220 beds and in the 1870s a separate smallpox hospital was added with 150 beds – a clear indication of the continuing presence of this dreaded disease. Belvidere treated a wide range of infectious diseases, from typhus and relaxing fever to smallpox and diptheria, but much of its work was treating the then common childhood diseases of scarlet fever, measles and whooping cough.

Ruchill Hospital

Three miles north-west from the Cross, this was the city's second fever hospital, opened in June 1900 with beds for 408 patients. In 1909 this figure had grown to 542, an indication of the need for the hospital treatment of what are now considered minor ailments. This need continued well into the Second World War, for in 1938 Ruchill still needed all its bed accommodation.

PARISH COUNCIL HOSPITALS

Stobhill General Hospital

In 1899 the City Parish Council issued a report showing that the City Poorhouse and Barnhill (later Foresthall) Poorhouse had between them hospital accommodation for only 698 sick poor. This was totally inadequate and it was decided to build a general hospital on the estate of Stobhill (adjacent to the district of Springburn on the north-east side of the city). The contract was awarded to the architects Thomson and Sandilands and work began at the end of 1900. The foundation stone was laid in September 1901 and by 1904 the new building had 888 patients out of an official bed complement of 1,867. For many years the fact that before being admitted to Stobhill Hospital patients had to acquire the status of paupers introduced a certain stigma, and to avoid future humiliation the birth certificates of babies born there bore only an address '133 Balornock Rd' with no institutional name. Because of this element of constraint, two policemen patrolled the hospital and its grounds to prevent patients from 'escaping'!

During the First World War Stobhill Hospital was requisitioned for the reception and treatment of wounded combatants as the 3rd and 4th Scottish Military General Hospitals. The presence of a railway line leading directly into the semi-underground boilerhouse area gave rise to the story that this line was built specially to allow troop trains to deliver the war-wounded unseen into the hospital. It took until spring 1920 for the building to revert to civilian use.

Shortly after the war the hospital acquired one of its best-known staff, when Dr Osborne H. Mavor was appointed a consulting physician. Later, under the pseudonym James Bridie, he became one of Scotland's leading dramatists; he said he made the move because he had heard that it was intended to change Stobhill from 'a dump for human wreckage to something like a voluntary hospital'. The occasion for this change from a poor law institution to a general hospital was the Local Government (Scotland) Act of 1929 by which Glasgow Corporation took over the poor law functions of the old Parish Councils for Glasgow and Govan. As a result, the Corporation Health Department found itself responsible for 17 hospitals (seven Corporation hospitals for infectious diseases and tuberculosis, 3,000 beds; four poor law general hospitals, 2,400 beds; three lunatic asylums, 3,000 beds; and three mental defective institutions, 1,300 beds). By 1939 the old stigma had disappeared for good and Stobhill General Hospital was one of Glasgow's five teaching hospitals (the other four being the Royal Infirmary, the Western Infirmary, the Victoria Infirmary and the Southern General Hospital).

The Govan Poorhouse, located originally in the old Cavalry Barracks in

Eglinton St, moved to Merryflatts (a site just to the west of Govan) in 1783, where a combined poorhouse, hospital and insane asylum was erected. When the old Parochial Board institutions were taken over by the Public Health Department of the Corporation, the Merryflatts building became the **Southern General Hospital**, serving the south-west part of the city.

Hutchesons' Hospital

George Hutcheson of Lambhill (*c.* 1558–1639) was a Glasgow writer (i.e. solicitor) and notary public who amassed a very large fortune by making extensive loans to many of the local nobility, including the Archbishop of Glasgow and Lord Blantyre – he has been described as the city's first banker. Much of his wealth went into land purchases, which included Barrowfield, Provanside, Ramshorn, Lambhill and Yoker. On his death-bed, he executed a Deed of Mortification which 'disponit a tenement of land to be edifiet and maid ane perfyte hospitall for eleven [later raised to twelve] poore aiget decrippet men to be placed thereinto'. His younger brother, Thomas (1590–1641), added to this charitable bequest additional funding to build and endow a school for 'tuelf maill children indigent orphanes or utheres of lyk conditioun'.

The Hospital to house the old men and young scholars was begun in 1641 and completed in 1660. It stood on the north side of the Trongate, and had a frontage of 70ft and a steeple about 100ft high. The steeple contained statues of the two brothers (by James Colquhoun, 1649) which were placed in 1824 in two niches of a new Hospital.

Not long after it was built the Hospital began to be diverted from its original purposes. In 1647 George Anderson, printer, set up his press in it, its lofts became public stores for victuals, the close was let for bull baiting, the gardens were used by nurserymen, the whole ground floor was let out as shop accommodation and the main hall became the resort of dancing and fencing masters.

In 1650 the Hospital Patrons set out a large part of its patrimony in purchasing the lands of Gorbals which involved them in grave financial difficulties. As a result very few pensioners were boarded within the Hospital, the school was forced to close for a while, and the building began to fall into disrepair. When it became apparent next century that the westward expansion of the city was considerably enhancing the commercial value of the site, the Patrons realised these assets in 1795 by feuing a new street and using the capital to build a new Hospital. The old Hospital was accordingly demolished to make way for the new street leading north from the Trongate to Ingram St (appropriately named Hutcheson St). In 1802 plans for a new Hospital were drawn up by David Hamilton, and the building was completed in 1805. Following a Glasgow architectural custom it was located so as to look directly down the new street.

The Hospital's regulations seem to have been fairly elastic, for in 1780 the pensioners consisted solely of five old women. Some changes were made, however – a 1773 regulation limiting entrance to burgesses was abolished in 1846 allowing pensioners to be drawn from 'any decayed citizens above fifty years known to have carried on a business as merchants or tradesmen, and to their widows and daughters'. The disappearance of the residential nature of the Hospital was inevitable, in face of the rapid increase in the number of pensioners: in 1800 there were 131 men and women; in 1880, 1,163; and by 1915 there were 195 men and 1,516 women.

A conspicuous feature of the new

building was its Great Hall, which seemed to have been something of a white elephant. From its opening until 1844 it was used to accommodate Stirling's Library, while in 1841 part of it was let as a reading room to certain gentlemen who had seceded from the Glasgow Exchange room on the question of Sabbath opening. When the gentlemen left in 1847 the Hall was taken over by the Glasgow banks as their Clearing Room, and in 1836 the National Security Savings Bank of Glasgow (better known by its later title of the Trustee Savings Bank of Glasgow) occupied premises on the Hospital's ground floor.

It was not until 1876 that the Hospital Patrons had full use of the Hall, when the whole building was extensively reconstructed. The original three storeys (ground, hall and intended schoolroom) were transformed into two by raising the hall floor 3ft and increasing its height to 30ft by entirely removing the third floor.

In 1984 the National Trust for Scotland inaugurated an appeal for funds to purchase the Hospital, pointing out that donations would go towards helping the Patrons of the Royal Incorporation of Hutchesons' Hospital to provide for its existing pensioners, then numbering 77. The appeal was successful and the building, now described as Hutchesons' Hall, has become the Trust's regional office for Glasgow and the west of Scotland.

Hotels

Along the Gallowgate, outside the East Port, lay the ruins of an old chapel, Little St Mungo's, founded in 1500. In 1754 the Town Council offered its 'old yaird, a burying-place' to Robert Tennent (brother of Hugh Tennent, the ancestor of the Tennents of Wellpark Brewery), vintner, gardener and owner of the White Hart Inn, on condition that he should erect on it a 'creditable' inn or hotel – the city had many inns and taverns suitable for the citizens but they lacked the polished gentility expected by visitors. As an inducement they offered him stones from the ruins of the Bishop's Palace, next to the Cathedral, and from the Gallowgate or East Port which was to be demolished. By the end of 1755 he had built the Saracen's Head Inn, which was to become in its fairly short life of some 37 years one of the best known of Glasgow's many inns or hotels. It consisted of three storeys with a 100ft frontage and had slightly protruding wings with a recessed central portion. The ground floor contained the general rooms while the first and second floors were private apartments. Some accounts describe an assembly room or ballroom in the middle compartment of the top flat, but most place it behind and separate from the main building, forming a group with a large court of offices and stables which could accommodate 60 horses. A carriageway was opened along the west side of the inn.

In his advertisement in the *Glasgow Courant* of October 1755, Tennent described the Saracen's Head as a 'convenient and handsome new inn . . . containing thirty-six fire-rooms . . . the bed- chambers are all separate [i.e. were entered without going through other rooms] . . . the beds are all very good, clean and free from bugs'.

'The Saracen's Head' was said to come from the sign of an old London hostelry in Snow Hill named after Thomas à Becket's maternal grandfather, reputed to be a Moor.

Poor Robert, however, did not prosper; he lost all his money and died about two years after his inn opened. It was then let to his widow, and on her death in 1768 was sold to a vintner, James Graham. After *his* death *his* widow became the proprietrix of the hostelry but was forced to relinquish it when her second husband became bankrupt.

During its heyday it was the chief rendezvous for all the distinguished visitors who had occasion to visit the city and for the local nobility and gentry. It was here that Dr Samuel Johnson stayed with Boswell on their return from touring the Hebrides in 1773, and met the College professors and other Glasgow notables. When the Lords of Justiciary visited Glasgow during their Western Circuit they always resided at the Saracen's Head, walking from there in procession to the Court Hall in the old Tolbooth at Glasgow Cross; and when William and Dorothy Wordsworth passed through the city on their way north it was here they lodged. The Saracen's Head Inn was the place selected for balls, country meetings and public dinners, and its reputation for well-prepared food was such that the young daughters of the city merchants were sent for culinary lessons from its head cook. It was a great posting house and it was here that the first London mail coach drew up on July 1788.

Over the years, however, the more centrally placed Buck's Head Inn and Black Bull Inn (both in the Trongate, close to the Cross) began to attract a growing number of the Saracen's Head's clients, and eventually in 1792 the building was bought by William Miller of Slatefield who converted it into dwelling-houses and shops. Its old inn sign was taken across the road for use by the New Saracen Head Inn about 1805. For about half a century the assembly room was used as a place of worship by various sects, after which it became a 'reading' school, which continued until its last schoolmaster, Alexander Fisher, retired in 1865. In 1904 the land was bought by Charles J. Anderson, who demolished the old building and built a tenement in its place. In the course of the demolition human bones were dug up from the old cellars, clear evidence that the site had indeed been an ancient burying-ground. Anderson also rebuilt the assembly room in what was described as the 'Norman–Elizabethan style of architecture' and used it for the social welfare of city youths.

The Inn area holds two other links with old Glasgow. Behind its site is an old draw well which carries the inscription: 'The ancient well of Little Saint Mungo, restored 1906 . . .', and also a large cast-iron fountain with the trade stamp of the Saracen Foundry. Walter MacFarlane, the founder of the firm (which moved to Possilpark), started in Saracen Lane in 1851. The present building includes a public house to which the name of the old inn has been given. Locally referred to as the 'Sarry (or "Sairy") Heid', it has borrowed a fair degree of its fame from its urbane predecessor.

In 1727 a group of 17 gentlemen, originally from the Highlands and settled in Glasgow (12 of whom bore the surname Campbell), set up the Highland Society. Its avowed purpose was to provide education, clothes and training in a trade for the children of poor Highlanders living in the city. About 1757 George Whitefield, an eminent English preacher, came to Glasgow and the Society asked him to preach in aid of their funds. This he did in the Cathedral yard, and the collection gathered on this occasion, with other funds belonging to the Society, enabled it to erect the Black Bull Inn on the north side of Argyle St near Virginia St. It opened in 1758, its first landlord having previously been in charge of a similarly named inn just across the road. It had a commercial room, a coffee room, a ballroom, nine parlours and 29 bedrooms, along with stabling for 38 horses. Its advertisement stated that 'great care had been taken to keep the bedrooms at a distance from the drinking-rooms'. The demise of the Saracen's Head Inn left it as one of the city's principal inns.

When the city began to expand westwards, John Murdoch, tobacco merchant and three times Provost, was one of the first to move outside the old West Port and in 1757 built his town-house on the south side of Argyle St in 1757. In 1777 it was sold to Thomas Hopkins, a Glasgow merchant. His son, James Hopkins of Dalbeth, sold it in 1790 to a vintner, Colin McFarlane, who opened it as the Buck's Head Inn. It and the Black Bull Inn benefited from the city's westward movement and became Glasgow's 'creditable' inns. The Buck's Head closed about 1830; on its site in 1862 Alexander 'Greek' Thomson erected his Buck's Head warehouse building.

The third of the city's hotels was the Tontine Hotel, built by the Tontine Society as part of the complex which took the place of the old Tolbooth at the Cross. It opened about 1780 and was probably the first such establishment in the city to be called a hotel – popularly known at one time as the 'Hottle'. Its gradual distancing from the westward-moving city centre, however, brought about its closure.

The hotel centre moved again in the early 19th century, this time to George Sq. The number of hotels which at various times surrounded it is extraordinary, and included (mainly on the west side) the Wellington, Star, Caledonia, Cranston's Hotel (formerly the Royal Horse, formerly the Edinburgh and Glasgow Railway Chop House and Commercial Lodgings), Franklin, James Watt, Sir John Moore, Waverley, Crow, Clarence and Globe. On the east side was the George Hotel, for long one of the city's best hotels. Demolished to make way for the City Chambers it moved to the north of the square, where it was associated with the adjacent Queen St station as the North British Railway Hotel. In 1986 it became the Copthorne Hotel, now the only hotel left in the square. The Royal Hotel occupied the north-east corner of the square till 1915. The building then became railway offices, eventually being demolished in the 1970s to make way for a nondescript block of office accommodation.

Hotels associated with the city's other main railway stations were the St Enoch Station Hotel (1880) and the Central Station Hotel (1883). The former was demolished in 1977, its site becoming the St Enoch Centre.

Still moving westwards, the city's newest international-style, multistorey hotels are mostly located at the extreme end of Argyle St, next to the west flank of the Inner Ring Road.

Two architecturally interesting city hotels are located at opposite ends of the town. The Beresford Hotel in Sauchiehall St was built in 1938 to receive visitors to the Empire Exhibition of that year. Its entire façade of ten storeys has faience tiles in red, black and mustard yellow applied to the walls, two drum towers and a set of fins. In 1952 it was leased to ICI as office accommodation, then sold in 1964 to

Strathclyde University who named it the Baird Hall of Residence for students. Unfortunately the coloured tiles have been obscured by paint.

The Great Eastern Hotel is an unusual relic of the city's textile era. Erected in 1849 as the Duke St Cotton Mill and originally five storeys high, with a façade in tooled ashlar with projecting end bays

and rusticated quoins, it measured over 210ft high. Its architect, Charles Wilson, designed it as a fireproof building with no inflammable material used in its construction. It was converted in 1907 to a hotel for homeless working men, a function it still performs.

See also TEA-ROOMS

Housing

An aerial view looking south from Rottenrow down the High St showing a jumble of tenements wreathed in smoke. The area at the top left-hand corner was the site of the University before its move across the city to Kelvingrove. The cleared site became the College Goods Station. (Thomas Annan, 1900, Mitchell Library)

During the last quarter of the 18th century when cotton-spinning factories were introduced into what was still largely a medieval Glasgow, the resultant population increase created an intractable housing situation which is still a problem for the city after more than two centuries of attempts to resolve it.

Traditional one- or two-storey buildings lining the streets, with public wells and open sewers, could cater, just, for the pre-industrial population; such simplistic arrangements were totally incapable of even beginning to meet the needs of the accelerating industrial population – during the 19th century it increased tenfold, from 77,000 to 762,000.

The *laissez-faire* solution to housing this population increase was simple: build over the long open gardens which stretched out behind the small houses lining the ancient streets. The resulting agglomeration of jerrybuilt tenements of three, four or even five storeys (the city's notorious 'Backlands') was accessed from the main thoroughfares by long wynds or closes, so narrow that neighbours could shake hands across them. Minuscule squares within this fetid mass were furnished with a single water stand-pipe and filled with the accumulated rubbish and excrement of the miserable inhabitants living round it. These middens were the landlord's perquisite, to be sold from time to time to local farmers. Sir Edwin Chadwick, the social reformer, said in 1840 that 'the conditions of the population in Glasgow were the worst of any we had seen in any part of Great Britain' – the city's central area was one of the most densely populated areas in Europe, with some 700,000 persons in three square miles.

The resulting insanitary conditions were such that throughout the 19th century the city's old centre was devastated by recurring outbreaks of various infectious diseases which maintained an annual death rate of 30 to 40 per thousand, rising at times to 50 or 60.

Up to the middle of the century ineffectual protracted discussions and innumerable pamphlets demonstrated that private enterprise could effect nothing and that the municipality itself would have to seek new and drastic powers and so, in 1866, under the guidance of Lord Provost Blackie, the City Improvement Act was passed. This innovative and pioneering act gave the Corporation (through Improvement Trustees) powers to acquire houses and lands compulsorily within certain designated areas, to alter, widen and divert existing streets, to form new wide streets, to take down existing buildings, to lay out lands so opened up and to sell or dispose of these grounds on lease or feu. Almost as an afterthought, the Act also empowered the Trustees 'to erect houses for mechanics, labourers and other persons of the poorer and working classes for let or sale'. The necessary funding was to be

Castlemilk, 1970. A typical scene in one of the city's huge post-Second World War housing schemes. (John S. Logan, Mitchell Library)

obtained by a tax on occupiers, starting at 6d. per £1. Although Blackie's proposals had initially received widespread support, the city's ratepayers showed their disapproval of these financial arrangements by refusing to vote him back into power.

The designated area covered some 88 acres, which carried a population of over 50,000 (about 600 persons to the acre, rising in places to 1,000). It was in fact the old city, which stretched up the Molendinar Burn from the Clyde to the Cathedral.

Twenty-six streets were widened and 30 new streets opened up, but the work of house demolition did not begin on any considerable scale until 1870. Unfortunately for the Corporation, the 1870s and 1880s were distinguished by the collapse of the property market and the Trust soon found that few if any private builders were willing to build on the cleared ground. Some progress was made in ameliorating the housing conditions of the very lowest elements of the population. Previously they had been forced into accommodation in numerous private lodging-houses of the very worst kind scattered throughout the old town, but the Trust managed to erect two model lodging-houses for them in 1870 and by the end of the century there were seven Corporation model lodging-houses, as well as a 'family house' of 160 single rooms where single families (such as widows' or widowers') could find suitable accommodation.

By the late 1880s the Corporation found itself compelled, reluctantly, to take on the role of house-builder. Up and down the Saltmarket and the High St, in Kirk St and the Calton, it erected handsome well-built red-sandstone tenements (many still

Main Street, Govan, 1872. Although by this date Govan was well established as part of the Clydeside shipbuilding complex, the thatched-roof cottages of a pre-industrial Govan still linger side-by-side with the newer tenement buildings. (William Graham, Mitchell Library)

standing and in good condition) of four storeys with one or two-room apartments. In addition, the Trust set up a public space, Alexandra Park, to the north-east of the city, and covered over both the Camlachie and Molendinar Burns.

The aims of the Trust, however, were scarcely being met. The displaced occupants, who had previously paid about £2 per year in rent, could not afford the £8 per year and upward for the Trust houses and were thus forced out into remaining old property; the occupants of the new buildings were not 'persons of the poorer

and working classes' but rather Corporation employees, 'well-to-do' labourers, shop-keepers, even minor 'professional men', all carefully selected. By the First World War only about 1,600 houses had been erected.

An interesting indication of the ruling power's mindset was the Trustees' decision to prohibit public houses in the Trust areas. This prohibition, extended in 1890 to all Corporation housing property, continued to be enforced throughout the vast Corporation housing schemes which later came to surround the central city, and it was not until after the Second World War that this 'big brother' decision was rescinded.

In an unusual attempt to combat the high levels of overcrowding throughout the city centre, the Corporation took powers under the Glasgow Police Act of 1866 to 'ticket' all houses not exceeding 2,000 cubic ft (later increased to 2,600) with an official and visible indication of the maximum numbers of persons they were allowed to house. These tickets were small oval metal plates screwed to the doors, setting out permitted levels of adults and children on the basis that each adult required 300 cubic ft of space and each child half that figure (in 1890 these figures were altered to 400 and 200 respectively). Eventually there were 75,000 'ticketed' houses in the city and it was said that during the activities of the inspectors during the hours of darkness the tenement roofs were covered with roused and illegal sleepers.

Although some working-class housing continued to be built up to the First World War, it was only with the passing of the 1919 Housing (Scotland) Act (sometimes known as the Addison Act) that far reaching developments in the provision of such housing began. Under this Act for the first time it became obligatory for local authorities to supply sufficient state-subsidised working-class housing for all its population, in particular by clearing slum areas and rehousing. One immediate and continuing effect of this was to transform Scottish local authorities into the sole suppliers of working-class housing by making it unprofitable for private developers to build affordable rented accommodation for the working class.

Glasgow's implementation of the Addison Act was based on a unique three-tier system of housing under which two departments became responsible for operating the system. The City Improvement Department (established in 1895 as a descendant of the original City Improvement Trust – it became the City Factor's Department in 1950 and the Housing Management Department in 1967) was concerned with management, factoring and rent collecting, while the Housing Department undertook all the necessary planning and construction work.

The first tier of this system was what the Corporation termed 'ordinary' housing schemes. These were low-density, semi-detached houses with gardens, constructed to a uniform design, and were located in a belt around the urban centre in Knightswood, Yoker and Scotstoun to the north-west, Carntyne, Riddrie and Shettleston to the east, Mosspark, Craigton and Carnwadric on the south and the south-west. These schemes were occupied largely by working-class élites and lower professional classes. The best of them was popularly considered to be the Mosspark Scheme, whose 175 acres had been bought by the Corporation in 1908 for a golf course. House-building began shortly after the war and its 1,510 houses were completed by 1924.

The second tier carried the name 'intermediate' and was intended for those who were too poor to pay the 'ordinary'

rents but who were not slum-dwellers. An example of this type was the Drumoyne Scheme of 42 acres, purchased in 1928 and accommodating about 800 houses.

The third tier was intended for the rehousing of central city slum-dwellers. The first slum clearance took place in 1923 when over 2,000 unfit houses were demolished in Anderston, Cowcaddens and Townhead, followed by another clearance in 1929 when 1,131 houses were demolished in Calton. The most conspicuous example of the perils of this type of rehousing was undoubtedly the notorious Blackhill Scheme, in the north-east sector. The ground was acquired by the Corporation in 1895 and for a number of years was used by the prestigious Glasgow Golf Club. The scheme was opened in 1935 but unfortunately there was an almost complete lack of community facilities and that, coupled with a disproportionate number of problem families moved *en bloc* from one area, meant that by the 1950s it had become the city's most stigmatised housing area.

In the interwar period Glasgow built some 50,000 council houses but this still did not satisfy demand. After the Second World War it was decided to build four enormous peripheral housing complexes in an outer zone beyond the earlier schemes. They went up on green-field sites and were mostly three and four-storey tenements, larger family terraced houses and some high-rise flats – to the east were Easterhouse, Barlanark and Cranhill, to the south Castlemilk, with Pollok and Nitshill on the south-west and Drumchapel on the north-west. By 1980 these huge schemes accounted for over 60 per cent of all municipal houses. They differed significantly from the earlier schemes; by this time much of the city's labour aristocracy had left the city under overspill arrangements and the new schemes almost inevitably became second-tier zones. This was aggravated by the lack of any planned infrastructure. Pollok, for instance, with its 50,000 population, had virtually no amenities, originally lacking adequate shopping centres, public halls, churches, cinemas, recreational facilities and even primary schools.

Because of the land shortage within the city and the speed with which they could be put up, Glasgow, like many other local authorities, built a large number of high-rise flats in the 1960s. By the end of that decade over 160 multistorey blocks were in use. The six Red Road 31-storey colossi in Barmulloch, housing 4,000 people on 22 acres, were remarkable for being, at 300ft, the highest reinforced concrete structures in Europe.

The land shortage was also responsible for the overspill policy – recommended in the Clyde Valley Plan of 1946 – where, by the transference of Glaswegians to new and existing towns, the housing demands of the city would be reduced. Two new towns were built, East Kilbride and Cumbernauld, and later Glenrothes and Livingstone entered the scheme, along with a few other established towns. Although the overspill scheme certainly reduced the housing demand within the city, it was found that it tended to draw away skilled rather than unskilled

workers, and so could be claimed only as a limited success.

As early as the beginning of the 19th century the polarisation seen in so many large British towns had begun to affect Glasgow, as the middle class moved west out of the old centre, leaving it to become a slum area, while the factories and their associated working-class housing spread east and north. The first move was to the immediate west, first around George Square, and then further west into the drumlin-dotted lands of Blythswood where William Harley and other speculators successfully took up feus of large areas. Next, the opening of the Great Western Road in 1816 led to a rapid (and almost linear) development along its north-west axis, in the form of the still existing splendid terraces and crescents of the city's merchant princes. These proved too expensive for the lower ranges of the middle classes who now looked to the undeveloped land south of the river. Soon its flat stretches were covered with high-quality red-sandstone tenements and free-standing villas. For a little while these districts remained outside Glasgow as independent burghs (for example, Pollokshaws, Pollokshields, Govanhill, Hillhead, and so on) but eventually all were incorporated into the city.

See also TENEMENTS

Illustrators

The earliest pictorial representations of Glasgow appear in a set of engravings published in London in 1693 by John Slezer. Slezer, a Dutchman and a draughtsman of some ability, was employed in Scotland on army matters and was persuaded by the Scottish Parliament to produce his *Theatrum Scotiae*, which consisted of 57 engravings of various Scottish burghs. The *Theatrum* contains three Glasgow views: (1) *Prospect of the town of Glasgow from the North East*, a view looking south towards the Cathedral, with the Molendinar Burn in the foreground; (2) *Prospect of the town of Glasgow from the South*, looking from the south bank of the Clyde, the outstanding features being the old Glasgow Bridge and the various spires and towers of the city; and (3) *The college of Glasgow*, an unusual bird's-eye view of the old University showing its two quadrangles, with the High St in the foreground and the College Gardens in the background.

A century later, the pupils of the Foulis Academy of Fine Arts produced a number of engravings of different aspects of the city, engravings which varied considerably in artistic quality. One of the finest is undoubtedly *A view of the Trongate of Glasgow from the east*. This much-reproduced view was drawn by Robert Paul, a very promising pupil who died in 1770 before finishing this engraving (it was completed by a fellow pupil, William Buchanan). It shows in detail a view of the city much admired by 18th-century visitors – looking west from the Cross of Glasgow along the Trongate, with the old Tolbooth and its steeple on the right. It also shows the adjacent new Town Hall with its arched piazza and its footpath separated from the road by a line of low pillars. This pathway (flagged after 1774 and hence called the Plainstanes) was traditionally said to be reserved for the perambulations of the city's rich merchants, in particular the Tobacco Lords. Of the other engravings produced by Foulis Academy, *View from the South* is a fine panoramic view of the city from the south

bank of the Clyde, stretching from the Broomielaw Quay on the west to St Andrew's Parish Church on the east, with many details of buildings and spires. *View of Glasgow from the South East* (1762) is a less fine panoramic view, depicting the run of the High St down hill from the Cathedral to the steeple of St Andrew's, as seen from open ground to the east of the city. *View of Glasgow from the South* (c.1762) gives a good impression of the old bridge, with net-fishing and clothes-washing taking place on the banks of the river at Glasgow Green. The originals of all of these views are now extremely rare, but in 1913 William Gemmell published a portfolio entitled *Early views of Glasgow, chiefly from the Foulis Academy of Fine Arts* which contains all those mentioned above and many others (including two splendid views of the harbours of Greenock and Port Glasgow, so closely associated with the city's trade), along with a useful separate book of descriptive notes.

At the end of the 18th and beginning of the 19th centuries, illustrated guides began to appear for the convenience and use of visitors to the city. The earliest of these is probably James Denholm's *An Historical Account of the City of Glasgow and suburbs . . . to which is added a sketch of a tour to Loch Lomond and the Falls of the Clyde . . . for the use of strangers . . . embellished with thirteen elegant engravings*, 1797.

Next is *The picture of Glasgow*, printed by Robert Chapman in 1806, with three engravings of the city and a map. This small volume (which ran into several editions) contains an interesting reference to Glasgow as being 'now placed in the conspicuous situation of the SECOND CITY within the British Isles'.

A similar but more lavishly illustrated visitors' guide was published under the title of *Glasgow delineated . . . with thirty-three engravings of its principal public buildings*. Succeeding editions increased the number of its rather small illustrations. It also, like Denholm's guide, described 'a tour to Loch-Lomond, Inveraray, and the Falls of Clyde', a clear indication of the city's early popularity as a place to visit.

In 1828 there was published *Select views of Glasgow and its environs, engraved by Joseph Swan, from drawings by Mr J. Fleming and Mr J. Knox* [and an] *introductory sketch by John M. Leighton*. This volume has 33 excellent engravings, surpassing all earlier efforts, probably due to John Knox (1778–1845), an accomplished local landscape artist.

A very similar volume followed in 1834 – *Glasgow illustrated in a series of picturesque views engraved by J. Scott*, [with text] *by John Cullan* – with 24 views rather similar to Swan's but exhibiting an individual and dramatic chiaroscuro effect.

'In 1835 David Allan published *Views in Glasgow and neighbourhood*, a series of original sketches of familiar views making full use of lithographic techniques. This publication is the first of four separate collections of lithographic city views, published between 1835 and 1849.

All the previous collections were printed and published in the city. In 1841 the Montrose publishers, J. & D. Nicol, put out *Nicol's cities and towns of Scotland illustrated, part III, Glasgow*. Also known as *Glasgow illustrated in twenty-one illustrations*, it took the form of a loose-leaved portfolio with a short introduction. The plates are lithographs and part of their undoubted charm comes from their very lively depiction of the multifarious activities of the city's street-life.

In 1847 the Glasgow lithographic printers, Robert Stuart & Co, brought out their *Views & notices of Glasgow in former times*. The text is illustrated by 27 lithographs, largely of the city's older buildings, both public and domestic, most of which were the unattributed work of the youthful William Simpson (see below).

Thomas Fairbairn (1820–84), a prominent local watercolourist, published in 1849 his folio volume *Relics of ancient architecture and other picturesque scenes in Glasgow*. Its coloured plates are lithographic versions of watercolour sketches and include views of the city's old closes, the interior of the Cathedral and the Glasgow Green.

Fairbairn marks more or less the last of the city's pre-photographic illustrators, but there is one collection which, although published in 1899, still represents a Glasgow of 60 years earlier. William Simpson (1823–99) who made his career in London and elsewhere as one of the earliest war artists (he became known as 'Crimean' Simpson for his *Illustrated London News* pictures of the Crimean War), was active in the city of his birth up to 1851. In the year of his death he was persuaded to publish a collection representing his early Glasgow watercolours under the title *Glasgow in the 'Forties'*. It contains 48 black and white reproductions of these watercolours with text written by himself.

The first of many collections of photographic views of the city (and probably pre-dating Thomas Annan's *Old closes and streets*) was published in 1869 with text by A. G. Forbes, under the title *Photographs of Glasgow with descriptive letterpress*. Each copy contains 13 actual photographic prints pasted on to its pages (the only method at that time of photographically illustrating books), the more remarkable for being by Thomas Annan.

There have been too many collections illustrating the face of Glasgow published this century to make a full listing possible (or desirable), but one or two are worthy of mention. In 1901 Sir Muirhead Bone (1876–1953), a draughtsman and a member of a well-known Glasgow family, collaborated with his brother, James Bone, and a friend, John Hamilton Charteris, to produce a little paperback, *Glasgow in 1901*. Bone's contribution to this was a remarkable series of 52 little vignettes and thumbnail sketches, all redolent of Edwardian Glasgow, along with 13 full-page photogravures (including some of his well-known illustrations of Clyde shipyards). Later, in 1911, he published a collection of city etchings, *Glasgow, fifteen drawings*, which, although somewhat neglected, no doubt for their lack of 'factuality', stand alone for their artistry and feeling.

David Small (1846–1927) was a local artist of some repute who published two well-illustrated collections, *Sketches of quaint bits in Glasgow* (1886) and *Bygone Glasgow* (1896), both, as their titles suggest, devoted to the city's older and more picturesque buildings. He also produced countless competent watercolours of Glasgow scenes, many of which are still extant in collections.

Two aerial views of the city deserve mention. The first is dated 1853 and depicts Glasgow as seen from a position several hundred feet above a spot somewhere near the south end of the Kingston Bridge. It is a lithograph and is consequently rather soft in its outline, but under magnification it displays remarkable details in the city's buildings, particularly those in the west end. The old city centre lies well to the east and is less distinct. The other aerial view is one of a series produced by the *Illustrated London News*; the Glasgow view is dated March 1864. It also takes as its viewpoint the south bank of the river but with the new Glasgow Bridge at its centre. It is in every way a less finished product than the lithograph (for instance, all the streets are widened out of all proportion) but most aspects of the city's physical appearance can be recognised, from Park Circus to the Cathedral in the background and from the crowded Anderston Quays to the Glasgow Green in the foreground.

Industries

COTTON

Linen manufacture, at one time an important Scottish industry, began to decline during the second half of the 18th century, but on its foundations developed an extensive trade in cotton manufacturing.

Based, like the linen industry, in Glasgow, its rise was helped by several local circumstances. The collapse of the city's tobacco trade made idle capital available to finance the new industry, there was a skilled workforce ready to move from linen to cotton, the Clyde had growing shipping capacity capable of dealing with the export of manufactured goods, and the region's humidity was ideal for spinning yarn.

One of the most famous of the early Glasgow cotton-spinners was David Dale, whose New Lanark mills (powered by the Falls of Clyde) had by 1793 become the largest of their kind in Britain. After him came the firm of James Finlay & Son, which under the ubiquitous Kirkman Finlay, developed into the largest textile concern in Scotland. James Monteith and his son Henry, prominent spinners and calico printers, set up a large mill in Anderston in 1780.

Until the 1790s water power was the prime source of energy, and the early mills (e.g. New Lanark, Blantyre, Catrine) were located on suitable rivers, but following James Watt's revolutionary improvement in the steam-engine, steam power rapidly took the place of water power and the mills could begin to move into centres of population, such as Glasgow and Paisley, and by the beginning of the 19th century there were over 100 steam-driven mills in the city. At first steam power was used in spinning, weaving remaining a domestic process, but by 1818 there were 18 steam weaving factories in Glasgow with 2,800 looms. The resulting unemployment among the handloom weavers was a main reason for much of the distress among the city's labouring population in the first half of the 19th century.

The extremely rapid growth in the number of mills in the city, mainly in Anderston, Bridgeton and Calton, brought about radical changes in several aspects of Glasgow life and society. Many of the mills were very large, employing up to 2,000 people, and it has been estimated that at one time one third of the city's workforce was employed in the textile industry. The natural growth of the city population could in no way have met this demand for labour and there was a great influx from outside. Many came from the rural districts around the city but the two most important sources of manpower were firstly the Highlands where many of the inhabitants found themselves caught up in the often forced depopulation of the area, and secondly, Ireland, where the natural emigration was hugely increased by the potato famine of 1845. It was the housing needs of this vast population increase which was largely responsible for the terrible late 19th-century slums of central Glasgow and the consequent social distress.

By 1854 the city's cotton manufacturing capabilities were proving as profitable a business as the tobacco trade had once been – out of almost two million cotton spindles in Scotland more than half were located in the city. However, expansion had begun to slow down as early as the 1830s – competition from Manchester (rapidly assuming a dominant position) and from overseas manufacturers began to increase. Both the application of new inventions and the need for continuing investment were neglected by the Glasgow manufacturers – their brutal response to competition was to cut labour costs. In 1837 they reduced the spinners' rates by 56 per cent and the ensuing struggle broke the power of the unions. The failure of the Western Bank in 1857, which had financed many of the large manufacturers, further weakened the trade's position. International events also played an important part: just as the American War of Independence (1775) had ruined the city's tobacco trade, so the American Civil War (1861), when the North's blockade of the South's ports had prevented the export of raw cotton, administered the *coup de grâce* to Glasgow's cotton industry. When imports were resumed in 1866 the damage had been done and the city continued to turn more and more to the products of its

plentiful supplies of coal and iron ore – shipbuilding, locomotive construction and other forms of heavy engineering.

LOCOMOTIVES

The Scottish locomotive industry began in Glasgow in 1831 when Murdoch, Aitken & Co built engines for the Monkland & Kirkintilloch Railway. Several other small Glasgow firms established themselves but the industry only became permanent in 1843 when Neilson & Co began building locomotives. The firm's earliest location had been in Hydepark St in Anderston, but in 1861 the works were transferred to a site in Springburn.

Several newcomers now appeared on the scene, Henry Dubs, a managing partner with Neilson, set up his own firm, Dubs & Co, in 1864, and in 1888 Sharp, Stewart & Co came north from Manchester to Glasgow. Shortly before this, William Neilson had fallen foul of his partners and, leaving them, had set up the Clyde Locomotive Co in 1884. It had not proved successful, and when Sharp, Stewart & Co came up they took over Neilson's new firm.

All these various parts came together in 1903 when Neilson & Co, Sharp, Stewart & Co and Dubs & Co amalgamated to form the North British Locomotive Co, which soon became the largest builder of locomotives in Europe. During the company's first decade it produced about 400 locomotives each year, and both World Wars brought it considerable and profitable business. With the passing of the years, however, steam as a source of locomotive power began to give way to diesel and electricity. This change began to affect adversely the North British between the wars, but the company had left making the transition to the new forms of propulsion until it was too late, and in 1962 it went into liquidation. During its existence it built over 28,000 locomotives and turned Springburn for a while into the world's leading railway metropolis – its departure took the heart out of the community.

POTTERIES

Beginning in about 1750, an important pottery industry developed in Glasgow, reaching its height in the 1850s with parts surviving into the 20th century. Early use was made of coarse local clay, deposits of which were found mainly in the east end of the city, but these were soon either worked out or built over and the continuing concerns imported their raw material mostly from Ireland or Cornwall.

The earliest manufactory on a large

scale in Glasgow was the **Delftfield Pottery**, believed to be the first in Scotland. It was set up in 1748 by Laurence Dinwiddie (1696–1764), a leading tobacco merchant, and his brother Robert. Knowing nothing about the production of delftware they engaged as their manager John Bird, a potter from London, who in turn engaged other London potters to work under him. The intention had been to use local clays, either from the Dinwiddie lands at

Glasgow's Springburn district was a major centre for
locomotive construction; this is an interior view of the North
British Locomotive Co's Hydepark Works. (Mitchell Library)

Germiston or from the Glasgow Green, but
both were found to be quite unsuitable and
Irish clay had to be shipped in. The site
chosen for the new pottery lay on the north
bank of the river near the Broomielaw
Quay, and the lane leading to it from the
Anderston Walk was called Delftfield Lane.
Early in the 1760s James Watt invested
about £200 in the venture and became a
partner. When he married in 1764 it was to
the pottery manager's house that he moved.
When the lane was widened in the mid-
1850s, it was renamed James Watt St in his
honour. White stoneware was produced
from 1766, cream-coloured earthenware
from 1770, and by 1800 it was producing
bone-china. The only piece positively
identified with the pottery is the Saracen's
Head Inn punch bowl, which carries the
inscription 'Success to the town of
Glascow' [sic] although other items have
been attributed to it. In 1810 the old site
was abandoned when the recently built
Caledonian Pottery was bought and the
business transferred there. In 1824 the
company ceased trading.

Although the **Verreville Pottery** was established as a flint-glass house in 1777 by Crookston and Colquhoun, by the late 1780s it was producing cream-coloured earthenware and soon became the most famous of the Glasgow potteries. Various changes of ownership and of types of pottery took place until 1847 when Robert Cochrane took it over. He soon abandoned the unprofitable decorated ware (a change several of the Glasgow potteries followed) in favour of domestic ware such as the utilitarian earthenware jam-pot. The pottery closed down in 1918.

Next was the **Caledonian Pottery**, first established by Reed, Paterson & Co in 1790 as the **Glasgow Pottery**. In 1807 it was taken over by Aitchison & Co, who gave it its better known name and who acquired for it the plant and goodwill of the Delftfield Pottery. The pottery was bought in 1840 by Murray & Couper, James Couper being the city's leading china dealer. Its attempts to produce bone-china were foiled by emissions from nearby ironworks in 1857, but it continued to produce a range of stoneware which included statuettes, flasks and jugs.

The **North British Pottery** was set up in 1810 to manufacture bone-china but ceased within ten years. Various stoneware potters occupied the premises until 1874 when they were acquired by Alexander Balfour who concentrated on strong, gaudily coloured graniteware for the African market.

Early in the 19th century the **Glasgow Pottery (2)** was formed by John and Matthew Bell to make fire-clayware, but by the middle of the century they were producing bone-china, parian ware and terracotta. They also produced sanitary ware; no other Scottish pottery was involved in such a wide variety of wares. This pottery closed down early in the 20th century. In 1869 the brothers Bell started to build North Park House, a magnificent mansion in Queen Margaret Drive, with special accommodation for their collection of paintings. It was their intention that the collection would come to the Corporation but John (Matthew had pre-deceased him) died intestate in 1880 and the collection had to be sold. Valued at £200,000 it realised only £50,256 at auction. The house lay empty till 1884 when it was taken over and set up as Queen Margaret College (the first college for women in Scotland). In 1893 it was handed over to Glasgow University. By 1935 the University had no further use for it and it was sold to the BBC, becoming (with numerous additions) the headquarters for BBC Scotland and Radio Scotland.

The **Victoria Pottery** was set up in Pollokshaws in 1855 to produce tableware and chimney ornaments in the Staffordshire style.

Robert Cochran, who had taken over Verreville in 1847 also established the **Britannia Pottery** in St Rollox in 1857 to mass-produce hard-fired ironstone china. This pottery's important position can be confirmed by the fact that at the end of the 19th century it employed about 1,000 workers. Because of the durable qualities of its ware it was a very popular line in both North and South America. It became Cochrane & Fleming in 1896, changing back to the Britannia Pottery Co Ltd in 1920, and concentrated on manufacturing semi-porcelains. It closed down in the 1930s' depression.

In 1875 the **Saracen Pottery** was established by Bailey, Murray & Bremner to manufacture Rockingham and jet ware.

The **Govancroft Pottery** is the only Glasgow pottery set up this century (1912). It began by manufacturing plain stoneware containers, jam jars, bottles and large storage jars, but when this gave way to glass containers the pottery changed to the production of coloured and decorated containers, as well as stoneware whisky flagons and acid containers.

TOBACCO

The English Navigation Acts decreed that cargoes from English colonies must be carried in colonial or English ships and must be brought to England before despatch to any other market. Until the 1707 Union this meant that Scottish traders could only take part in a very limited (and illegal) way in transatlantic trade. Now, following the Treaty, the markets of the North American colonies were open to them, and the Glasgow merchants eagerly seized the opportunity.

Because of the city's location on the west coast it had never been able to develop its trade with Scotland's traditional markets in Europe, but now it found itself in a position to become a centre for a growing transatlantic trade.

Glasgow's tobacco trade was slow in developing, partly due to opposition from the English merchants, but by the 1730s there were 20 or 30 ships involved. The city had two great advantages in trade with the colonies over the English ports. First, the voyage to North America from the Firth of Clyde by the north of Ireland was considerably shorter than via the English Channel (often an extra trading voyage per year could be made from the Clyde), and second, the northern route was free from the disruptions of war which frequently delayed ships using the Channel. Another advantage enjoyed by the Glasgow merchants was their ships' shorter turnaround period in America. Each ship from the Clyde was accompanied by a supercargo who had instructions to exchange his goods for enough tobacco (stored ready in warehouses) to fill the vessel and then to return home as quickly as possible. All these factors enabled the Glasgow tobacco merchants to cut their operating costs below those of their English rivals. The supercargos also had authority to extend credit to the planters – it was estimated that in 1775, just before the outbreak of the American War of Independence, the Glasgow merchants were owed the enormous sum of £1.3 million.

The cargoes on the outward journey consisted of those goods which the colonists had not yet begun to manufacture for themselves in quantity – linen and cotton goods, leather goods, shoes, stockings, ironware and so on, and the demand for these goods had the direct result of encouraging their manufacture in Glasgow.

The quantities of tobacco which reached the Clyde were enormous. In 1765 some 33 million pounds were imported and by 1771 this had risen to 47 million. Eventually more than half of Britain's tobacco trade went through the warehouses of the Glasgow 'Tobacco Lords' – in 1772, out of 90,000 hogsheads, almost 50,000 came to Glasgow. For most of this vast amount of tobacco (almost all in the form of leaf) Glasgow acted as an entrepôt, re-exporting it to France, Holland and Germany. Of the 47 million pounds shipped to the Clyde in 1771, 44 million was reshipped to Europe.

Although the trade brought great wealth to the city, it was largely concentrated in the hands of comparatively few merchants, probably less than 200 persons, involved in about 40 firms. When asked to explain the city's sudden prosperity, Provost Andrew Cochrane of Brighouse explained that it was due to four young men who started at one time in business in the city – James Cunningham of Lainshaw, Alexander Speirs of Elderslie, John Glassford of Dugaldstone and James Ritchie of Busby. The first three controlled over half the tobacco trade – Glassford alone owned over 25 ships and traded for above £500,000 sterling a year. It was said that Cunningham made his original fortune by buying tobacco, when the War of American Independence broke out in 1775, at 6d. per lb and selling it later at 3/6d. per lb.

The 1770s were the last years of Glasgow's prosperity in the tobacco trade, for the War of Independence put a sudden stop to the artificial advantage enjoyed by the British merchants under the Navigation Acts. Considering the prime importance it had for the city's economy its cessation was less harmful than might have been expected. There were several reasons for this. Although many tobacco merchants were bankrupted there were some who made and retained immense fortunes. Besides, the new United States of America eventually repaid most of the outstanding debts. Also, although the fortunate merchants spent large sums on setting themselves up as country gentlemen, they also invested much of their wealth in both established and new Glasgow industries – bottleworks, sugarworks, linen manufacturing, ropeworks, breweries and metal manufactures.

Four times Glasgow has risen from apparent disasters. When its thriving cotton industry was at risk during the American Civil War, it concentrated on heavy engineering; when its West Indian trade (sugar, rum, molasses) suffered from the declining fertility of the plantations, it turned to cotton. The start of this sequence was the efforts it made to escape from the disappearance of the tobacco trade, as the 'Tobacco Lords' gave way to the 'Sugar Dons'.

Language

Every community creates words particular to itself, and the larger the community the more likely this word hoard is to become a 'language', 'Glasgowese' is an important example of the effects of this tendency as demonstrated in a large industrial city (always an area of linguistic instability and change), and is perhaps only equalled by Liverpool 'Scouse' and London 'Cockney'.

Whereas in most Scottish cities and towns the inhabitants generally speak the dialect of the area, in Glasgow a unique tongue has developed, one recognised throughout most of Britain. Although based on West Mid Scots it has developed its own extensive vocabulary and its own grammar. Until recently criticism directed at it has been distinctly pejorative. Even the introduction to *The Scottish National Dictionary* describes it as 'impoverished and bastardised Scots', maintaining that 'owing to the influx of Irish and foreign immigrants to the industrial area near Glasgow the dialect has become hopelessly corrupt'.

It is only now that it has become an acceptable object of linguistic study and a medium for serious literature. Its origins are still unexplored, perhaps for the obvious reason that it is almost entirely an oral language and as such has a history extending back only three generations or so.

Traces of early authentic Glasgowese can be found in J. J. Bell's humorous tales of a Glasgow boy, *Wee Macgreegor*, and similar sketches by other less well-known writers, who published mainly just before the First World War.

It is essentially a language closely linked with the physical world – personal attributes, personal behaviour and actions, familiar objects and their descriptions. Its three chief characteristics are its pronunciation, its vocabulary and its rudimentary grammar.

Its notorious use of the glottal-stop has become almost a Glasgow trade-mark (despite its occurrence in many other languages and dialects) – *breid an bu'er, bo'alle a whusky*. The sound of 'ai', as in *fair* and *hair*, becomes *ferr* and *herr*. This idiosyncrasy even changes traditional Scottish pronunciations such as *mair* (more) or *flair* (floor) which become *merr* and *flerr*. Also to be noted is the unexpected absence of the initial 'th' which changes *that* to *at* and *there* to *err*.

Because the vocabulary of Glasgowese is large and is also constantly changing and growing, only a few examples are given below:

bahookie	backside
bampot, bamstick	an idiot or gullible person
boggin	smelly
boufin	stinking
chanty wrassler	a suspicious character (literally a 'potty' wrestler)
cludgie	toilet
crappy	afraid
dog	to play truant
dowt	cigarette end
dunny	a tenement cellar or stairs down to a back green
gub	mouth
hairy	a sluttish girl
hems	to put the hems on someone is to restrain or hold them back
hingoot	to spectate from an open tenement window
hoachin	full of or infested with
honk	to vomit
huckle	to remove someone
jukes	to keep something up the front of one's jersey or jacket, as in 'Pit this boax up yer jukes'
knock	to steal
lumber	a member of the opposite sex to go home with after a party or dance
malky	a safety razor used as a weapon, thought to come from Malcolm (i.e. Malky) Frazer
manky	dirty, grubby
mental	insane, enraged
ming	to smell obnoxiously
molocate	to batter or destroy (used mainly by children)
peery-heidit	someone who has lost their head

pochle	to get something by cheating
see	to pass, as in 'See me ower thon spanner'
stoatir	a desirable girl
wallies	false teeth

Glasgowese grammar is obscure but consistent:

Amur so represents 'I am indeed'

Amurny goin is 'I am not going'

Gony no dae that means 'Going to not do that' – 'Please don't do that'

The use of *see* as a preliminary emphatic pointer – *See him, seeis wee brither, thur baith mental* – Both him and his younger brother are definitely unhinged

The use of *but* in place of 'however' to indicate a contradiction – *It's no use you saying that but*

Them as an adjective – *Lookit them sodgers*

An adverb replaced by an adjective – *Run quick, talk quiet*

The intrusive definite article – *The wean's goat the measles*

Belong instead of *own* – *Who belongs tae this dug?*

Plural *you* – *youse*

The first extended use of Glasgowese in a work purporting to be serious literature was probably Alexander McArthur's *No Mean City* (1935), but its regular written use dates, roughly, from the 1970s. A TV programme of the 1960s (Stanley Baxter's *Parliamo Glasgow*) brought the language before a wider audience and may even have helped to establish some sort of regular orthography. Imitating an educational language programme it ran Glasgow phrases into a single word – such as *yekanniwhakram* for 'you cannot whack them'.

Being basically a spoken language, it is well represented by a number of plays – *The Bevellers* (1973) by Roddy MacMillan; *The Sash* (1974) by Hector MacMillan; *The Slab Boys* (1978) by John Byrne are good examples. A number of poets – Tom Leonard, Stephen Mulrine, Tom McGrath and others – have used it as representing their authentic voice and it appears as a matter of course in the works of several widely read novelists, including James Kelman, William McIlvanney and Allan Spence.

Libraries

Although several 18th and 19th-century Glasgow libraries were described as 'public libraries', it was only with the passing of the Public Libraries Act of 1863 that the establishing in Glasgow of rate-supported free public lending libraries became a possibility.

For over 30 years, various groups kept up pressure on the Corporation to adopt the Act, but despite the constant (and often acrimonious) agitation the Corporation took a long time to make up its collective mind. Certainly, early on it set up a committee to investigate the matter. Despite its report pointing out that Glasgow was far behind many smaller cities and towns in its provision of free access to books, the Corporation took no action.

In 1874 Stephen Mitchell's bequest to the city of a large sum of money to establish a free reference library was interpreted by some to cover the setting up of small book collections throughout the city. Although not a correct interpretation, it nevertheless re-awakened interest in public lending libraries and in 1876 a plebiscite was held; while 1,779 voted against adopting the Act, only 993 were for it. Another plebiscite was held in 1885 and this time the figures were 29,946 against, 22,755 for (only half the voting forms were returned). The result was described by one newspaper as 'a defeat of the working class by the shopkeeping class'. The advocates of free libraries tried a third time in 1888 and, showing a remarkable consistency, the figures this time were 22,987 against, 13,500 for (two-thirds of those entitled to vote did not do so).

After further fruitless attempts to have the Act adopted, the Corporation surprisingly agreed to seek a special Libraries Act for the city, but the opponents of free libraries managed to sink it on a technicality. But now a neat solution was found. A proposed Tramways and General Purposes Bill was being prepared and the Corporation took the opportunity to insert a few extra clauses. As a result, when the Glasgow Corporation (Tramways, Libraries, etc) Act was passed in 1899, it contained powers enabling the Council to borrow £100,000 and to levy a 1d. rate for the purpose of setting up a free lending library service.

Francis T. Barrett, who had been appointed the first Mitchell Librarian, was given the task of establishing such a service. His report of 1900 suggested eight locations for the new libraries – from Bridgeton to New City Rd, from Castle St

to Queen's Park. The first of these libraries was opened in the Gorbals in 1901 and there followed a remarkable period of rapid and intense development; by 1907 a complete network of branch libraries had been set up:

Gorbals (1901)	Springburn (1906)
Kingston (1904)	Parkhead (1906)
Anderston (1904)	Bridgeton (1906)
Woodside (1905)	Hutchesontown (1906)
Maryhill (1905)	Pollokshields (1907)
Dennistoun (1905)	Townhead (1907)

In 1901 Andrew Carnegie, ironmaster and philanthropist, offered £100,000 towards the cost of setting up the city's new libraries. Twelve were financed by his gift, and when the money was exhausted Carnegie gave a further sum of £15,000.

In addition, Kinning Park Library (presented to the independent burgh of Kinning Park by Andrew Carnegie in 1904) came into the Glasgow system in 1905 when the burgh became part of the city.

Under the will of Walter Stirling, a Glasgow merchant, a free reference library had been set up in 1791. Stirling's Library, as it was called, never really prospered, and several efforts had already been made to transfer its care to the Glasgow Corporation. This was finally achieved in 1912 when the collection became the Corporation library service's central lending library, opening in 1913 in a building in Miller St previously occupied by the Mitchell Library.

Also in 1912, two public libraries located outside the city were taken over as the result of the Glasgow Boundaries Act of that year – the Elder Park Library in Govan and the Couper Institute Library in Cathcart, both set up under bequests. Two years later another library came in under similar terms, the Campbell Library (which later became the Pollokshaws Library).

Next, Possilpark District Library was opened in 1913 and Langside Library in 1915. The latter was the first of the city's public libraries to be planned on the open-access system, and during the following decade all the other older buildings were similarly reorganised. That same year, parliamentary permission was sought to increase the levy to 1 fid.

To complete the city-wide service, it was decided to supply library provision for those areas brought into the city under the 1912 Boundaries Act – so, in 1925 Partick Library and Shettleston & Tollcross Library were opened.

The cutbacks resulting from the effects of the 1930s' depression affected the city's libraries and in 1932 five were closed – Stirling's, Gorbals, Dennistoun, Couper Institute and Pollokshaws. After representations from local inhabitants and organisations all but Gorbals were reopened in 1933. Gorbals actually came out best from this, as it moved into a brand new building when it reopened.

Between 1901 and 1933 every district and populated area of the city as it was then had been brought within easy reach of an efficient library system. Just before the outbreak of the Second World War, as an indication for the future, Riddrie Library was opened to serve one of the city's many interwar housing schemes.

In 1949 the Royal Exchange, one of the city's most prestigious buildings was bought by the Corporation for £105,000 and Stirling's Library transferred to it from Miller St. The formal opening took place in 1954. The new premises also housed the Commercial Library, opened in 1916 as the first municipal library of this type in the UK. In 1994 Stirling's moved to premises in Miller St.

Important changes were now taking place in the distribution of the city's population. Many of the old residential areas of the inner city were fast losing their inhabitants to the vast peripheral post-war housing schemes, and in 1946 it was estimated that branch libraries would be required in Drumchapel, Milton, Barmulloch, Barlanark, King's Park, Castlemilk, Pollok and Easterhouse. However, despite the removal of any limit on the library rate that same year, for some time financial stringencies permitted only the building of temporary libraries – Carnwadric (1947), Mosspark and Househillwood (1949), Milton (1954) and Barmulloch and Barlanark in 1956. In 1952 King's Park Library was opened in accommodation above a row of shops.

The reverse process was also taking place: it was becoming impossible to sustain some of the old inner city libraries; and those along both banks of the Clyde as it passed through the central city began to close – Hutchesontown in 1964 (later replaced by a shop library), Kinning Park in 1967, Anderston (1969), Kingston (1981) and Gorbals (1986).

It now became possible to build permanently in the new areas. Pollok Library was opened in 1967 (replacing Househillwood) and Drumchapel the following year (both replacements for temporary libraries). Pollokshaws Library was opened in 1968, replacing both the old Campbell Library and the temporary Carnwadric. Next came Cardonald in 1970 and Knightswood in 1971 (replacing an earlier library), Easterhouse Library also opened in 1971, with Darnley and Ibrox in 1979 and 1981.

Following local government reorganisation in 1975, a group of libraries in Lanarkshire now became part of Glasgow's service. Three of these (Rutherglen, Cambuslang and Baillieston) were located in centres of population, but the others

(Bankhead, Blairbeth and Halfway) were small service points and the first two were to close within ten years.

The present-day Glasgow District Council Lending Library service has over 260,000 registered readers (drawn from people working or living in the city) served through 43 libraries and one mobile library. As well as an up-to-date bookstock, all carry various non-book material: computer software for home use, educational and informational video cassettes as well as records and tapes (the latter on subscription). Most libraries also have public telephones and photocopiers, current newspapers and magazines, large-print books and community information files. Fax facilities are also available at some district libraries, and the Mitchell Library and seven others provide services for ethnic communities.

MITCHELL LIBRARY

The Mitchell Library owes its existence to Stephen Mitchell. For several generations the Mitchell family had been tobacco manufacturers in Linlithgow, but early in the 19th century Stephen Mitchell, in response to government regulations, moved the family business to Glasgow and set up business in St Andrew's Square. After his death in 1874 it was found that he had bequeathed the residue of his estate (almost £70,000) to 'form the nucleus of a fund for the establishment of a large public library in Glasgow'. The Town Council accepted it the same year and in a report the Town Clerk reiterated the donor's express wish that 'books on all subjects not immoral shall be freely admitted to the library and no book shall be regarded as immoral which simply controverts present opinion on political or religious questions'.

The initial stock was acquired by the purchase of three major Scottish book collections along with several donations, in all amounting to about 17,000 volumes. The library opened in November 1877 on two floors of a building at the corner of Ingram St and Albion St, under the charge of Francis Thornton Barrett, formerly of Birmingham Public Libraries' Reference Department. The stock was arranged in broad subject groupings, supplemented by a dictionary catalogue, and was primarily closed-access. Two major collections were initiated – the Scottish Poetry Collection (with a special emphasis on material by and about Robert Burns) and the Glasgow Collection (defined as the collection of 'all books, pamphlets, periodical publications, maps, plans, pictorial illustrations and generally all papers which in any way illustrate the city's life and growth').

In seven years the stock had quadrupled, and in 1891 the library moved to premises in Miller St, but the continually growing book stock soon required another move. With the money powers given by the Glasgow Corporation (Tramways, Libraries, etc.) Act, 1899, it was now possible to finance the designing and construction of a purpose-built library. The new site was in North St, off Charing Cross, and took the library right across the city. It was opened in October 1911 and proved more than adequate for its task for almost 30 years. A prophetic change took place in 1930 when its first open-access subject department, the Music Room, was established.

Once again, lack of book storage required action and an extension was begun in 1939, not to be opened (because of wartime conditions) until 1953.

A major change in the arrangement of the stock was initiated in 1960 with the adoption of the Dewey Decimal Classification in place of the old broad subject groupings.

In 1962 the city's main hall, the St Andrew's Halls (immediately adjacent to the library), was burnt down and three years later plans were prepared for the erection of a library extension on the vacant site. When it opened in November 1980 its design radically altered the running of the whole library, for the book stock was now divided into several self-contained subject departments, each staffed

and run as an individual library – these are at present Science and Technology (includes General Newspapers), Social Sciences (includes Philosophy, Psychology, Religion), Arts (includes Rare Books, Language, Literature), History and Glasgow Room, Business Information (includes a fee-based subscription service). The Mitchell Library's stock now exceeds one million items and in its third building it has become Europe's largest public reference library.

The building also houses the management and support services of the Glasgow District Libraries and, since 1984, as a separate institution, the Strathclyde Regional Archives.

STIRLING'S LIBRARY

Walter Stirling (d.1791) was a prosperous Glasgow merchant and Town Councillor. In his will he bequeathed to the city £1,000, his house in Miller St, his collection of books (804 volumes) and his share in the Glasgow Tontine Society to form and maintain a public library in the city. Its terms made it the first library in Scotland to which the public had the right of free access.

With various gifts and bequests Stirling's Library opened with a stock which soon amounted to some 3,000 books. Although the Directors did their best to carry out the terms of Stirling's bequest, it soon became apparent that its financial provisions were woefully inadequate. In an attempt to improve them they set up a subscription service which allowed books to be borrowed – Stirling's expressed intention had been that the library should allow free access for reference purposes three hours a day, an instruction not carried out till almost 50 years later! A life sub-

scription was three guineas and there were 202 subscribers the first year. In 1816 it was raised to ten guineas only to drop back to five guineas in 1833.

Most of the early librarians were ministers (which may account for the banning of Thomas Paine's *The Rights of Man* in 1794), and most of them proved to be remarkably inadequate; by 1842 the number of subscribers had dropped to 72. Ten years later, however, it had risen to 423, and in 1863 over 60,000 books were issued. In 1871 the Glasgow Public Library, a subscription library founded in 1804 with a stock of 13,000 books, amalgamated with Stirling's Library to form the Stirling's and Glasgow Public Library. The amalgamation did little to halt their joint decline, though – in 1880 there were only 339 members and an issue of 25,000 books. In an effort to attract new subscribers it was decided to arrange its stock, for the first time, in subject order!

In 1885 the library had 42,000

volumes but it was becoming more and more obvious that it could not maintain itself, and several unsuccessful attempts were made to persuade the Corporation to take it over. The opening of a network of rate-supported public lending libraries throughout the city in the early years of the 20th century effectively finished Stirling's Library, and in 1912 it finally passed into the care of the Corporation. It retained its old name, and in 1913 opened up in 21 Miller St in premises recently vacated by the Mitchell Library, becoming the central lending library of the city's new service.

During its long history Stirling's Library moved several times. Starting out in Surgeons' Hall in St Enoch Sq, it moved in 1805 to Hutchesons' Hospital in Ingram St. From there it went in 1844 to accommodation at the rear of Stirling's house in Miller St. By 1863 this had become so cramped that the old mansion house was demolished and a library building erected on its site. Next, in 1912, it moved across the road as one of the city's public libraries and then, in 1949, it transferred to the prestigious Royal Exchange building in Royal Exchange Sq. In 1993 it moved to Miller St, not far from Stirling's town residence.

Walter Stirling expressed a wish that the stock of his library would always contain items of rarity and value and this may be the reason why it eventually had 25 incunabula (books printed up to 1500) which now form an important part of the Mitchell Library's Rare Books Collection.

Literature

FICTION

While the Glasgow novel before the 1870s scarcely existed, in the 1930s there was a sudden flourishing (almost 40 are listed for this period in M. Burgess's authoritative *The Glasgow Novel*, second edition, 1986). There has been another burgeoning, this time dating from the 1970s, which for quantity and quality probably surpasses the earlier periods.

Sarah Tytler's (pseudonym of Henrietta Keddie, 1827–1914) *St Mungo's City* (1885) is the first Glasgow novel to tell an interesting story, to observe and

The 'Steamie'. In a smoky city of tenements, public wash-houses were a necessity and many of the Corporation's public baths had wash-houses (or steamies) attached to them. As places of gossip they have assumed an almost legendary place in the popular history of the city, as the phrase 'the talk o' the steamie' suggests. (Mitchell Library)

describe truthfully the manners of its times and to allow its characters to speak in something resembling their real accents.

Frederick Niven (1874–1944), despite long absences from Glasgow, cast an astringent glance over the middling Glaswegian of the pre-First World War city, particularly the commercial and business types connected with the city's many emporia. His easy documentary style, as exemplified by *The Justice of the Peace* (1914) and *The Staff at Simpsons* (1937), give him a high place amongst the Glasgow novelists.

Catherine Carswell (1879–1946) was Glasgow-born but left in 1912 to pursue a career as a dramatic and literary critic. Her autobiographical novel *Open the Door!* describes in moving terms the struggles of the heroine to escape from the stifling atmosphere of a middle-class Glasgow family.

Dot Allan (1892–1964) produced a remarkable range of Glasgow novels, from *Deepening River* (1932), a historical novel set in the early Clyde shipyards, by way of *Makeshift* (1928), describing a young girl's growing-up, to *Hunger March* (1934), depicting the events of one day in Glasgow during the depression years.

The Shipbuilders (1935) by George Blake (1893–1961) has a secure place in the canon of the Glasgow novel. An account of the tensions between a shipyard-owner's son and a riveter enables him to develop contrasting facets of the city in the 1930s.

In the *Dance of the Apprentices* (1948) Edward Gaitens (1897–1966) also deals with the depression years; its glimpses of the Gorbals of that time are some of the best-written accounts of a key period in the city's modern history.

James Barke (1905–58), in his *Major Operation* (1936), produced one of the first of the city's 'proletarian' novels, full of angry arguments between its two protagonists, a businessman and a workman.

George Friel's (1910–75) novels do not fit easily into the usual urban novel genres. His finest novel, *Mr Alfred, MA* (1972), is a grim account of the descent of a failed Glasgow teacher – the city is present only as a background.

A Very Scotch Affair (1968) by Robert Jenkins (*b*.1912) gives equal prominence to the city (in this case the Bridgeton district) and to the characters. It is near the top of any list of Glasgow novels.

Archie Hind (*b*.1928) in his *Dear Green Place* (1966) combines the 'proletarian' novel with a degree of romanticism, describing both the struggles of a young working-class writer and the tenement lifestyle which nurtures him.

Alasdair Gray (*b*.1934) has produced in his *Lanark* (1981) an extremely complex exploration of the city's life at two levels – a realistic account of a young man growing up in post-Second World War Glasgow, interlaced with a fantastic story of the city in a kind of parallel universe. A Glasgow novel like no other, it has become something of a cult classic.

William McIlvanney's (*b*.1936) *Laidlaw* (1977) is ostensibly a *roman policier* but is placed so firmly in an accurately observed Glasgow as to transcend that genre.

The unique patois of the city has always been an essential ingredient in any good Glasgow novel, but James Kelman (*b*.1946) has given it a new and realistic dimension in his *The Busconductor Hines* (1984). The language, continually coarse and vigorous, is almost as important as the chief character.

Alan Spence (*b*.1947) in his *The Colours They are Fine* (1977) links together a sequence of stories which trace the precisely observed deterioration of a Glasgow street-smart child.

Jeff Torrington's *Swing, hammer, swing!,* his first published novel, appeared in 1993, when the author was in his 50s, and won that year's Whitbread Prize. It describes life and work in contemporary Glasgow with a satisfying verbal exuberance and a confidence which serve to distinguish it from the more despondent atmospherics of other contemporary Glasgow novelists.

There are two writers of lesser consequence who nevertheless should be mentioned in any account of the Glasgow novel. John James Bell (1871–1934) was a newspaper journalist who created a pawky

young Glasgow boy, Wee Macgreegor. Although the epitome of the urban kailyard, the *Wee Macgreegor* sketches (1902) presented and have preserved a realistic Glasgow pre-First World War background. *No Mean City* (1935) considered as literature is a mediocre performance at best, but for many readers it has become *the* Glasgow novel; it has appeared in edition after edition and is still in print. It was put together by Alexander McArthur (1901–47), whose poorly presented manuscript was knocked into shape by a journalist, H. Kingsley Long. It presents a highly coloured view of the Gorbals in the 1920s but its many touches of accurate social detail can still animate its turgid pages.

POETRY

In the late 18th and early 19th century Glasgow truly found itself in its poetry, but the Muse then seems to have deserted the city. When George Eyre-Todd, Scottish man-of-letters, edited *The Glasgow Poets* in 1906, he listed more than 60 'poets' none of whom would now qualify as more than poetasters. The return of the Muse to the city, in the main after the Second World War, is amply demonstrated in Hamish Whyte's *Mungo's Tongues: Glasgow Poems 1630–1990* (1993). Its pages display more than 40 poets, most born in the post-war period, who are able to give their individual poetic shapes to the veritable city.

Any selection of Glasgow poets should include the following names:

John Mayne (1759–1836) was born in Dumfries the same year as Robert Burns. While in Glasgow he was employed as a journalist and as a printer with the Foulis Press. His *Glasgow, a poem,* in 17 standard

Habbie stanzas, successfully combines the elegance of late 18th-century syntax and versification with the vigour of an unexaggerated Scottish vocabulary and is thus able to present both the charm and the vitality of the pre-industrial city.

Alexander Rodger (1784–1846) was a weaver in Bridgeton and, like many of his trade, was a vehement radical. He was also a cloth inspector, a music teacher and a journalist – in 1819 he was the sub-editor of *The Spirit of the Union*, a radical paper – and in his last years worked as an editor of the *Reformers' Gazette*. Much of his verse consisted of strong (and sometimes indiscreet) protests on behalf of the labouring man. His economic and political satires, flavoured with anti-monarchial sentiments on occasion landed him in prison, such as his pastiche – 'Sawney, now the king's come' – of an adulatory poem by Walter Scott on the visit of George III to Scotland.

Alexander Smith (1829–67), from Kilmarnock, began as a lace pattern-maker in Glasgow, but later attempted a career as a poet and essayist. His celebration of the city in his poem *Glasgow* (1857) describes its post-industrial beauties as well as its horrors. Somewhat overpraised in his own time, he later suffered neglect but is now regarded as an exceptional early urban poet.

James Macfarlan (1832–62), a pedlar-poet and autodidact, led a tragic and disappointed life but he managed to express powerfully if imperfectly in his poetry the industrial city at its apogee – 'Peals the thunder throat of labour, hark! the deaf'ning anvils clash'.

An academic as well as a poet, the metaphysical wit and wide-ranging intellect of Edwin Morgan (*b*.1920) bring together, in a way no other Glasgow poet has attempted, the splendours and miseries of the city along with the world outwith its boundaries – always salted by an almost mischievous delight in the loom of language. His reputation, like his topics, extends far beyond his native city.

Much of the crystal-clear poetry of Stewart Conn (*b*.1936), neatly English in style and language, is firmly based on remembrance of a personal interwar Glasgow. Like several other Glasgow poets he has achieved some success as a playwright.

The unsurpassed ability of Tom Leonard (*b*.1944) to reproduce and exploit the authentic voice of the Glasgow working class in a sort of mad English – 'ma right insane yirra pape' – and to maintain at the same time a strong poetic impulse makes him an important Glasgow poet.

Liz Lochhead (*b*.1947) attended Glasgow School of Art for a while, and her poetry is informed by a keenly observing eye. Her poems are often about people, and help to temper the rather rampant masculinity of much Glasgow verse. She has written several plays.

Taught by Alasdair Gray's English teacher at secondary school and encouraged by Edwin Morgan at Glasgow University, Robert Crawford (*b*.1959) is preoccupied by Scotland's icons, past and present. Such 'tiny folded pictures' give weight and significance to his optimistic Glasgow poems.

Two song writers whose individual voices tell of a Glasgow perhaps not clearly seen by the poets are Matt McGinn (1928–77) and Adam McNaughtan, both, by an odd coincidence, at one time teachers. Born in the Calton, a totally working-class area of the inner city, McGinn played an important part in the folk and protest movement of the 1960s and 1970s. The music he devised for his simple verses moves easily from lyricism to a pile-driving vigour, from a lullaby to a union song. Adam McNaughtan successfully links the old Glasgow of the tenements and their back-courts, with the new Glasgow and its high-rise flats through the unchanging element of the child in his *The Jeely Piece Song* (1967), with its refrain 'Oh ye cannae fling pieces oot a twenty-storey flat'.

Maps

The earliest plan or map of Glasgow appears in *Blaeu's Atlas* of 1694. It comes from a 1596 survey by Timothy Pont of the nether ward of Clydesdale, but the scale is too small to show any detail of the city. In 1734 James Watt senior published a map entitled *The River of Clyde* in which the city is shown in detail sufficient to indicate only the major streets. In 1768 a map was prepared in connection with a lawsuit between William Fleming, owner of a sawmill on the Molendinar, and the Town Council, which shows in some detail the course of the stream from the College to the Clyde and the surrounding area.

The first plan to set out in detail most of the streets and important buildings was published in 1773 as an insert in Charles Ross's *Map of the shire of Lanark*. It was drawn to a scale of 6in = 1 mile. John McArthur's excellent *Plan of the City of Glasgow, Gorbells, and Calton* in four sheets (scale: 24in = 1 mile) was published in 1778. Its scope, accuracy and early date make it the first adequate map of the city. A reduced version in one sheet was published in 1779. In 1782 James Barry, surveyor, published his *Plan of the City of Glasgow, Gorbells, Caltoun and environs* (scale: 10in = 1 mile). Similar in style to McArthur's plan, it shows more of the areas to the north and south of the city. It also maps and numbers all the Royalty stones which marked the boundaries of the old burgh. Thomas Richardson's *Map of the town of Glasgow and country seven miles round* was published in 1795 (scale: 1in = 1 mile). Although the scale is too small for the city itself, the surrounding area shows all the local estates with the names of their proprietors. William Forrest's *The County of Lanark from Actual Survey* of 1816 (scale: 6in = 4 miles), like Richardson's, is particularly useful for the immediate surroundings of the city and gives estates and their owners as well as some early evidence of industrial activity such as coalworks, quarries, coal pits, and so on.

The desire and ability of the early 19th-century middle classes to travel for pleasure induced a demand for guide-books, and two which were produced for the city during this period both contain small-scale but useful fold-out maps. The first of these was the *Picture of Glasgow*, printed by R. Chapman, with three editions dated 1806, 1812 and 1818. Its companion was *Glasgow delineated*, also in three editions, 1821, 1824 and 1836.

In 1807 Peter Fleming, land surveyor, published his *Map of the city of Glasgow and suburbs* in six sheets (scale: 26in = 1 mile). Next, David Smith brought out a revised version of Fleming's map (1821), again in six sheets (scale: 21in = 1 mile). Then in 1842 a very large coloured *Map of the city of Glasgow, showing the parliamentary boundaries, parishes, police wards of the city and suburbs* (scale: 13in = 1 mile) was published by George Martin, civil engineer.

These three maps by Fleming, Smith and Martin depict Glasgow in considerable cartographic detail over a period of roughly 50 years, just as the city was beginning its extraordinary 19th-century expansion. Martin's map is particularly good for its coverage of the city's complicated administrative areas and has inserts showing police wards, *quoad civilia* parishes, parliamentary and municipal districts and Glasgow town centre in 1778.

The Glasgow Directory of 1847 included a *Plan of Glasgow and suburbs* (scale: 1in = 1000ft), the first of a continuing series, which was much improved in 1865 when its preparation was taken over by John Bartholomew FRGS at the scale of 6in = 1 mile. Although not as accurate or as detailed as the Ordnance Survey maps, those in the Directory have the distinct advantage of having appeared annually and can thus be used to chart the rapidly changing face of the city.

A successor to Richardson's map was published in 1852 by Edward Meikleham, covering ten miles around the city (scale: 1in = 1 mile).

By the early 1850s the Ordnance Survey began to publish sheets covering Glasgow in scales of 6in and 25in to the mile. These exhibited all the attention to detail and accuracy expected from the Survey, and from that date any mapping concerning the city has been inevitably based on its publications. The second edition of the Glasgow sheets was published at the turn of the century. It coincided with the city at its zenith depicting the complex layout of its late Victorian and Edwardian streets, railways, and buildings. In the 1890s the Ordnance Survey brought out a map of the city to the scale of 10½in to 1 mile – a scale which enables lamp-posts, tenement closes, individual trees and much more to be shown with meticulous accuracy.

This series of plans, all to approximately the same scale – Fleming (1807), Smith (1821), Martin (1842), OS first edition (1860s) and second edition (1880s) – offer an unparalleled opportunity to examine in detail the topographical growth of a major city.

There are a number of plans of the city which in origin and form differ from those listed above, all of them being modern reconstructions of various aspects of early Glasgow; the four publications which contain these fold-out maps are:

Charters and documents relating to the city of Glasgow, 1175-1649, 2 vols, 1897, 1906, edited by Sir J.D. Marwick.
Extracts from the records of the burgh of Glasgow, n.d., edited by Sir J.D. Marwick
Glasgow protocols, 1530-1600, 10 vols, 1894, 1900, edited by R. Renwick
History of Glasgow, 3 vols, 1921-1934, by R. Renwick and George Eyre-Todd;

The fifth source is a single map sheet:

Map of the city of Glasgow, showing the original area in the 12th century and the areas which have been added from that period, prepared by R. Renwick and A. B. McDonald in 1909.

Historic Towns, 1969, edited by M. D. Lobel, was intended to be the start of a series on European cities. It contains an informative article on the topographical development of Glasgow, illustrated by several excellently clear maps taking the city through to the end of the 18th century.

Merchant City

As Glasgow developed as a trading city in the 18th and early 19th centuries, its growing merchant community moved out of its old houses in the Saltmarket and the Bridgegate to a new development which began to spread west from the High St and north from the Trongate. This new part of the city, its streets unplanned but nevertheless consistently rectangular, has been called Glasgow's first New Town; its western edge, Buchanan St, marked the beginnings of the second New Town. Its residential life was brief, for by the 1820s the merchants had resumed their western march, leaving behind their warehouses and counting houses, their banks and public buildings.

The district continued to thrive well into the 1960s, with its wholesale distribution and light industry facilities. But with the departure of the fruit market to Blochairn in 1969, its single biggest user, the area went into decline and by 1980 many of its buildings were empty and deteriorating.

A decision was then taken by the Glasgow District Council and the Scottish Development Agency (later joined by the Glasgow Development Agency) to upgrade the district substantially, and in particular to restore its long-lost function as a high-quality, city-centre, residential area. These public bodies subscribed over £10 million, and the private sector over £60 million, to revitalise and, in a sense, to reconstruct this historically important section of the old town – the Merchant City.

In a single decade over 1,000 homes, 50 shops and 12,000 square metres of office space have been created, as well as eight restaurants to cater for the area's 2,000 residents and 9,000 daily incomers.

The quality and vision of the Merchant City has been recognised by a number of prestigious awards from bodies such as Europa Nostra, the RIBA, the Civic Trust and the Saltire Society.

The changes are not over – the City Halls (perched on top of the old Fruit Market) and the Sheriff Court (a city block-sized Greek Revival structure) are buildings looking for a use – but the Merchant City has proved itself, both as providing a wide range of facilities for its citizens, and also as a major tourist attraction.

Merchant Guild

Although the earliest Glasgow craft guild dates from the beginning of the 16th century, the Glasgow merchants were somewhat slower in setting up their own guild. After the Reformation had removed the Church from its ruling position in the city the organised craftsmen and the unorganised merchants fought for control of the burgh's administration. A resolution to this struggle was found in the Letter of

Guildry, 1605, which regulated both the city's craftsmen and, in the form of the Merchants' House, its merchants, and which fixed the form of Glasgow's government for the next 300 years.

In the beginning Glasgow's burgesses had been those with land within the burgh, but as this was used up there came to be a growing number of landless burgesses, some of whom did not even live within the city and none of whom was called upon to 'bear the burden' of government. One of the effects of this Letter of Guildry was to restrict these numbers, for henceforward a burgess must also be a guild brother, a qualification which was controlled by the Guildry, in the persons of the Dean of Guild (for the merchants) and the Deacon Convener (for the craftsmen).

The respective status of these two personages illustrates clearly the strong bias in favour of the merchants which existed till the 19th century, for the Deacon Convener of the Trades was never a magistrate, only a councillor. Although James VI had declared that the two sections of the Guildry, merchants and craftsmen, were to be equally represented on the Council, it so happened that the Provost, two of the three bailies, the Dean of Guild, the Treasurer and the Master of Works were always drawn from the Merchants' House.

The old hospital (now, under the Letter of Guildry, the Merchants' Hall) in which old, infirm and needy merchants were looked after was located in the Bridgegate (Briggait) at the foot of the Saltmarket. In 1659 it was entirely rebuilt, with a high central tower (still standing in the middle of the old Fish Market, now the Briggait Centre). Until the kickstart given to Glasgow's economy by the 1707 Treaty of Union, the activities of the Merchants' House were low key, but as the city's trading activities continued to grow it

began to take a significant part in the governance of the burgh. By virtue of its strong representation on the Council and in its own right, it became more and more involved in the town's affairs. Amongst other things it played an important role in the continuing struggle to make the Clyde a fully navigable river, it encouraged the building of the Forth and Clyde Canal, it constantly pressed the government for an improved postal service and it helped to recruit a Glasgow regiment to fight in the American War of Independence. It was largely due to the Merchants' House's best-known Dean of Guild, James Ewing of Strathleven (working with Kirkman Finlay of the Chamber of Commerce), that the nationwide campaign to break the trading monopoly of the East India Company was eventually successful.

The location of its Hall now began to give the Merchants' House concern. Its surroundings were, as one report put it, 'the residence chiefly of the inferior classes, with an awkward access and still more objectional vicinity', and so in 1817 the Bridgegate building was sold off (although the House retained possession of its steeple as 'an ornament to the city'). For some reason it was to be more than 25 years before another home could be found, and the House's meetings were held in the City Council's hall.

Part of the lands belonging to the Merchants' House lay on a rocky eminence directly east of the Cathedral. Known as Easter Craigs (later as the Fir Park), it had recently (1825) been graced by a monument to John Knox. In 1828 James Ewing made the bold proposal that it should be converted into a quality burying-ground. His idea was accepted; the Glasgow Necropolis was opened in 1833 and became a lucrative source of profit for many years.

The 1833 Scottish Burgh Reform Act,

which swept away 300 years of self-perpetuating burghal oligarchies throughout the country, also had the effect of loosening the strong link which for so long had bound the House and Council together. Although the Dean of Guild and the Deacon Convener still retained their places in the Council, all the other magistrates and councillors were now elected by the vote of all the citizens, not by the burgesses alone. In addition, the members of the Town Council no longer had to be drawn only from the ranks of the merchants and the craftsmen. As well as breaking the bond between the Merchants' House and the Town Council, the new legislation also did away with the by now more theoretical than practical belief that the two Houses (Merchants' and Trades) were one body under the Guildry.

In 1843 the Merchants' House moved into a new Hall. This new home formed part of a large block of buildings lying between Ingram St and Wilson St. The House was located between the City Chambers on the north and the Sheriff Court House on the south. By a happy chance the entrance to the new House faced due west along Garth St to the entrance of its old companion and rival, the Trades House in Glassford St.

Another diminution (a major one) in the powers of the Merchants' House now came about. There had been for several decades a growing neglect of the illegality of non-burgesses trading within the city, although the House had always drawn attention to any infringements of its rights. In 1846 this centuries-old distinction was done away with by an Act for the 'Abolition of the Exclusive Privilege of Trading in Burghs in Scotland' enjoyed by the merchants' guilds. The Merchants' House protested but to no avail, and it became clear that the chief purpose of the

House would henceforward be limited to increasing its funds, to administering them for the benefit of its members and for any other charitable purposes open to it.

The Merchants' House willingly took up its new role and throughout the remainder of the century there was a flood of gifts, donations and bequests – for example, James Ewing bequeathed £31,000, James Buchanan left £10,000, Samuel King £18,000, John Morgan £60,000, and the Inverclyde Bequest £184,000.

In 1877 the House moved for the third time. Joining the westward movement of the city's centre, it transferred itself to a handsome, custom-built building at the north-west corner of George Square to face its erstwhile companion of many centuries, Glasgow Corporation, in its magnificent Municipal Building.

The flow of bequests continued into the present century, and there was little doubt that the House's most important committee was now the Pensions Committee. One of its other committees, the Necropolis Committee, began to find it-self with very little to do, for the burying-ground no longer provided the House with any profit. So, in 1966, what had once been a useful investment was handed over into the care of the Corporation.

The last remaining link between the old Guildry and the Corporation now came under threat as several attempts were made to exclude the non-elected Dean of Guild and Deacon Convener from the Corp-oration. In 1965 it was agreed that in future these two personages should no longer vote in committee meetings, only in full council. This was only a halfway stage, however – with the reorganisation of Scottish local government in 1975 the final traces of these relics of the city's past were swept away.

See also   CRAFT GUILDS
MUNICIPALITY

Military History

Because of Glasgow's geographical position and physical layout it has never played a significant part in the country's military history. Invasion or civil strife invariably drew the protagonists to Edinburgh, the capital city, or to the ancient and powerful fortresses of Stirling and Dumbarton, and Glasgow came very low as a place of military importance.

Although the city had a whole series of gates or ports – Stablegreen Port on the north, Castle Gate across the Wyndhead leading to the Cathedral, Rottenrow Port and Drygate Port at the western and eastern ends of these two ancient streets, Gallowgate Port on the east, West Port across the Trongate, South Port (or Nether Barras Yett) at the south end of the Saltmarket and the Water Port next to the old Glasgow Bridge – these were not so much physical, defensible barriers as administrative control points; nor was there ever any proper city walls or other fortifications. Certainly there was a castle, the Bishop's Palace, and it was indeed defended and attacked by various factions at various times, but it was in no way a *place d'armes*. Nevertheless, the city was the scene of a number of military episodes and some fairly important battles were fought in the surrounding areas.

The first noteworthy event was the Battle of the Bell o' the Brae which was supposed to have taken place about 1297. In an early incident in the Scottish War of Independence against England, William Wallace destroyed an English force at the Barns of Ayr and rode north with a band of 300 followers towards Glasgow. Advancing up the city's High Street he attacked and overcame the English garrison at the bell (or brow) of the street as it ascended towards the Cathedral and the castle. Unfortunately, the only reference to this doughty deed is in the unhistorical pages of the metrical romance written in the 15th century by Blind Harry, and modern historians dismiss it as nothing more than a legend.

After this came a long period when no military happenings disturbed Glasgow's peace, although, like most other Scottish burghs, it sent a contingent of its citizens to fight at the disastrous field of Flodden (1513). The leader of the little band was Matthew, Earl of Lennox, the city's Provost; like many other Scots he never left the fatal field.

During the unsettled minority of James V, various military sorties plagued the city. In 1516 Mure of Caldwell took and plundered the Bishop's Castle (the spoils of war included 28 'feddir beds'!), and in 1518 it was again besieged by the Earl of Lennox.

More important than these minor skirmishes was the Battle of the Butts, 1544, when the Earl of Lennox set himself up in opposition to the Earl of Arran, the Governor of the Realm. Lennox occupied the city and Arran advanced against it. The opposing forces met on the Glasgow Muir, to the east of the town where the butts or targets for the wapinschaws stood. Lennox was defeated, about 300 of the citizens were slain, the castle was taken and the city given over to pillage.

The most important event in Glasgow's military history was undoubtedly the Battle of Langside, fought on 13 May 1568. After having abdicated in favour of her son James, Queen Mary escaped from Loch Leven Castle on 2 May and had set out for Dumbarton, whose castle was held by her supporters. The Earl of Moray, regent for the young James, was opportunely in Glasgow at this time and he assembled in the city a force of about 4,000 men (including 600 from Glasgow) to oppose the advancing army of the Queen. Learning of its westward movement along the south bank of the Clyde he occupied the small village of Langside and, in the ensuing conflict, defeated the Queen's forces. Although the numbers engaged were small, it was an important battle for its outcome settled the fate of Scotland and the future of England. It is said that the Regent was so pleased with the support he received from Glasgow that he granted to its baxters (or bakers) the Partick mills which from then on were known as the Regent Mills.

Following this, the city was once again fairly free from the alarums of war. Even during the tumultuous years of the Civil War Glasgow was spared any direct involvement. After Montrose's victory for King Charles at Kilsyth (barely ten miles away) in 1645, the Town Council, fearing a descent on them by his wild Irishmen and Highlanders, offered him £500 to spare the city. After his defeat at Philiphaugh that same year, David Leslie occupied the city with his Covenanters and it was ordained that 'the haill inhabitants of this burgh come out ilk Mononday of the weik' to cast up a 'trinch' or trench around the city – a

clear indication that no permanent fortification existed. The victorious Cromwell occupied the city on three occasions in 1650 and 1651, but the only warfare he engaged in was one of words. After being subjected to a virulent sermon by Zachary Boyd, the minister of the Barony parish, he avenged himself by inflicting on the fiery minister a prayer of three hours' duration.

Following the Restoration Glasgow became a military centre for the activities of the royal battalions against the Covenanters. In 1679 the latter forced the king's men to evacuate the city but, after only a few days' occupation, they were compelled to withdraw and met their doom at the Battle of Bothwell Brig (1679).

The next time the breath of war blew in upon Glasgow was during the first Jacobite rebellion in 1715. The citizens, staunch Hanoverians, raised a regiment of some 500 men which was involved, though not directly, in the Battle of Sheriffmuir. The 'lynes of intrinchment' were renewed and cannon placed in commanding positions. Although these temporary fortifications were never tested in action, they put the town to considerable trouble and expense – even to the 'kaill plants and leiks quhilk were destroyit by the trinches'.

The last occasion on which Glasgow was involved in actual warfare was during the second Jacobite rebellion in 1745. In September Prince Charles Edward Stewart, the Young Pretender, on his way south, demanded from the city £15,000 sterling. The Council pleaded poverty and had the sum reduced to £5,000 in cash and £500 in goods. In his retreat north after the collapse of his campaign in England, the Prince occupied the city in December. He was dourly received by the Whig citizens; as Provost Cochrane reported, 'Our people of fashion kept out of his way; few or none at the windows; no ringing of bells, and no acclamation of any kind . . . Our ladies had not the curiosity to go near him, and declined going to a ball held by his chiefs.' There was one exception to this lack of curiosity. John Walkinshaw of Barrowfield, one of the city's tobacco lords, had a daughter, Clementina, who waited upon the Young Pretender during his residence in the Shawfield Mansion. She became his mistress and when he escaped to France he sent for her. By her he had a natural daughter whom he legitimated as the Duchess of Albany a year before his death.

To clothe his ragged Highland army the Prince demanded from the city 6,000 short cloth coats, 12,000 linen shirts, 6,000 pairs of shoes, 6,000 pairs of hose, 6,000 waistcoats and 6,000 blue bonnets. He also carried away a printing press, a fount of type, printing paper and three workmen – no doubt to pursue the propaganda war! It was said that because of the churlish attitude of the inhabitants towards him he had resolved on leaving to give the city over to pillage, an outrage which would have taken place but for the plea for clemency from Cameron of Lochiel. Tradition has it that the magistrates in gratitude resolved that from then on any visit to the city by a descendant of Lochiel would be celebrated by the ringing of the town's bells.

The American War of Independence (1775–83) radically affected the city's tobacco trade. As practical assistance, private and public subscriptions raised within the city enabled a full regiment to be established in 1777 for service abroad. This was the 83rd Regiment of Foot or the Royal Glasgow Volunteers. One of its earliest duties was to quash an incipient mutiny at Leith in 1779, when some 50 Highland recruits objected to being enrolled in the Glasgow regiment and not,

as they had supposed, in the Black Watch and the Highland Light Infantry. The 83rd was short-lived, being disbanded at the end of the American war.

The outbreak of war with Revolutionary France in 1793 roused the city's burghers to a patriotic frenzy, involving them in much amateur military activities. Two batallions of infantry were raised. The first of these consisted of 350 men who clothed themselves but received their arms from the government. They served without pay and were naturally known as the 'gentlemen volunteers'. The second battalion (c.800) was clothed and paid for by the government; it was highly disciplined and ranked almost as a regiment of the line. There was also a squadron of light cavalry, the Royal Glasgow Volunteer Light Horse, about 60-strong, raised in 1796, whose members equipped themselves entirely at their own expense. It was regarded as a splendid corps – in appearance, at least. In addition a body of musketeers was formed, known as the Armed Association. Following the Peace of Amiens (1802) all these bodies were disbanded. A demonstration of the popular feeling aroused by the 'gentlemen volunteers' occurred when they stood down at the Merchants' Hall in the Bridgegate and were thoroughly bombarded and bespattered with filth and mud by the crowd.

With the resumption of war in 1803 new bodies of troops were set up. This time there were eight battalions, most of them distinguished by particular names. There were Trades (600 men) and Grocers (600) Battalions, a corps recruited from the Anderston district (900) and one from the Port Dundas area, known as the Canal Volunteers. There was a grand Highland Regiment of 700 men, all dressed in full Highland dress and led by 'Colonel'

Samuel Hunter of the *Glasgow Herald*. The élite corps were the Gentlemen Sharpshooters (700); the shortest-lived corps was 'The Ancients', 300 elderly gentlemen who were mercifully stood down in 1804. In all, some 5,000 defenders of their city took part in these largely otiose activities.

Before the establishment of an efficient police force, urban unrest throughout the 17th and 18th centuries and the first half of the 19th century could only be kept under control by the use of military force, both infantry and cavalry. Glasgow was no exception, and the city enjoyed – or suffered – an almost continuous presence of army units throughout this period. More than half of the 40 or so units stationed in the city were English and included county regiments from Suffolk, Kent, Lancaster, Essex and Shropshire. These regiments often paid repeated visits to the city. Half a dozen were Irish – the Iniskilling Dragoons (cavalry) visited the city eight times between 1824 and 1880, and the Irish Regiment of Foot four times between 1786 and 1850. The remainder were Scottish and almost every Scottish infantry or cavalry unit was stationed in the city at one time or another. The years 1820–50 saw the greatest number of units in Glasgow, with the object of acting as restraining forces during a period of unrest which included the Radical Rising of 1820 and the Bread Riots of 1848.

The 'Year of Revolutions', 1848, also saw the raising of a cavalry arm, originally known as the Glasgow and Lower Ward of Lanarkshire Yeomanry Cavalry and later as the Queen's Own Royal Glasgow Yeomanry. Its members all supplied their own horses, many of them being members of the prestigious Lanarkshire and Renfrewshire Hounds. Described as 'popular and decorative', they formed a guard of

honour during both Glasgow visits of Queen Victoria (1849, 1888). They sent a contingent to the Boer War of five officers and 115 NCOs and men. During the First World War they took part in operations in Gallipoli, Palestine, Syria and France, and in 1947 the Queen's Own was reborn as a unit of the Royal Armoured Corps.

Even as late as 1877 the Town Council was complaining to the War Office that there were '100,000 Irish (many Fenian) now in Glasgow', and asking for the garrison to be increased.

Until the building of the Infantry Barracks in 1795, the city's soldiers were billeted on the inhabitants. The only citizens exempt from this were those whose rent was under £2, were in receipt of charity, were spinsters or widows, clergymen or schoolmasters. Those liable were obliged to provide accommodation for two soldiers for periods ranging from two to eight weeks depending on the amount of their rental. The ill-feeling roused by this method became so strong and widespread that in 1795 infantry barracks were erected in the city's east end on the north side of the Gallowgate. The area chosen was known as the Butts, where the citizens had many years before held their Wapinschaws. The barracks cost £15,000 and could house 1,000 men.

By the mid-1800s the Gallowgate Barracks were in a deplorable state – more of its soldiers were admitted to hospital than those of any other barracks in Scotland – and it was decided to build new accommodation. Land was purchased at Garrioch (part of Maryhill) to the north of the city in 1868 and the new barracks (constructed from stone quarried at Huntershill, Bishopbriggs) were completed in 1872. These Maryhill Barracks were intended to be temporary; land had been acquired near Helensburgh for the erection of a permanent depot, but it was never constructed due to lack of funds.

The Maryhill Barracks covered 30 acres and was surrounded by a 12ft-high wall. It was intended to accommodate an artillery brigade of four batteries and an infantry battalion – in all about 1,000 men. At times of high unemployment and consequent unrest it also housed cavalry units. Until the end of the 19th century it was garrisoned by various regiments, mainly Scottish (Black Watch, HLI, Argyll & Sutherland Highlanders and the Gordon Highlanders). After the First World War it became the permanent depot of the Highland Light Infantry until they removed to the Churchill Barracks, Ayr, in 1958. The Scottish Special Housing Association

then acquired the land and built the Wyndford Housing Scheme on the site. This was completed in 1967. The perimeter wall, the main gate and the guardroom have been retained.

The Cavalry (or Horse) Barracks were originally at Hamilton but the considerable delay in bringing cavalry forces into the city in times of civil unrest persuaded the authorities to erect in 1821 new barracks at the head of Eglinton St just south of the river and with quick access to the city across the Jamaica St bridge. When the Maryhill Barracks opened, the cavalry was moved there and the vacant building acquired by the Govan Parochial Board for use as a poorhouse.

THE HIGHLAND LIGHT INFANTRY (CITY OF GLASGOW REGIMENT)

The regiment most particularly associated with Glasgow (despite its name) is the Highland Light Infantry, in its day the second senior Highland regiment. It is the proud possessor of 53 battle honours – more than any other Scottish regiment – and now forms part of the Royal Highland Fusiliers (Princess Margaret's Own Glasgow and Ayrshire Regiment).

Its two regular battalions both came into being in the 18th century. The 1st Battalion began as the 73rd (Highland) Regiment of Foot and was raised at Elgin in 1777. It was issued with the standard government tartan, to which was added red and white stripes; the regiment's first colonel was a Mackenzie and the altered tartan became known as the Mackenzie tartan. The regiment was also known as MacLeod's Highlanders after another early colonel, Major-General John, Lord Mac-

Leod. Later, in 1786, it was renumbered the 71st (Highland) Regiment of Foot, taking over the number previously borne by Fraser's Highlanders.

In 1809 it became a light infantry regiment under the name of the 71st (Glasgow Highland Light Infantry) Regiment of Foot, George III having graciously granted it the privilege of adding 'Glasgow' to its title. The change in style and name was accompanied by a significant change in uniform from kilt to trews (trousers), a change which only served to confirm (somewhat against its wishes) its identity as a non-Highland regiment; it was not until 1947 that permission to wear the kilt again was granted. Although still carrying the soubriquet 'Highland', most of its recruits came from Glasgow with its large Highland community and over 200 of its earliest recruits were from the city.

During the Peninsular War (1808–14) this Glasgow connection was used to good effect during the British assault on Fuentes de Onoro (1811), when Colonel Cadogan led the regiment into the attack with the cry: 'Forward! Forward, 71st! Charge them down the Gallowgate!'

In the thorough reorganisation of the Army in 1881 the regiment lost its separate identity, amalgamating with the 74th (Highlanders) Regiment of Foot, becoming the 1st Battalion, the Highland Light Infantry Regiment, with its depot at Hamilton, Lanarkshire. This integration was described as 'the marriage of MacLeod's Highlanders with Mar's Grey Breeks'.

What was to become the 2nd Battalion was raised at Glasgow in 1787 as the 74th (Highland) Regiment of Foot. Although nominally a Highland regiment associated with Argyll (Campbell country), its depot was in Glasgow. It also was issued with the standard Army tartan, with the addition of a distinguishing white stripe – a design which became known as the Lamont tartan. In 1881 it amalgamated with the old 71st to become the 2nd (and junior) Battalion of the Highland Light Infantry Regiment.

Separately and together, the constituent parts of the new regiment took part in all the major and minor outbreaks of hostility from the 18th to the 20th centuries, from the American Revolutionary War, the Crimean War and the Indian Mutiny to two world wars, by way of the many little wars of the British Empire. They were also frequently employed in preserving civil order in Ireland and Scotland. For example in 1848, the 'Year of Revolutions', three companies of the regiment were sent by night to police Glasgow, at the request of the civil authorities.

On the outbreak of the First World War the regiment was rapidly expanded. It eventually reached almost 30 battalions, most of which were recruited within Glasgow and district. Some of these wartime battalions became quite well known. For instance, Glasgow Corporation itself raised two battalions. The first of these, 1st Glasgow (15th Battalion), was made up almost entirely of employees of Glasgow Corporation Tramways Department. The department's manager, James Dalrymple, was probably the most efficient recruiting agent in Scotland: in the first 14 months of the war he persuaded 10,000 men to join up. The 1st Glasgow was said to have been recruited through his agency in 16 hours, during which time 1,100 tramcar drivers and conductors enlisted. The 2nd Glasgow (16th Battalion) was recruited almost entirely from former members of Glasgow's Boys Brigade companies, and was popularly known as the 'BB Battalion'. In similar fashion the members of the 3rd Glasgow (17th Battalion) were drawn from the Glasgow Chamber of Commerce. There were also a number of battalions made up from Militia and Volunteer forces, most of which were disbanded at the end of hostilities. The Territorial Army furnished two battalions which existed till after the Second World War. The 7th (Blythswood) Battalion, raised initially from an early rifle volunteer corps, eventually became part of Q (Glasgow and Blythswood) Battery of the 445 (Lowland) Light Air Defence Regiment in 1964, while the 9th (Glasgow Highland) Battalion, which began at Glasgow in 1868 as the 105th Lanarkshire (Glasgow Highland) Rifle Volunteer Corps, ended up after 1946 as the Glasgow Highlanders Battalion of the HLI. During the First World War about 80,000 Glasgow men served in the HLI's ranks; of these, 568 officers and 9,428 other ranks were killed.

After the cessation of hostilities the

regiment went back to its peacetime strength and took up quarters in Maryhill Barracks, and in 1919 was accorded a civic reception by the Corporation. The regiment's close connections with the city were further recognised in 1923 when it was redesignated the Highland Light Infantry (City of Glasgow Regiment).

After giving a worthy account of itself in the Second World War at Dunkirk, Eritrea, the Western Desert, Italy, Normandy and Germany, the regiment continued to contract and in 1948 the two battalions became one. The bond between the city and the regiment was further strengthened in 1949 when the Freedom of the City was bestowed upon it.

In 1959 the regiment finally lost its separate identity when it and the Royal Scots Fusiliers were brought together under the new name of the Royal Highland Fusiliers (Princess Margaret's Own Glasgow and Ayrshire Regiment) with its depot at Ayr. Despite its close connection with Glasgow, the HLI still thought of itself as fundamentally a Highland regiment and took it ill at being amalgamated with a Lowland one. Nevertheless, when it marched out of Maryhill Barracks – the last regiment to occupy these old barracks – it left the name of the old HLI behind it.

Mills

For most of its early history much of the city's meal and flour requirements could easily be met by mills located along the little stream which ran down past the Cathedral to the Clyde, the Molendinar Burn. There were three principal mills, which processed grain of various kinds, along with several smaller mills involved in other processes requiring water power, such as the preparation of flax, snuff and the slitting of iron bars. Until 1608 these mills belonged to different owners but in that year the Town Council bought up the rights to these mills, mainly to profit from the legal requirements which bound (or 'thirled') farmers in particular localities to use particular mills.

Farthest north was the Provan Mill, which lay on the north side of the Monkland Canal. It had a 22ft diameter water-wheel and was used for grinding both oats and peas. A little distance below it was the Flax Mill, latterly converted for processing barley and snuff. South of the canal and nearer to the Cathedral was the important Town Mill with its capacious pond. Then came the small Iron Mill (also known as the Pile Mill, the Old Malt Mill and the Snuff Mill), another grain mill. Closest to the Cathedral was the Sub Dean Mill. Although a charter of 1446 permits its erection, it must have existed in some form for many years before that date, and was doubtless associated with the nearby Cathedral. Its dam was located where the Bridge of Sighs now crosses Wishart Street. Its final form dated from 1810 and its 24ft diameter wheel was used to grind oats.

By the beginning of the 19th century the Molendinar mills could not keep pace with the growing needs of an increasing population, and attention was shifted to the waters of the Kelvin, a much larger stream, which enters the Clyde about three miles to the west. By the middle of the 19th century only two mills were left on the Molendinar – the Town Mill (destroyed by fire in 1857) and the Sub Dean Mill which was removed (following the implementation of the City Improvement Act of 1866) in order to allow the burn to be covered over and its valley converted into a thoroughfare, Wishart St.

The Kelvin's volume of water and fairly steep fall south into the Clyde offered a considerable source of water power, and there had been grain mills on it from an early period. These early mills lined the east bank of the river from where the Kelvingrove Art Gallery and Museum now stands, downstream to the 1895 bridge (Benalder St).

Bishop's Mill (Old Dumbarton Rd)

The oldest (and the furthest downstream) was the Mill of Partick, probably dating from the 12th century. It lay just below a natural weir, on the opposite bank from the Bishop's Castle, and belonged to the Church in the person of the Bishop, later Archbishop of Glasgow. It was sometimes known as the Bishop's/Archbishop's (Baronial) Mill and was the mill to which the local farmers were 'thirled'. In 1608 the Town Council acquired it, under the title of the Old Mill of Partick, from the Archbishop, in furtherance of their plan to gain the milling monopoly. The Council retained it until the end of the 18th century, when it was sold to the nearby Slit Mill. It burnt down in 1836 and was rebuilt in 1839 by William Wilson, grain merchant and miller, resuming its old name of Bishop's Mill. Towards the end of its useful life it was operated by electric power; currently, it has been converted to provide housing accommodation in the form of 20 apartments.

Scotstoun Mill (Partick Bridge St)

Next was the Scotstoun Mill, dating from 1507 when it was known as the Waulk Mill of Partick. Its early name refers to the process of preparing woollen cloth by wetting and beating it. It lay slightly to the north of the Bishop's Mill and was the only early mill to be sited on the west bank of the Kelvin. It took the name Scotstoun Mill from the family for long connected with it. About 1847 it became the property of John White (second Provost of Partick), who built part of the surviving structure and converted it to grain milling in 1877. It now serves as a warehouse for animal foodstuffs and as a mill producing white flour from wheat for Rank Hovis Ltd. At one time a small mill existed immediately below it, known as the Wee Mill.

Regent Flour Mill (Bunhouse Rd)

The Baker's Wheat Mill lying between the river and Bunhouse Rd had its origins in an incident during the west of Scotland campaign of the Regent Moray against the forces of Mary, Queen of Scots. After his victory at the Battle of Langside (1568), the Glasgow bakers supplied the Regent's army with emergency supplies of bread, and, in gratitude, he granted them the right to build a wheat mill on the east bank of the Kelvin. It later became known as the Bunhouse Mill from its proximity to a tavern, the Bun and Yill (ale) House. It was rebuilt in 1828, was destroyed by fire in 1886 and then rebuilt by John Ure. In 1903 it was taken over by the Scottish Cooperative Wholesale Society (for obvious reasons becoming known as the Regent Mills) who continued to use it until the 1970s when it was demolished.

Clayslaps Mill

The New Waulk Mill of Partick was located furthest north of all these early mills, on the east bank of the Kelvin where the Kelvingrove Art Gallery and Museum now stands. Around 1517 the mill was rented to a Donald Lyon and afterwards to his son Archibald Lyon, becoming known as Archy Lyon's Mill. He obtained permission to change it to a wheat mill in 1554, and in 1588 the Town Council bought it from its then proprietor, Walter Stewart, Commendator of Blantyre. By now it was known as the Clayslaps Mill. The Council in turn sold it to the Glasgow bakers in 1771. Finally, in 1874, it was conveyed for £13,500 back to the Council, who demolished it in the course of having the new Kelvingrove Park laid out.

Slit Mill

This latecomer on the scene was located on the east bank near where the Expressway now crosses the Kelvin. Built c.1738 by the Smithfield Iron Co, it was used to slit imported bar iron into rods for making nails and small tools. Shortly after 1780 it was converted to a grain mill. A large part of it was burnt down in 1815 and later rebuilt. In 1862 it was demolished to make way for a boilerworks.

Farther upstream a later group of mills developed, mainly in the 18th century. The most northerly of these were the **Dalsholm** and **Balgray** mills. The former was founded about 1783, eventually becoming the Dalsholm Paper Mills (Dalsholm Rd), closing in 1970. Balgray began in the 18th century as the Balgray Snuff and Paper Mill. Its name was later changed to the Kelvindale Paper Mills (Kelvindale Rd), and it closed in 1976.

Downstream were mills at Garrioch, North Woodside and South Woodside. The North Woodside mill (in Garriochmill Rd) was grinding barley as early as 1758. At one time it prepared gunpowder and was later rebuilt (1846) to grind the flints used in making pottery glazes. It closed about 1963.

Although several watercourses enter the Clyde from its south bank, the fall of the ground is not as steep as on the north side. Despite this, several mills were built on the White Cart river.

In 1690 Nicholas Deschamps, a Huguenot refugee who had been a paper-maker in the Loire region, found his way to Glasgow and set up a paper-mill on the Cart at Millbrae, Langside. The business prospered and was passed to his son-in-law James Hall who, in about 1729, transferred the mill to a site further up the river, at Millholm. In 1841 it was taken over by Robert Couper, a local man. (Couper left about £8,000 in his will to build a hall, a reading room and a library. The library, still known as the Couper Institute, is now part of the City of Glasgow Libraries.) Until 1853, when machinery was introduced, the paper was made by hand. The mill was sold in 1884, and in 1906 was taken over by Wiggins, Teape Ltd. It changed hands several times after that, finishing up in 1931 as the Linnwood Flock Co, and was demolished just before the Second World War.

Solomon Lindsay came to Cathcart from Penicuik in 1812 and began to manufacture cardboard in what had been the old Cathcart Meal Mill, by the side of the old bridge. A small part of the mill was also used to grind snuff. On his death in 1902 the Cathcart Paper and Snuff Mill came to an end. In 1976 the Cathcart Society saved the mill from demolition but a decade later the derelict building was sold to a property dealer.

Monuments and Statues

Albert, Prince (1819–61)

George Square.

Equestrian bronze statue designed by Baron Marochetti of Vaux.

Cost £6,000, raised by public subscription.

Inaugurated October 1866 by Prince Albert's son, the Duke of Edinburgh.

Arthur, James (1819–73)

Cathedral Square.

Standing bronze statue designed by G. A. Lawson (who never saw his subject).

The statue was paid for by subscriptions from former employees in Arthur's drapery business.

Unveiled July 1893 by Sir James King, Lord Provost.

Battlefield Monument

Battle Place, Langside.

Spirally decorated column with a lion on top, its paw on a cannonball, designed in 1887–88 by Andrew Skirving.

Celebrates the Battle of Langside (1568), when Mary Queen of Scots was defeated by the forces of the Regent Moray.

Burns, Robert (1759–96)

George Square.

Standing bronze statue on a granite plinth designed by local sculptor George Edwin Ewing.

Cost £2,000, raised by 400,000 public subscriptions. Unveiled on 25 January 1877 (the centenary of his birth) by Lord Houghton in the presence of about 30,000 people – Glasgow was slow in erecting a monument to the national bard.

The poet holds a detachable bronze daisy which it is said can be (and frequently is) removed, and a supply of replacements is kept handy. On the base are reliefs depicting 'Tam O'Shanter', 'The Cottar's Saturday Night', 'The Vision' and 'The Twa Dogs'.

Campbell, Thomas (1777–1844)

George Square.

Standing bronze statue in Regency dress on a granite base, designed by John Mossman. Erected by public subscription in 1871. Campbell, a poet, was elected Lord Rector of Glasgow University in 1826 and for two subsequent terms.

Carlyle, Thomas (1795–1881)

Kelvingrove Park.

Stone bust rising out of massive plinth.

Cenotaph

George Square.

Granite pylon designed by Sir J. J. Burnet, *c.*1922, with forespace flanked by lion sculptures by Ernest Gillick.

It was unveiled in May 1924 by Earl Haig.

Clyde, Lord (Sir Colin Campbell) (1792–1863)

George Square.

Standing bronze statue on a circular granite base, designed by J. A. Foley.

Unveiled in August 1868 by Sir James Campbell.

Dosser, Lobey

In 1949 Bud Neil (1911–70) started to draw a cartoon strip for the *Evening Times*, which ran for six years. The hero of the strip was called Lobey Dosser (*Lobey* for lobby or hall, *Dosser* someone asleep – meaning a tramp sleeping on the stair-landing of a tenement close) and his exploits took place in a piece of Indian territory called the Calton Creek. His two-legged horse was called El Fideldo and his evil opponent was Rank Bajin. A campaign to honour this important Glasgow character was organised by Tom Shields, *Herald* columnist, and in 1992 a bronze statue depicting Lobey on his steed with Bajin riding postillion was erected in Woodlands Rd. Designed by Tony Morrow and Nick Gillon, its £18,000 cost was largely raised by public subscription.

Elder, John (1824–69)
Elder Park, Govan.
Standing bronze statue (with a model vertical steam engine) on a granite base, designed by Sir J. E. Boehm (1887–88).

Elder, Mrs Isabella (1827–1905)
Elder Park, Govan.
Seated bronze statue on a granite base, designed by A. Macfarlane Shannan (1905).

Mrs Elder was the wife of John Elder, shipbuilder.

Gladstone, William Ewart (1809–98)
George Square.
Standing bronze statue depicting Gladstone in the robes of Rector of Glasgow University, on a granite base, designed by William Hamo Thorneycroft. The two bronze bas-reliefs show the Prime Minister in the Commons and felling trees at his home, Hawarden.

The sculptor carefully concealed Gladstone's loss of a finger from his left hand. The statue originally stood on the site of the Cenotaph, in front of the City Chambers.

Gladstone was greatly appreciated by the merchants and manufacturers of the city for the part he played in the success of the 'Free Trade' movement. He was given the freedom of the city in November 1865 and was elected Lord Rector of Glasgow University in November 1877.

Graham, Thomas (1805–69)
George Square.

Seated and gowned bronze statue designed by William Brodie. Gifted by James Young of Kelly, a former student and assistant of Graham. A scientist of international fame, Graham was Professor of Science in the Andersonian University and later the Master of the Mint.

Highland Light Infantry Memorial
Kelvingrove Park.
Seated figure of a soldier designed by Birnie Rhind, 1906.

Erected in memory of those killed in the Boer War.

Ibarruri, Dolores, *La Pasionara* (1895–1989)
Custom House Quay.
Standing bronze on a 10ft steel plinth, designed by Arthur Dooley (1980).

Ibarruri was a long-lived Republican heroine of the Spanish Civil War and a leading figure in the Spanish Communist Party. The statue cost £3,000.

Kelvin, William Thomson, Lord (1824–1907)
Kelvingrove Park.
Seated bronze statue depicting the famous physicist in academic dress, on a granite base, designed by A. Macfarlane Shannan (1913).

Kelvin Way Bridge
Four bronze symbolical figure groups, each end showing two figures: (1) *Peace and War* – a mother and a warrior; (2) *Progress and Prosperity* – a bearded sage and a woman musician; (3) *Navigation and Shipbuilding* – woman holding a model ship; (4) *Commerce and Industry* – woman with a money purse and man with mallet. Though designed by Paul R. Montford from a commission in 1914, the statues were not erected until *c.*1920. They suffered some damage during the Second World War, and were repaired by Benno Schotz.

Kennedy Monument
Kelvingrove Park.

Bronze group depicting a Royal Bengal tigress sharing a peacock with her cubs, designed by A. Cain in collaboration with Rosa Bonheur (*c.*1866).

It was presented by W. S. Kennedy of New York.

John Knox, the Scottish reformer, stands on his column high above the Necropolis, which he pre-dated by eight years. (George Oliver)

Knox, John (1513–72)

Standing stone statue, 12ft high, designed by William Warren and carved by Robert Forrest (1825), on top of a huge Greek Doric column designed by Thomas Hamilton.

Erected at public expense on the highest point of the Necropolis.

Lister, Joseph, Lord (1827–1912)
Kelvingrove Park.

Bronze statue of the surgeon in academic dress, designed by G. H. Parkin (1924).

Lister's discovery of the use of anti-septics in operations was made while he was working in the Glasgow Royal Infirmary.

Livingston, David (1813–73)
Originally erected in George Square in 1879 but moved to Cathedral Square in November 1959.

Standing bronze statue on a granite base, with bronze bas-reliefs, designed by John Mossman.

Lumsden, James (1778–1856)
Erected in Cathedral Square in December 1862.

Standing bronze statue, designed by John Mossman.

'The most popular as well as the most successful Provost [1866–69] of these contentious decades', James Lumsden, a stationer, pushed through the Municipal and Police Extension Act which vested municipal and police government in one authority.

Macleod, Revd Dr Norman (1812–72)
Cathedral Square.

Standing bronze statue on a granite base, designed by John Mossman.

Paid for by public subscription and unveiled by Principal Caird of Glasgow University in October 1881, near his church in Cathedral Square.

Macleod was Minister of Barony Church, 1851–72, and Chaplain to Queen Victoria.

Moore, Sir John (1761–1809)
George Square.

Standing bronze statue designed by John Flaxman.

Cost £4,000; unveiled in August 1819. The first monument in George Square, the statue is said to be cast from brass cannons.

Nelson, Viscount Horatio (1758–1805)
Glasgow Green.

Takes the form of a 144ft-high stone obelisk and plinth, designed by David Hamilton and built by Andrew Brocket, builder and mason.

It was erected in 1806 by public subscription of £2,000.

Shortly after its erection it was struck by a bolt of lightning (1810) and the damage caused is still visible.

Oswald, James, MP (1779–1853)
George Square.
Standing bronze statue on a granite plinth, designed by Baron Marochetti of Vaux (1855).

This statue originally stood at Charing Cross on what later became the site of the Grand Hotel, and was transferred to George Square in 1875. It is said that when sparrows nested in Oswald's conveniently placed top hat, a hole had to be made in it to drain away the stagnant water. It is also said that the same hat was the basis of an unusual game: contestants threw coins at the hat – the winner was the first to land a coin in it and his prize was all the coins on the ground which had missed the hat!

James Oswald is probably the least known of the various persons commemorated in George Square. He was a staunch Whig and was among the first Glasgow MPs elected to the reformed parliament of 1832.

Pearce, Sir William
Govan Cross.
Standing bronze statue on a granite base, designed by Onslow Ford (1894).

Peel, Sir Robert (1788–1850)
Erected in George Square in June 1859.
Standing bronze statue on a granite base, designed by John Mossman.

Prime Minister Peel was highly regarded in Glasgow, in particular for repealing the Corn Laws. He was elected Lord Rector of Glasgow University in 1836 and in January the following year a magnificent banquet was held in his honour in a special hall built for the occasion on a piece of ground off Buchanan St near the present Princes Court.

Reid, James, of Auchterarder
Springburn Park.
Standing bronze statue holding plans and papers, on a decorated plinth, designed by William Goscombe John (1903).

Roberts, Frederick S., Field-Marshal, Lord, First Earl (1832–1914)
Park Terrace.
An equestrian bronze statue on a sculptured plinth, designed by Harry Bates.

It was unveiled by his daughter, Lady Roberts, in August 1918.

Roberts had addressed three public meetings in Glasgow in 1913 advocating the need to form a Citizens' Army as a defence against attack by a continental power, and the statue was the result of the profound impression these speeches made on the city. It is a replica of a statue erected in 1896 on the Maidan, Calcutta.

Royal Faculty of Procurators Hall
Mandela Place.
The ground-floor window arches of this hall (the finest example of Charles Wilson's Venetian Renaissance style, 1854) are ornamented by 14 sculptured heads usually (but erroneously) said to be the 14 Scottish law lords. Some of the more eminent, reading from east to west are: (2) Henry Cockburn, Lord Cockburn (1779–1854). A persistent Whig when most judges were Tory. A friend of Jeffrey and Brougham; (3) Francis Jeffrey, Lord Jeffrey (1773–1850). One of the founders of the *Edinburgh Review*; (5) John Millar, Professor of Law at Glasgow University; (6) James Reddie, Town Clerk of Glasgow; (12) Henry Brougham, Lord Brougham (1778–1868). A radical law reformer. Raised to the peerage in 1830; (13) Earl of Mansfield, William Murray (1705–93). Chief-Justice of the King's Bench. An impartial but unpopular judge.

St George and the Dragon

St George's Cross.

A stone group depicting the mounted saint killing the dragon. It was originally on the roof corner of a building belonging to the St George Co-operative Society at the north-east corner of the Cross, and was re-erected in the centre of a small landscaped area in 1988.

St Mungo's Bird

Buchanan St pedestrian precinct.

A large bronze statue representing the legendary bird which the saint restored to life, designed by Neil Livingstone (1977).

Scott, Sir Walter (1771–1832)

George Square.

Standing stone statue on a column, designed by John Greenshields and executed by A. Handyside Ritchie. The Grecian Dorian column is by the Edinburgh architect David Rhind. It was erected in 1837, only five years after Scott's death, and was the writer's first memorial. It is interesting to note that Scott's plaid is worn on the right shoulder in the style of a Border shepherd, not on the left which was the Highland custom.

Trades Union Martyr Memorial Pillar

Located near the door of Maryhill Old Parish Church, Maryhill Rd (not the original site).

Cast-iron pillar with a vase finial, about 6ft high, bearing the inscription: 'To the memory of George Millar . . . mortally stabbed on the 24th of February 1834 by one of those put to the Calico Printing Trade for the purpose of destroying a Union of the regular workmen.'

Victoria, Queen (1819–1901)

George Square.

Bronze equestrian statue, designed by Baron Marochetti of Vaux.

It was initially erected at the west end of St Vincent Place on September 1854 to commemorate Queen Victoria's first official visit to the city in 1849; it was moved to George Square and set on a new pedestal in 1866 on the day of the unveiling of Prince Albert's memorial.

War Memorial, 1914–18.

Kelvingrove Park, near west end of Art Galleries.

Bronze group of charging soldiers, designed by I. Lindsay (1924). Erected in memory of the Cameronians (Scottish Rifles).

The bronze equestrian statue of the Duke of Wellington by Marochetti (1844) stands outside the Royal Exchange in Queen St, overlooked by the drab conformity of modern office blocks. (George Oliver)

Watt, James (1736–1819)

George Square.

Seated bronze statue on a granite base, designed by Sir Francis Chantry. It was unveiled at the south-west corner of George Square in 1832, one of the few statues to remain in the place originally suggested for it, and was paid for by public subscription.

The sculptor was asked to design a

'bronze equestrian statue', a request which he fortunately ignored!

Near the Nelson Monument in the Glasgow Green there is a large boulder said to mark the spot where James Watt first thought of the separate condenser for the steam engine.

Wellington, Arthur Wellesley, Duke of (1769–1852)
Queen St at Stirling's Library.

An equestrian bronze statue on a granite plinth. Designed by Baron Marochetti of Vaux. It was paid for by public subscription (almost £10,000) and was unveiled in October 1844.

The two large bronze panels on the plinth represent the battles of Assaye and Waterloo, while the two smaller ones depict 'The Return of the Soldier' and 'Peace and Agriculture.'

White, James (1812–84)
Cathedral Square.

Standing bronze statue, begun by James Mossman and finished by Frank Leslie.

Unveiled in August 1891.

White was a Partner in the Rutherglen chemical firm of J. & J. White.

William III, King (1650–1702)
Cathedral Square.

A bronze equestrian statue on a tall plinth, Glasgow's best known statue.

Its first position, in 1735, was opposite the old Tontine building at the Cross. In 1898 it was moved to the middle of the Trongate, where it was for long the focus of the city's New Year celebrations. It is popularly supposed that the horse's tail is attached to the body by a ball-and-socket joint which allows the appendage to sway in a high wind. It was removed during street alterations in 1923 and re-erected in Cathedral Square three years later. It was presented to Glasgow in 1735 by James Macrae, former governor of Madras, who was born in Ayr about 1677.

Municipality

For more than half of its recorded history Glasgow has been under the supervision of the Church. The terms of the founding charters of the city (dating from the 12th century) created it a free burgh, gave it a market, established its fair, and made it a Burgh of Barony with the Bishop of Glasgow as its feudal ruler – the city's freemen or burgesses were *homines episcopi*, the bishop's men. Although as a Burgh of Barony it was the least powerful of the three categories (the others being a Burgh of Regality and a Burgh of Royalty),

its lord had adequate powers; his courts disposed of all the civil business and petty disputes of his people and, in addition, dealt with those crimes which were not reserved for royal justice.

There was an old saying, 'Better under the crozier than under the lance', and Glasgow's relative absence from the stormier pages of Scotland's history is to a degree due to the fact that its ecclesiastical lord was less likely to seek to gather up treasure on earth than a lay lord. The See of Glasgow was the centre of an extensive domain, which stretched as far south as the border with England, and its power and riches no doubt materially assisted the slow but steady progress of the little medieval burgh.

To execute his justice and to regulate the trade and commerce of his burgh, the Lord Bishop appointed at will his officers or magistrates. The chief of these magistrates was called the *praepositus* (later to become the provost); the other magistrates were habitually described as bailies. These officers had no independent powers. Though the power of the Church buttressed and assisted the burgh, the latter's early comparatively low status (it occupied eleventh place amongst the Scottish burghs) in no way presaged the heights to which it was to rise.

There was no office of provost as we understand it till the middle of the 15th century when an indenture alludes to 'ane honorabyll man John Stewart the first provost that wes in the cite of Glasgow'. The reason for this claim probably arose from the city's elevation to a burgh of regality in 1450. The method of election of the chief magistrate was by the bishop's nomination, and the bailies in turn were appointed by the bishop choosing from a list presented to him by the magistrates.

The first major change in the burgh's government was in 1450 when a charter granted by James II raised the city from a burgh of barony to a burgh of regality. However, despite its higher rank, its magistrates still remained the bishop's men. Another charter in 1470, from James III, only served to confirm the status quo, laying down that the bishop had full powers 'to constitute and appoint provosts, bailies, sergeants and other officers . . . and remove to and from these offices such persons as he shall think proper'.

The effect of the Reformation in 1560

on Glasgow's government was profound. At first great confusion was caused as customs and codes which had prevailed for over 400 years were swept away. The last Roman Catholic archbishop, James Beaton, fled the country into France, taking with him the accumulated treasures and records of the Cathedral and the city. It was declared that search having been made for the Archbishop and his not having being found, it was agreed that the council should themselves elect, which they accordingly did, but this suddenly gained freedom was just as abruptly stripped from them.

The ending of ecclesiastical control had left a power vacuum. The Crown, the nobles and the great magnates began to transfer the land of the See into their own hands. In this scramble for land they were aided and abetted by the city's new Protestant archbishops, the 'tulchan bishops' (a *tulchan* was a calf-skin stuffed with straw, used to induce a cow to give milk), who obliging granted away Church property. These new superiors retained the age-old right to nominate the city's provost and bailies but, not surprisingly, we begin to find not citizens but more eminent personages such as the Earl of Lennox, Lord Boyd, Sir George Elphinston of Blythswood, Crawford of Jordanhill and the Stewarts of Minto occupying the position of chief magistrate. It has been suggested that the appointment of Lord Boyd, a peer, as provost (1577) introduced the fashion of addressing the chief magistrate as 'Lord Provost' (its first recorded use applied to a non-peer was in 1767 when the then holder of the office, George Murdoch, was so addressed).

By a charter of 1611 the city was erected into a burgh of royalty. The charter was directed not only to the archbishop but also to the magistrates, council and community of Glasgow, but again the right to nominate was retained, this time by the Duke of Lennox (11 years earlier he had been infeft in all the rights previously enjoyed by the archbishop). Then, in 1636, the Great Charter of Charles I confirmed and ratified the city as a Royal Burgh under the magistrates, etc (no mention of the archbishop) but yet again reserving to the Duke his heritable jurisdiction over the city. The thoroughly disturbed state of the city throughout this period was very injurious to its importance and prosperity and between 1660 and 1688 its population seems to have declined from 14,600 to 11,900.

With the removal of the old authority of the Church, two groups now began a furious dispute over who should govern the city – the merchants or the craftsmen. Intense rivalry between these two had long been general throughout the Scottish burghs, and little by little the merchants had managed to gain the upper hand. Local circumstances in Glasgow had made the contest more evenly balanced than elsewhere and to bring the matter to an end it was put to arbitration. The resulting Letter of Guildry (1605) brought about a complete revolution in the membership of the Council. It was now to consist of 12 merchant councillors, and 11 craft councillors, the Dean of Guild (merchant), the Deacon Convener (craft) and the Treasurer.

In 1637 it was enacted that 12 persons should now elect the Council. These were to be the new provost and his bailies, the previous provost and bailies, and the provost before him with his bailies. This was a neat and convenient way to ensure an agreeable continuity (agreeable, that is, to those in power), and thus was set up a thorough-going merchant-controlled olig-archy which endured right up to the Municipal Acts of 1833.

From now until the end of the century two families ruled the city, the Bells of Cowcaddens and the Campbells of Blythswood (with occasional help from the Andersons of Dowhill and the Walkinshaws of Barrowfield). About this time (the beginning of the 17th century) the Town Council found itself seriously embarrassed by increasing debts, and to remedy this situation it began to sell off burgh land (which formed a large part of the city's Common Good) to themselves and to neighbouring lairds.

The Glorious Revolution of 1689–90 brought at long last the missing power element to the Council, for the city now became a full Royal Burgh with power to choose 'Magistrats, etc. als fully and als freely in all respects as . . . any other Royal Burgh in the Kingdom'.

Having finally achieved full self-government, the merchants now settled down to run the city's affairs as equitably and as efficiently (for the merchants) as they could for the next 145 years. The Council was responsible for a wide range of activities – maintaining order, providing education, dispensing justice, conducting financial business, caring for the sick, keeping the city clean and wholesome, and directing the observance of public holidays. The magistrates seemed to have administered their justice in an alfresco manner – it was their habit to 'stand on the plaine stanes beneath the tolbuith, the place ordinarie for the Magistrats ther waiting and attending to heir the complents and grievances of the burgesses and utheris and to give them justice'. They had a proper care for their appearance: in 1720 it was decreed that the provost should wear court dress (abandoned about 1855), and in 1767 that he should be supplied with a gold chain – the first to wear it was Provost George Murdoch, on the occasion of the

Grand Masonic Procession at the laying of the foundation stone of the Jamaica St Bridge. The Church, although possessing only a pale shadow of its former authority, still oversaw certain matters such as the maintenance of public and private morality and the relief of the poor.

A new source of municipal power was introduced in 1800 when a Police Board was set up. The Council had hitherto exercised its powers mainly through common law and general custom, but now, with the Board, codified rules and regulations were introduced. The members of the Board were the provost, the bailies and 24 commissioners elected by the citizens. The existence of the latter group marked a first significant step towards a representative local authority. Its police powers were wider than the mere maintenance of public order for it was responsible for cleansing, sewers, street-lighting and, later, roads and bridges. Although ostensibly under the control of the Town Council, its extensive powers for a while appeared to threaten the older and more traditional powers of that body.

Between 1800 and the 1870s the city's boundaries were extended six times as the city grew, and so did the Council; in 1801 the important office of bailie was increased in number to five (three merchants and two trades). The main units of authority within the burgh were now the Town Council, the Police Board, the Dean of Guild Court (an old body which regulated the 'linings' or positions of all new buildings), and the Statute Labour Trust which was responsible for making and maintaining all roads and common sewers within the burgh.

Echoing the 1832 parliamentary reform, the Burgh Reform Act of 1833 brought a radical change to the entire structure of Glasgow's municipal govern-ment. Two Acts gave, for the first time, representative government to all royal and parliamentary burghs – the hegemony of the merchants had at last been broken. A third Act set up Commissioners of Police, responsible for crime-fighting, riot-quelling, street-lighting, paving, scaven-ging, water supply, prevention of infectious diseases, sewers and fire prevention – indications that local government was now expected to concern itself with providing a range of public services. The new franchise was extended to all £10 householders, and although for a few more years only burgesses could present themselves for election, the make-up of the new Corporation was beginning to alter out of all recognition. The burgh was now divided up into five wards, each supplying six representatives, which with the Dean of Guild and the Deacon-Convener (now both *ex officio*, and the only remaining links with the old closed corporation) gave a Council of 32 members. Two of each six retired each year so that one-third of the Corporation came up for re-election each year – a system which continued until local government reorganisation in 1975.

At the very first meeting of the reformed Council, Councillor McGavin witnessed the stirrings of a new attitude by remarking on 'the ridiculous nature and buffoon-like appearance' of the bailies in their customary costumes, and moved that three-cornered hats should be dispensed with and that the gold chains of office be sold. He found no seconder!

The districts which by this time surrounded and hemmed in the old Regality presented a picture of municipal confusion – on the south bank of the Clyde was Gorbals, an unfree 17th-century burgh of barony, and Bridgeton, a village with a Feuars Court; while on the north side Anderston in the west was an 1824 burgh of barony with parliamentary franchise and Calton in the east an 1817 burgh of barony with limited burgess franchise. This confusion was swept away in 1846 by the first of the city's many annexations when its boundaries were made co-extensive with the parliamentary constituency, thus bringing into it these four communities along with the districts of Dalmarnock, Parkhead (in part), Camlachie, Dennistoun and Garngad. This expanded city now had 16 wards, each returning three repres-entatives, which, plus the Dean of Guild and the Deacon-Convener, gave a council of 50 members (at the same time the bailies were increased to seven).

Four years later it was required that all magistrates and councillors be also police commissioners, thus removing the anomaly of Commission's separate powers – powers now enlarged to include the regulation of public baths, lodging-houses, slaughter-houses and food inspection. In 1872 the number of magistrates was increased to ten, and three years later they (and the Town Clerk) were suitably adorned with official robes.

Although the immediate circle of the older small authorities around the city had been annexed in 1846, the ever-increasing population, an efficient public transport system (rail, tramcar and ferry), and the rise of a well-to-do middle class had led to an exodus from the city to a growing circle of new suburbs. Under the Police Acts any centre of population of at least 700 inhabitants could, if it wished, become an independent police burgh, and nine of the city's new suburban areas quickly took advantage of this facility – Partick (1852), Maryhill (1856; pop. 2,800), Govan (1864), Hillhead (1869; pop. 7,738), Kinning park (1871; pop. 6,634), Crosshill (1871; pop. 3,798), Pollokshields West (1876; pop. 1,864), Govanhill (1877; pop. 14,399), and

Pollokshields East (1879).

From the 1870s onwards a struggle now began between these small inde-pendent burghs and the city. Glasgow claimed that almost all the inhabitants of these burghs were employed in the city and enjoyed its advantages without contributing towards their costs. Parliamentary battles raged, boundary commissions met, and the result was the City of Glasgow Act (1891) under which Glasgow took over Maryhill, Hillhead, Crosshill, East and West Pollokshields, Govanhill and a few other small areas. Under this Act the wards were increased from 16 to 25, making the number of elected councillors 75. In 1896 the wards, previously known only by numbers, received their familiar names (Calton, Park, Maryhill and so on). Further annexations took place – Kinning Park in 1905 and Partick, Govan and Pollokshields in 1912 – and the number of wards was increased to 37. Now the city began to refer to itself as 'Greater Glasgow'. Indeed, it was during the decades just before the First World War that Glasgow reached its apogee, a high point shared both by the city at large and by its municipality, for it was now that Glasgow Corporation came to represent to the world the proper theory and practice of municipal government, particularly in regard to its efficient control of so many of the city's public services. It had early on taken responsibility for its halls (1840), parks (1852), art galleries (1856), water supply (1859), housing (1866) and gas supply (1869). To these it now added baths and wash-houses (1878), a labour bureau (1886), electricity supply (1892), public transport (1894) and telephones (1901).

Until the 1880s the provostship had always been filled by men of social position and large means, but a problem arose in 1883 when no one with these requirements could be found to fill the post. Fortunately, Bailie William McOnie, a hitherto inconspicuous Council member (and an engineer by trade), was persuaded to take the office on being promised that he would be given every necessary assistance. The next holder of the post, James King of Levernholme, was not even a councillor when he was pressed to become provost. He was rewarded with a baronetcy in 1888 (the first Lord Provost to be so honoured), and it was remarked that from then on no trouble was experienced in filling the provostship! In 1893 the city was raised to the dignity of the County of the City of Glasgow, which gave it all the powers of a county. The Lord Provost acted as Her Majesty's representative and as Lord-Lieutenant. In 1912 he was further elevated, from being 'The Honourable . . .' to 'The *Right* Honourable . . .'

Until near the end of the century the Town Council had carried out its various civic responsibilities under a bewildering variety of names – as the Corporation it was responsible for the Common Good fund, the Tramways, the Municipal Building, the Libraries, etc; as Trustees its members looked after Parks, Markets and Housing (the City Improvement Trustees); as Commissioners they supplied the water, gas and electricity and as Police Commissioners they attended to the police, fire prevention, lighting, cleansing, baths, halls, streets, bridges and sewers. Most of these separate bodies disappeared in 1895 (the Police Commissioners' duties were transferred in 1904) and for the first time in its history the burgh was governed by, and only by, its provost, bailies and councillors as a corporation. In 1929 the Corporation added to these responsibilities education, poor relief and hospitals.

It is an interesting reflection on local democracy that throughout the latter half of the 19th century a surprisingly large number of citizens never used (or never had the opportunity to use) their votes. Over and over again prospective representatives were returned unopposed – in 1878 and in 1880 only one ward was contested. When there were contests they were on the old basis of Whigs *v.* Tories, and until Gladstone ran into trouble in the 1880s over the Irish problem, the Liberals generally were the dominant party.

After the First World War two circumstances, one temporary, one permanent, began to change electoral attitudes. First, in 1920, following post-war reorganisation, all representatives of all 37 wards came up for election at the one time, and secondly, party politics began to play an increasing role in local government. As early as 1898 the first Labour councillors (steelworker, publisher, baker, butcher, publican, engineer) had been elected, mostly funded by the Glasgow Trades Council, and by 1914 there were 19 Labour councillors in a Council of 113. The Labour Party was quick to set up local electoral machinery and in the first post-war elections it won 45 seats against its opponents' 66. These elections also saw the appearance of the first women councillors; the first four included Agnes Dollan (wife of the well-known Lord Provost, Sir Patrick Dollan), an important figure of the Left in her own right.

Labour's continuing success was due to their linking up politically with the city's Irish Catholic population (an interesting exception in European elections) which formed a considerable element of the city's workforce (in the middle of the 19th century 20 per cent of the population had been born in Ireland). After the settlement of the Irish question in 1920 the city's Irish were then free to turn from nationalist politics to local politics, and it was due in large part to their support that Labour remained in power. In 1918 Labour's backing for the state-funding of the city's separate Roman Catholic schools ensured the continuation of this support.

Control of the Corporation was achieved by the Labour group in 1933 (at first with the co-operation of the ILP, and from 1938 by Labour alone). The first Labour provost was Sir John Stewart (1935–38), and from then until reorganisation in 1975 they retained that control (with the exception of 1948–51 and 1968–71). Although sometimes associated with the 'legend' of the Red Clyde, Glasgow has never been a very left-wing city; its Labour majority has always concentrated on a limited range of parochial matters – municipal rented houses and the municipal ownership and control of major public services. Oddly linked with this has been that marked characteristic of the Scottish left – a strong moralistic element – exemplified by the Corporation's 1890 ban on public houses within its housing schemes (not rescinded till the 1970s).

Having reached the greatest extent of its responsibilities in 1929, the city now began to see its power dwindle as various functions were taken away from it. In 1947 the National Health Service (Scotland) Act transferred the hospital service to central control, and 'poor relief' was exercised by the National Assistance Board. That same year the Corporation Electricity Department was taken over by the British Electricity Authority, and the following year the Gas Department was transferred to the Scottish Gas Board.

In 1946 the boundaries of all but six of the then 38 wards were altered, resulting in a reduction to 37 wards. Redistribution of the city's wards in 1949 reconstituted the Corporation and for a while brought a Conservative administration – of the 111

seats, Labour took 56 and the Progressives 55, Labour refused office and the Progressives, with the help of the two *ex officio* members, the Dean of Guild and the Deacon-Convener, took charge.

Radical reorganisation of the city's municipal government followed the Local Government (Scotland) Act of 1973. The old Corporation disappeared and in its place was the new City of Glasgow District Council (the largest of Scotland's 53 new District authorities) with 66 councillors (one for each ward, elected for a four-year term). The first election under the new arrangements took place in 1974. The unsuccessful struggles at the end of the 19th century by the small burghs on the boundaries to keep out of Glasgow were now repeated, successfully, by Bearsden, Milngavie and Bishopbriggs to the north, and Newton Mearns and Giffnock to the south; by contrast, the ancient Royal burgh of Rutherglen, the burgh of Cambuslang and the village of Baillieston, all lying east of the city, now became part of it.

The Labour group was routed in 1977, largely on the basis of national circumstances, but resumed control of the District Council in 1980. Responsibility for large areas of Glasgow's corporate life hitherto directed by its civic fathers was now transferred to the new Strathclyde Regional Council (of which the city formed part) – transport, education, social welfare, police, fire brigade, water supply and sewage.

The responsibilities left to the District Council are carried out by a number of committees:

Policy and Resources Committee, which helps the other committees, and the Council, in choosing and developing objectives and priorities.

Area Management Committees, which review the effects of Council policy at local levels.

Art and Culture Committee, which oversees the activities of the departments of libraries, of museums and galleries and of performing arts and venues.

Building and Works Department Policy Control Board is concerned with maintaining in good shape the Council's large number of houses and buildings.

Economic Development Committee is concerned with creating jobs within the city and in attracting investments.

Environmental Protection Committee is responsible for the Cleansing Department, the Environmental Health Department and the Veterinary Department.

Finance Committee controls all the Council's financial affairs through the Finance Department.

General Purposes Committee's responsibilities cover a wide range of Council activities, including the Town Clerk's Office which co-ordinates and services the work of all the Council's committees, and attends to its legal matters. The department of Architecture and Related Services oversees building programmes, supplying technical and design services.

Housing Committee (Public Sector Housing). The Council is one of Europe's largest municipal landlords, with 138,000 houses, and its supervision is the responsibility of this committee.

The leisure pursuits of the city's inhabitants are supervised by the Parks and Recreation Committee. The facilities available include 70 parks, 15 swimming pools, 56 bowling greens, 7 golf courses, 57 tennis courts and 134 football pitches.

The Planning Committee is responsible for carrying out the Council's urban regeneration policies in co-operation with the Strathclyde Regional Council. Part of its remit is the care of over 1,200 'listed' buildings of historical and architectural importance.

See also   BURGESSES
COMMON GOOD
CRAFT GUILDS
MERCHANT GUILD

Murder Trials

Between 1856 and 1908 Glasgow was the scene of four celebrated murder cases. With the exception of the Pritchard case, they all presented problems which are still unresolved. Jack House brought the four cases together in one volume which he titled, quite truthfully, *The Square Mile of Murder*.

THE CASE OF OSCAR SLATER

In May 1909 Oscar Slater (born Oscar Joseph Leschziner in Germany of Jewish parents), went on trial in the High Court of Justiciary in Edinburgh charged with the murder of Marion Gilchrist, a spinster aged 83, at her first-floor flat, 15 Queen's

Terrace, a short distance west of Charing Cross.

Miss Gilchrist's body was discovered on 21 December 1908 in the sitting-room by her servant Helen Lambie (on her return from a ten-minute errand) in the company of the downstairs neighbour, Arthur Adams, who had been alarmed by noises from her flat. Before finding the body, and while they were still in the hall, a man came from one of the bedrooms, walked past Lambie and Adams and ran down the close stair. On the identity of this mysterious personage the whole affair was to hinge.

Miss Gilchrist had been killed by a series of blows about her head, and one of the legs of her chair was covered with blood. Documents were supposed to have been removed from the bedroom, and Lambie said a diamond crescent brooch was missing. Based on the somewhat diffident descriptions of the man by Adams and Lambie, the police issued a description which included the phrases 'slim built' and 'clean shaven'. A third witness, Mary Barrowman, a 14-year-old girl, came forward and gave a surprisingly detailed description of a man she had seen outside the close for only a few seconds on a dark rainy December night – she spoke of a tall, thin, clean-shaven man.

An attempt to pawn a diamond brooch by someone known as 'Oscar' led the police to arrest Slater, whose previous history had included earning his living as a gambler, club manager and bookmaker in Hamburg, Brussels, Paris, New York, London, Edinburgh and Glasgow. By this time he was in America, having travelled via Liverpool, under his own name and with nine pieces of luggage. The three witnesses were taken over to New York where the two women identified him, under most unsatisfactory conditions, as the man they had seen on the night of the murder –

despite the fact that Slater was in fact heavily built with a black moustache – and he was extradited to Scotland. The pawned brooch was completely irrelevant – nor were any of the many pieces of jewellery kept in the flat by Miss Gilchrist ever reported missing.

On the basis of nothing more than these two unsatisfactory identifications Slater was found guilty (the jury was out for one hour and ten minutes – nine found him guilty, one not guilty and five found the case not proven). So great was the public outcry at the injustice of the verdict that, in a short space of time, a petition signed by over 20,000 people asking for its overturn was presented to the Secretary of State for Scotland and on 25 May his sentence was commuted from death to penal servitude for life.

The publication in 1910 of William Roughead's account of the case in the *Notable British Trials* series attracted considerable attention, and Sir Arthur Conan Doyle entered the fray on behalf of Slater, publishing in 1912 a booklet entitled *The Case of Oscar Slater*. Nothing further came of these efforts until 1914 when John Thomson Trench, a Glasgow Police Force detective lieutenant involved in the case, averred that Helen Lambie had named another man as the mysterious stranger in the flat. The outcome of this action by Trench was that he was discharged from the Force with ignominy (for making statements without permission) and a special enquiry was set up to examine his statement. When the enquiry's report was published it contained several references to someone referred to only as 'A.B.' and whose activities were discreetly shrouded by a series of asterisks. It has been suggested that A.B. was Lambie's stranger, that he was a Dr Francis Charteris, putative nephew of Marion

Gilchrist, whose surgery was close by, and that he was the murderer. In 1920 Charteris went to St Andrews University as a professor and died there in 1964. When questioned in 1961 about his part in the affair he denied being the murderer, but said that having been informed by the police of the murder on the fatal evening, he went to tell his mother and on the way visited the flat at the moment when Lambie was being questioned by the police. Another theory says that Charteris's involvement was as an accessory. He and Austin Birrell, another relative, visited the flat that evening in order to retrieve some documents. Birrell, an epileptic, killed Miss Gilchrist while having an epileptic fit, and fled up the close stair to hide on the second-storey landing while Charteris walked out past Lambie and Adam.

At the instigation of Conan Doyle, William Park published in 1927 his *The truth about Oscar Slater* which made public Trench's theory about what had really happened at 15 Queen's Terrace. Questions were asked in Parliament, and in November 1927 Slater was released on licence. His case was brought before the Scottish Court of Criminal Appeal in June 1928 and his conviction was quashed on the grounds of misdirection by the presiding judge (who in his address to the jury had laid great stress on Slater's moral turpitude). Slater was given an *ex gratia* payment of £6,000, from which he grudgingly gave £250 towards the cost of his appeal, the bulk of which was paid by Conan Doyle.

Oscar Slater married and settled down quietly in Ayr. He died in 1948, aged 76.

SANDYFORD PLACE MURDER

John Fleming, a respectable Glasgow accountant, lived in a terraced house at 17 Sandyford Place, Sauchiehall St. He and his family were on holiday in July 1862, and the only inhabitants left in the house were his old father (also named John Fleming but usually known as 'Old Fleming', who was in his 80s) and a servant, Jess McPherson. When the old man's son returned home on the afternoon of Monday, 7 July, there was no sign of the servant, and her bedroom door was locked. Old Fleming said he had not seen her since Friday evening. When the bedroom door was opened, Jess McPherson's dead body was found inside – she had been severely assaulted about the head and arms with some kind of sharp weapon, perhaps an axe or a cleaver.

John Fleming senior was arrested on 9 July. Four days later, 'acting on information received', the police arrested Jessie McLachlan, a married woman aged 28 who had been a servant in the Fleming household, was a friend of Jess McPherson and was acquainted with Old Fleming.

Police investigation discovered that Jessie McLachlan had sent off by train to Hamilton and Ayr blood-stained clothing belonging to the dead woman. She gave a long, circumstantial statement regarding these garments which was shown to be completely untrue. During the course of the case Jessie was to make five statements – three before the trial which were all barefaced fabrications, one in court at the end of the trial after the verdict had been pronounced, and one while she was in prison.

Following the identification of the bloody print of a small naked foot on the deceased's bedroom floor as being Jessie's, the Procurator Fiscal, a personal friend of the Fleming family, arranged for Old Fleming to be released. 'Respectable' Glasgow (represented by the *Glasgow Herald*, which called Fleming 'the old innocent') regarded Fleming as a guiltless and respectable old gentleman; others pointed out Jessie's utter lack of motive and the complete lack of evidence connecting her with the crime (other than the clothes).

The trial began on 17 September. Whereas Madeleine Smith had been tried in the comparatively neutral venue of the Edinburgh High Court, poor Jessie had the misfortune to find herself in the Glasgow Circuit Court before a jury of 'respectable' Glasgow gentlemen. Old Fleming was dealt with very tenderly by the presiding judge, Lord Deas. Other witnesses were frequently questioned by him, whereas Old Fleming received his protection from awkward defence questions. The strangest part of the whole trial (apart from Jessie's 40-minute-long statement) was the incident of the milk boy who called at the house early on the Saturday morning after the murder. He was met at the door, unaccountably, by Old Fleming and asked where Jess was. When the defence lawyer asked Fleming why Jess had not gone to the door as usual, Fleming said, 'Jessie? We kent it was a' ower wi' Jessie afore that!'

The trial lasted three and a half days; the jury was out for a mere 15 minutes and unanimously found Jessie guilty. After saying his piece as a witness, Old Fleming left Glasgow for his son's house near Dunoon.

Before sentence was pronounced, Jessie's counsel read to the court a long statement by her which purported to be a true account of what had actually happened during that fateful weekend. Jessie said she had gone to the Fleming house on Friday, 4 July, and after sharing several drinks with Old Fleming and Jess, had gone out to buy more whisky. When she returned she found her friend bleeding profusely from a large wound on her brow. She attended to Jess's injury and washed the blood from her. Jess said that Old Fleming had tried 'to use liberties with her' (it was later disclosed that in 1852 the old man had undergone the disciplines of the church for the sin of fornication with a Janet Dunsmure by whom he had a child) and being repulsed had hit her. When Jess's condition worsened Jessie decided to get a doctor. She went upstairs (they were in the basement kitchen) to look out and see if anyone was stirring. When she went back down she discovered the old man killing Jess by striking her with a meat chopper. Fearing for her own life she helped Fleming to tidy up the room and agreed to say nothing. She also agreed to take away the bloody clothes and dispose of them. After the reading of the statement the judge gave sentence – Jessie McLachlan was to suffer death by hanging on 11 October.

There immediately followed a loud and long public outcry over the verdict. At a public meeting on 29 September a petition asking for a stay of execution was subscribed by nearly 50,000 signatures. A stay was granted and the Lord Advocate set up a private enquiry. Meanwhile Jessie, in the condemned cell, was supposed to have told a very peculiar story: under the influence of laudanum and drink, *she* had murdered Jess – an account which she later denied.

The enquiry's findings were that 'the prisoner was an accidental and constrained witness of the murder but not an actor in it. She can never be hanged'. However, 'having concealed and adopted it', she must be punished. On 7 November she was conditionally pardoned and sentenced to be kept in penal servitude in Perth Penitentiary for the term of her natural life.

Jessie McLachlan was released in October 1877 in her 44th year, with £30 which she had earned during her imprisonment. She emigrated to America, married again, and died in 1899.

EDWARD W. PRITCHARD

Edward William Pritchard (1825–69) was an Englishman who, after serving for several years as a surgeon in the Royal Navy, set up as a general practitioner in Yorkshire, where he met and married in 1850 Mary Taylor, daughter of an Edinburgh businessman. In 1860 Pritchard moved north and began to practise in Glasgow. His medical antecedents were doubtful and the city's medical profession never fully accepted him. Seemingly his character did not inspire confidence – a newspaper account would later describe him succinctly as 'fluent, plausible, amorous, politely impudent, singularly untruthful'. Of the four murders popularly described as happening in Glasgow's Square Mile of Murder (Madeleine Smith, Jessie McLachlan and Oscar Slater are the others) the circumstances of Pritchard's offer no mysteries whatsoever, and leave nothing unexplained.

While Pritchard and his family were living in Berkeley Terrace in 1863 a fire broke out in the servant girl's bedroom (both the doctor and his family were providentially absent from the house at the time) and the unfortunate girl was burnt to death. There were some suspicious circumstances and it was rumoured that the girl was pregnant, but after making enquiries the police authorities dropped any further investigation, accepting Pritchard's suggestion that while reading in bed the girl must have allowed a gas-jet to ignite the bed-hangings.

In October 1864 (they were now living at 1431 Sauchiehall St) Pritchard's wife took ill. Her symptoms appeared mainly after meals (which were usually prepared by her husband) and Pritchard put them down to gastric fever. When she visited her family in Edinburgh the symptoms disappeared only to return when she came back home. Eventually she became so weak that in February 1865 her mother came through from Edinburgh to nurse her, but she in turn became suddenly ill the same month and died, according to her son-in-law who made out her death certificate, of paralysis and apoplexy. Just before Mrs Taylor's death a Dr Paterson had been called in to treat her. His suspicions were aroused and after her death he informed the Registrar that 'death was sudden, unexpected and to me mysterious' but the matter was taken no further at that time. At the trial he explained to the judge that 'medical etiquette' prevented him from taking more direct action.

The following month Mrs Pritchard died and her death certificate, once again supplied by Dr Pritchard, gave the cause as gastric flu. On 20 March he took his wife's body to Edinburgh for burial. In the meantime the Procurator Fiscal received an anonymous letter which described the two deaths as suspicious and on Pritchard's return from Edinburgh he was arrested at Queen St Station on suspicion of murdering his wife and mother-in-law.

The police now began a full investigation. The interment of his wife's body was halted and a post-mortem disclosed the presence of the poison antimony. Then Mrs Taylor's body was exhumed and was also found to contain traces of the same poison. In July 1865 Pritchard was tried before the High Court of Justiciary in Edinburgh for the two murders. Evidence was produced to show that he had purchased large quantities of antimony and that his servants had exhibited the same symptoms as Mrs Pritchard when they had tasted the food prepared for her. Any character he may have had was destroyed when the servant, Mary McLeod, confessed to having been seduced by him. Dr Paterson gave evidence that Mrs Pritchard had shown symptoms of slow poisoning and was taken severely to task by the judge for not having disclosed this to the police. The trial lasted for five days, at the end of which the jury brought in the expected verdict of guilty on both charges. A hypocrite to the last, Pritchard spent much of his time before the execution in reading his Greek New Testament and enjoying the attention of clergymen of several denominations – to one of these he finally confessed his total guilt. A gallows was erected in front of the Justiciary Building at the foot of the Saltmarket, facing Glasgow Green, and on it, on 28 July, Pritchard 'died facing the Monument'. This was the Glasgow fashion of referring to a public hanging, for the last thing a condemned man would see before he dropped would be the obelisk of the Nelson Monument in the Green. It was estimated that a crowd of between 80,000 and 100,000 saw him die at the hands of William Calcraft, the public hangman. This was Glasgow's last public hanging.

MADELEINE SMITH

Madeleine Smith was the eldest child of James Smith, a well-to-do Glasgow architect.

Pierre Emile L'Angelier, the son of a French nurseryman, was born in Jersey in the Channel Islands. He was working in a Glasgow seedsman's office at 10 Bothwell St for 10/– per week when he caught sight of the 18-year-old Madeleine in Sauchiehall St and arranged to be introduced to her.

They seem to have immediately fallen in love with each other, and on April 1855 Madeleine addressed to him the first of a long series of love letters whose frankness was later to shock respectable, middle-class Glasgow. Forbidden by her father to associate with L'Angelier, Madeleine nevertheless defied him and continued to meet Pierre in secret. In her letters she soon began to address him as 'My own darling husband' and eventually, in the summer of 1856 in the garden of the family country house 'Rowaleyn' at Rhu (near Helensburgh), they consummated their passion.

About this time the family moved from their town residence in India St to Blythswood Square (the north-east corner – still extant). Madeleine's bedroom was in a basement room with a ground-level barred window, at which she and Pierre talked and through which she would pass him cups of hot cocoa. The separate flat upstairs was occupied by an eligible young bachelor, William Minnoch. Madeleine apparently began to see in him the chance of a more attractive future than she might have with Pierre, and in January 1857 she accepted Minnoch's proposal of marriage. For obvious reasons Madeleine wrote to Pierre the following month asking for the return of her letters. His disquieting reply was that as he considered her to be his wife (a possible interpretation of their position in Scottish law) he intended to keep the letters as proof of this and would show them to her father if necessary.

She now began to display an unusual interest in buying prussic acid or, failing that, arsenic – on 21 February, for example, she purchased a sixpenceworth of the latter, quite openly, at a local chemist. On the following day Pierre entered in his diary, 'Sun 22 Feb: Saw Mimi in Drawing Room . . . Taken very ill'. (This diary, which might have changed the outcome of the case, was not allowed in evidence.) It was subsequently shown at the trial that Madeleine made other purchases of arsenic – she claimed that she used it for cosmetic purposes.

In March he went to Bridge of Allan (from where Madeleine, unknown to him, had just returned to Glasgow after holidaying there) and in response to a letter from Madeleine (forwarded to him by his landlady), walked the 15 miles back to his Glasgow lodgings on 22 March. He went out about 9 p.m. and returned about 2.30 a.m. in great physical distress – it was never discovered where he had been during this time. By noon on 23 March he was dead, from a dose of arsenic sufficient to have killed 40 men.

When his belongings were searched, 198 letters from Madeleine to him were found and on 31 March she was arrested and charged with his murder by poison. Her trial opened in Edinburgh on 30 June (it was judged that feelings were running too high in Glasgow for her to receive a fair trial).

The trial lasted for nine days and captured the attention of the world, with reporters from many countries sending off daily accounts of the proceedings. The highlight of the trial came on the fifth day which was almost completely taken up with the reading out in court of 60 of her letters. These explicit declarations of sexual passion burst like a bombshell upon the respectable citizens of middle-class Glasgow society: here was a young, carefully educated, unmarried girl of excellent family who not only indulged in clandestine sexual intercourse, but actually wrote (incessantly) about how thoroughly she enjoyed it – as she euphemistically put it, 'What would I not give to place my head on your breast, kiss and fondel [sic] you – and then I am sure you would kindly love [sic] me'.

Her defence lawyer, John Inglis, made a brilliant speech; his successful defence was simply that instances of Pierre's attacks of sickness could not be linked with meetings with Madeleine, in particular with that on 22 March. The Lord Chief Justice summed up and the 15-man jury retired, taking only 30 minutes to deliver its verdict – 'Not Proven' (a singular Scottish verdict, which, it has been suggested, means 'Go away and don't do it again!') and the courtroom spectators broke into loud cheers. It can be assumed that the *Glasgow Herald* spoke for its readers when it declared, 'The awful tale of immorality and unrestrained appetite is concluded . . . the record of wantoness is closed'.

Now a free woman, Madeleine went south to England while the other members of her family left Glasgow for the decent obscurity of Bridge of Allan and later Polmont. In 1861 she married George Wardle, a drawing teacher and a supplier of dyes to William Morris. They settled down in Bloomsbury and had two children, a boy Tom and a girl known as Kitten. She became actively involved in the early socialist movement, becoming manager of the Central Democratic Club which had Sidney Webb on its committee and George Bernard Shaw as a member. After Wardle left her to go to Italy, little is known of her subsequent history, but in 1916 at the age of 80 she emigrated to the USA, where her son Tom had preceded her. She had married again and died in 1928; her tombstone bears her American married name – Lena Sheehy. To her existing great-grandchildren she was 'Great Grandmother Wardle' and nothing more; her secret remained her own.

This *cause célèbre* has continued to attract attention – in 1949 a film of the story, *Madeleine*, appeared starring Ann Todd and Leslie Banks, Smith featured in a TV production by BBC Scotland and many books have been written about this enigmatic young woman whose direct approach to sexual matters, unfeeling elimination of a lover and ice-cold composure when on trial for her life are still as mystifying to us as they were to her contemporaries.

PETER MANUEL

Although the murderer Peter Manuel and his eight victims all lived outside the city's administrative area, the places where the various crimes were committed were, for practical purposes, Glasgow suburbs.

In January 1956, Anne Kneilands (aged 18) was found murdered by blows to the head in East Kilbride (a Glasgow over-spill-town a few miles to its south-west) and a local small-time criminal and molester of women, Peter Manuel, fell under suspicion, but nothing could be proved.

In March, Manuel was freed on bail, following a charge of burglary at a local colliery, and in September a Mrs Watt, her sister and her daughter Vivienne (aged 16) were found dead in the family home in Burnside. They had been shot by a .38 revolver. Mr Watt, a baker, who had been absent from the house at the time, was arrested and charged but was later released.

In December of the following year Manuel was released after serving an 18-month sentence for the colliery break-in, and the same month a young girl, Isabelle Cook (aged 17), went missing. A thorough search was made but no trace of her was found. That same month Manuel, through

his solicitor, visited Watt and told him that his wife, daughter and sister-in-law had been shot by two men and a woman who had broken into his house intent on burglary and that they had given him the gun used to commit the crime which had been thrown into the Clyde.

In January 1958 the Smart family (father, mother and young son aged ten) were found shot in their house in Uddingston. Manuel now went to the police with information which he said would clear up several unsolved crimes in Lanarkshire, including the murders of Anne Kneilands, the Watts and Smarts and Isabelle Cook, and shortly after, in the presence of his parents, he confessed to having murdered these eight people. He took the police to where he had buried the body of Isabelle Cook and showed where he had thrown two guns into the river – they were both found after a prolonged and arduous search.

In May 1958 Manuel was brought before the High Court of Justiciary sitting in Glasgow and tried for the eight murders. After nine days he dismissed his counsel and argued his own defence. This was based on an old and largely unused form of defence – impeachment – under which he claimed that the crimes had been committed by another person, the unfortunate Mr Watt! The trial lasted 14 days and the jury returned after little over an hour with verdicts of not guilty of the Anne Kneilands murder, and guilty of the other seven. In his summing up the judge said that 'the accused has presented his own case with a skill that was remarkable'. Manuel was executed by hanging within Barlinnie Prison in July 1958.

After his execution, a coroner's court

in Newcastle found that he had been responsible for the murder of Sydney Dunn, a Newcastle taxi-driver, in December 1957. It also came to light that in 1946 he had been charged with attacks on women. He had defended himself but had been sent down for nine years (of which he served six). In 1955 he was tried for sexually assaulting a woman. Again he defended himself, this time more successfully, receiving a verdict of 'not proven'.

Newspapers and Periodicals

NEWSPAPERS

Glasgow led the way in Scottish newspapers with its short-lived *Glasgow Courant* which commenced publication in November 1715. Printed by Donald Govan 'for R. T.', it was considerably smaller even than the tabloids of today, being no larger than a small quarto book. Each issue consisted of 12 pages, and it came out on Tuesdays, Thursdays and Saturdays. Regular readers paid 1d., others 1½d. After its fourth issue it changed its title to the *West Country Intelligence*; it ceased publication after 67 numbers in May 1716. Its contents were mainly extracts from London and foreign newspapers and from London correspondents, some letters, a few poems and very few items of local interest – a style followed by its successors till the end of the century.

Reading the papers. The scowling gentlemen are reading the Glasgow Chronicle *(Whig), the* Glasgow Courier *(Tory) and the independent* Herald*, while their colleague smiles over the pages of the* Looking Glass. *(Glasgow Looking Glass, 1825, Mitchell Library)*

There was a considerable gap between the *Courant* and the next Glasgow newspaper, the *Glasgow Journal*, which was begun in 1741 by Andrew Stalker (a staunch episcopalian) and printed by Robert Urie. It was published once a week and apparently satisfied the public taste, for it continued till 1845, when it was absorbed by the *Glasgow Chronicle*. For its first 37 years it had the field to itself. In 1840 its circulation was 239, a figure not unusual for the early press, when Stamp Duty, Paper Duty and Advertisement Tax made early newspapers very expensive. Its politics, where discernible, were liberal, and it specialised in agricultural news. In 1745 Stalker found himself in difficulties over how to report the Jacobite Rising of that year. As an episcopalian – and hence as someone whose sympathies might be supposed to lie with the Pretender – he decided that 'considering the situation of affairs I cannot with safety publish so as to please the generality of my readers', and ceased publication till the affair was over.

What was to become the city's newspaper of record began in 1783 as the *Glasgow Advertiser*, soon changing its name to the *Glasgow Herald*.

In 1778 the *Glasgow Mercury*, a neat little well-printed paper, began publication. Printed by Chapman & Duncan it came out once a week changing to twice weekly in 1794 and ceasing in 1796.

The *Glasgow Courier* started in 1791. Its politics were distinctly High Tory. It sided with the West Indian planters (many of whom were associated with the city) in their support of slavery, fought against Reform, dabbled in Orangeism and in everything was a rival to the liberal *Glasgow Chronicle*. It was published on Tuesdays, Thursdays and Saturdays till 1860, when its declining fortunes and influence reduced it to a weekly. At one time it was on competing terms with the *Herald* and had a select circulation among the middle and upper classes, but the spread of liberal opinions reduced that circulation (in 1850 it barely reached 700). Its first editor was the poet William Motherwell, followed in 1835 by James McQueen, a virulent Tory. It ceased publication in 1866.

After the end of the Napoleonic Wars, Whig opinions began to spread among the intellectuals and the middle class, and the *Glasgow Chronicle* was established in 1811 as their advocate and as a confirmed opponent of all that the *Glasgow Courier* represented. Like its rival, it came out on Tuesdays, Thursdays and Saturdays. After the demise of the *Glasgow Journal* in 1846

it took over many of its features, including copious reporting of agricultural activities, and was the first Glasgow paper to publish theatrical criticisms. Although its circulation reached the thousand mark, its support fell away and it expired in 1857.

The first *Glasgow Free Press* (1823, Wednesdays and Thursdays), like the *Glasgow Chronicle* and the *Scots Times*, advanced strong liberal opinions and for a while was running second to the *Herald* in circulation figures. It only lasted till 1835, however.

Set up shortly after the *Glasgow Free Press* in 1825, the bi-weekly *Scots Times* was, despite its name, very much a Glasgow newspaper. In keeping with its Whig principles, one of its main aims was to reform the oligarchic Town Council. Its circulation began to drop and it stopped in 1841 when its readership had fallen to little over 100.

The *Scottish Guardian* (1832–61, bi-weekly, Tuesdays and Fridays) was somewhat unusual in representing not a political but an ecclesiastical point of view, being the organ of the Free Church in the west of Scotland. In 1851 it had reached the respectable circulation of some 1,000 but ceased publication ten years later.

A variety of political publications of a periodical nature appeared in Glasgow between 1831 and 1864, all carrying the word *Reformer* somewhere in their titles. They were all the creations of Peter Mackenzie, a Glasgow lawyer and political journalist. When the various newspaper taxes were still being levied Mackenzie tried (usually successfully) to evade them by passing off his publications as weekly (or even monthly) periodicals. His *Loyal Reformers' Gazette* started in 1832 as a 16-page weekly. It is typical of his idiosyncratic approach to politics that when

William IV seemed to be flagging in his support for parliamentary reform Mackenzie removed the *Loyal* from the *Reformers' Gazette*'s masthead. In 1833, to further confound the Stamp Office, he changed it to a monthly 32-page publication, and in 1837 changed it again to a more conventional format as the weekly *Scotch Reformer's Gazette*. In 1854 it became the *Glasgow Reformer*. He was particularly popular with the working class, but was read with relish, if not always with agreement, by all classes. His aim, he boasted, was to 'ferret out and expose frauds, impositions and abuses of all kinds' and he was to be as outspoken against the orthodox Whigs as the Tories. Mackenzie claimed a circulation of some 2,000, but at 2d. per issue it later lost out to the new penny dailies and ceased in 1864.

The *Glasgow Argus* was started in 1833 as a bi-weekly for 'the educated radical' and, as such, exhibited a moderate degree of liberalism. It was especially associated with a group of local politicians known as 'The Clique' (the group included James Oswald one of the city's first reformed Members of Parliament) which, it was claimed, ruled Glasgow for some 12 years. In 1840 its circulation was about 800 but its too close association with the city's rulers worked against it and it ceased publication in 1847.

The *Liberator*, one of the city's most radical newspapers, began in 1833, among the first newspapers in Britain to be financed and supported by a trade union. It was said that for a while its circulation equalled that of the *Herald*, but despite its popularity it ceased publication in 1838; only two issues are extant in Glasgow, both in the People's Palace.

The *Glasgow Constitutional* (Wednesdays and Saturdays) began in 1835 and was intended to counterbalance the high Toryism of the *Courier*. It represented the interests of the city's growing middle class and the Established Church, publishing lengthy reports on all the ecclesiastical courts. It ceased in 1855.

In 1842 the weekly *Glasgow Citizen* was started up by Dr James Hedderwick. It attempted, with some success, to be both a newspaper and a literary journal; in 1851 its circulation was over 2,000. In 1864, when the *Evening Citizen* started, the *Glasgow Citizen* changed its name to the *Weekly Citizen* and its contents to the purely literary. Its stable-mate, the *Evening Citizen*, was the city's first fid. evening paper and set out to be a family publication with a mildly Unionist tinge. It became known as the churchgoer's paper, for its Saturday edition listed forthcoming services in the city churches, as well as supplying articles and news stories on ecclesiastical matters. Of the three Glasgow evening newspapers (the other two being the *News* and the *Times*), it had the smallest circulation. From 1914 to 1924 it was known as the *Glasgow Citizen* – at one time or another all three evening papers had 'Glasgow' in their titles, but they all dropped it when their circulation reached beyond the city boundaries. It ceased publication in 1974.

The *North British Daily Mail* (1847) marked the beginning of a new epoch in Glasgow newspaper publishing. Under its main proprietor, Sir Charles Cameron, it was the first penny daily in the city. It espoused the cause of popular liberalism, it reported in detail the city's many trade union activities, it made a feature of its telegraphic news and local events coverage, and it published 'Special Commissions' (as it called them), mainly exposures of public scandals such as baby farming, shebeens and prostitution. Despite its radical approach it had many readers amongst the middle classes, and its large, daily circulation made it popular with advertisers. It was sold to Lord Northcliffe in 1901, changing its name first to the *Glasgow Daily Mail* and then to the *Daily Record and Mail*.

The *Glasgow Sentinel* started in 1850 (there had been two earlier *Glasgow Sentinels* – one which ran from 1809 to 1811 and apparently amalgamated with the *Glasgow Chronicle*, and another even more obscure one which was published 1821–23). It gave full accounts of labour matters and was popular amongst the 'operative class'. In 1866 it became the *Glasgow Sentinel and Journal of Industrial Interests*, and ceased in 1877.

In 1873 the *Glasgow News* was set up as a popular Tory daily, financially supported by James Baird, the wealthy iron and coal-master. It achieved some success, with a circulation of about 12,000, but the withdrawal of Baird's support in 1879 brought financial problems. It was rescued by the shipbuilder William Pearce, became the *Scottish News* in 1886, and expired two years later.

The *Evening Times* began life in 1876 as an evening daily. Of the city's three evening newspapers it generally has had the biggest circulation and is the only one which survived into the post-war era. Like the *Herald* it is still printed and published by George Outram & Co Ltd (formerly a subsidiary of the Lonhro conglomerate) but has recently been bought over by the management under the title of Caledonian Newspaper Publishing. For the last 10 or 15 years it has made a name as a crusading organ, particularly in connection with the social and economic conditions of the city and its surroundings. A short time ago it stopped publishing its regular Saturday edition, replacing it with a tabloid magazine, *Weekly Times*.

The *Glasgow Observer* (1885) could

be regarded as the city's Roman Catholic newspaper of record. In 1895 it changed to the *Glasgow Observer and Catholic Herald*, and eventually lost its city connection in 1939 when it became the *Scottish Catholic Herald*. There was an earlier Roman Catholic organ, the *Glasgow Free Press* (2) (1851). At that time the Irish RC influence in the city was struggling against the native Scottish priesthood, and the *Free Press* vigorously, not to say vehemently, took the part – political as well as ecclesiastical – of the Irish immigrants in the city. It eventually became so outspoken that in 1868 it was closed down in face of condemnation from Rome.

The *Daily Record & Mail* (½d., morning daily) dates from 1901 when Northcliffe took over the *North British Daily Mail*, changing its name first to the *Glasgow Daily Mail*, then to the *Daily Record & Mail*. It was said to be the first Scottish newspaper to use pictures. Its political inclinations moved to the right and by the 1920s it was unequivocally a Unionist paper. It dropped the *Daily Mail* from its masthead in 1954.

More a political journal than a proper newspaper, the *Forward* was a unique Glasgow phenomenon. Launched in 1906 by Tom Johnston, it was ostensibly the Scottish ILP's house journal, but it soon became a genuinely independent and non-sectarian forum for all and any left-of-centre writer. It had its own idiosyncrasies – no alcohol adverts, no gambling news – but its openness and freshness soon made it a commercial success; its pre-First World War circulation reached 10,000. Most of the major figures of the British left appeared in its pages, from Keir Hardie and John Maclean to H. G. Wells and George Bernard Shaw. It was banned for a month in 1915 when it attempted to give an exact account of the tumult roused in Lloyd

George's St Andrew's Halls audience when he attempted to speak against the activities of the Clyde Workers Committee. By the 1930s it was beginning to suffer from the disaffiliation of the ILP from the Labour Party, its circulation was dropping and it was struggling financially. In 1933 Tom Johnston passed over the editorship to Emrys Hughes. There was an abortive move to hand control to the *Daily Herald*, but, after struggling through the war years, it left Glasgow for London in 1956 and became absorbed into the *Socialist Commentary*.

In 1915 the *Evening News* was launched as the organ of the Conservative Party in the west of Scotland. Its predecessors were the *Glasgow Evening Press* (1866), the *Evening Star* (1875), the *Glasgow Evening News* (1888) and the *Glasgow News* (1905) – an excellent example of the extreme volatility of newspaper publishing in 19th-century Glasgow. It was one of the first UK newspapers to publish a special edition giving football results. Of the triumvirate of the city's evening papers (*Citizen, News* and *Times* as they were popularly known) it was the first to succumb after the Second World War, in 1957.

The *Bulletin* was launched as a morning newspaper in 1915. In 1923 it amalgamated with the *Scots Pictorial* and in so doing became a unique Glasgow newspaper. The *Scots Pictorial* (started in 1897) had been a 'society' periodical and was lavishly illustrated with photographs of society weddings, social functions, and so on. After the 1923 amalgamation, the *Bulletin & Scots Pictorial* continued and expanded this theme. Its front, back and centre pages were entirely given over to news photographs, which now included not only the activities of the Scottish middle and upper classes but many pictorial

aspects of daily life. In its heyday it was thought of, somewhat pejoratively, as a woman's newspaper (it included many special features on fashion, home care, children and cookery); it is now regarded as an excellent illustrated source for the second quarter of the 20th century. It ceased publication in 1960, but in 1980 its name and, for a while its masthead, were taken over by Glasgow District Council for its periodical news sheet.

During the period of the General Strike six Glasgow newspapers (the *Glasgow Herald, Daily Record, Bulletin, Glasgow Evening News, Evening Times* and *Citizen*) published several issues of a joint Emergency Press during May 1926.

In 1750 and in 1800 Glasgow had two newspapers, and in 1850, five. By 1900 there were seven (plus four weekly editions of daily papers and seven local suburban papers). In 1950 there were six, with two suburban papers, and by 1990 the total was down to three: two morning newspapers – the *Daily Record* (circulation *c.*760,000, distributed throughout Scotland, Mirror Group Newspapers) and the *Herald* (circulation *c.*122,000, Caledonian Newspaper Publishing) – and one evening, the *Evening Times* (circulation 164,000, a stable-mate of the *Herald*). It is probably no coincidence that the circulation efforts of all three are now reaching out well beyond the city boundaries.

As well as the general Glasgow newspapers, there were also many suburban newspapers which appeared roughly between the 1870s and the First World War, when the city became temporarily ringed by a number of small, self-governing suburban burghs. The following is a list of the longer-lasting of them (omitting their many name-changes and amalgamations):

Rutherglen Reformer, 1875–77
Partick Observer, 1876–78
Partick & Maryhill Express, 1881–85
Govan Press, 1885–1983
Pollokshaws News, 1885–1940
Tollcross Advertiser, 1885–86
Parkhead, Shettleston & Tollcross
Advertiser, 1892–96
Partick Star, 1892–1901
St Rollox & Springburn Express,
1892–1909
Glasgow Eastern Standard, 1923–61

The only one of note amongst these is the *Glasgow Eastern Standard*, begun by John Wheatley, Labour MP and Cabinet Member, and a fairly wealthy printer/publisher in Shettleston. The *Standard* continued to show his influence throughout its existence in its excellent reporting of local civic affairs and its consistent left-of-centre position.

THE HERALD

The Glasgow newspaper generally accepted as the city's paper of record is now known as *The Herald* and ranks as the oldest national newspaper in the English-speaking world (*The Times* is two years younger, *The Scotsman*, 33 years younger). It was first published in January 1783 as *The Advertiser*, a rival to the *Glasgow Journal* (1729–1845). At first its political stance was definitely right of centre and it soon became the valued voice of the Glasgow businessman; it has now distanced itself leftwards somewhat from its Conservative-Unionist roots. Until 1793 it appeared weekly, thereafter every Monday and Friday. Its first owner and editor was John Mennons (1747–1818), an Edinburgh printer who came to Glasgow in 1782. By 1802 he had given up the editorship and disposed of his financial interest in the paper. One of the new partners, Dr James McNayr, who acted as editor for only two months, left his mark by changing the newspaper's name to *The Glasgow Herald and Advertiser* in 1802 (in 1804 it became the *Glasgow Herald*, in 1834 *The Glasgow Herald*).

The next editor was Samuel Hunter (*d*.1839) an unsuccessful army surgeon who became the paper's best-remembered editor. His corpulent figure (he weighed 18 stone) was found at every civic or social function in the city. He was a vehement supporter of the Tory party, and demonstrated his views by forming the Glasgow Volunteer Sharpshooters (with himself as Colonel Commander) during the height of the Radical scare in the 1820s. He retired in 1836 and the partners appointed George Outram (1805–56), an Edinburgh advocate, as his successor. When he joined the partnership (as almost all the editors did) it assumed the well-known name of George Outram & Co.

By this time *The Herald* was well on the way to becoming the most substantial newspaper in the west of Scotland, with a circulation of some 3,500. In 1855, when the hated Stamp Duty was withdrawn, it began to publish a third issue on Wednesdays and reduced its price to 3d. In 1854 Outram's assistant editor, James Pagan (1811–70), took over the editorship to become the paper's first professional journalist to occupy that position. He was caught on the hop, however, by the *North British Daily Mail* which had for some time been a thorn in *The Herald*'s side. In 1858 *The Herald* began making preparations to come out daily at 2d. On the very first day of 1859 the *Mail*, without warning, changed its price to 1d. and *The Herald* was forced to follow suit. That same year the paper vacated its premises in Spreull's Court (off the Trongate) and moved to St Vincent Place. Ten years later it moved to Buchanan St.

Pagan was succeeded by William Jack, Professor of Natural Philosophy at Owen's University, Manchester. *The Herald's* circulation then stood at over 27,000 and his inability to materially increase it compounded with a drop in the annual profits, caused his resignation in 1875. During the time of his successor, J. H. Stoddard, the partnership started up an evening newspaper in 1876, the *Evening Times*, in response to the appearance of the weekly *Citizen*. The *Times* (selling at ½d.) was an immediate success, and its folksy approach to the news of the day soon gave it a circulation of 50,000.

All copies of the early files of *The Glasgow Herald* having disappeared, the date of its first issue was wrongly taken to be 1782, and its centenary was accordingly celebrated one year too early in 1882.

In 1888 Charles G. Russell took over as editor, and during his term of office the partnership changed to a private limited company. Later, in 1920, it became a public company. From 1893 to 1899 the rear of the Buchanan St building, which overlooked Mitchell St, underwent a major reconstruction in the design of which the young Charles Rennie Mackintosh, then an assistant with Honeyman & Keppie, Glasgow architects, played an important part. He was responsible for the curious slender octagonal tower, and he also designed several pieces of office furniture. It was said to have proved so unsuitable

and uncomfortable that over the years most of it quietly disappeared. The tower itself served for a while as a carrier-pigeon post, and later as a fire-watching post during the Second World War.

At the end of 1901 *The Herald* began to produce its Trade Review (originally as an eight-page supplement), in which it surveyed the year's work in the engineering trades. In 1907 it became a separate annual magazine which soon enjoyed a national, even international, reputation for its coverage of world shipbuilding activities. It is also worthy of note for the series of spectacular colourful pictures which decorated its front covers.

William Wallace followed Russell as editor and was succeeded in turn (after a short English interregnum) by Sir Robert Bruce in 1917 whose particular expertise lay in the field of political reporting. Under the next editor, Sir William B. Robieson, the paper continued to speak its mind in political matters. It regularly denounced the policy of appeasing Hitler and the editor was summoned down to London to be disciplined by a member of the Cabinet for his paper's intransigence – a vain hope.

Under his successor, James Holburn (Sir William had retired in 1958) *The Herald* shook off the last relic of its past – in October 1958 it began to display news articles on its front page, hitherto devoted to public announcements, advertisements and notices of births, marriages and deaths.

In the autumn of 1964 George Outram & Co became involved in a takeover battle between Hugh Fraser (later Lord Fraser of Allander) and Lord Thomson of Fleet (William Thomson) for both *The Herald* and its sister-paper, the *Evening Times*. After a long drawn-out struggle SUITs (Scottish and Universal Investments, which represented the Fraser interest) was successful and took control of the two newspapers at the end of 1969. After ten years the papers became part of the Lonhro empire which was eventually forced to put them on the market in 1992. Led by its managing director and its editor, Arnold Kemp, a successful bid of £74 million was made by the management under the name of Caledonian Newspaper Publishing. The new owners' first actions were to redesign the paper's appearance and to emphasise its new role as a national newspaper by changing its name from the *Glasgow Herald* to *The Herald*.

PERIODICALS

During the last part of the 18th century and for most of the 19th, a large and ever changing number of periodicals were published in Glasgow. The earliest of note was probably the *Glasgow Magazine and Review*. It ran for only two years (a common occurrence) from 1783 to 1784 and such was its popularity, even if short-lived, that it was eventually republished as a single volume of some 500 pages. Its verbose title page proclaimed that it covered the arts, sciences, entertainment, literature, history, poetry, biography, amusements, politics and manners, a prescient list of topics for most succeeding Glasgow magazines.

Several radical periodicals appeared in the 1820s and 1830s, none long-lived. Just before the famous Radical Rising of 1820, the *Spirit of the Union* came out in 11 weekly parts in 1819 and 1820. Its final issue carried an announcement why it was the last – the publisher had been 'apprehended on Monday last on a warrant from the Sheriff-Substitute for an alleged contempt of court'. In 1833 the *Agitator* argued in five issues for parliamentary reform, and the *Chartist Circular* (1839–42), published by the Universal Suffrage Central Committee for Scotland, continued the struggle between 1839 and 1842. The *Herald to the Trades Advocate* came out 1830–31 with the aim of providing 'a newspaper to air just grievances, to run until enough money to publish the *Trades' Advocate*' had been received – it never was!

The *Glasgow Looking Glass*, 1825–26, was unique amongst the city's periodicals. It was a lavishly illustrated satirical magazine published fortnightly in the form of a four-page lithographically produced broadsheet. It was entirely the work of an English draughtsman, William Heath (1795–1840), who had come north to Glasgow to paint some large panoramas, then very popular. Working with John Watson, an early Glasgow lithographic printer, he published 19 issues of the *Looking Glass* (it became the *Northern Looking Glass* after the fifth issue). In its pages he depicted items of current news (Scottish, English and European) along with graphic illustrations of the manners, fashions, politics and eccentricities of all levels of Glasgow society. Many of his illustrations give first-hand evidence of the appearance of the Glasgow of his day – and probably the best known of these is his lively depiction of the Glasgow Fair at the foot of the Saltmarket as seen from the roof of the Justiciary Building. Others show douce Glasgow folk disporting themselves in the waters of the Clyde supported by 'Macintosh's Waterproof Life Preservers', a prophetic view of birds dropping dead from the smoke-polluted skies above George Square, and vivid scenes of dissipation in the city streets after Hogmanay. The clever and discriminating eye he cast on Glasgow and its people may not have endeared him to the citizens; he left for London in 1826.

The latter half of the 19th century was particularly rich in short-lived periodicals – the *Bee*, *Sphinx*, *Chiel*, *Traveller*, *Detective*, *Prompter* and *St Mungo* were only a few of those which appeared. They all had illustrated jokes, gossipy notes (now quite unintelligible), romantic serials, political cartoons, reviews of pantomimes and plays and too much bad verse. As in so many other spheres, the First World War marked the demise of the local periodical. Efforts at resurrection seem to have been doomed – the *Glasgow Review* (1964) lasted ten years, the *Glasgow Magazine* (1982), only three.

Only one periodical developed any staying power. This was the *Bailie*, which ran from 1872 to 1926. Its coverage differed little from its ephemeral rivals but it was well written and apparently well sourced. In addition, it carried a great deal of commercial gossip and provided excellent coverage of the city's art world. Its chief claim to fame nowadays is its series *The Men You Know*. Each week some prominent Glaswegian was written up and illustrated by a full-page portrait. Although by today's standards these articles appear wordy and hagiographical, they contain useful and often unique accounts of well over 2,000 Glasgow personalities, at a time when the city was at its height – churchmen, academics, merchants, manufacturers, artists, politicians – making it an indispensable source for Glasgow biography.

Orange Order

The Orange Order, which began in Ireland at the end of the 18th century as an organisation of Irish Protestants, was introduced into Scotland before the beginning of the 19th century, and the second biggest lodge was set up in Glasgow by 1807. The oldest Glasgow lodge still in existence is said to be the 1813 Brunswick L.O.L. 106. An account of 1821 speaks of the city's three Orange Lodges, with their swords, emblems, flags and music, passing Glasgow Cross. By 1830 the number of Glasgow lodges had grown to seven, mostly in the Calton district. Processions in 1822 presented the threat of serious trouble and the following year the Glasgow magistrates

banned such processions, a ban not lifted till 1872. In 1836 the whole Order came into disrepute on account of various disturbances and was dissolved by Parliament. Despite the ban, William Motherwell, poet and editor of the strongly Tory *Glasgow Courier*, who had been appointed District Master of the Glasgow lodges in 1833, continued in office. It is reported that he had considerable trouble in exercising control over the members.

It has been suggested that in 1850 some Clydeside shipyard workers were sent over to Belfast for training and that on their return they reintroduced the Order into Glasgow. At any rate, the first Glasgow parade for many years (commonly called the Orange Walk) was held in 1872, when some 1,500 persons took part, accompanied by eight bands. The lack of trouble was supposed to be the result of banning 'party' tunes! From this period onwards, Glasgow became the focal point for Scottish Orangeism and of the 90,000 or so British members of the Orange Order, 15,000 were to be found in the city. Many of the city's small businessmen were attracted to the Order in the latter half of the 19th century and a strong link developed between the Order and the 'conservative-minded working class'.

By this time the lodge in Partick was reckoned to be the largest in Scotland, which may have been the reason why the burgh was the scene of serious sectarian riots in 1872. The local Roman Catholic community determined to celebrate the centenary of the Irish patriot, Daniel O'Connell, with a procession to the Glasgow Green. A riot developed before the procession had left Partick, when fighting broke out between those in the procession and the onlookers. The disturbance was brought under control by the police but the rioting began again the next day. The Riot Act was read, the

Volunteers were called out and order was restored, but extensive damage was caused to property and 60 people were arrested.

The Liberal Party's support for Irish Home Rule in the 1880s brought about a political alliance between the Glasgow lodges and the Glasgow Conservatives, an alliance which lasted till after the First World War. The period from the 1920s to the 1930s was marked by continued disturbances at the annual 'Walks' – physical assaults (it was said that the poles supporting the colourful lodge banners had a secondary use) and stone-throwing. They often attracted considerable support – the crowd at the 1925 walk in Shettleston was estimated to have reached 40,000 persons.

After the Second World War the Order in Glasgow, as elsewhere, found that its industrial base in the traditional working-class districts such as Govan and Calton had been largely eroded, and that although new lodges were appearing in the new peripheral housing schemes (Easterhouse, Castlemilk and Drumchapel), its old political influence in the city had waned and that its purpose was now primarily a social one. Significant of its decline was the recent sale of its hall in Cathedral St (built in 1914) to a Christian sect.

Parks

Like most Scottish burghs early Glasgow had around and within its boundaries stretches of land which belonged to the community and not to individuals. Their primary purpose was the pasturing of cattle and for the general uses of the burgesses.

Glasgow's common land extended from Springburn in the north down to the Clyde and from the Camlachie Burn in the east to St Enoch's Church in the west. In the 16th and early 17th centuries Glasgow Town Council regularly found itself in financial difficulties and in order to extricate itself began to sell off large parts of its common land, including parts which are now known as Glasgow Green. Then, in the late 17th and 18th centuries it began to buy back, piecemeal, some of what it had earlier sold, almost all of these repurchases being parts of what is now Glasgow Green. It was in this way that Glasgow's first and most famous public park came into being. It lies on the north bank of the Clyde, running east from the foot of the Saltmarket in a broad strip bounded on the north by the erstwhile village of Calton towards Bridgeton. In 1730 it amounted to 59 acres which was increased by purchase to 117 acres in 1810; in 1894 it finally reached 136 acres, its present size. Its unique historic position gives it a special place in the story of the city's open spaces.

The middle of the 19th century saw the start of a rapid increase in the number of the city's parks, an increase which was to continue up to the First World War, by which time 16 public parks had been opened. This trend was not peculiar to Glasgow, for as early as 1833 a Parliamentary Select Committee on Public Walks had been set up 'to consider the best means of securing Open Spaces in the Vicinity of populous Towns', and in 1859 the Recreation Grounds Act passed into the Statute Book. But the city's enthusiasm for setting up parks was such that eventually it could claim to have more public open spaces per head of population than any other town or city in the United Kingdom. Quality as well as quantity has always been represented: when figures for the number of blooms in the Royal Parks of Paris were published, it was found that a single Glasgow park had more flowers than all the Paris parks added together.

Glasgow's first step was in 1852 when the Town Council made the bold move of creating a park *de novo*. Despite strong opposition, some of which arose from the feeling that a great deal of money was being spent on the affluent west end at the expense of the east end and its historic Glasgow Green, the Council purchased 66 acres of land lying on the east side of the Kelvin a short distance above its entering the Clyde. The ground, which had cost over £77,000, was laid out following designs of Sir Joseph Paxton, and was named the West End Park. When Glasgow University moved in 1870 to Gilmorehill, a site overlooking the west bank of the Kelvin, the Council took the opportunity of extending the West End Park (now better known as Kelvingrove Park) over the river, increasing its size to 73 acres.

The park was the site of three of Glasgow's most prestigious exhibitions – the 1888 International Exhibition, the 1901 International Exhibition and the 1911 Scottish National Exhibition. The only prominent survivor from these is the Kelvingrove Art Galleries and Museum, situated on the south side of the park and built from the profits of the 1888 International Exhibition.

Kelvingrove Park probably has more interesting monuments than any of the other Glasgow parks. The Stewart Memorial Fountain, an elaborately symbolic piece, was erected in 1872 to commemorate the energetic activities of Lord Provost Robert Stewart of Murdostoun, who was responsible, against strong opposition, for the passing of the Loch Katrine Act which secured for the rapidly growing city an almost inexhaustible supply of pure water. There are also commemorative statues to Lord Lister (antiseptics and chloroform), Lord Kelvin (University professor and inventor) and Thomas Carlyle. The bridge over the Kelvin has remarkable groups of iron statuary, and on the skyline of the eastern heights is a magnificent monument to Lord Roberts of Kandahar. On the steeply sloping right bank can be found the Sunlight Cottages by James Miller, erected as part of the 1901 Exhibition; they are copies of workers' dwellings at Port Sunlight. On 20 April 1918, at the end of Kelvin Way, near University Avenue, there was planted the Suffrage Oak to celebrate the granting of parliamentary franchise to women.

Because of its hilly nature Kelvingrove Park has always been ill-suited for recreational purposes and has few areas devoted to athletic pursuits, which are located at the flat south-east corner. However, with its numerous winding walks and ornamental flower-beds it is an excellent example of a typical Victorian park landscape. Its setting adds considerably to its charms for it is surrounded by a ring of prominent buildings, all with architectural pretensions – the Art Galleries on the south, Glasgow University to the north, and the residential area of Park Circus to the east – which help to create a piece of urban landscape with few equals in the United Kingdom.

It has one more claim to fame, being commonly thought of as the locus of the well-known Scottish song, 'Will ye gang to Kelvingrove, bonnie lassie O?'. Unfortunately, the song actually refers to the Kelvin as it flows past the Botanic Gardens, slightly to the north.

Queen's Park

The city south of the Clyde was expanding and the Corporation began to look for a suitable site for a public park in this area. They soon found one in the lands of Pathhead Farm, and in 1857 bought its 143 acres for £30,000. Once again there was strong opposition, this time because the grounds were two miles beyond the city boundary (a position the new park retained for 30 years), and the project only went ahead on the casting vote of the Lord Provost. Once again Paxton was asked to advise on the layout, and once again much of the work in preparing the site was carried out by the unemployed. The park was formally opened in September 1862; despite being established in the heyday of the Victorian period, its name, Queen's Park, commemorates an earlier queen, Queen Mary, and her defeat at the Battle of Langside (1568) on the southern edge of the park.

The park's highest point, marked by an artificial mound, is 209ft above sea-level and affords a series of unsurpassed views which include the Kilpatrick and Campsie Hills, the Vale of Clyde as far as Lanark, the Cathkin Braes, Neilston Pad, Gleniffer Braes, Ballygeich, the Mearns muirs and Ben Lomond. Close to the summit is an ancient earthwork. When the extension of the city's boundaries brought it inside Glasgow, the adjoining Camphill estate was bought and added in 1894. This brought within the park Camphill House which was converted to a museum in 1896. (It is now a Museum of Costume.) Of all the Glasgow parks it is said to enjoy the purest and freshest air, for the prevailing south-westerly winds bring to it none of the smoke and grime of the city.

Alexandra Park

Despite the existence of the venerable Glasgow Green in the east end it was still felt that the west and south were being favoured, and so in 1869 the City Improvement Trust (a body concerned with the removal of the central slums) purchased some 30 acres in the north-east of the city and handed them over to the Corporation for a park; to it Alexander Dennistoun of Golfhill (after whom the district of Dennistoun was named) gifted an additional five acres which provided its principal entrance from Alexandra Parade. Once again the work of laying out the park was performed by 'unemployed starving artisans and labourers'.

Considerable difficulty was experienced in persuading trees and shrubs to flourish because of the high level of industrial pollution from the surrounding industrial sites, particularly the Blochairn Iron Works close by. Much of the early plantings of poplars and willows died out in less than 25 years, while in the more exposed parts only hardy thorn trees could be coaxed into growing – even the wire of the fences had to be replaced more often than in any other park!

Near the main entrance is a large, elaborate cast-iron fountain, made by Walter Macfarlane's Saracen Foundry for the 1901 International Exhibition. Its base has four female figures representing Literature, Science, Commerce and Art. In its early days it had an 18-hole golf course (later reduced to nine), and its other amenities included a model yacht pond – at one time no Glasgow park was complete unless it could boast (1) a bandstand, and (2) a model yacht pond complete with a large boathouse in which to store the yachts.

Rutherglen Park

The next addition to the city's open spaces was Cathkin Braes Park – the first of several examples of generous gifts from benefactors which Glasgow has been fortunate to receive. In 1846 two brothers Dick began to use gutta-percha or rubber in place of leather for the soles of boots and shoes and in the process achieved a considerable fortune. In 1886 James Dick bought Cathkin Braes, a piece of ground high above the southern edge of the Clyde Valley, and gifted it to the city – for a while it was known familiarly as the 'Gutty

Park'. It lies 1fi miles south of Rutherglen, about 5fi miles from the city centre and was in those days four miles outside the city boundaries. He made two stipulations, both somewhat unusual for the time, that 'as far as possible the natural features and configurations of the ground should be maintained and preserved' and that 'the land shall not be used for football, cricket and other similar games and sports'.

Extending to 72 acres, its highest point, Queen Mary's Seat, is 300ft above sea-level, affording a magnificent view which takes in Arthur's Seat and the Pentland Hills to the east, Goatfell on Arran to the south and Ben Lomond, Ben Ledi and the Cobbler to the north.

Maxwell Park

As the city's rapid expansion at the turn of the century continued, several established parks from outside the boundaries came into the care of the city. Maxwell Park (Glencairn Rd) was one such. Having been gifted to the Burgh of Pollokshields by Sir John Stirling Maxwell in 1878, it came into the city in 1891. Occupying only 21 acres it is one of the smallest of the city parks, and its attractions include a small boating pond and a peculiar white fountain erected in 1907 in memory of John Hamilton who shot game there when the park was little more than a bog. Constructed in Carrera stoneware it has suffered the usual dilapidation and vandalism which such structures usually endure.

Victoria Park

Victoria Park, although given to the burgh of Partick in 1886–87 by Gordon Oswald of Scotstoun, was to all intents and purposes a Glasgow park; it became one officially in 1912 when Partick was brought within the city boundaries.

Apart from its horticultural features it is famous for its Fossil Grove. When a path was being dug across a disused whinstone quarry within the park area, a group of about ten fossilised tree stumps (the largest over 3ft in diameter) was discovered. Identified as belonging to the Coal Measures of 330 million years ago, they are now projected by a glass-roofed museum building.

The fact that Victoria was one of the very few Glasgow parks to have a rugby pitch and that it once had a shinty pitch is a fairly clear indication of the city's sporting inclinations!

The route of the northern access road to the Clyde Tunnel removed a sizeable part of the eastern end of the park – unlike the successful campaigns against similar depredations which threatened the Green, a vigorous campaign to save Victoria Park came to nothing.

Botanic Gardens

In 1891 the Botanic Gardens (Great Western Rd) was opened as a park. Like the Glasgow Green it pre-dates the ordinary city parks; its original purpose was to provide medicinal plants for Glasgow University (*see* BOTANIC GARDENS).

Springburn and Ruchill Parks

Eventually the Council's attention returned to the north side of Glasgow when Springburn Park (Balgrayhill Rd) and Ruchill Park (Bilsland Dr) were both opened in 1892 within a couple of miles of each other. Their height and exposed position are not conducive to abundant floral displays, but Springburn's highest point of 351ft, as well as making it the highest of all the parks within the city boundaries, has made it a useful weather station since 1896.

Ruchill has the distinction of having a large artificial hill at its summit, constructed from 24,000 cart-loads of material excavated from the foundations of the nearby Ruchill Hospital, and given the nickname 'Ben Whitton' after the Director of Parks at the time.

Bellahouston Park

Bellahouston Park (Paisley Rd West), purchased in 1895, is chiefly remembered for being the site of the Empire Exhibition of 1938. Of the many exhibition buildings which filled the park the only remaining one is the erstwhile Palace of Art, now used mainly as an educational centre. It also houses the Bellahouston Sports Centre, one of the largest of the city's indoor sports complexes.

Govanhill Park

Govanhill Park, opened in 1896, has the unenviable fame of having cost over £3,000 for each of its four acres!

Tollcross Park

The industrial east end of the city, despite the Green to the south and Alexandra Park to the north, still had no convenient central open space until the mansion and grounds of Tollcross House, designed by David Bryce in 1848, were purchased in 1896 from Colin Dunlop, ironmaster, for £29,000 and converted into Tollcross Park (Wellshot Rd). Despite having had the heaviest deposit of soot of any Glasgow park, it boasts a wealth of timber including many magnificent specimens of chestnuts, elms and beeches.

Rouken Glen

In 1906 another generous donation to Glasgow when Lord Rowallan gave to the city the magnificent estate of Rouken Glen. Various subsequent additions increased the original area to 227 acres, making it the city's biggest park. With its large boating pond, its waterfalls, wooded glen, fine trees and walled garden (and, some might say, its absence of football pitches, bowling-greens and tennis courts!), it became one of the city's most attractive and popular parks, particularly as a venue for many summer Sunday School trips. Its position outside Glasgow's southern boundaries unfortunately became a cause for discussion between Glasgow District (which insisted that its maintenance costs were too great) and Eastwood District (in which the park lies). The outcome was that in 1984 the park was transferred into the ownership of Eastwood on a 125-year lease.

Elder Park

The city's second wave of expansion in 1912 brought in the Elder Park which had been gifted in 1885 to the Burgh of Govan by Mrs Elder whose family owned the famous Govan Fairfield's Shipyard. In the heyday of the burgh's independence it was surrounded by the Town Hall, the Library, the Cottage Hospital and the High School of Govan. As befits its shipbuilding background, it has a large model yacht pond as well as a fountain to the memory of the men who died when the submarine *K 35* sank in the Gareloch.

Balloch Castle

In 1906 the Corporation bought Balloch Castle and its policies (200 acres) on the south-east side of Loch Lomond, part of which consisted of parkland and gardens sloping down to the edge of the water. Special powers had to be obtained by the Corporation before this land, lying outside the city's boundaries, could be acquired on behalf of the citizens. Despite its beautiful setting, little use is now made of its amenities, possibly because most of today's tourists prefer to pass further up the loch in order to admire the Highland scenery at its northern end.

Linn, Dawsholm and King's Park

Between the wars the city acquired the ownership of the Linn (1919), Dawsholm (1921) and King's Park (1930). These were all good examples of the traditional type of open space, with contrasting woodlands and formal gardens, although both the Linn and Dawsholm broke new ground with their extensive nature-trails, the former as early as 1965. King's Park includes Aikenhead House, built in 1806, possibly from a design by David Hamilton. In 1986 it was divided into several residential flats. A change of direction was apparent in other acquisitions of this period such as Hogganfield Loch, Lethamhill Golf Course and Knightswood Park, for here the emphasis was on the provision of facilities for active recreation such as boating, tennis, bowling, golf, pitch and putt, and football. In addition, many other smaller spaces, too numerous to mention individually, were developed for amenity and recreational purposes.

Pollok Country Park

After the 1930s the city's urgent need for housing land made sure that additions to the city's open spaces were few in number and small in size. A notable exception to this was in 1967 when Mrs Anne Maxwell Macdonald generously gifted to the city a magnificently laid-out piece of land lying a little to the south of the river, a piece of land which has become without doubt the city's greatest park, Pollok Park. This land, the Pollok Estate, which had been in the possession of the Maxwells of Pollok from an early period, comprised some 360 acres of natural woodlands, farmlands and formal gardens. Pollok House itself, designed by William Adam in 1752, still has much of its original furnishings and decorations, and contains a superb art collection, particularly rich in paintings of the Spanish School. In addition, the park contains the prize-winning building which houses the world-famous Burrell Collection.

PARKS	Acquired	Acres	PARKS	Acquired	Acres
Alexandra	1866	104	Household Gardens	1950	61
Auldhouse	1918	19	Kelvingrove	1852	85
Barlanark	1954	7	King's	1930	98
Bellahouston	1895	175	Knightswood	1929	142
Blairtumock	1964	2	Linn	1919	212
Botanic Gardens	1891	44	Lochair	1967	15
Cardonald	1928	7	Lochlomond	1915	200
Castlemilk	1961	4	Maryhill	1922	23
Cathkin Braes	1886	72	Maxwell	1891	21
Cowlairs	1920	35	Milton	1954	5
Cranhill	1957	26	Newlands	1913	14
Croftcroighn	1959	9	Plantation	1912	3
Cross	1911	5	Pollok	1967	361
Dawsholm	1921	72	Queen's	1862	148
Dowanhill	1904	2	Richmond	1897	44
Drumchapel	1961	11	Ross Hall	1948	33
Elder	1912	35	Rouken Glen	1906	227
Glasgow Green	1852	85	Ruchill	1892	52
Glenconnar	1914	14	Springburn	1892	75
Greenfield	1950	53	Titwood	1895	14
Govanhill	1896	4	Toryglen	1965	41
Hogganfield	1920	124	Victoria	1912	58

RECREATION GROUNDS	Acquired	Acres	RECREATION GROUNDS	Acquired	Acres
Barlia Drive	1965	46	Penilee	1947	7
Dalmarnock	1947	23	Petershill	1948	14
Holmlea	1914	4	Smeaton St	1928	5
King George's Field	1937	34	South Pollok	1950	46
Langlands Rd	1935	3	Temple	1925	14
Lister St	1912	1	Westhorn	1935	20
Newfield Square	1955	3	Yoker	1926	2

BOTANIC GARDENS

When Glasgow University still occupied its old site on the east side of the High Street it had a small patch of ground, the Physic Garden, where various medicinal plants were cultivated. In 1818 a chair of botany was instituted, the first professor being William Hooker – later the celebrated Sir William Hooker, Director of Kew Gardens. Even before the increased requirements brought about by the new chair, it had proved impossible for the small garden to supply all the University's botanical needs, so in 1816 Thomas Hopkirk, an amateur botanist, formed a society to set up a proper botanic garden in Glasgow. With the financial support of the University and many wealthy citizens, about eight acres of land at Sandyford (located at the west end of Sauchiehall Street and Dumbarton Road) was purchased and laid out as a botanic garden in 1817. In 1819 the society was incorporated as the Royal Botanic Society of Glasgow and in the course of the next 20 years, largely through the exertions of Professor Hooker, the garden became a useful and popular institution with a valuable collection of plants.

The westward tide of the city's population finally forced it to forsake this site and move elsewhere. A fine piece of rising ground of 22 acres extent, lying between Great Western Road and the south bank of the Kelvin, was purchased in 1839, and by 1842 was opened as the new Botanic Gardens. Access was free to members of the Institution and their friends – the ordinary public was admitted on certain days on payment of 1d.

In 1871 an agreement was entered into by the Society with John Kibble of Coulport, Loch Long, whereby that gentleman's vast glass conservatory was removed from his grounds and re-erected in the Garden. It soon became clear that the burden of maintaining an area three times the size of the old ground was straining the Institution's finances, and it arranged a loan of £25,000 from the Corporation. Part of this loan was used to buy out Kibble's 21-year lease on Kibble Palace (as it was now known) and to return it to its original use as a conservatory. (While under Kibble's control it had been extensively used as a venue for all kinds of social and musical events.) Unfortunately, the Society's financial problems continued to grow until eventually it was forced into bankruptcy, and the Corporation, as the major creditor, took possession of the

Gardens and the Palace in 1887. Four years later, when the independent burgh of Hillhead (in which the Botanic Gardens were located) was annexed by Glasgow, the property was formally conveyed to the Parks Trustees as a public park.

There are many other ranges of hot-houses in the park which between them provide a world tour of many plants and shrubs, including a particularly fine collection of exotic orchids. In addition the Gardens continue to supply material for the use of the Department of Botany in Glasgow University.

In the northern part of the Gardens, past which the Kelvin flows, there was located one of Glasgow's most famous wells. It was a favourite place for picnics and admirably illustrates Glasgow's propensity for becoming involved in discussion over place names. Usually called the Pear Tree Well (despite there never having been any pear trees near it) it was also sometimes called the Pier Tree Well or even the Three Tree Well. Another form, Pea Tree Well, though not so romantic, is most likely to be the correct version, as the 'pea' tree was the Scottish version of the laburnum tree.

KIBBLE PALACE

John Kibble (1818–94) was the son of James Kibble, owner of a wire warehouse firm in Paisley Rd West. Little is known of his personal affairs – apparently a man of independent fortune he has been described as a botanist, an astronomer and an engineer. As he is known to have had a ship, the *Queen of Beauty*, built for him by T. Wingate & Co in 1843 which he used to demonstrate an unsuccessful propulsion device (an endless chain of paddle-floats), it is probable that he was indeed an engineer. It was said that he was the first and only man to cycle across Loch Long on a bicycle (fitted with floats). He was also well known as an amateur photographer of some eminence and constructed in 1858 what was for its time the world's largest camera – the lens had a diameter of 13in, and a focal length of 6ft, while each plate negative weighed 44lb. It was mounted on wheels and drawn about by a horse. Its most famous product was an extremely large print of the Broomielaw, of which no copy is known to exist.

About 1865, possibly on his retirement from business, he erected at Coulport House, his residence in Cove, Loch Long, a large iron-framed conservatory, designed by Boucher & Cousland, Glasgow architects, and erected by James Boyd & Sons, Paisley, horticultural builders. Costing £15,000, it consisted of a large circular dome connected to a smaller dome by a short passage. In March 1871 he offered the conservatory to Glasgow Corporation for re-erection in the Queen's Park. The unusual terms of agreement were that Kibble would pay the cost of removal, transport and re-erection (£1,500), would contribute £2,000 to £3,000 towards the cost of increasing the diameter of the main dome, and would retain the lease of the building for 21 years, during which period he would receive any profits accruing from the letting of the conservatory. After 21 years the building would become the property of the Corporation. The Corporation declined the offer; it was said that some Councillors had objected both to the 'immoral statuary' which ornamented its interior and to the intended provision of a bar.

In disgust Kibble then offered it in October of the same year and under similar terms to the Royal Botanic Society of Glasgow. The Institution, which had moved from a site in Sauchiehall St in 1842 to an area between Great Western Rd and the River Kelvin, accepted the offer with alacrity, and at the end of 1871 the dismantled building was towed on rafts down Loch Long, up the Clyde and the River Kelvin as near as possible to its new Botanic Gardens site. While it was being re-erected the large dome was enlarged to 146ft (the original 12 supporting twisted cast-iron columns were supplemented by an additional 24 which supported the extended circumference), the corridor connecting it to the smaller 60ft dome was lengthened, and two transepts were placed at the entrance, with the 60ft dome at the crossing. The enclosed area was now 23,000 square ft, making it one of the largest glasshouses in Britain. The formal opening took place in June 1873 and took the form of a promenade concert attended by over 2,000 people.

For several years the Kibble Crystal Art Palace and Royal Conservatory, as it was then called, became the venue for many city meetings and functions. Regular twice-weekly concerts were held in it and it was used for the inaugural speeches of both Disraeli (1873–over 4,000 attended) and Gladstone (1879) on the occasions of their installations as Lord Rectors of Glasgow University.

In 1881, with £10,000 of a £25,000 loan from the Corporation, the Botanic Society bought up the remainder of Kibble's lease in order, it was said, to prevent further damage to the plants and the building by its many visitors. They installed a heating system and returned the conservatory to its original purpose. Increasing financial problems forced the Institution into bankruptcy, however, whereupon the Corporation, as the major creditor, took over the building and the grounds in 1887. When the area became part of Glasgow in 1891, the Kibble Palace and the Botanic Gardens were handed over to the Parks Trustees for public use.

GLASGOW GREEN

To extricate itself from its financial troubles in the 16th and early 17th centuries, Glasgow's Town Council sold off much of its common land. By the end of the 18th century, however, it had repurchased much of what it had so recklessly alienated, in particular those parts belonging to Glasgow Green. This was the rebirth of what is without a doubt Glasgow's most famous open space. It lies on the north bank of the Clyde, running east from the Saltmarket in a broad strip bounded on the north by the old village of Calton and ending at the western outskirts of Bridgeton. In 1730 it amounted to 59 acres, increased by purchase to 117 acres in 1810, and to 136 acres, its present size, in 1894.

During the 17th and 18th centuries the Green was devoted almost solely to the utilitarian purposes of grazing cattle and washing and bleaching clothes. The reason for the latter activity (which continued well into the 19th century) was because the only plentiful source of water was the Clyde itself as it flowed past the southern grassy slopes of the Green.

By the beginning of the 19th century the Green was in a state of sore neglect. Its low-lying parts were much subject to flooding by the Clyde, and its western end was made obnoxious by the presence of numerous tan-works and slaughterhouses, while its hilly surface was divided by many swamps, ditches and burns. Thus between 1817 and 1826 a smoothing and civilising process was begun (the prime mover in the process being Dr James Cleland, Superintendent of Public Works) which was eventually to produce the present-day park. The laborious levelling, filling-in and turfing, which included the tunneling of the Molendinar and Camlachie Burns, was

mainly carried out by unemployed workers (hand-loom weavers, victims of early 'technological unemployment' caused by the introduction of the power-loom). This is an example of public works alleviating working-class distress, something which occurred several times in the Green's history. This process also marked the end of the Green as an arena for popular, disorganised sport. For instance, for over 400 years it had been the site, every Shrove Tuesday, of a rowdy game of football with unlimited players and minimal rules, but in 1819 the Town Council created a bylaw which 'strictly prohibited and discharged every person whatever from playing golf, cricket, shinty, football, or any other game whatever on the Green of the City'.

In 1857 the Green was formally taken over by Glasgow Corporation – it was now a public park, no longer the city's common green. Then in 1878, under the Glasgow Public Parks Act, it made the final transition, becoming totally financed by the ordinary funds of the Corporation. Another link with the past was broken in 1870 when the grazing of cows within its boundaries finally ceased, although a few enclosures were retained for sheep.

Despite a Town Council prohibition as far back as 1623 outlawing the washing of clothes anywhere other than in 'housis and privat placis', it continued as a common washing green until 1977, and iron posts for ropes to hang washing from are still visible on the northern side of the Green. By 1741 a large washing-house had been erected near the centre of the Green with a piped water supply. Even then so great was the demand for washing places that the banks of the Clyde where the river flowed past the southern edge of the Green were lined with little solitary fires on which water was heated by *alfresco* washerwomen. For English visitors to the city, the attraction of the washing-house was that the washerwomen agitated the washing by treading or tramping on it with their feet, displaying parts of their anatomy apparently seldom seen south of the Border! By 1879 this centrally placed wash-house had been moved north to near William St eventually becoming the Greenhead Public Baths and Wash-house – one of the earliest of the famous Glasgow 'steamies'.

The Green of Glasgow can be regarded as one of the most historically important pieces of urban parkland in Scotland on account of its age and its continued existence as a 'lung' for this industrialised area of the city. The Green never was, nor has it become, an 'ornamental' type of park; it has always remained the natural and favourite place for all kinds of games and sports. From an early date it had been used for the playing of golf; in 1792 the 'Golf Club' applied to the Town Council to be allowed to remove the old Herd's House or golf house and to build a new one. Earlier still, in 1675, the Council had organised 'foot raices' round the Green, offering the winner the generous prize of £1 sterling (£12 Scots). In the 19th century it had an open-air gymnasium for adults, and, later still, could boast of six bowling-greens, ten tennis courts and a hockey pitch. Football has always flourished on the Green – it has 22 pitches – and it was a group of young lads playing here who metamorphosed themselves into the famous Glasgow Rangers. Fishing and bathing in the Clyde were favourite pastimes; not surprisingly the rapid increase in the level of pollution in its waters put a stop to these pursuits, but it was not until 1877 that the Corporation removed the bathing huts and spring-boards

it had placed on the river-bank.

As the only large open space in the city the Green was often used for military parades and manoeuvres. It was here, for instance, that Prince Charles Edward Stewart reviewed his raggle-taggle army when he paid an unwelcome visit to the city in 1746, and where Moray assembled his army before defeating Mary Queen of Scots at Langside in 1568.

Glasgow Fair week, the great yearly occasion for popular celebrations and amusements, was for long associated with the Green. The park's western end, facing the Jail Square at the foot of the Saltmarket, was filled every July with a motley collection of temporary wooden constructions housing all sorts of theatres, circuses, curiosity shows, displays of wild beasts and boxing booths. Vast crowds from the east end attended these 'keek-shows' but unfortunately the authorities barely tolerated this outbreak of working-class ebullience, and in 1870 effectively rid the Green of these shows by decreeing that only for a short three weeks at Fair-time could any structures be erected on the Green.

It was realised early on that economic seams of coal lay below the Green and in 1821 the Town Council authorised boring to establish their extent, starting a lengthy struggle between commercial interests and the citizens who saw their treasured park under threat. In 1858 the Council needed money to finance its purchase of land for the West End Park and attempted to raise it by leasing the mineral rights to John McDowall ('Airn John'), owner of the Milton Ironworks in Northwoodside. The righteous indignation of the east enders knew no bounds – why should one of their few amenities be destroyed to pay for those of the west enders? A contemporary poem sums up their feeling of outrage:

Airn John, since that's your name,
Let me say this to thee;
Ye'd better try some ither scheme,
An' let the Green a be.
Look at it yersel, John,
Is't no dishonest wark
O' you, to sell the Glasgow Green,
To pay the West End Park?

The matter was allowed to drop only to rise again in 1869 and 1888 – fortunately, the Council eventually seemed to have realised the strong feelings that were aroused whenever the Green was attacked and nothing more was heard of the mineral wealth below its surface.

Any attack on the Green's integrity was always quickly repelled by those who lived around it. For instance, an early 19th-century Glasgow textile merchant, Alexander Allan, built a splendid mansion on the north side of the Green and, to have undisturbed access to the banks of the river, he diverted the public pathway along the Clyde into a pen or tunnel. So strong were the feelings aroused by this behaviour that weavers refused to work for him, bringing him near to ruin. Even nature took a hand in the affair, for a flood finally swept away Allan's Pen, as it was known. In 1847 The Glasgow, Monkland and Airdrie Railway Company wanted to bring a railway viaduct through the Green and the successful legal efforts to defeat it went all the way to Parliament. This 19th-century attack has a modern counterpart: the ring road which circles Glasgow to the north, west and south was intended to be completed by an eastern section which would have run straight through the Green – a piece of official vandalism so far kept at bay.

From time immemorial the Green had been an established locus for public speeches and demonstrations of all kinds, the equivalent of London's Hyde Park. Every Saturday and Sunday its western end used to be thronged with preachers and politicians, mountebanks and quacks, and it was a recognised entertainment to walk to the Green and listen to this multitude of speakers. From the vast Chartist demonstrations of the 1830s to John Maclean's advocacy of a Scottish Republic in the 1920s, the Green was a favourite sounding-board. When the Corporation began to find the Green's politics somewhat too far to the left of centre it resurrected an old bylaw of 1916 prohibiting singing, preaching, lecturing and demonstrating in public parks without permission. Guy Aldred (1886–1963), a local anti-parliamentary anarchist, fought this for ten years until finally the Corporation restored the freedom of speech previously enjoyed. Political customs were changing, though: the annual May Day parade was moved from the Green to Queen's Park, outdoor meetings no longer attracted crowds, and the Green has become a much quieter and less lively place.

Not aspiring to be a garden park the Green has attracted few monuments, and those it has, oddly, have mostly been borrowed from elsewhere. The oldest, and one of the few to have been specifically designed for the Green, is the tall freestone obelisk (143ft) commemorating Lord Nelson and his victories. Municipal and commercial Glasgow never wavered in its allegiance to the Crown and the city's 1806 Nelson monument (erected on the site of the Herd's House) was one of the first to be erected to the 'one-handed adulterer' – no one seems to have regarded it as a sign of Divine displeasure when the obelisk was struck and damaged by a bolt of lightning only four years after its erection.

In 1890 Sir Henry Doulton re-erected in the Green the Doulton Fountain.

Glasgow Green, 1947, with the exotic facade of Templeton's Carpet Factory in the background. From time immemorial the Green, the city's oldest open space, has been used for household washing and drying. (George Oliver)

Constructed in red terracotta, it had originally been gifted to the 1888 Glasgow International Exhibition by Sir Henry, the china-manufacturer. Crowded with a host of allegorical figures and surmounted by the figure of Queen Victoria, it is a splendid celebration of the British Empire at its height. The fragile nature of terracotta, and the monument's exposed and unmonitored position, has reduced it to a state of terminal vandalism – and its present abject condition is as symbolically appropriate today as its original state was then.

The only other large-scale monument in the park is the McLennan Arch, located at the Charlotte St entrance to the Green. It was originally the entrance to the Glasgow Assembly Rooms in Ingram St; it was removed from the building in 1894 and transferred first to Monteith Row and in 1924 to its present position.

One of the major attractions of the Green is undoubtedly the People's Palace. Centrally placed, it cost £18,000 – money received from the Caledonian Railway Company as compensation for allowing it

to run its line through a tunnel under the Green. It was erected as a palace of culture for the deprived east enders. It had recreation rooms, a museum, an art gallery and a superb winter-garden or glasshouse (said to have been built in the upside-down shape of Nelson's *Victory*!). It was opened in 1898 by the Earl of Rosebery, becoming Glasgow's local history museum in 1940.

The Green once possessed two famous wells. Robin's Well was celebrated for its bleaching qualities but it has long since disappeared without trace. The other – Arn's Well – was located halfway between the Nelson monument and the Humane Society House. It took its name from the arn or elder trees which grew near it, and its water was reputed to have been the best and purest in Glasgow and as such was in great demand for the preparation of tea and punch. It was close to this well that James Watt first thought of using a separate condenser for the steam-engine, an innovative invention which literally supplied the driving force for the industrial revolution.

The Green's long presence as an open

space located so near the built-up centre of the city has ensured its continued popularity as a park – in its heyday, on one August day in 1894, more than 78,000 people were counted entering its gates. As a result of the westward movement of Glasgow's centre of gravity it has become rather neglected, however. In addition, its future is threatened by rival and competing projects by the district and regional authorities. The former wishes to erect a range of 'leisure' structures, while the latter sees it as an opportunity to tidy up the city's motorway network by running roads through or under it. It is to be hoped that this centuries-old park will be able once more to call on the support of the citizens in preserving its historic place and style.

Parliamentary Affairs

Before the 1707 Union of the Parliaments, Glasgow was represented in the old Scottish Parliament by one member, chosen by the Town Council from its own numbers; he was often the Provost. The earliest mention of the city's parliamentary representative dates back to 1546.

After the Union the city lost its individual membership and became one of a group of Clyde burghs (Glasgow, Rutherglen, Renfrew and Dumbarton) who from amongst their several town councils elected one member to represent them all in the new British Parliament. (Out of the 29 members elected between 1707 and 1831, no less than 14 had the surname Campbell!) Each town council appointed a delegate who would cast a vote for his council's choice. The office of the returning burgh was shared in rotation and should there have been an equality of votes (not unusual) then the returning burgh had a casting vote, a device which led to a great deal of behind-the-scenes manoeuvring.

The Reform Act of 1832 swept away this centuries-old self-perpetuating system and made the city one single constituency returning two members. In the 1833 elections an electorate of less than 5 per cent of the population had a choice of six candidates – two lawyers, two merchants, a university professor and a retired East India company surgeon. Not surprisingly, the city's choice was the two merchants – James Oswald of Shieldhall, a strong Whig, and James Ewing of Strathleven, whose political allegiance was never quite clear. This choice of Whigs (or Liberals) was to be the city's preference until the end of the century.

By the Scottish Reform Act of 1868 the city's representation was increased to three. This Act also linked Glasgow's university with that of Aberdeen, in appointing a single university MP; it also introduced for the first time the secret ballot, and increased the proportion of those voting to 15 per cent.

It was not until the Redistribution of Seats Act in 1885 that recognition was given to the great increase in Glasgow's population. Now the city was divided into seven separate constituencies (each with an average of 15,000 inhabitants) – Blackfriars, Hutchesontown, Bridgeton, Camlachie, Central, College, St Rollox and Tradeston. (Only one name appears in this list *and* amongst the current constituencies – Central.) At the same time the suburban constituencies of Govan and Partick were formed but did not become Glasgow seats till 1918.

Post-war Glasgow had been considerably enlarged by the addition of a number of peripheral suburban burghs and districts, and this was recognised in the new distribution of seats, now increased to 15:

Bridgeton	Maryhill
Camlachie	Partick
Cathcart	Pollok
Central	St Rollox
Gorbals	Shettleston
Govan	Springburn
Hillhead	Tradeston
Kelvingrove	

This distribution was to remain undisturbed until 1948. The hegemony of the Liberal Party had disappeared, as far as Glasgow was concerned, when Gladstone tried to introduce Irish Home Rule in 1893, and it became clear that Labour was now the city's choice. This change was clearly signalled when Glasgow sent ten Labour MPs south in 1922; memories of the wartime reputation of the Red Clydeside led to expectations of great things from them. In the event, only one of them achieved anything – John Wheatley who, as

Minister of Health in the Labour administration, gave a significant impulse to the financing and building of working-class housing. During the whole of this period the average make-up of the city's representation was nine Labour to six Unionist.

After the Second World War Glasgow had its constituencies increased from 15 to 17, mainly to take into account the existence of its large new housing schemes. The 17 were:

Bridgeton	Maryhill
Camlachie	Pollok
Cathcart	Provan
Central	Scotstoun
Craigton	Shettleston
Gorbals	Springburn
Govan	Tradeston
Hillhead	Woodside
Kelvingrove	

In the next redistribution of seats (1974), Glasgow's significant population decline reduced its constituencies from 17 to 13:

Cathcart	Maryhill
Central	Pollok
Craigton	Provan
Garscadden	Queen's Park
Govan	Shettleston
Hillhead	Springburn
Kelvingrove	

By 1983 the seats had dropped to their current 11 with the removal of three – Craigton, Kelvingrove and Queen's Park – and the addition of one – Rutherglen, which had been brought into Glasgow under the 1975 local government reorganisation. The current (1994) state of the parties gives all seats to Labour.

Two Members of the European Parliament cover the city, one for Glasgow as such, the other for Strathclyde East, a constituency which covers part of south-east Glasgow.

People

BIOGRAPHIES

John Anderson (1726–96)

Born at Roseneath in Dunbartonshire (a son of the manse – his grandfather was the first minister of St David's (Ramshorn) Church, Glasgow), he was educated at Glasgow University. In 1756 he was appointed Professor of Oriental Languages at the university, taking up the chair of Natural Philosophy (physical sciences) there in 1760. He excelled in the art of teaching and throughout his academic career he delighted in giving classes in applied science to working-class audiences. In 1791 he visited France and presented a cannon of his own design to the revolutionary French government. His consistently radical views caused him to support the students when they presented a petition to Parliament asking for a Royal Commission to investigate the indolence and apathy of the university's academic staff. He was the only professor to show sympathy for the students' point of view and was roundly ostracised by his fellow professors. It is said that it was their treatment of him over this affair which caused him to draw up a scheme for what would now probably be called an 'alternative university'. It was set up after his death under the very elaborate terms of his will, and can claim to be the oldest technical school in Britain, if not in Europe. It has been known by various titles. He described its purpose and title as being for 'the improvement of science in an institution to be denominated Anderson's University'. It was also called Anderson's Institution, sometimes Anderson's College

or the Andersonian Institute. Whatever title it went by, it is the one and only progenitor of the present-day University of Strathclyde.

William Beardmore, Lord Invernairn (1856–1936)

Educated at the High School of Glasgow, he later attended Anderson's College, forerunner of the Glasgow and West of Scotland Technical College (now the University of Strathclyde), receiving a practical education befitting someone who was to become a giant of Scottish heavy engineering. After serving an apprenticeship at the Parkhead Forge, in the east end of Glasgow, he set up in 1879 in partnership with his uncle and went on to found the engineering firm of William Beardmore & Co. The company became world-famous as a centre for heavy engineering and shipbuilding, becoming in the process the largest single employer of labour in the west of Scotland. During the First World War the Parkhead Forge constructed many battleships, cruisers, destroyers and submarines, as well as aircraft engines for the Royal Flying Corp. Peacetime and the Depression of the 1920s affected the company adversely. Although the outbreak of the Second World War was to revive its fortunes somewhat, Beardmore himself broke his connection with the firm in 1929. The post-war period proved once again disastrous to Beardmore's and the Forge ceased to exist in 1973. Its original function is kept alive by the name of the shopping supermarket, The Forge, which occupies part of its old site.

Henry Bell (1767–1830)

Apprenticed at first to a stonemason Bell later became a millwright and a self-taught engineer. After a short stay in London he returned to Glasgow in 1790 and began experimenting with the use of the steam-engine as a motive power for ships. His endeavours met with little encouragement and he became a house builder in Helensburgh (Dunbartonshire). In 1812, however, his years of experiments paid off and in August of that year he launched into the Clyde what was to become the first practical sea-going steam-propelled vessel. Named the *Comet* after a comet seen in the skies the previous year, it was built for him by John Wood & Co of Port Glasgow, with a steam-engine by John Robertson, Glasgow engineer, and a boiler by John Napier. It was 43ft 6in long with a beam of 11ft 4in, a depth of 5ft 9in and a tonnage of 24½ tons. The engine (piston diameter 11½in, stroke 16in) developed a nominal 4 horsepower. The original design had two paddle-wheels on each side but this arrangement soon gave way to the more orthodox one wheel per side – at the same time its length was increased by 20ft. It plied between Glasgow and Greenock and later extended its run to include Helensburgh. It occasionally ventured further down the Firth of Clyde and beyond, and it was on one of these voyages that in December 1820 it was wrecked at Craignish, Argyllshire.

Dr Thomas Chalmers (1780–1847)

Although born in Anstruther (Fife) and educated at St Andrews University, it was in Glasgow that Dr Chalmers made his name as a social reformer. His first charge was at Kilrenny (Fife) in 1803, and it was

there that he convinced himself that the Church was still the best means by which the plight of the poor could be relieved. His fame as an outstanding preacher and orator brought him to Glasgow in 1815, first to the Tron Church, one of the most prestigious in the city. He claimed that the Tron was 'not calculated for his delicate habit' and asked for a charge further from the city centre. So in 1820 he moved to the newly created St John's Parish, located in one of the poorest of the city's east end districts, where he put to the test his belief that poor relief could best be administered by the 'old Scotch parochial economy' based on church-door contributions administered by church elders. That this voluntary system could ever have coped with the rapidly rising tide of a big industrial city's degradation and poverty is unlikely, although his ministrations in four years reduced the pauper expenditure in his parish from £1,400 to £280 per annum. In 1823 he returned to the academic life at St Andrews University. Later he achieved acclaim of another kind, when in 1843 he led 470 ministers out of the Church of Scotland in protest against the exercise of patronage in the choice of ministers – The Disruption – and set up the Free Church of Scotland.

James Cleland (1770–1840)

The son of a cabinetmaker, Cleland was considered by many of his contemporaries (and by himself) to be one of the most important personages in Glasgow. He was intimately involved in most of the activities of the municipality from 1806 to 1834. A bailie in 1806, he was appointed Superintendent of Public Works in 1814, the first non-councillor to hold that post. Amongst his many schemes, *c.*1819 he put the city's unemployed hand-loom weavers to work levelling and turfing the Green of Glasgow and culverting the Molendinar and

Camlachie Burns; he was involved in having the Town Council move from the Tolbooth down to the new Justiciary Building at the foot of the Saltmarket (and then bought the old site for £8,000); he designed the Bazaar in the Candleriggs; converted the ground floor of the Saracen's Head Inn to shops; drew up the plans for St David's (Ramshorn) Church and planned the new Post Office in Nelson St. He tried to standardise the country's weights and measures. He was an early (and avid) statistician, and was the Government census-taker in 1821 and 1831. His publications, *The Annals of Glasgow* (1816) and *The Rise and Progress of the City of Glasgow* (1820), are treasure-houses of indiscriminate facts and figures, from the price of coal in Glasgow to the probability of human life in the same city. In 1831 an old Glasgow lady, Mrs Agnes Baird, published a pamphlet, *A review of the historical and topographical works of James Cleland, LL. D.* [he had been given an honorary degree by Glasgow University] *containing a detection of numerous errors and misrepresentations of facts in his books and pamphlets* and her opinion has been confirmed by later Glasgow historians. When he retired in 1835, the sum of £4,600 was subscribed with which a tenement was erected at the top of Buchanan St bearing the inscription 'The Cleland Testimonial'. He was buried in crypt of the church he had helped to design, in a vault kindly presented to him by a grateful Town Council.

Andrew Cochrane of Brighouse (1693–1777)

Considered to be one of the city's greatest provosts, he left Ayr for Glasgow in 1722 and became a prosperous tobacco merchant and shipowner (three of his vessels were named *Cochrane*, *Murdoch* and *Prince William*). He was chief magistrate during the '45 Rebellion and it was his staunch opposition to Prince Charles that earned him his reputation. In his account of the affair he could claim that 'when for eight weeks the rebels had been masters of Scotland, not one man from Glasgow joined them' and that 'the prince appeared four times [in Glasgow] . . . without the smallest respect being paid him; no bells rung, no huzzas'. When the Prince demanded a list of all those in the city who had contributed to his defeat, Cochrane refused, saying that he would be the foremost on it. He journeyed to London in 1748 to persuade a reluctant government to recompense the city for its losses. After being kept waiting for almost half a year he received a grudging payment of £10,000. Cochrane St is named after him.

Patrick Colquhoun (1745–1820)

Colquhoun was born in Dumbarton and went out to Virginia when he was 16, learning at first hand all the necessary skills of a Glasgow merchant. After his return to the city in 1766 he became a prosperous tobacco and cotton merchant. He built a country house a few miles to the west of the city and called it Kelvingrove (where Kelvingrove Park now is) and was Lord Provost in 1782. He was the prime mover in setting up the country's first Chamber of Commerce and Manufacturers in 1783 and acted as its first chairman. He was involved in various schemes to improve the city's police force, its educational facilities and its poor relief. He also acted for a while as the Chamber's parliamentary agent in London. He seems to have found the city's attitude too restricting and too disregarding of his schemes for its improvement, for in 1789 he moved permanently to London where he became a police magistrate and published several important statistical and social works, including one on the resources of the British Empire and another on the reform of the River Police.

Billy Connolly (*b*.1942)

Glasgow has produced many great comedians but few, if any of them, ever ventured with success outside their home ground. Only one, Billy Connolly, has broken this seemingly impassable barrier, and has thus played an important role in representing to the rest of the world, if not the 'traditional' Glasgow, then a very vivid 'alternative' one.

Born in Partick in 1942, he and his family moved to Drumchapel when he was four – one of the four huge, anonymous post-war housing schemes exiled to the city's boundaries. Apprenticed as a welder, when he was 21 he quit his job and turned professional entertainer. For five years he toured, with his banjo and guitar, Scottish folk clubs, London pubs, Amsterdam *halles* and Danish beer gardens. In the early 1970s he was part of a trio called the Humblebums and when that broke up he returned to the circuit. His breakthrough came with an Edinburgh Festival revue, *The Great Northern Welly Boot Show*, which gave him an opportunity to show the public a hitherto unrepresented type of Glasgow humour – vulgar, uncouthy, lavatorial, blasphemous, outrageous, with a touch of the surreal – which became his trademark. As one of the earliest alternative stand-up comedians he trod on many toes and roused in many that infamous Glasgow put-down of home-bred genius: 'Him! A kent his faither!' His intelligence and outspokenness brought him the enmity of the media, and in the early 1980s he left Scotland. Within ten years he had taken his Drumchapel gallusness (and his unique brand of Glasgow oral history) to the United States and had become a superstar.

Helen Crawford (née Jack) (1877–1954)

Born in the Gorbals of a middle-class family, she early became involved in women's interests, joining the suffrage movement in 1900. In London in 1912 she was arrested and imprisoned for breaking windows, and her prison experiences made her into a militant. Back in Scotland she became an outstanding speaker for the Scottish Suffrage Movement. She was blamed for a bomb explosion in the Botanic Gardens which resulted in her fourth prison sentence and her third hunger strike. Her first-hand experiences of life in working-class Glasgow brought her into socialism, and she joined the ILP in 1914. She became an outspoken anti-war protester (an attitude which caused her to break with the suffrage movement), and worked for a while with John Maclean in his Scottish Labour College. She became a leader in the Glasgow Rent Strikes of 1915 as secretary of the Glasgow Women's Housing Association. Many wives in Glasgow whose husbands were serving as soldiers, found their rents escalating. Crawford said the 'fight was essentially a women's fight'. By careful organisation and swift local action the housewives waged a campaign (particularly in Govan and Partick), supported by the shop stewards' movement, which lasted for six months and finally forced the government into passing the Rent Restriction Act of 1915.

In 1918 she became vice-chairman of the Scottish Divisional Council of the ILP but became disillusioned with its policies. She was invited to the 2nd Congress of the 3rd Communist International in Moscow in 1920 and was greatly impressed by what she saw there. On her return to Scotland she left the ILP and joined the recently created Communist Party of Great Britain, eventually serving on its executive committee. She stood twice for Parliament but failed to be elected. As a Communist she gave her support to the Second World War. Throughout her life she was a dedicated fighter who brought a high intelligence to bear on everything she did.

David Dale (1739–1806)

Born in Stewarton (Ayrshire) into a simple farming family, Dale, after an apprenticeship to a Paisley weaver, became a weavers' agent, travelling about the countryside distributing yarn and collecting finished cloth from hand-loom weavers. About 1743 he came to Glasgow and laid the foundations of his prosperity by trading in imported fine French yarns. Later he seized the opportunity afforded by Richard Arkwright's new machines for the spinning of cotton, and in partnership with him set up the New Lanark Mills (1783–85) on the banks of the Clyde. They soon became the largest water-powered spinning mills in Britain, with 1,500 employees (more than one-third of whom were children under 14, working 12 hours a day). He went on to set up other spinning centres in Catrine (Ayrshire), Newton Stewart (Galloway) and Spinningdale (Sutherland). By the standards of his time Dale took good care of his workers – his beneficial efforts in this sphere have often been wrongly ascribed to his son-in-law, Robert Owen, the social reformer, who took over the management of the mills at New Lanark in 1799. Dale was also involved in the introduction of turkey-red dyeing into the Scottish textile industry and in 1783 became the first agent and cashier of the Glasgow branch of the Royal Bank of Scotland. He was a director of the city's poorhouse, the Town's Hospital and was known as 'The Benevolent Magistrate'. His religion was as self-made as his education; he early broke away from the established Church and set up his own under the banner

of the Old Scotch Independents, teaching himself Greek and Hebrew in order to carry out his duties as a preacher, which he did for 37 years. The erection of his church was financed by a friend, a candlemaker, so it was popularly known as the Caun'le Kirk. He built for himself an elegant mansion designed by Robert Adam in Charlotte St, next to Glasgow Green. Remarkable for Glasgow, it survived until 1953. In an age of formality and pride in ancestry David Dale had neither; he enjoyed singing the old Scottish songs and it was said that his rendition of *The Flowers of the Forest* could draw tears from his audience.

Patrick Joseph Dollan (1885–1963)

P. J. Dollan was born in Baillieston (a mining town to the east of Glasgow) to Roman Catholic parents of Irish descent. He worked for eight years in the pits as a youth and then became involved in socialism through his friendship with John Wheatley. He joined the ILP in 1908 and became a reporter for the *Forward*. About 1911 he severed his links with the Roman Catholic Church. He remained, like many of the old Left, a believer in total abstinence.

He was elected to Glasgow Town Council in 1913 and became increasingly involved in managing the Labour and the Roman Catholic vote in the city. In the 1920 municipal elections, largely due to his efforts, 45 Labour candidates were elected. In 1933 Labour gained control of the Council and Dollan became City Treasurer (1934–37). In 1938 he became Glasgow's first Roman Catholic Lord Provost (it is interesting to note that out of 116 councillors only six were Catholics). He received a knighthood in 1941, the same year his term as Provost came to an end. He then went on to become chairman of the East Kilbride New Town Development

Corporation from 1947 to 1958.

Throughout his political life he always preferred local politics, and Glasgow was the arena he felt most at home in. The only time he stood for Parliament (Ayr Burghs) he was not successful. His position was always right of centre, pragmatic and down-to-earth, an attitude which did not always endear him to his fellow Clydesiders, and one which became more pronounced as he got older. After leaving the Council he returned to the Church. His wife, Agnes Dollan, was a political figure in her own right, and was amongst the first women to be elected to the Town Council in 1921. She died in 1966.

Kirkman Finlay (1772–1842)

One of the most important figures in the mercantile history of the city, Finlay was born in the heart of old Glasgow, the Gallowgate. His unusual forename came from a radical London alderman admired by his father. He was only 18 when his father died, leaving him in sole charge of a thriving business, James Finlay & Son, the largest British exporter of cotton textiles into Europe, with extensive mills at Katrine and Deanston. When Napoleon's Berlin Decrees of 1806 attempted to blockade the British Isles, Finlay broke it by setting up depots at Heligoland, Gibraltar and Malta.

His manufacturing interests led him to take a principal part in two successful campaigns (1813 and 1833) to abolish all the trading monopolies enjoyed by East India Company in India and China; in 1834 it was one of his vessels, the *Earl of Buckinghamshire* (600 tons), which was the first ship to sail direct from Calcutta to the Clyde.

He was the first Glasgow-born MP for 70 years to represent the Clyde Burghs (1812 to 1818). At first he proved highly popular, but when he voted for the Corn Laws the Glasgow mob marched on his town-house in Queen St and smashed its windows. It was also about this time that he became involved in behind-the-scenes activity combatting a series of strikes amongst the Glasgow cotton operatives. In 1817 it was he who was instrumental in bribing a Pollokshaws weaver, Alexander Richmond ('Richmond the Spy'), to act as an *agent-provocateur* and prosecution witness.

He took a leading part in all of Glasgow's affairs – he was Lord Provost in 1812 and 1819, Governor of the Forth and Clyde Navigation Co, four times chairman of the Glasgow Chamber of Commerce and Lord Rector of the University. He was also highly regarded and much consulted at Westminster for his wide acquaintance with mercantile matters.

He eventually retired to his country estate, Castle Toward, in Cowal on the Firth of Clyde. The firm he developed is still working out of Glasgow, and still has interests in the Far East.

David Hamilton (1768–1845)

He has been described as the founding father of Glasgow architecture. Beginning as a working mason Hamilton finished up by designing most of the principal buildings in the city (and many in the west of Scotland). His favourite styles were the Classical Revival and the Italian Renaissance; and so great was his output that he became the unofficial 'City Architect'. He designed several banks, many churches, markets and other civic projects as well as country houses throughout the west of Scotland. His best known works include the Royal Exchange (1827–29), Hutchesons' Grammar School (1839, demolished), Aikenhead House (1806–23), the former Western Club

(1840), the British Linen Bank (1841, demolished), Hamilton Palace (1822–38, demolished), Lennox Castle (1837–41) and the Glasgow Green Nelson's Monument (1806).

William Harley (1770–1829)

When it became apparent that residential middle-class Glasgow was beginning to move west out of the old city centre, the Blythswood Estate (on the city's western boundary) rapidly became desirable property. One of the first to seize this opportunity was William Harley. He had come to Glasgow from Glendevon in the Ochils in 1790 and had become a successful manufacturer of turkey-red gingham. In 1802 he bought Sauchy Hall (built by Lawrence Phillips) as a family residence, along with the land about it lying in the Blythwood Estate (the house name was changed to Willowbank House, the anglicised version of the Saughy Haugh or Willow Valley; another version was used for the major east–west thoroughfare – Sauchiehall St). Realising the potentialities of the estate, he began to lay out roads through it. An old bleaching ground which had used the abundant local springs lay within his property. At this time the city's water supply came from a number of public wells supplemented by the river, neither of high quality, and Harley began to send tank-carts loaded with the spring water (which was collected in a reservoir at what is now West Nile St) through the city where it found ready purchasers. He charged ½d a stoup and was said to have realised £4,000 the first year.

The opening of the Glasgow and Cranston Hill Water Companies in 1807–8 reduced the demand for Harley's spring water and he moved on to a new venture. He had created a public pleasure garden at the highest point of Blythswood estate

(now Blythswood Sq) and to provide access to it he had laid down a road leading from the upper part of the old town, west to this garden. The new road crossed the southward-flowing St Enoch's Burn; here he built a bridge or embankment (near the top of West Nile St) and beside it he erected the city's first hot and cold public baths. There were four main pools: one for men, 40ft by 20ft and 4½ft deep; one for women, 20ft by 12ft; a boys' pool and a girls' pool (each 12ft by 10ft). Again his venture prospered – so popular were his baths that his road leading past them up to his gardens became known as Bath St.

Some of his invalid users appreciated a glass of warm fresh milk after their bath and for this purpose he began to keep a cow. When the novelty of his baths began to wear off he developed the dairy side and soon had a herd of some 300 cows on the site (it covered the ground between Bath St, Renfield St, Sauchiehall St and West Nile St). Once again his innovation was a success. It was largely secured by his meticulous application of 'regularity, order and cleanliness' – qualities almost entirely lacking in the city's more traditional milk suppliers. The Willowbank Dairy, or Harley's Byres, soon became an early tourist attraction and were visited by many of the city's distinguished visitors. In 1829 he published his *The Harleian Dairy System*.

Harley continued developing the roads within the estate (these included West Nile St, St Vincent St, Sauchiehall St, and Renfrew St) and went on to establish a bakery business. However, with the end of the Napoleonic Wars in 1815, Harley shared in the financial ruin which afflicted many of the city's entrepreneurs, but he managed to struggle on till 1827. Two years later the Tsar asked him to come to St Petersburg and start up a dairy there on his new principles. While passing through London *en route* in 1829 he caught a fever and died.

Lord Kelvin, William Thomson (1824–1907)

Born in Belfast, the son of the Professor of Mathematics at the Royal Institution, he came to Glasgow in 1832 when his father became Professor of Mathematics at the University. His academic prowess was such that after finishing his education at Glasgow University and Cambridge he was appointed to the chair of Natural Philosophy (Physics) in Glasgow at the age of 22. His many scientific interests included thermodynamics, electricity and magnetism, in all of which he made major scientific discoveries. He always sought practical applications for his discoveries and became a partner in a company which had been started up by James White to manufacture scientific instruments. As Kelvin & White it concentrated on producing his many electrical innovative devices, in the process making him a wealthy man. He was largely responsible for the successful laying of the first transatlantic cable in 1866, and his marine compass became the standard instrument for the Admiralty and most of the major shipping lines. He was created a peer in 1892 (his title comes from the name of the small river which flows past the university on its way to the Clyde) and after his death was interred in Westminster Abbey.

David Kirkwood, first Baron Kirkwood of Bearsden (1872–1955)

Born in Glasgow, Kirkwood's working life was largely spent at Beardmore's Parkhead Forge for which he seems to have had a love-hate relationship. Not long after starting work there he was sacked and banned after becoming involved in a strike,

but was back at the Forge in 1910, becoming chief shop steward. He joined the ILP and when the radical anti-war Clyde Workers' Committee was founded in 1915 he became its treasurer. After calling for strike action at Beardmore's in 1916 he was arrested, tried and deported to Edinburgh. When the deportation order was lifted he returned – to the Forge, where he was appointed foreman! He was elected to the Glasgow Town Council in 1919, representing the Mile-end ward, and in 1922 became MP for the Dumbarton Burghs, entering Westminster as one of famous group of Clydeside MPs. His impetuosity often carried him away in the House and he was twice suspended – in 1925 and 1937. He was re-elected in 1935 but spoke little. When the ILP disaffiliated he resigned and joined the Labour Party. In 1947 he became a Privy Councillor and in 1951 was raised to the peerage. He was always a typical 'labour aristocrat' – respectable, church-going, teetotal – and although he distanced himself considerably from the radical end of the Left spectrum, he made few enemies.

Sir Thomas Lipton (1850–1931)

Lipton was born in the Gorbals of Ulster parents who had come to Glasgow during the Hungry Forties. After a spell in New York working in a grocery store he returned to Glasgow and in 1871, on his 21st birthday, set up a grocer's shop in Stobcross St in Anderston, sleeping behind the counter. From the beginning he founded his enormous success on two things – no middle-man and adventurous advertising. His main trade was in bacon and cheese which he bought directly from Irish farms and he was thus able to monitor quality and cut prices. His fertile mind was responsible for many publicity stunts. He had a monster cheese containing gold sovereigns driven through the streets from the docks to his shop; he had two distorting mirrors outside his shop door: one which reduced was labelled 'Going to Lipton's', the other enlarging and labelled 'Coming from Lipton's'. He soon had shops in most large Scottish towns and in many English ones; his successes demonstrated the profits to be made from selling cheaply to the working classes through a chain of multiple stores. During the 1880s he began selling tea. Once again he cut out the middleman, buying his own plantations in Ceylon, and soon became famous for his Lipton's teas. So widespread did his shopping empire extend that in the 1890s his headquarters were transferred to London. He caught the public imagination even more strongly with his valiant but fruitless efforts to win the America's Cup for yacht-racing with his *Shamrocks*.

Benny Lynch (1913–46)

Benny Lynch, born in the Gorbals, was taught to box by a local Roman Catholic priest, Father James Fletcher. He turned professional in 1931 and fought regularly in Glasgow from then until 1934, showing early promise – in 1932, for example, he fought 29 times and lost only three fights.

His first step to the top came in 1934 when he fought and beat Jim Campbell to win the Scottish flyweight title. The following year he reached the top when 500 fellow citizens travelled south to Manchester to see him take the world flyweight title from Jackie Brown, who had held it for three years. In 4 minutes 42 seconds he had Brown down ten times, before the referee intervened, so becoming Scotland's first-ever world boxing champion. On his return to Glasgow the victor was met by a crowd estimated at 20,000.

He defended and retained his British

and World titles against Pat Palmer in 1936 but already the first warning signs of trouble began to appear; now that he had achieved his goal he felt less need to keep away from drink.

The Americans regarded Small Montana as the world champion and in 1937 Lynch fought him in London. He was pronounced winner after a 15-round fight, still regarded as the finest-ever flyweight match. That same year he fought Peter Kane at Shawfield Park, Glasgow, before a 40,000 crowd, scoring a knock-out in the 13th round. This was the last time he was able to make eight stone, the maximum for a flyweight, and it was said that he was no longer bothering to train hard. He fought Kane again in Liverpool, where a draw enabled him to retain his titles.

The end of his meteoric career came in 1938. He was matched to defend his title against the American Jackie Jurich, but at the weigh-in he was found to be overweight by 6½lb. The match went ahead as a non-title contest but although he knocked out his opponent in the 12th round he forfeited his world title. Later that same year the total collapse of his career was confirmed when, out of training, in very poor condition and weighing 9st 5lb, he was knocked out by a Romanian boxer in three rounds. He now found himself relegated back to the boxing booths of his youth and took solace in drinking. He sank deeper and deeper, until in 1946 he was picked up from the gutter dying from pneumonia.

Lynch was undoubtedly Scotland's greatest boxer and also its most tragic one. Built on a physique produced by one of Glasgow's worst slums, he was unique as a hard-punching flyweight matched with a perfect sense of balance, and his record remains – five world flyweight title fights, four won, one drawn.

James Macrae (*c*.1677–1774)

Macrae was born at Ayr and when his father died earned a poor living by herding cattle and running errands. He was befriended by an Irish fiddler, Hew McGuire, and at 15 went to sea. Nothing was heard of him for more than 40 years, but it transpired that by 1720 he had attained the rank of captain in the Honourable East India Company, and that he had been appointed Governor of Madras in 1725. In 1730 he resigned and returned to Scotland with the immense fortune of some £100,000 and settled down in his native Ayrshire. In 1735 he presented to Glasgow a bronze equestrian statue of William III in classical costume. For almost 200 years it stood at Glasgow Cross, a familiar sight to natives and an object of admiration to visitors, until it was moved to Cathedral Sq in 1923. When he died it was found that he had left his whole estate to members of the McGuire family.

Charles Macintosh (1766–1843)

His father came from the Highlands and in 1777 set up a factory in the Dennistoun district of Glasgow to manufacture cudbear (a purple or violet dyeing powder made from lichens). It was surrounded by a high wall and employed only Gaelic-speaking Highlanders and was consequently called the 'secret factory'. Charles, who succeeded his father, was interested in chemistry. Ammonia, used in the production of cudbear, became available in quantity as a by-product of the making of coal gas (1818). With this new and copious supply Macintosh began to experiment and soon discovered that in the form of naptha it dissolved rubber. When cloth was covered with this solution it became impermeable to water and could be used to make rain-proof garments. The new material, first introduced in 1824, became so popular that it soon became known as *Mackintosh* (note the intrusive 'k'). He was also associated with David Dale in developing turkey-red dyeing in Scotland and established the first Scottish alum works. He supplied much of the chemical knowledge which enabled Charles Tennant, at his St Rollox Chemical Works, to perfect his chemical bleach. He left Glasgow about 1840 and moved to Manchester in order to exploit the manufacture of his mackintosh cloth.

Charles Rennie Mackintosh (1868–1928)

Son of a police superintendent, Mackintosh began his career as an apprentice draughtsman in a Glasgow architect's office in 1884, at the same time attending evening classes in the Glasgow School of Art, which was then in the McLellan Galleries, Sauchiehall St. In 1889 he joined the architectural firm of Honeyman & Keppie, an association which lasted until he left Glasgow in 1914. Essentially he made his individual mark on three types of architecture – public buildings, private houses and tea-rooms.

The principal public buildings in which his influence can be best appreciated are Martyrs' School (1895–98), Scotland St School (1904), Queen's Cross Church (1897–99) which, since 1977, has been the headquarters of the Charles Rennie Mackintosh Society, and, above all, in the Glasgow School of Art (1897–99, 1907–9) where, able to pursue his own ideas, he created an entirely original blend of aspects of Scottish vernacular architecture, the Arts and Crafts movement and Art Nouveau. Following the success of his Art School design he became an equal partner in the firm (Honeyman, Keppie & Mackintosh) and received commissions for two private houses. Both of these are located outside Glasgow. The first was Windyhill,

Kilmacolm, commissioned in 1899 by William Davidson, a Glasgow businessman, and finished in 1901. The second design was for Hill House (Upper Colquhoun St, Helensburgh), considered to be his finest domestic commission. It was built (1902–4) for the Glasgow publisher Walter Blackie and is now the property of the National Trust for Scotland.

From the 1890s until shortly before he left Glasgow Mackintosh was associated with Kate Cranston, whose innovative mind brought into being the Glasgow tea-room. In her Buchanan St (1896), Argyle St (1897) and Ingram St (1900) tea-rooms Mackintosh converted existing premises, while in her Willow Tea-room (Sauchiehall St, 1903, still extant) he was given full freedom and fashioned a new type of interior design based on elegant and simple variations of Art Nouveau themes.

In 1900 he married Margaret Macdonald, a fellow art student. She and her sister Frances, along with Mackintosh and Herbert McNair (sometimes known as 'The Four') had worked and experimented together in a wide range of styles and designs and were a prominent influence on the development of the Glasgow Style. From about 1900 until the First World War Mackintosh enjoyed considerable critical acclaim, mainly on the continent, where he exhibited widely at various international exhibitions. His close attention to the Gestalt of an entire building, from its basic layout to its fireplaces, staircases, cutlery and clocks, brought him a growing reputation as an interior, as well as an architectural, designer. A good example of this aspect of his work can be found in the portfolio of designs he produced for a German international competition (1901) to design a 'House for an Artlover' (*Haus eines Kunstfreundes*). No first prize was awarded and his entry was disqualified on a technicality, but its merits were felt to be so considerable that he was awarded a special prize. It is now considered possibly his greatest domestic design and an important 20th-century work of art.

Despite this European critical acclaim, the lack of local recognition (and even more, of commissions) seems to have thoroughly discouraged him. Although Kate Cranston's tea-room commissions helped him financially through these lean years he suddenly resigned his partnership and in 1914 left for England. There he began to establish a new career as a designer of textiles and interiors, but no architectural commissions came his way (other than to design interiors for W.J. Bassett-Lowke in Northampton). In 1923 he and his wife settled in France, where he devoted himself to producing a remarkable series of flower studies and landscape watercolours. In 1927 he returned to London, where he died the following year.

Surprisingly, it has only been within the last 20 years or so that Mackintosh's seminal importance in modern architecture and interior design has been recognised in Britain – his high continental reputation never suffered a similar eclipse. The very large number of books and studies on every aspect of his work and the prices fetched by his furniture and other objects designed by him bear witness to this change of attitude. Even his designs for a 'House for an Artlover' is now becoming a reality in the city's Bellahouston Park, for in 1989 work began in the park on the site of Ibroxhill House (demolished 1910) to construct the House, as far as possible, from his design portfolio. Despite some delays, progress has been made; an Art Lover's House Trust has been set up and it is hoped to have it ready for use as an international post-graduate school for the Glasgow School of Art by 1994.

John Maclean (1879–1923)

Maclean was born in Pollokshaws, Glasgow, and after attending local schools he graduated from the Free Church Training College as a teacher in 1900. While occupying a full-time teaching post he studied part-time at Glasgow University and took an MA in 1904. In the early 1900s he became involved in many local socialist organisations, particularly those which had an educational aim. He regarded working-class education as an essential part of the Left's road to power, founding the Scottish Labour College in 1916 to further that goal. He objected strongly to what he saw as the capitalistic roots of the First World War and suffered several terms of imprisonment for his views. During his time in prison he frequently complained of being ill-treated, and popular feeling several times forced the authorities to release him before he had finished his sentence. His position as a major international socialist was emphasised when he was appointed, but not recognised, as the first Bolshevik Consul in Scotland in 1917. His combination of a belief in international communism and Scottish nationalism alienated him from mainstream British socialism, and his last years were spent in local election campaigns which brought him little support and which aggravated his feeble health and finally killed him. Despite his lack of influence on socialist ideology he has become an untouchable legend of the Scottish Left.

James Maxton (1885–1946)

From a middle-class background in Barrhead, a small Renfrewshire burgh near Glasgow, Maxton graduated MA at Glasgow University and, like John Maclean, taught in various Glasgow schools. He joined the Independent Labour Party, to which he gave unflinching loyalty through-out his life, and soon became one of its most powerful propagandist speakers. A conscientious objector during the First World War, he took a prominent part in the activities of the Clyde Workers' Committee (the source of the 'Red Clydeside' label) and was imprisoned on a charge of sedition in Edinburgh's Calton Jail, 1916–17. He stood as the ILP candidate in Bridgeton after the war but was defeated. He then became the Scottish organiser for the ILP until, in 1922, he was elected MP for Bridgeton (a seat which he held till his death – it was said his votes were not counted but weighed!). He was one of the ten Glasgow left-wingers who entered Parliament at this time and who became known as the 'Clydesiders'. The political cartoons of the time consistently show Maxton as a sort of pirate chief, and indeed his parliamentary career cast him in the role of a freebooter with little regard for what his colleagues saw as practical politics. Under his chairmanship in the 1930s the ILP moved steadily away from the official Labour Party line, finally breaking with the latter in 1932, dooming itself to a place on the side-lines. Despite his 'seagreen incorruptible' approach to politics, his essential humanity made him many friends amongst MPs of all persuasions.

John Millar (1735–1801)

Millar was Professor of Law at Glasgow University in 1761. His studies in the relationships between law, social structures, history and philosophy were very much in advance of the thought of his time. His *On the origins of the distinction of ranks*, published in 1771, is now recognised as one of the earliest modern approaches to the sociology of the family, occupations and property.

Thomas Muir of Huntershill (1765–99)

Born in Glasgow's High St, Thomas Muir was destined for the pulpit but turned to the law. After becoming an advocate in 1787 he was widely recognised as a radical champion of liberty. The onset of the French Revolution inspired hopes of parliamentary reform in Britain, and many local societies sprang up to further this end. However, as the conflict between Britain and France deepened, the government began to look with horror on such dangerous aspirations and in Scotland the full power of the law was used to stamp them out. Muir's advocacy of these views was well known and, while abroad in France, he was charged with sedition and in his absence 'put to the horn' – outlawed. On his return to Scotland in 1793 he was immediately arrested and became the main figure in a series of show trials stage-managed by the Lord Advocate, Robert Dundas, and Robert McQueen, Lord Braxfield, the hanging judge. At his trial his eloquent defence and defiant stance won him considerable sympathy, particularly in Glasgow, making him a martyr for democracy. Not all saw him in this light, however – Wolfe Tone, in some ways his Irish counterpart, declared that 'of all the vain blockheads that I ever met I never saw one his equal'. Muir was sentenced to 14 years' transportation, to Botany Bay, but escaped on a ship bound for America (said to have been sent for this purpose by George Washington). Captured by the Spaniards he was on his way to Spain as a supposed spy when the ship carrying him was attacked by the British navy. In the conflict he was seriously wounded and so badly disfigured that he was able to escape without being recognised and took refuge in France in 1798. Here he was hailed as a 'Hero of the Republic', but ill and partially blinded, he died the following year.

St John Ogilvie (c. 1579–1615)

After the Reformation the Roman Catholic Church sent missionary priests into Scotland to minister to the few remaining faithful souls and to work towards the restoration of the kingdom to the faith. The best known of these was the Jesuit John Ogilvie who came to Scotland about 1613 to 'unteach heresy'. He disguised himself as John Watson, horse cooper, but was apprehended in Glasgow in 1614 and was found to have on his person 'Three little Books containing directions for receiving Confessions . . . with some relics, with a Tuft of St Ignatius' Hair – the Founder of his Order'. He was imprisoned in the Tolbooth and there tried. In a letter smuggled from the jail 16 days before his death he said he had been kept without sleep for nine days and eight nights. The king, James VI, took a keen interest in the case and ordered that, if he was found to be a Jesuit and had said mass, he was to be banished from the Kingdom. However, when a series of questions were put to him regarding the competing authorities of the Pope and the King, his answers were taken to be treasonable and he was condemned to death. On 10 March 1615 he was executed by hanging at the Cross of Glasgow. His body, which was not quartered (as was the usual custom with those judged to be traitors), was buried: some say, in ground to the north of the Cathedral reserved for malefactors; others, near the chapel of St Roche outside the northern boundary of the city.

In 1929 the conduct of his life and the manner of his death caused him to be beatified. Then in 1965 a Glasgow man, John Fagan, was diagnosed as suffering from cancer. In 1967, as he lay dying, a medal of Blessed John Ogilvie was pinned to his night-clothes, after which he began to recover. By the following year he was back at work and upon examination no medical explanation could be given for his remarkable recovery. In 1976 John Ogilvie was canonised, becoming Glasgow's second saint. John Fagan died in 1993.

Alexander Reid (1854–1928)
Born in Glasgow, Reid first worked in his father's business, Kay & Reid, carvers and gilders. In 1887 he was sent to Paris to serve with one of the foremost art-dealers there. Theodore Van Gogh worked in the same establishment and through him Reid met his brother, Vincent Van Gogh, who painted two portraits of him – Reid was his only British sitter. It was only after Reid's death that their identity was established, for they had till then been accepted as self-portraits. In Paris Reid became familiar with the works of many famous French artists – Degas, Monet, Sisley, Pissarro and Gaugin. At that time these painters and the styles they represented were quite unknown back in Glasgow, to which he returned in 1889 to set up his own gallery, La Société des Beaux-Arts. He dealt in the older Scottish and English artists such as Reynolds, Gainsborough, Ramsay and Raeburn (particularly the latter) but he soon began to introduce his clients to the French Impressionists, putting on a large exhibition of them in 1892, as well as showing works by Fantin and Bourdon between 1897 and 1913. By the outbreak of the First World War he had become Glasgow's leading art-dealer.

About this time Reid became involved with a group of young Scottish artists, whose approach to colour somewhat resembled the Impressionists. This group, which became known as the Scottish Colourists, included Peploe, Cadell, Fergusson and Hunter. Reid was also interested in Crawhill (mounting a large exhibition of his work in 1894), Hornel and Henry (for whom he arranged a visit to Japan, 1893–94) and McTaggart. When clients came to him to buy French paintings he always took the opportunity to introduce them to the works of his artist friends, thus establishing them firmly in the contemporary art world.

From 1890 till his death Reid was one of the outstanding figures in art affairs in Scotland; it was his passionate commitment that so strongly influenced the art purchases of the affluent mercantile classes of the city. It was said that after he died there was no more serious art-collecting in Glasgow. He was no mean artist himself, excelling in watercolours and pastels.

Thomas Reid (1710–96)
Professor of Moral Philosophy at Glasgow University, where he succeeded to the chair occupied by Adam Smith, Reid was an influential exponent of the philosophy of 'common sense', attacking the sceptical ideas of his contemporary David Hume. Although to some extent a prophet without honour in his own country, his views were well received abroad, particularly in France and Italy, and were highly regarded by the philosopher Schopenhauer. Renewed interest in him has now given him a well-deserved position of importance in the history of 20th-century philosophy.

Sir Hugh Roberton (1874–1952)
Glasgow-born Sir Hugh Roberton combined business, politics and music, and is chiefly remembered for his creation of the famous Glasgow Orpheus Choir. In 1901 he became the conductor of the Glasgow Toynbee House Choir, which not only introduced him to music but roused his interest in radical politics. Dissatisfied with his subordinate role within the Toynbee House organisation, he left in 1906 to found the Glasgow Orpheus Choir, which through the years built up a worldwide reputation. This

reputation was largely based on Sir Hugh's ability to create a very distinctive and instantly recognisable harmonic 'sound' and in no small measure to his robust personality as a conductor.

In 1914 he established links, not only at a cultural level, with the Independent Labour Party, and became a life-long pacifist. Throughout the 1920s the choir travelled worldwide, so great was its popular appeal, and in 1931 Roberton was knighted. After the outbreak of the Second World War his pacifist views became a matter of controversy, and the BBC banned his choir from broadcasting because of his political opinions. He received much public support; the affair was raised in Parliament in 1942 and he was reinstated. After the war he decided to retire from conducting and, in line with his belief that the choir was the man, to disband the choir. Fortunately he was persuaded to let it continue under another name, the Glasgow Phoenix Choir, with himself as its honorary president. His outspoken comments and behaviour earned him the title of the Bernard Shaw of Scotland.

Adam Smith (1723–80)

Born at Kirkcaldy, Smith attended Glasgow University from 1737 to 1740 and then spent seven years at Oxford. In 1751 he was appointed to the chair of Logic at Glasgow University and the following year became Professor of Moral Philosophy. It was largely the lectures he gave from this chair that formed the basis for his *Inquiry in the nature and cause of the wealth of nations* (1776), which became the founding work of classical political economy. He was on friendly terms with the merchants of Glasgow (he was a member of the Merchants' Club) and it was his close contact with the city trade that helped him to test the theories he set out in his book.

He gave up the chair in 1764 but returned in 1787 as Lord Rector of the University. His *Wealth of Nations*, a seminal work of political economy, has been described as 'probably the most important book that has ever been written'.

David Stow (1793–1864)

Born in Paisley, Stow came to find mercantile employment in Glasgow. He was intensely interested in the education of young children and by 1816 had established a Sunday evening-school for poor children in the Saltmarket. He became an elder in Dr Chalmers' church. In 1824 he established a day-school for 100 children in the Drygate, with the assistance of the Glasgow Educational Society, and in 1826 he set up his own Glasgow Infant School Society. These developments soon led to a teacher training college which moved in 1836 to premises in Dundas Vale as the Normal School for the Training of Teachers, the first of its kind in the country – 'Normal' in the sense of the French *Ecole Normale*, a college for training teachers. He left the Established Church at the Disruption of 1843 and set up a new establishment, the Free Church Normal College, which later metamorphosed into the Stow College. So great was his reputation for training teachers that his students were eagerly sought by many English schools. In 1906 the two branches merged and in 1922 became the Jordanhill College of Education. Many of Stow's ideas were far in advance of his times – he advocated playgrounds, coeducation at primary and elementary levels, and opposed both corporal punishment and prizes.

Charles Tennant (1768–1838)

Immortalised by Robert Burns (in his *Epistle to James Tennant, of Glenconner*) as 'wabster Charlie', Tennant began his career as an apprentice weaver in the little village of Kilbarchan, and in 1788 opened a bleachfield. At this time the only practical method of bleaching linen was to expose it to sunlight, a laborious and inefficient process which could take months to complete. In 1787 James Watt had demonstrated that the recently discovered element chlorine had strong bleaching properties, although its application to textile bleaching proved difficult. Charles Tennant began experimenting with a combination of chlorine and lime, receiving much assistance from the formal chemical education of Charles Macintosh (of waterproof cloth fame). In 1798 they invented and patented a liquid 'chloride of lime', and a chemical works to manufacture it was set up at St Rollox (south of Springburn) under the name of Tennant, Knox & Co. The power of the liquid form was too evanescent to be useful, but a powder version proved exactly what was needed. It revolutionised the textile industry, and the St Rollox Chemical Works expanded rapidly – in 1799 it was producing 52 tons, by 1825 some 910 tons. In 1803 it began making soap along with the production of soda and sulphuric acid.

In 1815 Macintosh left the business, now known as Charles Tennant & Co. By 1830 the St Rollox Chemical Works covered nearly 50 acres and was soon the largest chemical factory in the world. It was also a powerful pollutant: acres of land were covered with its solid chemical wastes. In an attempt to dispose of its gaseous wastes safely a huge chimney was built in 1841 at a cost of £12,000. Popularly known as 'Tennant's Stalk', it dominated the city's northern skyline for many years. It was 455ft 6in from foundation to top (435ft 6in from ground level) and its diameter at foundation level was 50ft (40ft at the surface). It was built

originally to carry off muriatic acid gases, but shortly after its erection these noxious gases were collected and condensed without its aid. In 1903 part of the tower cracked, requiring it to be lowered by 30 to 40ft, and in 1922 it was demolished. (The neighbouring Townsend chimney, 1857–1927, was taller than Tennant's by several feet.) The works, which now specialised in the production of sulphuric acid, were taken over by United Alkali in 1892, but were already beginning to decline (the labour force was halved to about 600), as some of the chemical processes used were being replaced elsewhere by more efficient methods. The works finally closed under ICI in the late 1960s. Although he created a vast fortune and a dynasty, Charles Tennant remained true to his early opinions. He was always a leading spirit in the city's radical movement and turned down a knighthood the year he died.

James Watt (1736–1819)

Son of a blockmaker and ship's chandler in Greenock, Watt went to London in 1754 to learn the trade of a mathematical instrument-maker. On his return to Glasgow he was appointed by the University as their mathematical and philosophical instrument-maker and given accommodation and a workshop in the University building, a circumstance which gave rise to the erroneous belief that the opposition of the Glasgow Hammermens' Guild forced this action on him.

In 1763 he was given a model of a Newcomen steam-engine to repair by Professor John Anderson. In general use at the time, this type of engine required the cylinder (in which the piston moved) to be heated when steam was admitted, and then laboriously cooled to condense the steam – a process very wasteful in terms of time and coal. In 1765 while Watt was idly wandering through the Green, he had 'gone as far as the Herd's House when the idea came into my mind' (a spot now marked by a memorial stone) – he had, in fact, invented the separate condenser (which removed entirely the need for alternately heating and cooling) and had, incidentally, made the industrial revolution possible.

Watt had many other irons in the fire: he became a partner in the Glasgow Delftfield Pottery; as a civil engineer he surveyed the Forth & Clyde Canal, the Monkland Canal (and superintended its construction) and the projected Caledonian Canal; he gave his professional support to Golborne's scheme to deepen the Clyde; and he experimented with chlorine as a bleaching agent. As a hobby he constructed a number of musical instruments, including four organs. One he built in 1762, a little table organ with two stops, was for long erroneously supposed to have been the contentious organ installed in St Andrew's Parish Church and which was outrightly banned by the Glasgow Presbytery.

He lacked the finances to set up the manufacture of his new engine, so in 1774 moved to Birmingham, where Matthew Boulton (1728–1809) and his Soho Foundry supplied both the necessary money and the plant. Their first engine on the new principle was erected in 1776 and was a complete and resounding success (it was estimated that fuel costs dropped by 75 per cent) – by 1800 some 500 engines had been constructed and lucrative orders poured in. Till 1800 Watt and Boulton enjoyed the 'exclusive privilege' of manufacturing the new steam-engine although for a while they were considerably harassed by strenuous attempts to break their patent rights – Watt received £76,000 in royalties in eleven years. In 1784 he invented his governor, an ingenious device which enabled the engine by a simple feed-back system to regulate its own speed.

Thirteen years before his death the University of Glasgow conferred the honorary degree of LL B on him; in 1832 a bronze statue of Watt was placed in George Sq.

STREET CHARACTERS

Society has always had to deal as it thought best with those poor unfortunates whose physical or mental disabilities rendered them incapable of earning a living by ordinary means. In Glasgow's 18th and early 19th centuries it was the task of the Church and the Town's Hospital to provide a bare modicum of relief for these anonymous figures, 'the poor indigent children, the old decayed men and women, and others rendered unable to provide for themselves'.

A few of them, a very few, however, refused to become anonymous, refused to relinquish their individuality – and in doing so earned themselves the soubriquet of 'characters'. The names and careers of

about 20 of them have come down to us, these defiant nonconformists with whom even bailies and grand city magnates were not ashamed to indulge in verbal sword-play and whose sayings and actions amused and still amuse the citizens of Glasgow.

It is an ironic commentary on the whirligig of time that it is the once great men who are now completely forgotten, while the beggars, ballad-singers and chapmen live on.

Blind Alick

The best known of all these characters was Blind Alick. Born Alexander Macdonald in 1771 in the north of England, he was rendered blind by childhood smallpox. He had an excellent ear for the fiddle, however, and it was this talent which provided him with a living when he settled in Glasgow in 1790. He was regularly engaged to play at penny reels and weddings – 1/6d for the first two hours, then 1d for each reel after that. A blind poet, he was often called the Glasgow Homer, and celebrated his country's victories in verse which anticipated many of the felicities of the great McGonagall. Here is his account of a famous naval victory:

> We have gained a mighty fight
> On the sea at Camperdown.
> Our cannon they did rattle, lads
> And we knocked their topmasts
>   down;
> But the particulars you will hear
> By the post in the afternoon.

His love of the life of the city streets was surpassed only by his love of aqua vitae, for he would sooner take his reward in the shape of a dram than as two bawbees. Despite his hard life and hard drinking he lived to the ripe old age (for those days) of 59, dying peacefully in a hospital bed.

Hirstlin Kate

About 1812 this poor unfortunate creature could be seen creeping about the Glasgow streets between the Calton Mouth in the east and Jamaica Street in the west. Having lost nearly all use of her legs, she 'hirstled' along on a little low cart in a most peculiar manner. In one hand she held an old bauchle [shoe]; her good foot was shod with its partner, and by the dexterous use of these two limbs she propelled herself through the city streets. Her appearance was coarse, masculine and haggard, and her tattered and bedraggled skirts constantly swept the city's dirty cobblestones, yet this extremely unprepossessing figure was eagerly sought after by the children. She never begged but the breast of her ragged dress was stuck all over with pins, and for each one given to her she would sing in a cracked voice for her child audiences verse after verse of the old songs and ballads. One of her songs has come down to us:

> The cuckoo sits in yonder tree,
> He sings a song that pleases me,
> He sings a song that pleases me well
> I wish I were where the cuckoo doth
>   dwell.

Auld Hawkie

William Cameron, born at St Ninians near Stirling, was left with a crooked right leg following a boyhood accident while apprenticed to a tailor. He travelled through Scotland and the north of England as a hedge-preacher, strolling actor, toy-maker and china mender. He took to begging, then settled down in Glasgow in 1818 as a ballad seller and street orator. One of his successes was a chapbook called *The Prophecies of Hawkie, a Cow*, from which he took his nickname. Although his wares may have been ordinary, his eloquence was not – apropos of the Irish immigrants coming into Glasgow, he declared: 'They Irishers! We canna' get the use o' oor ain jyles fur them!' Peter Mackenzie, in his *Old Reminiscences of Glasgow*, describes him as 'one of the greatest and wittiest beggars that ever infested the streets of Glasgow'. He died in 1851 in the Town's Hospital, but his 'autobiography' was published in 1888, a curious work which provides an excellent insight into the world of the beggars.

Jamie Blue

Jamie Blue's proper name was James McIndoe, an old soldier who had been drummed out of the 71st Regiment. He was described as a 'dealer in hardware, leeches, spurious pepper and blue' and was also well known as a ballad singer and speech crier. His odd nicknames, 'Jamie Blue' and 'Blue Thumbs', he earned because of the colour of his hands from his trade in indigo-coloured buttons. He was an inveterate enemy and rival of Hawkie whom he strenuously maintained had stolen Jamie's position as Glasgow's 'Head Speech Crier'. He died in 1837 in the Govan Parish Poorhouse.

Bell Geordie

The bellman was an important person in the days when the local newspaper carried no local news. He perambulated the city thoroughfares, attracting the lieges' attention by ringing his bell then making his official announcements in 'a clear and audible voice'. At one time he might be forthtelling that James Hodge's wife's niece dressed dead corpses, at another that Mrs Lamont in the Stockwell Entry had soups ready every day from 12 to 2. The best known of these criers was undoubtedly George Gibson, alias Bell Geordie. As he walked through the city in his red livery coat, its gilt buttons decorated with the city arms, and his blue plush breeches, white stockings, buckled shoes and cocked hat, he was famous for his ability to announce his often pedestrian news in rough rhymes and for his caustic humour. The latter brought about his downfall for he claimed that the bailies were as much the town's servants as himself. Instantly dismissed, he ended his days, silent and stone blind, being led through the streets by a little girl, thankful for the smallest pittance.

The Rev John Aitken

The Rev John Aitken was a self-ordained 'minister' of Calton weaving stock. He had in his youth received a good education and used the remnants of it to deliver public 'preachments', generally at the entrance to

Glasgow Green from the Saltmarket. His style of pulpit oratory was celebrated in a contemporary stanza:

> Stop here, an' pitch a bawbee in my
>   Plate.
> I'll gie ye Gospel for 't, the best I can.
> I'm puir, unbeneficed an' cauld's my
>   Pate,
> My Kirk is space, my Hearers, any
>   man,

His equipment was extremely simple – a three-legged stool, a pewter plate and an old fir chair – and his sermons strong meat, full of fire and brimstone.

The Major and Mary

The poor Major's claim to fame was his appearance and his behaviour. Peter Mackenzie, in his *Reminiscences of Glasgow*, described him as 'round-shouldered, twisted, knock-kneed, splae-footed, his head projecting from the nape of his neck like a duck choking on a rebellious potato'. The Major sang over and over some doggerel lines while he 'accompanied' himself on two sticks, capering about in the queerest of contortions. Here again Peter Mackenzie has a telling phrase: 'a fair representation of an isosceles triangle gone mad'. The dance was actually a *pas de deux*. His partner was Coal Mary, so called from her earlier employment – carrying sacks of coal up the stairs of the Glasgow tenements. This gentle soul was captivated by the Major and in 1825 joined in his crazy cavortings – her dancing style was described as 'ae fit on the grund an' the ither never aff it!'. She got the 'big bawbees' (pennies) while the Major took the 'wee bawbees', of which many more were given! Apart from a penchant for dressing in blue and for carrying scraps of food about her person in many little pokes, history has nothing more to say about her.

Major and Mary were swept away within 48 hours of each other in the cholera outbreak of 1832.

Rab Ha'

Robert Hall was celebrated in his day throughout all the west of Scotland as Rab Ha', the Glesca Glutton. He had been a farm labourer but had early abandoned settled employment for the life of a vagrant, and was a constant attender at all the horse-races, fox-hunts and coursing in the district. So great was his appetite that no one who wagered on his gastronomic powers on such occasions was likely to lose his bet. It is recorded that only once was he beaten, and that by a most curious dish – a saucerful of oysters mixed with cream and ground lump sugar! He died in a hayloft in Hutchesontown in 1843.

Penny-A-Yard

Amongst the many ballad singers, blind fiddlers and vendors of small wares who frequented the Saltmarket, none was stranger than Edward Finlay, wire-worker, born about 1800. Over one shoulder he slung a coil of shining wire from which, with the aid of a small pair of pliers, he skilfully created long lengths of chain which he draped, ready for sale, over his other shoulder. Strange to say, these chains of his met with a ready sale amongst the Glasgow housewives and small traders, and his sales-cry – 'Penny-a-yard' – became the name by which he was known throughout the city. He also had a fair degree of ingenuity which he exercised by twisting his raw material into clever wire-puzzles. As another sideline, he often concocted arithmetical puzzles which he printed and sold, demonstrating their solutions with the aid of chalk and a board. His arms and chest were covered with tattooed Biblical quotations.

Wee Jamie Wallace

James Wallace caught the city's fancy and became elevated to the rank of a 'character'. He had the shoulders and torso of a Hercules but with legs sadly short. His chief claim to fame was his post as self-appointed 'officer' in the Scotch Fruit Market in Kent St. Occasionally he would retire for a while from his voluntary duties to seek the shelter of the Parliamentary Road Poorhouse. Then he would return to take up his superintendence of the gooseberries, plums, pears and apples from the Clydeside orchards.

Wee Willie White

William White was a blind street musician. In physique he was broad and stout, standing scarcely 5ft high. He patrolled the Trongate from the Steeple to Jamaica St, playing patriotic and popular songs on his tin whistle. He was a great favourite with everyone and many of the city notables would salute him as they passed. The sums he earned by his musical talents enabled him to live in what a contemporary account described as 'respectable poverty'. He died in 1858 and, a reflection on the mores of the society of the time, his admirers purchased a lair for him in the Southern Necropolis and decorated it with a carved representation of his tin whistle and the box he carried it in.

Big Rachel

Mrs Rachel Hamilton, born in the north of Ireland in 1829, was an outstanding woman who stood over 6ft tall. She was by turns a labourer with Tod & McGregor, ship-builders, a forewoman navvy at the Jordanhill Brickworks, and a worker on an Anniesland farm. During the Partick Riots in the early 1870s, she acted as a special constable. She died in Dumbarton Rd, Partick, in 1899, aged 70.

Old Malabar

Old Malabar was unique amongst the Glasgow characters by being neither a beggar nor an eccentric nor a ballad singer, but a street showman-entertainer. He was an Irishman, born in Sligo in 1800, under the name of Patrick Feeney. Over 6ft 4in tall, dressed in his colourful Oriental robes and accompanied by his faithful wife who looked after his props, he was always able to attract a street crowd. He juggled, he swallowed swords, but his *tour de force* was when he hurled a heavy metal ball high into the air and caught it in a cup bound to his forehead, an act which he prefaced with 'Three ha'pence more and up goes the ball'. He seldom indulged in ardent spirits; once he did, and during his next performance he failed to catch the ball properly in the cup. The result was a scar which he carried to the day of his death at 83 years of age in 1883.

The Clincher

The Clincher, alias Alexander Wyllie Petrie, was a barber by trade, but first and foremost he was a character of the purest water. A kenspeckle figure in his immaculate top hat, he was notorious throughout the city for the tongue-lashings he freely distributed, either verbally or through the pages of his very own newspaper, *The Clincher* (started in 1897), and mainly directed at his two constant enemies, the Town Council and the Police Department. Taken to the local asylum, he was released with a certificate, and thereafter he boasted of being the only Glaswegian officially to be declared sane! He died in 1937, aged 84.

VISITORS

The unanimity of the early visitors to the city as to its architectural beauty is a clear indication of Glasgow's pre-industrial appearance; from the beginning of the 19th century visitor's observations are more subjective, more personal and more critical.

1650: 'The Town of Glasgow, though not so big, nor so rich, yet to all seems a much sweeter & more delightful Place than Edinburgh.' (*Several Proceedings in Parliament.*)

1655: 'The inhabitants [of Glasgow] (all but the students of the colledge which is here) are traders and dealers: some for Ireland with small smiddy coales, in open boats, from foure to ten tonnes, from whence they bring hoopes, ronges, barrewll staves, meale, oates and butter; some from France with pladding, coales, and herring . . . for which they return salt, paper, rosin, and prunes; some to Norway for timber; and every one with their neighbours the Highlanders . . . with pladding, dry hides, goate, kid, and deere skyns which they sell.' (Thomas Tucker.)

1658: 'In Glasgow the Streets and Houses are more neat & clean than those of Edinburgh; it being also one of the chiefest Universities in Scotland.' (*The Perfect Politician.*)

1661: 'We went . . . to Glasgow, which is the second City in Scotland, fair, large, and well-built, cross-wise, somewhat like unto Oxford, the Streets very broad and pleasant.' (John Ray.)

1661: 'Glasgo is the second town in the kingdom of Scotland . . . The streets . . . are large and handsome, as if belonging to a new town; but the houses are only of wood, ornamented with carving.' (Jorevin de Rocheford.)

1689: 'Glasgow is a place of great extent and good situation; and has the reputation of the finest town in Scotland, not excepting Edinburgh, tho' the royal city. The two main streets are made cross-wise, well paved and bounded with stately buildings, especially about the centre, where they are mostly new, with piazzas under 'em . . . the nest of fanaticism, and the most factious town in all that kingdom.' (Thomas Morer.)

1669: 'At last we came to the renowned city of Glasgow . . . [which] for pleasantness of sight, sweetness of air, and delightfulness of its gardens and orchards enriched with most delicious fruits, surpasseth all other places in this tract . . . The city is governed by a Mayor [sic], and is very eminent for its trade and merchandize.' (James Brome.)

1682: Samuel Pepys (1633–1703) visited Glasgow in 1682 in the train of James VII and II when, as the Duke of York, the latter came north to Scotland. Pepys made a tour of the country, visiting Stirling, Linlithgow, Hamilton and Glasgow, which last he found to be 'a very extraordinary town indeed for beauty and trade, much superior to any in Scotland'. However, he also said that he had a 'dislike [of] their personal habits' and that 'a rooted nastiness hangs about the person of every Scot (man and woman)'. The Duke was enrolled as a burgess, the Town Council spending the enormous sum of £4,000 in entertaining him.

1724: Daniel Defoe (1660–1731), in prison for publishing an anti-establishment pamphlet, was released and sent to Scotland in 1706 as a secret government agent to promote the Union. In 1724 he published his *Tour through Great Britain* in which he gives a very detailed description of Glasgow based on several visits he paid the city. As an English Dissenter he seems to have found it a congenial place and has several perspicacious remarks to make about its trade and industry. He describes it as 'a city of Business' and says, 'The Union has indeed answered its end to them more than to any other part of the kingdom, their trade being new formed by it . . . they now send near 50 sail of ships every year to Virginia'. He also foresaw the convenience to the city of a Forth and Clyde canal, conjecturing that 'if this city could have a communication with the firth of Forth . . . they would very probably in a few years double their trade.' His general description of Glasgow is a worthy encomium: 'In a word, tis one of the cleanliest, most beautiful, and best-built cities in Great Britain.'

1723: 'Glasgow is the beautifullest little city I have seen in Britain; it stands deliciously on the Banks of the River Clyde, over which there is a fair Stone Bridge of eight Arches.' (John Macky.)

1725: 'Glasgow is to outward appearance, the prettiest and most uniform Town that ever I saw; and I believe there is nothing like it in Britain.' (Burt's *Letters*.)

1771: 'Glasgow is the most handsome City in Scotland, all the Buildings being of fine Free-stone. It consists of several spacious Streets, which, if they were uniform, would be extremely beautiful. Many of the Houses have their Gables to the Street, and are built over Arcades, but too narrow to be walked in with any conveniency.' (Spencer's *English Traveller*.)

1803: William Wordsworth (1770–1803), on his way north in 1803 to visit the Highlands with his sister Dorothy and his friend Samuel Coleridge, stopped off at the Saracen's Head Inn. In her journal Dorothy noted that she found the city's 'streets as handsome as streets can be . . . the New Town is built of fine stone, in the very best style of the very best London streets . . . but not being of brick they are greatly superior'. They had time to visit Glasgow Green where she remarked that the washing-house there contained 'a hundred, or two or even three' washerwomen.

1819: Robert Southey (1774–1843), poet laureate, visited Glasgow in 1819. What struck him most about the city comes in his description of his visit to the Cathedral: 'the seats are so closely packed that any person who would remain there during the time of service in warm weather must have an invincible nose'.

1829: James John Audubon (1785–1851), American ornithologist, came to the city in 1829 seeking subscriptions for his famous 2-volumed *Birds of America* with its 435 hand-coloured life-size pictures. He complained – 'One subscriber [the Hunterian Museum, in Glasgow University] in a city of 150,000 souls'.

1832: William Cobbett (1763–1835), the English radical journalist, visited Scotland in 1832 to see the effects of the Reform Act of that year. When he visited Glasgow he exclaimed: 'A city of the greatest beauty, a commercial town, and a place of manufacture ...Manchester and Liverpool in one.'

1841: Thomas De Quincy (1785–1850) lived most of his later life in Edinburgh, from where he visited Glasgow several times. He was keenly interested in astronomy and in pursuit of this hobby he stayed in Glasgow from 1841 to 1843, at first with his great friend, J.P. Nichol, Professor of Astronomy at Glasgow University, and afterwards with Edmund L. Lushington, Professor of Greek there. He also came to Glasgow in 1847, fleeing from his insatiable Edinburgh creditors, living first in Renfield St and then in the Rottenrow.

1847: Charles Dickens (1812–70) first visited Glasgow in 1847 when he was invited to be the principal speaker at the opening of the Athenaeum in Ingram St and afterwards to be the guest at a Grand Soirée in the City Hall. He remarked later: 'I have never been more heartily received anywhere or enjoyed myself more completely.'

He returned the following year as the leading actor in his Company of London Amateurs, who were touring the principal cities in order to raise money to purchase Shakespeare's house in Stratford-on-Avon. They gave two performances in the Theatre Royal, Dunlop St (Dickens played Slender in *The Merry Wives of Windsor*) and the receipts, £681. 17s. 8d., were the largest of the tour. Dickens gave some of the profits for the relief of the city's many unemployed.

In 1858 he was back in Glasgow, this time to give two of his celebrated readings from his works – he is reported to have received £600. He returned for similar purposes in 1861 and in 1868–69. *A propos* of his 1861 visit he said that 'it rains as it never does rain anywhere else . . . it is a dreadful place, though much improved, and possessing a deal of public spirit'.

1848: Frédéric Chopin (1810–49) came to Glasgow in 1848, just one year before his death, and gave a *matinée musicale* in the Merchants' Hall. A contemporary newspaper account reported that 'the audience, which was not large, was exceedingly distinguished', and noted that he was 'a man of weak constitution and seems labouring under physical debility and ill-health'.

1849: Queen Victoria (1819–1901) was the first British monarch to visit Glasgow since the 17th century. She arrived at Glasgow Harbour in August 1849 on board the Royal steam yacht *Fairy*, visited the Cathedral and the University, knighted the Provost and departed for Balmoral by way of the Royal Train from Queen St Station. She came back to the city in August 1888 to visit the Glasgow International Exhibition and took the opportunity formally to open the new City Chambers in George Sq.

1852: Harriet Beecher Stowe (1811–96) toured Europe in 1852 following the publication of her *Uncle Tom's Cabin.* She was especially welcomed in Glasgow, which had strong anti-slavery sympathies. During most of her visit to the city she felt unwell, not more so than during her visit to the Cathedral when she reported that the 'strain upon the head and eyes . . . have overcome, as I was told, many before me'.

1852: William Thackeray (1811–63), novelist, came to Glasgow in 1852 to give his famous lectures. 'What a hideous smoking Babel it is, after the clear London atmosphere quite unbearable!' He was also disconcerted by the number of Hirishmen [sic] and women.

1864: Giuseppe Garibaldi (1807–82), Italian patriot, is said to have visited Glasgow incognito *c.*1864 in order to recruit volunteers to fight in Italy, the city

being thought of as the centre of the Garibaldi movement in this country. The sympathy for his cause was so great that some of the Irish in the city volunteered to fight against him for the Papal States.

1874: D. L. Moody (1837–99) and I. A. Sankey (1840–1908), evangelists, visited Glasgow in 1874. Their mission lasted over five months and most of their meetings were held in a tent in Glasgow Green. The City Hall was also used on occasions. Tens of thousands attended their meetings and the closing service was held in the Kibble Palace. They returned in 1882 and in 1891. During the latter visit they used the St Andrew's Halls and on this occasion they were instrumental in founding the Bible Training Institute in Bothwell St.

1898: Joseph Conrad (1854–1924), novelist. In his early sea-going days Conrad served mainly on Clyde-built ships under Scottish shipmasters. After the publication of his first novels he developed bad writer's block and came to Glasgow in 1898, hoping to get command of a Glasgow ship. Fortunately for the English novel, his interviewee skills proved to be so bad that he returned south and resumed writing.

Photographers

John Kibble (1815–94) is probably better known as the owner of the vast circular conservatory, the Kibble Palace in the Botanic Gardens, but he was also an amateur photographer of some note, and published many technical articles in the professional journals of his day. He is now

probably best known as the constructor of a 'monster' camera. It had a 13in diameter lens and focal length of 6ft and could take glass plate negatives of up to 44 × 6in weighing 44lb. It was transported on a specially built cart and the operator customarily worked inside it when preparing the collodion coating before exposure. Its most celebrated print was a picture of Glasgow Harbour titled *General Terminus, Glasgow, and Shipping in distance* which measured 40 × 21in.

John Urie (1820–1910), born in Paisley, became one of Glasgow's most prominent early commercial photographers. In a somewhat similar fashion to Thomas Annan, he first exercised his artistic talents by setting up in the city as a wood-engraver in 1850, combining this in 1853 with 'photographist'. One of his claims to fame is a group photograph he made in 1857 of the family of a Glasgow architect, James Smith. Smith's eldest daughter Madeleine figures prominently in the photograph and later she had Urie take a photograph of herself which she exchanged for one of her lover, Pierre L'Angelier; that same year she was tried for his murder, escaping the gallows under the Scottish verdict of Not proven.

Local interest in **Thomas Annan** (1830–87) largely derives from his mid-19th-century recordings of Glasgow's old closes, but he has also achieved international fame as a pioneering and talented photographer in his own right, as a 'skilled technician, fine portraitist, recorder of the city and artist'.

In his early years he trained as a lithographer and copperplate engraver with Joseph Swan, the distinguished Glasgow engraver, an indication that his skills were not merely mechanical. Realising the potentialities of this new medium he set up in 1855 in the west end of Glasgow, advertising himself first as a calotype printer and then in 1857 as a photographic artist.

His firm rapidly became one of the leading Scottish photographic establishments, and the range of the facilities he offered was extensive – his business card reads 'Photographers of Engineers' and Architects' Drawings – Ships taken in the Stocks, or when Launched, or from Paintings – "Cartes de Visite" and large Portraits (Plain or Coloured) – Groups taken Out of Doors of Volunteers, Cricket Clubs, &c – Views of Gentlemen's Seats, and every Variety of Landscape Subjects'.

To his contemporaries Annan was best known for his photographs of the newly built residences of the newly enriched middle classes, for his reproductions of famous works of art and for his portraits; but now his place as a photographer is established by the remarkable prints he made of the old closes of central Glasgow around the 1860s and 1870s. The Corporation had established in 1866 the City Improvement Trust which had innovatory powers to acquire and demolish the old slum tenements which lined the High St and the Saltmarket and the closes and vennels leading off them. The Trustees wished to make a pictorial record of these buildings before they disappeared and they might very well have commissioned a series of engravings or watercolours. However, the Corporation had chosen Annan in the 1850s to record photographically aspects of the city's magnificent new Loch Katrine water supply (published in 1859 as *Views on the line of the Loch Katrine Waterworks*, second edition, 1877), and it may be supposed that his successful completion of this project caused the Trustees, in turn, to chose Annan to make for them another 'photographic record'. In three magnificent editions, entitled *Old Closes and Streets of Glasgow*, and containing over 50 prints, he captured the physical appearance of old Glasgow and produced one of the earliest series of urban photographs.

The first edition had no title or publication date but was probably produced about 1871 and contained 31 pasted-in albumen prints taken between 1868 and 1871. The second edition also had no date through its title describes its contents as 'taken 1868–1877'. It contained 40 pasted-in carbon prints. (Before the invention of the photogravure process the only way of illustrating a book photographically was by the pasting-in of individual prints, a laborious process in which Annan's firm was extensively employed and of which many examples have survived.) The third edition came out in 1900 and had 50 photogravure reproductions. The family firm added dealings in fine art to its photographic work and is still in existence, located not far from the site of its 1855 debut.

William Graham (1845–1914) lived most of his life in the Springburn district of Glasgow. Employed by the North British Railway Co, he was suspended following a railway strike in 1893. Photography had been a lifelong hobby and he now turned professional, with a little wooden studio in Springburn. Almost nothing is known of his commercial photographic work, but on a personal basis he combined his photographic abilities with a keen interest in the past and present of the city (he was a founder member of the Old Glasgow Club to whose transactions he often contributed) and he built up a large collection of plate negatives and prints devoted to relics of old Glasgow and to the busy life around him. His tastes were catholic – cathedrals and carthorses, churches and mansions, slums and shops (usually with the staff lined up in front), milk girls and ministers. After his death his collection of some 3,000 negatives and 450 slides plus two albums of prints came to the Mitchell Library. As a photographer his skills were no more than competent but nevertheless more than adequate to record the physical appearance of much of late 19th-century Glasgow.

James Craig Annan (1864–1946), son of Thomas Annan, spent his early years working in his father's printing factory and studio. Glasgow knows little of him; he moved away from the work that has made his father famous and became better known as a pictorialist, a composer of landscapes and genre scenes. He is reckoned a master of the photogravure process and was an early user of the hand-held camera.

Oscar Marzaroli (1933–1988). Marzaroli's family moved from Italy to Glasgow when he was two years old. He attended Glasgow School of Art but his studies were cut short by illness. Next he worked for a while in Stockholm and London as a freelance photo-journalist, returning to Glasgow in 1959, where he found employment as a freelance film cameraman. In 1967 he co-founded Ogam Films, a production company making documentaries. In the early 1980s he returned to full-time still photography and between then and his death produced a remarkable series of photographic albums, mainly about Glasgow. He was fascinated by the great changes being thrust upon the city in the 1980s, and as these changes were most noticeable in the east end it was there that his genius particularly flourished. There is not a 'meaningful abstraction' amongst his photographs – the ordinary Glaswegians, almost invariably an essential ingredient in his work, brought his prints to life and, by their mere presence, mutely criticised the uneasy overlapping of the old and the new Glasgow in which Marzaroli so carefully locates them.

Like Marzaroli, **George Oliver** (*d*.1990) also spent some time at the Glasgow School of Art. After freelancing in London, he worked for a while with the Scottish Committee of the Council of Industrial Design, but from the early 1960s he freelanced as a designer and illustrator as well as a historian of the motor-car and of photography. As a photographer he specialised in the visual and performing arts, transport and travel, but there were few aspects of built Glasgow which he did not record, and many of this book's illustrations have come from his camera.

Police

The preservation of order within the burgh was one of the duties laid on all burgesses – to 'watch and ward' – and as long as the town remained small, the night guard drawn from the ranks of the burgesses was sufficient to maintain the town's peace. It customarily met in the session-house of the Tron or Laigh Church from which it would periodically issue during the night to patrol the city's empty streets.

As the city and its population grew the inability of a group of elderly gentlemen to preserve order became obvious, and in 1778 an inspector, with a body of men under him, was appointed to police the streets. It was not legally possible to pay for this service from the town's revenue, and it lasted scarcely three years. In 1790 another attempt was made by setting up a night guard drawn from all male citizens, but this was not persevered with.

In 1800 a bread riot and some strikes persuaded the authorities to take the bold step of establishing a realistic and reliable police force. The 1800 Act vested the control of this new force in a body of trustees consisting of the Provost, the Dean of Guild, the Deacon Convener and 24 elected commissioners. For several reasons this act was epoch-making for the city. For the first time in the burgh's history the funding of a burgh activity was to come from a tax laid on all the citizens; in other words it brought into being the Glasgow rate-payer. For the first time the ordinary citizens were able to elect their own representatives (the Commissioners). It also marked the beginning of what was to become the city's Public Health and Sanitary Departments. At this time 'policing' meant more than keeping law and order – it also involved street cleansing, maintenance and lighting. A Chief of Police was appointed with three sergeants, nine officers and 68 watchmen. The latter were on duty during the night and were suitably equipped with greatcoats (numbered on the back), staves and lanterns (two candles were supplied, one lit). They also had the use of sturdy wooden sentry-boxes.

The assembly point was, once again, the session-house of the Tron Church, but after one or two moves a Central Police Office was erected in South Albion St in 1825. Although a very considerable improvement on the old 'ward and watch', the police were still incapable of dealing with large-scale civil disturbances, and in the event of riots recourse was always had to the military, usually in the form of cavalry forces from barracks in Eglinton St.

When the neighbouring burghs of Gorbals, Anderston and Calton were annexed to the city in 1846 their police forces were amalgamated with the Glasgow force. As provided for by the 1833 Burgh Reform Act, the Town Council was now freely elected by citizen vote, so it was now considered unnecessary to retain the separately elected police commissioners. Instead, the management of the police force was invested in the Police and Statute Labour Committee whose members were elected by the Council, but were not under its direct control.

In 1877 the responsibility for policing the city was vested directly in the Council itself sitting as police commissioners. By now the force had grown to over 1,300 men under a chief constable and seven superintendents, and its duties included statute labour, lighting, health, street improvements, public baths and wash-houses. After 1890 its powers were further extended to include sanitation and the licensing of theatres, public shows and billiard-rooms.

For the next 40 years or so much of the work of the police was involved in keeping pace with the rapid expansion of the city. In 1846 when Anderston, Calton and Gorbals were annexed to the city the force was divided into four divisions – Central (the old City of Glasgow), Western (Anderston), Eastern (Calton) and South (Gorbals). To cover the 1891 takeovers, two other divisions were added – 'C' (or Queen's Park) Division and 'H' (or Maryhill) Division – Maryhill, Hillhead and Kelvinside. It was following this annexation that a series of police boxes were set up throughout the city equipped with telephones and light signals – these boxes remained in use until they were replaced by an improved type in 1932. By the turn of the century the force was employing 1,355 officers (of whom 187 were Irish, 26 English and three were foreigners). Finally, with the 1912 expansion, the divisions were increased from nine to eleven by the addition of Partick and St Rollox.

Some progress was made in equipping the force for the 20th century. In 1921 two police cars were purchased. As these were for emergency use only, personnel were expected in ordinary circumstances to walk or take the tram. In 1926 an innovatory system was introduced which card-indexed the MO (*modus operandi*) of every persistent criminal in Glasgow.

The Glasgow force was now the largest in the country after that of London, but by the early 1930s its morale had been badly affected by various circumstances – the most obvious of which included the dire economic effects of the '30s depression (particularly severe in the west of Scotland) which had in turn led to a marked deterioration in the relations between the police and the unemployed, as well as corruption amongst some councillors (including the Police Committee Convenor) and the wrongful conviction of Oscar Slater in the 1920s *cause célèbre* murder case based on doubtful police evidence. So in 1931 a new broom was brought in – Sir Percy J. Sillitoe came from reorganising the Sheffield police force to be the city's Chief Constable. In one decade he applied his experience to all aspects of the Glasgow police and totally reorganised the force. He reduced the number of divisions from eleven to seven: 'A', Central; 'B', Marine; 'C', Eastern; 'D', Southern; 'E', Northern; 'F', Maryhill; and 'G', Govan. He closed down 13 police stations, many middle and senior ranks were done away with and retirement was made compulsory after 30 years. He also substituted civilian women employees as telephonists, typists and clerks. A Fingerprint and Photographic Department was set up and in 1933 a new radio transmitter enabled contact to be maintained between HQ and an increased fleet of police cars. He had acquired a reputation in Sheffield as a gang-buster and he now tackled the proliferating Glasgow gangs. He set up control centres equipped with maps, allowing the gangs no respite, anticipating their moves and laying ambushes ahead of their 'marches'. He picked off their leaders, and eventually drove them from the city streets. At another level he was responsible for breaking a 'graft' ring amongst the city bailies (in his ten years he sent five magistrates to prison on charges of corruption). It was said that he was known to patrol the city streets at night dressed as a workman. He introduced the chequered black and white hatband – the Sillitoe tartan, it was called – in use now by many other police forces. He was also responsible for setting up the so-called C Division Specials, a network of informers used in particular against IRA terrorists and what were described as 'extreme left-wing agitators'. In 1943 he left Glasgow to take control of the new Kent force, leaving behind a completely restructured system which is, basically, still today's force.

In 1945 a Scientific Branch of the CID was formed which included an Identification Bureau, soon expanded to cover all the Scottish police forces. The same year the minimum height (which had been for some 80 years 5ft 10in) was reduced to 5ft 9½in, later to 5ft 8in, and by 1955 the Glasgow Police Department was employing over 2,000 officers in seven divisions, with its headquarters at St Andrew's St in the Saltmarket. A centre for the receipt and dissemination of information was set up with five switchboards, four police switchboard extensions, two exchange lines and four teleprinters, and by 1960 it was receiving some 200,000 calls. The earlier use of civilians on routine tasks was now extended to fingerprint work, police car maintenance and radio control, freeing more policemen for street duties. The growing ability of criminals to move easily and swiftly in and out of the city introduced a regional aspect into crime prevention, and a Regional Crime Squad was set up. It was based in Glasgow and included the police forces of Dunbartonshire, Lanarkshire, Renfrewshire and the city. This proved to be so successful that two years later the squad was amalgamated with others to form the Scottish Crime Squad. Between 1965 and 1967 shortage of constables brought about the introduction of two-way radios for beat constables (one beat in the city centre where there had been ten), and of unit-beat policing (two officers and a Panda car replaced a foot-patrol of six).

The policing of the city was another of the age-old responsibilities lost to the civic fathers at local government reorganisation in 1973. Just before the handover, Glasgow's seven police divisions and their headquarters (still at St Andrew's St, but shortly to move to Pitt St) employed over 3,000 officers.

Population and Area

YEAR	POPULATION	YEAR	POPULATION
1300	1,500	1861	395,503
1450	2,000	1871	477,732
1556	4,500	1881	511,415
1600	7,000	1891	565,714
1660	14,000	1901	761,712
1708	12,000	1911	784,455
1740	17,043	1921	1,034,174
1755	23,546	1931	1,088,461
1780	42,000	1939	1,128,473
1791	66,000	1946	1,050,000
1801	77,385	1951	1,089,555
1811	100,746	1965	1,012,436
1821	147,043	1966	990,855
1831	202,426	1971	897,848
1841	255,650	1981	765,915
1851	329,096	1991	681,228

The population figures from 1300 to 1800 are only estimates, but they do indicate, by the slow regular growth of its population, the pattern of development of a small market town. There is one odd hiccup. In 1660 the population had doubled from 1600 (7,000 to 14,000) and then dropped to 12,000 in 1708. Various reasons have been suggested to explain this anomaly, such as man-made disasters – from 1640 to 1700 the kingdom was racked by religious and civil disturbances and it is quite possible that the Presbyterian majority refused to have their children baptised by Episcopalian clergy – or natural disasters such as the plague visitation in the 1640s and the two disastrous fires of 1652 and 1677. A simpler explanation might be that the estimates are out!

Starting with 1801 the certainty of the Census begins. The sharp increase between 1801 and 1831 is largely due to immigration from the Highlands and from the surrounding agricultural areas into the city's rapidly increasing number of factories. It was estimated that by 1831 there were approximately 163,000 Scots, 3,000 English, 36,000 Irish and about 500 foreigners in Glasgow.

Between the years 1841 and 1914 the population quadrupled, much of this increase coming from large-scale immigration of Irish during the 'Hungry Forties'. The bulk of these immigrants found employment in the city's thriving cotton industry. Over the century as a whole, Glasgow's population had increased tenfold.

From 1841, when the city was experiencing high birth rates, and high death rates (particularly high infant mortality), it moved with surprising swiftness by the end of the century to a situation of low births and generally low death rates. In spite of the annexation of populous areas to the city in 1846, 1891 and 1912, the population figures did not show the large increases which should have been expected, a clear indication that population growth was slowing down. From 1901 to 1911 there had in fact been a net outflow of 83,000 persons, and from then on the city's emigration has always exceeded its net immigration.

In the 1841 *Guide to the Glasgow & Ayrshire Railway* it was stated that 'Glasgow [is] now the second city in the Empire', a sentiment echoed ten years later by Robert Buchanan, a Glasgow minister, who said that Glasgow 'is now the second city of the greatest empire in the world'. The city was able to maintain this boast only to 1951 when its population of 1,089,555 was surpassed, just, by Birmingham's 1,096,000. Two reasons have been put forward for these 20th-century losses: first, the continuing emigration to England or overseas; and second, a movement (hastened by increasing access to private transport) away from the city and its suburbs to areas outside the city, such as Bearsden, Milngavie, Clarkston, Giffnock, Newton Mearns and beyond.

Despite this fall, the city's population was still large enough to create problems, particularly as regards housing. The 1946 Clyde Valley Regional Plan proposed overspill as the solution – that is, reducing the population even faster by assisting inhabitants to move out to other localities. Its final figure for the numbers involved was 500,000. The Corporation would not accept this and withdrew from the Plan, but eventually, by 1959, it had to admit that some overspill was necessary, and arrange with some 60 other local authorities and with the new towns of East Kilbride, Cumbernauld, Glenrothes and Livingston to take a sizeable part of the city's population. The projected population figure of Glasgow is expected to be 635,000 by the year 2002.

AREA

Original area: 1,768 acres

The original burgh boundary, which marked off the Royalty or Regality and which contained the city till the end of the 18th century. It followed a meandering course, north from the west end of Broomielaw Quay, then east along Argyle St and north following the line of the Glasgow or St Enoch Burn. Next it skirted three sides of the lands of Blythswood, then north and east to the High St. It then wandered back and forth, eventually reaching north of the Cathedral, from where it turned south to end up on the river at the east end of the Glasgow Green. From the beginning of the 17th century to the start of the 19th century the city's boundaries remained unchanged.

1800: 1,864 acres

Part of the Green and ground between St David's (Ramshorn) Church and St Enoch's Burn added 96 acres to the city. From this date to 1938 the city's area increased more than 22 times.

1830: 2,181 acres

The Necropolis on the east and the Lands of Blythswood on the west increased the city's area by 317 acres.

1843: 2,373 acres

The ground between Castle St and the Garscube Rd – north of the Cathedral added a further 192 acres.

1846: 5,063 acres

The burghs of Anderston and Calton, along with most of Gorbals added 2,690 acres to the city. This was the first annexation of a number of small contiguous burghs, a process which reached a climax at the end of the century. With the addition of Gorbals, the city for the first time included land on the south side of the Clyde. Also included were Bridgeton, Parkhead (part), Camlachie, Dennistoun, Garngad, Park, Woodside and North Kelvinside. The Kelvin marked its western boundary and Shettleston its eastern.

1872: 6,033 acres

The ground on which the new Glasgow University was built, Keppochhill and part of Alexandra Parade, to the north-east (a further 970 acres).

1878: 6,111 acres

Coplawhill and part of Gorbals (78 acres).

1891: 11,861 acres

The burghs of Govanhill, Crosshill, Pollokshields, East Pollokshields, Hillhead and Maryhill, and the districts of Mount Florida, Langside, Shawlands, Kelvinside, Possilpark, Springburn, etc added 5,750 acres to the city. This represents the much fought-over annexation of the little independent burghs which had sprung up on the city's south and west boundaries and which were no more than suburbs of the city, along with two districts to the immediate north of the burgh.

1896: 12,311 acres

Bellahouston Park, and Craigton extended the city westwards by 450 acres.

1899: 12,688 acres

Blackhill – a small area to the north east; Shawfield – another small area, at the east end of the Green together added 377 acres.

1905: 12,796 acres

Kinning Park, another of the small burghs, added 108 acres on the south bank of the river.

1909: 12,975 acres

Mosspark to the south-west increased the city's area by 179 acres.

1912: 19,183 acres

The burghs of Govan, Partick and Pollokshields and the districts of Shettleston, Tollcross, West of Govan, Cathcart, Newlands and West of Partick, Dawsholm, Temple and Knightswood (north). With this large takeover of 6,208 acres Glasgow had almost reached its modern boundaries. The historical burghs of Govan and Partick had earlier stood out against annexation. The other miscellaneous areas are located all round the perimeter, but Shettleston and Tollcross mark the first significant extension to the east.

1926: 29,509 acres

Lambhill, Robroyston, Millerston, Carntyne and Aikenhead, and Mansewood, Kennishead, Nitshill, Hurlet, Crookston, Cardonald, Scotstoun, Yoker and Knightswood together added 10,326 acres. Whereas the earlier large annexations had mainly been for the purpose of bringing suburban residential areas within the city, the bulk of these takeovers provided areas for Corporation house-building.

1931: 30,044 acres

Hogganfield, Carntyne (east), small areas on the east added 535 acres.

1938: 39,725 acres

Balmuildy, Auchinairn, Cardowan, Gartloch, Easterhouse, Queenslie, Linn Park, Jenny Lind, Darnley and Penilee; Drumry, Drumchapel and Summerston together increased the city's area by 9,681 acres. Fulfilled the same purpose as the 1926 annexations and included areas (such as Easterhouse and Drumchapel) which became vast post-war housing schemes.

1975: 50,038 acres
Under the terms of the Local Government (Scotland) Act, 1973, Rutherglen, Cambuslang, Mount Vernon and Baillieston (10,313 acres) became part of the City of Glasgow District.

1987: 50,111 acres
73 acres were added.

Postal Service

The city's early postal service was for many years concerned almost solely with traffic between Glasgow and Edinburgh – all mail from England reached the city via the latter. The Town Council minutes of 1630 refer to the appointment of 'ane trustie youthe' who would, on foot, carry the mail between the two cities. A horse was supplied in 1661 but withdrawn three years later. In 1687 an attempt was made to run a coach and six horses (carrying six passengers, preference given to burgesses), but this was soon abandoned.

In 1674 the person employed was given the official title of Postmaster, and 20 years later the service was upgraded to allow it to be used by others besides merchants and traders. In 1711, following the Union, the separate Scottish establishment was abolished when a General Post Office for Great Britain was set up.

In 1715 the frequency of the post was increased from one to three journeys each week, and finally, in 1717, a horse post was introduced. This left Edinburgh at 8 p.m. on Tuesdays and Thursdays, reaching Glasgow at 6 a.m. on Wednesdays and Fridays. About this time the city's first post office was opened, probably in the High St office of the postmaster, Robert Thomson.

In addition to the official letter-carrier, in 1786 the Glasgow–Edinburgh stagecoach (started in 1749) also began to carry mail. Two years later came the long-desired introduction of a direct mail coach service between Glasgow and London by way of Carlisle. In 1798 the three days a week service became a daily run. The mail continued to come to Glasgow by coach till 1848 when the Caledonian Railway Co took over the service.

In 1724 the Glasgow post office was

located in Princes St; from then until the middle of the next century it was constantly on the move – St Andrew St, Trongate, East Albion St and Glassford St all equally unsatisfactory. Finally, in 1856, a start was made on a new General Post Office building at the corner of George St and South Hanover St. This grew by alterations and accretions in 1876, 1892 and 1914 to become the present-day city-block structure.

Poverty

A single-end, with sleeping-places, and a lit candle to counteract the absence of natural lighting. This family is comparatively well-off in having a few pieces of furniture. (W. Mitchell, Rescue the Children, *1886. Mitchell Library)*

From the end of the 16th century to 1845 the relief of general poverty in Glasgow (as elsewhere in Scotland) was the joint responsibility of the parish church and the local heritors (i.e. landowners). The 'legal poor' were children, widows, the infirm and the elderly; no provision was made for the able-bodied unemployed. Because of Glasgow's size, its various parishes were organised into a single General Session whose business it was to allocate money, food and fuel to its constituent parishes for distribution. More specialised and limited relief was provided by the 14 Incorporated Trades of the city, from Hammermen to Bonnet Makers, who took care of their own indigent members and their families.

There also existed a large number of private charitable institutions and organisations, such as Bell's Mortification (1641), Aird's Mortification (1723), Bell's Wynd Society (1746, described as 'a rather primitive association'), the Lock Hospital (1805, 'the care of unfortunate women', i.e. the treatment of venereal disease), the Aged Women's Society (1811), the Old Man's Friend Society (1814), the Blackquarry Funeral and Mortcloth Friendly Society (1829), and the Weary Workers' Rest (1885, holidays for 'hard-wrought female workers'). Even as late as the beginning of the 20th century there were still over 200 such bodies in the city. Noticeable also were the many Scottish county societies in the city (over 20, from Orkney to Galloway, Argyll to Fife), which provided relief for their natives in want in Glasgow.

The growing burden of alleviating the city's poor was beginning to surpass the church's ability to deal with it, and in 1731 the General Session approached the Town Council for help. The response of the

Council was to erect, in 1733, the Town's Hospital on the edge of the Old Green. It was an all-purpose building, functioning as a workhouse (the work included picking oakum, weaving, spinning, knitting, tailoring and shoemaking), an old folk's home, an orphanage, an asylum and an infirmary. By 1815 it had over 500 inmates. Its funding came from the Town Council, the Merchants' and Trades' Houses, the General Session and from bequests. But even all these sources soon proved insufficient, and eventually an assessment had to be laid on the citizens. As the population increased the traditional charity of the church continued to fail to meet the demands on it, and the Town Council was forced to stent those with property valued over £300; the income from this tax was then passed to the General Session.

Several other factors reduced even further the ameliorative efforts of the Session. The growth of Secession churches (whose members were not entitled to Church of Scotland relief), the influx of large numbers of Roman Catholic Irish and, above all the degradation brought about by a rapidly industrialising city, required a new approach to the relief of Glasgow's poor. A valiant attempt to demonstrate that the church still had its part to play in poor relief was made by the Revd Thomas Chalmers in 1822. His appointment to the parish of St John's in 1822 provided him with a test-bed where he tried (and failed) to relieve the parish poor through voluntary church contributions.

By the 1830s some 18,500 persons were on poor relief in the city, and it was obvious that the task was now beyond the power of local authorities, so in 1845 central government passed the Poor Law (Scotland) Amendment Act – an Act of such far-reaching consequences that it remained on the Statute Books till the Second World War. Its main provisions were: compulsory assessment on Glasgow's citizens; administration by parochial boards composed of elected members; 'occasional' relief for the able-bodied out-of-work; medical relief for paupers in poor-law hospitals; asylums for the lunatic poor; and, most innovatory of all (though the Town's Hospital had shown the way), the provision of poorhouses (modelled on the English workhouses). These parochial boards answered not to their local authority but to a central supervisory board in Edinburgh.

Gorbals, 1975. Glasgow has always been a city of social contrasts – Rolls Royces and down-and-outs. (George Oliver)

Five years after the passing of the Act, Barnhill Poorhouse was opened on the north side of the city near Springburn. Although built initially for the use of the Barony Parochial Board, for almost a hundred years its name became a word of dread for the whole city's destitute population. Barony parish, which was estimated to be the most densely populated parish in Scotland (a population of 177,527 in 1861), had a greater pauper problem than almost anywhere in the country, with one pauper to every ten inhabitants. The poorhouse operated on draconian principles, its policy being to subject its inmates to a régime 'more irksome than labour'. So feared was it that 1,400 applicants who were offered admittance to it refused – five in every six paupers preferred to remain on meagre outdoor relief.

The City (i.e. Glasgow) Parochial Board took over the Town's Hospital, (which had moved to a vacated asylum building in Parliamentary Rd in 1843) as its poorhouse. Then in 1894 the Barony and

City Boards amalgamated, forming the largest Poor Law Union in the country. City closed its Parliamentary Rd building in 1901 and moved to share an expanded Barnhill with Barony. The result was Scotland's largest poorhouse with over 2,000 inmates, and in 1905 it became the city's sole poorhouse.

The 20th century brought about a change in society's attitude towards its poor and as a result the 1845 Act was drastically reformed. Under the Local Government (Scotland) Act of 1929, the provision of poor relief (now called public assistance) for the entire city passed from the Boards to the Corporation, which administered it through its Public Assistance Department, and many changes followed. The dreadful stigma of having to register as a pauper in order to gain admittance to the erstwhile poor-law hosptials was done away with in 1930. Then in 1936 the relief of the able-bodied unemployed was transferred to the newly established Unemployment Assistance Board. Next, during the Second World War, two other groups, the elderly and the widows, hitherto the city's responsibility, were similarly transferred. In 1943 the notorious Barnhill Poorhouse was transformed into the Foresthall Hospital and Home, to be demolished in the early 1970s. The Public Assistance Department was renamed the Social Welfare Department, and was run jointly by the Corporation and the Western Region Hospital Board till 1974, when its duties were transferred to the Social Welfare Department of Strathclyde Regional Council.

Printing

In 1638 the General Assembly of the Church of Scotland met in Glasgow and its members prepared a statement, *The Protestation of the Generall Assemblie of the Church of Scotland*, which was the first book to be printed in the city. The printer was George Anderson, who had been persuaded by the Town Council to leave his business in Edinburgh and establish himself in Glasgow. He died in 1647; ten years later his son, Alexander Anderson, came to the city and took over his father's business, but in 1661 he returned to Edinburgh. He was replaced by Robert Sanders, elder, and after his death in 1694 his son Robert Sanders, younger, began printing in the city, describing himself as 'one of His Majesty's Printers' and as printer to the University.

The work of these 17th-century Glasgow printers was very poor even by provincial standards, and was remarkable only for poor paper, bad type and lamentable press work. Their customers were drawn from the middle and lower classes and their output was largely standard religious works, along with some school textbooks and a little bad poetry. Not until the middle of the next century, with the appearance on the scene of Robert Urie and the Foulis brothers, Robert and Andrew, did the quality of Glasgow printing improve – an improvement all the more remarkable when compared with their predecessors and contemporaries.

By the beginning of the 18th century the printing needs of the city could not be met by only a single printer, and several now came forward. In 1718 James Duncan established himself as a printer and bookseller (until the 19th century the two trades were usually combined), typefounder (Glasgow's first) and papermaker. He was appointed the town's printer in 1719 and in 1736 printed the city's first history, John McUre's *A View of the City of Glasgow*. He also printed works in Gaelic (the Psalms and the Shorter Catechism).

About the same time Donald Govan, merchant, set up as a printer and bookseller but was active for only a few years. He is remembered as the printer of the city's first newspaper, the *Glasgow Courant* (1715–16), and as printer to the University.

Robert Urie began printing in Glasgow about 1740, continuing till his death in 1771. His output was so markedly superior to his contemporaries that he stands comparison with the Foulis brothers – in fact, the Foulis' first book was printed for them by Urie. Like the brothers, he also made use of the new type being cut by Alexander Wilson at his Camlachie Foundry. He was also able to get good paper locally from the Glasgow paper-maker, Edward Collins. There was no other Glasgow printer who published such a wide range of works as Urie – from his presses came works of theology, Latin and Greek classics, essays and *belles-lettres*, (including translations from the French), history, travel, poetry and drama – in all, over 300 items. His productions indicate a cultured and educated patronage; his customers included the Duke of Montrose, local nobility and gentry, university professors, ministers of religion, doctors of medicine, town councillors, merchants and traders. Probably his two most beautiful works are his printings of George Buchanan's *Psalms* and the Greek New Testament, both in 1750. Because most of

his output was in the smaller book sizes of octavo and duodecimo, rather than in the larger sizes of quarto and folio (for which the Foulis press was celebrated), he has been somewhat unjustly overshadowed by them. He even developed overseas markets, exporting his products to the West Indies.

Robert (1717–76) and Andrew (1712–75) Foulis were the sons of a Glasgow barber and wigmaker, Andrew Faulds (they changed the spelling of their surname to 'Foulis' in 1738). Robert was apprenticed to a barber in 1720 and his brother studied divinity at Glasgow University but both were fascinated by classical literature and by the books which contained it. In 1738 they toured the Continent and brought back six or seven hogsheads of books which, on their return, they sold at a profit. They repeated their successful trip the following year and back in Glasgow set up as booksellers within the College of Glasgow in 1741.

That same year Robert started his career as a printer by having a volume of Cicero printed for him by Urie, but in 1742 he began to print for himself. At this time printing in Glasgow was at a very low ebb, a situation which Robert was obviously determined to change. Every operation of his press's activities was carried out with meticulous care. Only the finest paper and the blackest ink was selected, and when Alexander Wilson was appointed type-founder to the University in 1748, Foulis was quick to make use of his considerable skills in creating new fonts. Departing from the current printing styles of his time, he eschewed the use of florid printers' flowers and rules, creating aesthetically pleasing pages by the careful choice and symmetrical spacing of the type alone and by limiting his title pages to capital letters from one font only. His close and friendly association with the University ensured high levels of editorial skills and proof-reading.

While none of his books were negligible, several were outstanding, even by his own high standards. In 1744 he published an edition of Horace; in an almost obsessional concern for accuracy he displayed round the College quadrangles each sheet as it was printed, and offered rewards for the discovery of errors. So accurate was the edition that it was called the 'Immaculate Horace' – later examination disclosed about six errors! A two-volume edition of Cicero in 1749 became so well known that it was usually referred to as the 'Glasgow Tully'.

The excellence of the Foulis Press reached its peak in its folio editions. Chief of these was undoubtedly its medal-winning Homer in four folio volumes – the *Iliad* in 1756 and the *Odyssey* in 1758. A double pica Greek font specially struck for them by Wilson was used and the result has been acclaimed as 'one of the finest monuments of Greek typography which our nation possess', and Edward Gibbon, the eminent historian, said, 'I read Homer with more pleasure in the Glasgow edition'. The final typographical achievement in folio was John Milton's *Paradise Lost* in 1770. Earlier, in 1768, the press had published a quarto edition of Thomas Gray's *Poems* which has been described as 'the most elegant piece of printing that the Glasgow press or any other press has ever produced'.

The total output of the press (it was continued for a few years after Robert's death by his nephew, Andrew) reached some 700 volumes. Most of these were scholarly editions of classical authors and other works of service to the University, but it also included books in French, Spanish, Italian and Gaelic. From 1754 onwards, Robert's obsession with further-ing his Academy of Fine Arts (*see* FOULIS ACADEMY) consumed what little profit the press may have made, and when he died in 1776 he left the considerable debt of £6,500. But he also left a reputation as a printer unsurpassed by the best of his own time or since.

An unusual Glasgow printer whose work was in complete contrast with the Foulis press, was Dougal Graham (1724–79). Not only did he print cheap and popular pamphlets, he was also a chapman or pedlar as well as brewing and selling his own ale. His occupation of city bellman or town-crier brought him the soubriquet of 'the literary bellman'. He was famous for having accompanied the forces of Prince Charles Edward Stewart down to Derby and back up to Culloden, and he wrote and published a poetical account of his experiences, *A full, particular and true account of the late rebellion in the years 1745 and 1746*. It proved to be so popular that it was still being printed 30 years later. He has the doubtful distinction of being one of the first to stigmatise, in his *John Highlandman's Remarks on Glasgow*, the Highlanders who were then beginning to flock into the city, by their idiosyncratic use of English:

> *Her nainsel into Glasgow went,*
> *An erran there to see't;*
> *And she ne'er pe saw a ponier town,*
> *Was stan'ing on her feet.*

Two apprentices of the Foulis brothers, Robert Chapman and Alexander Duncan, began printing on their own in 1775 and are best remembered for having printed, edited and published the *Glasgow Mercury*.

With the beginning of the 19th century, printing in the city lost, for better or worse, its provincial characteristics, and the output of most of its printers (now seldom combined with bookselling) became indistinguishable from UK publishing as a whole. Two printers can be singled out, however – Blackie & Sons Ltd and William Collins & Sons Ltd.

John Blackie (1782–1874), a weaver, turned bookseller in 1809 (later in partnership with his son, also John (1805–73), who was the city's provost in 1863 and 1864, and was the prime mover in setting up the City Improvement Trust). At first the firm sold books, mainly on religious topics, printed by others, but in 1811 it began printing for itself and in 1829 it acquired the premises and plant of Duncan, University printer.

In the second half of the 19th century the firm moved into general publishing, but with the rise of compulsory education in the 1870s it began publishing educational textbooks, the sale of which was soon extended into various markets in the British Empire. They also produced a wide range of children's books and annuals, and the embossed and coloured pictorial covers on many of these became almost a trademark of the firm.

Before the First World War the publishing side of the company began to outrun the capabilities of the printing side. Eventually, in 1929, the firm opened a huge (225,000ft square) custom-built and well-designed factory at Bishopbriggs, calling it the Villafield Press after one of their early Glasgow sites. About this time the firm began to move into the publication of technical and scientific works. Unlike most other publishers, Blackie largely ignored paperbacks. In the 1980s the Bishopbriggs factory was sold and the firm moved into much smaller premises close to Bishopbriggs Station. The factory building was demolished and the site used for a private housing development.

William Collins (1789–1853) of Pollokshaws, was a cottonmill clerk with a strong interest in evangelism. He was instrumental in bringing to the city in 1814 the Revd Thomas Chalmers, the popular preacher and lecturer. The two men became close friends and it was with Chalmers' financial help that Collins was able to establish the printing and publishing firm of William Collins & Co in 1819. Its initial success was due to it being in a position to publish Chalmers' bestselling religious and scientific works, and because Collins owned the presses that printed the books he sold. The firm undertook the printing of the Glasgow Post Office Directory in 1848 and, like Blackie, began publishing an increasing number of school books. Another boost to the young firm was its bible printing. By the 1850s it was turning out about 80,000 bibles each year and by the 1870s it had a *de facto* monopoly on bible printing in Scotland. William Collins II took charge after the death of his father in 1853. He played a conspicuous part in the political and social life of the city and was elected Lord Provost in 1877. He was a confirmed teetotaller and during his term of office was known as 'Water Willie'. The press now began to add scientific and educational texts to its output and, by the 1870s, was beginning to expand into the growing British Empire. In 1881 it began to publish a line which has almost become its trademark – Collins' diaries – and by the end of that century it was publishing 25 different kinds.

In the early 20th century its lists began to include cheap editions of the classics and a whole range of boys' adventure and school stories, with other forms of juvenile literature.

After the First World War the firm's production of cheap classics lessened and it began to build up a strong line in original, high-quality fiction, with authors like Henry James, Quiller Couch, Vita Sackville-West, Rose Macaulay and Walter

De La Mare. It also attracted a number of detective story writers, such as Freeman Wills Croft and, above all, Agatha Christie. It still maintains a good fiction list and continues to turn out bibles, school books, reference works of all kinds, children's books and stationery. It has been succinctly described as a 'quality publisher with a talent for mass sales'.

Prisons

The Justiciary Courts (High Court) at the foot of the Saltmarket, were erected, 1809–14, to provide accommodation for the municipal offices, court house and jail, previously located at the Cross. By the beginning of the present century the High Court became its sole occupant. The open space in front, between the Courts and the Glasgow Green, was formerly known as Jail Square, and it was here that public hangings were held till 1865. (George Oliver)

Before custodial sentences became an accepted method of punishing criminals, Glasgow had no need for extensive prison buildings and a few apartments in the Tolbooth served to hold the small numbers of those awaiting trial. More pressing was the need to deal with those who offended against social custom, and in 1635 (following the successful example of Edinburgh) the Magistrates opened a 'House of Correction' for vagrants and 'dissolute women' in the converted Manse of the Prebend of Douglas, on the south side of the Drygate. The 'corrective' procedure obliged inmates to work (spinning, weaving, shoemaking, etc) and the resulting profits went towards the expenses of the institution. It seems to have fallen into disuse for a time but was revived in 1726 and substantially extended in 1785 – its inmates still being mainly dissolute women.

Further accommodation being required, part of a granary at Shuttle St and College St (near the old Mealmarket) was converted in 1788 into a temporary Bridewell (this was the first use of 'Bridewell' in Glasgow – after a jail in London) with 14 rooms. As before it took in mostly women (and boys) but later men were admitted. It has been said that French prisoners-of-war were incarcerated here.

Perhaps because of official fears respecting the influence of French revolutionary ideas, perhaps because of the city's increasing population, the Town Council decided to build a custom-designed Bridewell. Erected *c.*1798 in the gardens of the old Correction House (which sloped down south to the recently opened Duke St), it was 106ft by 30ft and had 74 debtors' cells and 58 felons' cells. Although still mainly for vagrants and women it was also legalised to hold convicted felons whenever the old Tolbooth jail could not accommodate them.

By 1807 the latter's prison provision

had become quite inadequate – it had only 32 cells which were required to hold debtors, criminals (men and women) and those from the shires of Lanark, Renfrew and Dunbarton awaiting circuit trials. So in 1814 increased jail accommodation was provided in the new Justiciary Court House at the foot of the Saltmarket, facing Glasgow Green. It had 122 apartments but the increasing population of the city soon rendered even this number inadequate.

When the Gaol Act of 1823 assimilated the functions of Bridewells and jails, the city, in co-operation with Lanark County, decided in 1825 to build a new prison (again in the grounds of the old House of Correction in Duke St) which would take both the city's convicted criminals and those from the Lower Ward of Lanarkshire. It could accommodate over 300 inmates and although its first official title was the Town & County Bridewell it soon, under the General Prisons Act, became known as Duke Street Prison. When Barlinnie Prison opened in 1882, Duke Street Prison became largely a women's prison, remaining so until its closure in 1955 (demolished 1958). The last remaining link between the local authority and its prisons came in 1877 when central government, through the Prison Commissioners for Scotland, became responsible for prisons.

Until 1865 public executions took place in front of the Justiciary Building, facing Glasgow Green; after that date they were carried out inside Duke Street Prison till 1928 when they were transferred to Barlinnie Prison (last hanging in 1960).

Barlinnie Prison (popularly known as 'Bar-L') is now the only prison within the city boundaries and was opened in 1882. At the beginning of 1973 it became the test-bed for a most unusual prison régime when its Special Unit came into operation. Its essential approach is to place a very small group of long-term prisoners (15 years or more) inside a secure perimeter in a relaxed atmosphere. A self-styled therapeutic company in which the creation of a community spirit is considered fundamental, it offers its inmates a remarkable amount of freedom, responsibility and personal choice. The prisoners wear their own clothes, decorate their cells and are allowed to keep books and record-players. They can cook their own food and their mail is unrestricted and uncensored. The staff-to-inmate ratio is high and the usual formal prison hierarchy does not exist. The Special Unit has been much criticised and is still regarded as experimental, but it has had at least one success. James Boyle is undoubtedly its best-known graduate. Born in the Gorbals in 1944, Jimmy 'Babyface' Boyle was in and out of institutions from the age of 12, and by the 1960s the press were styling him Glasgow's worst-ever gangster. He was first charged with murder in 1964 but was found not guilty. He was again charged with murder in 1967 and found guilty this time. Sentenced to life imprisonment, it was recommended that he serve not less than 15 years. The Lord Advocate described his behaviour as being of 'almost unimaginable ferocity'; after a savage attack on the Governor he was transferred to Inverness. Further violence resulted in his being incarcerated in 'The Cages', small barred cells within cells which were designed to break the spirit of the most intransigent.

Then in February 1973 he became a member of the first intake of the Special Unit and under its unimaginable freedom Boyle changed. He became interested in sculpture (some of his works were exhibited in an Edinburgh gallery) and he collaborated with the playwright Tom McGrath in producing *The Hard Man*, a play based on his own experiences. Then he married a psychiatrist and prison visitor, Dr Sarah Trevelyan, and was released from prison in November 1982.

Provand's Lordship

Provand's Lordship is the late 19th-century name given to an old stone building on the west side of the High St facing the Cathedral. It is composed of two structures, the larger of which fronts on to the street, the other lying behind it.

The front portion consists of nine rooms, three on each of its three floors, almost identical as to size and to the position of doorways and windows. The eastern extremity of the south gable carries a much worn coat-of-arms of one of the medieval bishops of the cathedral, Andrew Muirhead (1455–73). It has been suggested that the main entrance to this building was originally on its western façade.

The rear portion can be dated by its architectural style as being later than the other part. It consists mainly of additional rooms and a central staircase which provides access to the various storeys of the older building. One of its crow-stepped gables bears the date 1670.

It was Bishop Andrew Muirhead who founded the Hospital of St Nicholas, a hospice for 12 old men, in 1456 or 1471, consisting of a central chapel on the west of the High St with buildings lying to the north and south of it. To the south was the hospital proper while to the north was the manse of the Master or Preceptor of the Hospital, and it is claimed that this manse should be identified with the present-day building. Certainly, the ground on which it stands was held in feu from the hospital's preceptor.

John McUre, in his history of Glasgow (1738), mentioned that the manse of the prebendary of Balornock (Balornock was a part of the better-known Barlanark, and hence the prebendarial land was usually referred to as Barlanark) was situated 'at the large house near the Stablegreen Port that now belongs to Mr Bryson', and indeed John Bryson did own the house in question. McUre's statement could mean no more than that Mr Bryson's house (the present-day Provand's Lordship) was *at* or *near* the site of the prebendal manse. However, towards the end of the last century, with little evidence, it was eagerly accepted that this old building was connected with one of the 32 Canons of the Cathedral. All these Canons were supported by various temporal revenues; one was maintained by the temporalities of the lands of Barlanark, a large area of land lying to the east of the city. Early documents referred to him as '*dominus prebende*', lord of the prebend of Barlanark; later this title became corrupted to '*dominus de provand*' and so his lands became known as the lordship of Provand. Finally, this land title was transferred to the house in the form of 'Provand's Lordship', the name by which it is now known.

Whether the Prebendary of Barlanark ever stayed in the building or not, it is undoubtedly a medieval house (with 17th-century additions) and as such is secure in its claim to be Glasgow's oldest dwelling-house, perhaps even the only domestic building of its period still standing in Scotland. It was saved and restored in 1906 by the Provand's Lordship Society which had been set up for that purpose. Sir William Burrell in 1927 assisted in the purchase and provision of a collection of 16th and 17th-century furnishings and fittings, and it is now a museum in the care of Glasgow District Museums and Art Galleries Department.

Public Health

The public health of Glasgow was from early times a concern of the Town Council, but it was not until the increase of medical knowledge in the 19th century that significant control of public disease became possible.

That most loathsome of all medieval diseases, leprosy, was dealt with by putting its victims furth of the city. When the first stone bridge of Glasgow was built in the middle of the 14th century, St Ninian's Hospital was erected at its southern end, in the Gorbals, by Marjorie Stewart, Lady Lochow, to take care of eight lepers. The Town Council ordained that the city's lepers 'sall haif clapperis and ane claith upoun thair mouth and face, they sall stand afar of quhill they resaif almous' – a clear indication of the almost superstitious fear generated by this affliction.

The pestilence, bubonic plague, was a constant visitor to the city up to the middle of the 17th century, its worst outbreak lasting from 1646 to 1648. The Town Council did its ineffective best to control it; the city gates were closed and guarded, the streets were patrolled by searchers, the holding of 'wakes' over the dead were prohibited, house-to-house visitations were made twice daily and it was ordained that 'all personis of this towne qha hes doggis or cattis athir kepe thame fast or hang

thame'. Glasgow University, more discreet than valorous, migrated as a body to Irvine in Ayrshire, remaining there till the plague had passed. A reawakening of the plague's eastern sources brought it back, surprisingly, to Glasgow in 1900, when 48 cases resulted in 16 deaths; a most unusual outbreak, attracting worldwide attention.

Whereas lepers had been exiled south across the Clyde, plague sufferers were thrust out of the city's northern gate where, on the Town Muir, a chapel and burying-ground dedicated to St Roche (later corrupted to St Rollox), the patron saint against the plague, was built. Plague victims were lodged in rough sheds thrown up round the chapel and the dead were buried in its cemetery.

James Cleland's pioneering vital statistics relating to the city in the first half of the 19th century (the first reliable figures on mortality and disease in any large British city) demonstrated that the public health problems of Glasgow were amongst the worst in Britain.

After the plague had waned, its place as an epidemic scourge was taken by smallpox, typhus and cholera. In 1801 the Faculty of Physicians and Surgeons of Glasgow started vaccinating the children of the poor gratis, and this effective prophylactic kept smallpox within fairly reasonable bounds. Extraordinarily, the two most significant smallpox epidemics in the city took place in the 20th century; in both cases the immediate cause was Glasgow's position as a major port. In 1901 an Indian seaman suffering from the disease was the source – there were 2,250 cases, of which 276 died. Following this outbreak the city was named as the Port Local Authority for the whole riverine area, with its Medical Officer of Health in charge. Again ship-borne, a second outbreak happened in 1920, resulting in 542 cases of which 113 died. A third, minor, outbreak took place in 1942 – 36 cases, 8 deaths. On this occasion, so great was the fear of a major outbreak that a general vaccination of the city's population was attempted. That same year saw what was taken to be an even greater threat when a message was received from a Glasgow-bound ship that it had '50 cases of smallpox aboard'. After large-scale arrangements for preventative measures had begun, a revised message revealed that the ship's cargo included '50 cases of small boxes'!

Typhus grew in strength with the rise of the city's industrial development. The first epidemic outbreak took place in 1818–19 and typhus remained endemic through the 19th and into the 20th centuries, major outbreaks occurring in 1831, 1837, 1846 and 1864. The average death toll was around 2,000, but the 1846 outbreak was more fatal and more pro-longed – 4,346 died (including over 30 of the medical and nursing staff). It made its final appearance in 1926, this time with only eight cases.

Cholera, with its swift attack and high mortality (as great as 50 per cent), was the most feared of all the 19th-century fevers. The first appearance in Glasgow of *cholera morbus* was in 1832. In its progress it had passed from Hamburg to Sutherland at the end of 1831, then to Newcastle, Hadd-ington, Edinburgh and, via Kirkintilloch, to Glasgow in February 1832. Spread mainly by polluted water, it was almost entirely restricted to those areas of the city dependent upon the old public wells – High St, Saltmarket, Gallowgate and Trongate. A tax (and subscriptions) raised £14,000 and a temporary Board of Health was set up, with eight or nine depots in working-class districts. When the epidemic had run its course (there was at that time no effective preventative), out of over 6,000 cases 2,842 had died, a death rate of 14 in 1,000. The 1848 epidemic brought an even higher mortality figure – 3,923 – along with a disturbing tendency to extend its attack into the more well-to-do districts. 1866 marked the last appearance of cholera as an epidemic disease – measures against it (mainly clean water) reduced its mortality to a mere 68 deaths.

Over and above these major epidemics there was a continuing death toll amongst the city's children from such diseases as measles, whooping cough (then known as chincough) and scarlet fever. In 1808 an outbreak of measles killed over 700 children and in 1855 it carried off 1,657. In that same year some 3,000 died from whooping cough (in 1872 more than 1,000 died), while scarlet fever was responsible for 1,719 deaths. It was not until well after the First World War that these figures began to drop, though even in 1921 deaths from measles and whooping cough were more than 2,000 for each disease.

Tuberculosis, one of the inevitable consequences of poor nutrition and overcrowding, remained a major health problem in Glasgow for almost 100 years. By the 1880s some 15 per cent of all city deaths were caused by it. After the First World War the provision of TB sanatoria and home treatment began to reduce the number of cases. Unfortunately, during the Second World War its incidence began to increase, but by 1955 the situation was once more under control.

For centuries the municipality's fatalistic approach towards community disease had been the usual one of 'may it please God to remove the heavy hand of pestilence', but the 19th century's increasing medical knowledge meant that effective community action could now be taken. Previously, for each epidemic, a temporary Board of Health had been set up and temporary hospital accommodation provided. Under the sanitary clauses of the 1862 Police Bill, however, the municipality acquired a permanent Medical Officer under a Sanitary Committee with far-reaching powers – the adoption of special measures to prevent epidemics and contagious disease, the provision of medical treatment and accommodation for sufferers, the compelling of owners and occupiers to 'cleanse, whitewash, ventilate and disinfect', the prevention of overcrowding, etc. – and in 1870 a Sanitary Inspector was appointed.

Although in the long run the introduction of an adequate supply of unpolluted water in 1855 helped to eradicate many of the city's health problems, in the short term it created a new one, for the increasing use of water closets (the 1890 Police Bill compelled landlords to install them in their tenements) meant that solid human waste, previously sold to local farmers as manure, was now being discharged straight into the Clyde, turning it into a stinking open sewer. The solution was a vast upgrading of the city's sewage system and the creation of the city's first sewage treatment plant at Dalmarnock under the new Sewage Purification Department in 1894.

Under a series of innovative and energetic Medical Officers of Health many long-standing threats to the public health of the city were now dealt with, and by the 1870s epidemics were being confined to much smaller areas; improved provision was now made for free medical treatment and the accommodation of sufferers; small pox, though not eradicated, was being kept under control; cholera had given way before Loch Katrine's supply of pure water; typhus was being tackled by the demolition of substandard housing and by the procedure of 'ticketing' dwelling-houses (occupation levels were established for each room of each house and were set out on a metal plaque or 'ticket' affixed to each door).

The increasing involvement of the Corporation in the cleansing of the city also played an important part in improving its public health. The first Police Act in 1800 had involved the police in the cleansing of the city's public streets but in 1868 a separate Cleansing Department had been established, responsible for keeping clean all the city's streets, public and private, as well as the many back-courts behind the city's tenements. These back-courts had, slightly earlier, been cleared of another nuisance. The Town Council, wishing to do away with the immemorial custom of using these courts and the closes leading to them as urinals, wanted to erect public conveniences. The landlords would not allow this on their properties so the Council, in the summer of 1852, began the erection of a series of public conveniences in the streets.

The work of the Medical Officer and the Sanitary Inspector continued to increase, and soon covered all aspects of general sanitation, control of infectious diseases, housing, inspection of food, smoke pollution and port sanitation. In 1920 the widening task of keeping the city healthy brought about the amalgamation of the Sanitary Department (independent since its creation in 1870) with the Public Health Department under the overall control of the Medical Officer. The Local Government (Scotland) Act of 1929, more than doubled the work of the Department for it now became responsible for school health services, maternity and child welfare services, general hospitals and poor law medical services.

The changes in Glasgow's death rate over a hundred years clearly show the inimical effects of the city's rapid industrialisation, and the success of the various methods used to combat them: in the 1820s the rate was 22 in each 1,000; by 1847 it stood at a peak of 56; had declined to 22 by the 1870s; and by the 1930s was down to 14.

Although Glasgow's public health has become since 1947 largely the responsibility of the National Health Service, the Environmental Health Department (under the District's Environmental Protection Committee) monitors hygiene and air and noise pollution, carries out health and safety checks, monitors houses in multiple occupancy and checks on the quality of food coming into the city through the Clyde Port. In addition the Committee, through the Cleansing Department, is responsible for the city's street-sweeping and refuse collection. In addition, a sub-committee on nuclear-free zones (the Council declared itself a nuclear-free zone in 1981) monitors local radiation levels.

Quarries

Until the 16th century Glasgow's only major stone structures were the Cathedral and the manses of its clergy. There is no clear evidence for the source of their building stone but it probably came from a quarry which lay between the Cathedral and George Square.

Two serious city fires in the 16th century caused the Town Council to insist that stone and slate must replace timber and thatch; in addition, the town's increasing importance began to make the prestige of stone buildings more desirable. Much of the city's surface has a sedimentary bedrock of good quality, light coloured stone which cut easily and could be found not far below the surface, and so quarries began to be opened up in various places.

The earliest recorded quarry (1573), the 'querrel hoil of Rammishorne', was located in the neighbourhood of St David's (Ramshorn) Church; another early one was the Black Quarry (1649) near North Woodside Rd which was worked till the end of the 18th century.

The later quarries were nearer the city centre; Dundas St ran between two of the largest. On the west was the Crackling House or Meadowflat Quarry (the Crackling House extracted tallow from hides for use in the Candleriggs candleworks). Its working span ran from the beginning of the 18th century till about 1789, when the development of Buchanan St required its closure. To the east lay Provanside or Bell's Quarry. It had the longest history of any of the Glasgow quarries, possibly back to the medieval period. It was one of the city's largest and was constantly being expanded – in some places the quarry face was as much as 60ft high. It closed in the 1840s, when Queen St Railway Station opened.

Further north were another two large quarries. Most of the area of Cowcaddens was one large quarry, which lasted till *c*.1825, while to the east lay the East or Little Cowcaddens Quarry, north of Parliamentary Rd. Its closure must have preceded the building of Buchanan St Railway Station in the 1840s.

Besides these major quarries, many smaller ones were opened up, often to supply a particular need – for instance, a quarry was opened up at Gilmorehill when the new University was being built. A belt of good limestone ran north-east from Kelvingrove to Bishopbriggs and supported many small quarries. The Huntershill and Crowhill quarries at Bishopbriggs, and those at Giffnock on the south side, were probably the last of the Glasgow quarries, continuing in production till the 1890s. Most of Springburn's now demolished tenements were built with stone from the Bishopbriggs quarries. After the Giffnock quarries were given up, their tunnels were used for a while for growing mushrooms.

The rapid expansion of the city was beginning to exhaust the older quarries and many of them were filled in for building purposes. The arrival of the railways in the 1840s enabled stone to be easily brought from any distance and large-scale quarrying in the city came to an end.

Railways

The railway age reached Glasgow in 1831 when the Glasgow & Garnkirk Railway opened. A parliamentary Bill had been obtained in 1826 for the construction of a railway from Glasgow to the Monklands, a district about ten miles to the east of the city and one particularly rich in coal, iron ore and other minerals. So unacquainted were the early promoters with the power of steam that horses and winding engines were seriously considered as motive units, but one year before the passage of the Bill the Stockton & Darlington Railway had proved itself a resounding success. So, as a result of a deputation to England, two of the new-fangled steam locomotives were purchased.

Highlanders living in the city used to meet down at the Broomielaw Quay (where the boats from the Highlands docked), but with the construction of Central Station, its Argyle St bridge became the new recognised meeting-place, under the name of the Highlandman's Umbrella. (William Graham, Mitchell Library)

In September 1831 the line was opened to scenes of wild enthusiasm, admirably portrayed in D. O. Hill's *Views of the Opening of the Glasgow and Garnkirk Railway*, Edinburgh, 1832. Although the line carried many passengers, it had been designed for the movement of goods and it was its success at bringing into the city at low cost coal and other minerals which started the decline of the Monkland Canal.

The next two lines to be opened were of greater magnitude and importance. In

August 1840 the Glasgow & Ayrshire Railway began operations between Bridge Street Station (on the south bank of the Clyde, near the Jamaica Bridge) and Ayr, via Paisley, Kilwinning and Irvine. It was the opening of this line which enabled Glaswegians to reach London in the hitherto unheard of time of 24 hours, by taking a train to Ardrossan on the Firth of Clyde, then a steamer to Liverpool, and from there travelling by train to London. The Glasgow & Greenock line was authorised at the same time as the Ayrshire (1837) and was opened in June 1841.

The fourth Glasgow railway, the Edinburgh & Glasgow, was the first trunk line in Scotland. The Act for its construction was obtained in 1838 and it was opened in February 1842. Its Glasgow terminus, Queen Street Station, was located at the north-west corner of George Square, and it ran, on some of the flattest land in the country, for 46 miles to Haymarket at the west end of Edinburgh.

With the appearance in the 1840s of the great Scottish railway companies – North British, Caledonian and Glasgow & South Western – the story of Glasgow's railway development becomes the account of the power struggle amongst these contending railways, a process which had the unfortunate result of leaving the city with an astonishing and embarrassing duplication of services, with no joint-owned central terminal, and above all, with no continuous north–south route through the city.

The several lines into the city from Ayrshire came together at Bridge Street Station (built in 1841). The various small companies which used it jointly eventually became reduced to two – the Glasgow & South Western and the Caledonian – and the rivalry between these two continued to grow and strengthen. Both wanted to bridge the river to the north side so as to obtain a central site near the city centre and thus be able to accommodate trains coming up from England. A proposal for a joint terminus on the north side was realised by the construction of St Enoch's Station (1876) by the City of Glasgow Union Railway, but it very quickly became dominated by the North British and the Glasgow & South Western railways to the exclusion of the Caledonian Railway – which had then to find its own solution to the problem. In 1873 it obtained an Act which allowed it to build a high-level bridge across the Clyde from Bridge Street Station, having somehow persuaded the Admiralty that an opening swing-bridge was not really necessary. Work began on the chosen site, between Gordon Street and the Clyde and in 1879 it was opened as the Central Station.

Until the building of Central Station the only foothold of the Caledonian Railway on the north of the Clyde was that Cinderella of all the Glasgow stations, Buchanan Street. Opened in 1849, it was situated quite close to the existing Queen Street Station and was used for the company's English traffic. When Central was opened its business fell away and its activities were largely limited to traffic going north to Stirling, Perth, Crieff and beyond. Its physical appearance was singularly lacking in any charm, resembling as it did a very large, very plain wooden shed, and its closure in 1966 met with no opposition.

CENTRAL STATION

In keeping with its name this is the city's most important station. Its complicated and extensive layout had several unusual design features, some of which, happily, have been preserved. Its 13 platforms are arranged in an echelon fashion so that platforms 1 and 2, used for the west coast expresses from England, are immediately next to the concourse, while platform 13 ('All stations to Largs') is unobtrusively tucked away in a distant corner. As well as being the terminus for the English expresses it also caters for the considerable traffic generated by the southern uplands, Ayrshire and Renfrewshire, including all the traditional Clyde holiday resorts spread out along the east coast of the Firth. One important and local aspect of Central is the circular route which moves south from it through Mount Florida and Cathcart, west through Shawlands and then back north by Maxwell Park to the station. Although simplified now from its early complexity of Outer and Inner Circles, it still serves the middle-class power-house of south suburban Glasgow – the land of the red sandstone tenement and the totally detached villa.

The Edwardian timber buildings in and around the gently sloping, triangular concourse are unique in their use of curved building lines and rounded corners, designed, according to the architect, 'to take account of the tendency for people to spread like flowing water . . . along the line of least resistance'.

Until quite recently train information was displayed on a 74ft spread of 13 large windows overlooking the concourse – one for each platform. Into these apertures teams of highly skilled personnel manhandled large destination boards which successively displayed full details of all the rapidly changing train departures; the absence of any such obvious human control behind the current giant yellow-dotted display-board does little for the confidence of present-day travellers!

Central, like Queen Street, has a low-level line. Much of its length is below ground, and in the days of steam locomotives, it was infamous for its smoke-filled and ash-burdened atmosphere. Disused for a while, it has now been restored. It runs eastwards out to Motherwell, while westwards it links up at Partick with services running west from Queen Street low-level and on to Dumbarton and Helensburgh.

The north-west side of the station is fronted by the Central Hotel which was opened in 1883 and which has over the years offered its luxurious hospitality to many visiting celebrities.

QUEEN STREET STATION

This is the city's oldest surviving station (it dates from 1842) and serves one of the busiest intercity routes in the United Kingdom. Completely unlike any other station in Britain, it is approached by only one set of lines which descend from Cowlairs to the north of the city down a steep 2,000 yards incline (a gradient of 1 in 42), ending dramatically in a half-mile of tunnel from which one emerges suddenly into a train shed with a superb single-span glass roof. It is this unique approach, combined with constantly increasing traffic and with the impossibility of expansion which has constrained its activities throughout its life. In its early days, when the under-powered locomotives were incapable of pulling their trains up such a steep slope, a rather unusual form of alternative propulsion was used. The trains were pulled out of the station by means of a cable attached to a stationary winding-engine placed at the head of the Cowlairs incline. At first made from hemp (239 cwts of it), and later from wire (1847), the cable could cope with trains of more than 20 carriages. The descent into Avernus was easier – two or more special brake cars (weighing some 20 tons) replaced the engines and carefully ran the train down the long slope. Accidents did happen when carriages careered out of control down into (and sometime beyond) the bumpers, but careful working spared the station from any major accidents. The increasing power of later locomotives enabled the use of the rope to be abandoned, and, in August 1909,

authority was given to remove the cable.

Like Central Station, Queen Street has its own low-level line which also runs west and east, at right angles to its upper level. The electric trains on this line (for long known from their colour as the 'Blue Trains', now gaudily painted in what could perhaps be called 'Strathclyde Orange') run a full 35 miles from Helensburgh in the west, on the edge of the Highlands, to Airdrie in the east, in the heart of Glasgow's industrial hinterland, serving the passenger transport needs of a great part of the Glasgow conurbation.

Religious Groups

Baptists

The earliest evidence of Baptists in Glasgow dates from 1770 when Archibald McLean, printer and bookseller, gathered together a congregation which met in a house in the High St; its earliest converts were baptised in the Clyde at Fleshers' Haugh. By 1802 the congregation's size (about 250) and its wealth enabled it to erect a proper church building in George St. These early Baptists were called 'Scotch' Baptists to distinguish them from the English Baptists. The latter set up a congregation in Glasgow in 1801. It had disappeared by 1806 but resumed its activities in 1820. The indigenous Baptists shared the Scottish tendency to divide, but came together and erected a new chapel in John St in 1845. By the 1860s, although

there were seven Baptist meeting-places in the city (three 'Scotch' and four English), their overall numbers remained small. However, by the outbreak of the First World War there were 27 churches and five missions, many of them located in the city's developing suburbs – Queen's Park, Hillhead, Partick and Maryhill. Membership had increased from about 1,000 in 1861 to over 6,000 in 1921. Thereafter membership began to decline, particularly in the inner-city churches and several of them had to move out. This process continued after the Second World War when the remaining churches closed – John Knox in 1959, Cambridge St in 1963 and John St in 1969. The current yearbook lists a total of some 20 churches in the Glasgow area.

Covenanters

During the reigns of Charles II and James II, several outlawed supporters of the radical wing of the Presbyterian Church were executed in Glasgow for their faith. Between 1666 and 1688 Robert Bunton, John Hart, Robert Scot, Matthew Paton, John Richmond, James Johnston, Archibald Stewart, James Winning and John Main suffered death at Glasgow Cross for their testimonies to the Covenant and were buried within the Cathedral burying-ground. John Wharry and James Smith similarly suffered in Glasgow in 1683 and have a monument at Inchbelly, between Kirkintilloch and Kilsyth. William Boik, who was executed in the city in 1683 has a memorial stone in the Campsie burying-ground.

The best remembered of these sufferers were the three commemorated on the Martyrs' Stone. James Nisbet (an Ayrshire farmer), James Lawson and Alexander Wood were executed at the Howgate, an execution site to the north of the Cathedral. A stone was erected in their memory at the top of High St near the place of execution. In 1818 it was removed to allow an extension of the Monkland Canal basin and the canal proprietors erected a duplicate stone. This tablet was remodelled in 1858, to be replaced by a larger one in 1862. In 1925 this was taken down and erected further south in the wall of the then new Carlton Picture House in Castle St. The construction of the Townhead Interchange has now removed all traces, and the site of their martyrdom now lies under a feeder road leading to the M8 – there is said to be a replica of the inscription on one of the motorway arches.

Episcopalians

After the accession of William and Mary in 1689, the inability of the Episcopalian bishops in Scotland to offer their unqualified support to the new sovereign rendered the loyalty of the Scottish Episcopalian Church highly suspect. The remnants of these 'Scotch' Episcopalian 'non-jurors' (i.e. who would not swear their allegiance to a Hanoverian monarch), led a fugitive life for many years. About 1703 those left in Glasgow met, more or less surreptitiously, in Corbet's Land in the Candleriggs and elsewhere in the city. Then the Revd Alexander Duncan, a staunch Jacobite, held services in a house in Bell St from 1715 to 1733; later services took place in the old grammar school in George St.

Episcopal clergymen ministering to English congregations in Scotland were, for obvious reasons, known as 'jurors'. In Glasgow before 1750 they mainly officiated to English troops billeted in the city. From 1746, after the Jacobite Rising, until 1792 (when the last of the Penal Acts were repealed) their churches were the only legal places of Episcopalian worship in Scotland. In 1750 St Andrew's-by-the-Green (i.e. Glasgow Green) was built by public subscription to minister to the English community in Glasgow. The builder was Andrew Hunter, mason, and so strong was the prejudice against the 'Piskies' (as they were popularly called) that the Kirk Session of the Shuttle St Secession Congregation (to which Hunter belonged), having failed to convince him of the 'great Sin and Scandal' of his behaviour, excommunicated him.

St Andrew's was the first post-Reformation church in Glasgow to use an organ in public worship – first a Schnezler, then one by Donaldson of York in 1792. Two early adherents were Robert Tennent, vintner and owner of the Saracen's Head Inn, and Andrew Stalker, bookseller and editor of the *Glasgow Journal*. The church's occasional visitors and 'sitters' (as they were called) included many local notabilities – the Duchess of Hamilton,

Lord Cathcart, Sir William Hooker (the famous botanist), the Speirs of Elderslie, Bogles of Gilmorehill and Houldsworths of Cranstonhill. In 1805 the two branches of the church, jurors and non-jurors, came together under William Abernethy Drummond, Bishop of Glasgow. After his death in 1809 the diocese was linked with Edinburgh till 1837 when Michael Russell became the Glasgow bishop – he is reported to have said that his whole flock 'could all be accommodated comfortably in a reasonably large drawing-room'! After meeting for a while in St Mary's, Renfield St, in 1893 they moved to the splendid St Mary's Cathedral in Great Western Rd.

Heretics

Heresy does not seem to have greatly troubled Glasgow and its neighbourhood. In 1503 in the chapter-house of the Cathedral accusations of heresy were brought against George Campbell of Cessnock and John Campbell of Newmilns, but no further action seems to have been taken against them. In 1538 'two very young men, Jerom Russel and John Kennedy, a young man of Air' were judged to be heretical and were burnt to death at the east end of the Cathedral. There is a doubtful reference to a James Resby who was burnt at Glasgow around 1407 for saying that the pope was not the vicar of Christ.

Methodists

Although John Wesley himself visited Scotland 22 times between 1751 and 1790 and often preached in Glasgow, there was no permanent Methodist Society in the city until 1765. This first society met in a room in the Barbers' Hall in Stockwell St for the next 20 years or so until new chapels were opened in John St (1787) and Bridge St, Tradeston (1813). Still later three more were opened, in Great Hamilton St (1817), Anderston and Parkhead. These buildings

were, unfortunately, so expensive for their small congregations (Bridge St cost £6,700) that they were forced to sell and disperse. The Great Hamilton St building was bought by the Town Council and became the burgh church of St James's in 1820. These financial disasters and the Scottish dislike of a non-settled and often lay ministry forced Methodism in Glasgow (and in Scotland) into a long decline, and their current handbook lists three Stations only in the Glasgow area.

Quakers

George Fox, founder of the Quakers, visited Glasgow in 1657 and a small society was set up in 1687. As elsewhere, they were subjected to very rough treatment. In 1691 a bailie of the city supported by some town officers broke into the Quaker meeting-house and damaged their benches, following which they petitioned for redress from the Privy Council. From 1716 they had a meeting-house and a burying-ground in Stirling St (about the time this burying-ground was closed the Society was presented with another one in 1711 in Partick which remained in use till 1857). They then moved to a rented room till 1815, when they began to meet in Portland St where they had accommodation for about 400. They were in Bath St for a while, then in Newton Terrace. Their beliefs would not allow them to observe the many public and sacramental Fast Days declared by the Church of Scotland and so those early Quakers who were shopkeepers frequently had their shops forcibly closed by the police. The best known of the Glasgow Quakers was probably William Smeal, grocer, who came to Glasgow in 1802 and played a prominent part in organising the influential Glasgow Anti-Slavery Association.

Roman Catholicism

After the Reformation the eclipse of the

Roman Catholic Church in Scotland was so complete that until the end of the 18th century there was seldom more than a score of Roman Catholics in and around the city, mostly poor Highlanders. There was no resident priest and their religious needs were catered for by the chaplain at Drummond Castle, Perthshire, who rode over once or twice a year to celebrate mass.

The earliest known meeting-place of this minuscule congregation was in a private house in High St. Despite the very small number of Roman Catholics in Scotland, their presence aroused such animosity that parliamentary efforts at the end of the 18th century to remove the penalties they laboured under caused 12,000 members of 85 anti-Popery Societies to petition against any relief. A Glasgow mob attacked their High St meeting-place in 1778, and the following year they were evicted by a similar riot from the house of Robert Bagnall, a Gallowgate potter (probably the city's only Roman Catholic of standing). About 1782 they began to meet in a small room in Blackstock's Close, near the Bridgegate.

In 1792 Alexander Macdonnel came to the city as the first resident Roman Catholic priest and the following year some of the penal statutes were repealed (now, for instance, Roman Catholics could be entered as burgesses and guild brethren). Largely through the influence and enterprise of Robert Monteith (heir of Henry Monteith of Carstairs, an extremely wealthy Glasgow textile manufacturer) the small community obtained a recognised meeting-place in a disused tennis court in Town's Court (off Mitchell St) belonging to the Duke of Hamilton. An eminent Protestant was said to have provided the little chapel with benches for 300 persons. Monteith was one of a group of several Scottish converts which included the Duchess of Hamilton and the Marquis of Bute. Next, in 1797, a chapel to hold 600 worshippers was opened in Marshall's Lane in the Calton opposite the Infantry Barracks.

Until the beginning of the 19th century Scotland's Roman Catholic centre had been around Enzie in Banffshire, where elements of the old faith lingered in obscurity. Now the centre of influence shifted south to Glasgow, moving from a rural to an industrial environment. It was priests from Enzie, Peter Forbes and Alexander Scott, who came south to the city – this choice of Scottish rather than Irish priests, it was hoped, would be more acceptable in the city.

Following the establishment of the city's first cotton mill in 1779, an influx of Irish workers (the majority of whom were, of course, Roman Catholics) began which was to continue and grow for the next 80 years or so. At one time the Highlanders had been at the bottom of Glasgow's social pyramid; that position was now occupied by the Irish. A few sections of the Protestant majority took a benevolent interest. In 1817 Kirkman Finlay built a Roman Catholic school for the children of immigrant Irish – but insisted that the Protestant bible be used. In 1819 several manufacturers formed a Catholic Schools Society, with five Protestants and five Roman Catholics, under Finlay's chairmanship; Finlay himself remarked that 'manufacturers of this country could never have got on without the assistance of the Irish weavers' and it was noticeable that the members of the Society were mainly employers of large Irish workforces.

When the Enzie priests came south to Glasgow in 1805 they had about 450 parishioners but so quickly was the Roman Catholic population growing that by 1814 the Calton Chapel's congregation had increased to 3,000 and a larger place of worship was an urgent requirement. A site was obtained on the riverfront in Clyde St and the grandiose St Andrew's Cathedral was erected on it (1814–17). For years its huge cost (upwards of £13,000) was a considerable burden on the church's local resources, and it was not until 1842 that St Mary's, the next church, was opened in Abercrombie St in the Calton.

From the 1820s until well into the century there was considerable tension between the aboriginal Scottish Roman Catholics and the incomers from Ireland, the latter claiming that positions and money were going to the former. The situation was considerably aggravated by a strong nationalist element amongst the first and second-generation Irish, but this tension between the city's old and new Roman Catholics was in great part removed by the appointment in 1869 of an Englishman as Archbishop, in the person of Charles Eyre.

The strong anti-Popery sentiments of most of the 'native' Glaswegians had always been fairly easily aroused, and these sentiments were further aggravated by the extraordinarily rapid increase of the city's Irish population. The peak, both of animosity and population increase, was probably about the time of the Hungry Forties and has been consistently but slowly falling since – in 1841 and 1851 the proportion of Irish in the city was 18 per cent, but by 1891 it had fallen to 10 per cent, and to 7 per cent in 1911. From the Irish side, the passing of the 1918 Act which set up separate but government-funded Roman Catholic state schools removed a major cause of discontent (Glasgow Labour's support for this Act did much to bring it the Irish vote) and the breaking of the nationalist link following the 1921 establishment of the Irish Free State allowed the Glasgow Irish to concentrate on local affairs.

Although Irish-trained priests still predominated they were leavened by the presence of priests from Italy, Poland and Lithuania. The rise of a Glasgow Irish middle class, as indicated by the establishment of the St Aloysius and St Mungo's academies, and the fact that by the 1970s more than 40 per cent of Glasgow Roman Catholics were marrying non-Roman Catholics, are only two indications of the continuing abrasion and softening of long-standing social and religious distinctions.

See also CATHEDRAL
CHURCHES
ETHNIC GROUPS
ST KENTIGERN

Riots

Shawfield Riot (1725)

Daniel Campbell of Shawfield was the Member of Parliament for the Clyde Burghs (Glasgow, Dumbarton, Renfrew and Rutherglen) from 1715 to 1734. It was rumoured that he and his friend on the Town Council had been as careful for themselves as for the burgh – it was said that when entrusted with uplifting in London £738 owed the city he had claimed over £300 in expenses, and he had added to his considerable fortune by farming the customs in the Firth of Clyde.

The common belief that his had been the chief hand in putting through Parliament an imposition of 2d. Scots on Scottish malt had caused a considerable outcry in the country. This feeling was so strong in Glasgow that on 22 June 1725 (the day before the tax was to be introduced) Campbell thought fit to convey out of his town-house, the Shawfield Mansion (built in 1711, located in what would become Glassford St), not only his family but all his money, banknotes and plate to his country house at Woodhall. In addition he arranged for two companies (about 100 men) of Lord Deloraine's Regiment of Foot under the command of Captain Bushnell to be sent through to Glasgow from Edinburgh.

The conduct of the citizens on 23 June (the commencement of the tax) prevented the Excise officers from carrying out their duties. The next day the soldiers arrived about 6 p.m.; they were to be stationed in the Town Guard House, but as their access to it was blocked they were billeted in private houses throughout the city. That evening Provost Charles Miller and his fellow magistrates, after waiting in the Tolbooth in case of trouble, retired to a tavern at 9 p.m. An hour later a large crowd marched on the Shawfield Mansion with hammers, axes and levers and thoroughly gutted the house from top to bottom. At midnight Captain Bushnell offered the assistance of his forces in quelling what had evidently become a riot, but the provost declined his help, pointing out that it would be impossible to bring together his men safely and quickly from all over the city.

The following day about noon the troops eventually took up their station in the Guard House but a crowd assembled and began throwing stones. Bushnell then turned out his men, formed them into a hollow square at the junction of Candleriggs and King St and ordered them to fire, killing and wounding several persons. The crowd then broke open the Town Magazine and the provost, fearing an armed riot, advised Bushnell to withdraw from the city. This he did, and on the way his men fired again at the mob – in all nine rioters were killed and 17 wounded. Eventually the troops found shelter in Dumbarton Castle, ten miles away.

When the news became known in Edinburgh the authorities (amongst whom was Shawfield's brother, Edinburgh's MP) chose to regard the outburst as an armed rebellion, and on 9 July General Wade entered the city accompanied by Lord Deloraine's Regiment, six troops of the Royal Scots Dragoons and of the Earl of Stair's Dragoons, a company of Highland soldiers and a train of artillery. After an investigation by the Lord Advocate, the provost and other magistrates, along with 19 other people, were arrested and taken to Edinburgh and imprisoned in the Tolbooth there. The magistrates, after being charged with 'partiality and maladministration', were later released; of the 19, two were banished, eight liberated and the rest whipped through the streets of Glasgow.

The following year an Act was passed which granted Shawfield £6,080 to make good the depredations he had suffered. The Act also ordered 2d. Scots to be collected for every pint of ale or beer sold in the city until this whole sum had been repaid to the Exchequer. With this money Shawfield bought the islands of Jura and Islay, and Glasgow knew him no more. He sold his mansion in 1727 to Colonel William McDowall of Castlesemple for £1,785.

It was said that the provost and his party, having managed to get rid of Shawfield's influence in the city, were not overzealous in defending his property, and that Shawfield, in turn, welcomed the opportunity to settle old scores.

Anti-Popery Riots (1778)

Until the influx of Irish immigrants in the 19th century, Glasgow had scarcely a score of Roman Catholics, mainly poor Highlanders. Despite this, when Parliament began to discuss a bill to remove some of the penal statutes affecting Roman Catholics, the whole of Scotland was roused to a pitch of religious frenzy and some 85 anti-popery societies were set up to defeat the bill. Feelings were particularly strong in Glasgow, and one Sunday in October 1778 a mob attacked and wrecked a house in the High St where Glasgow's few Catholics were accustomed to meet. The rioters (one account says they were mainly young boys) were dispersed by the magistrates. In February of the following year a more serious disturbance took place. One particular Tuesday having been declared a Fast Day, it was rumoured that workmen employed by a French potter, Robert Bagnall, a Roman Catholic, were continuing to work in contempt of the fast. It was also said that, following the destruction of their High St meeting-place, the city's Roman Catholics were now assembling in Bagnall's house in the Gallowgate.

A mob soon gathered and first set fire to his house and then went on to his shop in King St and destroyed its contents. So fierce was the mob that the magistrates were forced to enlist the aid of the Western Fencibles in maintaining the peace. Several of the rioters were imprisoned but later released – 'to prevent worse consequences'. Bagnall raised an action against the city, claiming damages amounting to £1,429.

The Calton Weavers' Strike (1787)

In 1787 the weavers in the Calton district of the city's east end went on strike. Their bargaining powers had been considerably weakened as the number of weavers increased, some of whom were willing to work for reduced rates. In protest 7,000 of the 20,000-strong Clyde Valley Weavers' General Association agreed not to accept these low wage levels, and in retaliation the masters instituted a lock-out. The affair dragged on for two months until in September some of the striking weavers cut out the webs of working weavers and paraded, with these as trophies, towards the city centre. When an attempt by the magistrates to stop them was defeated by a shower of stones, the military were called out (39th Regiment, the Dorset Militia) and succeeded in chasing the weavers back. In the course of a later attempt by the weavers to return by way of Duke St, the soldiers fired on the multitude, killing three immediately and mortally wounding three others. On the following two days the weavers again took to the streets, burning webs and wrecking looms but were finally dispersed without further bloodshed by the soldiers, who had been reinforced by the 56th Regiment (the West Suffolk Militia) from Ayr Barracks.

There was considerable sympathy for the plight of the strikers and the Calton Weavers bought a lair in the Calton Burying-ground in which three of the victims were interred. Stones commemorating those who had been 'Martyred by the Military under orders of the Civic Authorities' were erected over the grave in 1836; they were renewed in 1931 and 1957 by the Glasgow Trades Council.

The Radical Rising (1820)

After the end of the Napoleonic Wars in 1815, lack of employment, falling wages and government repression helped to create considerable discontent amongst the working classes, and in Glasgow brought about one of the city's best-known disturbances.

In 1819 the largest radical gathering in the city till that time took place in the Calton when it was noted that many of those present sported the French Republican 'cap of liberty'. The response of the Town Council was to have a cavalry force barracked in the city. Other similar rallies took place elsewhere in Glasgow but these were merely the preliminaries. On 1 April 1820 copies of a poster appeared throughout the city. Headed an 'ADDRESS to the Inhabitants of Great Britain & Ireland' it called upon them to refrain from labour 'from and after the FIRST of APRIL'. The workers of Glasgow had earlier suffered from the actions of an *agent provocateur*, Alexander Richmond, a Pollokshaws weaver, recruited by Kirkman Finlay, the city's Lord Provost and MP, and it is possible that this inflammatory placard (which made reference to English rather than Scottish history) was part of a further attempt to embarrass the operatives – it was even rumoured that a French army was on its way and would set up camp on the Cathkin Braes!

Whatever element of hoax may have been involved, the authorities took it seriously – the Rifle Brigade, the 30th/83rd Regiments, the 7th/10th Hussars, several regiments of yeomanry and the Glasgow Sharpshooters (a Glasgow volunteer force under the command of Samuel Hunter, editor of the *Glasgow Herald*) were all ordered out under arms.

Active reponse to the call was meagre, although many weavers, workmen and labourers stayed away from work. A band of some 100 men (which dwindled on the way to about 25) led by James Wilson, a 63-year-old weaver, set out from Strathaven bound for Cathkin, but finding no evidence of any support returned home;

Wilson was, nevertheless, arrested as having been the ringleader. In the belief that a force of English revolutionaries was advancing on the Carron Ironworks (an important centre of ordnance manufacture) near Falkirk, some 70 radicals armed with pikes, swords and muskets and led by Andrew Hardie, a Glasgow weaver, left the city to offer their support to their English comrades. By the time they reached Condorrat (where about ten weavers led by John Baird joined them) their numbers had considerably diminished. On finding no trace of the supposed English contingent, most of the little band dispersed, but near Bonnymuir the remainder, some 30 men, were attacked and rounded up by the 10th Hussars and the Kilsyth Yeomanry.

Eighteen of those captured at Bonnymuir and four others were charged with high treason at a Court of Oyer and Terminer held at Stirling. John Baird and Andrew Hardie (said to have been an ancestor of Keir Hardie) were convicted, hanged and beheaded at Stirling as ringleaders; of the rest, 19 were transported to New South Wales, Australia, and were eventually pardoned in 1835. In addition, the Strathaven weaver, James Wilson, was publicly hanged and beheaded in August in Glasgow's Jail Square, before a crowd of 20,000 spectators.

Baird and Hardie soon became (and have remained) popular martyrs of the working classes in the west of Scotland. In 1847 their bodies were quietly and discreetly exhumed from their burial places in Stirling Castle and reinterred on the summit of Sighthill Cemetery, Springburn, and surmounted by an elaborate monument known as the Martyrs' Memorial.

Queen Caroline Riot (1820)

A second disturbance took place in Glasgow the same year as the Radical

Rising, but of a quite different nature. Queen Caroline, the estranged wife of George IV, was extremely popular amongst the lower classes and, when divorce proceedings against her were dropped, demonstrations in her support took place all over the country. In Glasgow the populace's desire for a general illumination in her honour was frustrated by the city authorities. In revenge, crowds went to the Glasgow Green, pulled up two miles of palings, 'acquired' several tar barrels and made an enormous bonfire. When the fire brigade arrived on the scene, the mob pushed its engines into the Clyde. Eventually the ultimate urban peace-keeping force was summoned, but the cavalry from Port Eglinton Barracks found the city bridges held against them and were forced to detour by way of Rutherglen Bridge. The Riot Act was read, the cavalry trotted forward and the mob hurriedly dispersed. So many fled across a temporary wooden bridge at Hutchesontown that it collapsed under their weight. One man was drowned, the incident's only fatality.

Provand the Dyer Riot (1822)
In 1822 a mob attacked the house of one George Provand, a dyer, and completely gutted it. He occupied the Dreghorn Mansion in Clyde St and it was reported that a reddish liquid had been detected running from his premises, that two children had been enticed into his house and that he was a resurrectionist. Arrests were made and several members of the mob were transported, while one, Richard Campbell, a weaver, was publicly whipped through the city streets, the last time this happened in Glasgow.

Bread Riot (1848)
The year 1848 saw a number of revolutionary riots throughout Europe, and Glasgow was not spared. Sometimes called the Bread Riots, the city's weekend of street fighting in March of that year has been documented as the city's most formidable riot.

Glasgow was suffering from a great influx of starving people from the Highlands and from Ireland, and there were more than 15,000 unemployed workers in the city. Some attempts at relief had been set up – meal was distributed at the City Hall and soup kitchens were organised – but such efforts were not sufficient to stem the rising unrest. The Chartists had been organising a series of mass meetings on the Glasgow Green since February and at the beginning of March over 3,000 people who had assembled there proceeded to march to the City Hall. They armed themselves with iron railings taken from Monteith Row and on their way broke into gun-smiths and gun-dealers, as well as plundering food shops and jewellers. The police force was helpless against such numbers (the Chief Constable was obliged to resign on account of his inaction) and the Town Guard (made up mainly of armed pensioners) was called out. It fired into the mob and a number of marchers were wounded, some fatally; one, David Carruth, a miner, was killed outright. His body, carried on a shutter, was paraded through the streets to cries of 'Vive la république!' (an echo of the French revolution in February of that year). Barricades of planks and coal carts were erected in the Gallowgate and during the night 600 gas street-lights were smashed. Some 10,000 special constables were hurriedly sworn in, and the following day the 3rd Dragoons from the Eglinton Cavalry Barracks and the 1st Royals from the Gallowgate Infantry Barracks – assisted by two companies of the 71st Regiment, the Highland Light Infantry (rushed through by train from Edinburgh) – quickly cleared the streets of the rioters and their barricades; as a contemporary account relates, 'thereafter perfect tranquillity prevailed'. Thirty-five rioters were convicted, two of whom were sentenced to 18 years' transportation.

The government was seriously disturbed by the somewhat exaggerated accounts of this Glasgow riot (which gave rise to similar attempts in London, Edinburgh and Manchester) and for a while there was talk of a 'British Revolution'.

George Square Riot, 'Black Friday' (1919) Clydeside's reputation for radicalism, which it earned during the First World War, remained with the city after 1918. In 1919 the Clyde Workers Committee (an unofficial body not recognised by the official trade union movement but supported by the Scottish Trade Union Congress and the Glasgow Trades and Labour Council) began to conduct a vigorous campaign in support of a 40-hour week. It commenced with a 3,000-strong meeting in the St Andrew's Halls on Monday, 27 January. By Friday some 50,000 were on strike within and around the city and a protest group of about 10,000 persons marched from the Halls to George Square.

While a deputation headed by Emmanuel Shinwell, President of the Glasgow Trades Council, went into the City Chambers to put the Committee's case to the Lord Provost, the crowd in the square became increasingly restive. The Committee had previously pointed out to the civic authorities the danger of driving any tramcars (the municipal employees, including the tramdrivers, were not on strike) through the streets bordering the square during its occupation, but the warning was ignored, and an attempt to push a tramcar through the crowds is thought to have sparked off the riot and led to a direct and bloody confrontation between the strikers and the police. The strikers were eventually dispersed and that evening soldiers equipped with machine-guns and tanks arrived at the city's Buchanan St Station and took up strategic positions throughout the city centre – these forces remained in Glasgow for a week. Fifteen persons were charged with 'inciting a mob of 20,000 or thereby riotous and evilly disposed persons' and Shinwell, William Gallacher and David Kirkwood were sentenced to imprisonment for several months.

Roads and Streets

ROAD SYSTEM

It is probable that the city's earliest road system would have been a mile-long track running downhill from the vicinity of the burial-place of Kentigern, its tutelary saint, to the north bank of the Clyde. At its northern end two other tracks extended east and west from it to form a quadrivium or crossroads: east, the Drygate leading down to and across the Molendinar; west, the

London Rd in the east end of the city. The Glasgow Eastern Area Renewal programme has swept away most of these old tenement buildings. The graffiti are mainly concerned with Glasgow gangs and their members. (George Oliver)

Rottenrow, lined with the Cathedral clergy's manses. Another crossroads developed about two-thirds of the way down the central track, becoming in time *the* Glasgow Cross and the nucleus for a developing merchant community – the Gallowgate, the city's main exit to Edinburgh and the east, the Trongate, its exit to Dumbarton and the west. The top two-thirds of the central track became the High St and its southern continuation was the Saltmarket. Each of these throughfares had a multitude of little lanes, wynds or vennels, opening off at right angles to the main street.

This simple layout, a double cross, was sufficient for the needs of the city until the 18th century, when its rapid expansion, first as a trading and later as a manufacturing centre, broke the old medieval pattern, and by 1760 a number of new streets had been opened up on the western boundary of the old centre. Similar attempts to expand towards the east were unsuccessful. These new streets were aligned with the rectangular boundaries of the old burgage plots and rigs, and so initiated, more by accident than design, the city's gridiron pattern.

As Glasgow's westward expansion continued, an unco-ordinated layout of streets and squares now developed west of the grid between 1760 and 1800, extending to the lands of Ramshorn and Meadowflatts to the north and to the new Buchanan St in the west, a phase which continued until the beginning of the 19th century.

From 1800 to 1830 several 'new towns' carried the city's spread further west, and also, for the first time, took it south across the river. There Tradeston, Laurieston and Hutchesontown grew up around the old burgh of Gorbals. These new southern developments exhibited no particular road pattern, but the new town, which spread across the drumlins of the Blythswood lands to the west of Buchanan St, was laid out on a strict gridiron system (despite its undulating surface), thus ensuring that most of post-medieval Glasgow's road system consisted of right-angled intersections at roughly every 50 yards.

With the increasing use of motor transport during the 1920s and 1930s, this horse-and-cart layout began to seize up as

Glasgow Cross from the east. The Tolbooth Steeple stands isolated and forlorn amongst its much later companions. It and its associated group of halls and assembly rooms (the latter now demolished) served, from the 17th century, as the municipal and business centre of the city. (George Oliver)

most of the main thoroughfares leading out of the city were quite inadequate for the new transport situation. Paisley Rd and Dumbarton Rd (leading west out of Glasgow on the left and right banks of the river respectively) were much too narrow, and were further circumscribed by the ubiquitous and street-blocking tramcar; both the eastern exits – London Rd and the Gallowgate – were similarly limited. Only the more modern northern exits – west by the Great Western Rd and east by the Edinburgh Rd and Parliamentary Rd – could be regarded as adequate arterial routes.

After the Second World War things had become progressively worse, and Robert Bruce, the city's Master of Works and City Engineer, tackled these transport problems in a 1945 report which offered a radical, not to say macho solution. His overriding aim was at all costs to retain within the city's boundaries its current population. This aim was strongly opposed in the Clyde Valley Plan, which advocated an 'overspill' solution by relocating the population to a series of proposed new towns, East Kilbride, Cumbernauld, Bishopton and Houston (only the first two of which were actually built). Bruce's proposal envisaged the almost complete eradication of the central city area (including the razing, amongst much else, of the City Chambers, George Sq, the existing railway stations and Mackintosh's School of Art!) and resowing it with high-rise flats to accommodate the population. His transport layout was a purely theoretical exercise based on the unwarranted assumption that main roads, tram routes and railways all conveniently cross each other at accommodating intervals.

Although the Bruce Plan, fortunately, remained unexecuted, the growing problem of the city's antiquated road system still had to be dealt with. In 1952 the average speed of traffic through the city was 9 mph, and by 1957 it had sunk to 7 mph – the slowest of any UK city. In 1960 the Corporation began to investigate the possibility of relieving central traffic build-up by means of encircling the city with an extensive ringroad which would allow bypassable traffic to skirt it and permit other traffic access to it by radial feeders.

This sweeping solution became an actuality with the Corporation's 1965 Highways Plan and by 1980, with the completion of the northern and western flanks of the Inner Ring Road, and the demolition of some 7,000 houses, the average traffic speed to 11mph. Cross-river communication, always a problem, had been greatly eased by the multi-lane Kingston Bridge, a massive high-level structure which took the west flank across the Clyde.

The plans for the eastern and southern flank roads ran into trouble. Their meeting-place was, unavoidably, Glasgow Green, a centuries-old open space always jealously guarded against any encroachment. In addition, the eastern flank, also unavoidably, ran through all that was left of old Glasgow, from the Cathedral at one end, to St Andrew's-by-the-Green at the other. In 1974 it was proposed to tunnel around the Cathedral and below the Green, but by the late 1980s, after the construction of the Clyde Expressway along part of the north bank of the Clyde, the difficult problem of the eastern flank became less pressing and a £2 million enlargement of the city's already extensive one-way system promised a less contentious way of speeding up city centre traffic.

STREETS

A very rapid increase in the number of streets took place at the end of the 18th century, when the city's commercial and manufacturing activities took off. For instance, a contemporary account estimated that in 1791 'new streets and squares built, building, and feued for building in the city and suburbs within the last three years amount to near 50 in number'. This progress continued into the next century: in 1800 there were 30 miles of streets; by the middle of the century almost 100 miles.

The names chosen for these new streets reflected a change in the way the city regarded itself. The old names had been straightforwardly descriptive – the street going past the weighing machine (the Trongate), the way to the gallows (the Gallowgate), the road to the bridge (the Briggate or Bridgegate) – but now the more self-conscious 18th-century citizens began to follow the Paris fashion of naming streets after royalty, and so we get King St and Queen St, Hanover St, George St, Frederick St, York St, Cambridge St and Kent St, Charlotte St, Albany St, Regent St and Brunswick St. Descriptive names still persisted, however, as witness the

Broomielaw and Sauchiehall St, Bath St, Candleriggs, Clayslaps and Goosedubbs. Another influence which played a part was the flattering of powerful political figures, from which comes Argyle St, Dundas St and Pitt St, and, at the lower level of the city's own rulers, its Lord Provosts – Cochrane St, Ingram St and Watson St. John St, near the City Chambers, is said to be a portmanteau effort to honour the large number of city bigwigs christened 'John'. Another group of street names commemorate the various entrepreneurs who were instrumental in opening them up – Gordon St, Buchanan St and Dunlop St, for example.

As the city began to spread westwards, every opportunity was taken to demonstrate its patriotic spirit; from this impulse comes a picturesque group of street names all connected with the French wars at the end of the 18th century. There are sea victories: Camperdown St, St Vincent St and Copenhagen St; a battle – Havannah St; famous leaders – Wellington St and Duncan St; even a defeat – Corunna St. The city's trade and industry have also contributed a few of its street names: Jamaica St, Virginia St and Antigua St all pay tribute to its trade with America and the West Indies, while industry is represented by Muslin St, Cotton St, Forge St and Shuttle St.

As the city continued to spread, the mileage of streets grew. In 1849 there had been nearly 100 miles; by the end of the century there were 320 miles and the problems of finding names for all these new streets tended to bring out romantic tendencies in the namers. A good example of this is the district of Laurieston lying on the south bank of the Clyde. In an effort to establish a high-toned atmosphere the proprietors, the brothers John and David Laurie, gave the streets names suggestive of the English aristocracy: Oxford St,

Norfolk St, Bedford St, Cumberland St and Carlton St; all in vain, however, for the invasion of low-toned industries eventually turned the district into the infamous Gorbals slums.

The growth of huge housing schemes in the interwar years presented particular street-naming difficulties and the solutions give some indication of the favourite reading of the councillors; the Corporation Minutes for September 1925 set out some street names for the Knightswood housing scheme, among those chosen were Friarscourt Ave, Monksbridge Ave, Rowena Ave, Crusader Ave, Palmer Ave, Cedric Place and Priory Place. This Sir Walter Scott virus also attacked south of the river where we find Durward Ave, Peveril Ave, and Kenilworth Ave. Riddrie's scheme can boast of a good handful of Scottish rivers – Gadie St, Dee St, Eden St, Tummel St – while close by, an unusual tribute (for Glasgow) to Edinburgh, gives us Fettes St, Loretto St and Warriston Street. A little to the north, Scottish lighthouses come to the fore in Bellrock St, Startpoint St and Fastnet St.

Street nomenclature affords an unusual and unexpected method of determining the social standing of any Glasgow district: if *Streets* predominate then you are in a working-class district and probably north or east of the city centre; an abundance of *Avenues*, however, locates you south or west and in an AB area.

The streets listed below, with dates and descriptions, for historical reasons fall almost without exception within a period ending somewhere in the first half of the 19th century and within a space bounded by the High St and Charing Cross, Sauchiehall St and the Clyde. After that date the city's explosive expansion multiplied the number of new streets many times over and their names derive, with few exceptions, either from some literary work (by Scott or Burns, for example), from Scottish place names, from local dignitaries long forgotten or, ultimately, from a local whimsy, so that any attempt to list them would be otiose, boring and lengthy. The word 'gate' or 'gait', which occurs in several of the older streets, has the meaning 'way' 'route' or 'street', and had nothing to do with 'gate' meaning an opening.

Adelphi St (Hutchesontown) – to commemorate the brothers George and Thomas Hutcheson, 17th-century Glasgow lawyers and philanthropists.

Albany St (Bridgeton) – after the Duchess of Albany, daughter of Prince Charles Edward Stewart and Clementina Walkinshaw of Glasgow. The Walkinshaw family owned land in the neighbourhood.

Albion St, north and south (off George St) – 1808.

Alma St (Camlachie) – after the Battle of the Alma 1854, during the Crimean War.

Argyle St (west from the Cross) – a continuation westward of the Trongate. Originally called Westergait, it then became known as Anderston Walk. Finally, after the removal of the West Port (at the top of Stockwell St) in 1751, it became Argyle St (early spelling 'Argyll') to honour the powerful dukes of that name. Its importance was greatly increased when Jamaica St was opened at its western end, leading south to the second bridge over the Clyde.

Armour's Wynd (south from Trongate) – 1689. Located between the Old and the New Vennels.

Back Cow Loan – *see* **Ingram St**

Barrack St (Calton) – opened 1795. Takes its name from the Infantry Barracks erected in the area that same year.

Bath St (parallel to Sauchiehall St) – the first street to be opened in the Blythswood district (1800). Became fashionable because of (and took its name from) the popular bathing establishment set up at its southern end by William Harley.

Bellgrove St (Dennistoun) – originally the Witches Loan, supposedly from a apocryphal story that bewitched cattle were driven south down it from Craigpark to spell-free pastures beside the Clyde.

Bell St (off High St) – the western part of Bell's Wynd (1676, named after Sir John Bell, Provost, 1680)

Blackfriars St (off High St) – takes its name from the convent of the Dominicans (c.1246) located nearby.

Blythswood Square – situated on the highest point of the Blythswood estate (owned by the Campbells of Blythswood), the centre of the new town. Layout begun in 1821 by William Hamilton Garden, property speculator.

Bothwell St (off Hope St) – laid out in the 1820s as a residential street and linked to St Vincent St by a curving portion in 1854.

Bridgegate (off the Saltmarket) – one of the city's early streets, probably dating from the late 13th century. Its name comes from the fact that it joins the foot of the Saltmarket to the northern end of the old Glasgow Bridge.

Broomielaw – immediately to the west of the Glasgow Bridge, on the north bank of the Clyde. Its name means 'gorse or broom-covered slope'. Site of Glasgow's harbour.

Brunswick St (off the Trongate) – opened in 1790 as part of a development which included Hutcheson St and Wilson St; a Duke of Brunswick fought in the Seven Years War.

Buchanan St (off Argyle St) – first feued in 1777. Named after Andrew Buchanan, a maltster turned successful tobacco merchant. It became the fashionable shopping centre in the Victorian period, particularly for high-class ladies' outfitters, but was later overtaken by Sauchiehall St. Fought hard to keep the tramcars out, but its success brought congestion from motor cars. Pedestrianised in 1978.

Camperdown Place – *see* **West George St**

Candleriggs (off the Trongate) – *c.*1679. Takes its name from the candle-works (a smelly and dangerous trade) then located outside the town's built-up area. On the same axis as Stockwell St to the south, it served as a route north from the Trongate.

Carlton Place (Laurieston) – 1803. Named after the Prince of Wales' London residence.

Carrick St (off Argyle St) – 1800. Named after a famous Glasgow banker, Robert Carrick of the Ship Bank.

Charlotte St (Glasgow Green, west end) – feuing began in 1779. Named after wife of George III. Merchants' houses, very fashionable, closed off from the Glasgow Green by a gate.

Cochrane St (off George Square) – 1787. Developed as part of the Ramshorn lands. Provost Andrew Cochrane procured government compensation for Glasgow's losses from Prince Charles Edward's exactions.

Cow Loan – *see* **Queen St**

Drygate – one of Glasgow's early streets, it led off eastwards from the Cathedral, barely crossing the Molendinar before it came to an end.

Duke St (continuation east of George St) – 1794. Two sources are given for its name. One links it with the Dukes of Montrose whose 'Lodgings' overlooked

it. A more likely suggestion is that it was meant to honour Frederick, Duke of York. The street was suggested by the Carron Company, Falkirk, to act as a direct route to Falkirk via Cumbernauld.

Dundas St (west side of Queen St Station) – 1812. Lord Dundas played a prominent part in the construction of the Forth and Clyde Canal.

Dunlop St (off Argyle St) – 1772. Named after Colin Dunlop, Lord Provost.

French St (Bridgeton) – formerly Papillon St, after Pierre Jacques Papillon, who was brought from Rouen in 1785 by George Macintosh to superintend the setting up of a turkey-red dyeing establishment.

Gallowgate – one of Glasgow's four important medieval streets, the city's access road from the east. Described as *Vicus Furcarum* (*furca*, a gibbet) it led east to the Gallows Muir where the gallows were located, well outside the city.

George Square – named for George III. Laid out in 1781, but for a number of years it remained a hollow full of dirty water, its banks used for slaughtering horses. Between 1787 and the 1820s its edges were filled up with houses.

George St (east from George Square) – 1792. Opened up as part of the Ramshorn land. Named after George III.

Glassford St (city centre) – Laid out from 1786 on. Named after John Glassford of Dougalston, one of the city's foremost tobacco merchants.

Goosedubbs (off Stockwell St) – 16th century, under its latin name *Paluda Anserum*, a goose pond. For a time known as Aird's Wynd.

Gordon St (off Hope St) – 1802. Laid out by Alexander 'Picture' Gordon.

Buchanan St always managed to remain slightly aloof from its surroundings, even keeping free of the rather vulgar tramcar. All the best shops were here, and its pavements were lined with the motorcars of the affluent – some can be seen in this early 20th-century view. Now pedestrianised for most of its length, it still keeps its air of well-being. (Mitchell Library)

Charing Cross. This early 20th-century view (looking east) has the Cameron Memorial Fountain (Charles Cameron MP, and proprietor of the North British Daily Mail*) on the left in front of the Grand Hotel, with the magnificent sweep of the Charing Cross Mansions behind it. The passage (in a deep cut) of the western flank of the Inner Ring Road almost immediately in front of the Mansions brought about the removal of practically everything but the Mansions and the Monument, but the open view this produced has been spoilt by intrusive and insensitive office blocks. (Mitchell Library)*

Grace St (Stobcross) – in memory of the youngest daughter of John Geddes of Verreville, potter, who was burned to death while dressing for a ball.

Great Western Rd – a toll road set up by Act of Parliament in 1816. Glasgow's longest and straightest thoroughfare, lined along most of its length with trees, terraced houses and large villas.

Hanover St (city centre) – 1798. After the Elector of Hanover, a title borne by the British kings from George I to William IV.

Havana St (off High St) – Gavin Williamson used his prize money won at the capture of Havannah in 1762 to build the first tenement in the street in 1763. It was known in the 19th century as 'the home of the shebeener, thief and child-stripper'. Disappeared under the now demolished College Goods Station.

High St – for hundreds of years the spine of old Glasgow, from which the lesser thoroughfares branched off. *Via regis*, the King's Way, it led downhill from the Cathedral, south to the Cross. Its upper part, called the Bell o' the Brae, was very steep and almost impossible for horse-drawn vehicles. Twice in the 18th century and once in the 19th, it was successively sliced away to ease access to the top of the town. Until 1870 it housed both Glasgow University and some of the city's worst slums.

Holland St (off Sauchiehall St) – Lord Holland was an 18th-century member of the Cabinet; his wife had West Indian connections.

Hope St – formerly Copenhagen St and afterwards named after Sir John Hope, fourth Earl of Hopetoun, in recognition of his bravery in the Peninsular War. One of the five most opulent thoroughfares in the early 19th-century city, along with Buchanan St, Gordon St, St Vincent St and West George St.

Howard St (off Jamaica St) – after John Howard, prison reformer. Its western end was laid out in 1768, and it was extended east from St Enoch's Square in 1798.

Hutcheson St (off the Trongate) – 1791. Part of development which included Brunswick St and Wilson St. Named after the brothers Hutcheson.

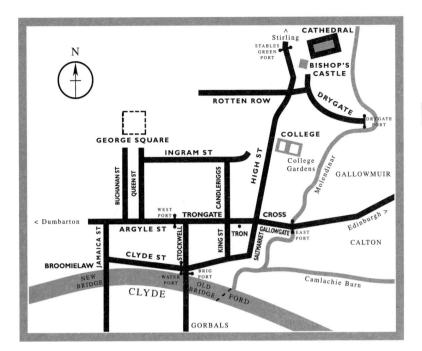

Inglis St (off Duke St) – after John Inglis, Lord Justice-General of Scotland, who defended Madeleine Smith in 1857 and the City of Glasgow Bank directors in 1879.

Ingram St (east off Queen St) – after Provost Archibald Ingram, laid out in 1772 along the line of the medieval Back Cow Loan, and was opened up in 1781. At first it reached only as far as Shuttle St but in the 1860s it was extended to the High St.

Jamaica St (south off Argyle St) – laid out between 1761 and 1763. Its name underlines the mercantile ties between the city and the West Indies. Important as the link with the second Glasgow Bridge.

John St (east off George St) – 1785. Named after John Campbell (Lord Provost), John Brown, jun., Baillies John Dunlop and John McAslan, John Nicholl (Bailie of the River), John Brown (Master of Works), John Wilson (Town Clerk), and John Orr (advocate).

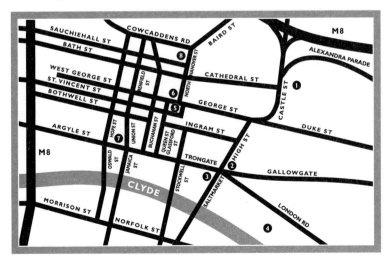

CITY CENTRE MAP
1 Cathedral
2 Cross
3 Tolbooth
4 Green
5 George Square
6 Queen Street Rail Station
7 Central Rail Station
8 Bus Station

Kent St (Calton) – 1802, Queen Victoria's family.

King St (south from the Trongate) – opened in 1722 and named in honour of George I. It matched Candleriggs to the north and linked the Trongate with the Bridgegate. The right-angled cross made by these streets helped to retain and extend the grid pattern as the new town developed to the north and west.

La Belle Place (western end of Sauchiehall St) – took its name from David Bell, who achieved local fame by reading out from the newspaper the first account received in the city of the passing of the Reform Bill in 1833. His unadorned name was considered too plebeian for the city's west end.

Miller St (off Argyle St) – Laid out in 1762 by James Barry on ground owned by John Miller of Westerton, maltman, but not opened up till 1773.

Monteith Row (north side of Glasgow Green) – the first terraces were erected in 1818, but the row was not completed till 1845. Now almost all gone.

New Vennel (east off High St) – 1666. Ran down to the Molendinar burn, north of the University.

New Wynd (south off the Trongate)– 1573.

North St (off Charing Cross) – Lord North was Prime Minister during the American War of Independence.

Peel St (off Dumbarton Rd) – Sir Robert Peel (Tory Prime Minister, 1834–35, 1841–46) was elected Lord Rector of the University in 1836. He attended a banquet in his honour in 1837, which was held in a large temporary building (127ft by 126ft) erected where Princes Square now stands. His constituency is remembered by the name of a small street in Bridgeton, Tamworth St.

Pitt St (off Sauchiehall St) – William Pitt the Elder, Lord Chatham, War Minister against the European powers in the Seven Years War. Before his death in 1778 he urged a conciliatory policy towards the American colonies.

Queen St (north off Argyle St) – after Queen Charlotte, wife of George III, laid out by James Barry in 1766. Formerly the Cow Loan, along which the town's cattle were driven to their pastures in the Cowcaddens.

Raglan St (Port Dundas) – named after Lord Raglan. Commander-in-Chief 1854–5 of the British forces in the Crimean War.

Rottenrow – one of Glasgow's early streets, it struck westward from the Cathedral along the high east–west ridge on the immediate north of the city. Its name has never been satisfactorily explained. Among many attempts have been: *roteran* 'to muster'; *ratounraw*, 'houses built of rattins'; *route de roi*, 'king's way'; *routine row*; *retinue row*; *vicus ratonum*, 'street of rats'; *rathad'nrigh*, 'king's road'; *rathad-an-ra*, 'road of going'; *rathad-an-rath*, 'road to the fort'; and *rawden-rhos*, 'meadow path'.

St Andrew's Square (off the Saltmarket) – planned round St Andrew's Church, 1787, and for a while a very fashionable address.

St Enoch's Square (city centre) – after St Thenew, mother of St Kentigern. Planned as a select residential area by the Corporation in 1768, but slow to get under way.

St Vincent St (west from George Square) – eastern end opened *c.*1804, western end in 1809. It was named after the famous naval battle of 1797.

Saltmarket (south from the Cross) – an early and important street. Formerly the Waulcergait, *Vicus Fullonum*, 'street of the fullers' (i.e. scourers of woollen

Waulcergait, *Vicus Fullonum*, 'street of the fullers' (i.e. scourers of woollen cloth). A fashionable place to live in the early 18th century.

Sauchiehall St (city centre) – *c*.1807. Its name means 'haugh or hollow meadow wooded with saughs or willows'. Became a fashionable shopping centre at the end of the 19th century, and could claim to be Glasgow's most famous thoroughfare. Originally, the eastern end of it was called Cathcart St. Now pedestrianised through much of its length.

Schipka Pass – a short passage from Gallowgate to London Rd, named after a Balkan pass important in the Russo-Turkish War of 1877.

Shitt Wynd – listed by McUre, the first historian of Glasgow, as lying on the south side of Argyle St.

Stockwell St (off the Trongate) – early street originally known as Fishergait then Stockwellgait. At the time it was the principal route to the river and its one bridge (till 1772), and home of many of the city's wealthy merchants.

Tamworth St (Bridgeton) – commemorates Sir Robert Peel's constituency and the 'Tamworth Manifesto' (*see* **Pitt St**).

Tobago St (off London Rd) – West Indian island taken from the French in 1803.

Trafalgar St (off Main St, Bridgeton) – Nelson's famous naval victory, 1805.

Trongate (west from the Cross) – one of the four main medieval streets, known as St Thenew's Gait (corrupted into St Enoch's Gate), from a chapel at its western end dedicated to St Kentigern's mother. It ran as far as the city's West Port. The first occurrence as Trongate comes about the middle of the 16th century (*c*.60 years after the city

West George St, looking east down the slope of Blythswood's drumlin. The back of St George's Tron Church (the front presents itself to George Sq) provides an eye catching climax, but causes problems for the city traffic. (George Oliver)

obtained the right to keep a free tron or weigh-bar which was located here). It lost its early importance to Buchanan St and Sauchiehall St as the city centre moved away from the Cross.

Union St (north from Argyle St) – laid out in 1815.

Vinegarhill St (off the Gallowgate) – perhaps named after a chemical works located here, but *fionna gabhar* ('white goat') is the presumed source of other Scottish Vinegar Hills.

Virginia St (north from Argyle St) – laid out by Andrew Buchanan, tobacco merchant, in 1753. The northern end was opened in 1796.

Watson St (north from the Gallowgate) – after Sir James Watson, Lord Provost.

West George St (west from George Square) – originally Camperdown St, after the famous naval battle of 1797.

World's End (Finnieston St) – in the 1850s it was on the extreme edge of the city's western boundary, now under the Clydeside Expressway.

York St (south from Argyle St) – laid out 1802. Named after Frederick, Duke of York.

TOLL BARS

The 1760s Turnpike Acts brought considerable improvements in the country's roads. The funds to make and repair roads constructed under these Acts came from charging tolls at barriers or bars across the highways, and by the beginning of the 19th century Glasgow was ringed by a dozen toll bars – Gallowgate, Gorbals, Shawfield, the Bridges, Cowcaddens, Inchbelly, Anderston, Whitevale, Paisley Rd, Greenock Rd, Port Dundas and Garngad. These bars increasingly annoyed the city's growing suburban population throughout the 19th century; they were finally abolished in 1883 under the Roads & Bridges (1878) Act whereby the Corporation became responsible for the upkeep not only of the roads within its boundaries but also for these country roads.

Royal College of Physicians and Surgeons

The beginning of an organised approach to the practice of medicine in Glasgow began with the arrival in the city of Dr Peter Lowe (c.1550–1610). By birth a Scotsman, he left the country about the time of the Reformation and spent some 30 years practising as a surgeon on the continent. In 1598 he returned to his native land and settled down as a surgeon salaried by Glasgow Town Council. In the following year he was instrumental in obtaining from James VI a charter in favour of himself and some others which established the Faculty of Physicians and Surgeons of Glasgow. Its powers included the licensing of all those wishing to practise as surgeons within the counties of Lanark, Renfrew, Dumbarton and Ayr. It also undertook the free medical visitation and treatment of the city's sick poor.

The close connection at that time between surgeons and barbers brought about an amendment in the charter which allowed barbers to become members of the Faculty – their powers, however, were limited and they could 'medill wt simple wounds annerlie [only]'. This traditional linkage was put under strain when the barbers achieved an incorporation of their own in 1656 and in 1719 the association was eventually broken.

In 1654 the faculty began to call itself the 'Facultie of Chirurgeons and Physitians' but by 1700 it had returned to the earlier form of its name.

The earliest training in medicine was given directly under the auspices of the Faculty, but when Glasgow University, at the beginning of the 19th century, began to turn out qualified surgeons, the Faculty fought with all its power to maintain what it considered its legal jurisdiction over all those wishing to practise surgery within its area. The dispute continued for over 40 years. The Faculty had the law on its side, but so great was the growing demand for qualified practitioners that in the end it abandoned its rights.

The first Faculty Hall was erected in 1697 on a site immediately to the west of the Tron Steeple in the Trongate (the building was demolished by the Town

Council in 1858). In 1790 it moved to St Enoch's Sq and again in 1860 to its present location in St Vincent St.

As an educational establishment the Faculty reached its height just before the First World War; thereafter the majority of its medical students went to the University, and the Faculty's influence decreased for most of the first half of the 20th century. It regained some of its influence subsequently and, now as the Royal College of Physicians and Surgeons of Glasgow, still holds examinations and grants qualifications.

Glasgow had other medical schools besides the Faculty and the University. Anderson's University (or Institution) was founded in 1796, largely in opposition to the University, and one of its original faculties, established in 1799, soon became a prestigious medical school. Its fame was such that up until the 1860s it was attracting more students than the University. One of its best-known students was the famous geographer and missionary, David Livingstone. In 1889 the school, now known as Anderson's College Medical School, moved to a site in Dumbarton Rd, adjacent to the University. Other medical schools in Glasgow included College St School (1796), Portland St School (1827), Royal Infirmary School, which was sometimes known as St Mungo's College (1876), and Queen Margaret College (1890).

Medical practitioners in the city whose pioneering influences extended beyond its boundaries include Joseph, Lord Lister (1827–1912), who became Regius Professor of Surgery in the Glasgow Royal Infirmary in 1860. While there he demonstrated that the deadly 'hospital gangrene' was caused by infection from micro-organisms and could be controlled by the use of carbolic acid dressings or sprays. This discovery of the antiseptic method effected almost as great a change in surgical techniques as did the earlier discovery of anaesthetics. Sir William Macewen (1848–1924), also an occupant of the chair of surgery at the Royal Infirmary (1892), extended Lister's antiseptic procedure to encompass the concept of asepsis – the complete exclusion of all contaminating micro-organisms. This enabled, for the first time, lengthy operations to be undertaken in safety, and he was one of the earliest surgeons to attempt operations on the brain. In 1863 William Tennant Gairdner (1824–1907), Professor of Medicine at the University, became the city's first Medical Officer of Health (on a part-time basis). When he resigned in 1871 he was followed by James B. Russell (1837–1904) as the first full-time MOH. Between them, Gairdner and Russell were responsible for many important changes in sanitary law and its applications. They thus played an important part in improving the health of the city's inhabitants and, incidentally, laid firm foundations for the efficient application of state medicine.

Royal Glasgow Institute of Fine Arts

One of the earliest of the city's art societies, the Glasgow Institution for Promoting and Encouraging the Fine Arts in the West of Scotland, was set up in 1821 by Alexander Finlay, print seller. Its first exhibition, of 253 works, was held in his shop, but the society soon foundered. Next came the Glasgow Dilettanti Society, founded in 1825. Its Argyle Arcade exhibition rooms opened in 1828, displaying 303 items, but lack of support brought about its demise in 1838. Then in 1839 the Artists' and Amateurs' Conversazione Society appeared on the scene, to be replaced the following year by the West of Scotland Academy. The latter struggled on for 13 years and an early Art Union was set up.

The next attempt to found an Institute of Fine Arts, of which Archibald McLellan, the art-collecting bailie, was a principal promoter, also failed, but after a few years the project was revised on more modest lines and opened in 1861 as the Glasgow Institute of Fine Arts. It held its first annual exhibition in the Corporation Galleries (now the McLellan Galleries, Sauchiehall St) with a remarkable display of over 800 pictures (of which 111 were sold). It attracted almost 40,000 visitors – now, over 130 years later, it is still mounting this annual event. It was never intended to be merely a display opportunity for local artists but was meant to bring examples of the best of modern painting to the city. Its popularity grew – in 1870 there were over 78,000 visitors. However, the Corporation now began to complain of having to clear away its own picture collection for four or five months every year to make way for the Institute and so the latter decided to build its own gallery. This was erected further east on the south side of Sauchiehall St, opening in 1879. In its new premises the Institute now became an established and major venue at a national level, a fact recognised by the award of a Royal Charter in 1896. Unfortunately, its ambitious and costly building venture, plus the added expense of having to organise a whole year's events, brought serious financial problems. These became so onerous that in 1902 the Institute went back to hiring the McLellan Galleries (the Corporation had now no objections as it had moved its picture collection to its new Art Gallery and Museum in Kelvingrove Park). It sold its building to the Pettigrew & Stephen's department store in 1912. This was destroyed by fire in the early 1970s and demolished.

The early Art Union, which had been set up in 1841, distributed £10,000 worth of art prizes on the basis of the sale of one guinea lottery tickets. This was superseded by a new Art Union set up in 1856; a later version, begun in 1884, ran until the low sale of tickets caused it to close in 1968.

With the passage of time the Institute's standards became more and more conservative, and by the 1940s few young artists were interested in exhibiting on its walls. Recent efforts, however, have been made to return it to its early, more eclectic policies. The gift of the John D. Kelly Gallery in 1965 has provided it with an excellent venue for small exhibitions by individual artists, and its annual exhibition is still the best-attended art event in and around Glasgow.

Sewage System

Before 1790 Glasgow had no sewers. The removal of surface water and domestic liquid waste was left to natural drainage which conveyed it, as best it could, by open

One of the unfortunate effects of the advent of the water closet was that by removing the back-court middens it added to the pollution of the Clyde.
(The Bee, *1874, Mitchell Library*)

ditches and burns into the river. Between 1790 and 1818 a start was made and over 5 miles of common sewers were laid along 45 streets.

The city's rapidly rising population and the increasing use of the water closet so enlarged the volume of untreated human waste being discharged into these sewers and into the river, that the Clyde became second only to the Thames for its thoroughly noxious state. Even after half a century, the total length of the sewers had reached only 80 miles – for a population of nearly half a million – and the raw sewage (which slowly oscillated up and downriver with the tides) made the river so offensive that travellers to the Clyde resorts preferred to take the train to Greenock rather than face embarking at the Broomielaw.

Much discussion took place from the 1860s onwards as to how best to deal with the city's effluent. Eventually the Corporation's hand was forced. The Caledonian Railway Co had obtained parliamentary authority to construct a railway tunnel for a proposed Glasgow Central Line under some of the city streets. When the Corporation protested that this would interfere with their existing (and inadequate) sewers, the railway replied that they would undertake to replan and reconstruct the disturbed sewage system – the area affected being the north-east and east parts of the city. Taking advantage of this forced modernisation, the Corporation arranged that the new sewers would deliver their contents to the city's first sewage purification works at Dalmarnock (opened in 1894). Using a system of screening and chemical purification, the effluent discharged into the river was such that the works manager boasted of having kept live goldfish in it in perfect health! In 1904 a similar sewage works was opened at Dalmuir to serve the rest of the city north of the river.

The lie of the land was not everywhere sufficiently steep, so pumping stations were erected, one at Pollok (1904) to serve Dalmuir and another at Kinning Park to serve a new purification works at Shieldhall (1910). By the middle of the century the length of the sewers had increased to 640 miles and several hundred million gallons of sewage were being treated each day. The Dalmuir and Shieldhall plants both produced large quantities of sludge, and in 1904 a specially built tank ship was launched to deal with this material. Another sludge-boat was added in 1910, the *Shieldhall*, capable of carrying 1,500 tons. Some of the sludge is still spread on land but these sludge-boats (the present ships are the *Dalmarnock* and the *Garroch Head*) carry over 2,000 tons of sludge a day, transporting it down to a deep-water dumping area between Bute and Arran. At the local government reorganisation in 1975, the control and management of Glasgow's sewers passed from the Corporation of Glasgow to Strathclyde Regional Council.

See also CLEANSING

Shipbuilding

Before the introduction of steam-powered ship propulsion very little shipbuilding took place along the Clyde; until the American War of Independence (1775–83) most of the sea-going vessels sailing from the Firth of Clyde were built in the shipyards of North America. After that event, however, a growing number of sailing ships began to be built at Greenock and Port Glasgow. A limiting feature at that time was the extreme shallowness of the upper reaches of the Clyde, which, as well as preventing sea-going vessels from sailing up to Glasgow, made the building of them upriver impossible. By the beginning of the 19th century, however, the deepening of the river by the Clyde Navigation Trust made it possible for ocean-going ships to reach right into the centre of the city.

The final impetus which started the Clyde on a course which made her yards and shipbuilders known to the world was the application of steam power to marine propulsion. Although by the middle of the 18th century the stationary steam engine was well established as a power source, it was not until James Watt in Glasgow invented the separate condenser that the engine's efficiency and weight/power ratio became such as to permit its use for marine propulsion. During the latter half of the 18th century several attempts were made in Scotland to use a steam engine to move a ship. In 1788 William Symington's steam-powered catamaran puffed across

Dalswinton Loch, and later, in 1803, the *Charlotte Dundas*, built to his design, made several successful journeys on the Forth and Clyde Canal.

Henry Bell (1767–1830), a native of Linlithgow and a mill-wright and mechanical engineer, was the first to make the steam boat practical and successful. In 1811, under his direction, John Wood, a shipbuilder in Port Glasgow, built a 43ft ship in which was installed a boiler from the works of John Napier & Son and a steam engine from John Robertson in Glasgow. The ship was named the *Comet* (after one which had recently appeared in the heavens) and on 6 August 1812 it successfully steamed from Port Glasgow up to the Broomielaw Quay in Glasgow in three and a half hours, making the *Comet* the first practicable sea-going steamer in Europe. It weighed 40 tons and could develop 3 to 4 horsepower. It steadily extended its service run until by 1819 it had reached Oban and Fort William. In December 1820 it was wrecked on Craignish Point, its lack of power preventing it from pulling clear of the rocks. Its engine was salvaged and can be seen in the Science Museum, London. Its place was taken by a second *Comet*, built in 1821, but this version also came to an unfortunate end when, in October 1825, it was run down near Greenock by another steamship, the *Ayr*, with considerable loss of life.

In the meantime, the *Comet*'s success

had encouraged others, and new engineering works were springing up all along the Clyde, especially at Greenock and Glasgow. Between 1812 and 1816 some 20 steamers had been built on the river and by 1818 no less than 17 paddle-steamers were running services from Glasgow. The routes now extended as far as Northern Ireland and Liverpool and the tiny vessels were reaching speeds of up to 8 miles per hour. However, growth was fairly slow until the 1840s – the annual tonnage built did not exceed 250 tons.

The next impetus came from two circumstances – it was now clear that steam propulsion on the open sea had proved itself, and the growing use of iron as the main construction element meant that hulls could be now made strong enough to bear the considerable vibration of the more efficient screw propeller. Glasgow was ideally equipped to take advantage of these circumstances. To the east of the city lay vast deposits of ironstone and coal, to the west the sheltered Firth of Clyde led on to the world's oceans, while the city's early expertise in building steam engines enabled the growing numbers of Clyde engineering firms to supply the demand for marine engines. Throughout the 19th century the Clyde shipyards continued to produce vessels of all kinds, from barges and dredgers to warships and liners. From an annual tonnage of about 50,000 tons in mid-century, their output had risen to 757,000 tons just before the First World War, a third of all British tonnage.

From a superficial viewpoint Clyde shipbuilding was in a healthy condition, but these high levels of output had little to do with the harsh realities of world economics, and were only maintained by the increased demand for warships. The First World War only served to increase this dependency, and the aftermath was a period of industrial depression in the 1920s which brought retrenchment and unemployment the length of the Clyde. The National Shipbuilders Security Ltd was set up to salvage what it could, and although it was unable to reinvigorate the industry its actions, brutal though they were felt to be at the time, may have saved the industry from worse consequences. On the Clyde 11 yards were badly affected but by 1936 the worst was over. The Second World War looked as if the river's great days had returned but the post-war period was once again fraught with problems, and the industry reached crisis point. Two of the great yards, Fairfield's and John Brown's, were in deep financial trouble.

The Geddes Report (1965–66) recommended that all British yards should be grouped into four regional sectors, two of these being on the Clyde – Port Glasgow and Greenock as the Lower Reaches, and Clydebank and Glasgow as the Upper Clyde. In response to this recommendation the Upper Clyde Shipbuilders Ltd was set up in 1966 and consisted of John Brown's, Connell's, Fairfield's and Stephen's, with Yarrow as an associate. It proved impossible for these yards to work together, however, and the scheme fell apart in 1971. Yarrow opted out and continued on its own, specialising in warship production. Another report suggested that a smaller, and hopefully more viable, successor should be constituted, mainly from Fairfield's along with Stephen's and Connell's, and this was done in 1972 under the name Govan Shipbuilders Ltd. John Brown's was sold to the Marathon Shipbuilding Co of Texas, and concentrated on oil-rig construction. In 1980 ownership passed to a French company, UIE Shipbuilding. The Govan Shipbuilders lasted only 16 years and was sold to a Norwegian group to form Kvaerner Govan Ltd in 1988.

Napier, 1821–1900

Lancefield, Govan Old, Govan East

Like many of the early Clyde shipbuilders, David Napier (1790–1876) came to shipbuilding from a background of general engineering and iron-founding, through his blacksmith father. It was under his direction that his father's firm, John Napier & Son, built the *Comet*'s boiler in 1812 and he installed his first marine engine in the *Marion* in 1816. He set up his first shipbuilding yard at Lancefield on the north bank of the Clyde in 1821 where his pioneering and inventive skills enabled him to set the course of shipbuilding for years to come. He built the first iron steamship in 1827, the *Aglaia*, a small craft which ran on Loch Eck. He also designed a compact form of engine (the steeple engine) which was for long a standard, and he increased the propulsive power of the engines by introducing 'feathering' of the paddles. He is even credited with setting up the first experimental tank (in the shape of the Camlachie Burn) and, as a result, was able to fine down the bows of his ships to a shape more suitable for the increased power of steam propulsion.

When he left Glasgow for London in 1836 the Lancefield yard was taken over by his cousin Robert Napier (1791–1876) who came from a similar background. Robert has been called the father of shipbuilding on the Clyde – he was so in an almost literal sense for many of the most eminent shipbuilders of later years learned their trade under him, and by 1827 he had come to be regarded as far and away the best engineer on the river.

Early in his career he became interested in the fast developing transatlantic steamship service. His meeting in 1839 with the Canadian Samuel Cunard, merchant in Halifax, had far-reaching consequences since he was given the contract to design and build the engines for the first ship of Cunard's new enterprise, the British & American Royal Mail Steamship Packet Co. Named the *British Queen*, 1,862 tons, 245ft long, 500hp, it was launched in May 1838 and sailed for New York in the July of the following year. In ideal conditions sailing ships took a month to cross the Atlantic; the new vessel took only 15½ days. So successful was the *British Queen* that Napier planned and engined the next four Cunarders, the *Acadia, Britannia, Caledonia* and *Columbia*. In turn their success convinced Napier of the need to move to a larger yard and he crossed the river first to Govan Old in 1841 and to Govan East in 1850.

In 1843 he built his first iron steamship, the *Vanguard* (700 tons), and about the same time acquired the Parkhead Forge in Glasgow's east end (later to become world-famous under William Beardmore as a supplier of armaments and armour-plating). Napier's attention to detail and his encouragement of experimentation brought him several commissions to build ships for the Admiralty. His best known Navy vessel was the *Black Prince* (1862), in its day the largest ship built on the Clyde.

In 1860 Robert retired, handing over to his two sons, under whom the yard began to decline until 1876 when A. C. Kirk (another Napier apprentice!) became the senior partner in the firm. His claim to marine engineering fame was the design and introduction (while employed by Fairfield's) of the compound engine. After some improvement under Kirk the business again began to decline towards the end of the 19th century, until in 1900 Beardmore of Parkhead Forge took over the yard so as to be able to install his naval guns and armour-plate in his own battleships.

Tod & McGregor, 1834–1873
Mavisbank Quay, Meadowside

Both David Tod and John McGregor had worked for David Napier but in 1834 they started up as engineers on their own. They soon moved into shipbuilding, first on the south side of the Clyde at Mavisbank Quay and later, in 1845, at Meadowside on the north bank at the mouth of the Kelvin. Their yard was the first to be set up for the exclusive production of iron vessels and, in its short history, was responsible for several innovations.

Their *Vesta* (1848) was the first Clyde-built sea-going ship to use screw propulsion, and the dry dock which they opened in 1858 was the first on the upper reaches of the river. It was 110ft long and remained in operation until 1962.

Their best known ships were undoubtedly those transatlantic vessels they built for the Inman Line of Liverpool. The first was the *City of Glasgow* and it was a significant venture in several respects. It was screw-propelled (the leader in this field, the Cunard Line, still depended on paddles), it accommodated the lower end of the passenger range, carrying many emigrants, it carried cargo and proved that it was possible to run a transatlantic service without government subsidy. Tod & McGregor continued to build ships for Inman, among them *City of Brussels* (1869 – the fastest ship of its time), and the *City of Montreal* (1872). But when Inman turned elsewhere for its North Atlantic liners Tod & McGregor's short but innovative life came to an end, with the yard being taken over by D. & W. Henderson in 1873.

Barclay, Curle & Co Ltd, 1844–1967
Stobcross, Whiteinch

The origins of Barclay, Curle go back to the earliest days of shipbuilding on the Clyde, when John Barclay began to build wooden sailing ships at Stobcross on the north bank of the river in 1818. His son brought in Robert Curle from an Ayrshire port, giving the firm the title of Robert Barclay & Curle in 1845. It began to build iron ships in 1847, at first buying in engines from A. & J. Inglis, but in 1857 began to make them itself.

One of the firm's early ships, the *Edina*, which had been built for service between Leith and Hamburg, achieved fame in later years as a blockade runner in the American Civil War. In 1855, in order to bid for the construction of bigger ships, the firm extended its yard space by acquiring land at Clydeholm (Whiteinch) which in 1874 became its sole shipyard. About this time the company began to specialise in combined passenger and cargo ships, mainly trading to India, and for second-class services across the Atlantic. It also became a specialist in ship repair, becoming eventually one of the largest in this field in Britain.

Barclay, Curle & Co began to expand into nearby shipyards but in 1912 was largely taken by the Wallsend firm of Swan, Hunter & Wigham Richardson. To try and beat the later years of depression it attempted to concentrate on building short-distance passenger ships but was defeated by the enormous increase in air travel and ceased shipbuilding activities in 1967; earlier, in the 1950s its repair work also ceased and in 1974 the company's dry dock facilities passed to Yarrow Shipbuilders.

A. & J. Inglis Ltd, 1847–1962
Anderston, Pointhouse

In 1847 the brothers Anthony and John Inglis, in the employ of Tod & McGregor, set themselves up as marine engineers at the Whitehall Foundry, Anderston. Later, in 1862, they took over the Pointhouse Shipyard of T. B. Sneath (who moved upriver to Rutherglen) and became general shipbuilders and engineers, constructing ships of all classes. They built over 40 steamers for the British India Steam Navigation Co and many well-known Clyde steamers. Thirteen of the latter were built for the North British Co and its successor, the LNER. The last of these, built in 1947, was the famous paddle steamer the *Waverley*. They also constructed the first commercially built Royal Yacht the *Alexandra* in 1905–7. Because of the yard's position on the river many of its vessels were launched by means of their patent 'marine railway'. Although the yard continued to build ships till 1962, the Inglis family sold it to the Harland & Wolff group in 1919. Its output was considerable and it has been estimated that it launched an average of five ships per year.

Alexander Stephen & Sons, 1851–1968
Kelvinhaugh, Linthouse

The Stephen family came to Glasgow from Burghead on the Moray Firth where their origins went back to 1750. Alexander Stephen came south in 1851 and took over the Kelvinhaugh Shipyard, moving to Linthouse in 1869. Although never a yard which led the way in technical developments it turned out many smaller passenger ships of distinction (over 547 vessels came down the slipways at Linthouse) including, in their early years, some vessels for the Anchor Line.

One of the worst disasters on Clydeside involved one of the yard's vessels. In July 1883 when the *Daphne* was being launched from the Linthouse Yard it capsized and sank, drowning 146 shipyard workers who were still working aboard the vessel.

From 1904 to 1949 Stephen's built a series of magnificent ships for Elders & Fyffes and the Imperial Direct West Indian Line for the banana trade, and during the Second World War supplied the Royal Navy with many craft – cruisers, destroyers, mine-sweepers, corvettes, the

aircraft-carrier *Ocean* (700ft long) and the sloop *Amethyst*, famous for its dash down the River Yangtse in 1949. The end of Stephen's as an independent yard came in 1968 when it became part of the Upper Clyde Shipbuilders Ltd.

J. & G. Thomson, 1851–1897
Govan, Clydebank

The careers of James and George Thomson illustrate yet again the considerable influence of Robert Napier on shipbuilding on the Clyde, for both brothers served under him at Lancefield. In 1847 they left and set up for themselves as J. & G. Thomson, engineers and boilermakers. In 1850 they added 'shipbuilders' to their title and opened a yard at Govan, naming it the Clyde Bank Shipyard.

Three of the yard's early paddle-steamers – all called *Iona* – achieved a certain fame, even notoriety. The first, built in 1855, was sold to the Confederate forces in the American Civil War as a blockade runner, but got no further than Greenock where it was run down and sunk. The second, built in 1863, was also destined as a blockade runner but she too sank, this time from the opening of strained seams off Lundy Island. The third *Iona*, built a year later, stayed at home, sailing down the Clyde then up to Oban and on to the Inner Hebrides, until 1935.

Forced to abandon their Govan yard, the brothers moved across the river to a greenfield site opposite the mouth of the River Cart, a situation which was to prove advantageous in later years. They took with them the yard's name, and from it the town of tenements – which sprung up in the surrounding fields to house the thousand or so of their workers – took the name of Clydebank.

They built many ships, both sail and steam, including several paddle-steamers for David MacBrayne's Western Isles services. They also built for the Inman Line (who usually used Tod & McGregor) two large and speedy ships, the *City of Paris* (1888) and the *City of New York* (1889); the latter was the first Atlantic passenger vessel with twin screws.

In 1897 the Thomsons lost control and the new management changed the yard's name to the Clydebank Engineering and Shipbuilding Co Ltd. Under this name the yard turned out over 30 ships in two years, but was brought over in 1899 by John Brown & Co Ltd of Sheffield who, like Beardmore's were looking for the shipbuilding facilities to enable them to make full use of their armour-plate.

Thomas B. Sneath, 1856–1902
Rutherglen

This small yard was unusual in being located upriver from the city, at Broomloan in the burgh of Rutherglen. Sneath had begun shipbuilding at Meadowside in 1853 but moved in 1856 to the Rutherglen site. The yard produced about 16 steamers (mainly for the Clyde and the Scottish lochs) as well as a number of other types including yachts, Sneath built the first six *Cluthas* (small passenger-carrying boats plying up and down the Clyde within the city) but probably the yard's most famous vessel was the paddle-steamer *Lucy Ashton*.

The weirs which lay between it and the open river restricted ship sizes to around 200ft in length and 500 to 600 tons, but despite this limitation Sneath built over 300 vessels. In 1902 the Clyde Navigation Trust erected a new type of weir which made work more difficult, so Sneath relinquished the yard to another concern.

Charles Connell & Co Ltd, 1861–1968
Scotstoun

Charles Connell, manager at Alexander Stephen & Sons, left in 1861 to found the Scotstoun Shipyard. Somewhat of an exception amongst the Clyde yards, it never manufactured the engines for its ships, limiting its direct activities to building and outfitting hulls. In its early years it built a number of sailing ships of note, many being designed for the China trade. These tea clippers were built for speed and endurance, for the profits went to the first ship to reach the London markets; one of Connell's ships, the *Taitsung*, took part in the famous race of 1866.

In its later period the yard built many carrying ships, such as the 5,600-ton *City of Chicago* (1883) for the Inman Line – considered at that time to be a very large vessel.

During the depression which followed the First World War, the yard closed its gates in 1931. In 1937 it reopened and went on to build 20 ships with a combined tonnage of 135,608 during the Second World War.

In 1968 Connell's became part of the Upper Clyde Shipbuilders Ltd. Following that ill-fated group's break-up, it joined with Fairfield's and Stephen's in 1972 to become Govan Shipbuilders. Managed as a separate company, Scotstoun Marine, it was finally closed in 1980.

Fairfield Shipbuilding & Engineering Co, 1870–1968
Fairfield (Govan)

John Elder (1824–69) set up a yard in 1870 which came to be one of the most important and innovative centres of shipbuilding on the Clyde. After serving his apprenticeship in Robert Napier's (where his father had been engineering manager for almost 40 years), and working for a while in England, Elder returned to Glasgow in 1852 and became a partner in the engineering works of Randolph & Elliot. (Charles Randolph was also a product of Napier's Lancefield Yard.) Assuming the name of Randolph, Elder & Co, from the beginning the partners showed exceptional engineering ability.

The first example of this was the installation in the *Brandon* (1854) of their new invention, the compound engine. This re-used the power of the piston-driving steam by passing it through one, two or even three additional low-pressure cylinders. The reduction in coal consumption realised by this device extended steamships' voyages, enabling them to surpass the sailing ships in sheer endurance.

In 1864 the company opened its own shipbuilding yard at Govan Old, moving in 1864 to Fairfield, Govan, where greater space enabled it to keep pace with its expanding order-books. The first four vessels built at the new yard were all blockade runners for the American Confederate forces. In all, during Elder's short period of ownership, 30 ships came down the slipways. After his death the new partnership was headed by Sir William Pearce (also a Napier-trained man) and in 1870 the name was changed to John Elder & Co. Pearce combined engineering expertise with a sound business sense and the firm continued to stay in the forefront of shipbuilding and marine engineering.

In the 1870s and 1880s Pearce built a number of Atlantic liners which combined speed with luxury. The first of these was the Guion Line's *Arizona* (1879), 5,146 tons, at that time the largest Clyde-built ship; it crossed the Atlantic in the record time of seven days, ten hours and 30 minutes, and remained at work until 1927, giving almost 30 years' service. Other similar vessels followed, such as the *Alaska* (1882), *Oregon* (1883), then *Umbria* and *Etruria* (1885) for the Cunard Line, and later still, in 1893, the liners *Campania* and *Lucania*. With a top speed of 22 knots they were the fastest ships on the Atlantic run.

Continuing improvements in its compound engines brought the yard's ships

success in the long-haul routes to India, South Africa and Australia. Following reconstruction in 1885 the firm became the Fairfield Shipbuilding & Engineering Co. The Cunarders of the 1880s and 1890s could be regarded as the high peak of the yard's history, for the limited length of the Fairfield berths took the building of a new generation of Atlantic giants across the river to the yards of John Brown's.

In 1907 after the death of Pearce's son (who had taken control after his father's death in 1888), the Northumberland Shipbuilding Co took control of Fairfield's. Although the yard weathered the depression of the 1920s it succumbed in 1935, but was rescued from its financial trouble by Sir James Lithgow, head of the great Lower Clyde shipbuilding firm of Scott Lithgow at Greenock.

Fairfield's had from its earliest days supplied ships for the Admiralty, and from the 1930s on it became increasingly involved in building naval vessels of all kinds – two of the most famous being the battleship *Howe* and the aircraft-carrier *Implacable*.

Then, suddenly, in 1965 the receiver was called in – an event which symbolised a turning point in the long history of Clyde shipbuilding. A rescue venture was carried out in the following year when a combination of government, business and union assistance set up a revivified yard under the name Fairfield's (Glasgow) Ltd. New techniques in the yards, the offices and the boardrooms were adopted and special attention was paid to industrial relations. But before the full effects of these profound changes could be measured Fairfield's merged into the uneasy experiment of the Upper Clyde Shipbuilders Ltd in 1968 and the story of a great yard seemed to have come to an end. But in 1972, along with Stephen's and

Connell's, it reappeared as the Govan Shipbuilders Ltd. After 16 years it was taken over by a Norwegian concern, to become Kvaerner Govan Ltd.

John Brown & Co Ltd, 1899–1968
Clydebank

John Brown's, a principal provider of armour-plating, had been for some time looking for a suitable shipyard where its plates could be used. This was found in the Clydebank Shipyard of J. & G. Thomson and Brown's bought it in 1899. This yard possessed two significant advantages: its berths were capable of extension, thus enabling really big ships to be laid down; and the mouth of the Cart, facing the slipways, could provide additional launching space for larger ships. Brown's added to these advantages a thorough-going programme of modernisation.

For more than two generations, nearly 400 cargo ships, luxury liners and warships – among them some of the largest ships ever built – came down Brown's slipways and made the name of Clydebank known throughout the world. The yard began by building three magnificent liners for the Cunard Line – the 14,281-ton *Saxonia* (1900) and the *Carmania* and *Caronia* (1905), both 20,000 tons. Probably the best known vessel of the yard's early days was the 32,000-ton Cunarder *Lusitania* (1907), which was almost 760ft long. It met a tragic fate in 1915 when it was torpedoed without warning by a German U-boat off the Irish coast.

During the 1930s several of Europe's industrial nations, including France, Germany and Italy, began to compete with each other by producing ever larger and more luxurious transatlantic liners. Britain was not slow in entering the competition and John Brown's was chosen to build this country's challenger. In 1929 the great hull of ship number 534 began to rise on its specially lengthened and reinforced berth. In 1931, however, caught up in the interwar depression, the company was forced to suspend all work on 534. The shock and dismay at this decision made the ship a poignant and long-remembered symbol of the powerlessness of Clyde shipyards in the face of world economics, and also provided a foretaste of the industry's fate after the Second World War. Work was in 1933 resumed with the help of a government subsidy and in September 1934 the completed vessel, the *Queen Mary*, was successfully launched. Weighing 81,000 tons and with a hull 1,019ft long, her slide into the narrow river was only possible by meticulous planning, by dredging the Clyde around the yard and by deepening the mouth of the Cart.

When the question of a companion ship arose, John Brown's was again chosen to build the new vessel. The *Queen Elizabeth*, laid down in 1937 and completed in 1940, was longer and heavier than her predecessor at 1,031ft and 84,000 tons. Without any preliminary trials or running-in period, trusting in her speed alone, she crossed the wartime Atlantic unmolested in March 1940. During the rest of the war she and her sister ship carried between them over a million Allied soldiers.

Two other mighty ships came from John Brown's yards. The first was the battleship *Vanguard*, the very last of that class to be built in Britain. She was completed too late to take part in the hostilities, easing her mammoth bulk down the specially dredged river in 1946. Costing over £9 million, she lasted barely 15 years and was broken up at Faslane in 1960. The second, *Queen Elizabeth II* launched in 1969, suffered one difficulty after another as labour troubles were followed by embarrassing engine malfunctions during her running-in cruises. There was no future in building more of these giant and expensive monuments to a past way of travel, and after an uneasy alliance with Fairfield's, Stephen's and Connell's in the Upper Clyde Shipbuilders Ltd from 1968 to 1971, the yards were taken over by the Marathon Shipbuilding Co of Houston, Texas, for the production of jack-up oil-rigs. In 1980 Marathon withdrew and the French company UIE Shipbuilding took over the yard's facilities.

William Beardmore & Co Ltd, 1900–1930
Govan, Dalmuir

The declining business of the Napier establishment at the end of the last century attracted the attention of William Beardmore's whose Parkhead Forge was well known for its production of heavy armour-plating and armaments. By birth a Londoner, Beardmore had been brought up in Glasgow, entering the forge, then owned by Napier's, as a boy of 14. Working his way up, he took over control of Parkhead in 1863 and followed this up by acquiring Napier's yard in 1900.

Under his ownership the direction of the shipyard's activities was decisively altered. No longer was it an innovative shipbuilding yard; instead it became a necessary adjunct which could provide a much needed outlet for the forge's armour-plate and guns, and the late 19th-century arms race, followed by the First World War, created an extremely profitable market for Beardmore's. In order to accommodate the huge bulk of the new warships the yard moved in 1905 across to an open-field site at Dalmuir, four miles down the river. One innovation was the setting up of the Dalmuir Dry Dock Co Ltd which built a gigantic dry dock which would have been capable of taking the largest of ships, but the scheme was not

persevered with and the company was later wound up.

The First World War kept the yard extremely busy and in 30 years it built over 60 Royal Navy vessels, from huge battleships like the *Benbow* and the *Ramillies* to seaplanes. It played a vital part in the war, but in order to fulfil the rush of wartime contracts, it both overstretched and over-diversified itself so that when the post-war industrial depression came its many new businesses had had no time to pay back their initial costs. The final blow was the cancellation under the terms of the 1922 Washington Treaty of orders for three Clyde-built battlecruisers. Three of the Clyde's greatest shipbuilding firms (Beardmore's, Brown's and Fairfield's) found themselves in deep financial trouble through these cancellations, and while John Brown's and Fairfield's survived, albeit it by the skin of their teeth, William Beardmore & Co Ltd went down for good in 1930.

Yarrow Shipbuilders Ltd, 1906–
Scotstoun

Yarrow's origins lay on the banks of the Thames. Begun in 1865 it early began to specialise in building fast torpedo boats for the Royal Navy and later moved on to the production of destroyers. Finding the Thames location somewhat limiting (and also, it is said, finding the Glasgow workforce prepared to accept lower wages), the firm moved north in 1906 to Scotstoun where it continued to specialise in fast naval craft. Although its business began to fall off between the wars it managed not only to survive but to flourish during and after the Second World War. Of the 400 vessels it has built at Scotstoun almost half have been Royal Navy craft. When the Upper Clyde Shipbuilders group came into being in 1966 Yarrow's joined as an associate member but secure in its continuing orders for warships (including many for foreign navies) it opted out and resumed independent operations in 1971, continuing its tradition as a builder of naval vessels.

Harland & Wolff Ltd, 1912–62
Govan

An early Clyde shipbuilding company, the London & Glasgow Shipbuilding and Engineering Co Ltd, took over a yard in Govan in 1864. About 40 years later Harland & Wolff's, a famous Belfast shipbuilding establishment then at its peak – having just built the world's largest ship, the triple-screwed *Olympic* – was seeking a place at the centre of the shipbuilding industry. The firm crossed the Irish sea and bought over the London & Glasgow and neighbouring yards (one of which, the East Yard, had belonged to Robert Napier's). Here it started a 50-year career as engineers and shipbuilders, concentrating on building tankers and cargo ships. It managed to weather the troubled interwar years, but by the 1960s it became apparent that the parent company in Belfast was the principal concern and the Glasgow yards closed in 1962. The doubtful honour laid at the door of its workforce was that it was the support of its strongly Ulster Protestant element that made Rangers Football Club the symbol of working-class Protestantism.

See also STEAMERS

THE QUEENS

QUEEN MARY

In the late 1920s the Cunard Line began looking for a new passenger ship to replace the ageing *Mauritania*, and in 1930 awarded the contract for a new liner to John Brown & Co, Clydebank. Work began immediately on what was for a long time known only as No.534, but in December of the following year the Depression stopped all work on her with 3,800 workers being laid off. However, with the aid of Government support, work was resumed in April 1934 and the £5,000,000 ship was launched as the *Queen Mary* in September of that year. One small problem was the existence of a Clyde steamer with the same name, but with a small amount of pressure the latter became *Queen Mary II*.

She was 1,019ft long with a gross tonnage of 81,235, which made her for a while the world's largest ship, until the French liner *Normandie*'s added superstructure brought her up to 82,790 tons. She carried 2,139 passengers with a crew of 1,101 and consumed 1,020 tons of fuel oil every day. Her normal service speed was 28.5 knots and from 1937 to 1967, as the last of the giant superliners of the pre-Second World War period, she was one of the fastest, largest and finest ships afloat. During the war she and her consort the *Queen Elizabeth* were converted to troop carriers (the *Queen Mary* could carry 15,000 troops each voyage) and from 1943 to 1945 carried over a million troops between them. During her career she travelled 3,794,017 miles and carried more than 2,114,000 people.

Although the *Queen Mary* resumed weekly commercial sailings in 1947, the increasing use of air travel rapidly rendered both her and the *Queen Elizabeth* uneconomic to run (the former was losing £2,000,000 each year) and both ships were withdrawn from service in 1967.

The *Queen Mary* was bought by the City of Long Beach, California, for £3,250,000 and was permanently moored at the Port of Long Beach as a hotel, a conference centre and the main attraction of a maritime museum.

QUEEN ELIZABETH

The *Queen Elizabeth*, the largest passenger liner ever built, was begun in John Brown & Co's Clydebank shipyard in 1936 and eventually launched in 1938. She weighed 83,673 tons and was 1,031ft long with a cruising speed of 28.5 knots. She was intended to complement her older consort, the *Queen Mary*, so that between them they would offer a weekly service in both directions across the Atlantic, but her fitting-out was interrupted by the outbreak of the Second World War and she left Britain secretly in 1940 to join the *Queen Mary* as troop-carriers.

Her first commercial transatlantic voyage was made in 1946 but in face of the growing air passenger transport competition she and her sister ship were laid off in 1967. In 1969 she was sold for £3,230,000, the buyers intending to convert her into a floating hotel and exhibition centre at Port Everglades, Florida. However, two years later she was sold again, this time to be converted into a 'university ship' but in 1972, before her refit was complete, she caught fire and sank in Hong Kong Harbour.

QUEEN ELIZABETH II

The building of the *Queen Elizabeth II* (more usually known as the *QE2*) was begun in 1965 by the Upper Clyde Shipbuilders and she was launched in 1967. She is 963ft in length, but her weight (by the extensive use of aluminium in her superstructure) is only 65,863 gross tons. She can carry 2,025 passengers and a crew of 920 at a service speed of 28.5 knots and consumes only half the fuel used by her namesake the *Queen Elizabeth*. Despite her state-of-the-art construction, she has been dogged by a series of mechanical troubles. She is the first ship to be deliberately designed to act both as a transatlantic shuttle and as a luxury cruise liner, but she crosses the Atlantic only a few times a year, earning her keep as a cruise ship.

The liner Queen Mary *on the stocks. During the Depression, all work on her stopped for several years, but eventually, with government financial support, she was launched in 1934. (*Weekly Illustrated, *Mitchell Library)*

Shipping Lines

Because of its position and its facilities, Glasgow was involved at an early date both in coastal and in transoceanic passenger and cargo shipping. Trade with the British Empire and the transportation of emigrants to North America and the Antipodes formed the mainstay of the larger Glasgow shipping lines up to the First World War and beyond. At one time or another, some 30 shipping companies had their headquarters in Glasgow, with fleets numbering from 30 down to one or two vessels.

Activities in the early part of the 19th century were mainly a continuation of the long-existing coastal trade. Of the many firms involved in this trade, the most successful was that belonging to George and James Burns who had started in 1824 trading to Ireland, Liverpool and the Western Highlands and Islands. Also operating on the Glasgow–Ireland route was the **Laird Line**, which dated back to 1814. (These two shipping lines amalgamated in 1922 as the **Burns & Laird Lines**.) The year 1969 saw the last direct sailing from Glasgow to Ireland.

In the 1840s George Burns joined in with the great **Cunard Line**, and David Hutcheson took over the company's Highland trade. In 1879 David MacBrayne became its owner and built up a network of passenger and cargo routes throughout the Western Seas.

The **Allan Line** was established in 1831 and was amongst the earliest to introduce a direct service from Glasgow to Montreal and Quebec. It has been claimed that the settlement of parts of Canada was made possible by the Scottish emigrants shipped by the Allan Line. By the end of the 19th century it owned 37 ships, one of the largest fleets sailing from the Clyde. It was taken over by the Canadian Pacific Steamship Co in 1915, but its ships continued to call at the Clyde till the 1960s.

The **Albion Line** was started by Patrick Henderson in 1840 and its sailing ships took many early emigrants out to New Zealand. It started a regular service to Burma (which lay on the route to and from New Zealand) and was responsible for

running the Irrawady Flotilla Co there from 1865. This developed into a very large inland water undertaking and was operating 650 ships when Burma fell to Japanese forces in the Second World War.

Regarded by many as the dominant shipping line on the transatlantic routes, the **Anchor Line** began back in the 1830s. Its first Glasgow to New York steamship ran in 1856, and by the end of the century it owned 22 vessels. David and William Henderson became managers in 1873 and from then till 1935 many of the Anchor Line's finest ships were built at their Meadowside yard. In 1911 it became part of the Cunard Line.

The **Donaldson Line** began in 1855, trading to South America. In 1870 it ran its first steamship and four years later it entered the Canadian passenger trade, becoming one of the best known of the emigration lines.

An indication of the volume of passenger trade from Glasgow can be estimated from the fact that, by the outbreak of the First World War, at least three large liners from the Allan, Anchor and Donaldson shipping lines respectively left the Broomielaw each week for America.

The **City Line** was operated by George Smith, a Glasgow merchant who found it more profitable to trade with India than with the West Highlands. His ships' names all began with the prefix 'City'. In 1901 the line was sold to the Ellerman group, but sailings continued from Glasgow till the 1970s.

Although the **Clan Line** began in Liverpool, it moved to Glasgow in 1880. Chiefly involved in trade to India and to South and East Africa, by 1914 it owned 56 steamers which made it one of Glasgow's largest ship-owners.

The shipping firm of **Burrell & Son** began cargo trading with the Mediterranean and India in the late 1860s. It has been said that their habit of naming all their ships with the prefix 'Strath' started a fashion. Not only from their trading, but from a judicious buying and selling of their fleets, the brothers William and George built up huge fortunes and let their shipping company die off till only one ship was left operating by the 1920s. Sir William Burrell amassed a priceless art collection and gifted it to the Corporation of Glasgow.

Glasgow continued to be an important centre for passenger and cargo ship traffic throughout the interwar years but several worldwide factors combined to extinguish it after the Second World War, including the growth of air transport, the rapid rise of cargo containerisation and the inability of the upper Clyde to cope with the increasing size of post-war shipping.

Shopping Centres

Glasgow is by far the largest shopping centre in Scotland and is the third largest after London and Birmingham. Before the recent rise of the shopping mall, Glasgow's principal shopping areas were formed by three streets which all led from one to the other – Sauchiehall St, Buchanan St and Argyle St.

Sauchiehall St, the furthest away from the old centre and hence the latest to develop, runs from east to west on the northern edge of the central area. It had its share of large department stores but these have practically all gone. Its eastern end, where most of the shops are, is pedestrianised, while its western end holds a higher density of ethnic restaurants than anywhere else in the city.

Buchanan St runs south from the eastern end of Sauchiehall St and was formed in the 18th century. It has always been famous for its *magasins de luxe* and still accommodates the last of the city's great department stores. It fought hard and successfully to keep itself free from the slightly vulgar tramcar, and old photographs show its pavements lined with expensive motorcars. It is now pedestrianised throughout most of its length.

The origins of **Argyle St** (which runs east from the foot of Buchanan St towards the Cross) are hidden in the city's early history and it has always been an important east–west thoroughfare. It has managed to retain some of the flavour of an older, less cosmopolitan, Glasgow, and until fairly recently many of the city's east-enders would go no further west for their town shopping.

The St Enoch Centre is built on the cleared site of the old St Enoch Station, between Argyle St and the Clyde. When it was built it was the largest glass-covered shopping mall in Europe and its L-shaped main hall contains a skating rink and two lengthy floors of shops. The mall is heated in winter by solar energy and heat from the mall shops, while in summer a system of shades prevents overheating. Its construction involved 2,500 tons of steelwork and over 300,000 square feet of glazing. It covers four acres, cost £65 million and was opened in 1989.

Princes Square, off Buchanan St, is

the unique conversion of an open square, enclosed originally by high office buildings, into a specialist shopping centre with over 50 shops, cafés and wine bars. It has been formed by roofing over the square (named after Prince (later King) Edward VII) and forming the interior into five shopping levels round a central courtyard. C. R. Mackintosh-type motifs are supple-mented by vigorous art nouveau iron-work. It cost £23 million and was opened in 1987.

The Sauchiehall Street Centre was opened in 1974 and revamped in 1987. It is equipped with the customary wall-climbing lift, fountains and pools, and mazes of mirrored surfaces. Some sense of locality has been supplied by the ubiquitous C. R. Mackintosh details.

ARCADES

Glasgow has had eight arcades, most of them dating from the middle of the 19th century or earlier; only one now survives.

Argyle Arcade

This arcade runs in a right-angled dog-leg from Argyle St to Buchanan St. It measures about 480ft and was constructed in 1827 by the architect John Baird senior. Its design was said to have been influenced by the Burlington Arcade, London, and from its earliest days it has always been able to attract high-quality shops, probably because it connects two of the city's best-known shopping streets. It has now lost whatever diversity it once had and is almost entirely given over to retailing jewellery, clocks and watches. One shop stood out from the rest: Galetti, a Glasgow seller of mirrors and optical glasses was an early tenant in the arcade; his son, John Galetti, took over in the late 19th century and introduced for sale models of yachts, locomotives and steam-engines. This line of business proved highly successful, and he whimsically named his shop The Clyde Model Dockyard. Sometime later, at the turn of the century, an Andrew McKnight took over and continued the tradition, providing a Mecca for Glasgow fathers and sons over several generations.

Wellington Arcade

Ran from Sauchiehall St north to Renfrew St. It is also said to have been designed by John Baird, and dated from before the middle of the last century. It was taken down in 1930 to make way for a Woolworths store.

Queen's Arcade

A continuation of the Wellington Arcade on the north side of Renfrew St, running north to Russell St. It was removed sometime after 1965.

Royal Arcade

Ran from the top end of Hope St (which then finished short of Cowcaddens Rd) to Cowcaddens Rd. Built about 1850 it was situated next to the Theatre Royal and provided access from the Cowcaddens to the city centre. It contained a market-place, a fountain and a bandstand. It was torn down in 1896 when Hope St was extended north to meet Cowcaddens Rd.

Milton Arcade

This arcade ran from Stewart St (off Garscube Rd) to William St, with a third entrance from the Cowcaddens. It was removed towards the end of the 19th century to make way for the Grand Theatre, later a cinema.

Hope St Arcade

Ran from Bothwell St to Waterloo St and was intended to be part of the Blythswoodholme Hotel by Peddie & Kinnear (1877). Eclipsed by the building of the Central Station Hotel opposite, it was reconstructed in 1890 as offices and the arcade disappeared.

Millar's Arcade

From the Saltmarket to King St. Dingy in appearance, it seems to have specialised in the sale of second-hand books, second-hand clothes and stucco images.

Campbell Arcade

Off the Trongate it was actually a cul-de-sac and was occupied mostly by grocery shops.

MARKETS

One of Glasgow's earliest charters (*c*.1176) granted its feudal lord, the bishop, the power to hold a weekly market every Thursday, and to use the fines and tolls generated by it to finance the city's activities. From an early date markets for different types of goods were set up in different locations – some in particular streets, some in various kirkyards and some in special buildings. Until the 19th century all foodstuffs were exposed for sale in markets rather than shops. For reasons no longer evident, these various markets changed localities with surprising rapidity, but the general course of their development is clear.

In 1577 markets for grass, straw and hay were held in the New Kirkyard (i.e. the Tron Church) south of the Trongate, and a Meal Market was located in the High St. The salt market had been moved from a site close to the river to the head of the High St but this had caused the Clyde fishermen so much trouble that in 1594 it was transferred back to its old site in the Saltmarket. In 1634 a horse market took place at the meeting of the Rottenrow and the Drygate, and markets for salt, horse corn, lint seed and hemp seed were located next to the College.

In 1700 a mutton market (12 stalls) was established in Bell's Wynd. Also known as the Country Market, it was unusual in being open to non-burgess fleshers. As its business increased, in 1754 it moved to larger quarters (26 stalls) in King St, along with the beef market (21 stalls) and the fish market (10 stalls). These market buildings in King St had paved courts, permanent stalls and their own supply of running water. The city butchers used this area and Skinners' Haugh (where the Town Council had erected a public slaughter house in 1744 – cattle had previously been slaughtered in the streets). The presence of this noxious trade so near the centre of the city eventually became such a public nuisance that in 1818 the Council erected a live meat market in Grahame Sq off the Gallowgate. In 1875 a dead meat market opened up in Moore St adjacent to Grahame Sq and in 1911 an abattoir was set up in the same area, considered to be one of the biggest in Europe. By the end of the 1960s it was decided to replace it but lack of funds meant that the third and final phase of the new abattoir was opened only in 1989.

In 1756 the Incorporation of Gardeners asked for the use of the old beef market in the Candleriggs, which then became the green (or herb) market. In 1808 the gardeners moved to a new green market on the site of the old Wynd Church in the

Bridgegate (opposite the King St fish market) where it remained till 1849.

The next major marketing activity was the opening in 1817 of the Candleriggs (or City) Bazaar, built on the site of an old bowling-green. It was designed by James Cleland, Superintendent of Works, and it concentrated a wide range of retail activities into one building – butter, second-hand books, poultry, cabbages, toys, fruit, eggs, flowers and so on. So successful was this venture that eventually the Council bought it for £3,000. The cheese market, originally located in Montrose St, moved to premises next to the Bazaar. As specialised markets and retail shops began to open up elsewhere in the city, the Bazaar now began to lose its miscellaneous character and by 1860 had become entirely a wholesale fruit and vegetable market with over 70 stances. The building was largely reconstructed in 1888 and made three times larger.

By 1914 Candleriggs was recognised as the main fruit and vegetable wholesale outlet for the whole of Scotland. A rival fruit market was established in Kent St, off the Gallowgate where, for some 50 years, the fruit-growers of the Clyde Valley brought their produce. In 1884 it moved closer to the city centre (off South Albion St) but it did not survive its proximity to the Bazaar for more than a few years.

The problems of running such an extensive market in the middle of a built-up area in the centre of a large town had become apparent as early as the 1890s, but almost 100 years were to elapse before the obvious remedy was adopted. By 1960 less than 30 firms were still using the Candleriggs premises and in 1969 the entire fruit and vegetable market moved out to a 30-acre, green-field location in Blochairn Rd, Garngad, on the site of the Blochairn Steel Works, and the emptied food-hall became a general retail market.

In the 1870s the City Improvement Trust cleared away most of the old buildings clustering around the Bridgegate, and in 1873 a new fish market was erected on part of this cleared site. It was enlarged in 1886 and 1903, but eventually, for the same reasons as the fruit market before it, it also moved out to the Blochairn site in 1977. The building was converted into an unsuccessful shopping centre.

The extensive market in second-hand clothing, popularly known as Paddy's Market, was located in various places at or around the south end of the Saltmarket (see PADDY'S MARKET).

An unusual market, located in Jail Square facing the west end of Glasgow Green, was the bird and dog market previously found in Cochrane St and then at the railings of St David's (Ramshorn) Church in Ingram St. It dealt exclusively in pet animals such as dogs, rabbits, pigeons and canary birds, an indication of the hobbies or pursuits of Glasgow's 19th-century working class.

THE BARROWS

Early this century there existed a street-market formed of hand-barrows (selling mainly second-hand bric-à-brac and old clothes) lined up along Clyde St. In the early 1920s these traders were evicted from their traditional stances, with no alternative accommodation. In 1923 Mrs Margaret McIvor and her husband, who hired out fruit and fish barrows to street-traders too poor to have their own, bought a piece of land in the Calton (enclosed by Gibson St, Moncur St, Kent St and the Gallowgate) and let sites on it to the displaced barrow-traders. Soon more than 300 barrows were using the site and it rapidly became a recognised Glasgow feature widely known as the Barrows. So popular did this market become that in 1926 it became necessary to erect a roofed structure open at the sides on one part of the site, which soon became filled with semi-permanent stalls (not barrows) mainly selling second-hand clothes. Contiguous with this structure was the famous dance-hall or ballroom, Barrowland, which for a long time was the venue for Glasgow's unsophisticated youth. The other part remained as an open-air site; many of its stalls or barrows sold new and second-hand tools of all kinds.

For long one of the city's attractions, it fell upon evil times in the 1970s and 1980s. Unfortunately, it lay on the intended route of part of Glasgow's Inner Ring Road and so suffered badly from neglect. In 1982, however, the stall-holders and other interested parties joined with the Scottish Development Agency to form the Barrows Enterprise Trust. Financed by a million pounds spread over three to five years, the whole set-up has been reorganised,

The Barrows. Although its original 'sales points' were hand-barrows, it now boasts permanent stalls dealing mainly in curtains, towels, crockery and talkative salesmen. (George Oliver)

revitalised and brought up-market. Streets passing through the area have been pedestrianised, decorative entrance gates have been erected, it has been awarded the accolade of its own official name, 'The Barras', and it is now said to be one of the biggest enclosed street-markets in Europe, with a thousand traders and a hundred shopkeepers.

PADDY'S MARKET

The foot of the Saltmarket, where the Bridgegate cut off to the west to meet the north end of the Glasgow Bridge, was for long the fashionable area of the city; but towards the end of the 18th century its merchant inhabitants began to move out to the west side where the air was cleaner. Their divided mansions (and hundreds of jerry-built tenements around them) soon became the slum-dwellings of the myriads of immigrants who crowded into the city at the start of the 19th century, mainly from Ireland – a flood greatly augmented by the

effects of the Irish Potato Famine of 1845. Soon there developed amongst these newcomers, for obvious reasons, an extensive trade in cast-off clothing, and by 1824 a group of Irish brokers set up some 40 shops largely given over to the buying and selling of old clothes. The location of this market was a hollow square of buildings in the Bridgegate, and the former nationality of the sellers and buyers soon gave it the name Paddy's Market. It was estimated that by 1831 there were over 1,600 hawkers and dealers in cast-offs,

Paddy's Market. From the early years of the 19th century, many of the dealers in second-hand clothes were Irish, living in and about the foot of the Saltmarket. The last remnants of this once-flourishing trade linger on, up against the walls of a railway viaduct near the Bridgegate. (George Oliver)

almost all of whom were Irish.

The trade continued to grow, for as well as the home market there was a lucrative wholesale trade, dispatching bales of old garments (too worn-out even for the Glasgow poor) to Ireland. In 1845 a petition of 60,000 signatures sought to have it moved, and about 1850 Jail Square, an area immediately north of the High Court building (facing Glasgow Green at the foot of the Saltmarket), became the new centre for the trade. Soon the Town Council, recognising its by now permanent nature, began to regulate the market, and in 1853 bought some ground to the south of the Bridgegate where it set up a public market-place exclusively for the sale of old clothes.

Paddy's Market remained there until 1869, when the whole area was cleared to make way for a railway viaduct leading into the Glasgow and South Western's new St Enoch's Station. For a while the market was accommodated in a square of covered wooden buildings (120ft by 160ft) at the north-west corner of Glasgow Green, but in 1875 a new market – the Glasgow Corporation Clothes Market – was erected in

Greendyke St under the control of a tacksman or lessee who paid £600 per annum for the tack; in 1900 the Council took over full control. Dealers regularly came over from Dublin to purchase entire cargoes of boots and shoes, clothes and bedding wholesale, and it was said as much as £500 could be cleared in a week. The retail side of Paddy's Market was largely kept going by the labouring part of the population, the wives of 'decent working men'.

Somewhat improved circumstances brought about a decline in the trade and the Greendyke site gradually fell into disuse. In the pre-First World War period the dealers began to drift back to the Bridgegate, either to shop accommodation or to the pavements, and by 1922 the Greendyke St building had been demolished. After the war the Bird and Dog Market, then located in the Jail Square, moved to another site and the second-hand clothes market moved in, complete with its own sign, 'PADDY'S MARKET'.

Once again, however, the peripatetic market had to move, when a new City Mortuary was opened on the market site in 1935. Some traders moved to shops in nearby Market St, but others leased the arches of the railway viaduct (which formed one side of Shipbank Lane leading from the Bridgegate to the Clyde). During the interwar years the market continued to specialise in clothing the city's poorest citizens (as well as large numbers of lascar seamen from the port), but after the Second World War, when it had contracted more or less to the viaduct arches and pavements and nothing more, it began to deal less in old clothes and more in second-hand domestic goods. Recently there have been several attempts to close it and a Shipbank Lane Tenant's Association was set up in 1984 for the protection of the few dealers who remain.

Slavery

By the middle of the 18th century Glasgow's increasing transatlantic trade enabled many of its merchants to develop links with the British West Indies. Some Glasgow merchants set up as sugar importers (particularly after the demise of the Virginia tobacco trade in the 1770s), and several of the West India sugar plantations had West of Scotland proprietors.

Such circumstances must have inevitably created a knowledge of or a degree of acquiescence in West Indian slavery, but hard evidence of the extent of its local significance is difficult to find. About 1650 the Glasgow Merchants' House displayed a board with various moral maxims of a business significance on it, one of which was 'Thirdly, do not buy men for slaves, this the Lord reproves in Amos, 2,6', evidence that slavery was not thought to be ordained of God.

An 18th-century painting of John Glassford of Dougaldston (an eminent Glasgow tobacco merchant) and his family has an odd black patch behind Glassford himself. Close examination reveals this to have been originally a black servant boy standing behind his master – who painted it out, and when and why, are not known. It is a reasonable assumption that other rich merchant families would also have had similar fashionable black boys – a close off the Gallowgate was known at The Black Boy Close – but their exact legal, or indeed social, status seems difficult to establish.

A landmark case in the 1770s made the Scottish legal position on slavery clear. In 1766 in the West Indies a John Wedderburn bought a young negro slave to whom he gave the name Joseph Knight Wedderburn brought Joseph Knight to Glasgow about 1771 as his personal servant, and not long afterwards Joseph fathered a child by the chamber-maid, Annie Thompson, who was immediately discharged. Joseph stayed on in his master's service but eventually left and married Annie in Edinburgh. Wedderburn, insisting that Joseph should return to his service, went to law and the Justices of the Peace decided in his favour. On appeal to the Sheriff by Knight, the JP's verdict was upheld. The case now went to the Court of Session (some Glasgow gentlemen had agreed to pay Joseph's legal expenses) and after some days' deliberation found for Joseph: 'the purchaser of a negro in the British colonies has no right to the perpetual service of such negro while in this country'. A fleeting glimpse in 1798 tells of a James Sommerville, cowfeeder (i.e. dairyman), who was charged with fracturing the skull of a negro.

Glasgow's best documented and strongest link with slavery was its Anti-Slavery Association. The 1820s and 1830s saw the formation of several anti-slavery groups throughout Britain, and Glasgow's was considered to be one of the most active. It was begun in 1822 by James Smeal, a Glasgow Quaker grocer, and remained active till 1876.

It may be that the city's attitude towards this matter was best expressed by a committee on slavery of the Glasgow Chamber of Commerce not long after the Chamber was established in 1783. Its report ended with the words 'since much difference existed between members, no decisive resolution was adopted, every member was left to take such part in the agitation [for abolition] as seemed proper to himself'.

St Kentigern

Glasgow's patron saint, St Kentigern, whose miracles are blazoned on the city's coat-of-arms, was one of that heavenly army of Celtic saints whose widespread missionary activities in the 6th and 7th centuries can be traced by the many churches dedicated to them.

Almost all that is known about Kentigern comes from two 12th-century lives, the earlier fragmentary and anonymous, the later written (sometime before 1185) by Jocelin, a Cistercian monk of Furness Abbey for the Bishop of Glasgow, another Jocelin. Apart from these two sources, along with a few additional scraps in two late-medieval breviaries, the only certain evidence from independent sources is that he died in 612.

Jocelin says he died aged 185, so assuming this to be a hagiographical inflation of 85, St Kentigern was probably born about 530. The sources all agree that his maternal grandfather was Leudonius or Loth, the eponymous king of Leudonia or Lothian. His father's name is a fair-sized mystery. Loth's daughter, variously named Thaney, Thenew or Teneu, firmly believed that her son had no earthly father. (In later years her name was corrupted into the form St Enoch, as in St Enoch's Square, and so on.) Jocelin throws cold water on such an heretical belief and suggests as a possible explanation that St Kentigern was conceived under an anaesthetic, while the fragmentary life says that his mother was violently raped by a certain Prince Ewen, son of the King of Cumbria, dressed as a woman. Thenew's condition becoming apparent, her father commanded that she be thrown from the top of a hill called Dunpelder (i.e. Traprain Law). Miraculously, she was unharmed by the fall, so her angry and violent father had her cast adrift on the Firth of Forth in a 'very little boat of hides' (i.e. a coracle). Carried safely through the waters she came ashore on the north side of the Firth at Culross, where she gave birth. A certain St Servanus or St Serf was attracted to the scene by the singing of angels and took the mother and the new baby into his care. He baptised the child under the name of Kyentyern a name with almost as many meanings as the word Glasgow itself. If it is Irish/Scottish Celtic then it probably comes from *ceann* ('head' or 'chief') and *tighearn* ('lord'), but the more likely etymology is a Cumbrian Celtic form, *cuno* ('hound') and *tegernus* ('lord'). St Servanus gave St Kentigern a pet name, Mungo. Jocelyn spells it 'Munghu' and glosses it as 'Best Friend', and says it was the name most often used by the common people whenever they invoked the saint's help. 'Dear Friend' is the customary translation, but recent scholarship suggests that it is actually a diminutive of Kentigern and means 'My Hound'.

When he was old enough, St Kentigern took his place with the group of youths being educated by St Servanus, but the preference shown to him by their teacher aroused the animosity of his fellow students. For instance, St Servanus had a pet robin and one day the boys handled it so roughly that its head was torn off, for which they blamed St Kentigern, who miraculously revived the bird and returned it to his master. It was the custom of the students to take turns through the night at keeping the church lamps alight, and once, on the eve of Kentigern's watch, they maliciously extinguished the fire. St Kentigern took a bough of growing hazel and caused it to burst into flames and from it relit the fire.

Eventually the jealousy of his colleagues drove St Kentigern away from Culross. As he journeyed westwards he chanced upon a venerable old man named Fergus who was on the point of death. The saint loaded the corpse on to a new cart drawn by two untamed bulls and turned them loose. 'By a straight road, along where there was no path, as far as Cathures, which is now called Glasgu,' the oxen and the cart went and stopped. At this spot there was an old cemetery consecrated long before by St Ninian in which St Kentigern buried the old man, the first fruit of that burial ground. Learning of his presence there the king of the area arranged to have him consecrated as bishop of a widespread diocese centred on 'a town called Glesgu, which is, interpreted, The Dear Family, and is now called Glasgu'.

There, beside the Molendinar Burn, a small tributary of the Clyde, he set up his little clay and wattle cathedral. Jocelin's history gives us many details of the saint's life, including a series of remarkable miracles. He was a vegetarian and an abstainer, he wore a hair-shirt next to his skin, slept on a stone, and recited the Psalter while immersed in cold water. At Mass a sweet-smelling cloud filled the church while a heavenly light shone round his head. He yoked together a stag and a wolf and, sowing sand, reaped wheat. In time of want he caused the flooding waters of the Clyde to bring to the Molendinar the corn-filled barns of Morken, a tyrant king.

It was the latter's continuing opposition which forced St Kentigern to flee to Wales, although Cumbria is more likely to have been his destination. After a sojourn there of some years he was recalled north by Rhydderch Hael, King of Alclud or Dumbarton. On his way he stopped at Hoddem near Dumfries where he performed a miracle which forms one of those depicted on the city's coat-of-arms; while preaching to the assembled people he caused the ground beneath him to rise up,

forming 'a little hill [which] remaineth there unto this day'.

It was following his return to Glasgow that he performed his best known miracle. Rhydderch's wife, Queen Languoreth, had cast her amorous eyes on a certain young soldier who was, as Jocelin says, 'easily induced to sin with her'. Very imprudently, she gave to her soldier lover a valuable ring she had been given by her husband. The king one day finding the soldier asleep on the banks of the Clyde secretly removed the incriminating ring and threw it into the river. He then demanded the ring from his unfaithful wife, casting her into a dungeon when no ring was forthcoming. In her despair she appealed to the saint for help; he instructed her to have a salmon hooked from the river. Naturally, when it was gutted, the ring was disclosed and the cuckolded husband hoodwinked.

His fantastical miracles continued to be performed in all their amazing exuberance. One Christmas a visiting Irish jester demanded as a gift from the king the unseasonable gift of a dish of mulberries, which St Kentigern obligingly produced. On another occasion a vessel of milk was upset into the Clyde and was changed into little cheeses. Once a follower of St Columba cut off the head of one of the bishop's rams, whereupon the head turned to stone and stuck to the culprit's hand – and that 'head turned to stone remaineth there unto this day'.

At length, in extreme old age, St Kentigern felt the chill of approaching death. A heavenly messenger announced that because he had suffered a life of martyrdom, he was to be granted an easy and gentle departure and that he should therefore be placed in a warm bath. The messenger also added that any of his followers who entered the bath would straightaway accompany his master. It is now supposed that this unusual 'bath' is a garbled account of the aged saint collapsing and dying while administering, as was his custom, total immersion baptism. The bath was prepared, St Kentigern placed in it, and the old man died peacefully on 13 January 612.

The popularity of the saint was manifested in his own day by the unusual course of giving him a nickname, Mungo. In a surprising way, despite the passage of centuries and despite the Reformation, he still retains that popularity, and the city's 1975 coat-of-arms still blazons forth his miracles – the salmon and the ring, the resurrected robin, the blazing hazel branch (transmogrified into an oak tree) and the little mound from which he preached his sermon, as well as the bell with which he summoned his flock to worship, all glossed in a children's rhyme:

Here's the Bird that never flew,
Here's the Tree that never grew,
Here's the Bell that never rang,
Here's the Fish that never swam

with the uncanonical addition of *'That's jist the drucken Salmon'.*

See also CATHEDRAL

St Mungo Prize

This award was instituted by Alexander Paterson Somerville, a Glasgow business-man (reputed to have invented the square-toed shoe) who set up a trust fund from which a gold medal and £1,000 was to be awarded every third year to someone who 'had done most for the good of the city, by making it more beautiful, healthier or more honoured.'

The first award was made in 1940 to Sir Patrick J. Dollan. He was the city's Lord Provost during the Second World War, an indefatigable worker for the city both at home and abroad.

1943	Dr Tom Honeyman, Director of Glasgow Corporation Museums and Art Galleries
1946	Sir William Burrell, shipowner, art collector, donor
1949	Sir Stephen Bilsland, businessman
1952	Dr Violet Roberton, public health and child welfare worker
1955	Mrs E. MacKenzie Anderson, Glasgow Tree Lovers' Society
1958	Councillor John D. Kelly, the arts in Glasgow
1961	Revd Dr Neville Davidson, minister of Glasgow Cathedral
1964	Revd Tom Allan, minister of St George's Tron Church, welfare
1967	Prof F. Anderson, Glasgow University, Chair of Geriatrics
1970	Sir Alexander Gibson, conductor and director, Scottish National Orchestra
1973	Mr Arthur Oldham, Director of the city's Parks Department
1976	Prof Sir Charles Curran, Principal of Strathclyde University
1979	Mrs Dorothy Henderson, environmental improvement
1982	Fred Paton, old folks' welfare
1985	Prof Gavin Arneil, Yorkhill Hospital
1988	Jack House, journalist and Glasgow historian
1991	Susan Baird, Lord Provost of Glasgow

Steamers

The *Comet* (built for Henry Bell by John Wood of Port Glasgow, 24½ tons, length 43½ft, speed 7 knots), the first sea-going, steam-propelled vessel, took to the waters of the Firth of Clyde in 1812; by 1820 there were almost 30 paddle-steamboats puffing up and down the river. These tiny ships were to grow greatly in size and number over the next hundred years or so, a growth helped by three favourable circumstances. First, there was the navigational advantage of the sheltered waters of the Firth of Clyde, combined with the tourist attraction of the magnificent scenery associated with its winding landlocked sea-lochs. Second was the continual advances in marine engineering made by the Clyde shipbuilders and, lastly, was the growing custom of city dwellers to leave the polluted urban areas now and then for a stay in the country or the seaside.

This efflux from the city had begun as early as the end of the 18th century when Glasgow's well-to-do citizens and their families flitted by coach and sailing vessel to the rural delights of Helensburgh and Greenock, but in little less than 20 years from the *Comet's* appearance, tiny villages and little hamlets were turning into trig townships with specially built and commodious piers to accommodate the ubiquitous paddle-steamers from Glasgow and their money-spending passengers.

Among the earliest locations were the little towns of Rothesay, Dunoon, Largs and Millport, with lesser establishments at Kilcreggan, Blairmore, Kirn, Innellan and Tighnabruaich. Substantial sandstone villas built by prosperous Glasgow merchants and businessmen soon began to spread out along the shorelines of these resorts, and so frequent and speedy were the paddle-steamers that a *pater familias* could commute weekly or even daily from and to his city place of business.

Until near the end of the century the vessels serving this growing trade were owned (and often captained) by individuals. At the beginning they usually ran from Bridge Wharf or the Broomielaw in the centre of Glasgow. Probably the first of these early vessels to undertake purely pleasure excursions was the *Leven*, built in 1823. By the middle of the century commercial groupings began to take over many of these individual holdings. One of the largest of these groups was that owned by George and James Burns, and their Castle Line ships sailed to Dunoon, Rothesay and Loch Fyne, while other fleets traded to Largs and the Ayr coast, Arran, Dumbarton, Helensburgh and the Gareloch, Lochgilphead, Inveraray and Ardrishaig, Campbeltown and Stranraer. The volume of traffic was such that it has been estimated that on one day during the Glasgow Fair weekend of 1851 about 25,000 people left the city by 42 sailings from the Broomielaw.

So lucrative was this trade (particularly on the Glasgow–Rothesay trip) that during the 1850s and 1860s the resulting competition between individual steamers became so intense that captain-owners frequently and recklessly raced and jockeyed for positions of advantage when approaching piers to the great inconvenience, discomfort and alarm of their passengers, a state of affairs which drove many timid holiday-makers to use the railways for part of their journey.

An innovation, ominous for the private owners, took place in 1841. The Glasgow & South Western Railway Co opened a line from Glasgow to the pierhead at Greenock and it soon became apparent that intending passengers often preferred the quick train journey that saved them time and spared them the exposure to the foul, miasmatic sewage which passed for water in and around the city. By the mid-1850s the North British Railway Co had established a successful north-bank line to Dumbarton and Helensburgh, while the Caledonian Railway Co and the Glasgow & South Western Railway Co went west and south respectively along the south bank. Another useful effect of the railways, with their need for strict timetabling was that they began to exercise a moderating influence on the erratic running of the old-style steamer captains.

It was during this period, in 1852, that the first Sunday service was introduced by the *Emperor* (built 1843 by Tod & McGregor, 78½ tons, 121½ft). As could be expected in Presbyterian Scotland, it met with very strong opposition and many piers were closed or barricaded against the Sabbath-breaking steamers. Predictably, however, this show of Sabbatarianism was soon a lost and forgotten battle.

The next major influence on the Clyde was the outbreak of the American Civil War in 1861. Both sides (but particularly the Southern States with their dependence on the export of raw cotton to Europe) had a pressing need for fast, manoeuvrable and shallow-draft vessels to act as blockade runners. The obvious, even only, source of supply was the Clyde paddle-steamer fleet, so as well as having new vessels built at the Clyde shipyards (usually under conditions of secrecy) many of the best of the operational fleets were sold to the Confederacy, denuding the Clyde of at least 16 of its best and newest vessels. One example of this traffic was the sale in 1862 of the magnificent *Iona* (1855, J. & G. Thomson, Govan, 174 tons, 17½ knots). She sailed in secrecy, without lights and was run down by another vessel off Gourock and sank in 13 fathoms. Strangely, a similar fate also overtook the second *Iona* (also built by J. & G. Thomson, 368 tons, 249ft, 17½ knots). She was sold to American Confederate agents for £20,000 in 1864, sprang a leak and sank in the Bristol Channel when *en route* for America.

It was an ill wind, however, for in the 1860s vessels of new and advanced standards were able to take the place of the worn-out remnants of the run-down Clyde paddle-steamer fleet. One early example of this new breed was the third *Iona* (1864, J. & G. Thomson, 141 tons, 255½ft, 17 knots, 1,400 passengers), of such quality that she continued to serve up and down the Firth for 70 years.

By the 1870s the increasing demand for passenger services (fuelled partly by the rise of the tourist trade and by the ability of the working class to afford and enjoy a trip 'doon the watter') had produced three paddle-steamers which are now regarded as the best ever made.

The first of these was the *Lord of the Isles*, built by D. & W. Henderson in 1877 (427 tons, 246ft) for the Glasgow & Inveraray Steamboat Co with a capacity for a thousand and more passengers. She ran between Greenock and Inveraray and her design reached new levels of elegance, comfort and speed. Towards the end of the century she went south to the Thames and became the *Lady of the Isles* (incidentally, an English misunderstanding of a historic Scottish title) and was broken up in 1904.

The second (and the *Lord of the Isles'* greatest rival) was the *Columba*, which entered service on the Glasgow–Ardrishaig run in 1878. Built by J. & G. Thomson, Clydebank (543 tons), she had a top speed of 21 knots, measured 300ft (the longest ever Clyde paddle-steamer), was the first Clyde steamer to be built of steel, and could carry 2,000 passengers. She was the first paddle-steamer to have her deck saloon comfortably carried over to the bulwarks, and had a little post office on board. The latter distinction earned her the right to label herself not merely PS but R[oyal] M[ail] PS. She sailed over the Royal Route (so named for having been travelled by Queen Victoria in 1847), one much patronised by the gentry on their way to and from their Highland estates. She carried out her duties on this run for 58 seasons, finally being scrapped at Dalmuir in 1935.

The third vessel was the *Ivanhoe* (282 tons, 225½ft), built in 1880 by D. & W. Henderson for the Firth of Clyde Steam Packet Co, carrying 1,200 passengers and sailing from Helensburgh to Rothesay via Greenock, then round Arran and back. She was unique for her time in being a temperance paddle-steamer. The drinking habits of the Glaswegians had been easily transferred to the bars of the paddle-steamers. These floating drinking dens were becoming so notorious that ordinary travellers preferred to avoid them and travel by train wherever possible, and the *Ivanhoe* was specially commissioned to counteract this undesirable state of affairs. As well as being teetotal, she also offered a high level of comfort and peace, making her very attractive to the 'douce' and 'bien' type of traveller. Her conspicuous drinking-fountain bore the proud and inspiring motto 'Ye may gang faur and fare waur'.

Until near the end of the century the encompassing railway companies were not legally able to operate their own shipping services and had to limit their activities to transferring their passengers to independently owned ships at their pier-heads. It was clear that the future of Clyde services lay with them, however, for the three major Scottish railway companies (Caledonian, North British and Glasgow & South Western) had far greater financial resources than those available to small fleet owners. The changeover began in 1889 when the Caledonian (the Caley), under the subsidiary guise of the Caledonian Steam Packet Co, began running its own ships. It further increased its attractiveness to passengers when, the following year, it transferred its south-bank Bridge St Station to the middle of the city at Central Station. One of its earliest ships was the *Caledonia* (244 tons, 200½ft, 16½ knots) built in 1889 by John Reid of Port Glasgow; it was the first ship with open engines (giving rise to the Glasgow drinking man's ruse, 'Ah'll jist awa' doon below, hen, an' watch the ingines!') and the first to use docking telegraphs. The G&SW retaliated with the *Glen Sannox*, (1892, J. & G. Thomson, Govan, 610 tons, 260½ft, 20 knots, 1,701 passengers), reputed to be the fastest ship on the Clyde, only to have the Caley reply with the famous *Waverley* (448½ tons, 235ft, 19 knots, 1,468 passengers), built in 1899 by A. & J. Inglis, said to have been able to take on any other paddle-steamer on the river as far as speed was concerned.

The disposition of the opposing railways at this time was that the Caley on the south side of the Clyde ran through to piers at Gourock and Wemyss Bay, with the G&SW serving their ships from the Largs and Fairlie piers. On the north side of the river the North British Steam Packet Co steamers left from Craigendoran pier which had been opened in 1883, taking the place of the pier at Helensburgh.

In 1901 an unusual steamer appeared on the Clyde. She was the *King Edward* (Wm Denny & Bros Ltd, Dumbarton, 502 tons, 250½ft, 19 knots, 1,966 passengers), the first ever turbine passenger steamer. She proved to be a very successful rival to her paddle-driven sisters and lasted for some 46 years. Other turbine vessels were built later but they never superseded the paddle-steamers whose extreme manoeuvrability and shallow draught made them eminently suitable for work in a crowded and sometimes shallow estuary.

It was around this time that the paddle-steamer reached its peak of perfection, with well over 40 vessels (the Caley had 10, G&SW 10, NB 9 and private owners 17) traversing the river in all directions. One could travel from Brodick in Arran to Glasgow in 80 minutes – today, with the most advanced car ferries, it takes 115 minutes! Such a superb service, however, in which the driving force was almost ruinous competition, was not particularly profitable to run, and the Caley and the NB were induced by falling dividends to pool their services with the result that several vessels were withdrawn from service.

After the First World War (during which many Clyde paddle-steamers went into action as mine-sweepers, a task for which their shallow draught made them particularly suitable) rationalisation continued. In 1923 the countrywide amalgamations of local railway companies brought the fleets of the Caledonian and the North British Steam Packet companies together under the LMS (London, Midland & Scottish), while the NB merged with the LNER (London & North Eastern).

During the interwar years some new steamers were built and some old ones withdrawn with the net result that at the outbreak of the Second World War the LMS fleet consisted of eight paddle-steamers and five turbine steamers, and the LNER fleet of four paddle-steamers. Once again the paddle-steamers were pressed into wartime service as mine-sweepers and support vessels. The LNER fleet was reduced to one ship, the *Lucy Ashton* (1888, T. B. Sneath & Co, Rutherglen, 234 tons, 190ft, 16½ knots, 903 passengers), the smallest and neatest vessel on the Clyde. She enjoyed a successful 63-year career, which included service in both World Wars. In 1949, instead of being broken up, her hull was used as a floating test-bed for Rolls Royce jet engines and for hull design.

A much later LNER vessel achieved fame very similar to the *Lucy Ashton*. The *Jeanie Deans* (1931, Fairfield Shipbuilding & Engineering Co Ltd., 635 tons, 258ft, 18 knots, 1,840 passengers) became, on the Arrochar run up Loch Long, one of the best known ships on the Clyde. In 1939 she was requisitioned as a mine-sweeper, and in 1941 was converted to an anti-aircraft ship as HMS *Jeanie Deans*. Withdrawn in 1964, she went south two years later and was put on the Thames as *Queen of the South*. Her performance proved so unsatisfactory that before the year was out she was towed to Antwerp and broken up. The saddest loss was the first LNER *Waverley*. She had come unscathed through the First World War but during the Second, while evacuating some 800 troops from Dunkirk in 1940, she received a direct hit and sank with the loss of 300 lives. By the end of hostilities the LMS fleet had been reduced to four paddle-steamers and four turbine-steamers, and the LNER to three paddle-steamers.

With the nationalisation of the country's railways in 1948, the Clyde steamer fleets passed into the ownership of British Rail (then known as British Railways). Then, in 1968, the British Rail Board handed over their Clyde steamers to the Scottish Transport Group. The Group soon found what had been evident for some time – a passenger fleet which only achieves its maximum use during a short period each summer is prohibitively expensive to run. Uneconomic ships were withdrawn, uneconomic piers were closed and, in 1970, a new vessel for new circumstances was found. The Group bought a four-year-old Swedish car-ferry (*Caledonia*, 1966, A/S Langesunds Mek, Verk, Sweden, 1156 tons, 202ft, 14 knots, 650 passengers in summer and 132 in winter, plus 50 cars) and put it into service on the Arran run as the Clyde's first roll-on, roll-off car ferry. So successful was this innovation that within four years the Scottish Transport Group had significantly altered the whole basis of ship services on the Clyde – for Clyde paddle-steamer read Clyde motor vessel car ferry.

One of the last paddle-steamers to be built for the LNER before nationalisation was a replacement for the old *Waverley*. She was built by A. & J. Inglis, Pointhouse, in 1947. She is 240ft long and can carry 1,350 passengers at a speed of 15 knots and is the last of the great paddle-steamers. She was withdrawn from regular service in 1973 and sold for the nominal fee of £1 to the Paddle Steamer Preservation Society. At first it was thought that the vessel would be preserved as a museum-piece but upon examination she was found still to be seaworthy. Thanks to public subscriptions and various grants the *Waverley* put to sea again as the last sea-going paddle-steamer in the world in May 1975 under the management of the Waverley Steam Navigation Co. Her career since then has been varied – mechanical and navigational troubles have made her future uncertain – but she is still afloat.

See also SHIPBUILDING

Streams

As it flows through the city the Clyde receives several tributary streams from its gently sloping south bank and its steeper north bank. The rapid spread of the city has meant that most of these burns, which once flowed through fields or between thatched wooden houses, now run obscurely underground (often no more than sewers) so that in many cases neither their source nor their route is definitely known.

The easternmost stream on the north bank is the Molendinar. Of all Glasgow's streams it most deserves to be called the city's tutelary stream for it was on its sloping west bank, about one mile north of the Clyde, that St Kentigern established his little Christian community near the end of the 6th century, and where the Cathedral dedicated to him was later built. The meaning of the name is probably from the Latin *molendinarius* – of, or belonging to a mill, but the interpretation of place-names is seldom certain, and another, somewhat fanciful derivation has been suggested: *meall an dhuinn*, the [stream] of the hill with the brown top. It rises in Hogganfield Loch (three miles north-east of the city), flows roughly west and then south along a narrow steep-sided valley between the Cathedral and the Necropolis. At one time two dams in this vicinity impounded its waters to drive the Town's Mill and the Sub-Dean's Mill – hence its name. In the 1870s it was covered over for most of its length, the part by the Cathedral becoming Wishart St. Flowing south, it passed under the Gallowgate close to where the Gallowgate Port stood. Its further course from there ran through an area occupied by tanners and butchers and the consequent pollution made the burn's disappearance underground a necessity.

It received one major and two minor tributaries. The Girth Burn, whose name may derive from a sanctuary garth close to the Cathedral, flowed east into the Molendinar past the Bishop's Castle, while, further downstream, it was joined by the Poldrait Burn coming in from the Gallowsmuir to the east. At the south-west corner of the church of St Andrew's-by-the-Green, the Camlachie Burn joined the Molendinar. Its source lay in the distant Provan Loch about six miles to the north-east, from where it flowed west to Shettleston, on to Parkhead, through Camlachie to Bridgeton Cross and then west across Glasgow Green to join the Molendinar. Until the beginning of the 19th century it ran undisturbed across the Green, dividing it north and south, and supplied the water for the Green's washing facilities – but it too was covered over. It once carried the odd name of the Reidclaith Gott.*

Further west was the St Enoch Burn. Rising near the Townhead district it flowed west, then south more or less along the line of Buchanan St, to reach the river at the Custom House. It was also at one time called the Glasgow Burn no doubt as marking the burgh's western boundary. Somewhere along its northern course it took in a very short stream called the Well Burn which rose near Cathedral Square.

A number of little streams ran south into the Clyde in this part of the city and exact knowledge of their courses has long since been lost. There was the Regality or Nameless Burn which entered the Clyde about Washington St, the Anderston or Greenhill Burn which came down from Garnethill and was intercepted by a sewer near St Vincent St, and still further west, the Finnieston Burn flowing south from Charing Cross.

The Clyde's last tributary on the north bank is the River Kelvin. It rises in the Kilsyth Hills, runs past Kirkintilloch, then through Maryhill and the city's West End to join the Clyde at Partick, a distance of some 20 miles. Its lower course used to mark the boundary between Glasgow and Partick and had a number of water-driven mills – flour, paper, gunpowder. At one time, from Maryhill on, it was very extensively polluted by industrial waste; more recently, however, its quality has been greatly improved. It has the further distinction of receiving the waters of the Pinkston Burn (rising in the St Rollox district), one of the few north-side streams which do not run directly into the Clyde.

On the south side of the river, the easternmost stream was the Polmadie Burn (also known as Jenny's Burn or Malls Mire Burn). From its origins near Aikenhead it ran through Mount Florida into the river just west of the Rutherglen Bridge. At one time it marked the south-east boundary of the city.

Further west was the Blind Burn or Sandiefield Burn, flowing south from Langside and entering the Clyde opposite the Saltmarket; it once indicated the boundary between the Gorbals and Lanarkshire.

Next came a stream with at least four names: Kinning House Burn, Shaws Burn, Mile Burn or Shiels Burn. From its origin near Strathbungo it flowed north to enter the river near the General Terminus Quay,

---

* gott – a drain or ditch

and marked the Gorbals' western boundary with Renfrewshire.

The westernmost stream on the south side was the Plantation Burn which, rising somewhere near Pollokshields, entered the Clyde at the old Harbour Tunnel. Confusingly, at one time it was also known as the Mile Burn.

Although the River Cart falls into the Clyde near Renfrew and so outside the city, one of its tributaries, the White Cart, runs through a large part of southern Glasgow.

See also THE CLYDE

Subway

In the 1880s a large proportion of the city's population still lived within two or three miles of its centre; in addition, within this same circle were located Glasgow's business community and its university, as well as its docks, railway stations and many of its industries. Such a situation made an underground passenger transport system (safe from adverse weather conditions and free of growing road congestion) an attractive and feasible proposal, and in 1888 a bill was presented to Parliament which set out a scheme for twin tunnels in the form of a circular track (entirely below ground) which, starting from St Enoch's Square, would swing north-west to the Botanic Gardens, continue south along the line of Byres Rd, pass under the Clyde at Yorkhill, turn east through Govan, turn north at Tradeston and finish back at St Enoch's. At first opposed by the Clyde Navigation Trust as preventing further deepening of the Clyde above the two river tunnels, it was finally passed in 1890 with one major alteration – instead of reaching out as far as the Botanic Gardens the route was diverted to the south of Great Western Rd. As finally built, the double tracks of the system, running in twin tunnels of 11ft

in diameter were approximately 6½ miles long and served 15 stations. The greatest depth of track (115ft) is below Glasgow St at Hillhead, while between Cessnock Station and Kinning Park Station (both south of the river) the depth is only 7ft.

Construction work began at the St Enoch Station site in 1891. North of the river the tunnels followed the lines of the main streets (Buchanan St, Cowcaddens St, New City Rd, Great Western Rd, and Byres Rd), a circumstance which enabled the 'cut-and-cover' method of tunnelling – i.e. cutting a trench from street-level in which to build the tunnel and then covering it over – to be adopted. This method was not possible south of the river where more orthodox tunnelling had to be used. Brick and cement were used where possible to line the tunnels, but where clayey soil threatened subsidence or where water-bearing strata were encountered (under the river, for instance) then cast-iron segments were used. The deepest station is Buchanan St (40ft), the shallowest is Kinning Park (14ft). At each station the two tunnels become one, rising some 18ft above track-level to form a station area about 150ft long. In order to assist trains to stop and start, each station is built on a slight hump. The original design called for the standard railway gauge of 4ft 8½ins, but this was subsequently altered to 4ft, a unique public transport gauge.

The enabling Act specified no particular form of transport (other than banning, for obvious reasons, steam power) but from the beginning cable power had been envisaged, and this was the method adopted. The power-house from which the two cables were driven was situated in Scotland St. Two giant steam-engines pulled the two endless cables (one for each tunnel) round the subway circle. There were four cables (two in reserve), each weighing about 57 tons. They were 1½in in diameter and 11,650 yards long. On the average they lasted about 7½ months. The engines, with their output of 2,000hp and their 50-ton flywheels, pulled the cables along at 13 mph – one complete circuit every 30 minutes – which allowed a transit time for the trains of 40 minutes including stops at stations. The workshops and the car-sheds were at Broomloan Rd, Govan, where the cars were lifted from the track through a 55ft x 28ft hole to the surface by a travelling overhead crane (12 tons in 1896, 22½ tons in 1935–77).

The most important piece of equipment on the train was the 'grip'. Mounted below the leading axle on the front bogie, it was controlled by the driver or 'gripman' so as to increase or decrease the speed of the train by gripping with more or less pressure the constantly moving cable as it ran along sheaves between the tracks, two inches above the rails.

The Glasgow District Subway ('subway' has always been preferred by Glaswegians despite efforts to substitute 'underground' in its place) was opened to the public on 14 December 1896. Early problems were mainly caused by the rush of curious passengers who packed the 30 cars well beyond their capacity. At first only single cars (40ft-long, non-smoking) ran, but in July 1897 25ft-long trailer cars were added – the sawdust on their floors and the spitoons under their slatted wooden seats made their use obvious!

At first a flat rate of 1d. was charged, mainly to try to meet the competition of the highly successful tramcars (taken over by the Corporation in 1894), a challenge considerably increased when the trams went over to electric traction in 1897. Other patterns of fare were tried, but the changes only served to underline the public's poor response to the system. In 1901 the flat rate changed to ½d. for one station, 1d. for two to five stations and 1½d. for more than five, returning to a flat rate in 1916, which was increased to 1½d. in 1919, then back to structured fares shortly after.

It was becoming clear that as a commercial undertaking the subway was never going to realise its promoters' hopes. Indeed, it is difficult to see why it should have for although its stations were located in a few densely populated areas it was of no relevance whatsoever to the rapidly expanding outer suburbs of the city, in particular those to the north and the east. Even though by 1918 it was carrying almost 21 million passengers per annum it was running into financial problems, and in 1922 it was decided to shut the system down. Negotiations were entered into with Glasgow Corporation as to a possible purchase, but when these broke down the subway was closed on 26 March 1922. The Corporation then increased its offer from £300,000 to £381,589 (an odd sum!), the company accepted it and the system reopened on 3 July 1922. The official opening took place on 1 August 1923, the Glasgow District Subway becoming a part of the Glasgow Corporation Tramways Department.

As early as November 1922 the Corporation began to investigate the possibilities of electric traction but it was not until 1933 that they finally decided to go ahead and convert all the cars to this method. The inner circle was tackled first, its first electric train running on 31 March 1935. The last cable car (on the outer circle) operated on 30 November 1935 and by 5 December that year the whole system was electrified. One lamented alteration was the change of name from 'subway' to 'underground', an official move which the people of Glasgow resolutely ignored.

The power for the electric running was taken at 600 volts AC from the Corporation's tramway power-station at Pinkston (taken over by the South of Scotland Electricity Board in 1958). The conductor rail which transferred the power to the coaches was supported vertically from each fourth sleeper on the side away from the platforms. The new form of traction enabled the running time to be cut from 39 to 28 minutes.

Alterations took place on the cars as well. In 1948 the passenger doors were converted from a trellis-work type to solid sliding doors and in 1954 the livery was changed from red with cream upperworks lined in black to all red with grey roofs.

In 1937 the possibility of extending the system was aired, the intention being to open up a branch line north to Robroyston and south to Kings Park, but the outbreak of the Second World War killed this proposal. Despite high expectations, the hoped-for increase in passengers did not happen. There was some increase during the war and for a while after, and a peak was reached in 1950 when the subway carried some 38 million passengers.

Once again extension of the system was considered. A report published in 1947 boldly tackled the neglect of the city's east end and proposed the construction of another circular route which would link with the existing circle at Bridge St, St Enoch's Square and Buchanan St stations. It would have reached north to Royston Rd then south through Shettleston and Tollcross turning west through Dalmarnock and so back to Bridge St. Despite the obvious need for such an extension it was finally ruled out by its prohibitive cost.

The early post-war years saw several surveys of the city's transport needs. Although all considered the subway system, beyond recommending its retention none advocated any radical upgrading.

Not surprisingly, by now the subway was fast approaching a terminal condition. Its running stock was thoroughly outdated and outworn – most of its passenger cars were museum-pieces, getting on for 80 years old, while many of the electric motors were nearly 40 years old and maintenance could only be carried out by continual cannibalising. The extensive clearing out of Glasgow's older residential districts had left many of its stations in the middle of drastically depopulated areas. The annual passenger journeys had declined from their post-war peak of 38 million to a mere 13 million, ironically a figure which had been reached only three years after the system's opening, and fares had risen at a rate almost double that of the bus fares.

Things took a new turn when the formation of the Greater Glasgow Passenger Transport Executive in June 1973 was the occasion for the announcement of an ambitious modernisation scheme for the subway, estimated to cost £12 million. (In May 1975, following the complete reorganisation of Scottish local government the ownership of the subway was invested in Strathclyde Region, but continued to be operated on their behalf by the Greater Glasgow PTE.)

There were serious problems in attempting to update a system built 86 years before: the sizes of the tunnels and the rolling stock were on such a very small scale, verging on the miniature as to put severe restraints on any new design; there was no possibility of extending or altering the route to take account of the patterns of city use; and it would be necessary to fit any redesigned system into the plans for a comprehensive overhaul of the whole area's transport needs.

Two major redesign projects were envisaged which would enable the system to slot into the proposed updating of the city's rail network. First, BR Partickhill Station (to be renamed Partick Station) was to be relocated to link directly with Merkland St subway station (renamed Partick Underground). Second, Buchanan St Station was to be linked by a moving pavement to the adjacent BR Queen St Station.

By July 1975 the estimated cost had increased from £12 million to £18 million but despite some misgivings the go-ahead was given in September of that year. Preliminary work began in February 1976 and the old system was completely shut down in July 1977. By December 1977 the estimate had grown to £27 million and many unforeseen construction difficulties had slowed up the work. But on 2 November 1979 the Queen opened the completely refurbished £53 million Glasgow Underground; teething troubles delayed the public use until 16 April 1980.

Its 33 brand-new coaches, each holding 34 seated passengers on bench seats along the sides of the cars and 56 passengers standing, are painted overall in a vivid orange livery, which the media, with their usual acuity immediately nicknamed 'Clockwork Oranges'. The journey time has been reduced from 28 to 22 minutes with a three-minute interval between trains at peak periods, and the number of users has increased from 9.9 million in the first year of operation to 14 million. The six busiest stations have separate platforms for both circles and the nine deep stations have escalators. The new car-sheds and workshops at Govan are accessed from the track by way of ramps. Eight new trailer cars now supplement the 33 motor coaches which enable three-coach cars to be run.

Three opportunities for extending the system have been identified: (1) a northern extension through Kirklee to Summerston; (2) a western extension to Glasgow Airport; and (3) an eastern loop via the High St. The extremely high costs plus the difficulties of obtaining rolling-stock to fit a unique gauge make any extension most unlikely in the foreseeable future.

Rolling Stock	
1896	Gripper cars 1–20 Oldbury Carriage & Wagon Co., Birmingham.
1897	Gripper cars 21–30 Length 40ft 9in; width 7ft 8in; height 8ft 9in. Capacity 24 seats.
1898	Trailer cars 31–54 Hurst, Nelson & Co., Motherwell. Length 25ft. Capacity 24 seats.
1901	Gripper cars 55–58
1902–07	14 trailer cars converted to 40ft 9in
1907–14	Remaining trailer cars scrapped.
c.1913	Gripper cars 59–60
1932	Experimental electric cars 60
1935	26 gripper cars fitted with electric motors.
1935	First electric train on inner circle, 31 March; last cable car on outer circle, 30 November.

Stations	Stations
Govan *(previously Govan Cross)*	St Enoch
Partick Underground *(previously Merkland St)*	Bridge St
Kelvin Hall *(previously Partick Cross)*	West St
Hillhead	Shields Rd
Kelvinbridge	Kinning Park
St George's Cross	Cessnock
Cowcaddens	Ibrox *(previously Copland Rd)*
Buchanan St	

Swimming

The city's recognised swimming place in the 18th century was the Clyde where it washed the banks of the Glasgow Green, and dales (or diving boards) were erected along its length. Fleshers' Haugh was the busiest section, while downstream Dominie's Hole was the resort of the more experienced swimmer. Another favourite spot was at the Gorbals, where a cotton mill discharged a steady stream of hot water into the river. However, by the second half of the century, the volume of untreated sewage and factory effluents had reached such proportions that river bathing became impossible and recourse was had to indoor baths.

Towards the end of the 18th century William Harley had set up his baths in what came to be called, for obvious reasons, Bath St. These were well patronised but catered more for the therapeutic than the recreational bather, so in about 1856 a group of 'public-spirited gentlemen' opened the London Rd Swimming Baths and in 1876 the city took them over.

Two years later the Corporation opened the first municipal pool, the Greenhead Baths and Wash-houses on the north edge of the Glasgow Green. Following this, in quick succession, the Corporation then opened baths at Woodside (1882), Cranstonhill (1883), Townhead (1884) and Gorbals (1885). The success of these baths brought about the closure of the London Rd baths in 1883. By 1914 the number had grown to 18. In the absence of adequate washing facilities in the city's tenements all these premises, as well as offering swimming pools (ranging from 73,600 gallons in Greenhead to 104,000 gallons in Cranstonhill) had large numbers of single baths – Greenhead had 32; Woodside, 34; Cranstonhill, 41; Townhead, 33; and Gorbals, 33. The latter also had kosher baths.

Despite the fact that the paternalistic Corporation provided these baths for 'the large mass of the poorer industrial population', the same Corporation had its suspicions that most users did not strictly belong to that class. It tried to catch the 'industrial population' when young but, as it complained, 'gentle compulsion continues to be necessary to induce the children of a humble grade to enter the swimming ponds'. Among those of a more elevated class, swimming was a popular sport and it was estimated that there were over 100 clubs in the city; Glasgow also became the leading centre in Great Britain for life-saving developments. The Council currently operates 13 swimming pools.

Most of these establishments had wash-house departments. Because of the lack of home facilities these 'steamies', as they were called, were well patronised by east-end housewives, transporting loads of washing back and forward in old prams or wheeled washing baskets. The steamies could accommodate from 44 to 78 washers, each with a stall, along with hot and cold water, wringers, centrifugal hydro-extractors (as mechanical clothes-driers were called) and, as an added extravagance, a mangle. As well as providing a useful facility the wash-houses were notorious for gossip – the 'talk of the steamie'.

The wash-houses have disappeared in the face of the home washing machine but the District Council presently runs 13 swimming pools throughout the city. The city has also had five private swimming baths, of which only two are still active – Arlington (1870), Western (1876), Victoria (1873–1939), Pollokshields (1883–1937) and Dennistoun (1884–1983).

Tea-Rooms

The trading monopoly exercised by the East India Company was broken in the early 19th century by the merchants of certain provincial ports, led by Glasgow. One of the first shipments to the city from India was a cargo of tea, and for a time Glasgow competed with London as a tea-blending centre. Stuart Cranston (1848–1921) was one of many blenders and tasters within the city. He and his sister Kate (1849–1934) came from a family involved in the hotel trade but Stuart broke away from family tradition and set up as a retail tea-taster in 1871. Four years later he had the novel idea of providing his customers, for a small charge, with a cup of tea and a choice of cakes, scones and biscuits. This innovation proved to be very popular and it marked the appearance of an unusual Glasgow invention – the tea-room.

The main reason for the success of this new idea was that it fitted in with a new social trend. Towards the end of the 19th century Glasgow middle-class wives found themselves with enough leisure-time and money to make regular shopping trips to the growing number of departmental stores in the city centre. There was one problem, however – unaccompanied women were not expected to frequent the city's old-style, licensed eating-rooms. The tea-room turned out to be the ideal solution, for it provided a clean, unlicensed, attractive venue where any respectable leisured female could go without rousing comment (not openly publicised, it also offered pub-licly available ladies' loos), and tea-rooms began springing up all over the city centre.

Kate Cranston, a woman with a fine combination of creative and managerial skills, decided to follow her brother's example and in 1878 opened up in Argyle St the city's first proper tea-room, the forerunner of several more. She opened another in Ingram St in 1886 and then, in 1897, devoted an entire building in

Buchanan St to a tea-room. The exterior was 'Pont St Dutch' but the interior made use of the artistic talents of two important practitioners of the 'Glasgow Style' – George Walton (1867–1933) and Charles Rennie Mackintosh (1868–1928). Walton was responsible for the furniture and most of the fittings, while Mackintosh's most striking contribution was a stunning stencilled frieze of giant white-robed women surrounded by stylised organic decoration. Despite its unusual appearance, the style of the tea-room met with general approval, so much so that it rapidly became one of the city's 'sights'. It is not too much to say that Kate Cranston's successful commissioning of these two young artists strongly influenced their future careers. The unique style became so well known that it even had its own adjective (in Glasgow at least) – 'Kate Cranstonish'!

The success of the Buchanan St tea-room encouraged Kate Cranston to commission Walton and Mackintosh to refurbish her expanded Argyle St premises. Once again Walton took the main part, but it is interesting to note an early appearance here of the famous (or notorious) Mackintosh high-backed chair.

Her continuing faith and support for Mackintosh brought a commission in 1900 to him and his wife, Margaret Macdonald, to work together in designing a room in the Ingram St tea-room – no Walton this time. The result was the White Luncheon Room. Although Mackintosh had used white paint before, this was its first use in a public place. Other prominent features were his high-backed chairs and the use of square decorative motifs.

In 1903 the Willow Tea Rooms were opened in Sauchiehall St (the tea-room's name came from the Scottish 'saughy haugh', the bank of willows). This proved to be the highest expression of his work

for, and co-operation with, Kate Cranston. He was responsible for every detail, from the exterior of the building to the cutlery. Its supreme achievement was probably its Room de Luxe, with its long low street window, its walls lined with purple silk and its glittering chandelier of pink glass globes. This was Kate Cranston's last major commission for Mackintosh. In 1913 he left the partnership of Honeyman, Keppie and Mackintosh and went south to London.

It is instructive to follow the fate of their buildings. After the death of her husband in 1917 Kate Cranston began to dispose of her tea-rooms. The Argyle St and Buchanan St tea-rooms were taken over and reconstructed by a shoe shop (1918) and a bank respectively. The Ingram St tea-room had a chequered history. In 1930 it was taken over by Cooper & Co, who continued to run it as a tea-room till 1950 when the Glasgow Corporation bought it for £23,000. It was acquired by Reo Stakis, the catering entrepreneur; in 1971, despite considerable protest, it was completely dismantled.

Fate has been kinder to the Willow Tea Rooms. In 1919 they passed into the hands of John Smith Ltd, restaurateurs, who changed the name to the Kensington. The building was then sold to Daly's department store in 1927, who used it as part of the store but fortunately left much of the structure intact. When Daly's moved out, the new owner was given planning permission on condition that restoration work was undertaken. This was done and and it reopened as a tea-room in 1983.

Kate Cranston and her brother were the prime innovators in the development of the tea-room in the city, but they were followed and imitated by a host of competitors, all of them now nothing more than names. Two early concerns moved into tea-rooms from the old-style eating-house –

William Skinner (1835) and Walter Hubbard (1848). James Craig (*c*.1910) was probably Kate Cranston's nearest rival with his Gordon tea-room in Gordon St and his unusual habit of hanging his establishments with works of art. About the same time the City Bakeries, pioneers in centralised bakeries, supplied a network of tea-shops and bakers throughout the city. Other names were R. A. Peacock & Son, A. F. Reid and M. A. Brown (popularly known as 'Ma Brown'). One of the latter's shops in Sauchiehall St probably has the dismal distinction of being the city's last traditional tea-room, closing down in the 1990s. Wendy's (1931) represented a slightly alien strand with the twee Englishness of its name and its resolutely ruralised interiors. It had a few imitators (easily distinguished by their possessive female forenames) and closed in 1972.

Following the Second World War the great Glasgow tea-room succumbed to the interlocking forces of takeovers of family firms by national groups and the deprovincialising of eating habits. A good example of this process is the Charing Cross end of Sauchiehall St which has become a diner-out's ethnic paradise.

See also HOTELS

Telephone Service

The name and the date of the earliest telephone system in Glasgow is disputed. It is usually claimed that David Graham set up an exchange in March 1879, a date which would make it the earliest UK exchange. It was called the Medical Telephone Exchange and its intended users were doctors, hospitals and chemists working in the city. Its Douglas St address became the exchange name, DOUglas. Soon after setting up this specialist system Graham went on to establish similar systems for lawyers and for stockbrokers, with an exchange in St Vincent Place.

On the evidence of newspaper advertisements, however, it has been claimed that Graham's system was not in fact operational till May 1880. If this be so then the earliest Glasgow exchange would be the Telephone Co Ltd (sometimes called the Scottish Telephonic Exchange) which was in business in Queen St by November 1879.

The rivalry between competing systems now became intense. In 1880 the Edison Telephone Co had two exchanges operating, one at 13 Royal Exchange Square, the other in mansard accommodation on the roof of the Royal Exchange building. About the same time, the Bell Telephone Co set up in Queen St (establishing BEL1 as another Glasgow exchange). These two merged in May 1880.

Next, the countrywide National Telephone Co, formed from an amalgamation of many of its local rivals, was set up in May 1881, taking over the former Edison accommodation in the Royal Exchange in 1883. However, the National system was the subject of so many complaints (out of over 4,000 subscribers, more than half complained) that a government enquiry was set up in 1897. As a result of this, Glasgow Corporation started up its own, rival system, the Municipal Telephone System, with an exchange in Renfield St and some 5,000 subscribers. Then in 1906 the Corporation system was taken over by the Post Office, to be followed six years later by the takeover of the National.

In 1909 the city's exchanges included Crosshill, Royal, Argyle, Tron, Hillhead, Bell, Douglas, Partick, Charing Cross and Central, Glasgow's first automatic exchange was opened in 1938 at Cardonald, as HALfway. Many complaints were received from local subscribers not getting through – this was solved by pointing out that the new exchange was spelt HAL not HAF!

Tenements

In an attempt to tackle the deterioration of the inner-city housing stock, over 90,000 demolitions were carried out in the various Comprehensive Development Areas – many bad tenement buildings went, but also did some good ones. (George Oliver)

By the middle of the 19th century central Glasgow (apart from its public buildings) was a city of tenements, and from this period till the First World War, one building style, one type of material and one architectural mode predominated.

The origin of the tenement style of housing has been attributed to many things, from climate to value of building land. There is little doubt that only the tenement could have provided sufficient housing to keep pace with the enormous increase in the city's population up to 1914, and its ubiquitous nature made it seem to Glaswegians to be Nature's way of providing shelter.

The classic form is a building of normally four storeys (although this could vary from three to five) with stone walls about 2ft thick and a pitched slated roof with as many as 16 chimney-pots on each gable. Each vertical group of houses is entered direct from the street through a public close or corridor. Halfway through,

the close becomes a stair ascending in a series of dog-legs and a continuation going on through to a back-court or drying-green, while each main landing provides access to the front doors of two or three individual flats. There are several variations on this basic pattern. Sometimes the ground-floor flats have their own outside doors opening on to little strips of ground bounded by low stone walls, once crowned with cast-iron railings removed during the Second World War. Sometimes the back-court is at a lower level than the tenement and that part of the close leading to it descends by a flight of stairs and a lower close often lined with cellar doors. This arrangement is called a 'dunny' (presumably a corruption of 'dungeon') and was traditionally the area for inter-sex relationships.

The early working-class tenements had no internal WCs, their place being taken by earth closets in the back-courts. After 1892 the stair landing between storeys either had added to it or was built

Bellfield St, Camlachie, demonstrates several facets of Glasgow town life. The ruler-straight, massive lines of the tenements with their hundreds of chimneys represent the basic 19th and early 20th-century Glasgow; the ruinous middens and wash-houses in the decaying back-courts signify the end of a way of life; the utterly bare foreground is symptomatic of its deliberate destruction. The gable-end painting (one of many in the city), by John McColl, is one small effort to create a new city. (George Oliver)

The quintessential Glasgow cityscape – the over-powering solidity of its four-storeyed, smoke-blackened tenement buildings. (George Oliver)

so equipped with a communal WC. Later still, bathrooms and WCs were brought inside the flats. Most of the early tenements were either one room (single-end) or two (room and kitchen). Bed recesses or box beds were common in both rooms and a cold-water sink (or jawbox) would be located in front of the kitchen window.

The tenements were commonly built in the form of a hollow square and the internal space was used for drying-greens, each close having its own green fenced off from its neighbours. These large units were spaced out along the streets and formed long, homogenous vistas. The outcome was that Glasgow became the tenement city *par excellence*, the most populous, most densely packed and most proletarian of European cities.

Each back-green had its own wash-house with a wash boiler and a fireplace below it. The ritual of passing on the wash-house key was a serious rite and could give rise to acrimonious debate. Each back-court also contained an odorous brick structure sheltering a number of metal bins for domestic rubbish. Commonly referred to as

'midgies' (i.e. middens) they were regularly trawled by 'midgie-rakers'.

Until the middle of the 19th century the tenement served as a class marker, but thereafter the form managed to accommodate itself to a fairly wide range of lifestyles – from the labourer in his single-end to the doctor or lawyer in his six or seven-apartment flat with its maid's room. The first of these high-quality tenements probably appeared in Garnethill, a district just to the north of Sauchiehall St, and spread north-west to Hillhead and Great Western Rd as well as crossing the river to Govanhill and Shawlands. These middle-class tenements had several distinguishing features. Whereas the lower-class (and earlier) tenements were generally built with local greyish sandstone, these superior tenements were usually built with red sandstone from more distant quarries. They were also more often three storeys in height with only two flats to a landing. From as early as the 1830s they had included WCs, and bathrooms from the 1850s. Often they had superior ground-floor flats with larger garden strips, and frequently they had bowed or splayed windows rising one above the other. The most commonly accepted characteristic of a high-quality tenement, however, was the presence of a 'wally' close, meaning a close and stairway lined with decorative tiles; added value was provided by the presence of coloured glass in the stair windows and decorative stencils on the stair walls.

After the First World War almost no new tenements were constructed. The Corporation's interwar policy of huge housing schemes militated against any private house-building, and the labour costs of building in stone had become prohibitive.

Though many of the earliest tenements were jerry-built, many were built to last, and they formed the basic Glasgow townscape. Their indiscriminate demolition during the 1950s and 1960s largely removed a Glasgow which had been the norm for over 100 years. The eventual realisation of their real human qualities stopped their wholesale demolition and has left enough to adumbrate some of the effects of the old Victorian city.

Glasgow is fortunate in having an actual tenement house whose contents, furniture, fittings and personal items have been preserved more or less as they were just before the Second World War. Garnethill, a district built on one of the city's ubiquitous drumlins, runs parallel to, and north of Sauchiehall St. It was part of the Blythswood Estate and, as such, its street pattern was laid out on the same rigid grid-iron pattern as the rest of the estate. By 1842 its first tenements were appearing amongst the small villas and by the end of the century only a few gap-sites were left. On one of these sites in Buccleuch St, a seven-close tenement was completed in 1893. It was a red sandstone building of superior quality, and number 145 included a hall, bedroom, parlour, bathroom and kitchen. The last occupant of the house was Miss Agnes Toward who, as a young child, in 1911 had moved into it with her widowed mother. From then until 1975 the house and its contents remained virtually unchanged, apart from the installation of electric lighting – now replaced by the original gas-lighting. Visitors to the house, which was sold to the National Trust for Scotland in 1982, are able to see (and appreciate) the material surroundings in which, until the 1920s, most of Glasgow lived.

See also HOUSING

Glasgow's tenements were constructed in an extensive range of styles, from simple, unembellished, four-storey 'room-and-kitchens' in Dumbarton Rd, for example, to red sandstone middle-class dwellings in Maxwell Park. The latter were invariably described as 'wally' closes, descriptive of their tiled close walls. (George Oliver)

Tolbooth

A tolbooth is a very common feature in most historical Scottish burghs. Such a building served several important purposes. It was, first and foremost, the meeting place of the Town Council, in it was held the various courts of law, it served as a prison and it also functioned, as its name indicates, as the place where the local tolls, custom dues and taxes were collected and stored.

From time immemorial the Glasgow tolbooth has been located at the north-west corner formed by the north–south-running High St and Saltmarket and the east–west-running Gallowgate and Trongate. As early as the middle of the 15th century the city records tell of 'The heid covrt of the burcht and citie of Glasgow' being held in the

The Tolbooth Steeple, with the High St tramlines running in front of it. The men are consulting copies of the Voters' Roll.
(William Graham, Mitchell Library)

'Tolbuithe thairof'. Very little is known of this early structure other than that its street-level accommodation was occupied by booths or shops.

The first reliable date is March 1626 when the erection of a replacement building began. It was completed by September 1627 and was described by a Commonwealth visitor as 'a very sumptuous, regulated, uniform fabric, large and lofty, most industriously and artificially carved from the very foundation to the superstructure, to the great admiration of strangers, and is without exception the paragon of beauty in the West'. It was a five-storey edifice showing a frontage of about 65ft along the Trongate, with a 126ft crowned square tower at its east end, on the corner formed by the High St and the Trongate. From the ground up its five floors were occupied by the Town Clerk's office, the Justice Court hall, the Town Council hall, the Dean of Guild hall and, right at the top (for reasons of security) the prison.

A conspicuous feature of the Glasgow tolbooth was the 'Great Stair', a monumental double flight of stairs leading up from the street to the entrance to the Justiciary Hall. It was on the platform of this stair that the burgh's dignitaries would assemble on festive or ceremonial occasions, such as the King's Birthday. As a strongly Hanoverian city this event was always enthusiastically celebrated – the city's notables drank toasts standing on the platform and threw the glasses down to the townspeople assembled below.

In 1665 a set of chimes which had originally been intended for the steeple of the Merchants' Hall in the Briggait were tradition of musical bells which was to continue into the 20th century.

Towards the middle of the 18th century the site began to display a bewildering series of architectural changes. The accommodation of the old Tolbooth was becoming cramped and so, in 1735, the Town Council bought a piece of land immediately to the west of their building and on it built a new Town Hall which was opened in 1740. Its ground floor was an assembly room, the first floor was the Town Hall (communicating with the old Tolbooth by an internal door) and the second floor was occupied by three municipal chambers for clerks and committee meetings. The assembly room lay behind a broad piazza and the keystones of its five arches were each ornamented with grotesquely carved stone faces by the structure's builder, Mungo Naismith.

In 1781 a syndicate which had set up a Tontine in Glasgow took over the piazzaed building, erecting at its back an elaborate suite of rooms (of the same size and width as the front portion) to be used as hotel, coffee house, reading room, assembly room, bedroom annexe and stableyard. The syndicate also took over a small building which stood at the west end of the Town Hall and which contained the Old Assembly Rooms. They neatly extended the façade of the Town Hall building on to this addition and matched it with the existing architecture. In extending the arches they increased their number to ten and to match Mungo's five faces they employed an unknown carver to decorate the new arches with another five – from then on the group of faces was popularly known as the ten Tontine faces.

In 1795 the Court Hall of the old Tolbooth (which had never been adequate for its purpose) was deserted, and for a few years the Lords of Justiciary held court in a High St building immediately to the north of the Tolbooth tower, known for obvious reasons as the Justiciary Court Land. In 1814 they moved to new quarters at the foot of the Saltmarket.

Once again the conglomeration of buildings at the Cross was proving inadequate. Instead of tinkering further with the existing building it was decided to move out completely. So the jail, court house, council chambers, clerks' chambers and all the rest moved lock, stock and barrel down to a site at the foot of the Saltmarket. The new building, designed in the Doric style by William Stark, an Edinburgh architect, looked across what came to be called Jail Square to the west end of the Glasgow Green. It was completed in 1814 and the vacated Tolbooth was sold to Dr Cleland, City Chamberlain, for £8,000, with the express provision that he erect in its place a new building conforming to a design by David Hamilton, architect, which was in a style similar to the old Tolbooth. It is interesting to note, keeping in mind the city fathers' future behaviour regarding old buildings, that they agreed by 15 votes to 9 to preserve, support and repair the crowned tower of the old building.

Although as far as administrative purposes were concerned the Town Council had now left the Cross, the Tontine Hall, as it was now known, continued in use as a public room until 1854 when its last public function was a banquet on the occasion of the inauguration of the equestrian statue of Queen Victoria (now in George Square). Later, in 1874, it was incorporated fully into the Tontine building by the City Improvement Trust. The famous piazza and its arches (including the equally famous Faces) disappeared, to be replaced by the shopfront of Moore, Taggart & Co, drapery warehouse.

Tontine

In February 1781 a Tontine Society was inaugurated in Glasgow. Lorenzo Tonti, a Neapolitan, devised a scheme in France in 1689 which involved loans given towards life annuities with benefit of survivorship, i.e. each subscriber named a person during whose life he received a proportional share of the profits accruing to the society. When only one nominee was left alive his or her subscriber then became the owner of all the property owned by the society.

There were 107 subscribers to the Glasgow Tontine; the shares cost £50 and no subscriber could own more than two. Most subscribers nominated a young son or daughter. A merchant named Peter Murdoch, for instance, nominated two of his daughters, Isabella and Lillias. A few, probably unmarried or childless, nominated children of relatives or friends – James Oswald nominated his nephew, also James Oswald. Singularly, one Glasgow merchant, James Finlay (father of the well-known Kirkman Finlay), possibly on the basis that she would be well looked after, nominated 'Her Royal Highness Princess Sophia, daughter of his present Majesty George 3d'. A total of upwards of £5,000 was subscribed and the final outcome was that Miss Cecilia Douglas (who had been named by Alexander McCaul) was both the last nominee and the last subscriber and fell heir in 1861 to an estate worth £7,000. She died the following year aged 90.

In those days 'bricks and mortar' were considered to be the only sure source of continued profit and so the money subscribed to the Glasgow Tontine Society went towards purchasing the whole building at the Cross which lay to the west of the old Tolbooth (except for the Town Hall) and on this property the society constructed a large coffee-room, and above it the Tontine Hotel. The coffee-room (built from a design by William Hamilton, architect) was constructed behind the piazza which ran west from the old Tolbooth and which was extended from 11ft to 27ft. It measured 74ft by 32ft and was 16ft high, and at its northern end a door led into the Tontine Hotel. It was opened in May 1784 and until Glasgow's centre began to move westwards it played an important part in the business, commercial and social life of the city. It was extravagantly praised by local guide-books as 'the most elegant of its kind in Britain, and, perhaps in Europe' and for a subscription of little more than £1 its members had access to all the Scottish newspapers, many of the London ones and some others from Ireland, Germany and France, as well as to a range of magazines and journals. The hotel was the first of its kind in the city and so unused were the populace to the word 'hotel' that it was for some time called the 'Tontine Hottle'. The coffee-room eventually became a newsroom and exchange, but suffered in popularity when the new exchange opened in Royal Exchange Square in 1829. It lingered on for a few more years as a sort of reading room until it was added to the shop accommodation of Moore, Taggart & Co about 1868.

The society also took over the Assembly Room without payment, on condition that they would maintain it until a new Assembly Room should be built. This the society agreed to, and from 1783 to 1796 the Assembly Room (which communicated directly with the adjacent Town

Hall to the east and which measured 47ft by 24ft and 24ft high) was used exclusively for all of Glasgow's public occasions.

Six years after the Tontine property passed to Miss Douglas it was sold to the City Improvement Trust for £8,750.

Several other Glasgow buildings were financed on the Tontine principle. One was the Glasgow Assembly Rooms in Ingram St which were set up in 1796 with 274 shares of £25 each. The Glasgow Athenaeum, which had taken over the Assembly Rooms in 1874, profited to the extent of £6,500 when the Rooms were vacated to make way for the General Post Office, a profit which enabled it to build new premises in St George's Place (now Nelson Mandela Place).

Tontine Faces

The Glasgow Tontine Society used its members' subscription to erect a building next to the existing Town Hall (which lay to the west of the old Tolbooth at the Cross and which had been built in 1740). The latter was fronted by a broad piazza with five arches. On each of these arches the mason and builder Mungo Naismith had carved grotesque stone faces and it was said that each one represented a particular Glasgow personage. The Tontine's addition (erected *c*.1760) at the west end of the Town Hall building was designed as a perfect match for the existing Town Hall façade. So each of *its* five arches were similarly ornamented with fantastic stone faces, and the group of ten heads became known and appreciated as the Tontine Faces.

About 1867, Peter Shannan, a builder, converted the Tontine building into a drapery warehouse and shop for Moore, Taggart & Co, in the process removing the piazza, its arches and their faces. The faces disappeared from sight for a while but reappeared in 1870 when they were found in Shannan's builder's yard. Hugh Fraser, the well-known warehouseman, then acquired them and had them fixed to that part of his new warehouse (rebuilt *c*.1872 after a disastrous fire) which was located in the lane at 10 Buchanan St. It was said that two extra faces were placed beside the ten originals.

Their adventures were not over, however, for a disastrous fire in 1888 caused the wall to which they were attached to collapse thus destroying, so it was supposed, six of them – the saved faces being all from the western wing of the Tontine building. All but one of the group supposed to have been destroyed were in fact saved. One went to Barlanark House, and four were taken to 'Craigiehall', Bellahouston, the residence of Thomas Mason, of Morrison & Mason Ltd, building contractors (later Sir Thomas Mason, Lord Dean of Guild).

See also TOLBOOTH

Topography and Geology

Glasgow, latitude 55° 52′ North (slightly north of Moscow and of Edmonton in Canada), longitude 4° 15′ West, lies at the western end of Scotland's Midland Valley. A down-faulted rift, this valley is a major geological feature some 50 miles wide and 120 miles long, stretching from the Firth of Clyde to the Firths of Forth and Tay, and separating the Highlands from the Southern Uplands. Its underlying rocks are formed from old red sandstone and carboniferous sediments, with many intrusions of lava flows and dykes. These bedrocks are covered by extensive glacial and post-glacial deposits of sand, gravel and clay. Of no importance during most of the city's history, these rock formations were to provide the essential ingredients (in the shape of coal, ironstone and limestone) for its later industrial development.

Glasgow's position has been described as lying in a vast, horseshoe-shaped howe or open space, hemmed in on the north, west and south by the bleak plateaux of weather-resistant lavas – the Campsie Fells, the Kilpatrick Hills and the Beith and Renfrewshire Hills – and open only to the east. The Clyde flows through this howe, the only major Scottish river to flow west into the Atlantic. Various land movements, caused by several glaciations, altered the level and course of the Clyde several times, and between Glasgow and Dumbarton its drowned channel is more than 200ft below sea-level. It has been the city's great good fortune that the river now flows through friable sand and gravel (and not the rock of its original channel) otherwise its artificial deepening, on which the city's prosperity has depended, would have been impossible.

The material left behind in the valley by the retreating glaciers – sand, gravel and clay – is the ground surface on which the city has been built. The disappearance of the glaciers left a prominent feature of the city's landscape in the form of its swarm of some 180 drumlins. These are hummocks or small hills which rise fairly abruptly from the plain – pearshaped, with their longer axis aligned with the direction of the glacier flow. Most of Glasgow's drumlins lie west of the cathedral (the eminence of the Necropolis, just east of the cathedral, is not a drumlin) and the most prominent include Garngad Hill (252ft), Partick Hill (179ft), Garnethill (176ft), Hillhead (157ft), Woodlands Hill (153ft) and Blythswood Hill (135ft). One singularity of the city's layout has been the imposition of a strict gridiron configuration on top of these eminences.

The alteration in sea-levels created raised beaches in many parts of Scotland, the highest being the '100ft' and an extensive intermediary being the '25ft' or 'Neolithic'. Both of these were important in the city's early development. Most of old Glasgow lies on a northern terrace of the '25ft', just above the flood-plain of the river, and its early northern limits were traced by the edges of the '100ft' beach.

At the beginning of the recorded history of the howe, five sites had established themselves within its shelter – on the south bank of the Clyde lay Rutherglen, Govan, Paisley and Renfrew, on the north, Glasgow. Two features connected with the topography of the area singled out the latter. First, it was the furthest upriver point at which the Clyde was fordable at all times, and second, it was the lowest downriver point at which it could be bridged. The city was thus located at a communication nodal point where the main lines of east–west and north–south traffic crossed. A third reason, much more imponderable than these two, was that the settlement possessed the burial-place of a holy man, St Kentigern, and even more important, that a cathedral came to be built around it.

Tramcars

In 1870 a General Tramways Bill was put before Parliament for the first time. Glasgow, as befitted the second city of the Empire, was amongst the first of the British cities to avail itself of new powers and had its own private Tramways Act passed on 10 August of that same year. Under this Act, after the Glasgow Tramway and Omnibus Co Ltd (a union of two rival groups) was set up, the Corporation then, under an 1871 agreement, built the necessary trackway by raising capital on the security of the Common Good Fund and leased it out to the Company for 23 years (to 1 July 1894). The Company agreed to pay the interest on the costs and all expenses connected with the undertaking, as well as 3 per cent per annum on the gross sum expended on capital account. In addition the company was required to hand over the tramways and the roadway between the lines in good condition at the end of the lease and to pay £150 a year for every mile of rail used for traffic.

Under the able management of Andrew Menzies (who had already made his name by successfully inaugurating a fleet of horse omnibuses in 1845) Glasgow's first trams were up and running on 19 August 1872. The first service was between St George's Cross and Eglinton Toll, and other sections quickly followed: Cambridge St/Royal Crescent; Bridgeton Cross/Candleriggs; Bridge St/Paisley Road Toll; Whiteinch/Royal Crescent; Whiteinch/Bridgeton Cross; St Vincent St/Dennistoun; Great Hamilton St/Camlachie Burn; New City Road/Sauchiehall St; Bridgeton Cross/London Rd; Eglinton Toll/Crosshill.

In 1887, despite the apparently onerous terms of the agreement, the Company asked for its lease to be extended another ten years. It believed, quite wrongly, that the operating Act did not permit the Town Council to run its own tramway system and that the Company could therefore bluff it into giving way. But the Council took legal advice, and changed its mind about the now obvious attractions of a tramway system. It began a campaign designed to return the system to the Corporation. Two municipal elections showed a strong popular demand for the municipality to take over the trams, and in 1891 the Corporation voted to do just that. Understandably, its attitude aroused much ill-feeling in the Company, and when it became clear that the Corporation intended to go ahead with the take-over, the former refused to hand over anything but the Corporation's own tramway lines! Thus the city fathers had to create a new fleet of cars, plant, stables, horses, and so on.

On Sunday, 30 June 1894, Glasgow Corporation became the first British municipality to own and operate its own public transport system. The new management had under its control 384 horse-drawn cars, 3,000 horses, nine depots and 31 miles of track. To the general surprise of everyone the change-over took place without a hitch, and Glasgow Corporation Tramways entered into a stewardship which was to go from success to success. During its first year of municipal operation the system carried 57 million passengers a total distance of over 5 million miles.

Glasgow is built on a series of drumlins or little hills, and it was early realised that horse traction, even along rails, could never cope with these conditions and that it was essential to introduce as soon as possible some form of mechanical traction. Many different motive systems were investigated, among them steam, third rail electric, continuous cable hauling, etc. By 1889 around 200 systems of overhead electric traction existed in the USA, demonstrating the viability of that method and it was this system which Glasgow adopted in 1897, when an experimental line running up and down the steep slope from Mitchell Street to Springburn was inaugurated. Its success signalled the change-over of the entire system to electric traction, the first regular route being introduced in time for the opening of the International Exhibition at Kelvingrove in May 1901. With the construction of a fleet of 500 double-decker 'Standard' tramcars between 1898 and 1902, Glasgow's public transport entered its golden age and, for over half a century, these vehicles' characteristic shape, colour, noise and smell became as familiar to Glaswegians as their living-room furniture.

Glasgow's tramway system was never particularly innovative. What it did have were managers who knew how to manage and a trained workforce capable of maintaining and operating a superb set of vehicles. It set a standard soon after taking over by instituting a ½d. fare, which accounted for 40 per cent of all fares and bred a race of passengers who could board and leave a moving tramcar from almost any position!

Slight indications of future discords began to show, however. There was considerable debate about whether there were any benefits in extending the service outwith the city boundaries, for example – by 1899 the system was running trams to Paisley, Cathcart, Rutherglen, Tollcross, Renfrew, Clydebank, Bishopbriggs and Cambuslang, and eventually it was possible (if not actually desirable) to travel all the way from Airdrie to Paisley for 2d. It was claimed that many of these more rural areas were being provided with a cheap service by subsidies from the fares paid by the city-dwellers. Another threat – the introduction of buses – was mooted as early as 1912.

The solidarity and comradeship which existed amongst tramway employees, and the paternalistic outlook of the manager, James Dalrymple, received a rueful confirmation early in the First World War when an entire HLI (Highland Light Infantry) battalion of over 1,000 volunteers was recruited from the workforce in 24 hours. Even wartime conditions could not affect the earning capacity of the tramways, however, and in 1917 the entire debt of the undertaking was cleared.

It has been Glasgow's strange fate to be saved, in industrial terms, by two World Wars and to experience hard times following each one. The tramways, unfortunately, shared this experience, and it could be said that their decline began almost immediately after the first conflict. In 1920, for the first time, its trading account showed a loss, as the first of many fare increases abolished the famous ½d. charge. The beginning of the end loomed as the Corporation introduced the first of its bus services; 1926 was probably the year of crisis. The General Strike, here as elsewhere a watershed, brought a new problem – labour trouble. After it was over James Dalrymple, refusing to carry out the instructions of his Committee to take back into employment a group of workers who had been on strike, resigned and went off to run trams in São Paulo.

Throughout the 1920s a phenomenon only too familiar nowadays began to show itself in earnest for the first time, namely the slow but irreversible escalation of fares. Questions also began to be asked about the age of the vehicles. Many of them were 20 or 25 years old. Despite frequent alterations and additions they were in no way examples of modern tramway vehicles. Particularly significant was the fact that the huge new housing schemes, which were springing up all around the city in the 1920s and 1930s, were being serviced by buses – the prohibitive cost of equipping them for tram services made this inevitable. Another foreboding event was the very first indication of the network contracting, when, in 1932, the tram service between Elderslie and Kilbarchan was abandoned to a bus service. It was becoming obvious that the tram's inflexibility compared with the bus could in no way be overcome. The growing numbers of motor vehicles in the city streets, both for private and commercial purposes, found themselves increasingly limited to single-line traffic by long strings of tramcars filling the centre of the road, and motorists were frequently brought to a standstill by intending tramcar passengers crossing from the pavement to the road centre.

Despite all these gloomy omens there was some sign of growth and change. Services were extended to Milngavie and to the west of Anniesland. Just as the 1901 International Exhibition had been the occasion for the introduction of electric traction, the 1938 Empire Exhibition made famous the 'Coronation' trams. Taking their name from the coronation of George VI, their streamlined appearance, remote-control equipment, separate enclosed driver's cab, and folding doors brought the city's tramcars belatedly but effectively into the 20th century. Another 'redding-up' was the abandonment of the 'coloured' routes, for so long a familiar part of the Glasgow street-scene, and their replacement by the more prosaic (but more practical) numbered routes.

Just before the outbreak of the Second World War these numbered routes were as follows:

1	Knightswood or Kelvinside/Airdrie
1A	Dalmuir West or Scotstounhill/ Springfield Rd
2	Provanmill/Polmadie
3	University/Mosspark (via Eglinton St)
3A	University/Mosspark (via Paisley Road West)
4	Keppochhill Rd/Renfrew
4A	Springburn/Linthouse
4B	Lambhill/Linthouse
5	Clarkston/Kirklee
5A	Langside/Jordanhill
6	Riddrie or Alexandra Park/Scotstoun or Dalmuir West
7	Millerston or Riddrie/Craigton Rd
8	Bishopbriggs (or Springburn) or Millerston (or Riddric or Alcxandra Park)/Newlands, Giffnock/Rouken Glen
8A	as 8, to Pollokshaws West, Thornliebank/Rouken Glen
8B	as 8, to Merrylee
9	Dalmuir West/London Rd or Auchenshuggle
9A	Dalmuir West/Scotstoun, Burnside
9B	Dalmuir West/Scotstoun, Rutherglen
10	Rutherglen/Kirklee
11	Maryhill or Gairbraid Ave/Sinclair Dr
12	Mount Florida/Paisley Road Toll
13	Mount Florida/Hillfoot or Milngavie
14	Milngavie, Hillfoot or Maryhill/Renfrew Ferry

15   Airdrie/Paisley (Ferguslie Mills)
15A Uddingston or Tollcross/Paisley
     (Ferguslie Mills)
16   Whiteinch/Keppochhill Rd
17   Cambuslang/Anniesland
18   Springburn/Rutherglen or Burnside
19   Springburn/Netherlee
20   Yoker or Clydebank/Duntocher
21   Provanmill/Crookston.

In 1948 the system reached its maximum strength, with over 1,000 cars in use. After this peak the descent was swift. By 1952 some 85 per cent of the trams were 35 years old (some even older), and services now began to be withdrawn. In 1956 services to Barrhead, Airdrie, Cambuslang and Milngavie were taken off, while the following year the Paisley area was abandoned. In 1958 the last trams ran to Govan and Mount Florida, and in 1959 Millerston, Bishopbriggs and Rouken Glen lost their trams. Then, in 1960, trams ceased to run along Great Western Road, and Rutherglen, Springburn and Maryhill became tramless in 1961.

At one time it had been thought that the trams would last until 1970, but by 1962 the three remaining services were withdrawn: 9 – Auchenshuggle (a name often thought, wrongly, to be fictitious!)/Dalmuir West; 15 – Anderston Cross/Baillieston, and 26 – Burnside or Rutherglen/Scotstoun. A long parade of old and new tramcars was held on 4 September 1962, when a crowd of 230,000 people turned out in the rain to say a last farewell to a transport legend.

List of the service at its height, January 1949

1   Dennistoun and Dalmuir West
2   Polmadie and Provanmill
3   Mosspark and University
4   Renfrew South and Keppochhill Rd
5   Clarkston and Kelvinside via Botanic
     Gardens
5A   Clarkston and Kelvinside via
     Hyndland
6   Riddrie and Scotstoun
7   Millerston and Bellahouston
8   Millerston and Rouken Glen
     (returning as Route 25)
9   Carmyle or Auchenshuggle and
     Dalmuir West
10   Rutherglen and Kelvinside
11   Sinclair Dr and Milngavie
12   Mount Florida and Linthouse
13   Mount Florida and Milngavie
14   Spiersbridge and University
14A Spiersbridge and Kelvinside
14B Carnwardric and Castle St
15   Airdrie and Anderston Cross
16   Scotstoun and Keppochhill Rd
17   Cambuslang and Whiteinch
18   Burnside and Springburn
19   Netherlee and Springburn
20   Clydebank and Duntocher
21   Elderslie and Anniesland
22   Crookston and Lambhill
23   Airdrie and Gairbraid Ave
24   Langside and Anniesland
25   Bishopbriggs and Rouken Glen
     (returning as Route 8)
26   Burnside and Dalmuir West
27   Renfrew Cross and Springburn
28   Renfrew Ferry and Spiersbridge
29   Broomhouse and Anderston Cross
30   Cambuslang and Blairdardie
31   Carnwadric and Lambhill
32   Elderslie and Provanmill
33   Springburn Circular via Springburn
     Rd, Sauchiehall St, Charing Cross
     and St George's Rd
34   Parkhead and Bridgeton Cross
     Circular
35   Dennistoun and Bridgeton Cross
36   Kelvinside Circular via Charing
     Cross, Bothwell St, Argyle St,
     Bridgeton Cross, Springfield Rd,
     Parkhead, Gallowgate, Bothwell St
     and Kelvinside

TRAMCAR TYPES

(1) Electrified Ex-Horse Cars
Around 1900 the rapid electrification caused a shortage of cars and 120 of the

horse-drawn cars were converted to electric propulsion. Many of them remained in service until 1923.

(2) 'Room and Kitchen' Cars

These were single-deckers built to negotiate low railway bridges. Their name came from the two sections (front and rear) with an entrance in the middle. They were also known as 'But and Bens'. Twenty-one of them were built at the Coplawhill Works. They were soon withdrawn, due to faulty design.

(3) Standard Car

The most famous of all designs, this type was first built in 1898. Many alterations and developments took place over the years. Four main designs can be distinguished:

(i)   Top deck unroofed
(ii) Top deck covered (1904–10)
(iii) Stair covered – over 1,000 built (1910–24)
(iv) Totally enclosed – the 'Standard' *par excellence*

(4) 'Coronation' Car

Early prototypes were developed in 1936.

(5) Ex-Liverpool 'Green Goddess' Car

Beginning in 1953, some 47 Liverpool tramcars were purchased by Glasgow at a cost of £500 each. They were longer than the Glasgow car and so were restricted to certain routes.

PRESERVED GLASGOW TRAMCARS

Glasgow Museum of Transport	7 cars
National Tramway Museum, Crich, Derbyshire	7 cars
Paris Transport Museum	1 car
Science Museum, South Kensington, London	1 car
Seashore Trolley Museum, Kennebunkport, Maine, USA	1 car
East Anglia Transport Museum, Lowestoft, Suffolk	1 car

Trolley-Buses

In April 1949 Glasgow became the last British city to adopt trolley-buses, and at its peak, in 1959, the service had 194 vehicles serving eight routes. The attraction of the trolley-bus was its combination of the immediate power of the tram with the manoeuvrability of the bus; it drew its power from overhead electric cables (like the tramcar) and could move freely across traffic lanes (like the bus), and great things were expected of the new service.

In 1954 the Corporation decided to stop any further expansion of its tram service, depending for future public transport on buses and trolleys. Out of ten tram routes discontinued at this time two were taken over by trolleys, both in the east end of the city.

For whatever reason they made no great impact on the travelling public. Almost their only claim to fame was their nickname – 'Silent Death' – given to them because of their ability to creep up soundlessly behind wandering pedestrians.

In February 1958 the Corporation decided to transfer its Pinkston Power Station (which had supplied power to its trams and trolleys) to the recently nationalised South of Scotland Electricity Board, a move which signalled the end of both the trams and the trolleys. By 1962 the latter had accumulated a large working deficit, partly due to changes in social patterns (shorter working hours, television, private cars) but also to the fact that its power costs were now greater than buses, and in May 1967 the last Glasgow trolley-bus journey was made.

Tunnels

Until the 1920s the Jamaica St (or Glasgow) Bridge was the furthest downriver crossing of the Clyde, apart from ferries. Attempts to bridge the river further downstream were always opposed on the grounds that the river traffic would be obstructed, so in 1890 the Glasgow Harbour Tunnel Co began excavating. When opened in 1895, the Harbour Tunnel ran south from Tunnel St in Finnieston under the river to Mavisbank Quay in Govan. Two rotundas on either bank marked the ends of the tunnel and from them vertical shafts 80ft in diameter gave access to three parallel tunnels each 16ft in diameter – two for north and south vehicular traffic and one for pedestrians. Access for carts was by hydraulic lifts, and for pedestrians by stairs. It was never a financial success; by 1897 the company was bankrupt and the tunnel closed. In 1913 the Corporation took it over and reopened it – free of charge – and in 1926 bought out the company for £100,000. By the 1930s pedestrians no longer had access to their own tunnel, and had to use the vehicular tunnels. In 1943 the lift machinery was removed, leaving pedestrians as the sole users till 1980. The vehicle tunnels were sealed off in 1986 and the access shafts filled in. For a while in the 1990s the north rotunda became a restaurant, and during the Glasgow Garden Festival of 1988 the southern one was transformed into a Dome of Discovery, a hands-on exhibition of science.

The problem of cross-river communication further downstream was greatly eased by the construction of a tunnel which took the west flank of the Outer Ring Road under the Clyde. In 1948 a parliamentary order gave permission for its construction but financial restrictions delayed its start till 1957 – the final estimate of costs was well over £10 million. Connecting Linthouse in Govan with Dumbarton Rd at Whiteinch, its two vehicular tunnels are 29ft in diameter with a minimum distance between tunnel top and river-bed of about 20ft. Construction progress was delayed by a year because of the difficult strata through which the tunnels were driven, ranging from hard rock to fine silt. Each carriageway is 22ft wide and accommodates two traffic lanes; the steepest gradient is 1 in 16. A bicycle and pedestrian tunnel runs below the vehicular tunnels. The west tunnel was opened by Queen Elizabeth in 1963 and the east tunnel the following year by Peter Meldrum, the Lord Provost.

The south approach road system was completed in 1967, the north in 1969. It was estimated that 9,000 vehicles would use it per day; early use had 22,000 in one tunnel alone.

Universities

Glasgow University, c.1672. Its two quadrangles are visible in this bird's-eye view, with the university's physics garden in the background. On the right is Blackfriars Church which at one time belonged to the university. The ornamental doorway in the High St was transferred stone by stone to the new site at Gilmorehill, to become the Pearce Lodge. (J. Slezer, Theatrum Scotiae, *1693, Mitchell Library)*

UNIVERSITY OF GLASGOW

The University of Glasgow was established by a papal bull granted by Pope Nicholas V to William Turnbull, Bishop of Glasgow, on 7 January 1451. What reasons may have moved Nicholas are, of course, unknown, but two which may have moved William can be guessed at. There was strong rivalry between the Sees of St Andrews and Glasgow, and as the former had managed to set up a university in 1411, Bishop William probably could see no good reason why Glasgow should not have its own university. Also a supply of trained and educated clergy must have been required to administer to the spiritual and temporal affairs of the extensive Glasgow see. The new University's members were divided into four nations – Clydesdale, Teviotdale, Albany and Rothesay (now Glottiana, Laudoniana, Transforthana and Rothesay) – and the principal control was put into the hands of a rector who was elected, even if somewhat indirectly, by the nations.

The University's dependence on the Cathedral is shown by its early meeting places – the Cathedral chapter-house and the altar of St Nicholas in the crypt. From its inception it was dogged by insufficient finances, and so instead of the usual four faculties – Arts, Theology, Medicine and Law – only that of Arts was set up.

As the influence and power of the Church waned and the dominance of the Faculty of Arts increased the need became apparent for closer control of the students; most entered the University at a very early age (between 13 and 15 years of age), and must have needed a fair amount of supervision. So there was founded a college or pedagogy which brought all the University members together in a common body. For a time it occupied a building in the Rottenrow which was known in later years as the Auld Pedagogy, but as early as 1453 the schools were apparently housed in a tenement on the east side of the High Street, a site which the College was to continue to occupy until 1870. In 1577 a new constitution, the Nova Erectio, put the College on a basis which was to endure with little change until 1858.

After two centuries the old college buildings must have been badly in need of replacement, and in 1631 a public subscription towards the expense of new buildings was opened. This was generously supported by the nobility and gentry, the clergy, University members, the merchants of the city and others. These others included Charles I, who entered his name for £100 sterling. It is no doubt in keeping with the characters of the two men that the king's entry is followed, after a lapse of some years, by one which reads: 'This soume was payed by the Lord Protector anno 1654'!

By 1661 most of the new college had been completed. It consisted of an Inner and an Outer Quadrangle. The west side fronted on to the High Street, while to the east the ground, pleasantly laid out, sloped down to the little Molendinar Burn and then up to the top of the Dowhill. It was this group of buildings which formed the 'Old College', familiar to so many students, visitors and travellers, and for long one of the chief ornaments of the city. Over the years other buildings were added: a Professors' Court (1722–80), a separate library (1732), the Macfarlane Observatory (1757) and a museum for the collection of the eminent surgeon, William Hunter (1804).

The teaching capacity of the University increased greatly during the early years of the 18th century. It now had about 400 students and one reason for this increase was that it had begun to enrol some students from England and even more from Ireland, for in these countries all but episcopalians were barred from the universities. Seven new Chairs were founded, the Faculty of Arts was reorganised and improved, and a beginning was made with Faculties of Law and Medicine. The University's function was no longer limited to preparing young men for the Ministry; it was now beginning to equip its alumni for a much wider range of liberal professions.

In 1727 wide-ranging reforms helped to usher in one of the most brilliant periods of the University's history. Many distinguished figures were associated with it at this time but perhaps three can be singled out as of particular importance and influence.

It was during this period that the University began to enter into the secular life of the community. Glasgow was an intensely 'clubbable' society. There were literally scores of clubs whose members dined, drank and discussed in every tavern of the city, and the presence in them of senior members of the University helped to bring professors and citizens together in fruitful intimacy. One such occasion was when Adam Smith, the University's Professor of Logic (1751–52) and Professor of Moral Philosophy (1752–54) became a member of a merchants' club begun by Andrew Cochrane, the Lord Provost. There can be little doubt that it was here that Smith acquired the detailed information on trade and commerce which helped to make his *The Wealth of Nations* the major work on *laissez-faire* economics.

Another intellectual light of the University was Joseph Black, lecturer in Chemistry and Professor of Medicine (1757–66). His classic experiments showing that air could be combined with and removed from solids laid to rest the ghost of the 'phlogiston' theory of heat. He also enunciated the concept of latent heat, of great general importance but also a fruitful idea in the development of his technical friend James Watt's steam-engine.

Thomas Reid, Professor of Moral Philosophy (1764–96), was an early and powerful exponent of the so-called 'philosophy of common-sense', which attacked the sceptical ideas of David Hume and exercised a profound effect on 20th-century British philosophy.

In 1858 a Royal Commission was appointed to reform all the Scottish universities. Although Glasgow's position was comparatively sound, the Commissioners undertook to do away with the hitherto entrenched positions of the 13 professors whose chairs were founded before 1800. They represented the College, and the powers they exercised often conflicted with those of the Senate. The principal changes were the creation of two new bodies, a General Council which represented the graduates and a University Court to supervise the financial administration of the University, leaving the teaching and discipline to a Senatus composed of all the professors. To act as a watch-dog of the new University there was created a Rector chosen by the students, and a Chancellor chosen by the graduates. With the adoption of the Constitution as set up by the 1858 Commissioners it can be said that the modern University had come into being.

The steady increase in the number of students seeking admission was only serving to emphasise the grave inconveniences of the old College, however – its limited accommodation and its crumbling walls. In addition, the city's impetuous and irresistible industrialisation and the concomitant slums were beginning to engulf the centuries-old buildings in filth and misery, while the garden walks and grassy slopes behind them were becoming increasingly 'darkened by smoke and polluted by chemical and other manufactories'. Not often were the Victorians (and certainly not those in Glasgow) 'sicklied o'er with the pale cast of thought', but a proposal in 1864 that the High Street site should be taken over by a railway company and the University moved to the west end was turned down. That same year a somewhat similar offer made by the City of Glasgow Union Railway Company was quickly accepted; their entry on to the site was only to be delayed until a new building could be erected on the heights of Gilmorehill, above the valley of the Kelvin in the city's west end.

With the advantage of hindsight this move can be criticised, for it brought about the total destruction of one of the city's most famous architectural and historical edifices. At the time, however, little regret was expressed – indeed there was little choice. The architect of the new University was George Gilbert Scott and the style he chose can best be explained in his own words: 'I adopted a style which I may call my own invention . . . It is simply a 13th or 14th-century secular style with the addition of certain Scottish features peculiar in that country to the 16th century.' This was all to the extreme displeasure of the city's own architect, Alexander 'Greek' Thomson, who particularly disliked all Gothic architecture. There is no evidence that Thomson ever submitted a design for the new building. The work went on apace but the surrender date came with the new University building still incomplete. Nevertheless, the inauguration took place on 7 November 1870, leaving the august halls to become a railway station – perhaps it was a sly joke on the part of the Union Railway to name it the 'College' Goods Station.

Two reminders of the Old College became parts of the new one. A famous staircase decorated with heraldic beasts – the Unicorns for Scotland and the Lion for England – was brought from the High Street building and now joined the College Buildings to the Professors' Court. And in 1888 the generosity of Sir William Pearce, a Clydeside shipbuilder, enabled a part of the main entrance of the old building to be re-erected as the Pearce Lodge at the northeast corner of the new site.

By degrees other now familiar features appeared. In 1882 the Bute Hall and the Randolph Hall completed the two quadrangles, and in 1888 the building acquired its characteristic spire and its clock. One necessary adjunct was not ready until 1874. The Royal Infirmary, which had stood close by the Old College, had for long served the University's medical school as a teaching hospital. Now three miles distant, a new hospital, the Western

Infirmary, began to rise on ground immediately adjacent to the west end of the University. It was opened in 1874.

Not long after the move the University was once again involved in constitutional discussions brought about by the setting up of the 1876 Royal Commission. The resulting Act (1889) is largely the basis of the modern University's constitution. The most important outcome for Glasgow was the great increase in the size and power of the University Court. It was now to manage all the University's property and revenue, and to appoint chairs as well as lecturers, assistants and examiners. One new feature was that the community of Glasgow was given a voice in University affairs by the inclusion of the Lord Provost.

In the session 1892–93 women students were allowed to matriculate for the first time – 131 of them that winter session. The beginnings of higher education for women had begun about 1867 when Mrs Campbell of Tullichewan persuaded some of the professors to give short lectures to ladies, in natural history, moral philosophy, English literature and astronomy. Ten years later the movement took practical shape by the formation of the Glasgow Association for the Higher Education of Women. Once again, similar courses of lectures were given along with tutorials in Latin, mathematics and the theory of music, and in 1883 the Association was incorporated under the name of the Queen Margaret College, after the saintly wife of King Malcolm Canmore. It established itself in North Park House (built for John Bell of Bell's Pottery, well known for his distaste for women) on the banks of the Kelvin near the Botanic Gardens. Eventually, the College buildings became too small for teaching purposes, and in 1935 they were sold to the BBC and now form the nucleus of BBC Scotland.

The outbreak of war in 1914 arrested all development and student numbers dwindled; compared to the 2,000 students in 1900, there were only 1,600 by 1916, most of whom were women. The post-war period, despite the depression, brought new developments, however: a Student Welfare Committee was formed which resulted in a new Union building; well-to-do, public-spirited citizens endowed 16 Chairs in a space of ten years as well as a number of lectureships; houses were given to be used as halls of residence and scholarships were endowed. Despite this increase in halls of residence Glasgow University, drawing as it does a large percentage of its students from the surrounding counties, has never developed a true collegiate life, but the increase at this time in the number of student societies (well over 70) did something to fill this want.

It was apparent now that there were many more non-professorial teachers than professors and yet they had no share in the academic councils, so in 1922 an Act was obtained which admitted lecturers or readers to the Senatus Academicus.

Once again the University's work was disrupted by war, and from 1939 to 1940 a depleted staff carried on as best it could – the problems were if anything greater than during the First World War for student numbers then did not fall to the same extent. Peace brought a large increase as students returned from the services, and by 1948 the student population had reached 7,496. A post-war building programme helped to accommodate most of this increase and many new Chairs were added, from Agriculture to Veterinary Medicine, and new departments such as History of Fine Art and Soviet Studies. One important piece of legislation initiated by the four ancient Scottish universities in 1966 has given the University a much greater degree of flexibility in establishing new degrees (such as M.Eng, M.Theol., B.Acc., and M. Phil.) and has increased the representation of non-professorial staff on the Senate.

Chairs (to 1934)

1637	Medicine
1640	Theology
1682	Humanity
1691	Mathematics
1704	Greek
1709	Oriental Languages (Hebrew and Semitic Languages)
1712	Law
1716	Ecclesiastical History
1718	Anatomy
1727	Logic
1727	Moral Philosophy
1727	Natural Philosophy (Physics)
1760	Astronomy
1815	Surgery
1815	Midwifery
1817	Chemistry
1818	Botany
1831	Materia Medica
1839	Forensic Medicine
1839	Physiology
1840	Civil Engineering
1861	Conveyancing
1861	Divinity and Biblical Criticism
1861	English Language and Literature
1874	Clinical Medicine
1874	Clinical Surgery
1883	Naval Architecture
1893	History
1893	Pathology
1896	Political Economy
1907	Mining
1923	Public Health
1934	New Testament Language and Literature (abolished 1947)
1934	Christian Ethics (abolished 1946)
1934	Systematic Theology

GLASGOW CALEDONIAN UNIVERSITY

In 1971 the Glasgow College of Technology was founded as the Scottish equivalent of the polytechnics in England and Wales, soon becoming one of the largest institutions of Higher Education in Scotland. It cost between four and five million pounds, was the first Scottish 'polytechnic' to be funded by a local authority, and helped to fill the gap created when the Royal College of Science and Technology became Strathclyde University.

In 1988 it changed its name to the Glasgow College (with the subtitle, 'or Scottish Polytechnic'). It now had about 7,000 students in three faculties – Business and Adminstrative Studies; Life and Social Sciences; Science, Engineering and Construction.

To celebrate its 20th anniversary it metamorphosed into the Glasgow Polytechnic, to take advantage of government funding which was available only to designated universities or polytechnics. Its roll was now 7,300.

Finally, in 1993, it was apotheosised into the Glasgow Caledonian University, becoming the city's third university, after Glasgow and Strathclyde.

UNIVERSITY OF STRATHCLYDE

John Anderson (1726–96) was Professor of Natural Philosophy (i.e. Physics) at Glasgow University from 1757 until his death. He held views unusual for a professor of the time (his nickname was – 'Jolly Jack Phosphorus'), and he was particularly interested in the application of theory to practical ends – he erected in the University steeple Glasgow's first lightning conductor and was instrumental in setting James Watt to work on the University's model Newcomen engine. Besides giving regular lectures he also set up courses in which the emphasis was on the practical application of science, courses which attracted many non-students, including working-men. This attitude, so much at variance with that of his fellow professors, did not meet with the approval of the University authorities and he was constantly engaged in altercations and disputes, many of which led to acrimonious lawsuits.

His will (May 1795) set out in meticulous detail how his estate was to be used to set up what he designated as Anderson's University, an institution which he intended to be 'for the good of mankind and the improvement of science'. It was to be managed by 81 trustees (ranging from artisans and farmers to lawyers and divines) and was to be divided into four faculties, Arts, Law, Medicine and Divinity. Whether his elaborate system would have proved practicable was never established for it turned out that his property was quite insufficient to finance his grandiose scheme. However, his trustees managed to raise enough money and something like his University was constituted in June 1796. It was decided to start on a small scale, limiting the teaching to natural philosophy and chemistry. The fledgling University's first professor was Dr Thomas Garnett, an Edinburgh graduate, and although he left after only three years he did much to establish the reputation of Anderson's Institution (as it now called itself) for practical science.

Its early meetings were held in the old Grammar School buildings in George St, a site which still forms part of the University's extensive campus. It later moved to its own premises in John St. The interests of several of the early professors lay in the field of chemistry and under them the 'Andersonian' became one of the most famous schools of chemistry in the country.

In 1799 a Medical School was formed. (In 1887 it was detached from the 'Andersonian' and established as the independent Anderson College of Medicine. In 1947, under the National Health Act, it was absorbed into the Medical School of Glasgow University.) At the beginning of the next century Chairs of mathematics and botany were established.

In 1823 some students attending the classes for mechanics broke away from the Andersonian and set up the Glasgow Mechanics' Institution – opened in November 1832. Some time later it took the name of the College of Science and Arts; in 1861 another institution for the instruction of artisans was set up under the will of Thomas Atkinson, bookseller and stationer in Glasgow, known as the Atkinson Institution.

In 1828 Anderson's Institution moved back to the buildings in George St and resumed the name of Anderson's University. During the 19th century many eminent scientists occupied its Chairs, including Thomas Graham (1805–69), chemist, physicist and Master of the Mint (one of his pupils was David Livingston), and James Croll (1821–90), geologist. Amongst the additional Chairs founded around this time, the most important was the Young Chair of Technical Chemistry, founded and endowed in 1870 by James Young (1811–83), who established the shale oil industry in Scotland.

Once again, in 1877, the Andersonian changed its name, this time to Anderson's College. A fifth change took place in 1886 when the Commissioners appointed under the Educational Endowments Act (1882) to reorganise the educational trusts of Scotland, decided that Glasgow, as a recognised centre of commerce and manufacture, ought to have an efficient technical college. They achieved this by amalgamating Anderson's College, the Mechanics' Institution, the Young Chair of Technical Chemistry, the College of Science and Art, the Allan Glen's Institute and the Atkinson Institution to form the Glasgow and West of Scotland Technical College. Its object, as set out by its first governors, was 'to afford a suitable education to those who wish to qualify themselves for following an industrial profession or trade'. Fifteen years after its foundation it had 596 day-school students and, interestingly, 4,394 evening-school students.

Although supervised by the Scottish Education Department, the college had close links with Glasgow University. In 1913 the Royal Technical College (as it had become in 1912) affiliated with the University, and in 1919 was accorded the status of a University College. The main result of this affiliation was that students following certain courses could sit the appropriate university examinations and thus obtain a degree.

Despite the high level of its teaching activities, during the first half of the 20th century the College continued to labour under the difficulties of this dual system of qualifications. In 1961, however, the University Grants Committee at long last recommended that the College should be granted university status. This momentous step became a reality when the new University of Strathclyde finally received its Charter in 1964. Its aims, as set out in that Charter, linked clearly both with those expressed by the 1886 governors – 'to advance learning and knowledge by teaching and research, particularly into the basic and applied sciences, and to enable students to obtain the advantages of a liberal education' – and with John Anderson's desire to promote 'the improvement of science'. In its first session more than 41,000 students were registered, and its campus now stretches north and east from its old founding site in George St for more than 26 acres.

The range and status of the new University were considerably enhanced by its amalgamation that same year with the Scottish College of Commerce in Pitt St. The origins of this institution go back to 1845 when a Glasgow Education Association was formed. In 1903, under its new title of the Athenaeum Commercial College, it was recognised as a Central Institution in Glasgow and the West of Scotland, and in 1915 its status was recognised by a new name – the Glasgow and West of Scotland Commercial College. In 1946 it set up the Scottish School of Librarianship, and in 1948 established the Scottish Hotel School at Ross Hall.

See also EDUCATION

Urban Myths

Glasgow has attracted very few urban myths; the few extant are mainly concerned with providing a popular explanation for some unusual circumstance.

One of the earliest is the folk etymology which explains the name Candleriggs (an area outside the town boundaries to where the noisome industry of candle-making had been banished) as being due to a local minister who was able to foretell bad weather, thus enabling his parishioners to illuminate their emergency night-harvesting of their *riggs* by *candle-light*.

The unusual name of a south-side district, Crossmyloof, is popularly explained as coming from the exclamation of Mary, Queen of Scots, after her defeat at the Battle of Langside, 1568: 'By the cross in my loof, I will be in Dumbarton tonight!' The place-name actually comes from the Gaelic *Crois Maoldhuibh*, the Cross of Malduff, an early Celtic saint.

A most persistent belief is that below Central Station lies a buried street, complete with shops and houses. When the station was erected the small village of Grahams-town, with its single thoroughfare, Alston St, leading down to Argyle St, was razed and the site built up to the level of the incoming railway tracks; there is no evidence for the existence of such a Scottish Pompeii.

The Art Gallery and Museum in Kelvingrove Park was erected in 1901, partly from profits made by the 1888 International Exhibition, and was a major feature of the 1901 International Exhibition. The valley of the Kelvin is the natural axis for buildings along its banks and the Art Gallery's north-facing main entrance is meant to face and counterpoint the Glasgow University on the other bank. Despite this, it is the common belief that the building was mistakenly erected back to front and that, on seeing the completed building, the ashamed architect killed himself.

There are another two myths of a similar nature, but on a smaller scale. For no obvious reason it is held that the equestrian statue of the Duke of Wellington in the Royal Exchange Square has its spurs on back-to-front, and Sir Walter Scott's statue on its central pillar in George Square is commonly believed to have its plaid on the wrong shoulder. This would be so for a Highlander, but Sir Walter, as a Borderer, wears his on the right shoulder.

Walkways

During the 1970s several walkways were established within the city, the two most important being the Clyde and Kelvin Walkways, each located on a river-bank.

With the end of the Glasgow Harbour as a working harbour the north bank of the river was cleared and landscaped for much of its length and the Clyde Walkway now passes along this area. It runs from the west end of the harbour (where the Scottish

Exhibition and Conference Centre stands) due east, entering Glasgow Green at the foot of the Saltmarket and continuing under King's Bridge into Fleshers' Haugh. It then leaves the Green, goes under Shawfield Rd at Rutherglen Bridge and follows the Clyde under Dalmarnock Bridge to Rutherglen and beyond to Cambuslang. After leaving the city it continues for a total of 37 miles to New Lanark.

The Kelvin Walkway starts near the west end of the Clyde Walkway and continues north-west along the course of the Kelvin. It passes the Museum of Transport and goes through Kelvingrove Park to finish at Dawsholm Park. It is intended that this walkway be extended so that it will join up with the West Highland Way.

There are other, lesser, walkways – the White Cart, the Levern, the Brockburn and the Victoria. The route of the Glasgow/Loch Lomond Cycleway also starts at the SECC, going through Clydebank and Dumbarton to reach Loch Lomond by way of the Vale of Leven.

Water Supply

Until the beginning of the 19th century Glasgow's water needs were easily satisfied by the River Clyde which washed its southern boundary, by its tributary streams and by the city's wells. However, even before the population explosion of the 19th century made the problem acute, early attempts were made to improve the supply. The first indication of the Town Council's interest was in 1574; thereafter references to it were frequent, being mainly concerned with the repair and maintenance of the existing facilities.

In 1636 we first hear of *piped* water, for there was a suggestion 'to set up pipes or conduits for conveying water to any place in the burgh', although there is no evidence of any action being taken. One reason for particular anxiety was the almost complete lack of water for fire-fighting – two great fires in 1601 and 1652, which had raged unimpeded through Glasgow's wooden houses, destroyed large areas of the city. Towards the end of the 18th century various attempts were made to augment the supply. In 1775 an engineer was appointed to search for fountains, springs and water of good quality in the contiguity of the city'. Another one in 1788 found only two new sources worthy of consideration, the Garngad Burn (supplemented by the Monkland Canal) and the Forth and Clyde Canal. Such was the rapidly growing inadequacy that the citizens became vocal and active, and in 1798 they held a public meeting to voice their complaints. Another survey, in 1800, put before the Town Council five different sources from which water might be supplied. A census of 1801 revealed a population of almost 100,000 with only 30 public wells – one for every 3,000 persons! This was obviously quite inadequate – apart from queues and daily disturbances, many of the wells were considered to be unhealthy.

The only consistent attitude shown by the Council over the years towards these various proposals had been apathy, but they were not entirely to blame, for the crux was the inability of the authority to raise the necessary finance. So, private enterprise took over, in the person of an eminent and philanthropic citizen, William Harley. He owned land in the Blythswood area of the city and constructed waterworks there. On his estate of Willow Bank, near Charing Cross at the west end of Sauchiehall Street, there were numerous springs which he channelled into a small reservoir near West Nile Street. The impounded water he then conveyed throughout the city in large barrels, charging ½d. per stoup. It is said that he made a profit of £4,000 each year. The water was also used to supply his hot and cold public baths as well as four small swimming-pools – hence the name Bath St.

In 1806 came the first serious attempt at introducing a general supply, when a parliamentary Bill was obtained sanctioning the setting up, with the advice of James Watt and Thomas Telford of the Glasgow Water Works. The intention was to pump water from the Clyde into reservoirs at Dalmarnock (about two miles upriver from the city centre and hence fairly unpolluted). After filtration the water would be pumped to reservoirs at Sydney Street, Drygate and Rottenrow, and from there to the city and its suburbs. The system came into operation in 1807, but could supply only inadequately the western end of the city. So, in 1808, a second Act was passed which established the Cranstonhill Water Works. Located near Anderston, on the west of the city, it managed for a time to supply a somewhat better service for the area around it. Ominously, however, in less than ten years it had to move, lock, stock and barrel, to Dalmarnock in the east, a short distance away from its rival, the Glasgow Water Works. The reason for this enforced move was that the combined effluents of an increasing population and industrial activity were turning the river passing through the city into an open sewer.

In 1834 we hear of the very first proposal for a *public* water supply, when a motion was put before the Town Council that 'it would be for the benefits of the public that the works for supplying the City with water should be conducted by the Corporation'.

The Cranstonhill establishment, proving neither successful nor profitable, was amalgamated with its rival, and the entire piped water supply of the city was now in the hands of the Glasgow Water Works. Although it was now supplying about six million gallons a day (about 26 gallons per person), the situation was deteriorating. The demands on it were now so great that often, to maintain the supply, the necessary filtration was either reduced or omitted so that Glasgow water often resembled sherry in colour. In addition, many parts of the city, particularly the poorer areas, still had no piped water whatsoever. The alternative supply, the 48 public wells, was becoming, like the river, unfit for human consumption and the two cholera outbreaks of 1832 and 1848 had indicated that the health of the city's population, rich as well as poor, depended on a city-wide supply of good water.

The pressing anachronism being obvious – the polluted river and wells – the search for new sources was speeded up, and the Town Council began an eight-year search for better water. Several new sources were suggested by private sponsors – the Earn Water (a tributary of the White Cart), the North Calder (near Airdrie), the Clyde at Stonebyres and at Hyndford Bridge, the Avon below Stonehouse, the Rowbank and Cowdenmill Burns (near Loch Lebo), Loch Lomond, the Kelvin, and the Endrick and Allander Waters – but none found favour with the Town Council.

The south side of the city still lacked

an adequate water supply and in 1848 the Gorbals Gravitation Water Company began to supply Gorbals, Pollokshaws, Govan and places intermediate and adjacent in the counties of Lanark and Renfrew with pure and wholesome water. The source was 350ft up on the lower slopes of the Renfrewshire uplands, about six miles south-west of the city boundaries. The year it started was also the year when the Gorbals became an integral part of the city, and seven years later the Corporation took over the Gorbals Water Works.

'The benefit to the public' convinced the Corporation that it should now search out on its own behalf the best possible supply for the city. It appointed John Frederick Bateman, CE, of London and Manchester for this purpose in December 1852, and the following autumn he reported that 'Loch Katrine seems to stand alone in the field. No other will meet all the requirements of the case.' But the Bill to sanction Glasgow's use of Katrine water ran into considerable and surprising opposition. The Gorbals Water Works opposed it, the ratepayers opposed it, the landlords opposed it; but what brought it to a halt, for the moment, was an unexpected report from Dr Frederick Penny, Professor of Chemistry in the Andersonian University, Glasgow. The soft Katrine water, he said, 'if led and stored in lead pipes and cisterns would be exceedingly hazardous to use and indeed highly poisonous'. It would appear, in the light of latter-day knowledge, that the doctor was a prophet before his time. A bevy of professional gentlemen were found who proved beyond all shadow of scientific doubt that Penny's conclusions were completely without foundation. The opposition to the next attempt to push the Bill through came from an unexpected quarter. The Admiralty claimed that the abstraction of Katrine water by Glasgow

Corporation would interfere with the navigation of the Firth of Forth which, it claimed, was the only war port north of the Humber. Recourse was had to the most famous of all engineers, Isambard Kingdom Brunel, who roundly declared that 'the Loch Katrine project is decidedly to be preferred' and the Bill, which had cost the Corporation over £25,000, received the royal assent on 2 July 1855. Much of its final success was due to the Lord Provost, Robert Stewart of Murdostoun, and his services were later remembered by the erection in Kelvingrove Park of the Stewart Memorial Fountain in 1871.

At the ceremonial commencement of the work in May 1856, the Lord Provost was presented with the tools for the job, described as follows: 'The steel of the hammer and the drill are made from Scotch iron, the handle of the hammer from a piece of oak, part of the old Glasgow Bridge, and the box to contain them is made of the oak of the Glasgow Cathedral.' A work which surpassed for the first time the building of the great Roman aqueducts took only three years. From Loch Katrine, 360ft above the Clyde at Glasgow, the 8ft-diameter aqueduct ran for a distance of about 34 miles to the northern outskirts of Glasgow with a fall of 10in in the mile. The water was fed into a service reservoir (62 acres, capacity 548 million gallons) at Mugdock, near Milngavie, and was then distributed throughout the city by 46 miles of pipes.

It was found, however, that because the aqueduct could only deliver 40 million gallons per day (instead of the expected 50 million), an extension of the system was urgently required. This extension took the form of increasing the capacity of Loch Katrine, adding to it water from Loch Arklet, building a parallel aqueduct and constructing a second reservoir at Craigmaddie, all of which allowed 110 million gallons per day to be drawn. This ambitious addition was completed by 1885. It was not without problems, though: the nature of the underlying rock at Craigmaddie required the digging of a 195ft trench – it took six years to complete and two serious fall-ins of the trench killed 20 navvies.

In a move which would have delight-

ed (and justified) Dr Penny, the eradication of lead piping was begun in 1979, replacing it with cast-iron and PVC pipes.

The Glasgow Corporation's responsibility for supplying clean water to its citizens ceased in 1968; the present water supplier is the Strathclyde Regional Council – distributing more than 2 million gallons to over 250,000 households.

WELLS

Until the beginning of the 19th century Glasgow's water supply came from the river and from a large number of wells, both public and private. Amongst the earliest recorded is St Ninian's Well in St Tenew St (i.e. the Trongate) in 1433, and the Deanside Well (1530) off Rottenrow in Balmanno St. St Mungo's Spout (1556) was located near the Gallowgate; St Kentigern's Well (1572) was probably the same well under the saint's proper name – it was located behind the Saracen's Head Inn. The Town Council minutes of 1574 refer to the Gleghornis Well, complaining that it had become 'fillit up with stanes'. The Trongate Well (1630) was a slated and pumped well – the first mention of a *pump* well rather than the usual *draw* well. A new well was opened in the Stockwellgate in 1638 and the Stinking Vennel had its well in 1655.

In 1664 the Council ordained that the Barrasyett Well (at the foot of the Saltmarket) was to be 'heightit twa stanes higher round about, for preservatioune of childerin falling therin'.

About 1730 all the draw wells began to be replaced by pump wells. Despite this, by 1822, the public wells had become so inefficient that it was proposed to tax the showmen at the Glasgow Fair so as to supply the cost of fitting cast-iron pump frames, and by 1834 only 14 wells, out of 30, were in good repair. An 1848 report

lists 41 wells, of which 38 were located in the city centre, the east end and south of the river, with only three in the west end (two of which were out of repair).

There were four important Glasgow wells. The twin-spouted West Port Well, located in the Trongate (probably the earlier Trongate, St Tenew's or St Ninian's Well), Virginia St, was the most used of all the city's public wells, and those wanting to draw water could often wait several hours before their turn came. The next most frequently used was Bell's Wynd Well in the High St, followed by the Spout Mouth in the Calton (perhaps St Mungo's Spout) and the Lady Well in Ladywell St, Drygate. Use of the latter was discontinued, for obvious reasons, when the first graves were dug in the bank of the Necropolis immediately behind it.

Two of the best-known wells were the Pear Tree Well in Kelvingrove Park and the Arne Well in Glasgow Green. The name of the former is doubtful – other forms were Pier Tree Well, Three Tree Well or Pea Tree Well. Its proper name may be indicated by a sketch of the well by Thomas Fairbairn which shows a laburnum or *pea* tree growing next to it. The Arne Well (*arne*, an alder tree) was said to supply the best water of all the Glasgow wells and was always in demand for preparing the celebrated Glasgow cold rum punch. The recipe for this required rum, cold water, sugar, lemons and limes. The sugar (one tablespoon to each lemon) was melted with a little water (as cold as possible) in a large bowl. About a dozen lemons were squeezed into the bowl which was then filled up with more water. This was known as sherbet and the final quality of the punch depended on this stage. Rum was now added (about one to seven) and finally a few limes were cut and squeezed into the mixture.

Witches

Like the rest of the west of Scotland, Glasgow suffered little from accusations of witchcraft, and there are only a few sporadic references to it in the city: A certain Sibyll Dowe, about the middle of the 16th century, rubbed a man's shoulder with a 'houlet hart' (an owl's heart) in order to cause him to fall in love with her. She was brought before the Glasgow Presbytery but was not punished. One of the first recorded cases, in 1597, came about when Margaret Atkin of Balweary informed on 'divers innocent women' in Glasgow. Through the credulity of the minister, Mr John Cowper, these poor folk were condemned and put to death. In 1676, Sir George Maxwell of Nether Pollock was suddenly taken with a fever while in Glasgow, said to be the result of witchcraft. Six persons were accused, of whom five were strangled and burnt. The Bargarran or Renfrewshire witchcraft trial of 1697, produced so many accused that Glasgow's Tolbooth had to be used to keep some of them in custody, and the Glasgow Town Council complained bitterly of the expense of feeding them.

A track which ran down from what is now Dennistoun to the Clyde used to be called the Witch Loan (now Abercrombie St). Supposedly this name was given to it because cattle grazing at its northern end came under the spell of a witch and only recovered when they were driven down the Loan to lusher pastures on the river-bank.

Zoo

In 1938 the Zoological Society of Glasgow and the West of Scotland acquired a site for a future zoo by purchasing for £1,850 the 112-acre Calderpark estate at Broomhouse (on the extreme edge of the city's eastern boundary). Construction was delayed by the Second World War but the zoo finally opened in 1947, and by the 1960s its attendance figures were reaching substantial levels. In 1983 the society changed the name from Calderpark Zoo to the Glasgow Zoo and, with the help of £2.3 million from the District Council, it began a ten-year period of major reconstruction. Recession and a growing general 'anti-zoo' attitude have caused attendances to fall away, despite the zoo's winning several awards for its successful breeding of rare species.

Bibliography

For convenience, the 210 entries in this short and selective list have been grouped together in broad subject arrangements. Those items which are thought most likely to be of general use or interest have been indicated by an asterisk*

ARCHITECTURE

Doak, A. M., and Young, A. Mc., **Glasgow at a Glance: An Architectural Handbook**, rev. ed., 1977

Esher, Viscount, L. G., **Conservation of Glasgow: A Preliminary Report**, 1971

Glasgow District Council, **Glasgow Heritage** (conservation)

*Gomme, A., and Walker, D., **Architecture of Glasgow**, rev. ed., 1987

McKean, C., et al., **Central Glasgow: An Illustrated Architectural Guide**, 1989

Reid, P. (ed.), **Glasgow: The Forming of the City**, 1993

*Williamson, E., et al., **Glasgow: The Buildings of Scotland**, 1990

*Wordsall, F., The Tenement, 1979

Wordsall, F., Victorian City, 1982

ART

Buchanan, W., 'State of the Art: Glasgow', 1855, in **Hist. Photography**, 13/2/1989

Glasgow Corporation, **Catalogue (Illustrated) of the Paintings and Drawings in the Old Glasgow Room**, 1927

Glasgow District Council, **Glasgow Style, 1890–1920**, 1984

BIOGRAPHY

Anderson, J. R., The Burgesses and Brethren of Glasgow: 1573–1846, 2 vols., 1925, 1935

Anderson, J. R., **Provosts of Glasgow from 1609 to 1832**, 1942

Innes Review, 'Career of St Kentigern', xxxvii, 1986, pp. 3–24

Knox, W. (ed.), **Scottish Labour Leaders, 1918–39: A Biographical Dictionary**, 1984

MacKenzie, P., **Glasgow Characters: Memoirs and Portraits of One Hundred Glasgow Men**, 2 vols., 1857, 1886 (beggars and other street characters)

Oakley, C. A., **Our Illustrious Forbears**, 1980

*Strang, J., **Glasgow and its Clubs**, 1864

HEALTH

Blackden, S. M., **Development of Public Health Administration in Glasgow, 1842–1872** (unpublished thesis), 1976

Christie, J., **Medical Institutions of Glasgow**, 1888

Dow, D. A., **Rottenrow: The History of the Glasgow Royal Maternity Hospital, 1834–1984**, 1989

Gibson, T., **Royal College of Physicians and Surgeons of Glasgow**, 1983

MacGregor, A., **Public Health in Glasgow, 1905–1946**, 1957

McQueen, L., and Kerr, A. B., **Western Infirmary, 1874–1974**, 1974

Patrick, J. A., **Short History of the Glasgow Royal Infirmary**, 1940

Robertson, E., **Yorkhill Story: The History of the Royal Hospital for Sick Children, Glasgow**, 1972

Slater, S. D., and Dow, D. A., **Victoria Infirmary of Glasgow, 1890–1990**, 1990

Watt, O. M., **Stobhill Hospital**, 1971

HISTORY

Berry, S., and Whyte, H. (eds.), **Glasgow Observed: A Documentary Anthology, 1773–1986**, 1987

Brogan, C., **The Glasgow Story**, 1952 (impressionistic account of Glasgow culture)

Brown, A., **History of Glasgow**, 1795

Chapman, R. (pub.), **Picture of Glasgow**, new ed., 1812 (guide)

*Cleland, J., **Annals of Glasgow**, 2 vols., 1816

Cleland, J., **Description of the City of Glasgow**, 2nd ed., 1840

Cleland, J., **Rise and Progress of the City of Glasgow**, 1820

Cowan, J. (pseud. Peter Prowler), **From Glasgow's Treasure Chest**, 1951 (popular miscellany of history, persons and places)

*Cunnison, J., and Gilfillan, J. B. S., **Glasgow: Third Statistical Account of Scotland**, 1958

*Denholm, J., History of the City of Glasgow, 1797

*Gibb, A., **Glasgow: The Making of a City**, 1983

*Gibson, J., **History of Glasgow**, 1777

Glasgow Delineated: An Illustrated Guide, 1821

*Gordon, J. F. S., **Glasghu Facies: A View of the City of Glasgow . . . Comprising Every History Hitherto Published**, 1872

*Gunn, J., and Newbiggin, M., **City of Glasgow: Its Origin, Growth and Development**, 1921 (includes facsimile early maps)

*Kellett, J. R., **Glasgow: A Concise History**, 1967

King, E., **Hidden History of Glasgow's Women**, 1993

*Lobel, M. D. (ed.), **Historic Towns**, vol. 1, 1969 (pre-industrial Glasgow, maps and text)

*McDowall, J., **People's History of Glasgow**, 1899 (popular encyclopaedic-style account)

MacGeorge, A., **Old Glasgow**, 1880

*MacGregor, G., **History of Glasgow, From the Earliest Period to the Present Time**, 1881

MacKenzie, P., **Old Reminiscences of Glasgow and the West of Scotland**, 1865

McUre, J., **City of Glasgow**, 1736 (city's first history, reprinted 1830)

*Marwick, J. D. (ed.), **Charters and other Documents Relating to the City of Glasgow 1175–1707**, 3 vols., 1897–1906

*Marwick, J. D. (ed.), **Extracts from the Records of the Burgh of Glasgow**, 11 vols., 1876–1916

Marwick, J. D., **Early Glasgow**

Marwick, J. D., **River Clyde and the Clyde Burghs**, 1909

*Miller, R., and Tivy, J. (eds.), **The Glasgow Region**, 1958 (general survey)

Muir, J. **Glasgow Streets and Places, Notes and Memoranda**, 1899

Muir, J. H. (pseud. James and Muirhead Bone and John Hamilton Charteris), **Glasgow in 1901**, 1901

*Oakley, C. A., **The Second City**, 4th ed., 1990

*Old Glasgow Club, **Transactions**, 1907–1955

Pagan, J., **Sketch of the City of Glasgow**, 1847

Primrose, J., **Mediaeval Glasgow**, 1913

*Reid, R. Senex, et al., **Glasgow, Past and Present**, 3 vols., 1884

Regality Club, **Series I to IV: 1889–1912** (miscellany)

*Renwick, R. (ed.), **Abstracts of the Protocols of the Town Clerks of Glasgow, 1530–1600**, 11 vols., 1894–1900

*Renwick, R., Lindsay, J. and Eyre-Todd, G., **History of Glasgow**, 3 vols., 1921–34 (to 1833)

Words and the Stones, Glasgow's Glasgow, People Within a City: The Words and the Stones, 1990 (published for Glasgow's City of Culture year)

HISTORY – Districts

Adams, G., **History of Bridgeton and Dalmarnock**, 1990

Brotchie, T. C. F., **History of Govan**, 1905

Castlemilk Local History Group, **The Incomplete History of Castlemilk**, 1993

Dow, D., and Moss, M., **Glasgow's Gain: The Anderston Story**, 1986

Gartshore, A., **Cathcart Memories**, 1938

McCallum, A., **History of Pollokshaws**

Morton, H. B., **A Hillhead Album**, 1973

Napier, J., **Notes and Reminiscences Relating to Partick**, 1873

Ord, J., **Barony of Gorbals**, 1919

Smart, A., **Villages of Glasgow**, vol. 1, 1988 (Glasgow districts)

Taylor, W., **Glasgow, N. W.: (Lambhill, Possil)**, 1976

Thomson, A., **Maryhill, 1750–1894**, 1905

HISTORY – Social, Economic & Political

*Bell, J., and Paton, J., **Glasgow: Its Municipal Organisation and Administration**, 1896

Cage, R. A. (ed.), **The Working Class in Glasgow, 1750–1914**, 1987

*Checkland, S. G., **The Upas Tree: Glasgow 1875–1975** (industry and politics), 1976

Damer, S., **Glasgow: Going for a Song**, 1990 (study of working-class Glasgow)

*Damer, S., **Social History of Glasgow Council Housing, 1919-1965**, 1991

Edward, M., **Who Belongs to Glasgow?**, 1993 (immigrant groups)

Fraser, W. H., **Glasgow Trades Council**, n.d. (introduction to microfilm copy of Council's archives)

Gemmell, M., **Societies of Glasgow**, 1904

Glasgow Corporation, **Facts and Figures, 1925–1974** (annual information of a statistical and financial nature)

Glasgow Herald, 'Municipal Centenary Number, 1835–1935, 1935

Grant, D., **The Thin Blue Line**, 1973 (Glasgow police force)

Jackson, A. M., **Glasgow dean of Guild Court: A History**, 1983

Jephcott, P., **Homes in High Flats**, 1971

Keating, M., **City that Refused to Die**, 1988 (political urban regeneration)

Leneman, L., **A Guid Cause**, 1991 (Scottish women's suffrage)

MacLennan, D., and Gibb, A., **Glasgow: No Mean City to Miles Better**, n.d. (city's housing study)

McShane, H., **Calton Weavers' Memorial, 1787**, n.d. (18th century strike victims)

Mann, B., **The New Scots: The Story of Asians in Scotland**, 1992

Middlemas, R. K., **The Clydesiders: A Left-Wing Struggle for Parliamentary Power**, 1965

*Murray, D., **Early Burgh Organization in Scotland**, vol. 1: Glasgow, 1924

Reid, J. M., **History of the Merchants House of Glasgow**, n.d.

Slaven, A., **Development of the West of Scotland: 1750–1960**, 1975 (economic history)

Steven, C., **Proud Record: The Story of the Glasgow Fire Service**, 1952

ILLUSTRATIONS

Allan, D., **Views in Glasgow & Neighbourhood**, 1835 (letterpress by J. M. Leighton)

*Annan, T., **Old Closes & Streets of Glasgow**. v.d. (photographic prints, three eds, 1871, 1877, 1900, new ed. 1977)

Bone, M. **Glasgow: Fifteen Drawings**, 1911

Buchanan, J., et al., **Old Country Houses of the Old Glasgow Gentry**, 2nd ed., 1878 (Annan prints)

Fairbairn, T., **Relics of Ancient Architecture and other Picturesque Scenes in Glasgow**, 1849

Forbes, A. G., **Photographs of Glasgow**, 1869 (Annan prints with descriptive letterpress)

*Gemmell, W., **Early Views of Glasgow: Chiefly from the Foulis Academy of Art**, 2 vols., 1913

Marzaroli, O., **Shades of Grey: Glasgow 1956–1987**

Nicol, J. D. (pubs.), **Glasgow Illustrated in Twenty-One Views**, 1841

*Scott, J., **Glasgow Illustrated: Drawn and Engraved by J. Scott** 1834 (text by John Cullan)

Simpson, W., **Glasgow in the Forties**, 1899 (views)

Slezar, J., **Theatrum Scotiae**, 1693 (includes three Glasgow views)

Small, D., **Bygone Glasgow**, 1896 (illustrations and text)

Small, D., **Sketches of Quaint Bits in Glasgow . . . In the Year Eighteen Hundred and Eighty-Five**, 1896 (illustrations and text)

Stuart & Co. (pub.), **Views and Notices of Glasgow in Former Times**, 1847

*Swan, J., **Select Views of Glasgow and its Environs**, 1828 (engraved by Joseph Swann, introduction by John M. Leighton)

INDUSTRY & COMMERCE

*Devine, T. M., **Tobacco Lords** c. 1740–1790, 1975

Fleming, J. A., **Scottish Pottery**, 1923

Glasgow Corporation, **Scottish Railway Locomotives: A History**, 1967

Hamilton, H., 'Founding of the Glasgow Chamber of Commerce', **in Scottish Journal of Politics and Economics**, 1/1/1954

Hughes, G. B., **English and Scottish Earthenware, 1660-1860**, n.d.

*Hume, J. R., **Industrial Archaeology of Glasgow**, 1974

Kinghorn, J., and Quail, G., **Delftfield: A Glasgow Pottery, 1748–1823**, 1986

McLean, A., **Local Industries of Glasgow and the West of Scotland**, 1901

Nicolson, M., and O'Neill, M., **Glasgow: Locomotive Builder to the World**, 1987

JUDAISM

Collins, K. E., **Second City Jewry: The Jews of Glasgow in the Age of Expansion, 1790–1919**, 1990

Hutt, C., and Kaplan, H., **A Scottish Shtetla: Jewish Life in the Gorbals, 1880-1974**

LANGUAGE

Macafee, G., **Glasgow**, 1983 (varieties of Glasgow dialect)

*Munro, M., **The Patter: A Guide to Current Glasgow Usage**, 1985

LITERATURE

Craig, C., **History of Scottish Literature**, vol. 4, 20th century, 1988

Royle, T., **Mainstream Companion to Scottish Literature**, 1993

LITERATURE – Fiction

*Burgess, M., **The Glasgow Novel**, 2nd ed., 1986, (bibliography and guide)

LITERATURE – Poetry

Eyre-Todd, George. (ed.), **Glasgow Poets: Their Lives and Poems**, 2nd ed., 1906

Whyte, H. B., **Glasgow Poets and Poetry: A Representative Bibliography, 1950–1975**, 1976 (unpublished Glasgow Room guide)

*Whyte, H. (ed.), **Mungo's Tongues, Glasgow Poems, 1630–1990**, 1993

MISCELLANEOUS

Berry, J. J., **Glasgow Necropolis**, n.d.

Black, B. J. (ed.), **Excursion Guide to the Geology of the Glasgow District**, 1973

Community Education Service (Strathclyde Region), **Old Games and Rhymes of Glasgow**, 1986

Curl, J. S., **Burial Grounds in Glasgow**, 1974

Dickson, J. H., **Wild Plants of Glasgow**, 1991

Kinchin, P., **Tea and Taste: The Glasgow Tea-Rooms, 1875–1975**, 1991

McCarra, K., **Scottish Football: A Pictorial History**, 1984

MacDonald, H., **Rambles Round Glasgow**, 1854

MacGeorge, A., **Inquiry as to the Armorial Insignia of the City of Glasgow**, 1866

McGinn, M., **McGinn of the Calton**, 1987 (biography, songs and music)

MacLean, M. (ed.), **Archaeological, Educational, Medical and Charitable Institutions of Glasgow**, 1901

McVicar, E., **One Singer, One Song: Songs of Glasgow Folk**, 1990

Rafferty, J., **One Hundred Years of Scottish Football**, 1973

Third Eye Centre, **St John Ogilvie, S. J., 1579–1615**, 1979

*Willing, J. A., and Fairie, J. S., **Burial Grounds in Glasgow**, 1986

PARKS

Glasgow District Council, **Leisure in the Parks**, 1980

King, E., **People's Palace and Glasgow Green**, 1985

McLellan, D., **Glasgow Public Parks**, 1894

Pattison, W. C., **History of Glasgow Green**, 1845

PUBLISHING/LIBRARIES

Blackie, A. A. C., **Blackie & Son, 1809–1959**, 1959

Cowan, R. M. W., **The Newspaper in Scotland: 1815–1860**, 1946

Duncan, W. J. (ed.), Notices and Documents Illustrative of the Literary History of Glasgow, 1831

Gillespie, R. A., **List of Books printed in Glasgow, 1701–1775**, 1967

Glasgow University, **Robert and Andrew Foulis: An Exhibition in the Hunterian**, 1958 (printing)

Hendry, J. D., **Social History of Branch Library Development with Special Reference to the City of Glasgow**, 1974

Keir, D., **House of Collins**, 1952

Mason, T., **Public and Private Libraries of Glasgow**, 1885

Phillips, A., **Glasgow Herald: Two Hundred Years of a Newspaper, 1783–1983**, 1982

RELIGION

Brown, J., **Religious Denominations of Glasgow**, vol. 1, 1860 (vol. 2 was never published)
Chalmers, P., **Cathedral Church of Glasgow**, 1914
Eyre-Todd, G. (ed.), **Book of Glasgow Cathedral**, 1898
*Fawcett, R., **Glasgow Cathedral**, 1987
Gallagher, T., **Glasgow: The Uneasy Peace: Religious Tension in Modern Scotland**, 1987
*Herron, A., **Historical Directory of Glasgow Presbytery**, 1984 (brief accounts of all Glasgow churches)
Scott, H., **Fasti Ecclesiae Scoticanae**, new ed., vol. 3, 1920 (Chuch of Scotland ministers, 1560 Glasgow volume)

SHIPBUILDING & THE CLYDE

Browning, A. S. F., **History of Clyde Shipbuilding**. 1991
Johnston, J., **Forty Years of Dreadnaughts Built on the River Clyde, 1906–1946**, n.d.
MacLeod, I., and Gilroy, M., **Discovering the River Clyde**, 1991
*Marwick, J. D., **River Clyde and the Harbour of Glasgow**, 1898
Riddell, J. F., **The Clyde: An Illustrated History of the River and its Shipping**, 1988
*Riddell, J. F., **Clyde Navigation: A History of the Development and Deepening of the River Clyde**, 1979
*Shields, J., **Clyde-Built: A History of Shipbuilding on the River Clyde**, 1949
*Walker, F. M., **Song of the Clyde: A History of Clyde Shipbuilding**, 1984

THEATRE

Baynham, W., **Glasgow Stage**, 1892
Coveney, M., **The Citz: 21 Years of the Glasgow Citizens Theatre**, 1990
Hay, M. H., **Glasgow Theatres and Music Halls**. 1980 (unpublished Glasgow Room guide)
House, J., **Music Hall Memories**, 1986
Irving, G., The Good Auld Days, 1977 (Scottish music halls)
Mackintosh, **Stage Reminiscences**, 1870

TRANSPORT

*Duckworth, C. L. D., and Langmuir, G. E., **Clyde River and other Steamers**, 3rd ed., 1972
Glasgow Corporation, **Glasgow's Trams**, 1964
Grieves, R., **Glasgow Bus Scene**, n.d.
Johnston, C., and Hume, J., **Glasgow Stations**, 1979
Kelly, P. J., and Willsher, J. D., **Glasgow Subway, 1896–1977**, 1977
Lindsay, J., **Canals of Scotland**, 1968
Little, S., **Handbook of Glasgow Corporation Motorbuses, 1924–1971**, 1971
McCrorie, I., **Clyde Pleasure Steamers**, 1986
Millar, A., **British PTEs: 1. Strathclyde**, 1985
Oakley, C. A., The Last Tram, 1962
Stewart, I., **Glasgow Tramcar**, 1983

UNIVERSITIES

*Coutts, J., **History of the University of Glasgow**, 1909
Glasgow University, **University of Glasgow: Gilmorehill Centenary**, 1979
Glasgow University, **University of Glasgow Through Five Centuries**, 1951
Mackie, J. D., **University of Glasgow, 1451–1971**, 1954
Sexton, A. H., **First Technical College**, 1894 (origins of Strathclyde University)

UTILITIES

Glasgow Corporation, **Glasgow Electricity Supply: A Historical Account**, 1935
Glasgow Corporation, **Glasgow Corporation Gas Department: A Brief Account**, 1949
Glasgow Corporation, **Water Supply of Glasgow: A Century of Public Ownership**, 1955
Hunter, R. (ed.), **Water Supply of Glasgow**, 1933
Marwick, J. D., **Water Supply of the City of Glasgow**, 1901
Thomson, R. D., and Penny, F., **Public Wells of Glasgow**, 1848

Index